ABORIGINES, LAND AND LAND RIGHTS

ABORIGINES, LAND AND LAND RIGHTS

Edited by Nicolas Peterson and Marcia Langton

Australian Institute of Aboriginal Studies
Canberra 1983

Published in Australia by the Australian Institute of Aboriginal Studies, PO Box 553, Canberra City, ACT, 2601.

Sold and distributed in North and South America by Humanities Press Inc., 171 First Avenue, Atlantic Highlands, NJ 07716.

The views expressed in this publication are those of the author and not necessarily those of the Australian Institute of Aboriginal Studies.

AIAS New series No. 42

National Library of Australia
Cataloguing in Publication data:

Aborigines, land and land rights.

Bibliography.
ISBN 0 85575 145 2.
ISBN 0 85575 143 6 (pbk.).

[1] Aborigines, Australian — Land tenure. I. Peterson, Nicolas, 1941- . II. Langton, Marcia, 1951- . III. Australian Institute of Aboriginal Studies.

333.2'0994

Typeset by Canberra Times Print, ACT

Printed in Australia by Ruskin Press, Melbourne 83 06 4000

CONTENTS

PART THREE
Modern structures

PART FOUR
Mining

PART FIVE
Canadian perspectives

CONTRIBUTORS

Jeremy Beckett
Senior Lecturer, Department of Anthropology, University of Sydney, NSW

Diane Bell
Research Fellow, Department of Anthropology, Research School of Pacific Studies, Australian National University, Canberra, ACT

Colin Bourke
Former Director, Aboriginal Research Centre, Monash University, Vic.

Maria Brandl
Visiting Fellow, Centre for Resource and Environmental Studies, Australian National University, Canberra, ACT

Peter Carroll
Principal Research Officer, Department of Aboriginal Affairs; on leave from July 1981 to work as a consultant in Department of the Chief Minister, Darwin, NT

Hans Dagmar
Institute for Cultural and Social Anthropology, Catholic University of Nijmegen, The Netherlands

Noel Dyck
Assistant Professor, Department of Sociology and Anthropology, Simon Fraser University, Canada

Geoff Eames
Legal Service Commission of South Australia, Adelaide, SA

Bill Edwards
Department of Anthropology, University of Adelaide, SA

Harvey Feit
Associate Professor, Department of Anthropology, McMaster University, Canada

Constance Hunt
Professor, Faculty of Law, University of Calgary, Canada

Sue Kesteven
Research Fellow, Social Impact of Uranium Mining, Oenpelli, NT

Marcia Langton
Research Officer, Australian Institute of Aboriginal Studies, Canberra, ACT

Robert Layton
Reader, Department of Anthropology, Durham University, England

Kenneth Maddock
Senior Lecturer, School of Behavioural Studies, Macquarie University, Sydney, NSW

Paul Memmott
Architect and Consultant in Aboriginal Projects, Department of Architecture, University of Queensland, Brisbane, Qld

Bette Moore
Research Officer, Department of the Secretary to the Cabinet, Parliament House, Melbourne, Vic.

Howard Morphy
Lecturer, Department of Prehistory and Anthropology, Australian National University, Canberra, ACT

Richard Moyle
Lecturer in Ethnomusicology, University of Auckland, Auckland, New Zealand

Kingsley Palmer
Anthropologist, Northern Land Council

Nicolas Peterson
Senior Lecturer, Department of Prehistory and Anthropology, Australian National University, Canberra, ACT

Meredith Rowell
Anthropologist, Central Land Council, Alice Springs, NT

John Stanton
Curator, Anthropology Research Museum, University of Western Australia, Perth, WA

David S. Trigger
Site Recorder, Department of Anthropology and Sociology, University of Queensland, Brisbane, Qld

Daniel Vachon
Anthropologist, Pitjantjatjara Council, Alice Springs, NT

Philip Vincent
Solicitor, Perth, WA

Michael Walsh
Lecturer, Department of Linguistics, University of Sydney, NSW

Nancy M. Williams
Research Consultant, Australian Institute of Aboriginal Studies, Canberra, ACT

PREFACE

This volume arises from the Aboriginal Land Rights Symposium held as part of the Australian Institute of Aboriginal Studies Biennial Meeting on 21-22 May 1980. The precirculated background papers on the land rights situation throughout the continent prepared for the symposium have already been published by the Institute under the title *Aboriginal Land Rights: a handbook*. This volume includes a selection of other papers prepared for the symposium.

The symposium brought together over 250 Aborigines, anthropologists, lawyers and people associated with the various land trusts and land councils throughout Australia; and in addition six Canadians participated—two lawyers, the president and vice-president of the Native Council of Canada and two anthropologists who have worked for native American organisations. The proceedings were opened by Senator Chaney, then Minister for Aboriginal Affairs, and closed by Mr Justice Woodward.

The symposium was a great success, despite the high feelings and what seemed to be insufficient time for the many papers that were delivered. Most importantly, people were brought together from all Aboriginal organisations with day-to-day involvement in one or other aspect of land rights, enabling links to be forged between them and the many lawyers and anthropologists who were similarly involved.

It would not have been possible to hold the symposium or prepare the papers for publication without an immense amount of help and work by many more people than can be mentioned here. However, mention must be made first and foremost of the Australian Institute of Aboriginal Studies, which sponsored the symposium and this publication, and of all the Institute staff who worked to make the symposium possible. Important assistance was also received from State and Territory land councils and the Aboriginal Study Grants Scheme. We are indebted to the following people: Peter Ucko, Warwick Dix, Ken Colbung, Alex Barlow, Patricia Allen, Hilary Cousins, Anita Campbell, John Millar, Garnet Wilson and Ossie Cruse. For help in preparing the manuscript for publication, our thanks are due to the staff of the Institute's Publication Section and Les Hiatt.

Nicolas Peterson
Marcia Langton

INTRODUCTION

Land rights was the major issue for Aborigines in the 1970s, culminating in the passing of the *Aboriginal Land Rights (Northern Territory) Act* 1976, and is certain to remain a major issue of the 1980s since this legislation applies only to the Northern Territory. Although it is neither the first nor only piece of land rights legislation in Australia, it is much the most significant, for unlike other legislation it not only transfers substantial areas of land to Aboriginal people but also provides them with a basis for independent action by establishing statutory bodies that are adequately and independently financed. By recognising that meaningful land rights are not just concerned with property rights, but also with regaining some fraction of the personal and group autonomy which existed prior to colonisation, the Northern Territory legislation marks a major watershed. Yet white thinking about land rights remains circumscribed. Rarely does it rise above the political, legislative and administrative constraints that have limited the range of options to those immediate, practical and expedient solutions which have favoured and justified white transgressions of Aboriginal rights in land. In particular, there remains an immense reluctance to acknowledge the impact of colonisation and to give recognition to the creative adaptations of the pre-contact land-tenure system by which many Aborigines have ensured the continuity of relationships to country. The failure of the Northern Territory legislation to recognise these adaptations, forced upon the people by invasion and the consequent disruptions, is its weakest point.

Since 1971, when Mr Justice Blackburn handed down his decision on the first legal test of whether Aborigines had rights in land recognisable under Australian law (see *Milirrpum and Others* v. *Nabalco and the Commonwealth of Australia),* official thinking has been dominated by concern with 'traditional' rights, even though these had no legal standing. Mr Justice Blackburn ruled, partly on the basis of eighteenth century legal commentaries and partly on ethnographic evidence, that although Aborigines did have a system of land tenure it could not be recognised as legal title under Australian law. He went on to say that, 'it seems likely that in primitive communities there was no conception of title at all'. He argued that 'desert and uncultivated', the eighteenth century expression that described, amongst other places, the continent inhabited by Aboriginal people, has 'always been taken to include territory in which live uncivilised inhabitants in a primitive state of society' (Milirrpum, etc., 1971:61). Thus Australia has been considered a ceded rather than a conquered colony because of the European view that there was no unified political and legal system or authoritative representative with whom to negotiate a settlement and the terms of colonisation. This legal decision was a crushing blow, not only for the people from Yirrkala but also for Aborigines throughout the continent who were hopeful that finally justice would be forthcoming from the legal system.

The Australian Government overcame this legal set-back by executive decision two years later in 1973, when it established the Aboriginal Land Rights Commission under Mr Justice Woodward. The Commission's terms of reference were not aimed at determining whether or not land rights should be granted, but how they should be granted. Woodward concentrated his reports (1973, 1974) on the Northern Territory, partly because of the time factor but more importantly because of his concern to establish certain principles relating to the granting of Aboriginal land rights, which could only be easily done in the Northern Territory where the Commonwealth could legislate directly.

The first draft of the legislation, based on Woodward's reports, was presented in the Australian Parliament in 1975. A dramatic change of government then intervened only hours after the Second Reading of the Bill. The Bill was reintroduced in 1976, considerably amended. Missing from the legislation was the possibility of Aboriginal people claiming land on the basis of need as well as by traditional right, a major point in Woodward's recommendations. Also counter to the spirit of his recommendation was the granting to the Northern Territory of the right to legislate on the day-to-day workings of the Act in respect of entry onto Aboriginal land, sacred sites, Aborigines on pastoral properties, and closure of the seas adjacent to Aboriginal lands. The most significant consequence of these changes was that those Northern Territory Aborigines who have borne the brunt of dispossession could not easily make claims, and the town dwellers now had to find their way through a maze of government departments to attain town leases. The concern to deny the right to land or compensation to such displaced Aboriginal populations emerged in the debates on the Bill. One speaker justified the emphasis on traditional ownership because it would keep the Aboriginal 'carpet baggers from the south' out. Thus, the onus of proof of even 'traditional' attachment to land was placed on the Aboriginal people, the very people whose land has been appropriated.

Not all Aborigines had to prove traditional ownership under the Act, only those whose land lay outside the former reserves on unalienated Crown land, and who sought its return. It was as a result of preparing these land claims that anthropologists and linguists, along with lawyers, came to constitute the main body of expert consultants to the Aboriginal land councils in the Northern Territory and to the Aboriginal Land Commissioner under the Act.

Currently, Aborigines have gained freehold title to over 28% of the Northern Territory; 18% through the direct transfer of former reserves and 10% through land claims. Although not all the papers in this volume deal with the Northern Territory legislation and its implementation all the Australian papers discuss issues that arise directly out of that legislation or the Aboriginal Land Rights Commission reports. Because land rights are very much 'in process' at the moment, both in the Northern Territory and elsewhere in Australia, it is too early for definite indications to emerge as to the long-term effects and significance. What the papers do present is a series of case studies on particular aspects of the impact which collectively touch on many of the major issues raised by land rights. Because the majority of authors are anthropologists, the emphasis is on the impact and significance of events for Aboriginal society and anthropological understandings. A striking omission, however, is the absence of substantial Aboriginal authorship: only two contributors, Bourke and Langton, are Aboriginal. The subsuming of Aboriginal views under fieldwork belies the active and crucial role they are playing in directing the legal and political process.

The papers have been grouped into five sections. The first deals with traditional principles of land tenure, the second with the consequences of the interactions between black and white for land tenure systems, the third discusses modern structures established in association with land rights, and the fourth deals with issues raised by mining. The fifth and final section presents a Canadian perspective on some land rights issues.

TRADITIONAL PRINCIPLES

The preparation and presentation of land claims have rekindled anthropological interest in Aboriginal land tenure and considerably advanced our understanding. The possibility of such claims arises because land rights were granted by statute rather than on the basis of recognition of prior Aboriginal entitlement. Since there were no prior rights, there was no concern to extinguish title in return for formal recognition of rights to some limited areas, as has happened in Alaska under the *Alaska Native Claims Settlement Act* 1971. Instead, it was much more open ended. While all unalienated land in the Northern Territory could have been handed back automatically, and as was suggested a reversionary interest granted in the pastoral leases that cover 55% of the Territory, a more restricted course was chosen. It was decided to hand back unalienated land only where there were demonstrated traditional owners, and to leave people to purchase leases on the open market. Apart from the political difficulties obvious in granting a reversionary interest, there were also seen to be practical ones. At the end of the lease the improvements have to be purchased from the leaseholder, often at considerable cost, such that it was felt the likelihood of the Aborigines or the Government having, or being prepared, to put up the money for them all was remote. A reversionary interest would therefore raise many false expectations and postpone them till around the year 2010, when most of the leases fall in.

Preparation of claims has focused attention on two issues: (1) a practical concern with the adequacy of the statutory definition of traditional owner, and (2) a more ethnographic interest in the regional range and variation of rights and interests in land that has expanded to embrace the whole continent. It is with the second aspect that the papers in this section deal.

Layton's paper on the Pitjantjatjara system is a good example of the extent of the advance of understanding that has come from a close analysis of the nature of rights and interests in land. He provides the first really clear analysis of their system, which he shows to be ambilineal rather than patrilineal, as has been maintained for so long. This paper, together with the work of Myers (1976) has extended the known range of systems of land tenure in Australia while indicating that these desert systems are transformations of the more clearly lineal systems in the tropical north.

The second paper links the ecological interest in Aboriginal life stimulated by the prehistorians during the 1960s and 1970s with the concern to decompose land ownership into its component rights. Memmott attempts to reconstruct the pattern of land use and ownership among the Lardil of Mornington Island at the time of contact, focusing on the wide range of factors structuring space use from the island as a whole down to the camp. By contrast, Moyle focuses narrowly on teasing out the complex relationship between song lines and rights in land among an Arandic-speaking group.

It is the relationship between land use and land ownership that has been the focus of theoretical debate since Hiatt (1962) demonstrated that the Radcliffe-Brown model of the land-using group—namely, the male members of the patrilineal clan plus their wives and their unmarried sisters—was wrong. Hiatt made a crucial distinction between religious ties to land and economic use but failed to provide an adequate general model for how the two related outside one or two limited areas. However, as far as the general public was concerned, the prevailing view was that Aboriginal relationships to land were so strongly and purely religious that the question of the actual use was largely unconsidered. As Williams shows in her contribution, this emphasis on the religious ties played an important role in the Yirrkala land rights case. Blackburn ruled that Aboriginal concepts of property were religious not economic, but Williams argues that this is to misunderstand the Aboriginal situation and that their concepts are both religious and economic, the relationship between them being mediated by the political process. The Yolngu, she argues, maintain the immutability of the religious basis to land tenure in daily discourse. However, daily life consists in gaining control over the myth-based symbols that translate as rights in land. The entailment of her argument is that the frequently quoted axiom, that the clan belongs to the land rather than the land belonging to the clan, is a superficial and inaccurate understanding of the nature of Aboriginal relations to land.

Morphy also writes about the Yolngu, arguing that the people of Galiwinku, unlike most Aboriginal people, have been concerned to draw Europeans into an equal relationship by revealing their most sacred objects which all relate to land. Although the Europeans misunderstood what the Yolngu were trying to do, the revelation created the basis on which other Australians came to recognise their special relations with land.

Peterson seeks to provide a general model of the processual aspect of traditional landownership. Because of the small size of landowning groups, it is inevitable that they died out from time to time, long before Europeans arrived, yet it seems no land was unowned. Succession to such areas was apparently achieved by converting one of the wide range of non-patrilineal rights in an area into a patrilineal interest where the original owners died out. The transition was and is mediated primarily by long-term residence in the new area, with its consequences for succeeding generations being conceived there and the older generation holding and integrating their ceremonies into the local religious system.

INTERACTIONS AND ADJUSTMENTS: ABORIGINES, LAW AND ANTHROPOLOGY

Two significant, but quite different, aspects to interaction and adjustment between black and white in respect of land rights are dealt with by the papers in this section. The first six papers focus on the consequences of disease, depopulation and dislocation on regional land tenure systems and how people have responded to these. The last two papers deal with a more subtle aspect: the way in which the interactions are influenced by our conceptualisation and cultural values which intervene to create difficulties in understanding both the traditional and the transformed systems in their full complexity.

Brandl and Walsh discuss the maintenance of identity and links to land despite traumatic upheavals in the Darwin area. Their concept of 'mixing' describes the intricate interconnectedness of all the activities of people in the area claimed, including shared experiences, whether or not labelled, lingual and other self-identification, and the shared social principles of association to land. Social integrity is perceived, not by isolating social structures but by examining the interconnectedness of individuals through land, language and kinship. Thus an anthropologist and linguist, working on a land claim, have found it necessary to explore their own ethnography and develop new concepts to make sense of Aboriginal associations to land.

In the eastern goldfields of Western Australia, where no land rights legislation exists, Aboriginal sustaining ideals, as expressed in mythological associations, have been adapted to deal with migration, succession and massive depopulation through disease and other factors. The newcomers to Mt Margaret have elaborated on the earlier mythological associations of the area through extension of their own Dreaming associations along with modification of beliefs about birth and conception, so that they have come to gain rights and control in their adopted home. Palmer discusses a similar case in the Pilbara of Western Australia where there are 'effective' and 'ineffective' owners. The problem posed to immigrant Aboriginal people in this area, as Palmer describes it, is how to occupy land they do not own and come to terms with local land-owners. Again traditional action is elaborated through the importation and trade of sacra as symbols of land-owning status and through rights established by marriage or conception.

In the Gascoyne region of Western Australia the impoverished fringe dwellers of Carnarvon sought to re-establish their ties to the land and their enjoyment of the bush by taking advantage of a new government policy initiative, begun in 1971, to purchase land for Aboriginal groups on the basis of need. The conjunction of this policy with recommendations made by Woodward led to the establishment of the Aboriginal Land Fund Commission in 1974 to purchase land throughout Australia. Dagmar documents the five attempts by the Gascoyne people to obtain a pastoral property between 1972, when the funds were handled by the Federal Government Department of Aboriginal Affairs, and 1976. All of the attempts were unsuccessful. He clearly demonstrates the full extent of the structural weakness of the Gascoyne people's position and their complete inability to mobilise the bureaucracy to act effectively and expeditiously on their behalf.

Despite recent changes to the Queensland legislation, Aborigines still have no secure rights in the reserve lands. Trigger discusses the issue of historical associations to land developed since the forced removals from traditional country to reserves, and from reserve to reserve. He argues that adequate land rights legislation in Queensland, should it ever come about, must pay attention to modes of attachment to land developed by Aboriginal groups in the historical process of surviving the impact of institutional segregation.

The Torres Strait Islands have been the traditional home of Melanesian peoples who were also brought under the same administrative control as the Queensland Aboriginal population. Beckett argues that community control has increased over traditional rights in these islands. Although the notion of estate remains valid in the contemporary situation, its significance has altered. The cessation of cult activity and the reorganisation of residential patterns have reduced the importance of traditional groupings, with the consequence that community council control and individual ownership of tracts of land have superseded the traditional system.

Maddock and Layton deal with some of the issues raised by the interaction between anthropology and law in the context of land rights. Maddock discusses the varying social relationships to land in the Northern Territory, the range of Aboriginal English terms applied by Aborigines to these relationships, and the conflicting anthropological and jurisprudential interpretations of Aboriginal rights in land. He argues that because a narrow definition of property rights has been enshrined in the legislation the numbers of people able to benefit as traditional owners may be limited. This has come about, he suggests, partly because of the history of anthropological understandings and partly through the uncritical acceptance of Aboriginal English usage, which refers to members of patrilineal descent groups as 'owners' in certain circumstances, leading to such important interests as those of sister's children in their mother's country being ignored. 'Conflicts of interpretation', he suggests, 'are only to be expected when important material interests turn on the precise way in which ideas and relations are conceived in English legal terms'.

Layton addresses the question of whether the adversary context of a court hearing is the best way to get at a full understanding of traditional land tenure for the assessment of a land claim. He deals with the problems of matching concepts expressed in legal writing with those of a traditionally non-literate society; of making verbal statements of implicit principles; and of getting Aboriginal witnesses to draw attention to features of their own social life that are often more apparent to an observer than a participant.

He explains how apparently conflicting evidence on sites and the identification of estates, such as was put during the Uluru (Ayers Rock) land claim, arise from the personal experiences of Aboriginal witnesses and the criteria they may use in a specific context or in answering a specific question, and how it was only during the hearings themselves that he clarified his own understanding of how the system worked.

MODERN STRUCTURES

The papers in this section focus on problems related to creating appropriate new administrative structures in the context of land rights. This matter became a major issue prior to the passing of the *Aboriginal Land Rights (Northern Territory) Act* 1976 when a number of people questioned the suitability of councils as structures for Aboriginal organisations. Some argued strongly against the statutory establishment of the land councils on the grounds that such structures did not mirror existing social arrangements among Aborigines, would be stressful and an imposition. Others argued that new situations and problems required new solutions even if this meant some strains were created, provided the new structures were flexible, forward looking and related to meeting the demands being placed on Aboriginal society.

Woodward recommended that regional land councils be established throughout Australia and provided with independent legal assistance and administrative help to enable them to formulate their ideas and claims. Victoria was the only State outside the Northern Territory in which a government-recognised and sponsored land council was established for a period, although there are now several other land councils operating without recognition from either a State government or the Commonwealth Government.

Moore documents the history of the Victorian Aboriginal Land Council, a consultative rather than a statutory body, and examines the reasons for its failure to produce the statement of land needs requested by the government. The central problem arose from the Aboriginal desire for self-determination, which seemed so accessible after decades of paternalism and assimilationist policies, but was fundamentally at odds with the concerns of the Commonwealth Government in respect of the Council. The Government's apparent failure to understand Aboriginal aspirations in those heady days of reform thwarted its stated intentions of allowing Aboriginal people in Victoria to ascertain their land needs because it failed to recognise the importance of some autonomy for group action, underlining that land rights are about more than property. This point was lost on the Victorian Government for subsequently, we learn from Bourke's paper, the relevant State Minister argued that the fundamental land rights issue in Victoria was assistance with home ownership. As Bourke emphasises, this is a gross simplification taking no account of the issue of cultural identity. Nor does it recognise that legal incorporation in some form of locale-specific identities is crucially important to Aboriginal people.

Rowell, an anthropologist employed by the Central Land Council, discusses the way in which the great preponderance of males in that Land Council, combined with the prevalence of male anthropologists, have led to the neglect of Aboriginal women's concerns, rights and views. She documents how Aboriginal women claimants have striven for, and partially achieved, a recognition of their distinctive role as claimants and witnesses by presenting evidence in ritual form, winning respect for their gender-specific knowledge and relationships to land.

The genesis of Central Land Council and its efforts to retain autonomy are described from a particular and personal point of view by the solicitor who assisted the process. Eames focuses on aspects of the political relationship of the Land Council to the Commonwealth Government and provides a view of the Aboriginal leadership in Central Land Council at that time.

Bell's 'Politics of protection' is an explanation of the operations of the Northern Territory sacred sites legislation and the protection authority in relation to a case study and its ramifications in the Alice Springs area. In this case, it is shown that the Aranda mode of site protection conflicts with the legislative mode, leading to consequences for Aborigines and local and other levels of government. Some consequences so far have been the introduction of amendments to the legislation, Northern Territory Government requests for compensation from the Commonwealth Government, ultimatums from the Northern Territory Government and constant repetitions by the Aranda of their case and their gestures of goodwill in an attempt to ensure that the area will not be desecrated.

In the final paper of this section, Edwards outlines the history of the Pitjantjatjara Council from the point of view of their minutes secretary and translator. He provides an informed interpretation of the evolution of the Council and the problems the Pitjantjatjara have in understanding the whites' lack of understanding. He emphasises the significance of the process of creating the Council and pushing for land rights in strengthening the resolve and understanding of the people, which is a point that applies to the land rights movement generally.

MINING

Integral to any discussion of land rights is the question of how control over land returned may be preserved in the face of mining proposals and activities. The degree of control hinges, of course, on the nature of the rights Aboriginal people have in relation to minerals and their exploitation. The strongest rights in minerals are held by Aboriginal people in New South Wales, but these are of little significance since they relate to less than 120 square kilometres of land broken up into tiny parcels. The most consequential rights are those in the Northern Territory where the Aborigines, although they do not own the materials, can veto prospecting on their land. Only in 1982 has the opportunity to veto prospecting arisen for during the previous nine years there has been a freeze on new exploration on Aboriginal land. The other State in which Aborigines have substantial rights in minerals is South Australia where, although there is no veto, mining companies have to negotiate with the people to establish mutually satisfactory conditions for prospecting. The papers in this section deal with some of the many issues raised by mining activity and negotiation.

Vachon & Toyne, the first an anthropologist and the second a lawyer, describe two different approaches to dealing with the relations between Aborigines and miners within the context of the economic and political ramifications of transnational mining activity in Australia. They contrast the procedures developed by the Pitjantjatjara Council, for whom they both work, with the approach taken by the Western Australian Government at Noonkanbah. They describe the strengths and weaknesses of the Pitjantjatjara approach to negotiating with mining companies and how they are able to work to protect sites, even on land not held by them. It was the Western Australian Government that chose the path of confrontation in the Noonkanbah affair, for the Pitjantjatjara approach could have operated there to avoid the disruptive confrontation.

The Noonkanbah pastoral lease was acquired by the Yungngora Community in 1976 through the Aboriginal Land Fund Commission in an attempt to reconstruct a viable community life after a long experience of conflict, violence and exploitation in the pastoral industry. Vincent, until recently a solicitor with the Western Australian Aboriginal Legal Service, provides a general history of the conflict between the community, Amax Pty Ltd, and the Western Australian Government. The specific focus of the dispute was protection of places of significance but the more fundamental issue was Aboriginal desire for autonomy and proper consultation, which it is evident cannot be guaranteed in the absence of land rights.

The Alligator Rivers region of the Northern Territory is one area where land rights and legally binding agreements exist. Carroll documents the history of land interests in the region particularly as it relates to uranium mining and the Kakadu National Park, and discusses the main features of the Ranger agreement in an appendix. His paper makes it clear how massive and rapid the developments have been in this area over the last 10 years and how they have greatly influenced Aboriginal people's lives. Matters are now further complicated for Aboriginal people by the need to organise association and settlements between themselves in relation to royalties. It is this issue that Kesteven, a member of the Australian Institute of Aboriginal Studies' Social Impact of Uranium Project, deals with in her paper.

The financial income to Aboriginal groups and individuals from the Ranger and Nabarlek agreements has wide ramifications both socially and politically. The structures for dealing with these monies have been imposed from outside and because two different bodies, each with their own and different agreement, are involved there has been much confusion in respect of rights and expectations. The bureaucratic side of handling the money and the opportunities for acrimony and jealousy have all created a high level of stress. Kesteven discusses these problems, the way people use the money and the consequent effect on existing services. It makes clear the scope of the obstacles in the way of self-management and some of the difficulties which follow from agreement to mining.

Langton introduces her paper with an examination of the findings of various government inquiries and commissions on Aboriginal rights and interests where mining has been proposed on Aboriginal land and concludes with a number of suggestions on how negotiations may be organised to protect Aboriginal interests and avoid debilitating conflicts and the possibility of improper or inappropriate mining activities. She builds her case for a firm set of guidelines for mining companies to observe in relation to dealing with Aborigines, on the basis of a study of the controversial 'agreement' between the Mandangala Community near Turkey Creek in Western Australia and CRA Pty Ltd. Many Aboriginal people affected by the proposal and the 'agreement' perceived improper dealings in the negotiations and felt cheated by the final outcome, so that it was not satisfactory to the Aboriginal people involved nor did it improve relations between Aborigines and other mining companies in the region.

CANADA

The worldwide surge in mineral exploration that began in the early 1960s has resulted in land rights being an issue in Canada and the USA as well as in Australia. The Canadian situation is the closer to our own for historical reasons, even though it is distinguished by the existence of some ill-defined Aboriginal entitlement to the land. Feit's two papers deal with the James Bay Agreement in northern Quebec made between 10 000 Cree and Inuit (the Eskimos' preferred term for themselves) and the Provincial and Federal Government. He provides a detailed account of the history of the negotiations and the intense pressure involved over a 2-year period. His account carries a number of lessons for Aboriginal people in Australia, in particular it underlines the extent of the organisation, research and professional expertise they need to mobilise if they are to eventually draw the States into meaningful negotiations.

Feit's second paper deals with an aspect of the negotiations, the innovative income security programme. This programme, which has some similarities to the Community Development Employment Payments Scheme currently working in many outstations, is directed at getting away from the negative and demoralising aspects of unemployment payments, which keep people hanging around in a passive role, by making it economically feasible for them to pursue certain traditional activities to gain income. For the Cree this takes the form of a daily allowance paid to both men and women who spend more than 90 days a year out bush and at least a further 30 days on fur-trapping and food harvesting related activities in their base village. This allows the people to maintain their hunting activities, which are at the core of the social fabric and personal identity in the face of rising costs that make hunting and trapping impossible.

Dyck discusses the land rights negotiations in Saskatchewan. He goes to the heart of one of the key problems surrounding negotiations: there is always a feeling that one might have been able to do better with a different strategy, prolonging the process or taking a tougher line. An achieved negotiated agreement always carries within it the potential for bitterness. The reasons for this are not difficult to see. Negotiations require tactics and political judgement, both of which are ultimately based on opinions and assessments that can be wrong or could be better. Further, since negotiations involve compromise, they are always open to criticism by some party once finalised. Dyck describes how a key aspect of the Saskatchewan negotiations was the assessment that the climate was getting less favourable, and that if the people did not settle with the Government at this stage they would do worse in the future. He argues that the only substantial erosion of treaty rights that has taken place has been where people were placed under just such a pressure and brought to an agreement on the grounds of it being the last opportunity to gain concessions. This kind of criticism has been levelled at the Pitjantjatjara negotiations in South Australia, where an agreement was reached which denied Aborigines an absolute veto over mining.

It is an easy criticism for people to make since there is never any likelihood of their having to demonstrate another outcome, and it is clearly something any negotiated agreement has to live with as the Cree and Inuit well know. Negotiations also raise the question of how fourth-world people are to make these political judgements when they involve a great deal of social and cultural information about the dominant society they may not have. Such political judgements are difficult enough for people born into a culture to make let alone those outside it, and there is no doubt but that Aborigines in remote Australia are very well aware of the problem. Under such conditions of uncertainty, even about the validity of the judgements and opinions provided by their advisers, they often choose the course suggested by the adviser they know or like best. For the advisers it is not much easier: under conditions of uncertainty when the costs of a wrong decision may be high and when the grounds for making decisions are being suggested for other people, the rational course is a minimax strategy emphasising the least uncertain course of action, which usually ends up being among the more conservative.

The final paper by Hunt allows us a glimpse of how others see us, in this case a Canadian lawyer who has been involved in land rights work, and the image is not unattractive. She comments favourably on the comparative speed of implementation of land rights in the Territory, the amount of land involved and the degree of recognition of aspects of Aboriginal culture as compared with Canada. She observes, however, that by contrast with Canadian peoples the Aborigines are underdeveloped politically, a point that strikes many visitors from North America.

CONCLUSIONS

Shifts of property and the power that goes with it rarely take place without conflict, and the changes associated with land rights are no exception. The papers published here are an initial contribution which deal with land rights from the point of view of people who have worked with or for Aborigines and do not detail the views of those individuals and groups with the greatest reservations about such restitution. Together they document some crucial aspects of land rights in process and will prove valuable in the future when seeking to assess the impact of the boldest and most radical shift in the social and political structure that outback Australia in general and the Northern Territory in particular is likely to experience.

It is not only the discipline of anthropology that will benefit from this review of our present understandings of the issues raised by land rights, but also the legal fraternity and government administrators. It is important to emphasise that these benefits have been achieved within the context of a dialogue between Aboriginal Australians and those others whose involvement has drawn them into this arena.

While the benefits to Aboriginal people have, to a great extent, been identified in these papers, the Aboriginal feedback to the academics and consultants is still insufficient. Although more literature by Aboriginal commentators appears each year, it may be another decade before a truly indigenous critique of the interactive process between Aborigines and their chroniclers becomes established. By that time new issues and questions will have arisen, and it is likely that the information published here will have come to play some part in formulating new options and resolutions for what is inevitably going to be a problem that will occupy the nation for some time to come. In the future problems to do with land management, the political economy of land rights and resource exploitation and the development of land councils will be among the issues drawing attention. Within a decade the full implication of the granting of land rights should be much clearer. Already, however, it is obvious that where substantive rights have been granted, land rights have done more to right the injustices of the past and to bring Aborigines into the mainstream of Australian life, while at the same time helping them to achieve substantial autonomy and self-determination, than any other policy during the past two centuries.

Marcia Langton
Nicolas Peterson

REFERENCES

Hiatt, L. R. (1962) Local organisation among the Australian Aborigines. *Oceania*, 32: 267–286.

Milirrpum v. Nabalco Pty Ltd. and the Commonwealth of Australia (1971) 17 Federal Law Reports.

Myers, F. (1976). *To have and to hold: a study of persistence and change in Pintupi social life.* Unpublished Ph.D. thesis, Bryn Mawr College, USA.

Woodward, A. E. (1973) *Aboriginal Land Rights Commission: first report.* Canberra, Australian Government Publishing Service.

Woodward, A. E. (1974) *Aboriginal Land Rights Commission: second report.* Canberra, Australian Government Publishing Service.

PART ONE

TRADITIONAL PRINCIPLES

1 AMBILINEAL DESCENT AND TRADITIONAL PITJANTJATJARA RIGHTS TO LAND

Robert Layton

The purpose of this paper is to outline aspects of Pitjantjatjara social life which are relevant to the requirements of the *Aboriginal Land Rights (Northern Territory) Act*. A second paper in Part II draws on the material presented here in discussing the problems of documenting and proving a land claim under the Act, exemplified by the Pitjantjatjara case.

The section of the Act most relevant to these papers is that which defines Aboriginal traditional ownership. It states (Section 3, para 3):

> 'traditional Aboriginal owners', in relation to land, means a local descent group of Aboriginals who—
>
> (a) have common spiritual affiliations to a site on the land, being affiliations that place the group under a primary spiritual responsibility for that site and for the land; and
>
> (b) are entitled by Aboriginal tradition to forage as of right over that land

This definition sets out certain criteria to be satisfied in proving a land claim but does not specify how they are to be satisfied. Each claim presents unique problems of analysis in deciding how best to match the Act's criteria against local institutions. The forms of descent by which the land-owning group is recruited are not defined. The group, however recruited, must then be shown to have certain rights and responsibilities vested in it but, at least in the spiritual sphere, the nature of the responsibilities is explicitly left open. Generally speaking, land claims have shown that the right to forage extends over a wider area than that in which the group has overriding spiritual responsibilities and so subparagraph (a) has been the critical one.

ESTATES

Among the Pitjantjatjara rights to land are held by groups of people linked through common descent in ways which will be examined later in the paper. Each group holds rights to an area of land which can be called its *estate* (Stanner, 1965:2). The estate is focused on a base camp, and derives its name either from the reliable water source near that camp or from the central area within which the camp lies. Uluru takes its name from Uluru rock hole above Mutitjulu (Maggie's Spring); Apara—in the Musgraves—from Apara soak in the bed of a rushy creek surrounded by river red gums. Other estates acquire their name from conspicuous hills; Katatjuta ('Many Heads') from the Olgas; Aputjilpi ('Grey Rocks') from the Kelly Hills. I have termed these points the *reference places* for the estates. In addition to a base camp, each estate takes in a number of less reliable, peripheral water sources. To learn the extent of an estate, one can ask for a list of the places that belong to it. Such a list may vary in length, but each one will plot the area included. There is good correspondence between lists provided by different people. Two lists of sites in the Atila (Mt Connor) estate illustrate this. One was provided by Paddy Uluru: Atila is adjacent to the Ayers Rock estate and lay within the subsistence range of people based at Uluru. The second list was given by Toby

Nangina, whose own country is Atila. Both are reproduced in the order they were given. Location of the sites is given in Fig. 1. and through grid references to the 1:250 000 map series.

Paddy Uluru's list

Tjulu (SG 52-8 483853)
Ilanula (SG 52-8 490828)
Marutjara (SG 53-5 535837)
Anari (SG 52-8 494825)
Witapula (SG 52-8 486815)
(collected 8 December 1977 at Witapula)

Toby Nangina's list

Anari
Amarari (SG 52-8 507835)
Ilanula
Tjukulatjara (SG 52-8 493836)
Witapula
Tjulu
Iyarrka (SG 52-8 494851)
Marutjara
Wilpiya (SG 53-5 529876)
(collected 6 March 1978 at Ayers Rock and 31 March 1978 north of Mt Connor)

This way of defining an estate is a convention. In practice, the land between water sources is as important as the water itself, and is often still regularly exploited for food.

Where peripheral sites were shared by two or more groups, then their estates overlap. This emerges clearly when lists of places belonging to adjacent estates are collected. Tjapiya, the most northerly estate in the Musgraves, belongs to both Uluru and Kulpitjata. Patji is shared by Uluru, Kulpitjata and Apara. Paddy Uluru remembered meeting Tjalkalyiri Tiger (now an elderly man) at Patji, when both were children. Tjalkalyiri had come up from Apara 'riding on his father's shoulders'. The hill Yulpartji (SG 52-12 388754) is shared by Apara and Ulkiya. Fig. 2 combines all the information obtained about the ownership of places that can precisely be located on

Fig. 1

Places in Atila Country. Those specified by Paddy Uluru are indicated by squares, those specified by Toby Najina by circles.

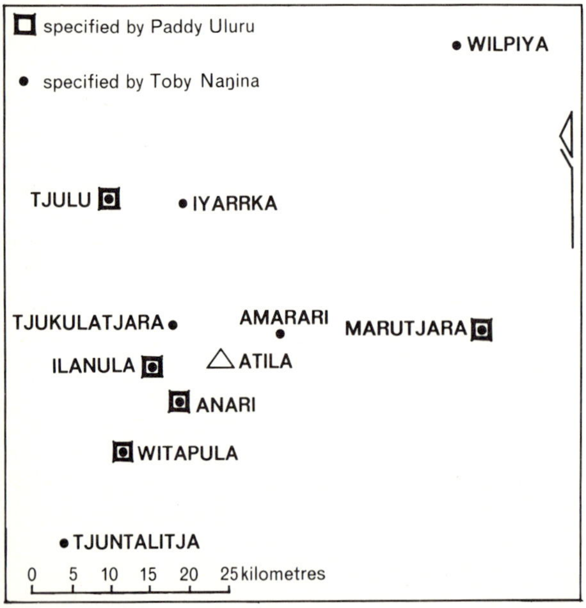

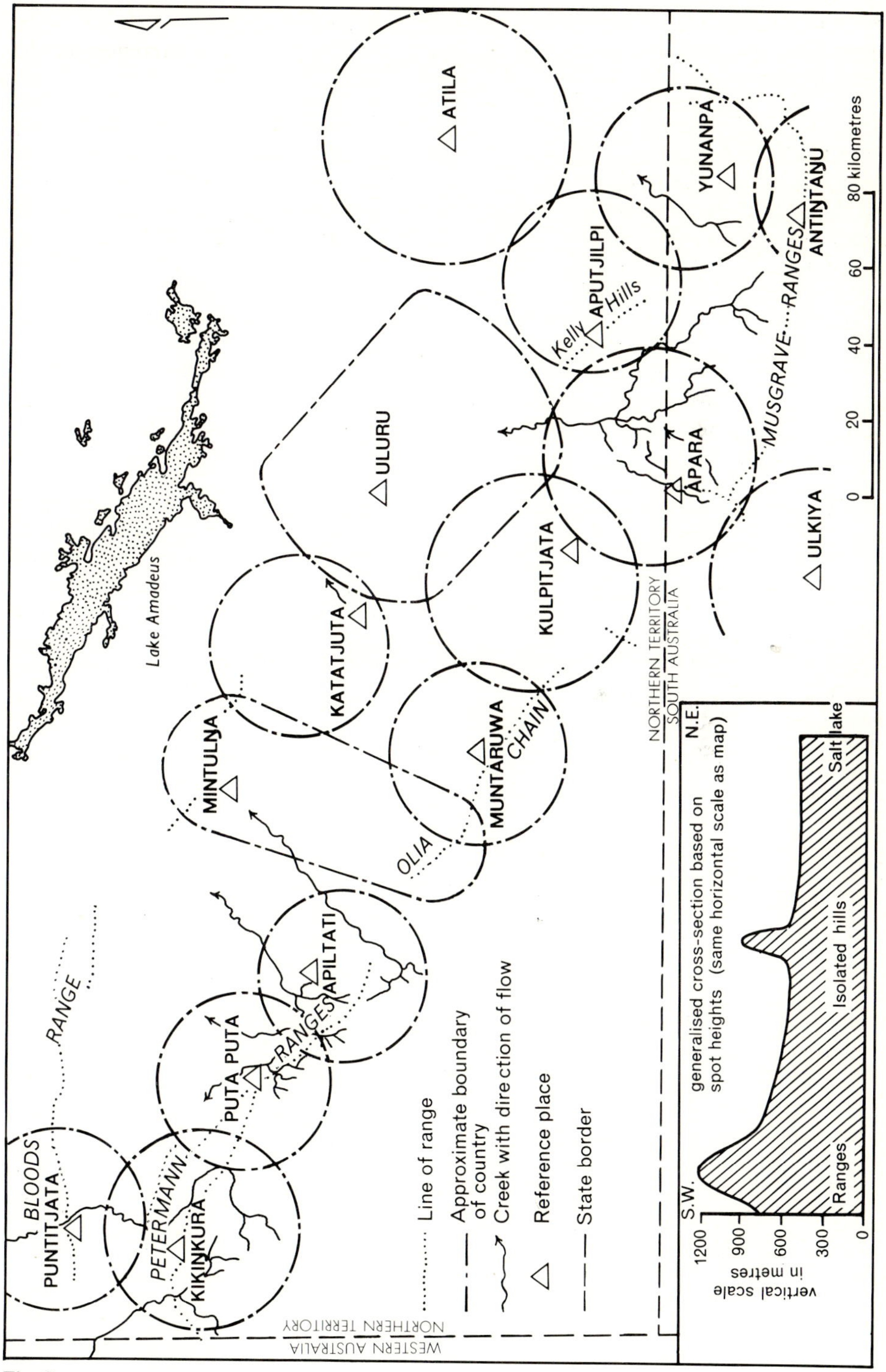

Fig. 2

Approximate boundaries of estates. *Inset:* generalised cross-section based on spot heights.

the map. It shows that overlap on the edges of estates is a common occurrence. This may exist even when the members of the two estates belong to different dialect groups (Pitjantjatjara/Yangkuntjatjara and Yangkuntjatjara/Matuntatjara).

A special comment should be made on the position of Uluru as an estate. Both Harney and Mountford believed that its ownership was divided between two groups. Harney seems to have reached this conclusion after he was told that the south side of Ayers Rock belonged to the 'Shade Side' people, the north side to the 'Sun Side' people (Harney, 1969:76–77). Harney thought that a man inherited membership of one of these two categories from his mother (op cit., p.77) but they are in fact generational categories—that is, all the people in one generation belong to the 'Sun Side', all their children to the 'Shade Side', and their grandchildren to the 'Sun Side' again (cf. Gould, 1969:106; Munn, 1965:7). In men's ritual, members of either category may sit and work together, but it is obvious that any of the descent groups owning an estate will contain representatives of both. Mountford recognised that the categories were generational divisions, although he quotes a different pair of names for them (Mountford, 1977:19,96). He was led to believe that the Rock was divided between two descent groups because he thought the individual's personal dreaming, the one he acquires from his 'birth' place, was something he inherited from his father. One family was thus supposed to all have Mala (Hare Wallaby) totems, the other all Kuniya (Python) totems. It is true that most Mala sites occur on the north side of the Rock and most Kuniya sites on the south, but detailed information on personal totems shows that they are not the exclusive property of groups who trace descent from father to son. Paddy Uluru's Dreaming was Minkiri (Rodent Mouse) from Yunanpa (Mitchell's Knob)—his country of birth, even though he was born during a brief visit by his parents to attend ritual.

Fig. 3
Places at Uluru (outline taken from Northern Territory Reserves Board map).

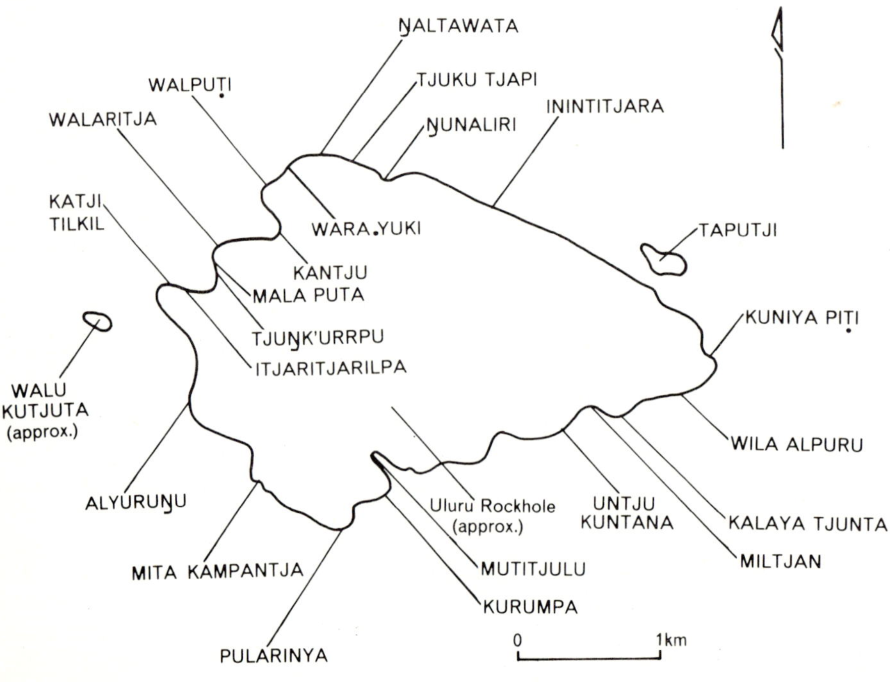

His father's Dreaming was Lungkata (Blue-tongue Lizard) from Ayers Rock. His father's sister had as her Dreaming the *kuniya* who severed the nose of the Liru (poisonous snake) at Mutitjulu, while his older brother had the left-handed mala who speared Tjinta-tjinta, the willy-wagtail at Ininti. Nipper Winmati's Dreaming is *Kuniya,* but his brother Palingka had both mala and kuniya Dreamings; Palingka was Mountford's main informant for the mala story at Uluru (Mountford, 1977:18). A genealogy for the group owning Uluru is given in Fig. 5.

On different occasions I collected lists of places which Paddy and Nipper attributed to the Uluru estate. These show without question that both men considered Ayers Rock as a unity (see Fig. 3).

Paddy Uluru's list

Mutitjulu
Kulpi Turrmil (Kulpi Mutitjulu)
Kurumpa
Alyurungu
Kapi Yularanya Tjukutjuku
(SG 52-8 387862)
Inintitjara
Tjuku Tjapi
Kantju
Walaritja
(collected at Ayers Rock
22 November 1977)

Nipper Winmati's list

Mutitjulu
Kala.ya Tjunta
Wila Alpuru
Kuniya Piti
Taputji
Inintitjara
Tjuku Tjapi
Kantju
Mala Wipu (the climb)
Walu Kutjuta
Mutjunranpa (near Walu Kutjuta)
Lungkata Waru (Mita Kampanitja)
Pularinya
Patji (see above)
Kapi Yularanya Pulka
(SG 52-8 389866)
Kapi Yularanya Tjukutjuku
(collected at Areyonga
23 March 1978)

It is not realistic to draw precise boundaries around estates. In contrast to the Aranda and Warlpiri, Pitjantjatjara people do not recognise exact points at which one leaves one estate and enters another. In effect, each site has a circular zone of bush accessible to exploitation from it, and is linked to other sites by the corridors along which people moved. The point at which bush became inaccessible from a given base would depend on weather conditions, the stamina of the individuals, etc. Other anthropologists who have studied territorial organisation in the desert areas of central Australia have come to similar conclusions (see Berndt, 1972: 182 and O'Connell, 1976: 5, who suggests viewing an estate as a cluster of points in space). Stanner's original discussion of estates also recognised that overlaps might occur (Stanner, 1965: 11-12). Nor do the Pitjantjatjara or Yangkuntjatjara have the ritual 'hand over points' i.e., places where control over song-line changes, characteristic of Warlpiri culture.

Since the existence of reliable water at a base camp is crucial to the persistence of an estate as a discrete unit, estates tend to be concentrated in the ranges, where outcrops yield more rock holes and where creeks capture surface run-off after rain to store in soaks along their normally dry, sandy beds. In all, 9 of the 15 estates in the Ayers Rock region lie along the chain of hills created by the Petermann and Bloods ranges, the Olia Chain and the Musgraves. In the ranges, the centres of estates also lie closer together (see Table 1). Where there is no break in the hills the average distance between reference places is about 30 kilometres. Mintulnga, the last estate in the Petermanns, stretches north to the Kulapurrinya Hills, across intervening sandhills.

Table 1. Distances between adjacent reference points

Reference points	*Distance (km)*
(a) Distance measured along continuous ranges	
Kikingkura–Untulyu	47
Untulyu–Wangkari	27
Kikinghkura–Puta-puta	47
Puta-puta–Piltati	27
Kukpitjata–Apara	30
Yunanpa–Antintangu [a]	20
Average	33.0

Reference points	*Distance (km)*
(b) Distance measured across intervening sand hills	
Kikingkura–Puntitjata [a]	27
Piltati–Mintulnga	52
Mintulnga–Katatjuta	53
Katatjuta–Uluru	30
Uluru–Kulpitjata	50
Muntarurra–Kulpitjata	55
Muntarurra–Katatjuta	45
Apara–Ulkiya	45
Apara–Aputjilpi	45
Aputjilpi–Yunanpa	50
Aputjilpi–Kulpitjata	50
Aputjilpi–Atila	70
Average	47.5

[a]It was not possible to establish with certainty whether Antintangu and Puntitjata were the reference points for estates.

Muntarurra (Butler's Dome) lies in an area where the ranges break down into individual hill masses, while the most isolated reference places are those situated in sandhill country between the ranges and the centre of the Lake Amadeus Basin—Katatjuta, Uluru and Atila. Duguid, writing specifically of the Haast's Bluff area, claimed 'Aboriginal practice was to avoid desert and move from waterhole to waterhole in the Ranges' (Duguid, 1972: 118). This is obviously an oversimplification. Explorers' reports, and the existence of Aboriginal place names around Lake Amadeus, show that the desert sandhills were used; but it is true to say that the ranges were the focus of Aboriginal settlement.

The distribution of reference places is not dictated solely by natural conditions. There is a distinct regularity in their spacing (see Table 1) which shows that Aboriginal behaviour and culture has imposed their own order on the landscape. None the less, the use of a place as a base camp depends on the reliability of its water. During drought some estates had to be abandoned. It was recognised that in harsh seasons people from Katatjuta would move to Uluru, those from Kulpitjata to Apara, and those from Aputjilpi to Atila. It is possible to see here an underlying process through which the culture could adjust to long-term changes in the climate by assimilating one estate to the territory of another. Certain areas, such as Mount Currie (Mulya Iti), half way between Katatjuta and Mintulnga and geologically identical to Uluru, Atila and Katatjuta, suggest themselves as potential reference places, where conditions were more favourable.

Foraging range

Pitjantjatjara and Yangkuntjatjara use the general term *ngura* or, in English, 'country' to refer to estates, but both *ngura* and 'country' are also used to refer to other kinds of territorial unit. In its most specific sense, a *ngura* is a camp. A base camp is a *ngura pulka* (big camp), a peripheral one a *ngura tjukutjuku* (small camp). The term is also used to describe what Stanner called a group's range (Stanner, 1965: 11–12):

> The range was the track or orbit over which the group . . . ordinarily hunted and foraged to maintain life.

In the Ayers Rock region a group's range included its estate, but also took in the territory of neighbouring groups. After rain (*Ukiri Pulkannga* green time, the time after rain) people travelled between each others' base camps, foraging and camping in the intervening bush. To enter neighbouring estates unaccompanied, people had to know the mythology and location of sites in those estates. Older men are well-versed in such knowledge, which they develop and express in ceremonies, but beyond a certain point one would reach 'foreign' country out of one's regular range. Unless authorised and accompanied by local people, one would not travel or forage in such an area. This seems to be what some of the Kikingkura men meant when they told Harney they could not stay at Uluru until admitted to local ritual knowledge (Harney, 1969: 53; 'Windralga' is Harney's spelling of *Wintalka*). During hearings for the land claim on country around Ayers Rock, one local man was asked in court whether someone from Indulkana could camp at Uluru. His reply, as translated by Daniel Vachon, acting as the interpreter, was that 'he (the visitor) would be embarrassed, and because he would be embarassed he (the local man) would teach him the Dreaming' (transcript of evidence, p. 612).

A land-owning group's range is referred to as *ngura kaputu*. This expression was first recorded by Munn in her work with Pitjantjatjara men whose estates lie in the Petermann Ranges (Munn, 1965: 3) and more recently has been obtained by Vachon from Pitjantjatjara men at Indulkana (Vachon, personal communication). Munn understood *kaputu* to mean 'round' or 'closed' while Vachon interprets it as a general term for plant foods. Speaking in English, people sometimes refer to their group's traditional range as its 'run', an analogy with the movement of cattle on a pastoral station.

Fig. 4 illustrates the ranges of people from Uluru and Kikungkura, as specified by Paddy Uluru and Leslie Mintjantji, both men who grew up before the 1930s. Both pointed out that to attend ritual, groups would travel further. Leslie spoke of walking from Kikingkura to Apara, while Paddy's father attended ceremonies at Yunanpa (where Paddy was born) and Ilturr, south of the Musgraves.

Rights and responsibilities of the land-owning group

An estate is thought of as a unit with reference to the named places that fall within it (see discussion of Uluru and Atila above). These sites lie on the ancestral tracks which pass through the area. Each estate contains sections of two or more major tracks, every one associated with a string of sites recording incidents in the ancestor's travels. There are song verses related to these sites, which are drawn from the *inma* cycles retelling each ancestral saga. Vachon, who recently carried out research at Indulkana (a Pitjantjatjara community across the South Australian border), recorded the phrase *ngura inmanguru,* or 'country from the *inma',* as a specific term for an estate (as opposed to *ngura pulka, ngura kaputu,* etc., referring to areas of land defined in other ways). Among the major traditional rights and responsibilities of the land-owning group are the maintenance and transmission of the sacred knowledge belonging to their estate. Such knowledge relates to the collectivity of ancestral beings who entered and structured the estate. At Uluru, for instance, it includes the Mala and Kuniya; at Atila the Wati Nyinnga (Ice Men) and Kungarangkalpa ('Seven' Sisters). It is incorrect, therefore, to think of the land-owning group having a single totem or supposing itself to be descended from a single mythological ancestor. While some senior men may have particularly profound knowledge of the lore associated with a specific track, the whole group shares responsibility for the total body of knowledge belonging to the estate. When *inma* are performed at collective ceremonies, members of the group start the singing of the verses belonging to their country. It is the group's responsibility to transmit this knowledge to its children, and to instruct members of neighbouring

Fig. 4
Sites on approximate limits of regular foraging movements for people living at Kikingkura and Uluru in traditional times.

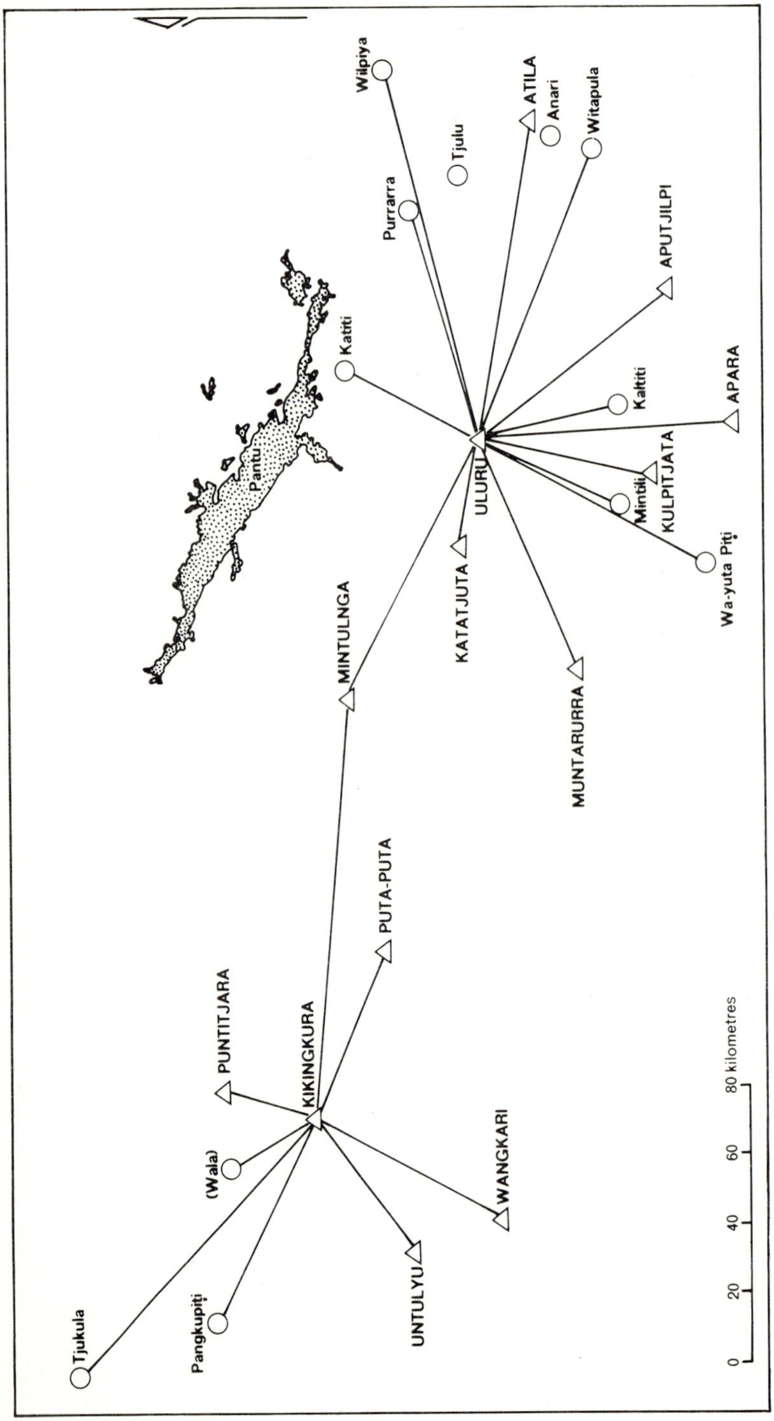

estates. It is also its responsibility to protect sites to which access is forbidden to women or children, and to prevent revelation of sacred knowledge to the uninitiated. Traditionally, serious offences might result in execution. There was an incident Paddy Uluru knew of, which Mountford also recorded, when a few generations ago a woman was speared for picking wild figs in a sacred area at the foot of Ayers Rock (see Mountford, 1977). If the owners failed to exact punishment they would themselves be at risk for ignoring their responsibilities. Ritual knowledge is still jealously guarded today and it continues to provide the core of Aboriginal identity within a living culture. Women have their share of knowledge, which relates to the same ancestral traditions but which develops different aspects and events within the narrative.

Children begin to acquire their part in the group's responsibility when they are old enough to be initiated. It would, however, be wrong to see initiation as itself admission to the adult knowledge guarded by the local group. Initiation is more of a general step which qualifies one to begin learning deeper levels of knowledge, not just in one estate but in both mother's and father's groups, as well as in estates around that where the child has grown up. Gould's use of the term 'Cult Lodge', when he writes of Western Desert initiation, a term he borrowed from Meggitt's work on the Warlpiri, could be misleading (see Gould, 1969:109). A Pitjantjatjara man acquires a progressively wider knowledge of the traditions throughout his area as his seniority grows.

From the 1930s many families in the Ayers Rock region left their own estates to live for part of each year on a mission or cattle station. This did not destroy the continuity of traditional knowledge. People found time to travel back to their own estates by camel or on foot with their children. Many young adults now recall such expeditions as the start of their traditional learning. One of Paddy Uluru's sons described how he had first seen Ayers Rock when, as a boy, he came up from the Ernabella mission with his family: 'What's that big sandhill?', he had asked his father as Uluru became visible above the horizon. 'That's my country', his father replied.

During court hearings for the land claim, a number of people spoke of showing their estate to their children, and teaching them its traditions. 'They will come up and they learn the place, and then with their memory that will give them some reason to come and live here . . . you show a person the country, a nice looking place, and they will feel in their hearts that they want to come and live here' (Vachon translating Tjalkalyiri Tiger, transcript of hearings, p.524). 'The old men bring them (their children) up to love the country; to know the country' (Bill Okai, transcript, p. 558). One of the senior women, when asked, insisted 'we train the children too' (Tirnpula, transcript, p. 689).

In some instances, men assumed the responsibility of adopting and teaching the sons their wives had had by white men, and these sons are now full members of the Aboriginal community.

The rights of members of neighbouring estates

The owners of an estate are not the only people with a traditional interest in its ritual knowledge or natural resources. Pitjantjatjara and Yangkuntjatjara people are most resistant to the idea that someone's rights might be confined to his own estate or that the estate's owners should have an exclusive prerogative. This view was forcefully expressed to members of the South Australian working party studying land rights among Pitjantjatjara communities across the border, and resulted in the South Australian Government of the time drafting legislation very different to the Act applied in the Northern Territory.

A major force mitigating the estate's exclusivity is the network of ancestral tracks. While the estate draws together sections of several tracks, each track (*Iwarra*) has the complementary effect of linking sites in a series of estates. Knowledge of tracks extends for many kilometres and gives members of those estates a common interest in maintaining the ancestral tradition. They should attend ceremonies performed in each others' countries and join together in singing the *inma*. There were, for instance, a number of occasions when I heard men from Kikingkura and Uluru sing together the *inma* verses describing the Mala tradition. Those verses describing the actions of the Wintalka men were begun by representatives of the Kikingkura group, those related to events at Ayers Rock by the Uluru men. Such a common interest is certainly recognised over a distance of up to 160 kilometres. On a number of occasions when the fathers of now-elderly men took up permanent residence in their wives' estates, this has been justified in terms of a common ancestral track which linked the couple's countries. The fathers of Pompy Wanampi and Pompy Douglas provide examples. Both left estates in the Petermanns to settle at Apara in the Musgraves. If there were no owners available to perform the songs of a certain estate, then this responsibility would pass to the members of an adjacent one on the same track. Were the group owning an estate to die out, it was said that people from an adjacent country on the same track would take over responsibility for the appropriate *inma* verses.

A second factor which reduces the autonomy of the land-owning group is the practice of regularly foraging over adjacent estates, and the requirement that adults who do so first know the traditions of those neighbouring countries. Members of neighbouring estates will tend to meet and interact at ceremonies even where they do not share a single ancestral track. Senior men are proud, and are acknowledged to possess an outstanding knowledge of all the *inma* in their area. After Paddy Uluru's death the task of completing his sons' teaching passed to an *Atila* man, and at the time of the land claim hearings it was he who initiated many of the Mala verses.

Composition of the land-owning group

Estate was the term Stanner used in his analysis of Aboriginal territorial organisation, to describe 'the traditionally recognised locus . . . of some kind of patrilineal descent group' (Stanner, 1965:2). Although the Pitjantjatjara and Yangkuntjatjara recognise named areas of land that correspond to estates, the owning descent group is not exclusively patrilineal. While the typical pattern in Australia is for everyone to inherit membership of their father's land-owning group, in the Ayers Rock region the group which holds an estate is made up of some people who have inherited membership through their father, and some who have inherited membership through their mother. At birth, each individual has rights in the land-owning groups of both parents, but during his or her lifetime they come to exercise these rights predominantly in one or the other group, and it will be membership of the selected group which the individual transmits to his or her children. People speak of choosing, *ngurkantjangkuku* (see especially transcript of evidence for land claim, p.472). This gives rise to ambilineal rather than patrilineal descent.

Generally Pitjantjatjara or Yangkuntjatjara children join the group that owns the estate in which they grow up. One example can be taken from the Aboriginal evidence (transcript, p. 699):

> Mr Hiley: Stanley, I think you said that your sister Nellie — her country is Apara . . . why is her country Apara?
> *Stanley Kumintjara:* Her mother took her there and she grew up there in Apara.

(There is another example on p.700.)

If they are brought up in their father's estate, they exercise and transmit rights in his group; if they grow up in the mother's estate then it is her group to which they are assimilated. Noel Wallace has also recorded cases in which a younger brother participated in his mother's group to avoid a position of lower ceremonial rank in the father's group. His finding has been that where a father has an eldest daughter rather than a son, then the daughter's sons may take precedence over a younger brother's son in seniority within the group (unpublished notes, quoted with permission). There are also cases where a child has joined an estate belonging to a more distant relative, but generally adjacent to that of one or other of the parents (see Table 2). A number of senior claimants gave evidence during the land claim that they belonged to their mother's land-owning group and had transmitted that membership to their children (see transcript, e.g., pp. 561, 703,704).

Since the ritual responsibilities which belong to the land-owning group can only be fully exercised by adults, children's membership of the group is based to some extent on their right to undertake such responsibilities *when they grow up*. Mr Lawrie, QC appearing for the Traditional Owners in the land claim, used the term 'inchoate rights' to describe the position of children. After initiation, the individual will start to assume his responsibilities. The community recognises his position by allowing him to do so.

Even if a person joins his mother's land-owning group, he continues to have rights and responsibilities toward his father's estate. Sometimes, if the father had moved a great distance at marriage and if drought or early death prevented him taking a son back to his (the father's) country before he died, the son may lose these rights—but it is something the son regrets, should it occur. Other members of the father's descent group may take over the dead man's task of instruction. It is possible, then, for an adult to belong to both his mother's and father's groups, but if he lives and raises his children in his mother's estate he is unlikely to pass membership of his father's group on to his children. The emphasis on the value of a man keeping links with his father's estate gives the ambilineal descent system a bias toward patrilineality. If he can, it appears that a man will try to continue living in his father's estate (see Table 2). Those land-owning groups, like the one holding Kikingkura, which are largely patrilineal take a pride in the fact. It seems to be forces like major droughts, or local overpopulation, which in many cases cause people to assume membership of their mother's group. Some anthropologists who have written about the Pitjantjatjara have described the desert system as being 'patrilineal with exceptions', but there are a number of reasons why this seems inadequate (see discussion following).

Table 2. Transmission of membership to land-owning group

Transmission	*No.*	*%*
Through father	79	69
Through mother	23	20
Through more distant relatives:		
parent's sibling	9	8
grandparents (not via parent)	3	3
Total	114	100

During hearings for the land claim many questions were asked of Aboriginal witnesses to try and establish whether it was enough for a person to have inherited rights to membership of a land-owning group through a parent, or whether he had to have taken up those rights to count as a member of the group. It was clear that people recognised a distinction between children who had not yet returned to the parent's estate and those who had; but the witnesses insisted that even those children who had not returned still had a duty to learn, and the older members of the group a duty to teach them about the estate. The following exchange illustrates this (transcript, pp. 462-63):

> *Mr Eames:* If those children did not come back, if they stayed out at Hermannsberg, would they properly belong to Katatjuta then?

Peter Bulla: Yes
Mr Eames: That is if they had not come back, if they had not learnt?
Peter Bulla: Yes. He do not learn but he must know.
Mr Eames: If they do not learn, what does that mean. . .?
Peter Bulla: Then family could take a stick (to make them learn?) what their idea of Katatjuta.

Bill Okai, when asked to comment on Peter Bulla's evidence, said (transcript, p. 557): 'Those children who go and live somewhere else, they still think of Katatjuta and Ayers Rock. A long time ago a person's mother or father might have taken them away from this area but they will still think about this place as being their country from their mothers and fathers.'

Susan Woenne in her evidence, distinguished between *kulira* (understanding) the word that would describe having been taught about a country without visiting it, and *nyinti* (knowing) that would describe first hand knowledge of an estate; but she denied that a person who only possessed the former would have lost their rights of ownership. The possibility is always open for them to return, even when already adult, to become *nyinti* (transcript, p. 954). Only after their death could a person be said definitely never to have taken up their rights in an estate. While a person will generally exercise his rights primarily in one estate, and hence transmit those rights to his children, he therefore continues to hold rights (which he will generally not transmit) in the estate of his other parent. The determination of which estate the person will choose is, moreover, a gradual process.

Not all members of the group holding an estate can always trace common descent with one another through known ancestors. For this reason, it is preferable to talk of the land-owning group as a *clan* made up of several (1-4) lines of descent. All members of the group address each other as if they were related, calling members of the same generation 'brother' and 'sister', and members of the generation below 'son' and 'daughter'. Their unity is defined by their joint ownership of the estate, so that they collectively form what the Northern Territory Land Rights Act calls a 'local descent group'. The component lines of descent can be said to be linked by putative (or imputed) common descent.

Figs 5-9 illustrate the composition of the clans holding estates in the vicinity of Uluru. Where the same individual appears on two genealogies they are identified by key letters. Generally speaking, people can only remember specific ancestors to the level of the grandparents of senior living men, and even at this level there appears to be selection—people who had no children, or whose children joined other clans, are unlikely to be remembered. Each genealogy thus takes the shape of a pyramid contracting to the key ancestors who define links between living members. Beyond this, actual ancestors are absorbed into the legendary community of the Creation period. It is, in fact, a tenet of Pitjantjatjara religion that on death, the individual becomes the personal Dreaming he incarnated.

The average population of the land-holding group is about 30, ranging from 8 members of a single family in the case of Aputjilpi to 45 members of seven families in the case of Apara. The average area of the estate is about 15 000 square kilometres; half the average area of the seven nearest cattle stations (as recorded on the Northern Territory pastoral lease map; I have included the small Middleton Ponds lease to balance the vast size of Erldunda). The traditional population density may therefore be assessed at approximately one person per 50 square kilometres.

Other writers' conclusions on the basis of affiliation to countries

Other anthropologists who have worked with groups from the Petermanns have presented patrilineal descent as the principal, but not the only determinant of local group membership. Yengoyan reported (in Berndt, 1970: 83), on the basis of fieldwork between September 1966 and March 1967 with 'tribal elders who formerly inhabited the Petermann and Rawlinson Ranges', that:

> The resident group was loosely organised and flexible as regards membership. Yet in each case a patrilineal core of kinsmen was recognized. It was this core which possessed and transmitted a detailed knowledge of the area of exploitation for each group.

Against this generalisation must be set his specific comments on Malu Piti (Mt Davies), which had recently become a centre of chrysoprase mining, causing a variety of people to claim traditional rights to the country (op. cit., p. 84):

> One of the factors is that the Mt. Davies country belongs to only those individuals who can claim either one of the following factors:
> 1 born in the Mt. Davies area
> 2 have a malupiti dreamtime (sic; i.e. a malu dreaming)
> 3 kinship relations with one who is from the area.

Yengoyan explains that the last criterion frequently refers to matrilineal or affinal links. Notice the patrilineal descent is not mentioned here. Munn writes of the Petermanns that 'the basic type of local group consisted of a relatively small number of male and female agnates' (Munn, 1965:5). She cites the case of a place called *Utantja,* 'just south of the Petermanns and slightly east of the Hull River' (Munn, op. cit., pp. 3, 5):

> I was able to identify 7 adults born before the exodus from the Petermanns (to Areyonga etc.) who claimed Utantja as their ancestral estate. . . These people are related to each other as full and half siblings and as patrilineal parallel cousins. At Kikingkura, however, the local group consisted of a more complex amalgam of agnatic links, the members of the different units being linked by ties of *classificatory* kinship. These different 'families' seem to have moved into Kikingkura at various times. The classificatory ties defines between them were not all patrilineal. [Munn's emphasis.]

One instance concerned a man whose father was from a site southwest of the Petermanns, whose 'father remained after marriage with his wife's family at Kikingkura'. Although I did not meet this individual it is clear that Munn is describing the same process as that illustrated above through the cases of Pompy Wanampi and Pompy Douglas. It seems possible that the complexity Munn saw in her data may have resulted from her inclusion of countries on the fringe of Kikingkura proper, such as Untulyu. None the less, both her observations and those of Yengoyan underline the error of treating patrilineal descent as the sole determinant of local affiliations. Munn (op. cit., p. 5) writes of the man whose father married into the Kikingkura area:

> [He] is said to have grown up at Kikingkura without becoming familiar as well with his father's country. For this reason, informants explained, he had no rights in his father's country but was considered a member of the Kikingkura land-owning group. . . Pitjantjatjara claim that rights over a country can be maintained only if the individual concerned is familiar with the area, this is to say, he has spent some time there.

Myers (1976:320) has more recently referred to the significance of residence as a determinant of the exercise of rights among the Pintupi: prolonged residence in a country, he writes, 'makes one a countryman of sorts, and people are said to be "from" the country they are most likely to return to, especially during those periods when only major waterholes retain water'.

Berndt, who works with the hypothesis that patrilineal descent determines land rights throughout the Western Desert, has some difficulty applying this explanation to

Fig. 5
Uluru genealogy.

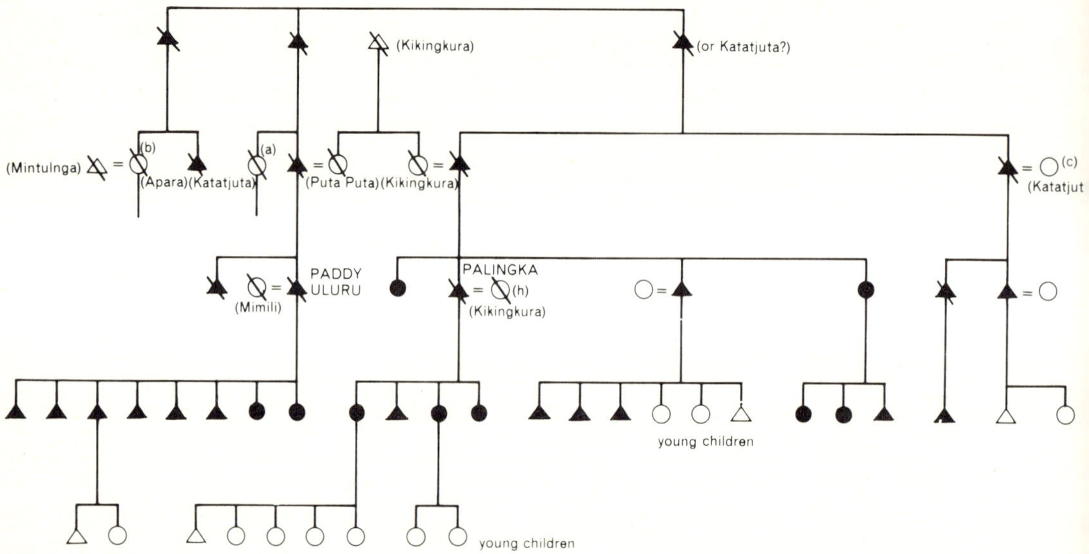

Fig. 6
Katatjuta genealogy.

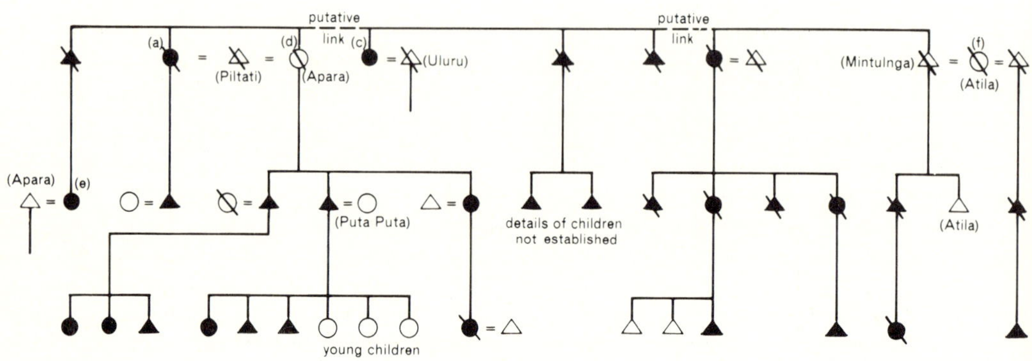

Fig. 7
Atila genealogy.

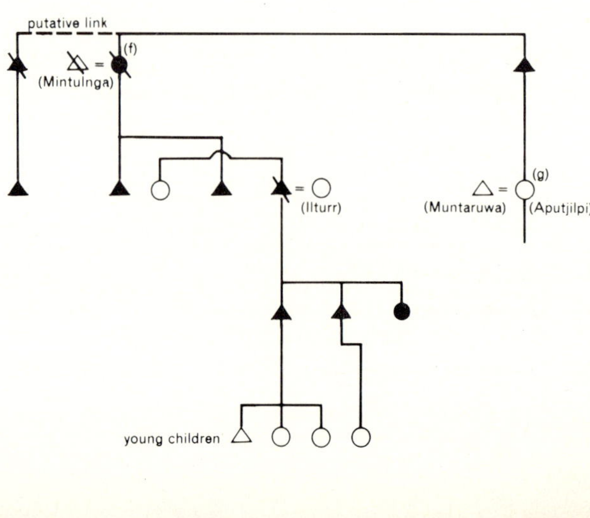

Fig. 8
Apara genealogy.

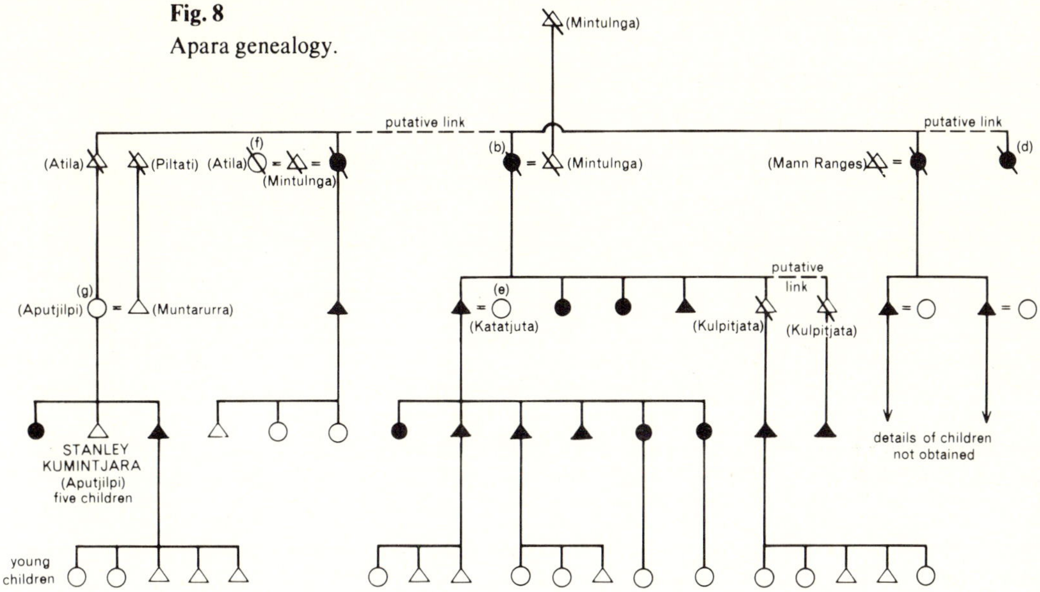

Fig. 9
Kikingkura genealogy.

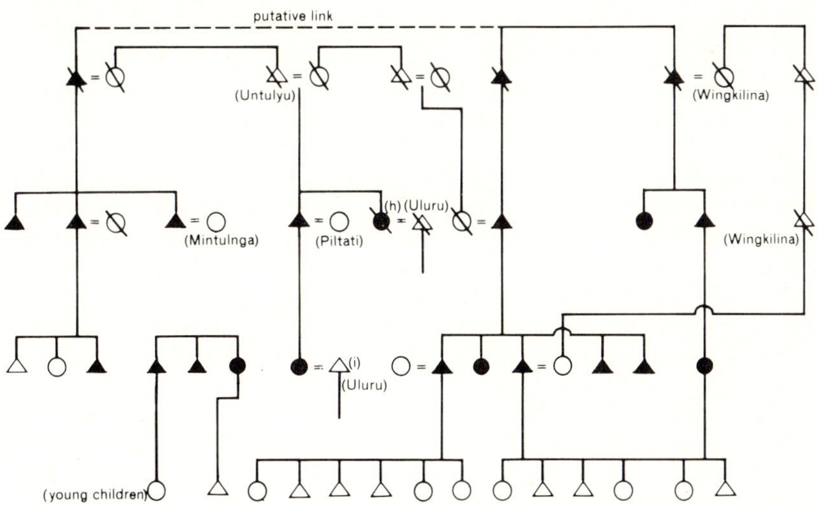

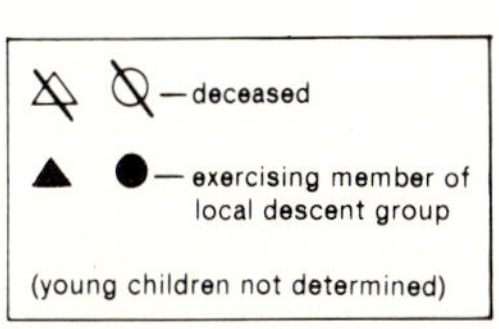

his ethnographic material. In the only example discussed by Berndt (1972:192), he concludes:

> What we are actually faced with are four local groups [i.e., not one patrilineal descent group] focussed on Luwana. . . . However Luwana is regarded as 'one country'.

In an earlier account of the social systems of Western Desert tribes (including the Pitjantjatjara and Yangkuntjatjara), Berndt (1959:96) documents the importance attached, in Aboriginal statements of the norm, to affiliation by birth, although taking the patrilineal recruitment of groups as axiomatic.

> He writes: in this whole region there is a *bias* toward patrilineal descent, and a desire that a child should *be born at or near a particular sacred site,* or constellation of such sites, with which his father is closely associated, *to facilitate inheritance* of his totemic affiliations [my emphasis].

At times he writes (op. cit., p. 98) as though affiliation by birth and by patrilineal descent tended to be synonymous: 'the "country" in which a person is born is in a sense unique' (although linked with other countries on the ancestral track), 'and is connected (ideally) with all members of the patrilineal descent group'. Elsewhere on the same page, he is more emphatic: 'Those persons united by common patrilineal descent, who share a given site or constellation of sites, constitute the local group, that is the land-owning group'. But later this is again qualified: 'Because local groups have been more of less constantly on the move, in many cases, both past and present, the important point seems to have been birth along the cult totem track of the father's totem, rather than at the specific waterhole or patrilineal local group ground.'

While one might take the view that the Pitjantjatjara Yangkuntjatjara system is a patrilineal one whose perfect operation is thwarted by the harsh conditions of the Western Desert, there are a number of features in the social system which suggest rather the emergence of a distinctive system exhibiting positive structural adaptations to the desert context. The kinship terminology of the Pitjantjatjara is one in which blood relatives in one's own generation on both the mother's and father's side (the children of one's parents siblings) are classified as brother or sister; the principle category to which they stand opposed is that of brother- or sister-in-law, applied to relatives by marriage in one's own generation. The terminology does not distinguish relatives in the father's line from relatives in the mother's line (see Scheffler, 1978: 90–91 and Rose 1965:49), it therefore differs from kinship terminologies of Arnhem Land and the Kimberleys (see, e.g., Warner, 1958:48 and Blundell & Layton, 1978:232). The absence of individual names for each of the groups in which ownership of land is vested further distinguishes the Ayers Rock region from Northern Australia (see, e.g., Warner, 1958:40; Fox et., al., 1977:278; Blundell & Layton, 1978:237). The Pitjantjatjara do not possess patrimoieties or the dependant ritual offices of 'owner' and 'manager'. Nor does it seem plausible to attribute the system described here to white contact since genealogical material shows the fathers of men now in their seventies or over taking up permanent residence in their wives' estates, and the sons inheriting and transmitting membership in their mother's estates. Intense contact did not begin until the 1930s.

Particularly relevant to the question of ideology and ecology is Peterson's paper (1979) discussing points in common between Australian Aboriginal and Kalahari hunter-gatherer cultures. Here, the !Kung San system of inheritance to rights in land is summarised as ambilateral (op. cit., pp. 115, 117):

> Ownership rights to a *n!ore* (estate) are usually acquired from either the father or mother. According to both Marshall and Weissner, a person becomes an owner of the *n!ore* in which the parents are established and with which they are identified.

Peterson develops a comparison made earlier in the Warlpiri claim book (Peterson et al., 1978: 4–7) between Aboriginal cultures in rich and poor environments. It is argued that an ideology of patrilineal descent masks variations in group composition that place desert Aborigines closer to the San than might otherwise be supposed (Peterson, 1979: 118). Figures quoted by Peterson (op. cit., pp. 115–17) suggest that among the San succession to the mother's and father's estates are more evenly balanced than among the Pitjantjatjara-Yangkuntjatjara, and that more people are assimiliated to an estate different to that of either parent. None the less, it appears that while the Warlpiri sustain an ideology of patrilineal descent which is translated into behaviour in the ritual offices of 'owner' and 'manager', etc., Pitjantjatjara-Yangkuntjatjara culture has similarities with the San even at the ideological level. Myer's work suggests that this may also be true among the Pintupi.

ACKNOWLEDGEMENTS

The material contained in this paper is largely taken from the Ayers Rock claim book (Layton & Rowell, 1979) and from evidence given during the course of hearings of the claim on vacant Crown land adjacent to the Rock. I would like to acknowledge the stimulation I received from working with the Central Land Council during this case, particularly in discussions of the material with Rod Hagen and Daniel Vachon. The genealogies presented here are the result of joint research carried out by myself, Meredith Rowell and Vachon. It will be clear from the paper that both Vachon and Noel Wallace have been generous in passing on the results of their own research. I think, however, that we have all reached slightly different conclusions about how the Pitjantjatjara system 'really works', and the analysis given here presents my own opinions. Many of the bush trips made to locate and learn about sites were carried out jointly with Bill Edwards, who was then the Uniting Church minister at Amata. I am especially grateful for the amount of time he was able to spare to make these joint expeditions and his help in collecting and understanding the material.

I would also like to acknowledge the long hours senior Aboriginal men spent with me explaining aspects of their culture and taking me to sites. Paddy Uluru, Nipper Winmati, Pompy Wanampi, Pompy Douglas, Toby Nangina, Bill Okai, Peter Bulla, Stanley Kumintjara and Charlie Wiliyati were especially helpful.

REFERENCES AND NOTES

Berndt, R.M. (1959) The concept of the tribe in the western desert of Australia. *Oceania*, **30**, 81–107.

Berndt R.M. (ed.) (1970) *Australian Aboriginal Anthropology*. Perth, University of Western Australia Press.

Berndt, R.M. (1972) The Walmadjeri and Gugadja. In: M.G. Bicchieri (ed), *Hunters and Gatherers Today*. New York, Holt, Rinehart.

Blundell, V. and Layton, R. (1978) Marriage, myth and models of exchange in the west Kimberleys. In: J. Specht and J.P. White (eds) *Trade and Exchange in Oceania and the Pacific*.

Duguid, C. (1972) *Doctor and the Aborigines*. Adelaide, Rigby.

Fox, R.W. et. al. (1977) *Ranger Uranium Environmental Inquiry, Second Report*. Canberra: Australian Government Publishing Service.

Gould, R.A. (1969) *Yiwara: foragers of the Australian desert*. London, Collins.

Harney, W.E. (1969) *To Ayers Rock and Beyond*. Adelaide, Rigby (1st ed. 1963).

Layton, R. and Rowell, M. (1979) *Ayers Rock–Mount Olga National Park and Lake Amadeus Traditional Land Claim: Claim Book*. Alice Springs, Central Land Council.

Mountford, C.P. (1977) *Ayers Rock: its people, their beliefs and their art*. Adelaide, Rigby (1st ed. 1965).

Munn, N.D. (1965) *A report on field research at Areyonga*. Australian Institute of Aboriginal Studies document 65/280.

Myers, F.R. (1976) *To Have and to Hold: a study of persistence and change in Pintubi social life.* PhD. Thesis, Bryn Mawr.

O'Connell, J.F. (1976) *Report on investigations of Alyawara land claims.* Department of Prehistory, Research School of Pacific Studies, Australian National University.

Peterson, N. (1979) Territorial adaptations among desert hunter-gatherers: the !Kung and Australians compared. In: P.C. Burnham and R.F. Ellen (eds), *Social and Ecological Systems.* London, Academic Press, 111–29.

Rose, F.G.G. (1965) *The Wind of Change in Central Australia.* Berlin, Akademie Verlag.

Scheffler, H.W. (1978) *Australian Kin Classification.* Cambridge University Press.

Stanner, W.E.H. (1965) Aboriginal territorial organisation. *Oceania,* **36**, 1–26.

Warner, W.L. (1958) A Black Civilization. New York, Harper & Row.

2

SOCIAL STRUCTURE AND USE OF SPACE AMONGST THE LARDIL[1]

Paul Memmott

The Lardil people are a group of Australian Aborigines who reside in the North Wellesley Islands in the south of the Gulf of Carpentaria. They occupied Mornington Island (*Kununa*), and two smaller islands, Sydney Island (*Langungantji*), and Wallaby Island (*Lingungantji*). Their traditional lifestyle of hunting, fishing and gathering was interrupted in 1914, when they began to concentrate in a mission settlement on the south-west end of Mornington Island.

This paper deals largely with the period of time just prior to this contact, namely, *c.* 1900–1914. At that time the Lardil classified themselves into social categories using a variety of criteria. A number of these social categories were accompanied by a spatial definition, and such association of a group with a space is referred to here as a sociospatial or sociogeographic unit. People identified themselves and each other as belonging to such units. They carried out repeated patterns of behaviour in these spatial domains, which demonstrates how social properties were attached to specific places in organised ways. This paper aims to elucidate the nature of the sociospatial structure of the Lardil at a number of interrelated levels.

First a brief examination is made of the Lardil as a tribe, and the extent of their tribal lands is defined. This is followed by a description of a class of sociospatial subdivisions of the tribe, that of patriclans and their coastal countries. Analysis is made of the mechanisms of (a) patriclan leadership; (b) rights of resource control in countries, and shifts in such controls; and (c) shifts in country boundaries. On a larger scale than that of patriclans is the division of the Mornington Island coastline into four segments, each comprised of a number of patriclan countries. Analysis of these four sociogeographic units deals with the problems of understanding their social and environmental meaning, given certain dynamic properties of their spatial definition. Finally, the sociospatial structure of Lardil camps is considered.

Before commencing examination of the social phenomena it is necessary to provide a short description of the physical environment of the North Wellesley Islands, so that some cultural properties can be later correlated with it. This is done using the concept of 'land system' units. These are characteristic landscapes produced by the interaction of soil, climate, flora, fauna, and sea. The dominant land systems[2] of the north Wellesley Islands consist of:

- Several landscape units of tussock grasslands[3], open low grassy eucalypt woodlands and open and closed scrublands based on the Mornington plateau[4]—a gently undulating formation, the surface being eroded from the lateritic sediment below. These units comprise what can be termed 'the interior land systems' as distinct from the coastal land systems which have been derived from far more recent activity of the sea and other forces.

- Open tidal flats, consisting of soil carried from the plateau, sorted alluvially and deposited as a mixture of sand and silt. These are located above the normal high tide level but are inundated at times of high spring tides in conjunction with tidal surges generated by summer cyclones. The flats are dissected by tidal estuaries with mangrove communities on their banks. Downdrift from the estuary mouths, mangroves may also be found on sheltered parts of the coastline as low closed forests.

- The sand-based land systems, comprised of sand ridges, sand dunes and sand platforms. Some coastal parts of these units have been lithified to form beach rock platforms, outcrops and cliffs. The oldest sand platforms support low and tall woodlands with some vine thickets, and contain many broadleafed plant species which yield edible fruits and nuts. The water-table rises sufficiently high in places for wells to be dug by the Aborigines.
- The sand-based coastal systems are interspersed with sections of laterite cliffs, boulder beaches, off-shore wave-cut platforms and reefs produced by the destructive action of the sea on the exposed edges of the Mornington plateau.

The Lardil classify their island land systems into two categories, using the terms 'inside country' and 'outside country'. The 'inside country' consists of the interior land systems (see the first land system described above), whilst the 'outside country' consists of the coastal land systems (see the second, third and fourth land systems described above). It will be seen later that the coastal forms contain the favoured camping sites as well as a concentration of geographic and magico-religious properties.

THE LARDIL AS A 'TRIBE'

The Lardil people traditionally associated with one another and shared a common culture. They could rightly be called a tribe according to a recent set of criteria formulated by Turner (1976:180–81). They shared the following characteristics.

- They spoke a common language called *Letil*[5], which differed from that of their neighbours on Denham and Forsyth islands and the South Wellesley Islands.

  They occupied a well-defined common territory, exploiting it for their economic needs. The physical nature of islands allows such a precise geographical-based unit to be defined. The Appel Channel forms the boundary between the Lardil territory and neighbouring tribal group, the Yangkal. All of the Wellesley Islands to the north-west of this channel are claimed by the Lardil, with the exception of the Bountiful Islands. (Refer to Fig. 1, which is a map of tribal lands in the Wellesley Islands.)

  They referred to themselves using two names, which were also used by their neighbours to refer to them, namely, *Letil* and *Kununamenta*. *Kununa* is the name of Mornington Island, and *Kununamenta* literally means 'people of Mornington Island'.

  They shared a common culture. It differed from that of their neighbours in at least two significant ways:
  1. the Lardil exploited only island resources. (The Yangkal had access to mainland resources as well as island resources), and
  2. they had only one contiguous tribe with whom they could directly interact and trade. Mainland tribes had from three tribal neighbours up to nine or more, (e.g., the Walpiri had 10 according to Tindale's tribal map (1974)).

- Their members interacted and co-operated on a more or less regular basis. Subtribal groups may have had disputes from time to time, but usually meetings of people from such groups occurred regularly for feasting, dancing and ceremony, as well as for the resolution of such disputes.

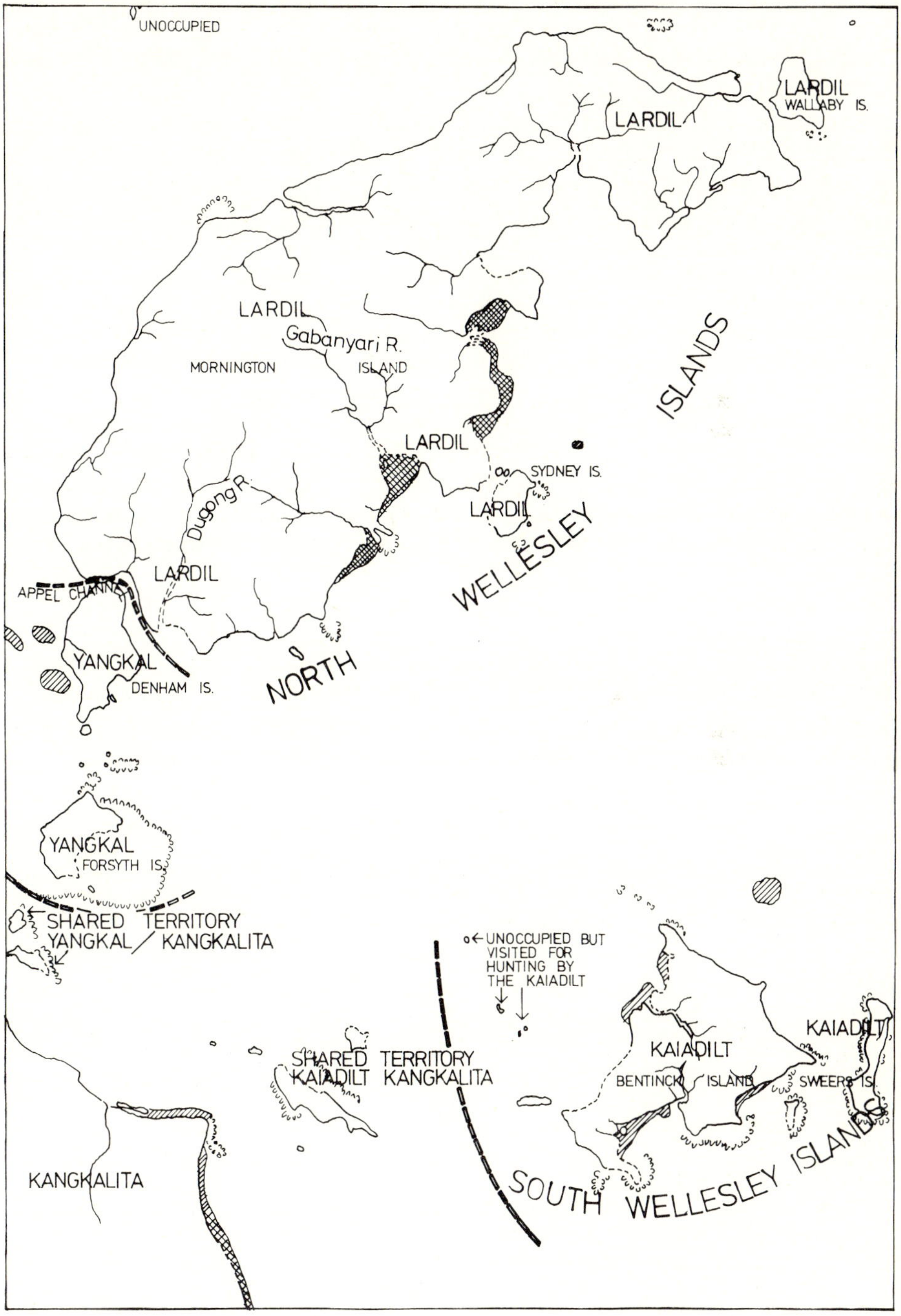

Fig. 1
Tribes of the Wellesley Islands.

- They exhibited a measure of political autonomy. A number of elders (largely male, but some female) comprised a governing body controlling allocation of important economic resources, maintenance of behavioural codes, trade and feud with neighbours, male initiation ceremonies, expression of religious and cosmological knowledge to manipulate the behaviour of people and activity in the natural environment.

The size of the Lardil tribe in *c.* 1914 is in doubt, since early reports conflict. Howard (1910) reported 400 people on Mornington Island in groups of 40 or 50 (i.e., from 8 to 10 groups). It will be demonstrated later that the size of local groups was variable, dependent upon seasonal and social factors. It is also likely that Howard's presence around the island made an abnormal impact on population distribution since many individuals would have travelled to observe his party and vessel. In 1914, Hall surveyed the island on horseback and estimated population size at 200 (Hall, 1915). One can extrapolate Tindale's findings on the environmental density of the neighbouring Kaiadilt tribe[6] (Tindale, 1962a:304) to obtain a third estimate somewhere between the first two—approximately 250. It seems then that the population at the time of first contact was between 200 and 400.

The social cohesion of the Lardil as a tribe was maintained through economic solidarity, a common social structure and language, a food-sharing ethic, familiarity with their lands and fear of other lands and strangers, although interaction with the Yangkal was acceptable and necessary. Shared ethnoscientific knowledge and religion, and typical Aboriginal ethnocentrism concerning such knowledge, were additional factors contributing to social cohesion (Memmott, 1979:Ch. 5). These factors have been well noted in a general sense by Peterson (1976a:4,8,10) in his examination of the concept of 'tribe'.

Lardil people had pedestrian access to all of their land. The channels separating Wallaby and Sydney islands from Mornington Island could be traversed on foot at low tide. In contrast, the channel between Denham and Mornington islands is too wide and deep to cross by foot. The Appel Channel was suited for defence, its natural properties permitting good boundary maintenance.[7] Its width is approximately 750 metres at the narrowest part and its length some 6 kilometres. This permitted ease of observation from high vantage points of people crossing by raft, except when nights were moonless and dark. Relations with the Yangkal were normally friendly, permitting exchange of resources, objects, wives, dances and knowledge. Rafts were used to effect boundary permeability. The Appel Channel was an important source of marine food, and it is probable that bands consisting of members from both tribes hunted and feasted together in peaceful conditions. Informant C.M.,[8] recalling his initiation, said that he and another Lardil man underwent the ceremony with three Yangkal men at a place on the Appel Channel (this occurred in *c.* 1918).

COUNTRIES AND PATRICLANS

In 1935 Sharp carried out research at Mornington Island mission on the social structure of the Lardil. He reported (Sharp, 1935, 1939) that among the Lardil there were eight segments or subsections which combined to form larger categories, namely, four unnamed semi-moieties and two unnamed moieties (Sharp, 1935:158, 162, 163). However, this represents only one dimension of the traditional Lardil social structure. Another set of social segments are land-holding units. They were briefly described by Sharp (1939:456-67) as being small and unnamed, and consisting of a 'few siblings or parallel cousins and their known descendants, the patrilineage or joint family. Its solidarity rests primarily on kinship bonds and a common interest in territory which consists of a number of usually contiguous named countries of varying size . . .'[9] 'Country' is the term used today by the Lardil to refer to these land units. A map of one country and of part of another is shown in Fig.2. 'Common interest in territory' was focused on the joint hunting-gathering activities of the group. The agnatically related land-holders of each 'country' will be referred to as a 'patriclan'. Each patriclan contained males from three or four generations. The unit was exogamous—women normally married into patriclans other than their own and came to identify with their husband's country.[10] From Sharp's definition the patriclan might be seen to consist of a fixed number of families displaying patrilineal affiliation and having common identity with a fixed area of land.

This land-holding patriclan was not, however, the residential group. As elsewhere in Aboriginal Australia, the residential group fluctuated in size and composition. Individuals travelled extensively outside of their patriclan countries for social as well as economic reasons (Memmott, 1979: 157–59). Although the majority of the occupants of a country were normally members of the patriclan, other individuals might be affiliated with the group for varying periods of time through a variety of ties such as patrilineal and patrifilial ties; affinal and matrifilial ties; friendship; ties of trade, e.g., with Yangkal tribesmen; ties of loyalty to a 'big man'; political ties arising from conflicts between patriclans and larger social groups; ties through common patricipation in dances and ceremony. All of these factors carried relative structural importance in the composition of local residential groups.

In addition, the changing size and membership of the band was partly controlled by principles of hunter-gatherer ecology such as conservation of effort, seasonality and scheduling, division of labour, imminence of diminishing returns, desire for mixed diet, and the sharing ethic (after Peterson, 1976a:8–12). Social factors such as internal conflicts, joining together for dance, etc. also caused the transformation of band groups.

Debate on the validity of the concepts of 'clan', and 'band' (or 'horde') is common in the Australian Aboriginal literature (see especially Hiatt, 1962; Stanner, 1965; and Peterson, 1976b). It is argued here that both of these units existed amongst the Lardil. The Lardil bands were population units of variable size and distribution. They might range from a single family to almost the whole tribe and did not necessarily correlate with the unit of patriclan. An individual might call on friendship, kinship, or political bonds, and so take advantage of an abundant food resource that might become available for exploitation at a particular place. Alternatively an individual might decline to participate in such a large scale activity and choose to operate within a small band context. Thus there was often the opportunity to select from a number of economic and social options.

'Nuclear families'[11] and single men might reside in a number of countries during a year and would camp with members of the home patriclan in each of those countries. Such individuals would normally maintain an indentity with their own (or father's) country, and express this relation by returning there from time to time to live with their agnates.

The residential group in a country, i.e., members of the patriclan together with outside visitors, were normally presided over by a senior male of the patriclan or by several senior persons (brothers, step-brothers, widows). In the absence of a strong male leader, a woman occasionally obtained this status. Reference to countries in speech is usually made today using the name of this leader,[12] e.g., 'Gully's country' or 'Fred's country'. Geographic data collected by the investigator indicate that the countries were not named in any other manner, although popular geographic place names are often used to refer to whole countries by loosely extending their proper spatial context to designate larger areas of land.

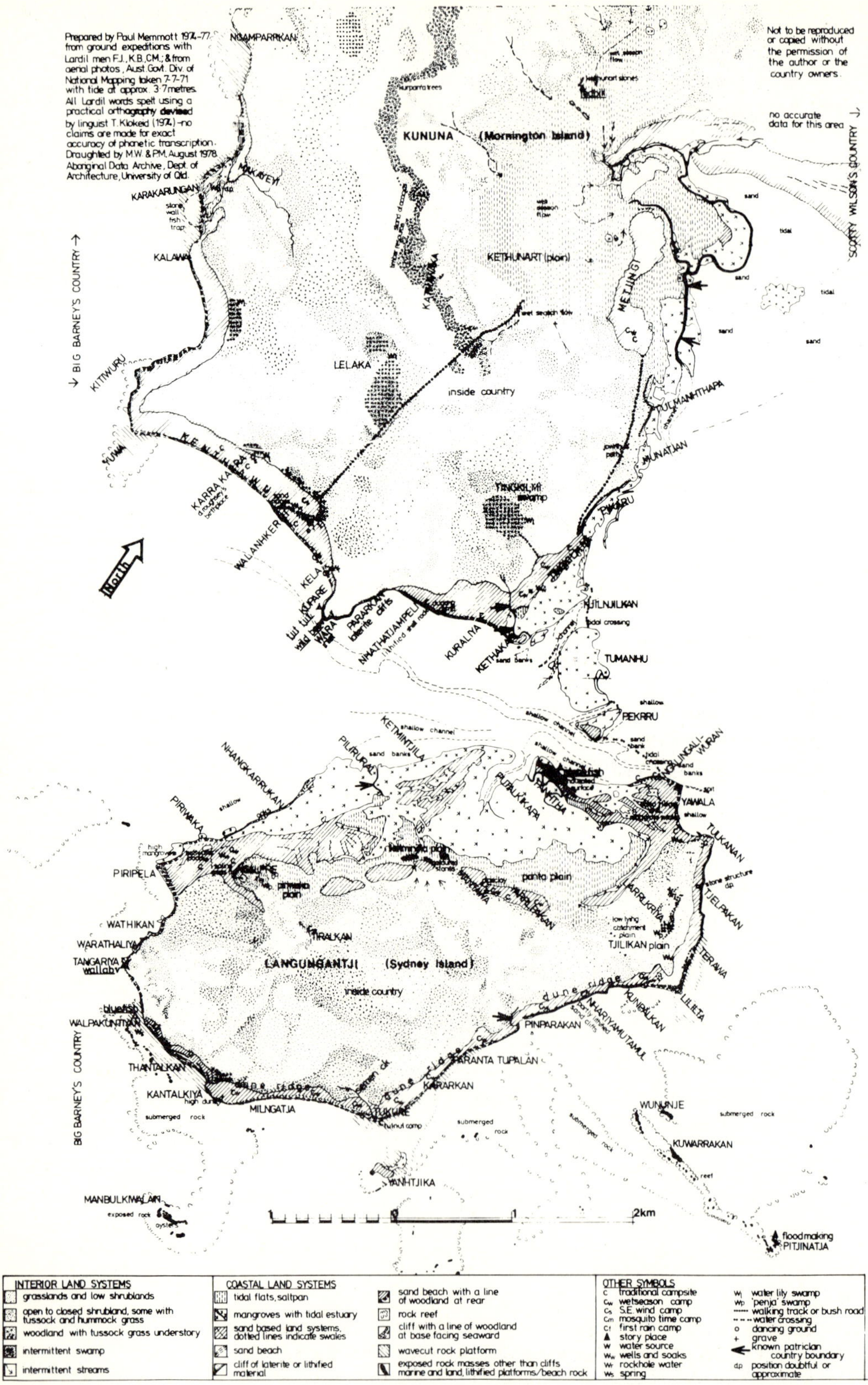

Prepared by Paul Memmott 1974-77 from ground expeditions with Lardil men F.J., K.B, C.M.; & from aerial photos, Aust. Govt. Div. of National Mapping taken 7-7-71 with tide at approx. 3·7 metres. All Lardil words spelt using a practical orthography devised by linguist T. Klokeid (1974) - no claims are made for exact accuracy of phonetic transcription. Draughted by M.W. & P.M. August 1978. Aboriginal Data Archive, Dept. of Architecture, University of Qld.
Not to be reproduced or copied without the permission of the author or the country owners.
no accurate data for this area
SCOTTY WILSON'S COUNTRY
BIG BARNEY'S COUNTRY
North
KUNUNA (Mornington Island)
NGAMPARRIKAN
KETHUNART (plain)
LELAKA
inside country
METJINGI
PULMANHTHAPA
MUNATJAN
TINGKILMI swamp
KARAKARUNGAN
stone wall fish trap
KALAWA
KITIWURU
KENTHUWU
KARRA KARRA
WALANHKER
KELA
PARARKAN laterite cliffs
NHATHATJAMPELI
KURALIYA
KETHAKA
KUTJUNUILKAN
tidal crossing
TUMANHU
PEKRRU
shallow channel
sand banks
KETMINTJILA
PILIRURAI
NHANGKARRUKAN
PIRIWAKA
PIRIPELA
WATHIKAN
WARATHALIYA
TANGARIYA wallaby
bluefish
WALPAKUNTIYAN
THANTALKAN
KANTALKIYA
MILNGATJA
submerged rock
TUKURE
PINPARAKAN
KARARKAN
dune ridge
LANGUNGANTJI (Sydney Island)
inside country
panta plain
TJILIKAN plain
low lying catchment plain
YAWALA
TULKANAN
TJELPAKAN
TERAWA
LILIETA
KUNBALKAN
NHARIYAMUTAMUL
WUNUNJE
KUWARRAKAN
reef
YANHTJIKA
MANBULKMALAN
exposed rock
oyster
flood making PITJINATJA
1
2km
INTERIOR LAND SYSTEMS
grasslands and low shrublands
open to closed shrubland, some with tussock and hummock grass
woodland with tussock grass understory
intermittent swamp
intermittent streams
COASTAL LAND SYSTEMS
tidal flats, saltpan
mangroves with tidal estuary
sand based land systems, dotted lines indicate swales
sand beach
cliff of laterite or lithified material
sand beach with a line of woodland at rear
rock reef
cliff with a line of woodland at base facing seaward
wavecut rock platform
exposed rock masses other than cliffs marine and land, lithified platforms/beach rock
OTHER SYMBOLS
c traditional campsite
Cw wetseason camp
Cs S.E. wind camp
Cm mosquito time camp
Cr first rain camp
▲ story place
w water source
Ww wells and soaks
Wr rockhole water
Ws spring
Wl water lily swamp
Wp 'penja' swamp
walking track or bush road
water crossing
o dancing ground
+ grave
known patriclan country boundary
dp position doubtful or approximate

The title given to these patriclan leaders was *tulmata*. In general, the *tulmata* was an elderly man with important social and legal authority. After the death of a *tulmata*, the *tulmata*-ship was normally passed down the patriline to an eldest son, grandson, brother's son, etc. In the absence of a mature male the role of 'country boss' may be carried out by other relatives of the deceased, e.g., a wife or daughter. A *tulmata* may nominate a specific individual as the person to take over as the holder of country upon his death. This individual may not be the most eligible person in the patriclan, or occasionally may not even be a member of the patriclan. Such situations were likely to cause serious disputes after the death of a *tulmata*.[13] Informant J.J. stated that the *tulmata* may have chosen to pass his country to a 'law man with a strong tongue' (i.e., a man of authority), rather than to a son whose authority was weak. Thus Big Peter and Billy *Waka* gave J.J.'s father *tulmata*-ship over their countries. Evidence collected by McKnight[14] suggests that the holding of countries by specific patriclans changed from time to time.

Population growth and internal conflict within a patriclan may have resulted in the division of a country into two.[15] Alternatively, the decline of the numbers of a patriclan due to death and infertility may have resulted in the amalgamation of a country into a neighbouring country under its *tulmata*. In such cases strongly individualistic Lardil men forced their claims by carrying out necessary 'square-up'[16] fights with challengers. Individuals were probably more interested in acquiring land to gain politico-magical powers rather than economic rights. Traditionalists make claims in the belief that power comes from being intimately associated with magico-religious sites ('story places' in Aboriginal English).

Thus over a time scale of several generations occasional fusions and fissions of countries may have occurred[17] in association with demographic fluctuations. The role of the *tulmata*[18] was not one of absolute land ownership and control, but involved only limited economic duties. He was in charge of a number of favoured seasonal plant resources, namely, *pentja* corms *(Eleocharis dulcia)*, water-lilies *(Nymhaea* species), *pena* or nail fruit, pandanus nuts or *kuriyal* (including *Pandanus spiralis)*, and palm tree nuts or *watat* (a *Cycad* species). These were consumed at organised feasts. The *tulmata* was responsible for preventing people from taking any of the natural harvest until it had properly ripened. He then sent invitations to favoured people from outside of his country who would come and participate in the feast with members of his own patriclan. The number of people invited was appropriate to the size of the harvest, and it was allocated by the *tulmata* to those families present. G.P. (in A.D.A.:F3) describes these procedures: 'Boss belong to water-lily looks to see first if bulbs big enough, try him, see if everybody can join . . . then go for *pentja* after water-lily . . . all together . . . then down here, Horses's Flat, have to ask boss of that *pentja* place first, *Kwita*, he gotta try *pentja* first . . .'[19]

Although the *tulmata* was in charge of these plant resources any Lardil individual had free access across all Lardil lands to more widely dispersed resources such as fish, oysters, timber, freshwater, etc. One important rule which had to be observed while not in one's own country was to allocate specific cuts of meat from any dugong or turtle which one might catch to the *tulmata* of that country, or to his closest relative in the case of his absence.[20] The *tulmata* was also in charge of 'story places' in his country. Simple behavioural procedures could be carried out at these places at any time to bring about the fertility of the creature or plant whose spirit was said to reside at that place.

◀ **Fig. 2**

The geography of a Lardil patriclan country belonging to Fred Jaurth, Lindsay, Dick and Tim Roughsey and Alick Hills (deceased), and part of another country that belonged to Big Barney (deceased).

Such places constituted an important level of environmental control which was largely the responsibility of the *tulmata*.

Available evidence does not suggest that the *tulmata* had any other roles or privileges other than those above. When informants describe the nature of the *tulmata* in Aboriginal English they normally use expressions such as 'boss belong that country', or 'boss belong that *pentja* place'. The suggestion is that the *tulmata* does not so much own the country, but is charged with the obligation of respecting and protecting it, and ensuring the proper use of all resources, both material and magico-religious. This is a different mode of land tenure to outright possession which must be borne in mind when discussing Lardil attitude to land.

An alternative means existed for an individual to obtain rights of use over resources. If a person was born near a resource, then that individual had similar rights to those of the local *tulmata* and the country was known as his or her birth country. Elsie Roughsey (1972:9,10) mentions this: '. . . water-lilies were grown in large swamps, when the green leaf turn yellow, its time to be rooted up. The person who was born there owns[21] that part of the place also owns the swamp too. So when the boss is there he gives order to his people, they can go down to lily swamp and dig them out . . . when they come in their camps, they give half of the big share to the person who owns or claims the water-lily swamp'; and again: 'even in the pandanus palm tree you cannot pluck any nuts off the tree or even from the ground when it full . . . when the harvest time is come, everybody is allowed to help themselves, order were always given by the man who own the place, where he was born . . .'

A *tulmata* of a patriclan country is therefore obliged to share his environmental rights and controls with those who were born in his country. This right allows individuals to make additional land claims outside of their patriclan country. Thus K.B. maintains that Lardil man, Angus Roughsey, is boss of *Nguira,* his birthplace, which is on the north-west side of Mornington Island. However, Angus's patriclan country is located on and near Sydney Island which is on the opposite side of Mornington Island. Another consequence of one's place of birth is that a person inherits the local place name as a personal name. For example, Dick Roughsey can be addressed as *Karrakarra* after the place where he was born in Big Barney's country, as well as by his tribal name of *Kupalathaltan*.

The most significant relation one can have with one's birth place is that of a totemic affiliation. This occurs if a birth occurs in the vicinity of a 'story place'. Of the different Lardil place types, story places emerge as having the most complex set of properties. Unfortunately, it is not possible to deal with all of their properties here. Discussion must be brief and largely limited to those relevant to the theme of this paper.

LARDIL STORY PLACES

Story places are marked neither by artefacts nor by structures, and even their natural characteristics are not necessarily outstanding visually, yet their invisible properties are intense according to Lardil belief. Each story place is inhabited by an individual entity who yields energies from its particular site. The entity reproduces there, under or inside the ground or sea, and simple actions performed by Aboriginal people can catalyse the reproduction or fertility process. Some of these places generate plant or animal species, whilst others yield meteorological phenomena, e.g., at the wild grape story place in K.B.'s country. '. . . if you want black grapes to ripe, you brush them with bush, any bush.' (K.B. in A.D.A.:F29). Other common methods include hitting or poking a particular story place with a stick and shaking bushes at places (e.g., at the barracuda, mudcrab and goanna story places).

Energies are transmitted from story places to humans who are born or conceived near a story place, or who preside over and regularly occupy the locale (e.g., the *tulmata).* These humans then possess a close identity with their story place and its occupants. The totem entities provide personal subjective links into an invisible but co-existing religious world, making everyday life experience both profound and personalised.

Furthermore, by frequenting a story place locale, individuals may receive gifts of knowledge via dreams from other entities in another cosmic dimension referred to as the 'Dreamtime'. Such pieces of knowledge appear to be qualitatively different at each particular story place. Together, this class of places comprises the geographic source of the Lardil cosmology. The pieces of knowledge obtained are often in the form of songs with accompanying dances. From each patriclan, there is likely to be at least one, perhaps several songmen. These men are in charge of the songs (and hence knowledge) dreamt by individuals from their group, individuals from both past and present generations.

Thus, in the politics of Lardil 'law' knowledge, there is sometimes ethnocentricity demonstrated between the song men and the law men from the different patriclans. A song man will claim the songs dreamt by past and present members of his social group, as being the contribution they have made to the tribal 'pool' of knowledge, the law. A lead song man may quite likely design a public dance programme with the majority of songs dreamt by members of his own group, and say that this is because these songs are the most important in the Lardil law. At a large dance where there are a number of song men from the different groups, rivalry and jealousy can occur. Severe political tensions may arise if the authority of one song man is not agreeably established over the others, thus allowing someone to be the lead song man and take the responsibilities of that role. The ideal song man in such a situation would ensure that the programme of songs and dances were derived from all groups, to provide a socially and intellectually balanced presentation. Such a balance implies contributions by the donor entities from all parts of the Lardil land, and the inherent systematic completeness of the knowledge represented therein.

Story places are the source of powerful gifts and energies for local group members, and so there is established yet another relation between people and places, involving a territorialisation of knowledge. The identity of individuals with their patriclans is reinforced at public dances, through their participation in those dances belonging to their own clan land, and in the celebration of the sacred knowledge inherent in some of these dances.

THE PATRICLAN COUNTRIES AND THE SEMI-MOIETIES

At this point it is necessary to carefully consider the relationships between a number of the constructs under discussion. Sharp's evidence (1935) suggests that there are important structural links between:

- a semi-moiety, i.e., an aggregate of patrilines,
- a patriclan or several patriclans occupying one or more countries,
- the totems of the semi-moiety (listed by Sharp, 1935:172–74),
- the totemic centres in the countries occupied by the patriclan(s).

Sharp claimed (1939:457) that 'totems associated with countries of the *dulmar*[22] are normally those of one's own semi-moiety, totems associated with homeland countries constitute a small constellation within the semi-moiety totems and tend to become particularly related to the patrilineage which thus assumes a certain totemic character'. 'Totems associated with countries' can only be interpreted as referring to Lardil 'story places'. These are special places in the landscape in which totemic spirits reside. Sharp is asserting that the totems which have their resident places in the country of a patriclan are the same as some of the totems of the semi-moiety to which the male members of the patriclan belong. It follows that the passing down of totems from father to child through the subsection system occurs within a spatial locale in which there are fixed places that contain the energies of those totems.

However, my evidence suggests that for given individuals there is not a neat correlation between the totems of one's semi-moiety and those that reside in one's patriclan country. There appear to be two separate systems of totemic affiliations.

If Sharp's argument was plausible, it should also be possible to divide the Lardil into their four semi-moieties and clearly associate the male members of each semi-moiety with fixed tracts of land consisting of several patriclan countries (not necessarily contiguous). However, this is not the case. A number of reasons can be put forward to explain why such arguments do not hold. It has been pointed out that if a *tulmata* died without an heir, his country would be amalgamated with a neighbouring country under a new *tulmata* who may belong to a different semi-moiety to that of the deceased *tulmata.* Thus the story places come under the control of a *tulmata* with a different 'skin' [23] to that of the previous one.

The Lardil also subscribe to additional and alternative marriage rules to that normally permitted under the Mara and Aranda type of semi-moiety systems (Sharp, 1939:456; 1935:162). According to Sharp, this permits a male to acquire a wife by placing himself in a semi-moiety not of his father's, i.e., his subsection is determined from that of his mother. This lack of uniformity in acquiring one's subsection would not make for easy comparative analysis of the 'skins' of the occupants of countries.

Still other factors complicate normal practices of land inheritance. A man may be permitted to take up permanent residence in a new country because of conflicts with relatives in his father's country, or because he simply prefers the social company of that group. If such a residential shift results in an ongoing identity with the new homeland, the man's children may eventually rise to challenge the *tulmata*-ship. Such seems the case in the country in which *Tjaurt* was *tulmata* in *c.*1920. Today *tulmata* -ship is claimed between not only *Tjaurt's* two sons, but also the sons of *Kiwalpitja*— the Roughsey brothers. These claimants belong in opposite moieties and comprise two patrilines, not one. Another method exists by which one can claim rights of *tulmata*-ship outside of one's father's country, that is, in one's birth country as described before.

As an individual example, we can examine the case of brothers K.B. and C.M. both *Kamarangi* subsection. [24] The story places to be found in their patriclan country are rock cod, wallaby, moon, wild grape, cyclone. Sharp's list of totems for the *kamarangi -puralangi* semi-moiety contains that of rock cod but none of the others. There are a further 17 totems in his list, none of which have their story places in K.B.'s and C.M.'s country; nor do any from his list of nine which he associated with their moiety. He classifies wallaby amongst *kangala-yekamari* subsections, and moon amongst *ngarilipangi-pangaranyi,* and makes no mention of wild grape or cyclone. The evidence thus suggests that the totems of one's semi-moiety as defined by Sharp are not necessarily those located in one's patriclan country.

COUNTRY BOUNDARIES

Patriclan countries are separated by clear boundaries that run approximately at right angles to the coast and the coastal land systems. (A boundary between two countries is coincident with the boundary between two locally named places.) These boundaries are

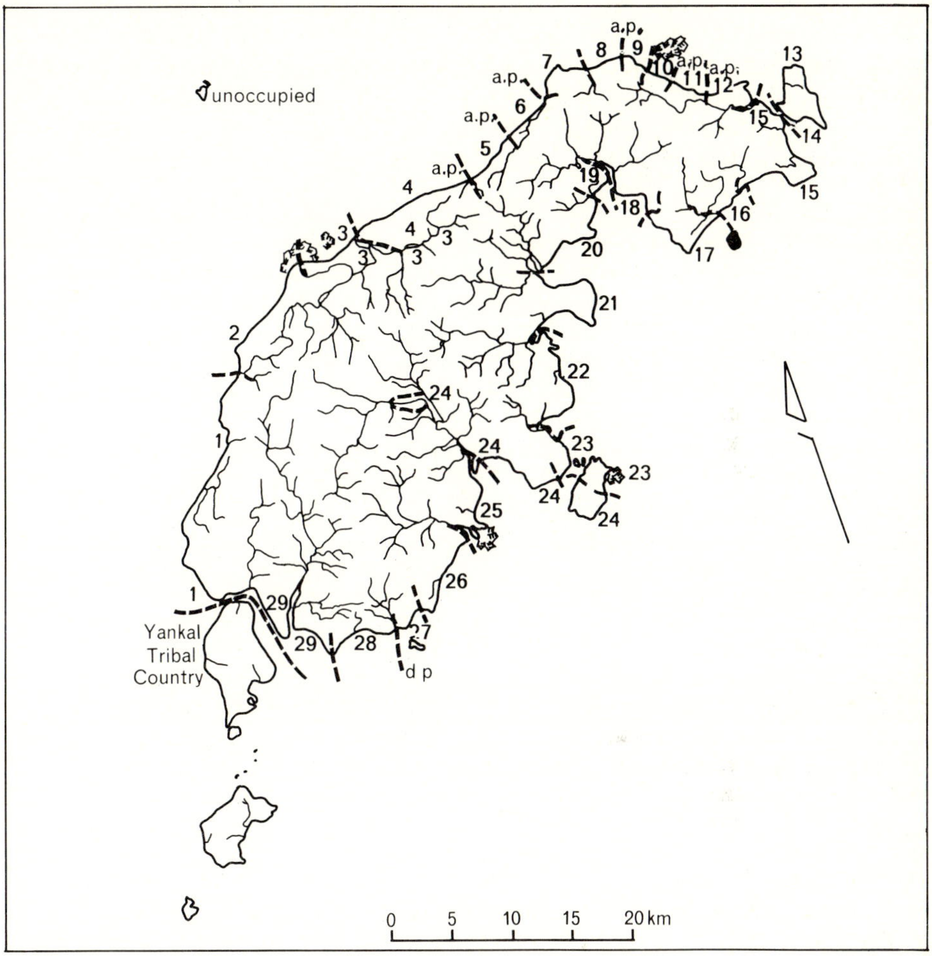

Fig. 3

Lardil patriclan countries; reconstruction *c.*1914.
ap = approximate position; dp = doubtful position.

List of Tulmata *or country custodians*

1 Kulthukalkan (previously Munkaletja)
2 Tjekartja (tall Peter)
3 Kanturelka
4 Malathurunku
5 Kamarangi (Johny)
6 Tjirnpitharrunku
7 Tjunkunirrkatja
8 Tjepalarr
9 Pimineetja (female)
10 Wangal Kelitja
11 Pungkal Walankru
12 Kupunku
13 Nithakanhmu and Pultapul
14 Quack, Doctor and Jock
15 Tipriti (followed by Panpatji)
16 Tjurpan (followed by Tenmiyaru)
17 Tuturemin and Yiriyil
18 Kemin (preceded by Tarin)
19 Taltjirrurungalin and Malarr
20 Parrapurr (followed by Paramparra)
21 Lunguri (followed by Wangalkelitjerr)
22 Petangalin and Pentangalin (the two Terrys)
23 Tjaurt
24 Thungaingilitja
25 Kununkurr (preceded by Kungkalkatnalin)
26 Kulthawangalku (followed by Kalalatiyan)
27 Tungunmu and Rekilrunkurr
28 Terin and Kalthaparrkurunkru
29 Wakatja (or Punch)

today referred to as 'cut-off lines' in Aboriginal English. Thus a 'place cuts out the end of the country'. This system of division clearly separates all of the coastal land systems into patriclan countries. The boundary lines extend out into the sea for an indefinite distance and thus marine resources are also allocated. Behind the coastal land systems the boundaries extend indefinitely into the interior land systems. Inland resource centres are usually found on watercourses which drain the higher interior zones. Isolated resource places such as a swamp or a stand of important trees can also occur in these interior land systems (e.g., *Acacia alleniana* which was used for manufacturing many artefacts). All such resource places located in the interior land systems are claimed by the patriclan occupying the nearest coastal land systems. Evidence suggests that there are no clear boundaries defining the interior limits of countries. [25] The interior zone, excluding resource places, is not considered to be in the charge of any *tulmata*. It is regarded as freely accessible environment for hunting wallaby, goanna and for obtaining 'sugarbag' and vegetable roots, i.e., resources whose locations are not permanently fixed.

The investigator has mapped the boundaries of the Lardil patriclan countries on two maps (Memmott, 1979: figs 10,11), together with information on the *tulmata* of the time. One map is a construction of this aspect of the sociogeography during 1975 whilst the other is a construction for c.1914, the year when the mission was founded and traditional Aboriginal culture was largely intact. This latter map is reproduced in the accompanying Fig. 3.

Cawte has also published a map showing the Lardil countries during the mid-1960s (Cawte, 1973:109). Comparison of his map with that of the investigator indicates a number of differences, the most outstanding of which is the inclusion of interior boundaries of countries on his map. Cawte spent a rather short time at Mornington Island [26] and it is unlikely that he had sufficient time to thoroughly explore the interior of the island. He would, of course, have readily been able to circumnavigate the island in a boat. He obtained some degree of accuracy with his coastal boundaries of countries, but it will be argued here that his internal boundaries are erroneous. Attempts were often made by the investigator to obtain information on Cawte's internal boundaries, both by interview [27] and during field trips into specific countries. Coastal boundaries were found to be fixed and their positions mutually agreed upon by informants. However, no linear boundaries were located in the interior land systems; only resource centres were claimed as belonging to individual *tulmata*. This aspect of Cawte's map cannot be readily supported by the investigator's fieldwork. [28]

FURTHER LARDIL SOCIAL DIVISIONS: THE *LARUMPENTA*, THE *TJIRRKARAMPENTA*, THE *LILUMPENTA*, THE *PALUMPENTA*, [29] AND THE WINDWARD AND LEEWARD

The Lardil people also subdivide and classify themselves into a small number of sociogeographic categories. According to Dick Roughsey (1971b:16) there are four: 'My people own Mornington, Sydney and Wallaby Islands. We are divided into four groups by direction. The western group is called Balumbanda, the north Jirrgurumbanda, the east Lelumbanda, and south, my own group, Larumbanda.' In the contemporary settlement various behavioural expressions of these units are often seen, e.g., in dancing, pre-initiation ceremony, and fighting. These categories may rightly be called groups after the definitions of Scheffler, Keesing and other social anthropologists.[30] They represent an important level of social structure. However, their exact definition does not appear to be as clear as Dick Roughsey suggests.

When applying this fourfold classification, in conversation with informants, confusion and contradiction arises concerning the number of land segments by direction, their geographic extent, and the identity of various individuals within these groups. The problem is particularly confusing with respect to the identity of the *palumpenta.* Were these people a Lardil group living at the south-west end of Mornington Island; or were the *palumpenta* the Yangkal people of Denham and Forsyth Islands; or were they both these groups?

These apparent contradictions are partly explained through a semantic analysis which recognises that the terms *larumpen, tjirrkarampen, lilumpen, palumpen,* are each polysemic.[31] There are several discrete meanings of each term that are related through their sharing a distinctive property. This suggests that the derivation of each meaning is from this shared property. All informants confirm that the terms *larumpen, tjirrkarampen, lilumpen, palumpen* mean the directions of south-east, north-west, north-east, south-west, respectively.[32] These four directions comprise the cardinal points of the Lardil 'cognitive compass'. Intermediate directions are *larumpen-lilumpen* (eastern), *lilumpen-tjirrkarampen* (northern), *palumpen-tjirrkarampen* (western), *palumpen-larumpen* (southern).

Some evidence exists to suggest why these four directions are the orientating directions of the Lardil, as distinct from some other set of directions (e.g., an east-west orientation based on where the sun rises and sets). On the map in Fig. 1, one can observe that there are two lengthy pieces of coastline on Mornington Island, roughly parallel, on opposite sides of the island, and differing in their physiography and microclimates. These coastlines are aligned approximately at right angles to the seasonal prevailing winds—the south-east trades and the north-west monsoons. The Lardil call the south-east coast the windward side of the island and the north-west coast the leeward side of the island. The nomenclature 'windward/leeward' refers to the strong south-east winds blowing from April to November. The Lardil preferred to live on the coast for most of the time, depending upon marine food resources. Their coastal economy was severely interrupted by the cycles of strong south-east winds, which, when peaking in strength, forced the people to temporarily seek food in the interior land systems of Mornington Island (Memmott, 1979:157-59). The Lardil living on the south-east side of the island were identified as windward people, and those on the north-west side as leeward people. This classification continues today: 'Why we call them *tjirrkarampen* [people] is because they're on the leeward side,' (K.B. in A.D.A.:F7).[33] The Lardil words meaning the people who live on these two pieces of coastline are *larumpenta* and *tjirrkarampenta.*

It appears that the original sense of these two terms may have been (a) *larumpenta* —people who live on Mornington Island on the coast exposed to the strong-blowing summer winds, and (b) *tjirrkarampenta*—the people who live on the opposite coast, and partly sheltered from those winds. The people who live in the directions in between these two principal directions were called separately by the names *lilumpenta* and *palumpenta.* Thus a division of Lardil land can be made on the basis of geographic and climatic criteria (as opposed to social criteria) in the following way:

- *larumpen* land—land occupying most of the south-east coast (windward side of the island),
- *tjirrkarampen* land—land occupying most of the north-west coast (leeward side of the island),
- *palumpen* land—land contiguous to the Appel Channel to the south-east.

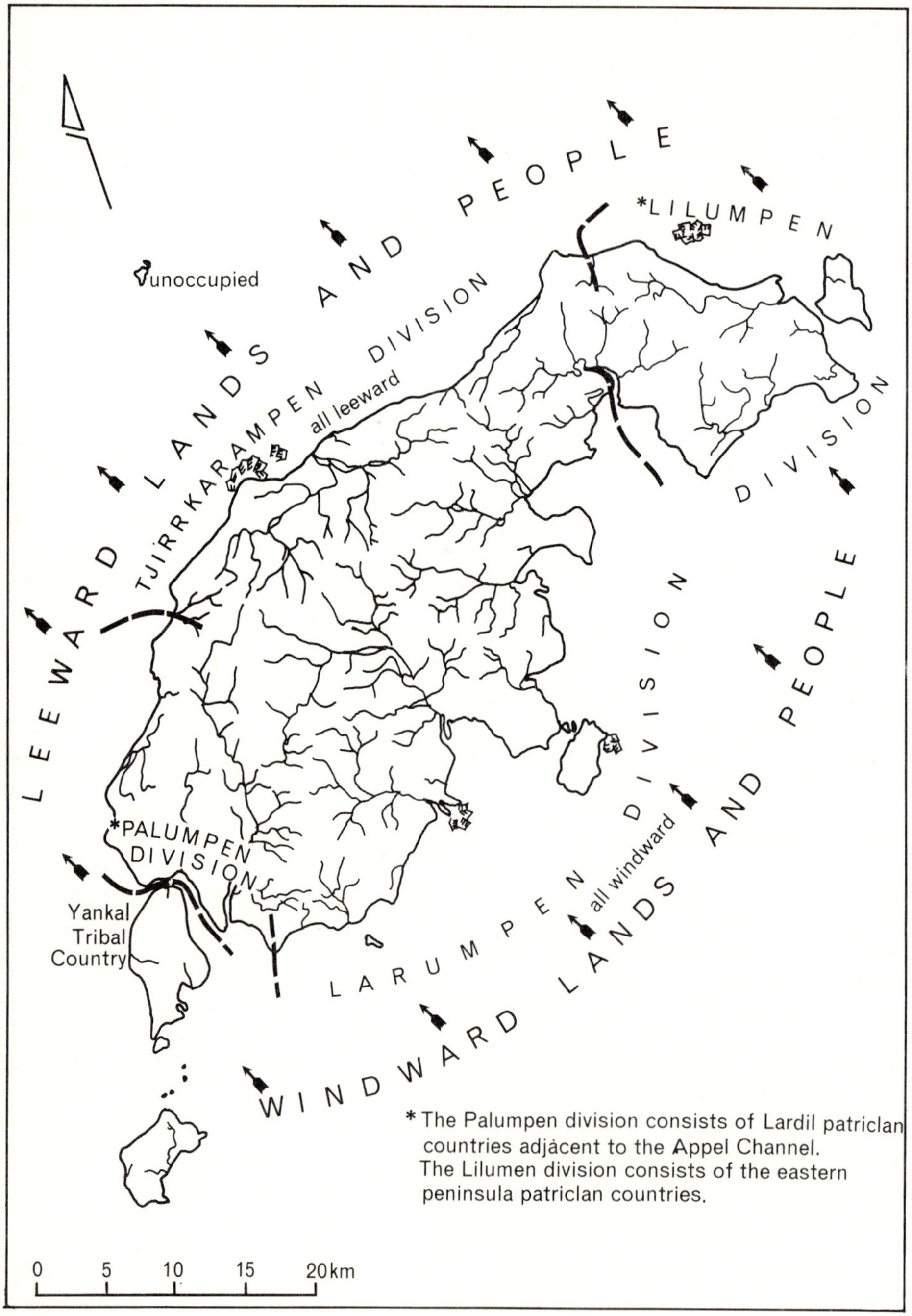

Fig. 4

A division of Lardil lands by direction, based on climatic and geographic criteria. Arrows indicate the direction of prevailing winter winds.

This division is shown in Fig. 4. The boundaries between these units are shown to coincide with patriclan country boundaries. This enables members of each patriclan to be clearly classified into geographical categories. It can be hypothesised that the semantic structure under discussion was derived from associations of people with spatial directions based on the nature of prevailing winds and the geography of the coastline. In time, the terms may have undergone a widening of reference by being applied in a variety of spatial contexts yet still conserving the spatial properties of direction. This hypothesis appears more than plausible particularly when supported by the fact that in certain social situations all of the Lardil people will identify as either windward or leeward people. These situations usually involve rivalry or antagonism between the two groups, e.g., during traditional dancing or fighting. Others have observed this social polarity within the Lardil people. Elsie Roughsey, for instance, has stated: 'I never noticed my father and mother living together. I was more on my father's people side . . . leeward people . . . in those times . . . it was very hard for them to get together . . .' (*c.*1943). A missionary[34] observed that '. . . there is constant tension between the North (leeward) and the South (windward) groups which makes for disharmony at times, though this is often transmitted into healthy competition . . .'

Ambiguity in the use of these Lardil sociogeographic terms by informants necessitated a semantic analysis of samples of speech data. Taking first the terms *larumpen* and *larumpenta:* in its primary sense (or significatum) *larumpen* can be said to mean 'in the direction of, or pertaining to the direction of south-east, with respect to a given point of reference or locale in space'. *Larumpenta* means people of the south-east. When used in various speech contexts the sense of *larumpen* can be narrowed by explicitly or implicitly selecting a specific reference point and/or spatial locale at which one chooses to apply the term. Likewise with the other directional terms. Thus if one is speaking of the people on Mornington Island, those who live on the south-east side are the *larumpenta,* on the north-west live the *tjirrkarampenta,* the *palumpenta* live on the south-west, and the *lilumpenta* on the north-east coast. By natural association, the *larumpenta* are the windward people, and the *tjirrkarampenta* are the leeward people.

If however one is speaking of people who live on the south-east side of Denham Island, then within that locale they are also windward people, or *larumpenta,* although they are not Lardil. Similarly, the people who live at the south-west end of Denham Island can be called *palumpenta.* The people who live on the mainland of the southern Gulf of Carpentaria are also *palumpenta* from the geographical viewpoint of those on Mornington Island. Dick Roughsey (1971a:39) employs this sense when referring to the first immigrants to the Wellesley Islands: 'The Bolamandoo first came by raft from the West and made these islands.' The people who camp on the south-west side of a camp are also referred to as being on the *palumpen* side of the camp. The four terms can be used correctly in any of the above modes. However, there is a more restricted meaning of the term *palumpenta.* It can mean the people to the west of Mornington Island who identified as the Yangkal tribe, and who inhabited Denham, Forsyth and other islands.[35]

Two important Lardil men who lived at the south-west end of Mornington Island in the early mission period were Punch or *Wakatja,* and Robert, son of *Kulthukalkan* (countries 1 and 29 in Fig. 3). Informants will agree that they are *palumpenta,* but some will say that Robert is *tjirrkarampenta* and that Punch was *larumpenta.* Punch and Robert are *palumpenta* in the sense that they live in the south-west part of Mornington Island—this is the simple directional sense. The second classification is based on a different level of meaning, a level that is not only geographic but social as well. In this context Punch is socially identified with the *larumpenta,* the south-east group of Lardil people, and Robert is socially identified with the *tjirrkarampenta,* the north-west group of Lardil people. This classification is at a subtribal level of group identity. The main technique of eliciting data on such group affiliation was to get informants to systematically name the group identity of given Lardil persons. In general, data collected in this way support the existence of only three major sociographic groups amongst the contemporary Lardil: the *larumpenta,* the *tjirrkarampenta* and the *lilumpenta.* The extent of land presided over by these three groups in current times is indicated on the map in Fig. 5.

No modern evidence for a *palumpen* social group was elicited but this does not preclude the existence of such a group in early or pre-mission times. The elder of one country contiguous to the Appel Channel, Punch or *Wakatja* is deceased with no male heir. His *palumpen* neighbour, Robert (son of *Kulthukalkan*) has a large part of his country's coastline located on the leeward side of the island and socially identifies with the leeward or *tjirrkarampenta* people in many circumstances. It is quite probable that the *palumpen* Lardil were once strong enough in numbers and leaders to be a recognisable and acknowledged social group. Some evidence does suggest this. Henry Peter (a *tjirrkarampen* man) told the investigator that a Lardil women, Big Mary, was an important individual presiding over land from Gold Cliff to Timber Point, i.e., on both windward and leeward sides of the south-west end of Mornington Island. A church observer said in 1967 that 'there used to be two further divisions (as well as windward and leeward), East and West, but these have merged into North and South respectively' (in *Encounter,* 1967:7).

SHIFTING GROUP AFFILIATIONS

Another level of dynamics in sociogeographic group identity has been identified which complicates method and analysis further. This is a level of group dynamics which appears to be political in nature. Families who lived in proximity to one of the boundaries between the groups may have found it advantageous to identify with both groups at different times. Such political shifts would have been necessary to maintain friendly neighbourly relations, to obtain wives and to participate in joint hunting, feasting and ceremonial activity. Although at times Robert and Punch may have identified as *tjirrkarampen* and *larumpen* respectively, they would have to also maintain a degree of cooperation and group identity with the Yangkal people on the opposite side of the Appel Channel. This channel is an important resource centre suitable for catching schools of fish and dugong by setting nets across the deepest parts. It was also a vital crossing point where Lardil people carried out trade activity for mainland commodities.

A further example of shifting identities can be seen in the *lilumpen* group of Lardil who preside over land, part of which is on the windward side of the island, and part on the leeward side, although it is all in the north-east and east of the Lardil tribal lands. A *lilumpen* family living on the leeward side of its group territory may have affiliated with the *tjirrkarampen* group if it was to their mutual advantage. In this way the *tjirrkarampen* could attempt to increase their membership during conflicts with the windward people. Such an identity shift or displacement could be justified by arguing that the family lived on the leeward side of the island, and thus must be leeward people also. Similarly, members of the *lilumpen* group living on the south-east coast of their territory might be said to be windward by the *larumpenta.* It is worthwhile noting that the investigator has never heard a man of the *lilumpen* group, as defined geographically on the map in Fig. 5, identify himself as either *larumpen* or *tjirrkarampen.* For example, K.B. identifies himself as *lilumpen*; G.P. identifies himself as *tjirrkarampen,* but identifies K.B. as *larumpen,* and the *lilumpenta* on the leeward part of the *lilumpen* territory as *tjirrkarampen.*[36] K.B. asserts (in A.D.A.:F30)

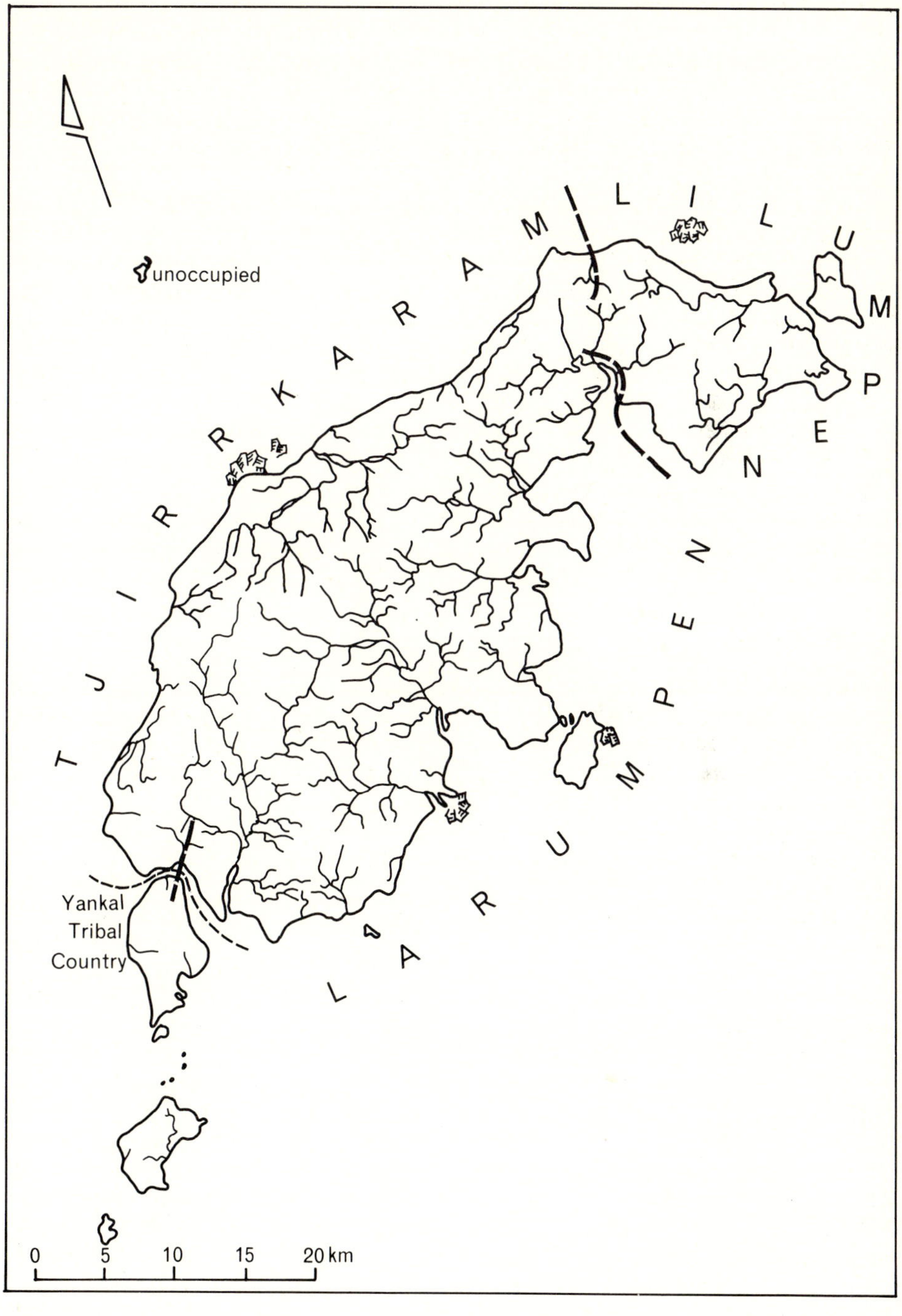

Fig. 5

A division of Lardil lands into three contemporary sociogeographic divisions.

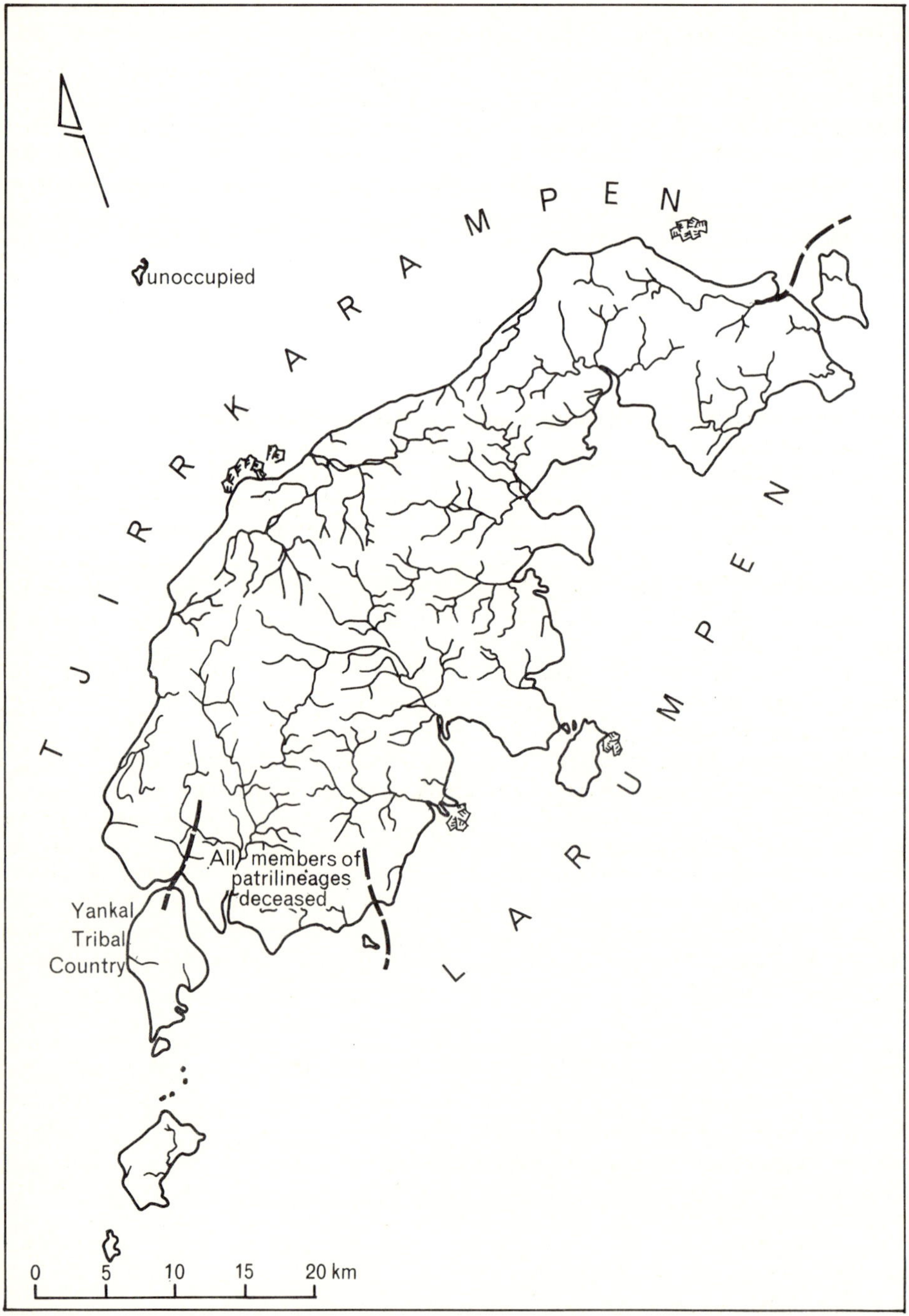

Fig. 6

A division of Lardil lands into contemporary sociogeographic divisions by informant P.J.

that his people all belong to 'one country, all *lilumpenta.* We all share this country right up to Elizabeth Creek . . . around *nguira.*' (K.B. in A.D.A.:F7).

Although the *lilumpenta* maintained their group identity, it often suited them to temporarily affiliate with the other groups and it is likely that they were involved in a history of such affiliations. Whether permanent transformation of group identity occurred can only be surmised. Affiliations still continue between groups today. The phenomenon can be described as displaced group identity, temporarily maintained for socioeconomic advantage, and made acceptable at a semantic level by purposely confusing the polysemic properties of the terms of identity, i.e., the directional and group senses respectively of the four relevant terms. The map in Fig. 6 shows an example of a classification of land and people into sociospatial groups that involves displaced group identity. The data were offered to the investigator by a *larumpen* man, P.J.

This analysis began with the property of spatial direction as the primary sense (significatum) of the four terms under discussion. It proceeded to generate two more levels of meaning for these terms by narrowing the conditions of reference or usage: firstly by fixing spatial parameters to the context of usage, and secondly by associating some of these spatial references with groups of people definable through social and economic activity in space. This analysis has been devised by the investigator to satisfy the sense(s) of the data collected—it was not proposed by the informants. Nevertheless, it has been found to be generally acceptable to the Lardil through the investigator's use of the terms in everyday speech contexts as well as in structured interview situations.

The foregoing discussion has demonstrated that there is an intensity of some geographic properties in the coastal land systems as opposed to the interior land systems. The boundaries between patriclans and the larger sociogeographic groups are well defined on the coast but not in the interior of the island. Similarly, there is a concentration of place names on the coast—no part of the coastal systems are unnamed (e.g., see Fig. 2). In comparison, the interior land systems contain relatively few place names; those that there are occurring at important resource places—chiefly perennial water sources (Memmott, 1979:84-86). The coastal land systems also contain all of the Lardil magico-religious sites (story places) except one (Memmott, 1979:123-25). Such cultural phenomena can be regarded as forms of adaptive behaviour that complement the socioeconomic importance of the coastal land systems. A brief discussion on coastal camps and resources will make this point clearer.

THE IMPORTANCE OF COASTAL CAMPS AND RESOURCES

For the Lardil, camps were not only places to sleep, eat and perform other domestic functions, but were also places of major social interaction and the base for economic activity. Their properties were multiple and varied, and must be left for extensive discussion elsewhere. The association of behavioural traits and artefacts with the natural properties of camp sites and their environs leads one into differentiating between seasonal shelters, forms of seasonal food exploitation, specialised food processing methods, specialised tools for carrying out economic tasks, and thus between different types of camps. Special camps were also used for social and ceremonial activities. Camps were all fixed places but the time, frequency and purpose of use, and the number of occupants varied. The decisions about when to shift camp and where to locate the next camp, were made many times by each Lardil family throughout the seasonal year, under varying social and personal circumstances, as well as within the economic context of seasonal food resources.

Given a choice of camp sites, two properties were always considered as criteria of fundamental importance: to camp on the beach and to camp where there is a freshwater supply.[37] Most water sources are only usable at certain times of the year, this being one of the many seasonal factors influencing the choice of where to camp. Seldom would one camp distant from a water source. (To carry quantities of water large distances in open bailer shells was not an easy task.) An exceptional circumstance was carrying water to exposed sand spits and bars that were used as camps to avoid summer mosquito plagues and from which to conduct dugong hunting at night. The most plentiful supplies of easily obtainable, all-year surface water are located in the centre of Mornington Island in the interior land systems. However these interior camp sites were only used when the strong south-east winds were blowing, causing sea hunting to be difficult and poor. Most of the time the people were camped on the coast.

A primary advantage of coastal camps was ease of access to food resources. Any coastal camp was within daily range of most of the land and marine systems. The diversity of these geographic units ensures a great variety of habitats for many animals and plants. The staple diet of the Lardil was composed of seafoods: dugong, turtle, fish, mudcrabs, mudshells and oysters. The coastal land systems contained an abundance of resources—food, water, and raw materials for artefact and shelter manufacture (Memmott, 1979:90–94).

The coastal camps were sited on the beach or on the first sand dune or ridge behind the beach, except for a few located in mangroves for mudshell feasts, and the few on sand spits and bars mentioned above. The Lardil enjoy most of all to camp on sand. The beach provides a clean soft surface free from the threat of snakes, centipedes, scorpions and grass fires. Such sites provide clear visible access to the movements of the sea and to the activities of its inhabitants who provide the staple meat foods. The most popular camps had shade trees: individual clumps or lines of *wunhan,* oak trees (*Casuarina equisetifolia*), at the top of the beach, and a variety of broad-leafed, fruit-bearing species behind.

Lardil camp sites were fixed and permanent but were not always in use. Distribution of population in Lardil lands varied from time to time, and some camps were more popular than others. The number of residents of a camp varied from a single family to large groups, sometimes the majority of the tribe. With Yangkal visitors this may have numbered between 200 and 400 according to the early population estimates by Europeans. This variable was largely dependent on both seasonal and social factors.

Although Mornington Island could be easily crossed on foot (the most athletic men could travel its length in a day), there was a tendency for people to stay on the coast for reasons discussed. In this sense the population was geographically extroverted, oriented to the sea from the island perimeter. This was expressed in settlement use as well as geographic properties. The entire island could be described as a 'sociofugal space'. This term was originated by Osmond (1969) to describe spaces which cause people to move to their periphery. Social interaction was more often in a circumjacent direction, travel being along the coast. Thus the members of a patriclan were often to be found in their own coastal lands or moving up and down the immediate coast in the countries of neighbouring patriclans who belonged to their own sociogeographic group defined by direction (*larumpenta* or *lilumpenta,* etc.).

The ethnocentrism of these sociogeographic groups was also expressed through fighting and in ceremony. Elsewhere the author has discussed how these groups were likely to transform cosmological knowledge to suit their own geographical perspective (Memmott, 1979:ch.5). This social ethnocentrism and outward spatial orientation was countered by other factors causing social networks to cross, and so reinforced group identity at the tribal scale: factors such as use of interior camps in winter (south-east wind time), joint seasonal exploitation of rich resource centres, large feasts, exchange of wives, large public dances and initiation ceremonies. An individual was able to associate himself or herself with resource centres and story places other than those in his or her own country, through cognatic and agnatic ties, and through the multiple totemic system operating amongst the tribal group.

THE INFLUENCE OF SOCIAL FACTORS ON THE SETTLEMENT PATTERN OF CAMPS

Lardil informants describe three principal types of domiciliary groups in traditional camps: the nuclear family consisting of a man, wife or wives, young children, uncircumcised sons, unmarried daughters; single men, unmarried initiated males, mostly young adults but some middle-aged and elderly individuals also—boys left their parents' domiciliary group after initiation to join the single men's groups; widows. (Alternatively a widow became the wife of another man or slept in a son-in-law's camp.) A reconstruction of some seasonal camp types illustrating these groups is shown in Figs 7–10.

The division of camp occupants into these three types of domiciliary groups, is often mentioned in the Australian literature,[38] e.g., Meggitt (1965:75–77) for the Walpiri, Smyth (1878: vol 1, 124) for Victorian groups, Mathew (1890:391), Thomas (1906:75–76) and Massola (1971:96) for eastern groups.

Other structural principles underlying camp layouts have been mentioned by Australian ethnographers. Some central Australian Aborigines camped in two spatially separate groups, each consisting of the males of one moiety and their nuclear families according to Thomas (1906:74–75),[39] or in four groups each consisting of the males of one semi-moiety and their nuclear families according to Spencer & Gillen (1899:31). The groups were well separated by a natural feature and control of socially

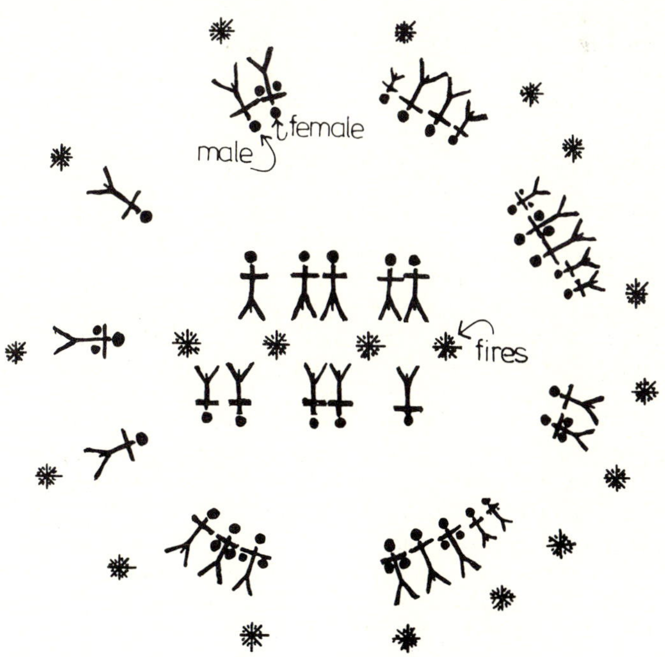

Fig. 7

Mosquito Camp layout, sketched by C.M. and K.B. in A.D.A.:F17.

Fig. 8

Alternative types of windbreaks and sleeping behaviour of single men.

prescribed avoidance behaviours between the members of the various subsections was spatially facilitated. Reser (1977:77) reports similarly for some Arnhem Land groups. Moiety divisions probably helped to maintain avoidance relations in camps.

At the same time one could argue that the division of camps into semi-moiety or section groups derived directly from the strength of parent-son relationships rather than from in-law avoidance relationships. Reay (1962:111) reported this amongst groups at Borroloola: personal kinship relations between son and father, or son and father's brother dictated the choice of company when selecting one's camp site.

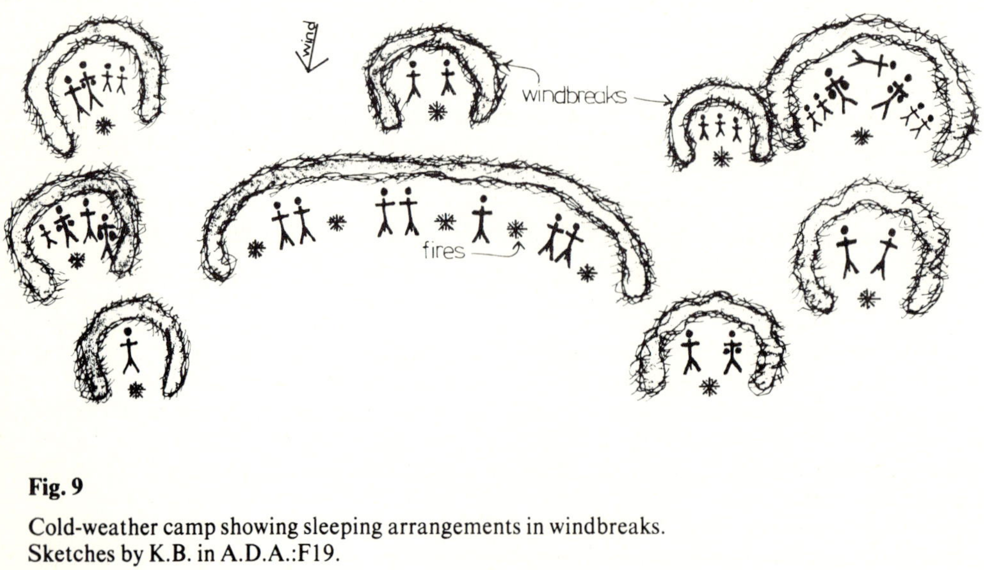

Fig. 9

Cold-weather camp showing sleeping arrangements in windbreaks. Sketches by K.B. in A.D.A.:F19.

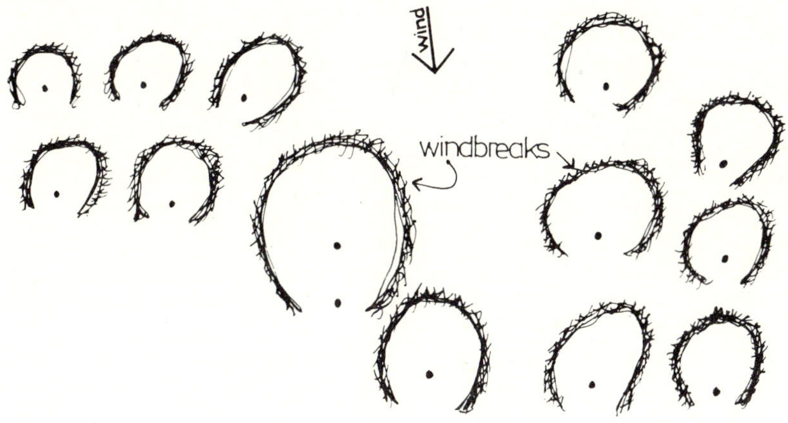

Fig. 10

Plan of Lardil cold-weather camp of windbreaks (dots indicate fires). Drawn by Wanyi tribesman Don Robertson.

Nevertheless, the semi-moiety system was also influential. According to Reay (1962:111), 'if a man has no actual father or father's brother living he may camp with a man who is a classificatory father by virtue of subsection membership'. In general, then, close parent-son relationships, semi-moiety and section affiliations, and avoidance relations between in-laws, could be said to be mutually supportive controls in camp spatial behaviour.

Amongst the Lardil, location of one's camp site or shelter was also influenced by in-law avoidance relations. K.B. reports (in A.D.A.:F50) that a married male chose his family's nocturnal camp site at a good distance from his parents-in-law. However, there is no evidence to suggest that camps were divided into the moieties or semi-moieties. People camped next to whomever they wished, given the above limitation. In general, preferred camp location was near close relatives, and the association of domiciliary groups was generated from the affiliations of the members of the patriclan and of members of spatially contiguous patriclan countries.

Nevertheless, it was probably common for a nuclear family to camp near the wife's mother at times depending on the personal nature of individual relationships and immediate circumstances. Such reasons have been noted by fieldworkers for other groups (especially Biernoff, 1974:5) and could include: (a) obligations to wife's family after marriage;[40] (b) dislike of internal fighting within husband's patriclan; (c) quarrels between the wife and members of the husband's patriclan; (d) to seek help from the mother-in-law in looking after small children or the wife when pregnant; and (e) when a woman's husband is from a neighbouring or distant tribe that does not have significant representation in the camp.

Two literature references, Mathew (1890:391) and Thomas (1906:75)[41] describe groups who located their camp sites in a spatial structure based on close kin relations of both an affinal and agnatic nature, e.g., '. . . a man and his wife were on the west; five paces north-north-east from them was his married son; ten paces south-east, close together, his wife's married brother, and his father's sister, if she were married; twice as far away north-east were his father and mother and his married brother . . .', and so on.[42] There is no evidence to suggest that the Lardil observed such a rigid custom of camp location.

Another well-reported factor exerting influence on the spatial structure of large camps containing groups from different tribal and/or subtribal divisions is that of

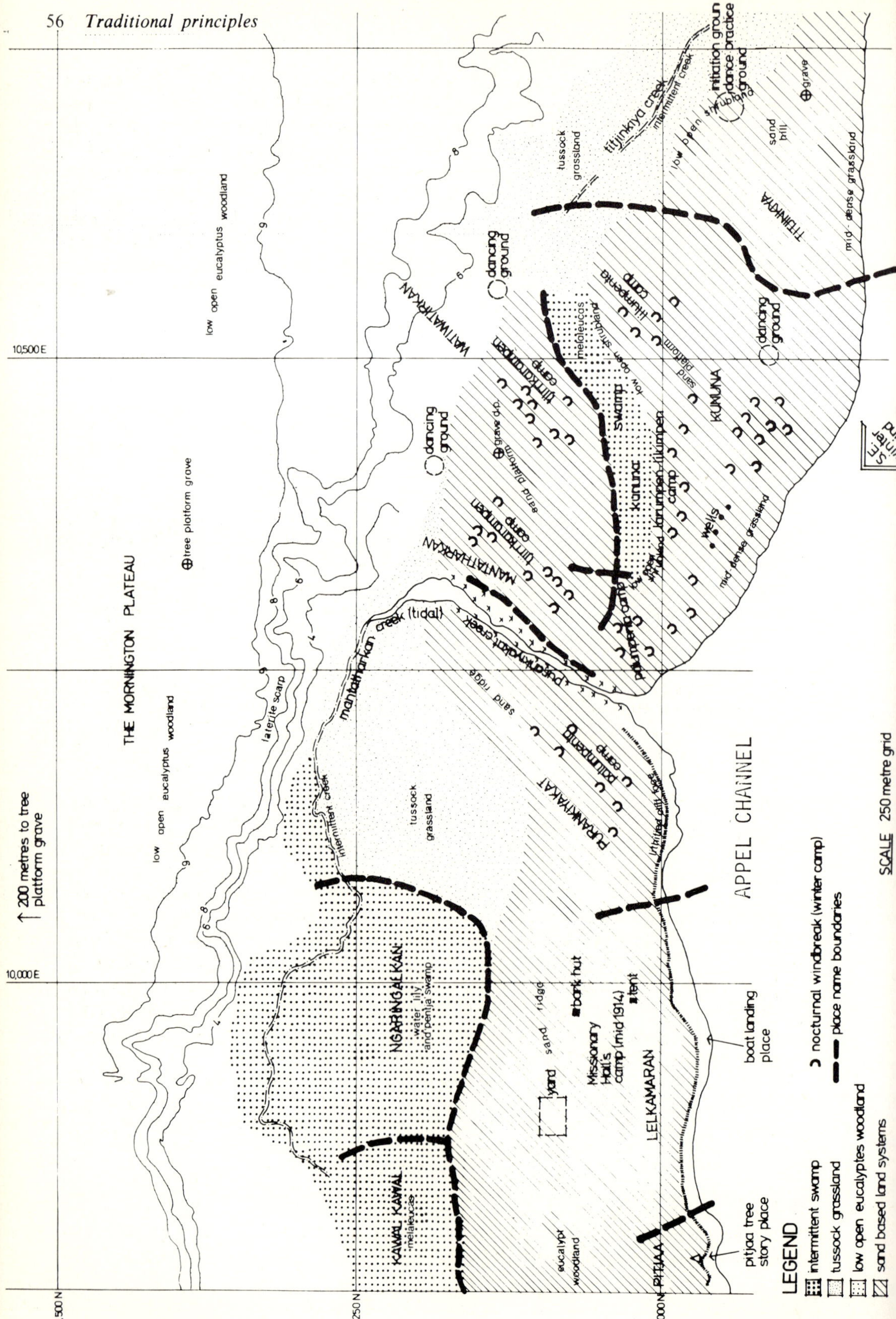
THE MORNINGTON PLATEAU
low open eucalyptus woodland
tree platform grave
200 metres to tree platform grave
laterite scarp
mantatharkan creek (tidal)
intermittent creek
tussock grassland
NGARINGALKAN
water lily and pentja swamp
KAWAL KAWAL
melaleucas
eucalypt woodland
PITJAA
pitjaa tree story place
LELKAMARAN
Missionary Hall's camp (mid 1914)
yard
sand ridge
bark hut
tent
boat landing place
APPEL CHANNEL
PURANKIYAKAT
sand ridge
MANTATHARKAN
WATIWATIRKAN
dancing ground
sand platform
swamp
melaleucas
low open shrubland
KUMUNA
wells
mid-dense grassland
TITJINKIYA
titjinkiya creek
intermittent creek
initiation ground
dance practice ground
grave
sand hill
tussock grassland
LEGEND
intermittent swamp
tussock grassland
low open eucalyptes woodland
sand based land systems
nocturnal windbreak (winter camp)
place name boundaries
SCALE 250 metre grid
10,500 N
10,250 N
10,000 N
10,000 E
10,500 E

camping in the direction of one's homeland. Curr (1886, vi:98) noted that 30 yards of space was left between such tribal campsites. Roth (1897:134) observed it in Boulia, and Thomas (1906:75) in central Australia—'the southern men . . . camp to the south and the northern men to the north.' Smyth (1878:vol. 1, 124) provides an example of a Victorian camp of about 800 people representing eight tribes which were arranged 'as if they had been set by compass,' McConnel (1934:335), whilst speaking of the Wik-Munkan and their neighbours in Cape York Peninsula, maintains that 'in any large camp met together for economic or ceremonial purposes, tribes will take up their position according to the direction whence they came—N.S.E. or W. Similarly, within the camp families will group themselves nearest those most intimately related, usually by clan ties . . . This relative intimacy largely corresponds to the local proximity of inter-marrying clans and tribes on their own grounds.'

Downing (1974:5) mentions that this pattern is a contemporary phenomenon at Haast's Bluff as does Reser (1976:18) at Maningrida, Milingimbi, Ramangining, Nungalala; similarly, Gould (1969:173) for the Ngatatjara who consider the custom as 'traditional desert etiquette', and camp with up to 300 metres between tribal groups. It has been said that Aboriginal people carry out this practice so that they can make a speedy retreat back to their countries should a serious quarrel or fight arise. No firm evidence has been provided to support this hypothesis. The literature does not provide any detailed maps of such camps and the phenomenon is generally poorly described.

The architect and anthropologist Peter Hamilton provides insights (personal communication, 25.8.78) that generate an alternative hypothesis on the function of this spatial convention. He discusses Victorian Desert groups arriving at a camp occupied by the traditional occupants of the locality to whom he refers as the 'home team':

> I have been in an advance party [of travellers], determining where they will settle and this concept [of camping in the direction of homeland] does not appear to apply as the motivating force. Rather they stop at a threshold between being 'too close' and 'too distant' from the 'home team' . . . The direction of the approach will be retained, but the distance will be modified by local topographical features, and availability of building material. In no case did an approaching group pass through, or go around a settled group, to get to what might be a good camping area in some other location.

This suggests that significant factors influencing camp layout may be (a) concepts of crowding and privacy between groups, and (b) an etiquette of approach behaviour.

The Lardil acknowledge that they observe the practice of camping in spatially separate groups, both when camping amongst other tribes and when members of the different sociogeographic groups came together. It was possible to reconstruct, with elderly informants, the sociospatial features of the Lardil/Yangkal trading camp at the Appel Channel as it was in 1914 upon the arrival of the first missionary (see Fig. 11). It can be seen that there is a clear division of camp space amongst the *larumpenta,* the *tjirrkarampenta,* the *lilumpenta* and the *palumpenta,* the latter group consisting of both *palumpen* Lardil and Yangkal men. The groups camped with a space of neutral territory in between[43] but within audible distance of each other. Informants could not give any explicit reason as to why they adhered to this custom.[44]

Although this Lardil camp was divided into sociospatial divisions, each group was not necessarily positioned in the exact direction of their homeland. Such an arrangement necessitates a flat site fairly free of obstacles. Most Lardil camps were

◀ **Fig. 11**

Mornington Island Aboriginal Mission settlement. Site plan reconstruction, 1914 (from informants' data).

situated on the beach or on sand dunes whose physical character often necessitated a longitudinal arrangement of camps (e.g., at *tingkilmiya* in F.J.'s country). People usually arrived from only two directions—either end of the beach (the 'bush road'). This spatial division of people did not represent a total classification of all individuals; rather, it was only one amongst other generating principles underlying spatial structure. Some individuals may have chosen not to camp with their homeland group for a variety of reasons involving sociopolitical affiliations and disputes. The separate camps contained a majority or a 'core' of individuals from one sociogeographic group together with persons from other groups with different forms of social ties.

In summary, then, the main social factors influencing the settlement pattern of Lardil camps seem to have been (a) the division of the inhabitants into domiciliary groups based on the units of the nuclear family, single men and widows; (b) the division of large camps into spatial units containing a core of members from the Lardil sociographic groups defined by direction.

LARDIL SOCIAL AND SPATIAL STRUCTURE, GEOGRAPHY AND SETTLEMENT

The traditional economic orientation of lifestyle to the sea, and the geography that reflects this orientation, generated the dichotomy of inside/outside country on Mornington Island. In the outside country the distribution pattern of places is regular in that examples of the different Lardil place types (camps, wells, dance grounds, initiation grounds, fighting places, story places, etc.), occur at more or less consistent intervals as one moves along the coast. One finds that the Lardil sociogeographic units largely coincide with the outside country, and their boundaries coincide with other boundaries that divide particular named places in the outside country.

In traditional hunter-gatherer life, boundaries between tribal and subtribal units were permeable—individuals could normally travel freely around all of the coastlines of the North Wellesley Islands (except possibly at times of feuding). There was a flow of people, things, customs ceremonies and songs into Yangkal land. The territorial relation of patriclans to their countries was not so much through land possession, boundary maintenance and the exclusion of outsiders, but through custodianship and control of key resources (control was maintained via rights settled through 'square-up').

The boundaries of Lardil territories were not usually articulated with any special markers or built structures. They were simply natural features whose significance was taught to the young as they experienced local movement in the environment. Extensions of country boundaries to seaward or into the inside country were easily made for economic gain if such a situation necessitated. Another type of shift was associated with changes in social identity amongst individuals as they daily participated in different sociopolitical situations. These shifts were achieved through redefining the extent and boundaries of sociogeographic units—a type of polysemy in place knowledge.

Although this regular coastal distribution of geographic naming and place types included camp sites, it did not necessarily follow that there was a corresponding regular and even distribution of people in coastal camp site locations. Nevertheless, such a distribution was probably approximated from time to time. Patriclans broke up into nuclear families ranging daily to obtain food from the variety of camps in their individual countries. This would usually occur in good fishing conditions, free of any interruptions such as caused by large catches of seafoods, exploitation of an important seasonal resource, major social events, or inclement weather.

It was at times of such extensive distribution that elders were most likely to be in their own patriclan countries and in the vicinity of a story place site. These individuals (both male and female) were then most susceptible to receiving dreams from cosmic entities in the Dreamtime dimension. Thus, a further responsibility of the *tulmata* and patriclan elders was the acquisition of 'ethnoscientific' knowledge.[45] This phenomenon provided a territorialisation of knowledge and knowledge sources amongst the Lardil. They still classify important songs according to the locale of their origin. It could be argued by the ecologically minded that regular attendance at such places in traditional times constituted a territorial spacing mechanism, but it must be also remembered that island travel was the norm for most.

The interruptions listed above occurred frequently, however, at least every few weeks for most of the year. Numerous people were then to be found travelling outside of their patriclan countries. The concept of the patriclan is thus inadequate to describe the nature of everyday, population units—a separate socioeconomic concept of the 'band' has been defined. In summary, then, population distribution varied continuously from spatially compact (e.g. at interior camps located near perennial waterholes), to the occupation of coastal camps of varying population size, ranging from a nuclear family to a geographic division or two. Distances between neighbouring camps that were occupied, also varied.

In pre-mission times (1900–1914) there existed multiple structures underlying social organisation in the North Wellesley Islands. Through various activities, group definition was achieved at the level of tribe (synonymous with language group), sociogeographic groups by direction, patriclans, resource exploitation bands, patri-moieties, semi-moieties, subsections, and domiciliary units. A number of these phenomena have been outlined in some detail, and shown to have a spatial, as well as a social, definition.

Social organisation did not so much occur as coexisting social structures, but rather as opportunities for participation in alternate social structures. For example, during the enactment of initiation ceremonies individuals gathered in groups of different sizes and compositions to conduct a series of activities, . . . male hunting bands; female gathering parties; nuclear families whilst in the camp, contained within a sociogeographic based structure; moieties during pre-ceremony games of handball; separate male and female divisions for body decoration prior to the ceremony; subsection divisions for specific roles in the ceremony; etc.

Changing behavioural, economic and political contexts brought about changes in group membership, and accompanying changes in group identity. Individuals moved in and out of group situations, taking on an appropriate identity and the appropriate behavioural norms. Forces operated to maintain or cohere individuals as groups, as well as to disperse individuals and so break down large group activity. Some factors encouraging cohesion amongst individuals were:

- use of common language,
- large-group participation in feasts, dances and initiations,
- trade,
- freedom to travel and have open access to many resources,
- a sharing ethic,
- common use of a limited number of interior camps during windy winter periods.

Some factors encouraging dispersal of individuals were:

- diminishing returns in hunter-gatherer activity,
- quarrels, fights and feuds,

- local custodianship responsibilities in particular countries, as well as responsibilities,
- to gain knowledge from dreams at story place sites,
- ethnocentrism and rivalry in use of law knowledge,
- fear of other peoples and strange (perhaps dangerous) lands,
- fear of sorcery practices.

The relations between population groups and use of space changed in some ways upon contact with Europeans. In 1914 the Lardil began to spatially concentrate in a camp adjacent to the newly founded mission centre. As demonstrated before, the camp was divided into the four sociogeographic divisions of the Lardil, the *larumpenta, lilumpenta, tjirrkarampenta* and *palumpenta.*

The author has studied the history of the mission camp and its development into a village in the 1950s and 1960s. A sociospatial analysis of the village domiciliary zone was carried out in 1975 (Memmott, 1979:336–45). Unfortunately, there is insufficient room here to discuss the detailed methods of this analysis, but briefly, the findings were that members of the four sociogeographic divisions still occupied the same zones as they did in 1914 and maintained a social identity with such spaces; and that residential clusters were definable and contained largely agnates who were descended from the pre-mission patriclans. These resident groups were presided over by a head person who also claimed ongoing rights of *tulmata*-ship. Despite this, *tulmata*-ship control of resources was not observed, owing to the shifts in social control and authority and the concentration of population. Nevertheless, *tulmata*-ship is still a topical subject and its importance is frequently expressed in discussion on Aboriginal law matters.

Within the settlement in 1975 each Lardil person had social interaction with most other individuals in some form or another. Each person knew everybody else, and all were related to one another through the eight subsection system as well as through complex genealogies. It was likely that each individual would encounter most members of the community every few days, even though avoidance behaviour norms may have demanded immediate behavioural adjustments upon many such meetings. (This social structure is similar to the 'multiplex' society defined by Hillier et al. (1976:181)). When these encounters were lasting, i.e., when individuals gathered together for periods of time for conversation and other exchanges sociospatial patterns were again seen to emerge that were based on traditional social structure. Important examples are briefly, as follows:

- Many public settings and events (such as the pictures, public meetings, attending the dance ground and visiting the store) involved patterns of sitting groups that displayed a generative sociospatial structure based on traditional sociogeographic units, namely, tribal groups, patriclans and the four divisions by direction.
- Fighting behaviour often involved people choosing to identify with an area of land, e.g., windward versus leeward, Sydney Island 'mob' versus Namie Island[46] 'mob', etc.
- Individuals and groups of dancers displayed different dress, symbols, and dancing artefacts to express particular roles in a dance, which were associated with either a totem, a moiety or semi-moiety, an ancestor or a supernatural being. These in turn may be associated with a story place, a piece of land or sea, or a patriclan.

Despite the population concentration that has occurred within the settlement since first mission contact, one must conclude that social identity was still being maintained in 1975 within the context of the traditional sociogeographic groups.

As economic dependence on the missionaries increased during the 1950s and 1960s, inter-island movement diminished, and local travel became largely limited to the coastal resource places in the area of the mission. In the last decade however, this trend has begun to be counteracted by improved technology (aluminium dinghy and outboard motor) and by the construction of roads on Mornington Island for motor vehicle usage. Many individuals travel away from the settlement to various parts of the North Wellesley Islands for daily trips, as well as for longer periods of weeks and months. Contemporary reasons for such decentralisation include: to hunt dugong and turtle and to obtain bush resources; to avoid personal conflicts; to escape the settlement during excessive drinking and fighting behaviour; to take children camping and teach them bush skills and Aboriginal geography, including knowledge of sacred sites; and to visit patriclan countries for nostalgic reasons. During all of these visits bush foods and water supplies are exploited. Nevertheless, the socioeconomic role of the settlement and the new hunting and transport technology have created local movement patterns that differ markedly from those of pre-mission time.

CONCLUSION

Culture change has brought with it some new patterns in the use of space for the Lardil, although aspects of traditional sociospatial organisation still prevail. An understanding of these processes may provide a clearer role for architecture and town planning in the support of social structures through the planned design of housing and settlement layouts. Heppell (1979:3) has recently emphasised the need for further in-depth research on how Aborigines

> . . . organize their camps and the spatial areas within a camp, how a camp supports those social institutions which operate within it, the ways in which a group changes its social institutions to adapt to the changed circumstances of a housing scheme and the stresses experienced by individuals and families during the transition period of adaptation to a house.

At present the Mornington Islanders are having to adjust to such change. Since the devastation of Cyclone Ted on Mornington Island in December 1976, the Queensland State Government has so far constructed some 84 new houses. More are expected. Most of the old village occupants have taken up residence in these new houses. It is too early yet to systematically report on what new sociospatial patterns are emerging, and what stresses are arising as a result of the disruption of the old sociospatial patterns, as well as the moving of people from their self-constructed domiciles into houses designed by Western architects.

It has been demonstrated in this paper that some of the relations with land and space amongst the Lardil have a tradition of being structured through a number of social processes. However, there are many other forms of people-environment bonds that have not been discussed in detail here, e.g., hunting and gathering activity; totemism; belief in the occupation of parts of the environment by ancestral ghosts; the control of some behavioural norms by invisible environmental entities, etc. The depth of people-land relations can best be indicated with a statement by the late Mornington Shire Council Chairman, Larry Lanley (*The Advertiser,* Adelaide, for 12 September 1978):

> If our Dreaming and our laws and languages and our way of living die then that will be the end of Aboriginal people . . .
>
> It all goes back to the land, that is why land rights are so important to us.
> We need the land to be Aboriginal in our minds—that is why Governments must give back the land if we are to keep our culture.

Take away our land like the Queensland Government is trying to do and we're nobody, we will die out, finish. The land gives the true meaning to Aboriginal life.

At the heart of everything is land—it is the way we feel and think about the land that makes us Aboriginals, . . .

It is the only way to keep our culture, and without it we are scattered into a country that is not ours, where we feel hunted, like wild kangaroos and dingoes.

Our bodies must keep doing the dances and living in the bush—we must teach in schools and get our people to perform dances for others.

These are the things we need to help us keep the head and body alive until we are given back our land, and the land can make us whole again.

NOTES

1. I am indebted to David Trigger for his critique of an earlier draft of this paper, as well as to Nick Peterson for his comments on the last draft. The research for this paper was carried out between 1973 and 1976 as part of my doctoral programme. Data collection methods included participant and naturalistic observation, structured interviewing, photographic and mapping techniques, genealogical construction and literature study. A detailed account of the interrelated use of these methods is available in my thesis (Memmott, 1979: ch.2). The data are held at the Department of Architecture, University of Queensland, in a data archive titled 'Aboriginal Data Archive: Aborigines and their Ethno-environment'. Reference is made throughout this paper to tapes of interviews located in the archive, using the following style of abbreviation: 'in A.D.A.:F4' where 'F4' indicates the cassette reference number.

2. After Stewart et al. (1954:113):

3. Structural forms of vegetation cited here, such as life form, density and height, follow the terminology of Specht's system of units in CSIRO (1970).

4. This term follows Grimes (1974:6).

5. Lardil words are italicised and spelt using a practical orthography devised by T. Klokeid (1974). No claims are made for the accuracy of phonetic transcription.

6. The Kaiadilt occupied Bentinck and Sweers islands in the South Wellesley Islands. These islands have similar geography, climate, flora, and fauna to the North Wellesleys.

7. Although the channel is a physical boundary, there are no exact boundary points or lines on the water surface or sea bottom that informants can point to. In this sense it is similar to boundaries between the islands of the Tiwi as reported by Pilling (in Lee & DeVore, 1972:156,157).

8. In this paper the names of informants are abbreviated as follows: F.J., Fred Jaurth; G.P., Gully Peter; E.R., Elsie Roughsey; K.B., Kelly Bunbujee; P.J., Phil Jack; C.M., Charlie Marme; L.R., Lindsay Roughsey; J.J., Jackson Jacob; D.R., Don Robertson.

9. Tindale (1962b:273) describes a similar land-occupying unit among the Kaiadilt as an unnamed hordal territory claimed by descendants of a common ancestor in the male line.

10. '. . . wives stay with their husband's people' (D.R. in A.D.A.:F22).

11. N.B. The term 'nuclear family', as used in this paper, is defined as comprising a man, his wife or wives, their children, and unmarried daughters.

12. Similarly, Tindale (1962b:273) notes that the countries of the Kaiadilt were referred to by the contemporary or immediately past 'boss' (eldest member of the patriclan).

13. Tindale (1962b:273) also mentions disputes over territorial claims amongst the Kaiadilt.

14. Personal communication, London, February 1975.

15. The idea of a hunting party growing in size until it becomes ecologically unstable, and then splitting into two distinct bands has been examined by Bradfield (1973:454) in his discussion on baboons. The first symptoms of such a split might be when the males separate into two groups for daily hunting.

16. A number of different behavioural events of the Lardil were commonly referred to as 'square-up' in Aboriginal English or *thalti* in Lardil. They were enacted according to fixed legal rules and social models. Their common characteristic was that they all aimed to settle or even up over a debt or grievance. They represented a sharing of emotions. A redistribution of resources was often made by a group to repay the emotional gestures of another group towards the first. Lardil *thalti* is directly comparable to the 'kopara' custom of the Lakes groups of Aborigines in South Australia (Elkin, 1931).

17. In certain ways this process is ongoing today. Hiatt (1965:18) also reports of the amalgamation of land holding units amongst an Arnhem Land group, the Gidjingali.

18. Evidence bearing on this subject is recorded in A.D.A.:F30,F31 with K.B. Also see Dick Roughsey (1971a:98).

19. A similar custom is observed by the Wik-Munkan (McConnel, 1934:335).

20. Dick Roughsey says the cuts were tail and head of dugong, flappers, chest and head of turtle. (1971b:50).

21. 'Owns' here, means having the same interests and rights of control as those of the *tulmata*.

22. Sharp's spelling of *tulmata*.

23. The term 'skin' is used by the Lardil to refer to 'subsection'.

24. In contemporary Lardil, the names of the subsections are *puralangi, kangaln, yekamari, kamarangi* in one moiety, and *ngaripilangi, pulanyi, pangaranyi,* and *palyarinyi* in the other.

25. The absence of hard territorial boundaries is not uncommon amongst other Australian Aboriginal groups (Hiatt, Pilling, in Lee & deVore, 1972:157).

26. During a university vacation (Cawte, 1972:8).

27. e.g., refer to K.B. in A.D.A.:F7 (units 738–755).

28. Several more anachronisms noted on his map by the investigator, are as follows:
   (a) Informants were unable to locate exact boundaries that divide the littoral zone into segments guarded by *malkri* totems, yet Cawte's map indicates such boundaries.
   (b) Cawte assigns a parcel of land to Clara Reid that consists of all interior land systems. All informants agree that Paddy Marme, her father, was the *tulmata* of coastal lands. The orientation of all of the patriclan countries to the sea is a point that will be returned to later.
   (c) Despite a detailed field study of *Panpatji's* country by the investigator, using his three sons (youngest approximately 68 at the time) as guides and informants, no night dove story place (i.e. *malkri* place) was found to exist, as is indicated on Cawte's map.

29. Klokeid's orthography is used again in the spelling of these Lardil words. It is more common in the Wellesley Island literature to see these terms spelt using a *b* for a *p*, a *d* for a *t*, and a *g* for a *k*, etc.

30. See Holy (1976:126).

31. After the definition of 'polysemy' by Scheffler & Lounsbury (1971:6).

32. Dick Roughsey's directions of south, north, east, west appear to be a simplification for European readers of his book.

33. Also note Elsie Roughsey's observation (1972:108) . . . 'they lived as one individual race, although they had two tribes of people, Winded and Lewit'. (1972:108).

34. In the Australian Presbyterian Board of Missions (1967:7). Presumably, the Rev. D. Belcher.

35. Some information on these people can be found in interviews with F. J. and C. M. in A.D.A.:F5, F18.

36. G.P., personal communication.

37. Emphasised by P.J. and D.R. in A.D.A.:F28 and F22 respectively.

38. Rapoport (1972) has also reviewed some of this literature.

39. Reser (1976:18) also reports this for contemporary Arnhem Land groups camping near Maningrida, Milingimbi, Ramangining and Nungalala.

40. Strehlow (1970:100) reports that in the Western Desert, a male slept in his in-laws' camp after marriage, before returning to his patrilineal core group.

41. Thomas is discussing the Wurunjerri and the Kurnai.

42. Thomas (1906:75) for the Kurnai. McConnel (1934:335) also mentions that amongst the Wik-Munkan, parents and parents-in-law may attach themselves to the camp of a son or son-in-law.

43. Biernoff (1974:10) reports a space of 30 metres between lineage clusters and 50–100 metres between clans in the larger traditional camps of the Nunggubuya.

44. One middle-aged Lardil man, Kirk Jacob, told the investigator that he had not recognised that such a structure existed in a contemporary camp on Denham Island. However, once it has been brought to his attention he agreed that it existed, and added that he only notices such things when Western observers point them out to him.

45. In contemporary times old men occasionally blame the cause of some forms of social disorder upon one another, for not spending time in their countries to obtain their contribution of social knowledge from their personal story place locales.

46. 'Namie Island' is a local name for Forsyth Island, which was part of Yangkal lands. One of its most important male residents in the early mission period was called Namie.

REFERENCES

The Australian Presbyterian Board of Missions. *Encounter,* September 1967, pp.7–9.

Biernoff, D. Pre and post European designs of Aboriginal settlement: the case of the Nunggubuyu of eastern Arnhem Land. *Man-Environment Systems,* 4(5): 273–82(1974).

Bradfield, R. M. *A Natural History of Associations: A study in the meaning of community.* London, Duckworth, 1973. (2 vols).

Cawte, J. E. *Cruel, Poor and Brutal Nations.* Honolulu, University of Hawaii, 1972.

Cawte, J. E. *Medicine is the Law: studies in the psychiatric anthropology of Australian tribal societies.* Honolulu, The University Press of Hawaii; Adelaide, Rigby; 1973.

Commonwealth Scientific and Industrial Research Organization. *The Australian Environment,* ed. G. W. Leeper, Melbourne University Press, 1970.

Curr, E. M. *The Australian Race:* its origin, languages, customs, places of landing in Australia, and the routes by which it spread itself over that continent. Melbourne Government Printer, 1886 (4 vols).

Downing, Rev. J. Traditional Aboriginal camp layout and town planning. *Aboriginal News,* 1(8):4–9 (1974).

Elkin, A. P. The Kopara, the settlement of grievances. *Oceania,* 2(2): 191–98 (1931).

Gould, R. A. *Yiwara, Foragers of the Australian Desert,* New York, Charles Scribner, 1969.

Grimes, K. *Mesozoic and Cainozoic Geology of the Lawn Hill Westmoreland, Mornington and Cape van Diemen 1:250,000 Sheet Areas, Queensland.* Canberra Bureau of Mineral Resources, Geology and Geophysics, Department of Minerals and Energy, 1974 (Record 1974/106).

Hall, R. Starting a mission station on Mornington Island: Gulf of Carpenteria. *Our Missionaries at Work.* Melbourne. Presbyterian Church of Victoria, October 1914, pp.15–24; April 1915, pp.4–12.

Heppell, M. *A Black Reality: Aboriginal camps and housing in remote Australia.* Canberra, Australian Institute of Aboriginal Studies, 1979.

Hiatt, L. *Kinship and Conflict, a study of an Aboriginal community in northern Arnhem Land.* Canberra, Australian National University Press, 1965.

Hiatt, L. Local organization among the Australian Aborigines, *Oceania,* 32(4): 267–86 (1962).

Hillier, B., Leaman, A., Stansall, P. & Bedford, M. Space syntax, *Environment and Planning B.,* 3:147–85 (1976).

Holy, L. Kin groups—structural analysis and the study of behaviour, *Annual Review of Anthropology,* 5:107–31 (1976).

Howard, R. B. *Annual Report of the Chief Protector of Aboriginals.* Brisbane Queensland Government Printer, 1910.

Klokeid, T. J. Case Assignment in Lardil. Unpublished paper delivered at the Symposium on Grammatical Categories in Australian Languages at the Biennial Conference, Australian Institute of Aboriginal Studies, Canberra, June 1974.

Lee, R. & DeVore, I. (ed). *Man the Hunter.* Aldine, USA, 1972.

McConnel, U. The Wik-Munkan and allied tribes of Cape York Peninsula, N.Q. *Oceania,* 4(3):310–67 (1934).

Massola, A. *The Aborigines of South East Australia As They Were.* William Heinemann, Australia, 1971.

Mathew, Rev. J. The Australian Aborigines. *Journal of the Royal Society of New South Wales, 23,* for 1889 (1890).

Meggitt, M. J., *Desert People, a study of Walbiri Aborigines of central Australia,* 2nd ed. University of Chicago Press, 1965.

Memmott, P. Lardil Properties of Place, An ethnological study of man-environment relations. Unpublished Ph.D thesis, Department of Architecture, University of Queensland, 1979.

Osmond, H. The relationship between architect and psychiatrist. In: C. Goshen (ed.), *Psychiatric Architecture.* Washington, D.C., American Psychiatrists' Association, 1969.

Peterson, N. Introduction. In: N. Peterson (ed.), *Tribes and Boundaries in Australia.* Canberra, Australian Institute of Aboriginal Studies, 1976a, pp.1–11.

Peterson, N. (ed.), *Tribes and Boundaries in Australia.* Canberra, Australian Institute of Aboriginal Studies, 1976b.

Rapoport, A. Australian Aborigines and the Definition of Place. In: W. J. Mitchell (ed.), *Environmental Design: research and practice*. Proceedings of the 3rd EDRA Conference, Los Angeles, vol. 1, 1972, pp.3.3–1 to 3.3–14.

Reay, M. Subsections at Borroloola. *Oceania*, 33(2): 90–115, (1962).

Reser, J. A matter of control: Aboriginal housing circumstances in remote communities and settlements. Canberra, Australian Institute of Aboriginal Studies (document no. 76/2041), Sept. 1976.

Roth, W. E. *Ethnological Studies among the North-West-Central Queensland Aborigines*. Brisbane, Queensland Government Printer, 1897.

Roughsey, D. Unpublished draft manuscript of the book 'Moon and Rainbow', and other notes and miscellaneous writings. Fryer Library, University of Queensland 1971a.

Roughsey, D. *Moon and Rainbow: the autobiography of an Aboriginal*. Sydney, Reed, 1971b.

Roughsey, E. Aboriginal mothers craft, culture and customs. Unpublished manuscript, Mornington Island, Queensland, dated Aug. 14 1972. (Quarto pages are numbered 1–197, followed by a revision on foolscap pages numbered 1–17 (introductory chapter), then followed by foolscap pages numbered 120–152. The foolscap sections are cited using the index ('N.S.'.). To be published by McPhee Gribble, Melbourne, 1983.

Scheffler, H. & Lounsbury, F. *A Study in Structural Semantics*, the Sirioni kinship system. New Jersey, Prentice Hall, 1971.

Sharp, L. Semi-Moieties in North-Western Queensland. *Oceania*, 6(2): 158–74 (1935).

Sharp, L. Tribes and totemism in north-east Australia, *Oceania*, 9(4): 439–61 (1939).

Smyth, R. B. *The Aborigines of Victoria*. London, John Ferres, 1878 (2 vols).

Spencer, W. B. & Gillen, F. J. *The Native Tribes of Central Australia*. London, MacMillan, 1899.

Spencer, W. B. & Gillen, F. J. *The Northern Tribes of Central Australia*. London, MacMillan, 1904.

Stanner, W. Aboriginal territorial organization: estate, range, domain, and regime. *Oceania*, 36(1):1–26 (1965).

Stewart, G., Christian, C. Perry, R. The Land Systems of the Barkly Tableland. In: *Survey of the Barkly Region, Northern Territory and Queensland, 1947–48*. Melbourne, Commonwealth Scientific and Industrial Research Organization, 1954, pt.viii.

Strehlow, T. G. N. *Geography and the Totemic Landscape in Central Australia: A functional study*. In: R. H. Berndt (ed.), *Australian Aboriginal Anthropology*. Published for the Australian Institute of Aboriginal Studies by the University of Western Australia Press, 1970, pp.92–140.

Thomas, N. *Natives of Australia, the native races of the British Empire*. London, Constable, 1906.

Tindale, N. *Aboriginal Tribes of Australia: their terrain, environmental controls, distribution, limits and proper names*. University of California Press, 1974.

Tindale, N. Some population changes among the Kaiadilt people of Bentinck Island, Queensland. *Records of the South Australian Museum, 14*(2):297–336 (1962a).

Tindale, N. Geographical knowledge of the Kaiadilt people of Bentinck Island, Queensland. *Records of the South Australian Museum, 14*(2):259–96 (1962b).

Turner, D. H. Levels of organization and communication in Aboriginal Australia. In: N. Peterson (ed.), *Tribes and Boundaries in Australia*. Canberra, Australian Institute of Aboriginal Studies, 1976, pp.180–91.

3

SONGS, CEREMONIES AND SITES: THE AGHARRINGA CASE

Richard Moyle

The relationship between musical life, or rather musical ownership, and land ownership among the Alyawarra is such that the two exist as links in a chain of reasoning which the Alyawarra themselves adopt in discussion. The chain may be represented as follows:

- There are people who are said to own songs; it is to such people that others in a community go for permission when they want to sing the songs.
- The people who own the songs also own the ceremonies in which the songs feature. (There is no category of Alyawarra song which has no associated ceremony.)
- The songs in the ceremonies have texts which relate to events and people from the Dreamtime *(altjirra)*; in every case, these events were localised at specific, named sites, most of which are known to present-day Alyawarra. The ceremony-owners also own the particular sites associated with each Dreamtime myth.
- Collections of such myths owned by members of the same patriline cover tracts of land which those members claim as theirs. In short, those who own the songs own the land.

This situation is not unique to the Alyawarra, and has been known to anthropologists for some time, but the published literature does not appear to contain case studies in which the credentials possessed by a particular community are examined in detail. And while there are numerous illustrations of Dreaming lines among anthropological writings, nowhere have these been localised precisely and presented as the determinants of a group's claim for ownership of a particular area of land.

By contrast, this paper presents detailed information on the portion of Alyawarra land called Agharringa Country, the means by which its inhabitants validate claims to ownership and by which ownership was established and is being perpetuated.

THE LOCATION AND CONSTITUTION OF ALYAWARRA TERRITORY AND AGHARRINGA COUNTRY[1]

The people who call themselves and their language Alyawarra consider a block of some 17 000 square kilometres to be their traditional country; this land lies around 200 kilometres north-east from Alice Springs in the Northern Territory, and is bounded by the Akaya, Pulanya, Akara, Eastern Aranda, Anmatjirra, Walbiri and Kaititja people (see Fig. 1). Of these, the Pulanya speakers are now extinct, and the Akaya (sometimes referred to by non-Alyawarra speakers as Wakaya) number perhaps less than a hundred.

While most Alyawarra live within this area, there are small but established groups attached to nearby cattle stations—Murray Downs, MacDonald Downs, and also Lake Nash, some 300 kilometres to the east, as well as Warrabri settlement. A few

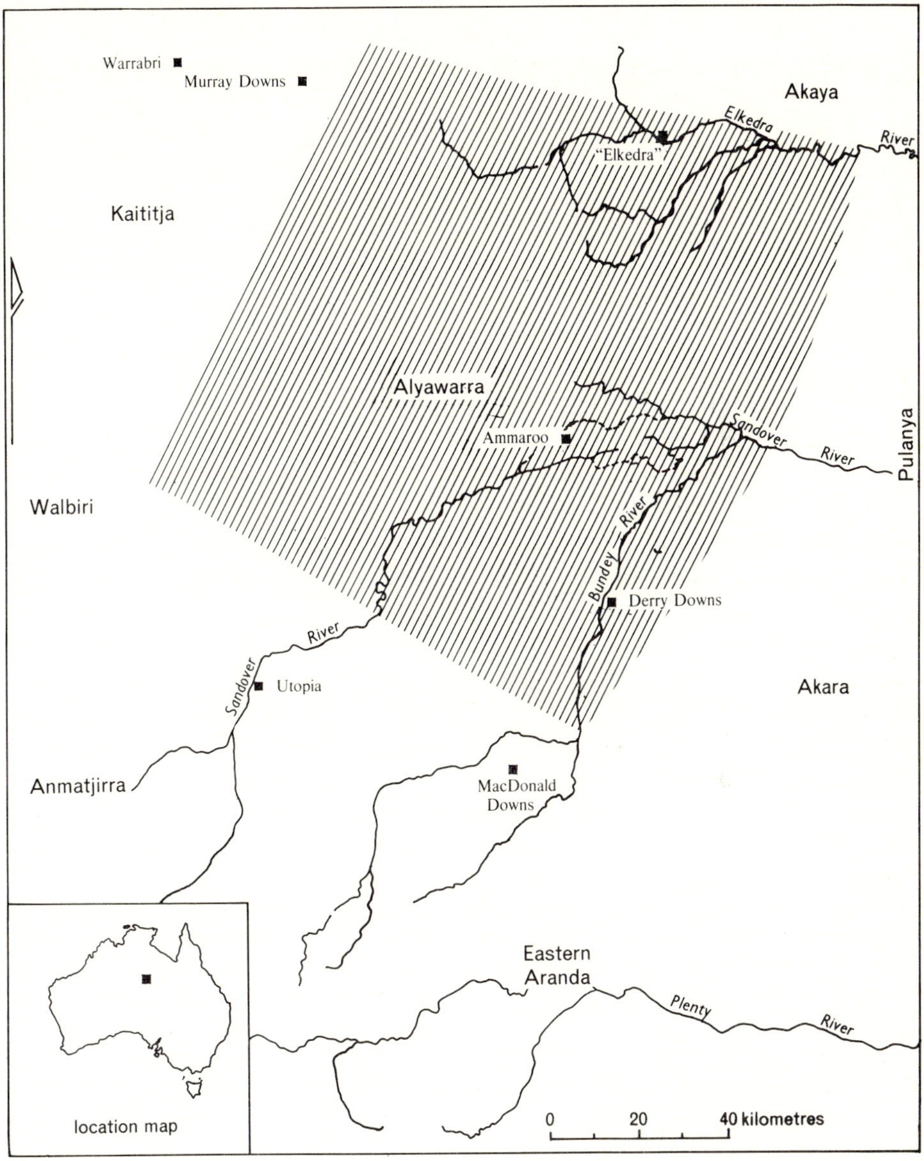

Fig. 1

The location of the Alyawarra, and station homesteads and Warrabri settlement.

individuals are said to be living permanently further away, e.g., at Alice Springs and Tennant Creek (some 100 kilometres to the north).

Alyawarra Territory is divided into a number of smaller units, which the people refer to by the English term 'Country'. In most cases (possibly all, although my informants were unsure in some instances), the Country name derives from the name of the site of principal religious significance within its boundary, e.g., Agharringa soak, Urriltja hill, Antaringinya soak. Fig. 2 shows the approximate location of these Countries in relation to Agharringa Country, whose area appears shaded.

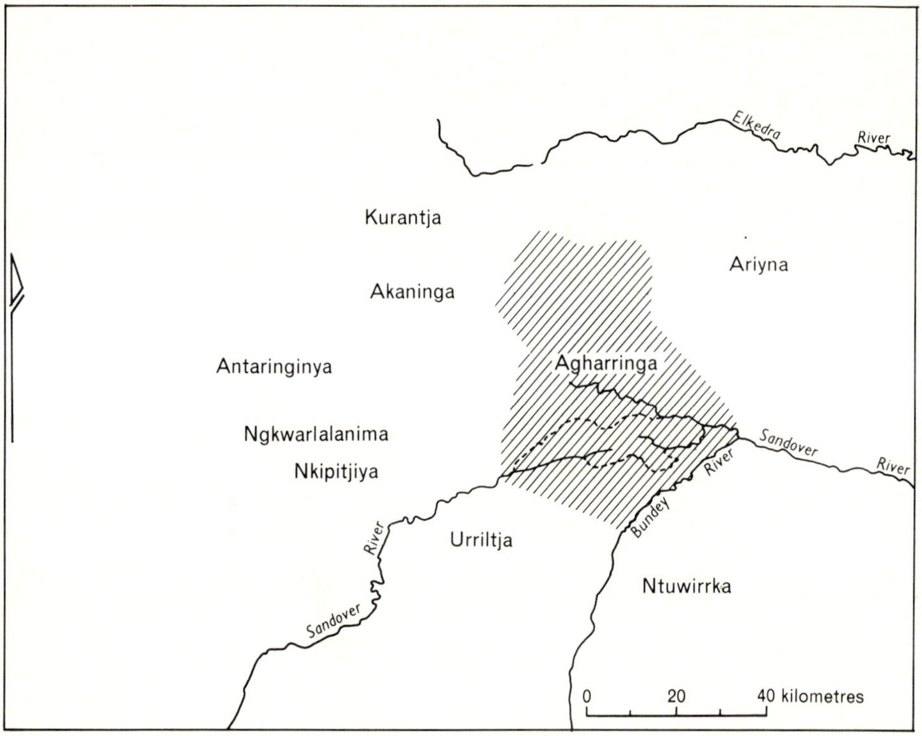

Fig. 2

The position of Alyawarra Countries relative to Agharringa Country.

It appears that the common use of the term 'Country' by the Alyawarra derives at least partly from European presence over the past 80 years or so; such people's interest was, and to a large extent still is, more in the land than in its traditional inhabitants. Discussions between Europeans and the Alyawarra therefore have focused on the land in the first instance, necessitating the use of a term for the area to which particular groups of Alyawarra had an attachment. However, there is no Alyawarra term even approximating 'Country', and in a traditional context there appears to have been no need for any. Certainly, the Agharringa men say they cannot conceive of any situation requiring it.

By contrast, O'Connell is reported as claiming that such terminology does exist (Toohey, 1979:6):

> Alyawarra territory is divided into a series of discrete named units called nguralungkwa or atcherunga, or in English 'countries' or 'blocks'.

Much discussion occurred during fieldwork over the meaning of the terms *ngirtilingkwa* and *atjurrunga* (to use Yallop's orthography), and I will only comment briefly on their meaning here.[2] *'Atjurrunga'*, say the Agharringa people, is an Anmatjirra word, although it is in common use throughout Alyawarra Territory. Its meanings are summed up well by Strehlow (1947:xiii), in dealing with the same word among the Aranda:

> In this book I have used the Aranda term tjurunga in two ways, always differentiated by their spelling. When spelt tjurunga it refers to the sacred stone or wooden objects

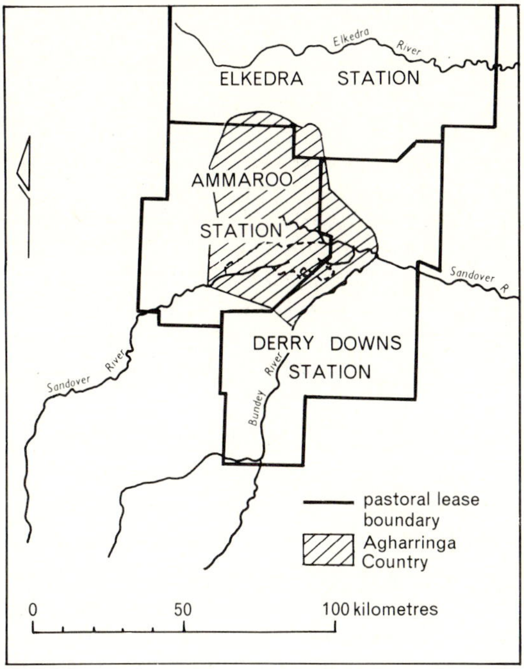

Fig. 3
The location of Agharringa Country in relation to pastoral leases.

> which figure in their religious life . . . The other spelling, tjuruŋa shows that the word is being used in its wider native significance, which embraces not only the stone or wooden objects already referred to, but also the ceremonies and chants and practically everything intimately associated with the sacred ceremonies.

'Ngirtilingkwa', say the Agharringa, is the exact Alyawarra equivalent of *'atjurrunga'*. Admittedly, *ngirtilingkwa* ceremonies are linked to the land, but not in the sense of whole areas, as claimed by O'Connell.

The location of an individual's affiliation with the land, determined by the site where conception is held to have occurred (this is discussed in detail later), is expressed in the suffix *arrinya*, which translates as 'belonging to' or 'a person of'. Thus we find typical references in conversation to Agharringarrinya—a person of Agharringa; Urriltjarrinya—a person belonging to Urriltja. As mentioned above, the name of the principal site in a given area is applicable in relevant context to the area as a whole and all people conceived inside it. The translations above also illustrate the fundamental difference in attitude towards land which exists between the Alyawarra and Europeans. It would appear there has been no need for a separate term approximating 'Country' in the Alyawarra language, although this situation does not imply that the boundaries of influence exerted by such principal sites are vague or unimportant, as is shown later in this book.

The Country claimed by the Agharringa people as theirs spans three cattle stations —Ammaroo, Derry Downs and Elkedra, as shown in Fig. 3.

There is some evidence that within Agharringa Country itself there are certain areas, each centring on a named site, which constitute subgroups; people personally associated with such areas have autonomy in the ceremonies localised within their own area. There are signs of a division into four, with centres at Aringkapungka, Agharringa, Alithila and Nkitingkuna.

Several Dreamings either pass through or end at these sites, and collections of ceremonial objects being the metamorphosed bodies of characters from such Dreamings are kept in storage areas in the vicinity of each one. If all the Dreamings localised in part or whole within Agharringa Country are superimposed on a single map, it is apparent that on the one hand a clustering effect would result around the four sites, while on the other hand there is little or no contact (in terms of Dreaming lines) between them. It would thus appear that the relative importance of these four sites is directly related to the amount of Dreamtime activity localised there. The Agharringa men say of these sites that they 'attracted the individual Dreamings' *(ngirtilingkwa anyintamanyintuwala akaralika),* so that the notion of totemic centres (to use T. G. H. Strehlow's term) is not foreign to them.

The status of the collections of objects near these sites appears to be twofold.

- That of final proof of the authenticity of myths as expressed in oral tradition and song series. In several cases, the objects are said to be the very bodies of named Dreamtime ancestors celebrated in the myths.

- It was the practice among earlier generations of Alyawarra for men's 'bush names' to be those of the Dreamtime ancestors associated with their conception sites. Although my information lacks enough time-depth for an accurate survey, the practice appears to have declined somewhat, and only six Agharringa men have such names at present. When the objects are displayed in the course of revelatory gatherings of men, the emotional attachment of these men is evinced with the same sort of tearful reaction seen when the memories of recently deceased relatives are evoked. Because the link between the Dreamtime ancestor and the present man either with the same bush name, or the senior owner of the associated Business, is held to be one of direct descent, the identical nomenclature is considered further proof of the validity of the present ownership.

It is a common way of referring to a man from Agharringa Country to attach the suffix *-arrinya* to one of the four sites mentioned above when specifying his area of particular influence. Such influence may derive from his conception locality or that of the Dreaming(s) owned by his father and passed on or about to be passed on to him. It is therefore possible, for example, for a man to classify himself as both Agharringarrinya and Aringkapungkarrinya—that is, a man of Agharringa Country with particular links to Aringkapungka. In appropriate context, such a statement is entirely unambiguous.

Of the four sites, Agharringa soak is considered of greatest importance, such that it has given its name to the Country as a whole, and the Dreaming from which its own name derives *(aghirra*—kangaroo) is the most important in the local repertoire. When or why this ranking occurred is something the present-day Agharringarrinya consider as deriving from the Dreamtime, and is therefore not open to question.

In much the same way that Agharringa soak is considered dominant among local sites even though the associated Dreaming line does not encompass the entire Country, so too the presiding control of the senior member of the dominant patriline, Frank Morton, extends over all the *ngirtilingkwa* and other men's Business for Agharringa Country, even though he does not have personal links with particular sites in the way other men may have.

The whole question of groups within groups is one requiring detailed attention; my own work with the Agharringa community barely scratches the surface.

THE EXTENT OF AGHARRINGA COUNTRY

The term 'boundary' is perhaps misleading in the context of Aboriginal land in that it has connotations of a line, real or imaginary, delineating the limits of property. The outer limits of Agharringa Country consist of 10 named locations, portions of two creeks in which a further 17 sites are localised, one range of hills which is named and another which is not. Only in the case of the creeks and hills is there a visible boundary in the European sense of the word. Elsewhere, demarcation focuses on series of individual sites wherein any particular site may or may not be visible from its nearest neighbour. It is therefore foreign to Alyawarra thinking to consider the boundary area even as points capable of confirmation by means of visual survey from a single position on the ground.

The individual sites owe their existence to the activities of various Dreamtime characters who created them when they camped or rested or emerged from the ground or departed into it or performed some otherwise noteworthy act there. When Alyawarra men recount the travels of any particular Dreamtime being, they invariably make a depression in the earth with one finger to denote a named site, then indicate travel from that site to the next named site in the myth by tracing an unbroken line in the earth away from that depression and terminating in another, this process continuing until the route of the myth is traced in its entirety. However, when discussing the boundary of Agharringa Country, the men would indicate specific sites with separated jabs in the earth, but did not join them. The series of linking lines are called *ingka,* the footprints or tracks of the ancestors, and because the points on the Agharringa boundary were created in more than one Dreaming and by more than one character, it is considered inappropriate to link them in such a manner.

In the course of fieldwork, groups of men took me to the various sites constituting boundary points for Agharringa Country. In addition to one or more senior men, a few younger men usually came along, and in some cases they were shown places for the first time. While the principal objects were to locate sites, explain their mythological significance and if necessary repair any stone arrangements that might be there, the positive qualities embodied in them were brought into even sharper relief by contrasting them with the surrounding terrain, and in this respect, two aspects were frequently emphasised.

On the one hand, almost all the boundary points were water sources—that is, soaks or rockholes—but there was not a single case where such a water source existed between any two boundary points and was not itself also a boundary point. On the other hand, relatively little religious significance is attached to land between boundary points, and no ceremonies exist to celebrate such places specifically. Dreamtime characters may have travelled through there in some cases, but they left no visible signs of their passage. The boundary sites therefore not only represent the most distant locations over which the Agharringa people have exclusive religious control, but are also ecologically reliable outposts beyond which the location, quality and quantity of drinking water cannot be consistently guaranteed in any given direction or within any given distance.

Fig. 4 identifies the boundary of Agharringa Country, with the named sites identified.

Generally speaking, for sites that are forbidden to women and children, sight is the means by which safe and dangerous distances are differentiated. For if a particular site should not be visited by these people, then it follows in Alyawarra thought that it should not even be seen by them. By this means, it is possible to warn away the women and children merely by indicating the region to within, say, 100 metres or so. No indication of the nature of the contents of such a region need be given nor indeed is

Fig. 4

The constituent points on the boundary of Agharringa Country.

given, as this in itself would be to divulge restricted information. Secrets are to be kept, or told selectively.

In the case of forbidden hills which, after all, may be visible from several kilometres away, women may approach to within two or three hundred metres for some legitimate purpose (e.g., to obtain water from a nearby but 'safe' source); this appears to be the only modification of the 'if you can see it, then you're too close' rule.

In the case of sites that are water sources, the perimeters are determined fairly easily. Waterholes cannot expand indefinitely no matter how much rain falls; as the surrounding earth is absorbent, a well-defined outline eventually forms. Although the ground in the immediate vicinity of such places is referred to as being 'at' such-and-such a site, close questioning reveals that the surrounding land is not incorporated into the site name. The locative suffix *-ila* normally meaning 'at', and also the allative suffix *-uwala,* normally meaning 'towards' are more accurately translated in such situations as 'in the vicinity of' and 'towards the vicinity of' such-and-such a site. Rockholes similarly are defined precisely by the contours of the rock itself, and soaks too have limits (although these may be found only by a hit-and-miss process). By coincidence or otherwise, all water sources inside Agharringa Country are available to everybody, so that the question of defining the physical extent of such sites is not linked with the matter of restricted access.

The perimeters of sites that are not water sources tend to be less precise, at least in European terms. If the site is freely available to all the attitude is that there is no need for a painstakingly accurate formulation. In every such site inside Agharringa Country there is a certain point or area of land about which there is unanimous agreement as to its geographic classification, e.g., that it is a sand hill, or a hill. In the course of conversation, each site may be described in two ways:

- in terms of the associated myth, in which case it will invariably be referred to as an *apmira* (camp site);
- in terms of its geographical classification.

Just as for sand hills and mountains about which there may be no associated mythology, so too for named sites there is no discussion about whether a given spot on the ground is part of the named feature or is part of the surrounding terrain; the issue is irrelevant. Mythological characters who metamorphosed into the land are said to have 'become a hill' *(apurtirika)* or 'become a sand hill' *(akulpirika),* and so on. In changing from characters into sites, and becoming part of the natural landscape with essentially the same visible composition as other similar but unnamed physical features, they are subject to the same conceptualisation concerning their perimeters.

Between the surrounding terrain and each site is a strip about which individual opinions may vary, some claiming it to be part of the one, others that it is part of the other, but most saying that they simply don't know. As remarked earlier, the issue is considered largely irrelevant in the absence of any Dreamtime precedent or guidelines.

Some Alyawarra Dreamings are not localised within a single Country, or within the Territory as a whole. These are of several types.

Type A Dreamings

There are some which either begin or end inside Alyawarra Territory, but over which the Alyawarra have no control and about which they have very little information at all. If the body of the Dreamtime character(s) metamorphosed into what is now a feature of the physical landscape, then that feature is afforded the same sort of respect given to similar features associated with locally owned Dreamings. No prohibitions of access apply, however. Those which concern Agharringa Country are shown in Fig. 5. The local people have no ceremonial authority over the myths or their respective rituals, neither is their knowledge of the myths' routes outside Agharringa Country detailed. (Only in one case, see point *k* in Fig. 5, do the Agharringa men know the associated songs, having attended performances of the complete ceremony at Warrabri.) In some cases the first or final sites of the Dreaming lines are known by name, although their precise locations may be a mystery. In other cases neither the sites nor even the Territories may be known. Within Agharringa Country itself, however, the location of the Dreamtime characters' travels are readily identified. Some contain arrangements of rock but most are features of the physical landscape.

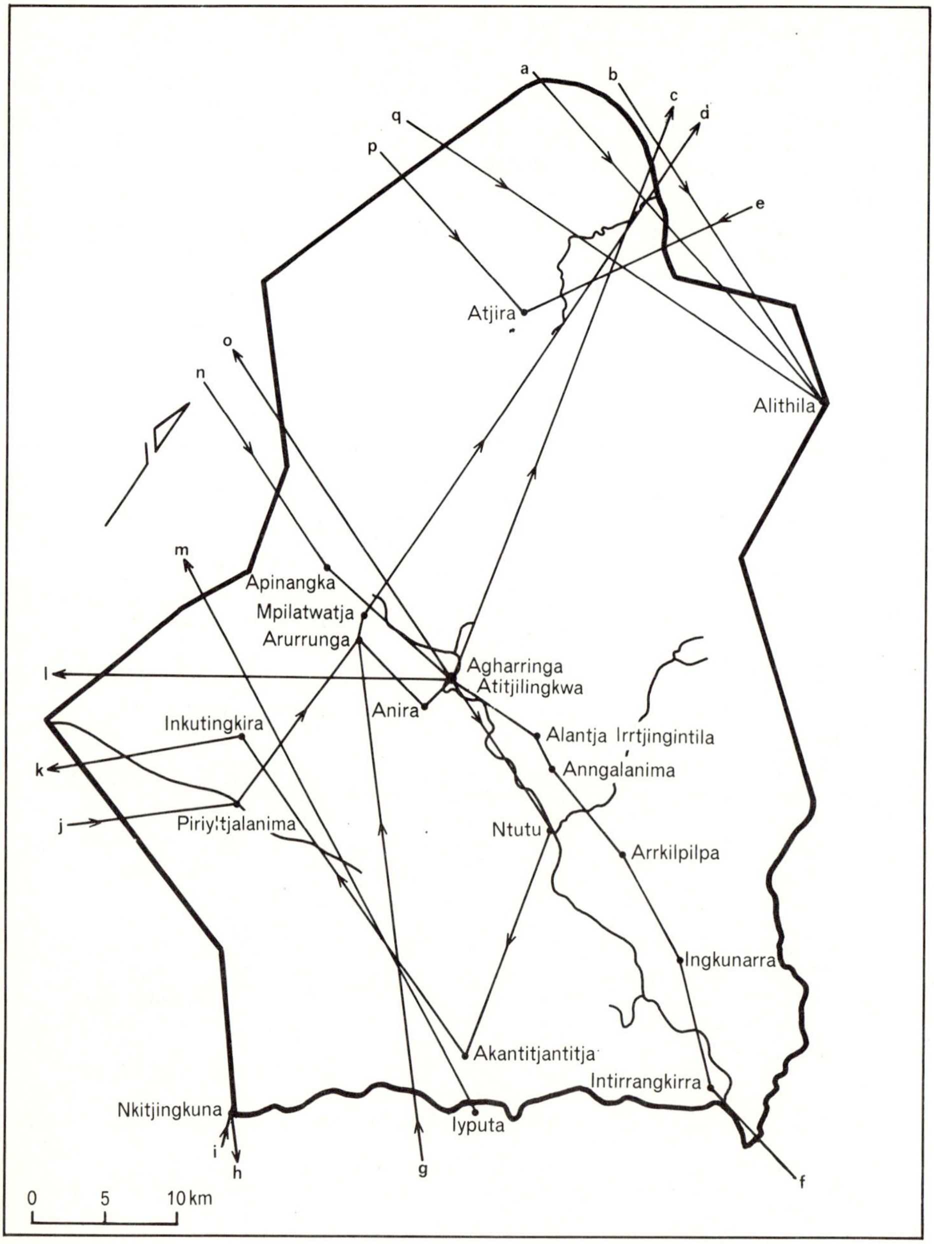

Fig. 5

The routes of Dreaming lines inside Agharringa Country travelling to or from non-Alyawarra Territories.

Legend to Fig. 5

a The route taken by a group of characters travelling to Alithila from Arapinya somewhere far to the northwest) via Intitjawila and Nguralirra (see *q* below, and *d* in Fig. 6).

b The route taken by a being going to Alithila from Tarla, near the present Peko Mines area, close to Tennant Creek.

c The exit direction of the character entering Agharringa Country originally from Atnungirrpa through point *j*.

d The exit direction of a being *en route* for Intapagharra, somewhere inside Warramunga Territory. The Dreaming line enters Agharringa Country west from Itarlintja on the Bundy River (see point *g*), and travels via Arurrunga and Mpilatwatja.

e The entrance direction of a character from the Barkly Tablelands area *en route* for Atjira soak.

f The entrance direction of two beings originally from Akiritjina, *en route* for Agharringa soak, via Intirrangkirra, Ingkunarra, Arrkilpilpa, Anngalanima, Alantja Irrtjingintila and Atitjilingkwa (see also points *l* and *o* below).

g The entrance direction of a character travelling from Ntuwirrka Country to Arurrunga and Mpilatwatja before passing north into Warramunga Territory.

h The direction taken by a character which arose from Nkitjingkuna soak and headed south-west.

i The entrance direction of a being which flew to Nkitjingkuna from Amuwala, somewhere to the south and entered the soak there.

j From Atnungirrpa a character travelled to Piriyltjalanima, thence to Arurrunga, Anira and Agharringa before heading north to an unknown locality, exiting at point *c*.

k The exit direction of two beings who entered Agharringa Country further north (at point *n*). Travelling ultimately from Kaititja Territory, they stopped at Apinangka, Agharringa, Ntutu, Akantitjantitja and Inkutingkira before leaving the Country, heading for Arrkala in Urriltja Country.

l The exit direction of one character. Starting originally at Akiritjina far to the east in the company of a different character, the Dreaming line enters Agharringa Country at Intirrangkirra (entrance point *f*), proceeding through Ingkunarra, Arrkilpilpa, Anngalanima, Alantja Irrtjingintila and Atitjalingkwa before arriving at Agharringa soak. Here, the second character went underground (see point *o* below), while the first continued alone, direct to Athiliya Country.

m The exit direction of a character which arose at Iyputa; it travelled direct into Kaititja Territory.

n The entry point of two beings from Kaititja Territory (see *k* above).

o The exit direction of the character originally from Ikiritjina, who, in the company of another being, travelled to Agharringa soak; while this other being continued on to Athiliya Country, the first one went underground to Awulaminintja soak, somewhere inside Atjaratjara (Walbiri) Country.

p The entrance direction taken by a character *en route* to Atjira soak from Walungkana inside Warramunga Territory.

q The entrance direction of a character to Alithila from Intitjawila, somewhere far to the north-west.

Type B Dreamings

By contrast, there is one Dreaming starting from Ikiritjina somewhere east of Lucy Creek (outside Alyawarra Territory) and heading north-west, following close to the present Sandover Highway for the last 110 kilometres and ending inside Agharringa soak. Agharringa men own and sing the entire line, even though they are not aware of the precise location of some of the sites outside their Country. (The particular Dreamtime character travelled in the company of another being of a different species (see point *f* in Fig. 5 above); despite this, the Agharringa people make no ownership claims to this other character's activities, or indeed to the present character after it reaches Agharringa soak.) Fig. 13 shows the route of this Dreaming.

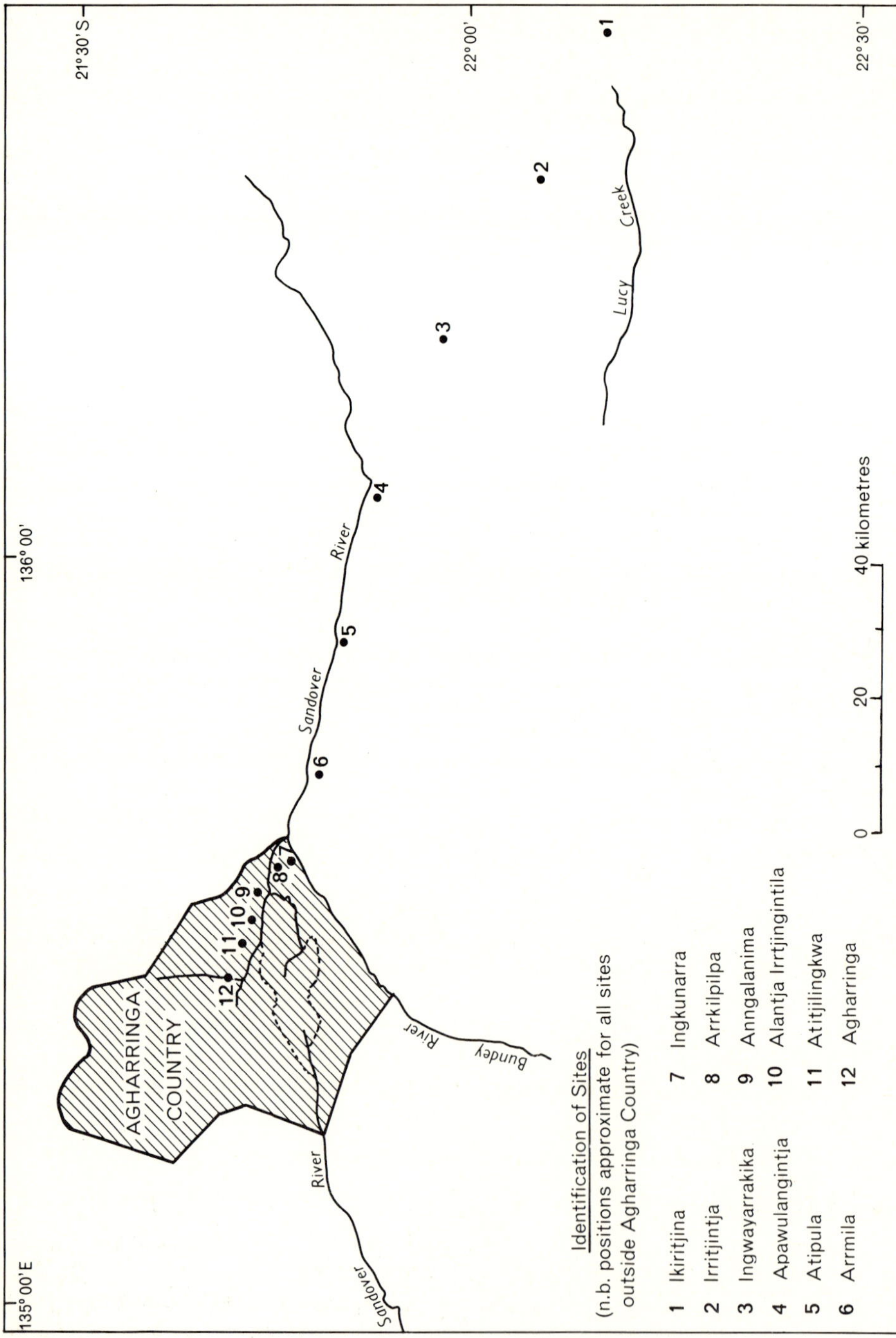

Fig. 6
The Dreaming line from Ikiritjina to Agharringa soak.

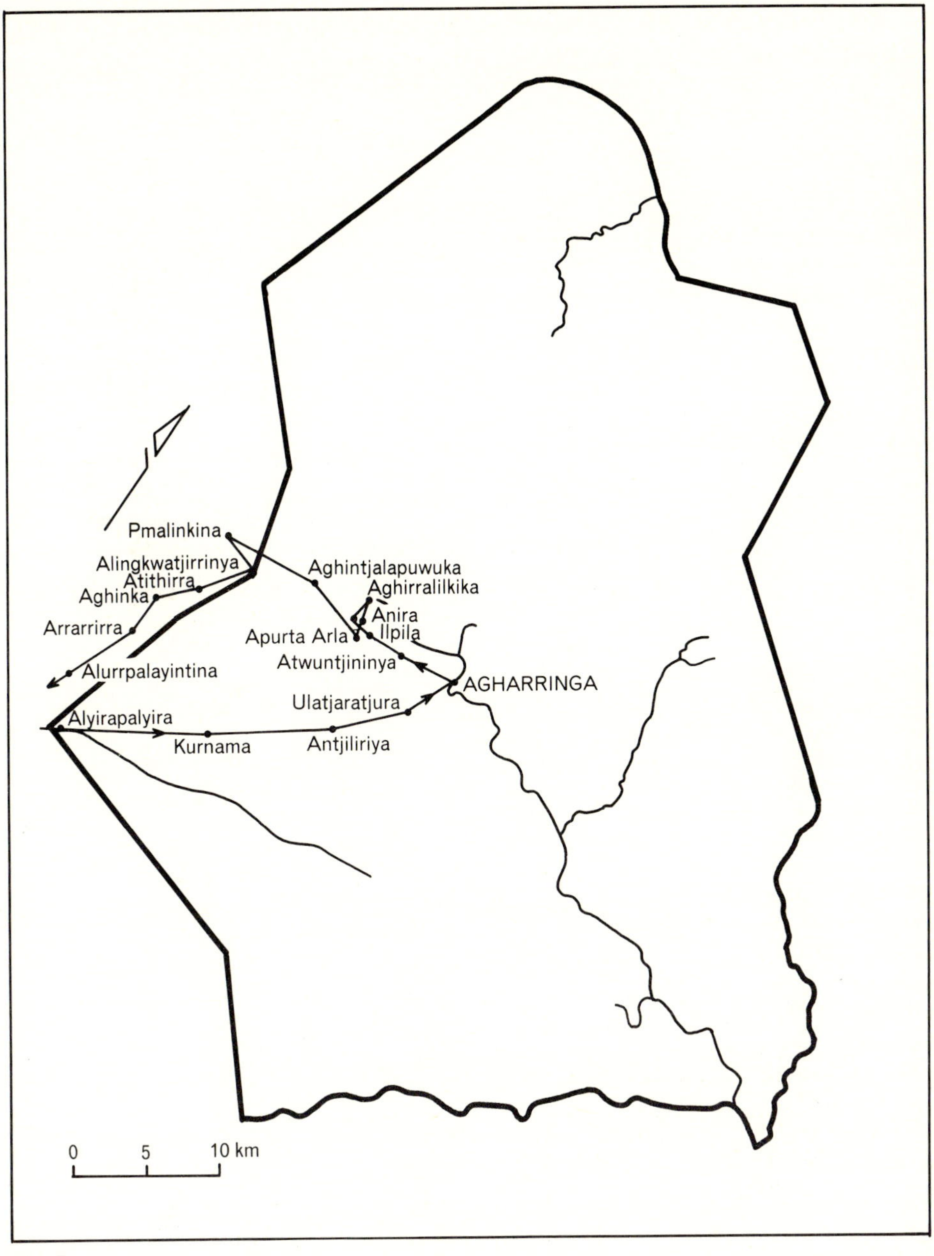

Fig. 7

Part of the route of an Agharringa Dreaming line which travels beyond Alyawarra Territory, later returning to its point of departure.

Type C Dreamings

There are some which are owned by one Country and which travel outside Alyawarra Territory. For example, the Agharringa people own a particular Dreaming which starts from Agharringa soak and passes through Anmatjirra and Aranda Territories *en route* to a certain named site. On reaching this point, the characters turn around and return home by a slightly different route (see Fig. 7). The Agharringa men performed the associated ceremony at Arurrunga in 1978.

Fig. 8

Three Agharringa Dreaming lines which briefly enter neighbouring Countries.

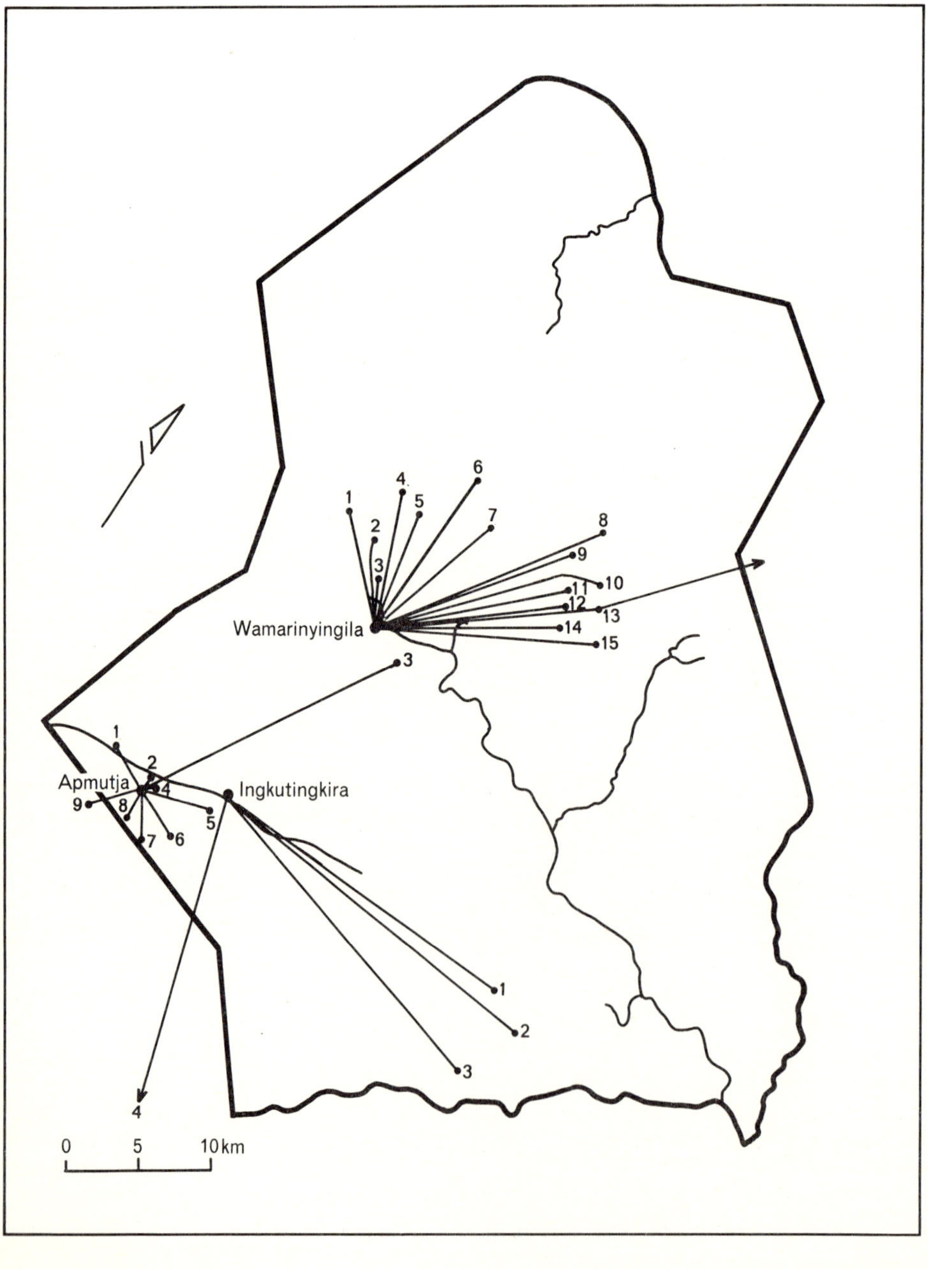

Type D Dreamings

There are those which are owned by one Alyawarra Country and which travel briefly outside that Country but remain inside the Territory as a whole. Three separate examples are found in the Agharringa repertoire. In each there is a site constituting a kind of home base from which sorties were made in search of food. Although all the base sites are celebrated in the form of shield designs, seen during *apulha* ceremonies, and the sorties are recounted in details in spoken form, yet there are no associated ceremonies or songs (see Fig. 8).

Type E Dreamings

There are a number of Dreamings which enter or leave Agharringa Country; the origin and location of these, over which the Agharringa people have no claims of ownership but whose sites they respect, is shown in Fig. 9.

It should be repeated at this point that the Agharringa people exercise no control at all over the type A Dreamings; apart from being aware of their existence, and of their routes (with varying degrees of certainty), and taking care not to disturb any stone arrangements which might be at the various sites, they show little interest in them. As mentioned earlier, only in the case of one Dreaming which starts at Alikuranga inside Warrabri settlement do the men profess any knowledge of the associated songs; however, their knowledge is bounded by the extent of the characters' travel inside Agharringa Country. Through extended residence at Warrabri a few men have gathered information and songs from other parts of the Dreaming line, and one man claims to be a 'boss', but all performances are said to occur within Kaititja Territory and with Kaititja men leading the proceedings.

Turning to Agharringa-owned Dreaming lines, four broad categories may be distinguished:

(1) As mentioned already, those which comprise a kind of 'home base' from which a number of trips are made, always returning to the point of departure;
(2) those whose route is circular, eventually returning to the point of departure after having passed through a number of other sites;
(3) those which consist of travel from one site to another, with or without passing through other sites *en route;*
(4) those which have no associated travel, and are not linked to any other site(s).

Turning to specific cases of each category, we find there are three Dreamings of the 'home base' type, in which these bases are respectively Wamarinyingila, Apmutja and Inkutingkira (Fig. 8). (I have deliberately omitted names and other details of the myths in accordance with the Agharringa men's wishes.)

There are three examples within the second category of Dreaming lines shown in Figs 7 and 10. As stated above, the line presented in Fig. 14 relates to the initial and final stages only of a myth figure travelling far beyond Agharringa and even Alyawarra land, but which is said to be the exclusive property of the Agharringa men.

Dreaming lines of the third category are far more numerous than for any other category, and are shown in Figs 11, 12 and 13. In Fig. 12 a further line occurring entirely within the Bundy riverbed cannot be shown clearly on a map, although the relevant locations have been given. The Dreaming arises at Walakuta, and travels by way of Nkitjingkuna, Alpatjakina, Alturatjirra and Apurta Alilkina, before ending at Nkitjingkuna. Fig. 13 shows part of Ilbumric Creek, in the north-eastern section of Agharringa Country in which a number of sites are clustered.

Dreamings within the fourth category are not celebrated in ceremonial form. The mythology attached to each site is similar: a being of one description or another emerges from the ground, moves away up to a radius of perhaps fifty metres in the course of finding food, then returns into the ground at the point of emergence. Unlike sites contained in Dreamings of the other three categories, there does not appear to be

Fig. 9
The routes of Dreaming lines inside Agharringa Country travelling to or from other Alyawarra Countries.

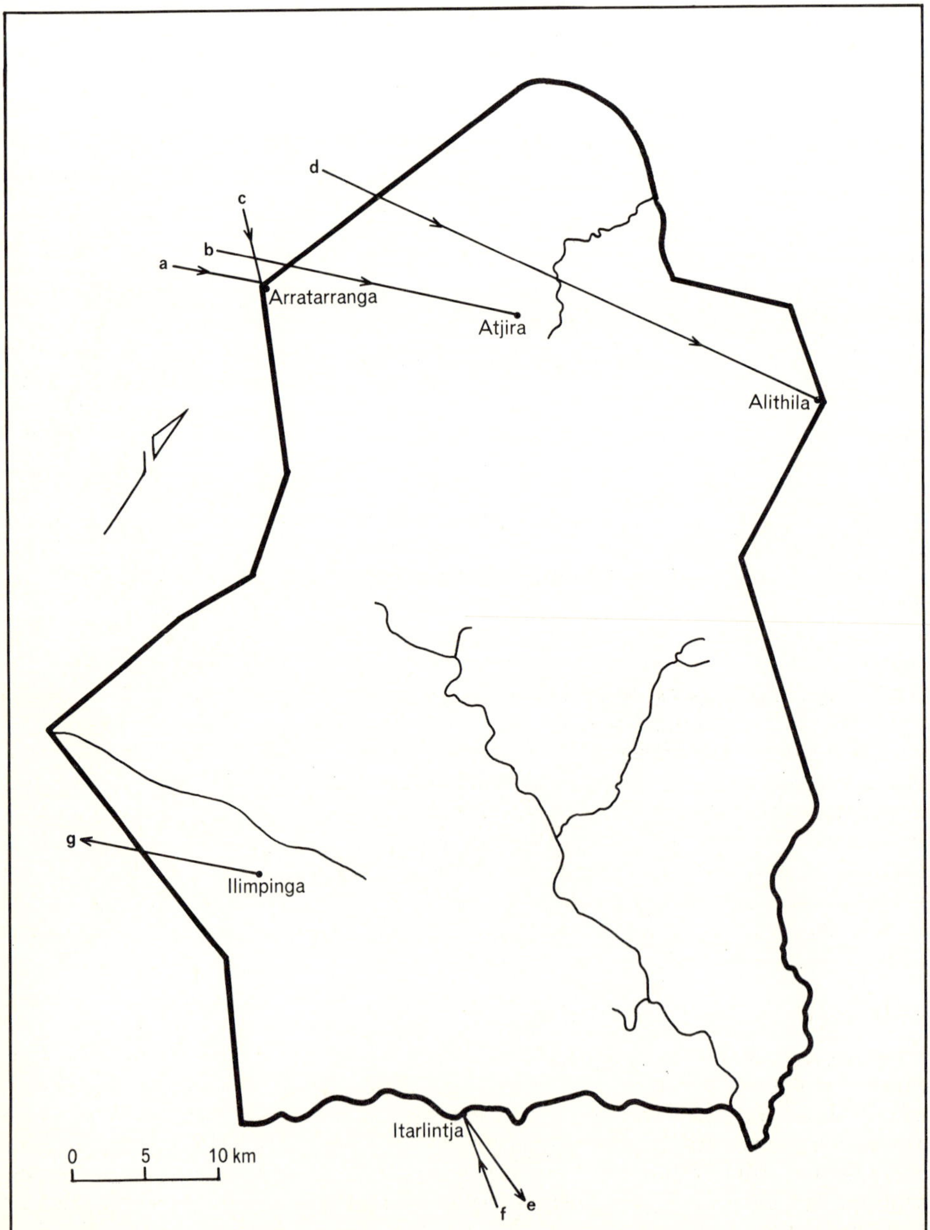

Legend to Fig. 9

a The entrance direction of a being travelling to Arratarranga from Ngkwarlalanima Country.

b The entrance direction of a being travelling to Atjira soak from Ayiynya, inside Antaringinya Country.

c The entrance direction of a character going to Arratarranga from Akaninga Country.

d The direction taken by a character from Nguralirra, inside Nkipitjiya Country, *en route* for Alithila soak.

e The exit direction taken by a being from Ntuwirrka Country going to Itarlintja soak.

f The entrance direction of this same being.

g A being arose at Ilimpinga and headed west into Urriltja Country.

---

any interest or desire on the part of the Agharringa people in maintaining the physical condition.

How typical the variety of Dreaming lines inside Agharringa Country is in relation to the other Alyawarra Countries is not known. The only work on Dreaming lines in the region has been in association with land claims, appearing in the claim books for the Alyawarra and Kaititja Claim of 1978 and the Utopia Claim of 1979 prepared by Hagen and Rowell. However, due to shortage of time, in neither of these cases did the authors visit all the sites about which they presented information, and as a result many of them could not be localised precisely.

Figs 15 and 16 present in simplified form the information given earlier in Figs 5 and 9. These tend to confirm Yallop's point (1969:197) that links with neighbouring Territories to the east are noticeably absent. The Agharringa people have no reasons or theories as to why this is so, apart from noting the present absence of Pulanya and Akara speakers to their east and south-east.

In contrast with all of the above categories in which individual groups possess exclusive ownership of complete Dreamings, there are two further series belonging to the men which are owned only in part by the Agharringa. In both cases, ownership of part or all of the rest of the Dreaming is imputed to specific groups outside Alyawarra Territory.

The first of these is Restricted (f), and the degree of secrecy surrounding it is such that the details of its route may not be divulged; suffice it to say here that the Agharringa begin singing from Luridja Territory and trace the travels through Walbiri Territory until finally reaching Alyawarra Territory.

The second, Restricted (g), is referred to solely by the name of its principal character. Ownership is said to be by the whole body of Agharringa men rather than any particular group or individual. The Dreaming arose in the north-eastern corner of Agharringa Country then moved south, eventually reaching a site said to lie somewhere inside Akara Territory. At that site, which the character himself named, a meeting occurred with another character of the same type, and the Agharringa have no further knowledge of the Dreaming, although they believe that the Akara people take it over. Fig. 17 shows the portion of the route inside Agharringa Country.

ACQUISITION OF OWNERSHIP

Ownership, or more precisely, co-ownership of men's ceremonies of the *ngirtilingkwa* category is determined by patrilineal descent.[3] However, not all sons of a given father inherit all his Business; separation in such cases is on the basis of the location of the conception site in relation to the site(s) associated with a given *ngirtilingkwa*. To take one example from Agharringa Country—Jupiter Barnes and Bob Nelson are full brothers, but, because of his conception site in the northern part of the Country Jupiter has inherited the Businesses associated with Alithila, Aringkapungka, and other less

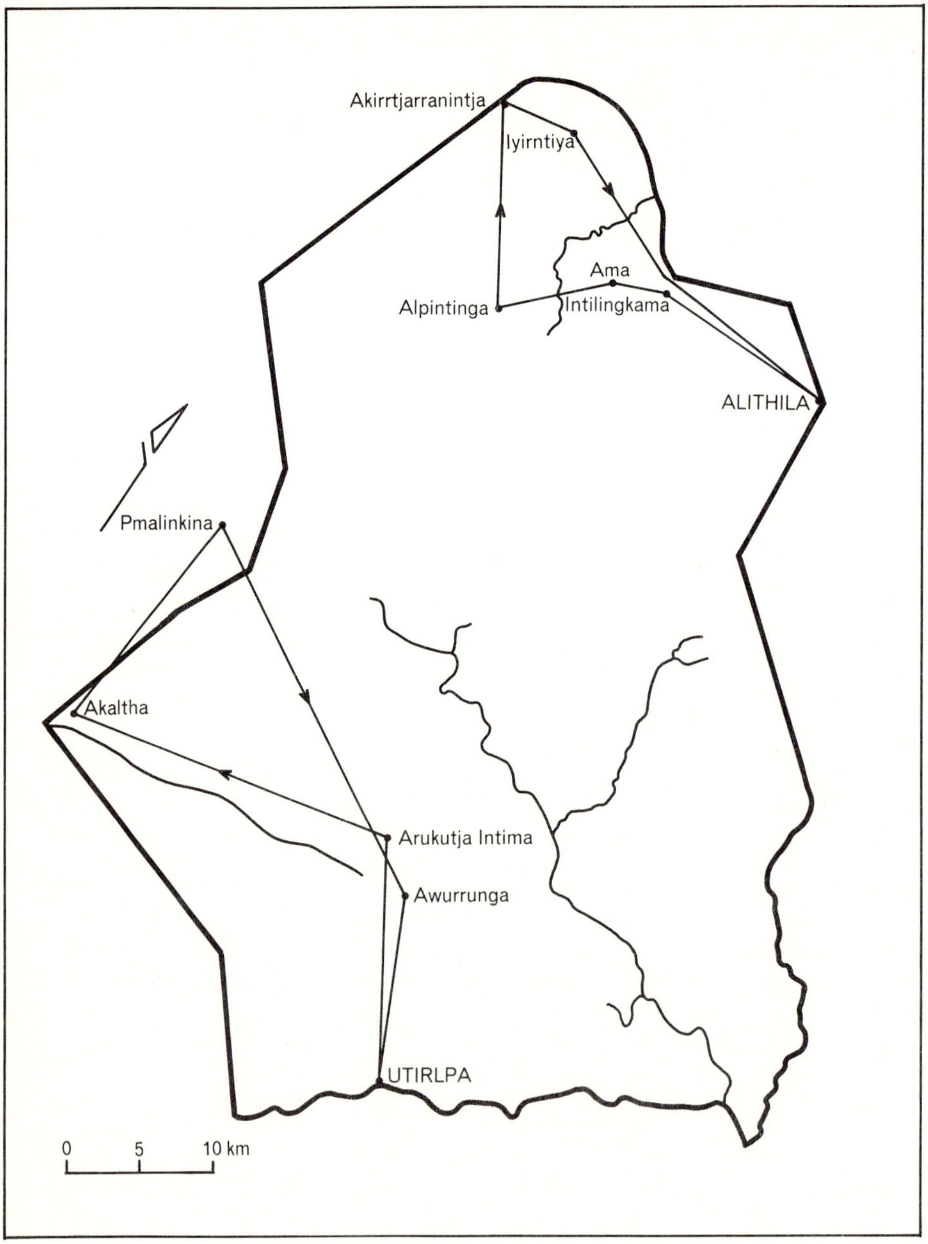

Fig. 10
The location of Dreaming lines of category (2).

important sites in the vicinity. Bob, on the other hand, has acquired ownership of ceremonies relating to Nkitingkuna, and other lesser southern sites.

Ideally, the inheritance of *ngirtilingkwa* ownership begins with the eldest son, thence to the second, third and so forth. There are a number of exceptions to this sequence, however.

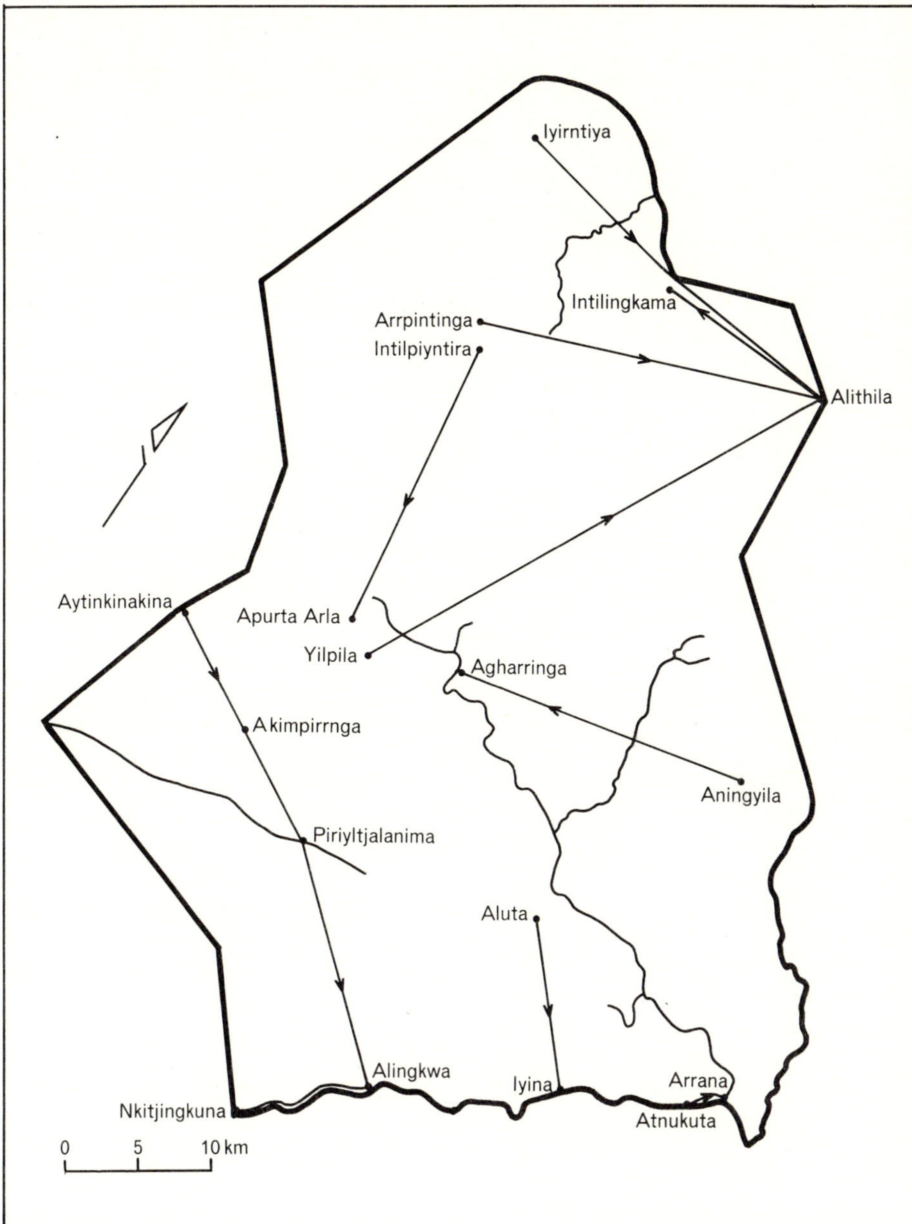

Fig. 11

The location of Dreaming lines of category (3).

- Perhaps the most obvious is where a senior owner has no younger brothers or sons, he may then adopt a son and in due course pass on the ownership to him. This practice is said to apply only where three conditions are met: where the adoptee's real father is dead, where the father was himself an Agharringa man, and where the stepfather has cared for the son since his boyhood. The Agharringa men discussed

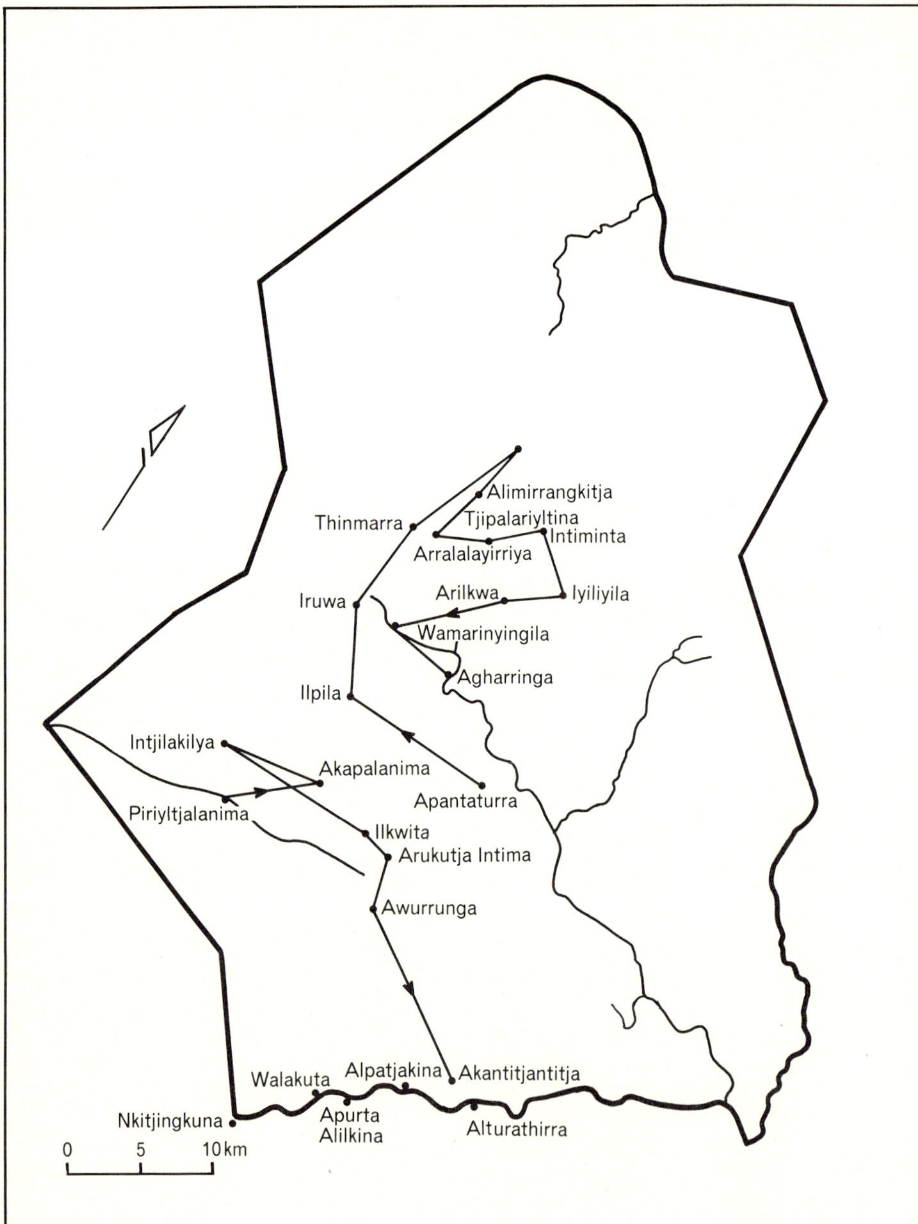

Fig. 12

The location of further Dreaming lines of category (3).

this situation in theoretical terms only, as no cases have occurred in their own Country within living memory.

- Where a man is considered unfit to receive it because of his temperament, ownership will be withheld until he can demonstrate sustained trust-worthiness. The

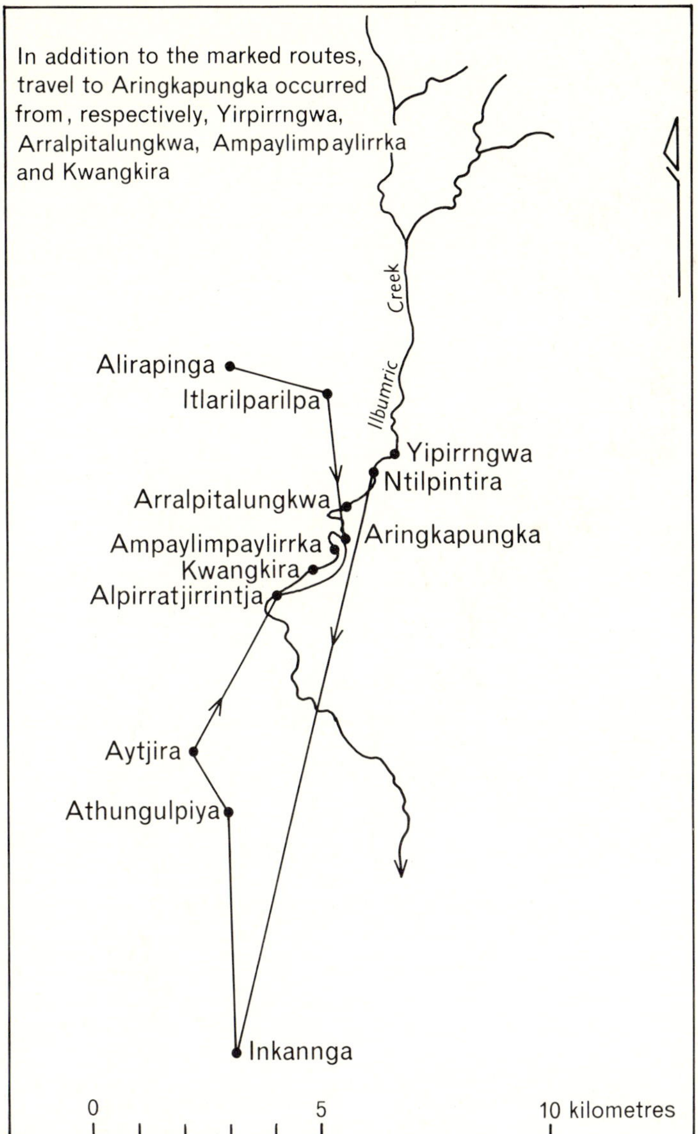

Fig. 13

The location of further Dreaming lines of category (3) occurring in the Ilbumric Creek area.

Agharringa men point out a certain individual who, in 1978, was barred from further instruction in a particular *ngirtilingkwa* following what was considered disgraceful conduct at another ceremony.

- Where a man is sole owner of a particular *ngirtilingkwa* and has no real or adopted sons, his death signals the end of that Business. In real life, performances would have been continued for as long as the owner believed he could interest some other close relative in assuming ownership, and at least one example of this is in progress locally.

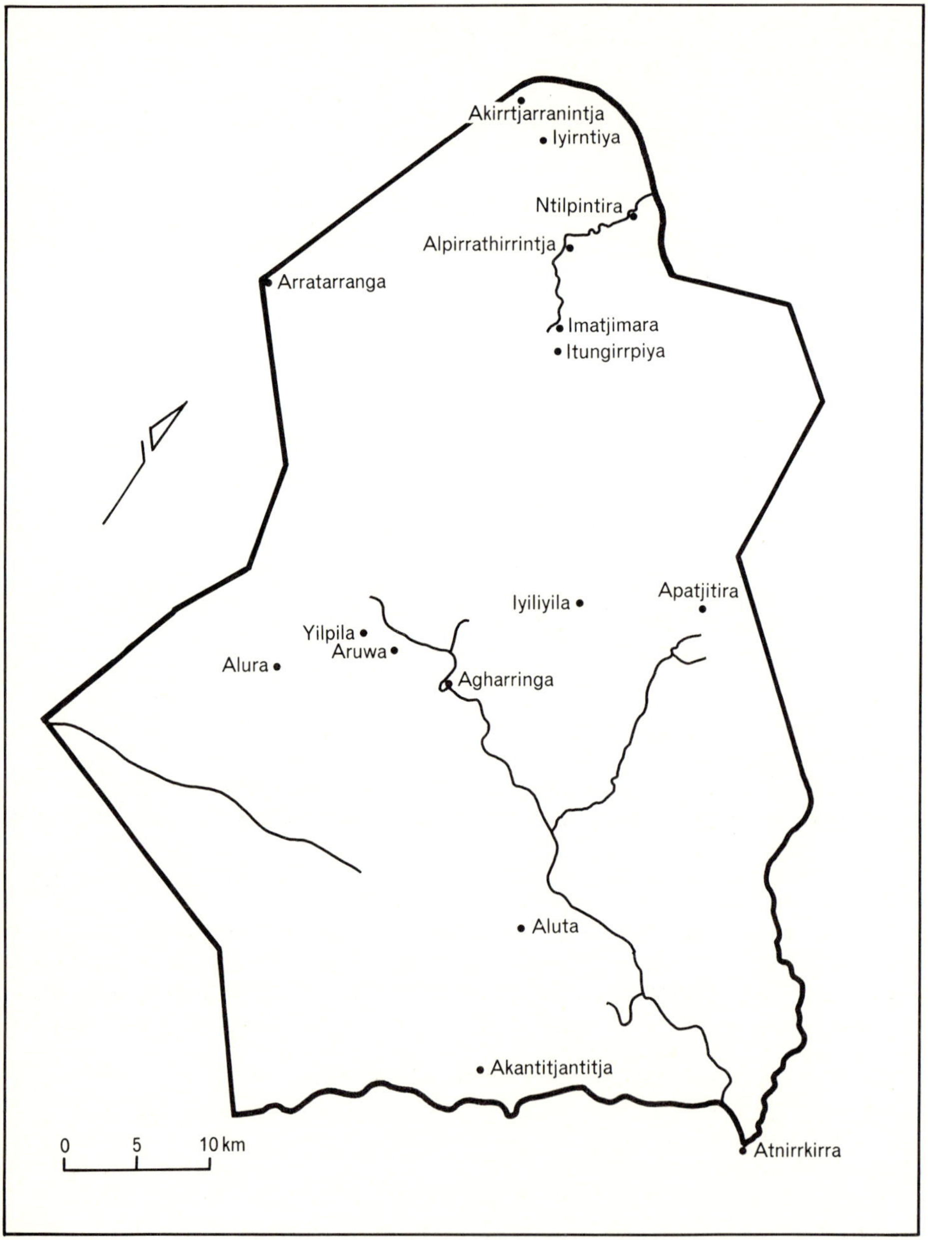

Fig. 14
The location of sites of category (4) Dreamings.

Despite these exceptions, the most common form of acquiring owner status in Agharringa Country is by direct inheritance in the male line. Ranking exists within the circle of owners on the primary basis of age. However, executant ability is also an integral factor in the ranking, and the eventual onset of debility associated with old age spells a corresponding weakening of ceremonial authority. Frank Morton is the present

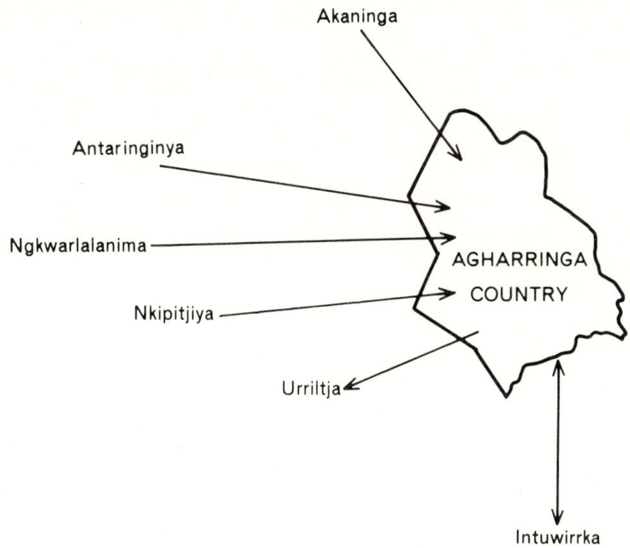

Fig. 15

A simplified diagram of non-Alyawarra Dreaming lines originating at, passing through, or terminating inside Agharringa Country.

acknowledged 'boss' of Agharringa Country, his paternal grandfather and father, and he himself, being eldest sons. There is general agreement about the line of succession within Frank's own generation, given that older men will die before younger ones; the line begins with Frank Morton, Slippery Morton, Alec Peterson, Peter Peterson, and Edward Morton, in that order.

Frank himself occupies his presiding position for the simple reason that he has a unique credential—he is the oldest living eldest son in the patriline. Although his conception site is Alpirrithirrintja, in the Ilbumric Creek, he is said to be an owner of every *ngirtilingkwa* inside Agharringa Country. However, certain other individual owners have closer personal associations with particular Dreamings because of their conception site affiliations, and the eldest owner with such a link generally takes executive control in performances of the respective Businesses.

Each *ngirtilingkwa* performance is followed by a teaching session in which younger men gather around the ground-painting and/or ceremonial objects and are lectured on their significance by one or more senior owners and *kutungurla.* The sessions are formal, solemn silence being observed by the audience, as one by one the pictorial or material representations of aspects of the myths are detailed together with verbal accounts of the particular episodes being celebrated. It is on occasions such as these that Frank's overall superior knowledge and social standing are most apparent, as together with a senior *kutungurla,* he leads the exposition. Junior owners periodically offer brief comments of agreement or emphasis, while non-owners remain silent throughout.

The mechanics for acquiring owner status are identical for each individual *ngirtilingkwa.* After the existing owners decide that a particular eligible owner has had sufficient experience in the preparation and enactment of one of their *ngirtilingkwa,* and provided that he has been regular in his *tjinkirra* food-gifts to the owners on previous occasions, they agree to extend ownership to him on the occasion of the next performance. When that occasion arises the ceremony is performed as usual and at its

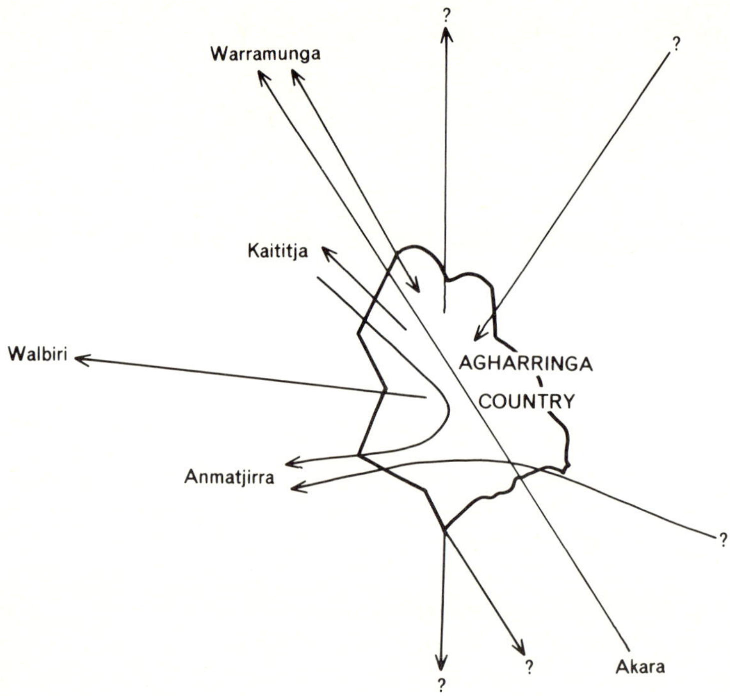

Fig. 16

Dreaming lines to and from other Alyawarra Countries which leave or enter Agharringa Country.

conclusion the existing owners summon the one they have agreed to admit. In the course of each ceremony a number of objects are manufactured; the larger types of these are either ground-paintings or constructions attached in some way to the human body. When admitting the newcomer, the owners instruct him either to sit in the middle of the ground-painting, or to sit on the ground with the constructed object in his lap. By so doing, he is said to 'secure the site' (*apmira inturrkwutjika*). It should be pointed out that each performance of a *ngirtilingkwa* ceremony celebrates a particular site from the original myth. Even though all the songs from the relevant series may be sung, and perhaps even though the objects manufactured are identical in appearance to those relating to one or more other sites in the Dreaming, yet it is maintained that the individual performances celebrate individual sites rather than the myth in its entirety. The site thus being celebrated at a given performance is the one which the newcomer is said to be 'securing'. By so doing, however, he acquires ownership of not just that one site, but the *ngirtilingkwa* in its totality—that is, the act does not have to be repeated for each successive site in the Dreaming: once suffices for all.

The older owners lean over the seated newcomer, telling him, 'You've got to take on that one now. Don't forget the details—that's your Business now. When this Business is performed at the next *apulha* [initiation] time, we ourselves won't play an active part —that's your responsibility now', and so on. This last comment is not in fact taken literally, but represents an agreement that the newcomer may participate more fully in future performances.

Vital though it is that this act occur as a conferral of ownership, of almost equal importance is the presence at the conferral of as many non-owners as possible to act as witnesses (*artwa akaltja*—experienced men, or *inkirrka akaltja*—experienced

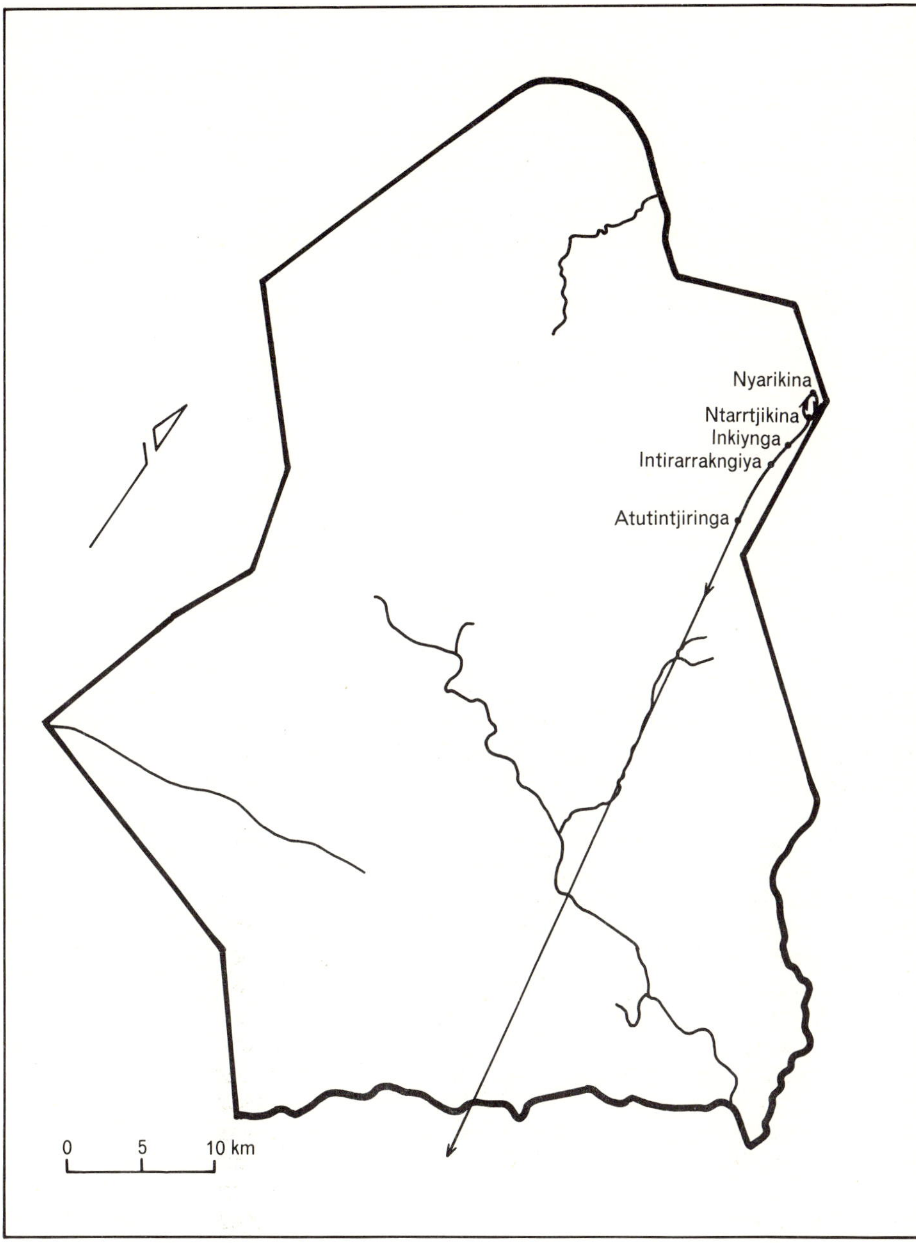

Fig. 17
The beginning of the Restricted (g) Dreaming route.

onlooker; the English term 'witness' is also frequently used), to ensure widespread knowledge that the appropriate formalities were observed and to support any later claims the newcomer may take in relation to ceremonial privileges regarding that *ngirtilingkwa*.

There is considerable variation in the age of the new owner at the time of conferral.

For example, in 1978 two Agharringa men were made owners of different *ngirtilingkwa;* one is in his early 30s, the other is more than 10 years older.

In cases where a particular site is associated with more than one Dreaming line (e.g., where two or more Dreamings cross, or begin or end at the same site), and is celebrated in a ground painting, the painting will include details relating to each Dreaming. Should a man sit on such a painting, ownership is thereby bestowed for all the Businesses.

On the death of an Alyawarra adult, performances of the major *ngirtilingkwa* of the deceased's Country are immediately stopped. For a man the period of suspension is one year, and rather less for a woman.

The first performance of a local *ngirtilingkwa* following the death of a senior patriline member, be it male or female, is called *ngirtilingkwa iyparima*—setting free the Business. The mechanics of the ceremony are identical to any other performance, except that the man who is now the new senior owner personally dominates the preparation and enactment, taking the lead role in any dancing or kinetic display, and himself being foremost in the teaching session afterwards.

Female members of the patriline are active in the teaching of domestic rather than ceremonial matters to their children, who are, after all, members of the opposite moiety and stand in a different relationship to the Country. In contrast to the men, who receive from other men a formal education in the Dreamings of their particular Country, the women remain largely ignorant of such matters and indeed may be ignorant of their own conception Country. The primary role of female patriline members is to be the means of providing *kutungurla.* The term *kutungurla* expresses a custodial relationship to land, in that one is *kutungurla* for one's mother's Country.

On certain occasions female patriline members partake, albeit in a minor way, in the *ngirtilingkwa* ceremonies associated with the patriline's Country. If decorated shields are used in these ceremonies they will be given to the most senior woman owner in camp, who takes them back to her own camp site, storing them temporarily on top of her brush shelter. No outward emotion is registered, and the other women show no obvious curiosity or even interest. The woman may be told by the men, 'This one is from your Country', as she receives the shield for the first time, otherwise no words are exchanged at the handover. Some women, especially the older ones, know the name of the *ngirtilingkwa* ceremony with which each shield is associated, and a few are familiar with the details of the designs.

Later that day, or on the following day, the woman, together with any others from the same Country, collect leafy branches and brush the decorated surface of the shields as they lie on the ground causing the ochre with which they are covered to partially disintegrate. The act is said to make the *ngirtilingkwa* (translated as 'seed' in this context by the people themselves) disseminate over the whole Country. After a few seconds of this, the surface of the shields is wet with water and the designs wiped off altogether; the shields are then stored in their customary places inside the camp.

The same women who partook in this brief act then set about preparing a food gift (called *tjinkirra)* for the senior male owners, to reciprocate for the men's efforts in performing the *ngirtilingkwa* ceremony on the women's behalf as well as for themselves. Formerly, this food gift consisted of seed cake and yams, although nowadays it comprises billies of tea and damper.

THE STATUS OF SONGS

Although I have not dealt directly with songs thus far, it will be apparent to those familiar with central Australian culture that with few exceptions songs are integral to ceremonial enactment. In terms of ownership, songs and ceremonies are inseparable.

The ceremonies called *ngirtilingkwa* form the basis of the Agharringa people's claim to ownership of Agharringa Country.[4] The total number of such ceremonies in the local repertoire is said to be 19, but it is apparent that some of these have fallen into disuse as a result of a lack of knowledgeable personnel to instruct younger patriline members. During the Dreamtime the *ngirtilingkwa* characters created and/or named more than three-quarters of the sites in Agharringa Country.

The songs associated with each *ngirtilingkwa* ceremony are believed to have been created by the Dreamtime ancestors in the course of their travels and other activities. In some cases, the words are expressed in the first person, e.g., 'I am dancing . . .', 'I can see someone approaching . . .', and the Alyawarra believe that these constitute the very words spoken by the ancestors. In other cases the texts are worded in the third person and assume a more narrative style. However, whatever the style of their texts, they are held to have been transmitted faithfully and with total accuracy through numberless generations to the extent that they have the status of an ultimate authority in matters of ceremonial detail or in what are considered historical facts. In addition, when travelling to or near a particular site celebrated in a ceremony, or when discussing among themselves details of the Dreamtime account, the men often break into song to illustrate or emphasise a point. Insofar as the Dreamtime myths are localised to precise areas of land which are still recognisable today, they embody information about land ownership. And insofar as this information is crystallised in song texts, the songs themselves represent the earliest statements about land ownership —a kind of original land claim.

Nobody who has witnessed a *ngirtilingkwa* ceremony can doubt the genuineness of the performers' enthusiasm, or the fervour with which the senior owners elaborate on the details of the myth. However, the details of the actions, and indeed the structure of the society as a whole, is founded on the belief that present-day ceremonies follow exactly the pattern as shown by successive generations of ancestors, and deriving from the teaching to the first generation of Alyawarra men at an indeterminate period in the past, and by an undefined means. While our current research methodology may not allow us to probe beyond the precontact past, it is possible to test such a belief in more recent times. All observable changes result, either directly or indirectly, from European presence in the area.

In the course of performance, a number of non-traditional items may be seen. These innovations are openly admitted the stated reason in most cases being greater ease of access. The material objects which have not changed are those of obvious antiquity kept in secret storage areas, the smaller wooden objects now fashioned with steel rather than stone implements, and the non-permanent creations made with materials readily available (e.g., ochres, saplings, antbed, earth). When men gather to explain *ngirtilingkwa* ceremonies to the younger number among them, they generally do not remark on the material constituents of the various objects. The prime concern is with the non-material aspects of the ceremony, such as the dance actions, songs, various prescribed movements and sequences. It is clear that these are the sorts of things which the Agharringa people believe are unchanging. Also included as indispensable and unchangeable are the order of ceremonial events, details of events not requiring the use of material objects, the timing of performances, and the various responsibilities and social relationships existing among the participants. In teaching sessions, it is these elements of ceremonial life which are emphasised; they came from the Dreamtime and have been faithfully perpetuated by successive generations of ancestors and must continue in the same manner. When an Agharringa man says, after a particular ceremony, 'this is the correct way; this is how we have always done it', he is not referring to the cotton wool, glass, steel and other non-traditional elements which may have featured, but to the organisation of non-material aspects of the performance. To him these are of primary concern.

By contrast, the published literature contains no cases of changes to the *ngirtilingkwa* songs. Comparison of recordings made in the 1930s with more recent versions shows an exact coincidence of song words, sequential order and overall melodic contour. In short, there is no reason to doubt the accuracy of Alyawarra claims that the songs are as they always have been. The reaction to attempts to insinuate changes in the musical content of ceremonies is that such attempts would be instantly recognised and rejected as *urrtjarrintja* (rubbish) and *nuwalinga atnuwurrnga* (not a Dreaming). With the exception of charms, Alyawarra singing is a group activity, and familiarity with the established contents of a given song series is such that, according to the Agharringa men, it would be impossible for anyone to change part of any text, or add or remove any song from a series.

The sole variation in song performances observed during the fieldwork period concerned the order of succession in which the individual songs in a given series were sung. Some series may be sung 'straight' *(arratja)*—that is, with the order of succession fixed—while others are 'crooked' *(ampirrampirra)*—in which the order of succession is more loosely organised. To omit any song in a 'straight' series and proceed to the next is called 'jumping over' *(atnanpika akuturrpa)* and labelled as an error. It is usually rectified by one or more knowledgeable men placing a restraining hand on the accompanying instruments of the offending singers, thus halting the singing. In practice, as well as principle, the Dreamtime precedent is faithfully followed.

On one level of observation, there are certain differences between individual performances of the same *ngirtilingkwa* songs—overall pitch and speed, numbers of repetitions of individuals songs before the singers proceed to the next in the series, identity of the song leader(s), and so on—but these in no way effect the Alyawarra's view of 'sameness'.

While spoken accounts of the same myths may vary in their points of emphasis or even omit particular sections, song texts are considered inviolate, and their contents the highest order of proof to which one may have recourse. To give one example of the extent to which this belief is maintained: in 1978 rumour reached Agharringa Country that a large group of *tjilkatja*[5] men from somewhere far to the south of Alice Springs had been seen little more than 160 kilometres away and that they were forcibly removing young men from various communities in order to initiate them. Hurriedly, men from four other Alyawarra communities were assembled, particular care being taken to include younger men, and the Alyawarra ceremonies associated with initiation were rehearsed over a period of several hours. The *tjilkatja* men, they said, had no authority inside Alyawarra land, and if they tried to abduct any young Alyawarra men they would be met, not with a show of violence, but with a performance of this particular Alyawarra ceremony as proof of their right to conduct their own initiations, a right conferred by Dreamtime precedent and given verbal expression in song texts. (As it happened, no *tjilkatja* men came anywhere near Alyawarra land on this occasion.)

Executant ability in singing the songs from a *ngirtilingkwa* ceremony is perhaps the first ceremonial achievement of a young Agharringa man, although it may be many years before he is told the meaning of the texts, which contain a combination of everyday and specialised words, as well as changes to the morphology to accommodate patterns in the musical rhythms. One of the factors considered by the older owners when deciding whether or not to extend ownership to a particular young man is his level of proficiency in singing the songs.

While other aspects of ceremonial activity may vary from one enactment to another, all Agharringa men agree that the appropriate songs must be sung, and that they must be sung unchanged. The rigidity with which this rule is being maintained clearly indicates the vital importance of song. Without the land, which their Dreamtime ancestors gave to them, the Agharringa have no self-identity and no means of spiritual selfdetermination. And without the songs which recount the Dreamtime activities, they have no claim to the land.

REFERENCES

Moyle, R. (1983) *Alyawarra Music.* Canberra, Australian Institute of Aboriginal Studies (in press).

Strehlow, T. G. H. (1947) *Aranda Traditions.* Melbourne University Press.

Toohey, J. (1979) *Land claim by Alyawarra and Kaititja. Report by the Aboriginal Land Commissioner Mr Justice Toohey to the Minister for Aboriginal Affairs.* Canberra, Australian Government Publishing Service.

Yallop, C. (1969) The Aljawara and their territory. *Oceania,* 29:187-97.

Yallop, C. (1977) *Alyawarra: an Aboriginal language of central Australia.* Canberra, Australian Institute of Aboriginal Studies.

NOTES

1. In this article I use the word 'Territory' to refer to the largest area of land over which groups of Aborigines calling themselves by the same name claim ownership. A Territory is divided into a number of 'Countries' over which each individual group claims autonomy in religious activities. I use the Aboriginal English term 'Business' to refer to any restricted ceremony. All three words have capital initial letters to distinguish them from the same words used in other contexts.

2. Fieldwork was carried out over 17 months between 1977 and 1980 at Arurrunga and Mpilatwatja camps, inside Agharringa Country, as part of a study of Alyawarra music. The contents of this article derive from parts of three chapters of that study (Moyle, 1983).

3. An owner will call another owner of the same Dreaming *atjina piltja*—my fellow-countryman; occasionally, the English term 'countryman' is heard.

4. Of those Dreaming lines presented earlier in the paper, those shown in Figs 6, 7, 8, 10, 11, 12, and 13 are *ngirtilingkwa.*

5. A term used for a novice about to be circumcised and his accompanying guardians when on their tour gathering people for the actual ceremony.

4 YOLNGU CONCEPTS OF LAND OWNERSHIP

Nancy M. Williams

The decision in the Yirrkala land case in 1971 affirmed European principles based upon the rights of individual economic man (see *Milirrpum v. Nabalco* (1971) 17 F.L.R. 141, per Blackburn, J.). Yolngu land use was examined as a system of ownership and possession (see Stanner, 1969:6) and was found wanting: the court held that the Yolngu system lacked concepts of property that existed in other legal systems; Yolngu ownership was a matter of religious belief but not of economic significance and therefore not law. I argue here to the contrary that Yolngu notions of proprietary interest in land are equally religious and economic. Yolngu do not separate 'economic' and 'religious' attributes, but rather join them in a fashion that requires their mediation by political process. The fact that European notions of property are fundamentally or exclusively economic may have invited anthropologists as well as lawyers and judges to find that economics or religion but not both defined Aboriginal relationships to land, or to find both present but that one was completely subordinate to the other.[1] This dilemma is at the heart of Mr Justice Blackburn's statement (1971:270–71) that

> . . . [I]t seems easier, on the evidence to say that the clan belongs to the land than that the land belongs to the clan.

In order to see how Yolngu articulate economics and religion in their system of land tenure, it is useful to see how scholars have separated them in the past. Mr Justice Blackburn's assessment of the evidence put before him in 1970 during hearings of the Yirrkala case provides the best data for this purpose. Following presentation of those data I focus on the secular, economic aspects (in European terms) of Yolngu land ownership. In concluding sections I discuss the mechanisms of political process by which religious and economic considerations are joined in the Yolngu system.

YOLNGU LAND TENURE 1970: EMPHASIS ON RELIGION

'The Aboriginal evidence', as it was called, was presented to the court in Darwin in 1970 as was also a great deal of the anthropological evidence. The Yolngu leaders who were witnesses perceived the court situation less in adversary terms than as one where they had an opportunity 'to explain', and they attempted to explain their ownership of land in terms that they thought the English-speaking court could understand. To explain meant also to demonstrate: they revealed some of their sacred objects, which their counsel had equated with title deeds to their lands, to the judge in his chambers. Because for the Yolngu the court situation was marked by explanation and understanding, they found it difficult to accommodate defence counsel's mode of questioning, of attempting to elicit from them inconsistent or contradictory responses. And in their emphasis on establishing their title to land, the Yolngu leaders left tacit a great deal of background information about the rules governing land utilisation, the 'economic' aspects of the system. In this connection, for example, they left largely implicit the procedures of seeking permission to use the resources of lands owned by other groups (Williams, 1982, n.d.*b*.). The Yolngu men did make statements about permission but, perhaps because of the form in which they were expressed, the court appeared to comprehend them imperfectly or to ignore them. In the interest of presenting a system comprehensible to English speakers they left implicitly or incompletely interpreted important categories of subsidiary rights in land, including those of inheritance (entailed in the kin-defined *märi-gutharra* relationships which I discuss briefly below).

Mr Justice Blackburn's summary description of Yolngu society and culture in his reasons for judgment (1971:166–167) contains a thoughtful statement of the religious basis of the Yolngu relationships to land as this was generally understood in 1970.

> In the aboriginal belief, all things in the physical and spiritual universes (and the difference between them seems not to be important) belong to one or the other of two classes called 'moieties'. The names of the moieties are Dua and Yiritja. It is in the unchangeable natural order to things that every human being, every clan, every animal and plant species, and every inanimate thing, belongs to one or the other of the moieties.
>
> The people themselves believe that they are descendants of certain great spirit ancestors whose names and deeds are well known; they arrived at identified places and they moved about the land doing various things at various places. Whether or not they were the creators of the physical world, they were certainly the ordainers of the system of life which the aboriginals accept. Foremost in this system is the principle of the clan . . .
>
> . . . [T]he fundamental truth about the aboriginals relationship to the land is that whatever else it is, it is a religious relationship, . . . the physical and spiritual universes are not felt as distinct. There is an unquestioned scheme of things in which the spirit ancestors, the people of the clan, particular land and everything that exists on and in it, are organic parts of one indissoluble whole . . . [E]ach clan regards itself as a spiritual entity having a spiritual relationship to particular places or areas, and having a duty to care for and tend that land by means of ritual observances. Certain sacred objects . . . are at once symbols of the continuity of the clan, and tangible indications of the relationship between the clan and certain land. These sacred objects are closely guarded and shown only to those who may properly see them, and then only with due solemnity . . .
>
> The clan, then, had a religious basis, it had a connexion with land, and the principle of its existence was patrilineal descent. But its relationships with other social phenomena were far from simple . . .

In the continuation of his summary description, the judge deals with matters relating to political organisation and to economics (1971:167–168), but here his characterisations are negative or are at least hedged with doubt.

> The clan had no internal organization of its own, or at any rate none relevant to this case. No chieftain ruled over it; rather, apparently, decisions affecting the whole clan may have been made by a consensus of the older men. The clan had little significance in the economic sense; indeed, it was a matter of dispute whether it had any such significance. The economic relationship between the aboriginals and the land is not easy to describe. It seems that at any given time there would be various groups of aboriginals in various places about the land, each group living in a particular area, hunting animals, obtaining vegetable food, getting materials for clothing and ritual observances and moving about from area to area as the economic exigencies required. Each group consisted of a number of adult men, some with their wives and children and some unmarried. The composition of any given group at a given time could not be predicted, and did not, for any fixed or recognized time, remain constant; indeed, one group might not be recognizable as such over a period of one year or even less, or might persist for a longer period. Changes in the personnel of the group would occur not only

> by reason of births, deaths and marriages, but for purely economic reasons such as sufficiency of food supplies, and also because of ritual requirements at special sacred places at particular times . . .

In view of his decision in the Yirrkala case, it is worth mentioning that Mr Justice Blackburn found that clans owned (in a non-technical sense) tracts of land, not merely sites separated by areas of unowned land as the defendants, the Commonwealth and Nabalco Pty Ltd., had argued.[2]

The judge also referred to Professor Berndt's agreement with Warner's (1958:389) interpretation of the economic aspect of clan ownership of land:

> The clan's so-called 'ownership' of the land has little of the economic about it. Friendly peoples wander over the food areas of others and, if their area happens to be poor in food production, possibly spend more of their lives on the territory of other clans than on their own. Exclusive use of the group's territory by the group is not a part of the Murngin idea of land 'ownership' (1971:170).

Further commenting on evidence given by the ten Aboriginal witnesses the judge said (1971:170) none gave any explicit indication 'that in the days before the Mission he lived chiefly in his clan territory and to a lesser extent in territory of other clans'.

Permission

Further analysis of the nature of the relationship of clans to their estate was taken up by Mr Justice Blackburn in a series of questions relating to 'the permissive use of land' (1971:181-183). His findings on the issues whether a clan had or exercised the right to exclude others from its land, whether specific rules governed others' use of a clan's land, and whether the use rights of others were vested in individuals or in clans as corporate entities bore directly on his conclusions concerning proprietary interests in land. Here the first specific question he posed was whether there was any requirement that another clan or an individual member of another clan seek permission before travelling on or using land not its/his own. His answer was prefaced by the reminder (1971:181) that 'aboriginals did not cultivate land or practice animal husbandry; they took what grew naturally'.

> The evidence shows that bands moved freely about the subject land, and that no permission was required for a band to go anywhere. (1971:181).

The judge did find however, that:

> care was taken that approaches to sacred sites were made only with the knowledge of the clan concerned: and that *participation* in ritual was, or might be, by invitation of the clan concerned. It also—though less certainly—shows that if an individual went by himself, for a purpose such as hunting, on land related to a clan of another moiety, he would take care that a responsible person of the appropriate clan was informed . (1971:181-182)

Mr Justice Blackburn found only one instance of permission being refused and was inclined to think that perhaps this indicated the influence of white attitudes about property (1971:182).

These findings unfortunately reflect inadequate interpretation of Yolngu modes of seeking and granting permission as well as the court's apparent refusal to accept at face value a good deal of explicit evidence on the existence of such requirements (see Williams (1982) on Yolngu modes of seeking and granting permission).

Relation to land through time

In examining the evidence of the relationship of clans to land through time, Mr Justice

Blackburn first mentioned the absence of any 'direct evidence . . . of what the links were between any clans and any areas of land at any time before that to which the statements of the deceased ancestors of the [Yolngu] witnesses related' (1971:183). By direct evidence Mr Justice Blackburn meant written records (1971:183-184):

> the aboriginals have no written records or anything corresponding to them; that [certain sacred objects] are, among other things, charters to land, is a matter of aboriginal faith; they are not evidence, in our sense, of title . . . [and] the earlier anthropologists . . . made statements in general terms about land-holding systems, but did not attempt to produce anything resembling a "register of titles".

At another place Mr Justice Blackburn noted (1971:176), 'Apart from the sacred [objects] which, I understand, do not purport to convey precise descriptions of land, there is nothing in the aboriginal world which in any way corresponds to title deeds or registers'.

Mr Justice Blackburn discussed the evidence which counsel for the defendants had put forward in challenging the Yolngu contention that the 'links between the actual clans and the actual pieces of land' were the same in 1935 as they had been in 1788, a contention the Yolngu had to prove. Passages in publications by Webb (1933), Warner (1958), Chaseling (1957), Berndt (1951, 1952, 1955, 1964), Hiatt (1962), and Stanner (1965) were cited. The court emphasised that all these works make statements of shifts, moves, or migrations of people implicitly or explicitly. Mr Justice Blackburn mentioned, for example, that in 1965 Stanner had written (1965:12):

> long-term shifts of estate or range . . . may have been more common than has been supposed.

and at the hearing Stanner said of this view (transcript, p.1003; 1971:187):

> I have no reason to change it, except that long-term is long-term.

A proprietary interest in land?

In reaching his decision in the Yirrkala land case, Mr Justice Blackburn examined a great deal of historical material, including cases from other common law jurisdictions and he commented on their bearing (or lack of bearing) on the Yirrkala case. In the quotation that follows I have added emphasis to the phrase that I believe provides the clue to his failure in 1971—and to the continuing failure of others—to find any interest recognisable as 'proprietary' in Aboriginal relationship to land. The judge refers here (1971:213; emphasis added) to cases decided by Chief Justice Marshall of the United States Supreme Court in the nineteenth century.

> In my most respectful opinion, these statements of law by the great Chief Justice do not affirm the principle that the Indian "right of occupancy" was an interest which could be set up against the sovereign, or against a grantee of the sovereign, in the same manner as an interest arising under *the ordinary law of real property*.

In considering the question whether a clan's relationship to land was 'proprietary', Mr Justice Blackburn divided the evidence into two categories; the Aborigines' beliefs about their land and the clans' use of their lands. Concerning the former, he said (1971:270), 'With great respect for the plaintiffs' beliefs, I do not think that they help me to decide the issue before me'. The plaintiffs' argument based on what the judge labelled belief had failed because he found no resemblance in them to the concept of property with which he was familiar (1971:270):

> In my view, my proper procedure is to bear in mind the concept of "property" in our law, and in what I know of other systems which have the concept . . . and look at the aboriginal system to find what there corresponds to or resembles "property".

The 'spiritual relationship' of the clan to its land, on the other hand, he said had been 'well proved'. It appeared to Mr Justice Blackburn that the Aborigines' feeling of obligation to the land was 'more cogent' than their feeling of ownership (1971:270).

The solution to the problem of the clans' relationship to land, Mr Justice Blackburn decided, was to consider what he termed 'the substance of proprietary interests rather than their outward indicia' (1971:272):

> I think that property, in its many forms, generally implies the right to use or enjoy, the right to exclude others, and the right to alienate.

Applying this standard to the plaintiff clans, the judge went on to say (1971:272),

> I do not think that I can characterize the relationship of the clan to the land as proprietary.

His conclusion in this matter was, finally (1971:273), that:

> [T]here is so little resemblance between property, as our law, or what I know of any other law, understands that term, and the claims of the plaintiffs for their clans, that I must hold that these claims are not in the nature of proprietary interests.

Proprietary rights in land, in Mr Justice Blackburn's analysis, can only be vested in individuals. His first mention of clan and first (provisional) definition occurs on the first page of his reasons for judgment (1971:146), and here he shows concern because not only is a group asserted to own land, but its very composition is unstable.

> [T]he clan is an indeterminate group in the sense that births and deaths, occurring from the indefinite past to, and after, the commencement of the action, are assumed not to affect the identity of the clan . . . [T]he plaintiffs are thus members of a class which is subject to continual changes of membership . . .

He never saw the clan as more than an indeterminate collection of individuals, and no statute provided for the vesting of title in such a group. Similarly, since Aboriginal 'beliefs' about the ownership of their land had no element of 'economics' about them —so Mr Justice Blackburn found—he saw the beliefs as unhelpful in his search for what might be proprietary about the clans' interest in land.

The proposition that the clan has no 'significant economic relationship with the land' (1971:270) follows from the principles that underlie European concepts of property. These concepts have come, in historical terms rather recently, to be wholly secular and to refer to individual rights of possession and alienation. Exclusion (i.e., the power to exclude others) is then simply the logical complement of the protection of possessory rights of individual owners.

SECULAR ASPECTS OF YOLNGU LAND TENURE

The Yirrkala land case in 1970 produced numerous instances of the problems caused by an artificial separation of 'the religious' and 'the economic'. In the following sections I discuss Yolngu concepts of grouping in relation to land and inheritance of land, because in these topics I believe we have significantly expanded our understanding of the secular aspects of Yolngu relations to land since 1970. In concluding sections I am then able to deal with how political process mediates religious and economic attributes of Yolngu proprietary interests in land.

Corporateness in relation to land

For the Yolngu the most important corporate groups are those that are corporate with respect to land. These groups have names, and they are corporate by virtue of 'holding in their hands' the ritual property that constitutes title to the land.[3] They continue in time through agnatic succession; they are patrilineally recruited. Thus they may appropriately be called clans. One should not assume of course that clans in Aboriginal Australia are everywhere identical in structure, size, derivation of names, or possession of a unique language (or dialect).

Warner (1958:16–29, 388–92) calls the land-owning group throughout the Murngin area a clan, and says (1958:16) that a clan is made up of those 'individuals who possess a common territory'. Thomson (1949:11) states that in Arnhem Land 'The clan is the territorial or land-owning group'. Hiatt (1967:472), referring to a group in the westernmost part of Warner's Murngin area, writes, 'The Gidjingali have named patrilineal descent groups possessing corporate rights in land . . .' Peterson defines (1972:30, fn8) the clan as the smallest land-owning group. Berndt (1964:266), in his publication on the Gove dispute, calls a *mada-mala* pair the land-owning unit in northeastern Arnhem Land: 'Together the *mada-mala* pairs constitute the land-owning, land-tending units'. Later, Berndt & Berndt (1977:139) designate the land-owning group in northeastern Arnhem land *'mada-mala* (dialectal unit—"clan") combination'. It is like land-owning groups throughout Australia, a 'local descent group, . . . defined . . . in relation to patrilineal descent,' and also like all others, it 'can be easily defined in relation to territory. . .'

In 1972 Peterson stated (1972:15) that 'the only corporate property of the clan is the estate and the sacred songs, rites and paraphernalia that constituted the title deeds to it'. This seems to imply that the clan as a corporate entity logically and/or historically precedes its common property, a statement of the kind of relationship between 'group' and 'land' that has been most commonly expressed in the literature on Aboriginal Australian land ownership. But land is not a property conferred on groups that are already corporate with respect to property of other kinds. Corporate groups do not search for land to own; Yolngu groups are made corporate by their ownership of land. There is no Yolngu tradition—either conceptually, historically, or in myth—of the corporateness of groups preceding their relationship with land. In Yolngu cosmogony, estates were defined and vested in named groups of people along with the property symbolizing the corporateness of the group in its ownership of an estate.

Names comprise an important category of a land-owning group's property not only because they symbolise relationships that are rooted inland but also because they constitute a full description of the group's land. Peterson (1972) enumerates sacred paraphernalia, rites, and songs as title deeds. While the recitation of names is an integral aspect of the performance of sacred songs and rites, yolngu also use those names, as well as others, in non-ritual contexts to indicate details of the estate and all its resources. (Yolngu, I would like to suggest, do not have to rely on paper and ink to guarantee the exact description of the land to which they hold title, as do members of societies that lack highly developed and sophisticated techniques of memory storage and retrieval.)

The development of the concept of corporateness in English law has been marked by a particular kind of change. As one legal scholar has it (Stoljar, 1973:182) 'the classical development of English law . . . has not been in search of juristic persons [to define corporations], but in search of separate property entities . . .' Yolngu, by contrast, begin with 'separate property entities' in defining their relationship to land. In English history changing social and economic factors are also related to the shifting cluster of ideas that jurists regard as historical developments in the notion of corporateness. By the twentieth century the cluster, containing some ideas that were ancient, defined formal incorporation in terms of its now ' "classic incidents" . . . namely, perpetual succession, the right to hold land, the right to a common seal, the power to make by-laws, and the capacity to sue and be sued' (Stoljar, 1973:33). These 'incidents', *mutatis mutandis,* characterise Yolngu land-owning groups.

Defining a group as corporate with respect to the ownership of land facilitates understanding how stability and continuity can be maintained while change occurs. It focuses on the processes that enable social and economic viability in terms that are consistent with Yolngu explanations of land ownership. To make this clearer still, another function of group names must be examined. This function produces effects that have in the past sometimes puzzled ethnographers and resulted in confusing or contradictory reports of 'correct' names (and sometimes allegations of 'incorrect' ones) for particular groups.

Names and contexts of their use. Yolngu have many ways of defining groups. Very frequently in discourse they wish to convey precise information about groups of people in relation to land. They can draw on a large number of lexical items and combine them to signify the composition of groups, their location in space and season, and their activities. Combined as names, a single term may convey all that information. Yolngu use names to cultivate, to maintain, and to strengthen ties that are of the greatest importance to them in interpersonal and intergroup relations. These are ties that have practical effect in long term demographic and economic viability, and they can be enhanced by emphasising connectedness through shared names or names that show relationship because they are drawn from a common myth.

In all communication Yolngu speakers can, of course, assume they all share a vast amount of detailed background information. A further factor influences Yolngu use of names just as it does their discourse in general: they derive intellectual and aesthetic pleasure from the use of language—including forms such as metaphor, hyperbole, and oblique constructions.[4]

A large number of names of differing orders of inclusiveness and relatedness and from different cultural domains are available. Principles also exist by means of which new ones, or recombinations of old ones, can be created, to indicate particular sets of people. The result is that inclusion or exclusion can be very precise. A speaker can, of course, also choose to use terms so general that they create ambiguity—the kind of ambiguity that masks contradiction and facilitates amicability in human relations (at least temporarily) by playing down conflicts of interest. Inclusions can occur at any range of social distinction, but are most frequent at the level of least inclusiveness—that is, at the level where fewest individuals and least property is involved. In other words, in contexts marked by informality these inclusions are most common.

Names are always available to indicate the unity of otherwise separate groups on the basis of something shared. A speaker may indicate the unity of a group as a courtesy, as an expression of solidarity, or as a tactic in the strategy of maximising potential advantage for himself or his group (see Sutton (1982) on this and related topics). As long as focusing on a unity is the intention, he will use names that indicate the common boundary of the grouping rather than what might set its components apart. For example, Balamumu is a particular kind of group name that Yolngu may use to indicate unity composed of Djapu clanspeople, their uterine kin, and their affines. Another example illustrates how the unity of *märi-gutharra* groups may be indicated. Rirratjingu clanspeople are *gutharra* to the Mandalpuy clan, and a Rirratjingu man once said to me, 'We are the body of the Mandalpuy and when we are with them we call ourselves Mandalpuy'. He did not mean to imply in any way that with this use of their *märi*'s name the Rirratjingu would cease being Rirratjingu, or that they would abandon their own language name or deny their identity as Rirratjingu. Yolngu would understand that the speaker was not compromising Rirratjingu corporateness with respect to their estate. He did convey the existence of the link between Mandalpuy and

Rirratjingu which Yolngu would understand to entail inchoate[5] rights of inheritance.

For Yolngu at least, there is no inherent contradiction or inconsistency (that is, unless it is intentionally created) in the many ways groups may be named. On the contrary, they use their conventions of naming to achieve a wide range of desired effects that I have only suggested. Some of these effects are related to the stability and continuity of land-owning groups. In that context names are used to signify jurally defensible claims to land. One outcome in Yolngu expectation is that there is always a viable group of people who have a basis for legitimating a claim of corporate status in relation to land.

Land and the structure of authority

Land-owning groups are viable groups, and viability depends on certain critical relations between absolute numbers of people to land area, and resources. Viability also depends on the abilities of leaders of these groups in spheres of politics and governance. When people at Yirrkala relate the myths that tell how land was vested in their ancestors, they often name spirit leaders of the first spirit Yolngu.

Each land-owning group also has other narratives that tell of later hero ancestors and designate those who were leaders—they often were innovators or teachers of some important technology or ritual practice. In myths that designate language-named groups as those groups corporate with respect to land ownership the first spirit leaders are often two. They symbolise the existence (or potential existence) of localised subgroups; and the relationship of these spirit leaders as elder brother and younger brother or father and son symbolises the principles of patrilineal succession and the ranking of the leaders.

People were not brought into being to multiply on their lands without leaders. On one occasion, when an old leader told me a series of names of spirit human beings and the first true people of a particular country, I asked their meaning. He told me simply, 'They are the leadership for that land'.

The head of a clan is defined in English as 'the first son of the first son'. If the first-born son is not regarded as mature enough to assume the headship of the clan on the death of his father, succession will pass to a younger brother of his father (ideally, second in birth order to his father). The succession may pass through a series of a deceased head's brothers before reverting to his own son, his own line. Younger brothers regularly succeed to their older brothers' positions, jurally replacing them and assuming all the rights, obligations, and liabilities of their older brothers.

A third principle, based on absolute age, operates in defining the headship of a clan. The head of a clan should ideally be (and usually is) its oldest male member. The oldest man is, of course, not always the most senior man of the senior lineage. When the oldest man is head of a junior lineage it is good custom for the head of the senior lineage to defer to the oldest man. An explicit agreement to this deferral should be confirmed by all the senior members of the clan as should the understanding that on the death of the oldest man the headship will revert to the senior lineage. These are the principal jural rules that define leadership and their ultimate sanctions are religious. There are of course subsidiary rules and pragmatics which generally operate to justify the Yolngu assumption that people in positions of leadership are effective leaders.

The hierarchical model that Yolngu at Yirrkala use to conceptualise the relationship of all parts of a clan's estate as a single entity also orders and validates the structure of authority. The model is also pyramidal. The site said to be most important in a myth is the most sacred, and it is the focal site of a clan's estate. Other sites, subsidiary sites within the estate, are articulated to the 'apical' site. Sites symbolise ownership of the areas in which they are located. They are ranked in sacredness, and the areas on which they are located are ranked accordingly. Ideally the allocation of sites to the mature men of a clan coincide with the rank of the men as determined by birth order and with the ranking of their lineages, which is based also on birth order. Thus the head[6] of a clan is ideally the most senior man of the senior lineage, and has responsibility for the site of greatest importance to his clan. He has, according to the ideal model, sole authority with respect to that site and superordinate authority with respect to all other sites within the clan estate.

A postulate of the hierarchical arrangement of the portions of an estate, based on the importance of the sites within the estate, is that the hierarchy remains unchanging. The estate, so structured, is a kind of tangible model for adjustment and resolution of anomalies and sometimes of disputes that may result from the inherent structural contradictions of the principles of primogeniture, succession of brothers, and absolute age.

The ranking of sites in the myth also affects the relations of groups linked by myth. Precedence should be accorded the head of the clan whose land contains the site acknowledged by all the linked groups to be most sacred. This ranking of authority is likely to be most salient and to prevail when groups are gathered together for the performance of ritual associated with the myth that links them. At other times, and in general, Yolngu recognise the precedence of the clan owning the land on which any group of people is residing, whether for the performance of ritual, for the purpose of joint economic enterprise, or for some other reason. Yolngu expect that people will defer to the head of this group and all its elder men in decisions pertaining to the entire group.

Succession and inheritance

For Mr Justice Blackburn property meant private property (see p.98). One rarely finds the term inheritance used in discussions of change in Aboriginal relations to land, especially change in ownership (Peterson et al. 1977 is a notable exception) for the same reason: it is very difficult for European legal systems to envisage proprietary rights in land except they be vested in individuals. And in European thinking inheritance of land has become linked with assumptions about private property.

Succession remains, for English speakers at least, a more general term than inheritance. In European legal systems inheritance refers specifically to the passage of property on death. Succession refers more broadly to a transmission of rights from one person (or entity) to another concomitant with a change in position or social identity. Time is implicated since both succession and inheritance involve change through time. But inheritance has come to apply more narrowly, as its derivation from the Latin *heres* (heir) suggests, to an individual or individuals on whom property devolves following a death. More narrowly still, in European legal systems, inheritance has come to connote the execution of a will or the operation of statutes of intestacy. We may appropriately use succession, I think, as a neutral term to refer to a change in rights of, between, and/or among persons in relations to property. Moreover, since changes in rights correlate with changes in role, succession entails readjustment of role relationships in which property is the pivotal feature.[7]

Succession is, further, probably best reserved in Aboriginal contexts for use in situations where transfer of ownership rights in land has been accomplished or is proceeding under some shade of right that the groups involved regard as appropriate in traditional law, and both (or all affected) groups acknowledge the process as one of succession. A situation which illustrates why I think this is so occurred in the Finniss River land claim hearing in Darwin in 1980 where two groups each claimed to be traditional owners of a particular area. One group was at some remove from land neighboring Aborigines attributed to them as their 'proper country', and the available historical material bore out the neighbouring groups' testimony. No group directly or tangentially involved referred to this contending group's claim in terms of what I have defined above as succession. Nobody publicly acknowledged change in ownership in terms of Aboriginal traditional law, either legal or illegal. I have been unable to find any comparable account in the literature I have searched. The anthropologist assisting counsel for the contending group was probably correct in using the phrase 'takeover marked by conflict' to refer to the basis of their claim. I am not so sure that he was correct in stating that this kind of 'change in ownership' has been recorded anywhere else in Aboriginal Australia.

In the context of Yolngu land tenure I think it is useful to distinguish between presumptive rights of succession, which are patrilineal, and subsidiary rights of succession. Yolngu acquire certain rights in a direct, patrilineally determined way; that is, each one has certain rights by virtue of membership in a patrilineally defined land-owning group. These are presumptive rights. Subsidiary rights are acquired by other routes than membership in a patrilineal group. Some subsidiary rights are inchoate rights and some are potential rights.[8] In the Yolngu system of land tenure, the most important subsidiary rights are those inchoate rights based on alternate generation relationship (the *märi-gutharra* relationship) and those potential rights arising from the relationship of groups joined in myth as 'sister' groups (sometimes called a company relationship), which may provide the basis for their fusion. These two categories of subsidiary rights may overlap.

I use the terms presumptive and subsidiary rights rather than primary and secondary rights because I wish to avoid implying the existence of an automatic or fixed hierarchy of rights in land that numeric terms may convey. Yolngu treat the various categories of rights in land as complementary, and although complementarity does not automatically preclude ranking, cases of changing tenure in land involving succession must be assessed individually to determine whether or not various bases of claim are being rank-ordered.

What the court was looking for in the Yirrkala land case was 'an explanation of the fact that groups speaking the same language can be found linked to discrete areas of land, separated by areas linked to people of other languages. . .' It then wanted to know whether the hypothesis 'that at some time in the past there has been migration or movement from one area to another' should be accepted as the most likely explanation (Milirrpum, 1971:186). Given the unchallenged reified status of *mala* and *matha* and the absence of an explanation of Yolngu mechanisms of succession and inheritance during the hearings, Mr Justice Blackburn's own deductive hypotheses (1971:196) were certainly unexceptionable:

> The first possibility is that a particular mata-mala pair may have become extinct. In every case, of course, it would be the death of the last surviving male which either caused, or foreshadowed with certainty, the extinction of a mata-mala pair. But the event could represent one of the following possibilities:
>
> 1. The last surviving male was the last representative of a mata as well as the last representative of a mala . . .
> 2. The last surviving male may have been the last surviving member of a mata, there being other members of the mala associated with another mata.
> 3. The last surviving male may have been the last surviving member of a mala, there being other malas associated with the mata . . .

Unfortunately, nobody explained to the court that many factors other than population movement or extinction may be involved in language variation, among them, for example, the very simple one that all human languages change continuously. It is not necessary therefore to postulate movement of people to account for divergence over time. More important, nobody explained to the court—our knowledge was not yet sufficient—how Yolngu defined the boundaries of the social groups relevant to the processes of succession. In fact the evidence that Peterson et al. (1977:6) referred to as 'One of the best documented . . . cases' of the process of inheritance of Aboriginal land they drew from the Yirrkala land case: the very evidence that had been instrumental in the defeat of one clan's claim. That claim was one of Gumatj clan succession to Lamamirri clan land.

In terms of the principles of Yolngu land tenure, a group of people whose *matha* was Lamamirri had been corporate with respect to the ownership of the land in question. They held radical title to that land, and a number of other groups named during the course of the hearing had subsidiary rights of ownership in the land by virtue of common myths that linked them and their lands to the Lamamirri. Together they were reciprocally 'sister' groups, but the Lamamirri were referred to as *ngurrungu* (first), or *bunggawa* ('boss'). Alternate generation *(märi-gutharra)* relationships existed within the linked sister groups. The Lamamirri were *märi* to several Gumatj patrilines, including that of the patriline which succeeded to nominal ownership (ultimately on behalf of the larger Gumatj *matha*-defined group).[9]

A number of the Yolngu witnesses referred to the procedures by which the Gumatj *gutharra* succeeded to ownership of their Lamamirri *märi* estate. Their descriptions clearly indicate that the procedures were generally known, were based on recognised rights, required explicit arrangement including the concurrence of others whose rights were affected, and account-keeping by witnesses.[10] Moreover, the evidence showed that the procedures were initiated before the death of the last male Lamamirri heir with a direct right of succession. That the land continued to be recognised as Lamamirri involved more than 'new traditions' filling Yolngu thought or 'myth dying hard', to use Warner's (1958:17–19) terminology. Two Lamamirri land-owners were still alive at the time of the hearing: two women who lived with their husbands at Elcho Island. One Yolngu witness, the oldest person living at Yirrkala, said that arrangements were begun a generation before the maturity of the then head of the Gumatj clan. The evidence also made it clear that it was inconceivable to Yolngu that they would not arrange succession to the ownership of land.

In fact, as *gutharra*, the Gumatj had always been responsible for 'looking after' their *märi* Lamamirri land, as had other groups of Lamamirri *gutharra*. With extinction of the Lamamirri as a viable land-owning group foreshadowed, Yolngu leaders would have put negotiations for succession in train. To assume that negotiations proceeded during this lengthy period to settlement and confirmation in the absence of any conflict of interest would be as naive as to assume that in any European jurisdiction an estate of great value will be automatically settled on an heir without a challenge. In this paper I do not document these conflicts of interest, which flow from two basic factors, but simply note them: land is the most valuable of all entities to Yolngu and with respect to virtually all parcels at least two land-owning groups can claim equal if not identical subisidary categories of rights.

Yolngu have devised other means of creating continuity in the relationship of groups to land. I do not deal with them here but simply indicate that they include, for example, the custom of allowing one group or its leaders to give names to other groups. Gifts of names, or more frequently exchanges of names, may accomplish several purposes, but they all result in extending or intensifying links between the groups involved, and may therefore be material to pressing rights in the process of succession.

THE CLAN OWNS THE LAND

We require a particular approach to translation if we are to understand the way in which Yolngu express the relation of religion and economics in their concepts of land as property. As Stanner (1969:2) puts it,

> In [A]boriginal understanding land was much more than property in our sense; ownership was more intrinsic; title, right and possession were embedded in different doctrines; and use and occupation were articulated into a highly distinctive body of social habits; but there was a sufficient coincidence between their underlying ideas and ours in relation to all these matters to justify the use of European terms, provided there are accompanying explanations.

I have followed Stanner's (1969) analysis in describing and attempting to translate the Yolngu concepts into terms familiar to people whose legal systems are derived from those of Europe in the summary that follows. After setting out the summary translations of these concepts, I deal with the process that articulates them.[11]

First, ownership under right of title is established and recognised as such by myths that bestow land on named groups. Title is vested in a patrilineal descent group; all members of this group are joint owners of the estate to which the group has title. Subsidiary categories of ownership are implied by virtue of links specified in the myth. Several categories of such inchoate rights exist and the most important has been mentioned. Through time some may be exercised, while others may lie dormant. The major myths, always narratives, are charters of land bestowal. The framework of the narrative is travel; the journey of spirit beings through lands and across seas in the distant past.[12]

Second, the right of possession flows from the myth of land bestowal and finds its expression in many forms ranging from the assumption of right by owners to be present on their land and to defend it against unauthorised entry by others, to symbolic expression in several modes such as certain named components of bark paintings and ritual song. Rights of possession also underlie the forms by means of which subsidiary rights of possession may be granted, such as that of a small area to a man of another land-owning group because his spirit came from that place.

Third, rights of occupation and use are assumed to rest on ownership and possession, hence to be inherently related to them. The fact that certain categories of rights with respect to possession, occupation, and use reside in persons other than owners, most notably in uterine relatives of owners, and that their exercise of these rights may over-ride the owners' rights in certain matters in no way impairs the title of the owners or diminishes the notion of ownership.[13] Instead, the rights of uterine relatives, which also entail specific duties, give additional precision to the right of title by spelling out their complementarity in terms of an elaborate system of checks and balances.

The relationship between ownership, possession, and use and occupation is further expressed in the rules requiring that the owners' assent is required to enter or utilise the resources of land of which one is not an owner. This rule applies in principle to uterine descendants of land owners, but for this category of individuals it is easier than for any other to negotiate an agreement with the owners that permits them to enter and use resources on a regular or continuing basis without having to obtain explicit permission each time. A body of rules defines categories of rights of occupation and use, all of which are contingent on the recognition of possession of an estate by a patrilineal descent group.

Order in changing allocation of proprietary interests to land over time is ensured by three means: the joint nature of rights acquired at birth in a patrilineal group; succession (entailed in the *märi-gutharra* relationship); and fusion of groups linked in a common myth (sister clans or subclan groups, those in a company relationship). Since ownership in an estate is joint, it does not actually pass by inheritance between generations but remains the property of extant members (cf. Stanner, 1969:8). So long as a viable patrilineage exists, title to its estate remains vested in that patrilineally defined group. Viability is determined by a number of factors, principally demographic and political.[14] Mechanisms of fusion based on the existence of links between groups defined in a common myth may be used to incorporate an estate (or part of an estate) of a patrilineal group near the limits of viability in that of a linked patrilineal group. When no male members of that group remain alive, another patrilineal descent group may succeed to the title through provisions of the *märi-gutharra* relationship. Those provisions enable a process of succession that leaders of the groups ideally commence when the threat of extinction cannot in any way be obviated.

'Religious', 'economic' and political process

Yolngu political process mediates myth and the 'historically real'. Political process for the Yolngu inheres first of all in the structure of rights and duties that they cite as binding particular individuals and groups at any point in time. This structure defines religious duty in the pragmatics of economics, explains economic rationale in sacred idiom, and makes them both immediately and eternally valid among kinsmen.

Yolngu, like other people, provide themselves with a moral framework of certainty; they accomplish this by positively valuing immutability, and thereby enable themselves to maintain that everyday affairs are predictable. Stanner (1956:62) wrote that Aborigines 'place a very special value on things remaining unchangingly themselves'. I am not as sure as Stanner was that Aborigines are unique in this respect, but I underscore a comment that follows (Stanner, 1956:62): '. . . they are not simply a people "without a history": they are a people who have been able, in some sense, to "defeat" history . . .'.

They have defeated history in the sense that is appropriate to land ownership by maintaining that the religious basis of the social foundation of land tenure continues to exert the same force as it did when the spirit beings bestowed land on the first real Yolngu. At the same time contemporary Yolngu are responsible for continuously recreating their relations to other people in respect to land. Control over the myth-based symbols that translate as rights in land is a crucially important aspect of these relations. As Stanner (1976:34) puts it,

> a 'property' relation is a direct relation between a person and an object only in an elliptical way. It is a relation between persons *in respect* of an object: and this is vastly different. It is at the least a triadic, not a dyadic relation. What we see in the Aboriginal world is a relationship between the members of a patrilineal local clan, or similar group, jointly and the whole world of other persons, single, joint, or common: a relationship expressed as a claim of right, with well-understood 'incidents', in respect of a finite territory, and all its symbols. It approximates to a covenanted relationship, entered into by, and multilaterally agreed to amongst, the ancestral founders of Aboriginal society, and raised by religious tradition to sacramental status.

Stanner is arguing explicitly against the proposition that 'the land owns Aborigines' as a number of people have put it, including, as I began this paper by noting, Mr Justice Blackburn in his decision in the Yirrkala land case.

To argue that the simple conclusion land owns Yolngu is inaccurate is, I believe, a necessary step in demonstrating the proprietary interests that Yolngu have in their clan estates. It is not to argue that Yolngu do not also perceive themselves as being from or part of their land in something more than a metaphorical sense: owning the land and being owned by it are not necessarily contradictory or mutually exclusive (Reay, personal communication).

Yolngu proprietary interests in land are morally grounded in religious belief and their everyday use and management are stated in religious idiom. This is not to say that Yolngu cannot discuss them in purely secular or economic terms. They can and do when Europeans want to discuss them in such terms. But most commonly, and I believe in their terms most appropriately, in an entirely Yolngu context they negotiate economic interests in religious terms. At least in matters relating to all categories of ownership rights, especially their transfer, Yolngu believe they must ultimately justify them in terms that articulate with the founding lineaments of their society.

ACKNOWLEDGEMENTS

I conducted the study on which this paper is based in the area of the Aboriginal community centred in Yirrkala on the Gove Peninsula in north-eastern Arnhem Land between the years 1969 and 1978. I was first a guest of the Yirrkala community from the end of 1969 to the end of 1970 while I was studying problems of social control and was funded by a US NIMH Training Grant (1 T01 MH12242-02 CUAN), adjunctive to US Public Health Service Predoctoral Fellowship (5 F01 MH 46168-02).I was able to continue my study in the Yirrkala area from 1974 through 1978 while I was the recipient of a Research Fellowship awarded by the Australian Institute of Aboriginal Studies. I would like to thank Dr Peter Ucko and Dr Myrna Tonkinson for their comments on an early draft of this paper. I owe a special debt to Dr Marie Reay for her criticism of the penultimate draft.

NOTES

1. Baxi (n.d.), a jurisprudential scholar, finds in a number of ways parallel to mine here that Mr Justice Blackburn's separation of religious and economic attributes was crucial to his judgment. Baxi's detailed and interesting critique of the judgment in his discussion of the legal issues he identifies relies on an analysis of legal relations modelled on that developed by an American scholar of jurisprudence, Hohfeld (e.g., 1964).

2. It may also be worth pointing out that in 1974 Mr Justice Woodward's definition of sacred sites (in paragraphs 517–20 in the second report of the Aboriginal Land Rights Commission, p.96) included the comments that 'no clear dividing line can be drawn between [sites] which are sacred and those which are not. Land generally has spiritual significance for Aborigines. . .'

3. European observers early noted the great importance of sacred ritual objects. I wish to note but do not demonstrate here, that their importance derives from their status as tangible symbols of land ownership, something I think Europeans have only recently understood. Among other indications of their importance is the consistently observed stringency with which these objects are guarded and the severity with which persons are punished for offences involving them. The same importance attaches to related categories of property, both noncorporeal and corporeal, that symbolise ownership of land. Peterson (1972:24) comments on the jealousy and secrecy with which they are guarded, adding that, 'The secrecy surrounding performances and the constant concern over who has the right to make or perform particular rites are further evidence for the strength of the ownership rights associated with totemic rituals'.

4. Peterson (1972:20) comments on this, citing Warner's earlier noting it (1958:180 fn). Stanner (1956) had also noted these kinds of linguistic creativity.

5. The concept of inchoate rights in the context of Aboriginal land tenure was, I believe, first introduced by Lawrie in the Ayers Rock land claim (opening address 4 April 1979, transcript p. 149) and was subsequently taken up and developed by the Aboriginal Land Commissioner in his report on that claim (1979:5, para. 27). Analytically it is important to distinguish inchoate rights from potential rights. The latter exist only in possibility but not in fact; they may be expected to come into existence at some future time, but do not now exist. The former actually exist now as rights but require some particular act to be activated or realised. Myers does not use the term but discusses the grounds of inchoate rights in land among the Pintubi (see for example, Myers 1982).

6. I use 'head' to refer only to the man whom Yolngu at Yirrkala recognise as the most senior of a clan (or subclan) group, the man with superordinate authority in decision-making in matters that affect the clan or

subclan. 'Leader' refers to all senior men whose authority Yolngu acknowledge regardless of the grounds on which it is legitimated.

7. The legal historian Vinogradoff in an article on succession remarks (1929:793) that succession deals with cases in which a will cannot be expressed and in such cases 'represents the view of society at large as to what ***ought to be*** the ***normal*** course of succession in the readjustment of property after [the] death. . .'. There can be, he asserts (1929:794) however, no succession proper where there is no individual property to begin with.

8. The concept of inchoate rights in the context of Aboriginal land tenure was, I believe, first introduced by Lawrie in the Ayers Rock land claim (Opening address, 4 April 1979, transcript p. 149) and was subsequently taken up and developed by the Aboriginal Land Commissioner in his report on that claim (1980:5, para. 27).

9. This case demonstrates the fact that it is more useful to conceive Yolngu land ownership in terms of categories of specific and differing rights rather than in unitary terms of either/or. It also shows how control over land is (or may be) held by one of the ranked lineages in a clan (or localised subclan) yet how the *matha* name is the indicator of the largest group which may be corporate with respect to ownership of the land.

10. What I have elsewhere described as the keeping of 'standing accounts' (Williams, n.d.*a*).

11. These summary statements are normative; as formulations of ideal behaviour they are of course like prescriptive statutes (and perhaps more like a code book of civil law than a proscriptive criminal code). I do not discuss here the rules of dealing with disputes.

12. See pp. 17–18 above for the political correlates. Many published accounts of these myths exist, the best known are those of Warner (see for example 1958) and Berndt (among others 1951, 1952, cited above). Where Warner (1958:389) observes that 'The land is not outside the clan but is an integral part of it', and also that 'The names of the country, the names of the wells, and the list of totems as well as the mythological ancestors all form fundamental parts of the clan unity', he indicates the Yolngu explanation with this quotation (1958:389): ' "Wongar [ancestral or spirit beings who travelled through the land] made it that way and that's why we have these things today".'

13. Briefly these rights, as well as others set out in the following paragraph, rest on rights of granting (or withholding) permission to enter, be on, and/or use the resources of land as well as on exercising certain rights over ritual property and performance. To request permission is of course tantamount to acknowledging the rights of others. I have spelled out these rights in more detail and described some of the contexts of their use in 'A boundary is to cross: observations on Yolngu boundaries and permission' (1982). Myers, 'Always ask: resource use and land ownership among Pintupi Aborigines of the Australian Western Desert' (1982), discusses the significance of not having to request such permission (among other related rights).

14. These factors and their interrelationships are both complex and relative. To the greatest extent they depend on leaders' abilities to organise effectively whatever followers they can muster, these numbers in relation to the strengths of like groups and of course the leaders' perceptions of the tasks (both religious and secular) involved and their abilities (and/or motivations) to fulfil them.

REFERENCES

Australia. Aboriginal Land Commissioner (1980) *Report on the Uluru (Ayers Rock) National Park and Lake Amadeus/Luritja land claim.* Canberra, Australian Government Publishing Service.

Australia, Aboriginal Land Rights Commission (A. E. Woodward, Commissioner) (1974) *Second Report.* Canberra, Australian Government Publishing Service.

Baxi, U. (n.d.) The Lost Dreamtime: now forever lost; a critique of the Gove land rights decision (mimeo, 65 pp.).

Berndt, R. M. (1951) *Kunapipi.* Melbourne, Cheshire.

Berndt, R. M. (1952) *Djanggawul.* London, Routledge & Kegan Paul.

Berndt, R. M. (1955) 'Murngin' (Wulamba) social organization. *American Anthropologist,* 57:84–106.

Berndt, R. M. (1964) The Gove dispute: the question of Australian Aboriginal land and the preservation of sacred sites. *Anthropological Forum,* 1(2):258–95.

Berndt, R. M. & C. H. Berndt (1977) *The World of the First Australians,* rev. ed. Sydney, Ure Smith.

Chaseling, W. S. (1957) *Yulengor: nomads of Arnhem Land.* London, Epworth Press.

Hiatt, L. R. (1962) Local organisation among the Australian Aborigines. *Oceania,* 32:267–86.

Hiatt, L. R. (1967) Authority and reciprocity in Australian Aboriginal marriage arrangements. *Mankind,* 6(10):468–75.

Hohfeld, W. N. Fundamental Legal Conceptions as Applied in Judicial Reasoning. W. W. Cook (ed.), New Haven, Yale University Press (essays first published 1917, 1919).

Milirrpum v. Nabalco Pty Ltd and the Commonwealth of Australia (Yirrkala (Gove)) (1971) *Federal Law Reports* 141–44. Judgment of the Honourable Mr Justice Blackburn (reported by A. J. Leslie).

Myers, F. R. (1982) Always ask: resource use and land ownership among Pintupi Aborigines of the Australian Western Desert. In: Nancy M. Williams & Eugene S. Hunn (eds.), *Resource Managers: North American and Australian Hunter-Gatherers, AAAS Selected Symposium 67. Boulder, Colorado.* Westview Press for the American Association for the Advancement of Science.

Peterson, N. (1972) Totemism yesterday: sentiment and local organisation among the Australian Aborigines. *Man* (n.s.) 7:12–32.

Peterson, N., Keen, I. & Sansom, B. (1977) Succession to land; primary and secondary rights to Aboriginal estates. A submission to the Ranger Uranium Environmental Inquiry prepared on behalf of the Northern Land Council, February 1977 (mimeo, 14 pp.).

Stanner, W. E. H. (1956) The Dreaming. In T. A. G. Hungerford (ed.), *Australian Signpost.* Melbourne, Cheshire.

Stanner, W. E. H. (1965) Aboriginal territorial organization: estate, range, domain and regime. *Oceania,* 36:1–26.

Stanner, W. E. H. (1969) The Yirrkala case: some general principles of Aboriginal land-holding (mimeo, 12 pp.).

Stanner, W. E. H (1976) Some aspects of Aboriginal religion. *Colloquium Journal of the Australian New Zealand Society for Theological Studies,* 19–35.

Stoljar, S. J. (1973) *Groups and Entities: an enquiry into corporate theory.* Canberra, Australian National University Press.

Sutton, P. J. (1982) Personal power, kin classification and speech etiquette in Aboriginal Australia. In: Jeffrey Heath, Francesca Merlan & Alan Rumsey (eds.) *Languages of kinship in Aboriginal Australia.* Oceania, Linguistic Monograph No. 24.

Thomson, D. F. (1949) *Economic Structure and the Ceremonial Exchange Cycle in Arnhem Land.* Melbourne, Macmillan.

Vinogradoff, P. (1929) Law of succession. *Encyclopaedia Britannica,* 14th edn, vol. 13, pp. 793–95. Encyclopaedia Britannica Inc., New York.

Warner, W. L. (1958) *A Black Civilisation,* rev. ed., New York, Harper & Brothers (first published 1937).

Webb, T. T. (1933) Tribal organization in eastern Arnhem Land. *Oceania,* 3:406–11.

Williams, N. M. (1982) A boundary is to cross: observations on Yolngu boundaries and permission. In: Nancy M. Williams & Eugene S. Hunn (eds.), *Resource Managers: North American and Australian Hunter-Gatherers, AAAS Selected Symposium 67.* Boulder, Colorado. Westview Press for the American Association for the Advancement of Science.

Williams, N. M. (n.d.*a.*) On Aboriginal decision-making. In: D. Barwick, J. Beckett, M. Reay (eds.), *Metaphors of Interpretation: essays in honour of W. E. H. Stanner.* (Forthcoming).

Williams, N. M. (n.d.*b.*) The Yolngu and their land: principles of a system of land tenure and the fight for its recognition. (Forthcoming).

5

'NOW YOU UNDERSTAND':[1] AN ANALYSIS OF THE WAY YOLNGU HAVE USED SACRED KNOWLEDGE TO RETAIN THEIR AUTONOMY

Howard Morphy

> Good evening ladies and gentlemen. My name is Narritjin Maymuru . . . the artist fellow. I have been here now for two and a half months . . . that's when I did all these bark paintings . . . All these paintings have got meanings. It doesn't matter whether it's the littlest thing or the biggest . . . All got meaning, their own story. Everything has been done here in order to teach the Europeans in Canberra, so that they can understand the way we are travelling and why we are carrying on and the way and why we are living. And that's all my message.
>
> And this painting I am going to give to Canberra. Nobody has to pay. I just give to Canberra my painting: the biggest one from my Manggalili clan. A present back to you in this country. That's all my message.[2]

In 1957 at Elcho Island (Galiwinku) in north-east Arnhem Land, a set of carved and painted sacred objects were erected in a public place alongside the church. Many of the objects were *rangga,* sacred objects, that had previously been secret and which were only revealed to initiated men in the context of restricted phases of ceremonies (see, e.g., Warner, 1958:343). This public revelation of sacred objects was part of what Berndt (1962) refers to as the Elcho Island adjustment movement.

The decision of the leaders of some Yolngu clans to open up certain sacred knowledge was a significant and potentially revolutionary step, with possible consequences in both the religious and political spheres. The system of restricted knowledge is a central organisational structure of Yolngu society. Not only is it related to differential control and participation in religious events on the basis of an individual's status and group affiliation but it is also integrated within the political structure of the society. Keen (1978:384ff.) argues that the devaluation of secret knowledge by opening it up to all members of the society would undermine the authority structure by altering the relations between old men and young men in favour of the latter, and that it would finally result in a breakdown of the marriage system by ending gerontocratic polygyny. It seems that the leaders of the Elcho Island movement were aware of these possible consequences and that they were involved in a conscious attempt to change aspects of the structure of their society or, in Maddock's terms, to remodel their society in a particular way.

As far as changing the internal structure of their society was concerned Berndt's account indicates that the leaders of the movement had two main aims. One was to alter certain 'traditional' institutions to make them more appropriate to the changed context of mission life and to make them accord more closely with European values and practices. Bearing in mind Keen's conclusions, it is interesting that some of those involved in the movement were concerned to change the marriage system by ending polygyny and enabling people to marry among their peers. 'The feeling seems to be that since the traditional marriage rules do not seem to have the same force as they did . . . then the best thing to do is to marry according to Australian-European procedure,' (Berndt, 1962:74).

The second aim was to create a wider basis of alliance among Yolngu clans so that they could present a united front in their negotiations with Europeans. Displaying the objects of different clans together, publicly, outside the context of restricted ceremonies, could be seen as a means of breaking down clan solidarity and establishing unity at a community level. According to Berndt (op.cit.:73) there was a conscious attempt to widen the scope of leaders' responsibilities from a clan level to a regional level.

In these respects it can be seen that the leaders of the adjustment movement were involved in an experiment in social change guided almost by Durkheimean principles. They were concerned to resolve contradictions in the structure of Yolngu society that had become more apparent as a consequence of European contact: contradictions between clan solidarity and unity on a wider societal basis and contradictions between a system of gerontocratic polygyny and the pressures from young men to marry earlier and to marry someone of their own age. Although these contradictions clearly existed in the structure of the pre-contact society they took on a different significance after European colonisation. For example, in the case of marriage, European missionaries not only offered an alternative model but also provided the means for young people to revolt against the traditional system of bestowal by giving sanction and sanctuary for those who opted out of it.

These issues of central concern to leaders of the adjustment movement continue to be of central concern to Yolngu people and continue as sources of conflict within the society. Because the adjustment movement failed to resolve the contradictions it would be naive to conclude that it had failed totally. What it did was to dramatise the issues and place within a single frame (both temporal and spatial) and with a central focus, a series of unresolved and perhaps unresolvable problems that were themselves only loosely interconnected. The *rangga* (sacred objects) as the ideological 'foundation' of Yolngu society could be thought of as central to or connected with all aspects of society and as representing an almost archetypical sign for Yolngu discourse. The goals of the movement were not, however, shared at a societal level, almost by definition, since they were seeking solutions to problems that were the product of structural contradiction and sectional interest. It is also likely that unintended and undesired consequences of the means chosen to resolve the problems became apparent to the participants after the objects had been revealed. In particular, the objects, revealed precisely because of their power, lost part of that power through being revealed, and their actions in revealing the objects were interpreted by other Yolngu as well as by European missionaries as a desacrilisation of their *rangga* and a denial of basic cultural values rather than an assertion of the fact that the solution to their problems was to be found through them. If the leaders adopted a Durkheimean approach they had certainly not read Simmel. It must however be noted that the breach of secrecy was neither total nor final. The majority of Yolngu clans did not commit themselves to the movement by revealing their sacred objects and those that did held much back including all but the most public meanings of the objects. As Maddock (1972:5) writes, 'the rank and file were thus divided by the partial retention of male privilege'.

So far I have only considered those aims of the movement concerned with the internal restructuring of Yolngu society, albeit a restructuring that was in response to outside or introduced pressures. The movement was also concerned with outsiders in a more direct way in attempting to set up negotiations with European colonists over a number of demands. It is this aspect of the movement that I will now turn to and which is most central to the topic of this paper. The idea of the leaders of the movement was that they could set up an exchange relationship with Europeans that would bring them certain benefits. By showing Europeans their most sacred and valuable possessions, the *rangga,* it was hoped to get in return 'education, economic security, employment and more control over their own affairs' (Berndt, 1962).

On the surface it seems unlikely that white Australians would grant political autonomy and certain material benefits in exchange for sacred objects from an alien religious system. In this respect Maddock (1972:2ff.) refers to the movement as 'deluded' and 'misguided' as 'it proposed an improbable exchange'. Berndt (1962:89ff.) argues convincingly that from a Yolngu perspective their action and expectations were perfectly rational but felt that they were unlikely to be successful and indeed that the movement 'may well have the opposite result to what is intended' (p.92). He suggests that, atypically, the nature of the missionary process in north-east Arnhem Land resulted in a mutual respect of European and Aboriginal spiritual beliefs and of the sources of spiritual power that the respective groups have access to (see, e.g., Chaseling, 1956:167ff.). Because the main contact Yolngu had had was with missionaries, the particular missionary world view became a false typification of that of Europeans in general. Hence an environment was created in which Yolngu could expect Europeans in general to recognise that in displaying to them their sacred objects they were offering something of considerable value. Berndt (op.cit.:91) concludes that Yolngu were therefore not in a position to assess realistically the kind of response their *rangga* offer would be likely to meet from Europeans in the wider Australian society to whom the offer was primarily directed.

While I think Berndt's argument is very much along the right lines, it seems that with hindsight the Yolngu were employing a strategy that was much more 'realistic' than it might have seemed at the time. I will argue that the aim was not to set up an exchange relationship in which valuable goods or rights were exchanged between groups; rather, it was to exchange perceptions of value. Yolngu had in a sense already accepted their part of the exchange by accepting the missionaries and some of their goals. The movement for example as well as asking for greater political autonomy and control over access to their land, sought better 'education' for their children and better employment opportunities. What they were demanding in return for their acceptance of certain European values was the recognition of the value of Yolngu culture by white Australians.

In some respects the external aims of the movement seem to contradict the internal ones. Whereas on the one hand Yolngu were concerned with remodelling their society in relation to white Australia on the other hand they were demanding political autonomy. However, the contradiction only exists if it is assumed that the desire for autonomy must be associated with the maintainance of a particular cultural difference.[3] However, there is always the danger that the means chosen to pursue external goals may change the internal conditions of existence. The Elcho Island movement involved an assertion of the value of the participants' culture to outsiders by attempting to share with Europeans their own valuation of the *rangga*. By trying to demonstrate the value of their *rangga* to white Australians through displaying them in public the possibility exists that they will be devalued as far as their own culture is concerned.

My aim in the remainder of this paper is twofold. Firstly, to show that the principles employed by the leaders of the Elcho Island adjustment movement for negotiating with Europeans have been applied by Yolngu people in different contexts over a long period of time. And secondly, to show that the means chosen, sacred objects and in particular painted designs, were an ideal way of demonstrating to Europeans the fact that Yolngu had their own systems of land tenure and law. This latter, of course, depended on European authorities adopting a cultural relativist stance and accepting the value of the Yolngu evidence. At the time Berndt was writing this must have seemed improbable. However, with hindsight it can be seen as no less probable than Australian law accepting spirit conception as a basis for claiming land ownership or than a demonstrable desire to return to live on clan lands being a means to acquire a motor vehicle. The fact that this situation has changed I think requires a re-evaluation of the strategy adopted by the Yolngu.

Although the Elcho Island Memorial has been treated in the anthropological literature as an almost unique occurrence it in fact represents in dramatic form a kind of transaction between Yolngu and Europeans that is almost commonplace. From the beginning of intensive European contact in north-east Arnhem Land in 1935, Aboriginal people have allowed some European people access to sacred and sometimes secret knowledge. Early on it was primarily anthropologists and missionaries who were involved in these exchanges. Subsequently the participants widened to include lawyers, schoolteachers and politicians of all political parties. I refer to them as exchanges even though for a long time Aborigines perhaps had no clear idea of what they sought in return and the Europeans had no idea that they were expected to reciprocate. A part of the return gift sometimes involved material goods, until recently tobacco or some other consumable, and increasingly since the 1960s, money. But I do not think that from the Yolngu viewpoint this completed the transaction nor was it the main motivation for releasing the kind of information that was given. Clearly, innumerable factors intervened in determining the form of the exchanges, including individual friendships, internal political affairs and evidence of the physical domination of Aborigines by Europeans elsewhere in Australia. However, it seems that for most of the period since European contact Yolngu have thought themselves free to withhold information but have chosen in certain circumstances to release it.

Within months of the establishment of Yirrkala Mission in December 1934, the Rev. Wilbur Chaseling was shipping crates of bark paintings to museums in southern Australian cities. Many of the paintings were public ones, secular in their content, some however were sacred clan paintings though few were secret. Chaseling's aim was to provide a source of cash income for the mission. Over the same period of time the anthropologist Donald Thomson made a large collection of paintings and sacred objects from the clans of the Caledon Bay and Milingimbi area. Many of the things Thomson collected were secret clan-owned objects or designs. He, like Chaseling, appears to have paid for them mainly with supplies of tobacco.

Subsequently such exchanges have continued at increasingly regular intervals and have developed distinctive forms. The exchanges of art for tobacco have become formalised within a developing art and craft industry which has continually presented the Yolngu with problems of what can or cannot be sold to an 'open' market, one over which Yolngu still have relatively little control (see Morphy & Layton, 1981). The presentation of gifts to missionaries and white advisers has developed a particular ceremonial form. Departing Europeans who have worked for any time in the area are given paintings and carvings in the context of ceremonies held in their honour. Such an honour is also extended to visiting church dignitariess, lawyers and parliamentarians and on one occasion, that we witnessed, to members of the Northern Territory police force who had rendered a service to the community.[4]

Paintings have also played a role in other transactions with Europeans that are more explicitly concerned with political objectives or are concerned with asserting Yolngu cultural identity in a more general context. The Elcho Island Memorial is one such example. Others include the bark petition sent to the Commonwealth Parliament in 1963 by the people of Yirrkala to ask the Commonwealth to intervene on their behalf to prevent bauxite mining on the Gove Peninsula (E. Wells, 1981) and the panels of clan paintings produced for the Yirrkala church (A. Wells, 1971; see also Morphy & Layton, 1981). Not all such transactions involve the public display of paintings and objects. Stanner (1979:278) reports that he and Purcell, the solicitor for the Yirrkala people in the Gove land rights case, were shown in secret, sacred objects and paintings in order that they should 'understand' how the Yolngu owned their land. At the time the intention was expressed to show the objects to the judge at the court in Darwin.

Clearly, we are dealing with a number of very different events and the specific motives and objectives of the transactions vary from occasion to occasion. The primary motive in one case might be economic, in another the expression of thanks, and only in a very few cases are the motives expressly political. However, it would seem that two general motives or perhaps presuppositions underlie the giving or the display of art objects to white Australians: one is to teach them about Aboriginal culture, to make them 'understand'; the other is to assert the value of the things they give. The two objectives are probably complementary, and perhaps the latter even has priority over the former; it is necessary for white Australians to believe that Aboriginal culture has things of value before the majority will show any interest in learning about the significance of those things.

In a sense this reverses the dictum that understanding comes through knowledge: people will not be motivated to know until they are oriented towards understanding. Aboriginal land rights in the Northern Territory would never have come through white Australians learning about Aboriginal systems of land tenure.[5] Rather, they came through political action by Aborigines and the continual assertion by Aborigines of their attachment to their land, as well as through the changed historical circumstances of Australia in the second half of this century (see Peterson, n.d.). The value of Aboriginal land to Aborigines only became a value to white Australians when it became inappropriate for them to continue expropriating Aboriginal land in the simple way they had done previously: by invasion. Only when white Australians learnt that Aboriginal land was something of value to Aborigines, *something that they had to take into account in their relations with them,* did knowledge of Aboriginal land tenure become relevant to white Australians. Only then did lawyers, judges, politicians and mining company executives begin to learn something of the way in which Aborigines owned their land.

The release of knowledge to Europeans, the giving and display of sacred objects and paintings can all be understood at one level as political actions which involved an assertion of the value of Aboriginal land and culture and which attempted to get Europeans to negotiate on the basis of those values. The effect at the individual level was to bind certain Europeans to Aboriginal groups in respect of those values. A further effect was the use of those Europeans as intermediaries in the communication of those values to wider society. At a wider level it introduced Aboriginal symbols into European discourse.

It is impossible to say what motivated the early transactions between Yolngu and Thomson and Chaseling involving secret knowledge and sacred paintings and objects. Today senior Yolngu claim that Wonggu, the leader of the Caledon Bay people, who in the years prior to the establishment of Yirrkala mission had been involved in violent conflict with Europeans and other intruders, made a deliberate decision to make peace with the invaders and teach them to understand Yolngu culture. Certainly, it is likely that both Thomson and Chaseling presented themselves as protectors of Yolngu rights, mediating between them and other white Australians.

By the time of the Elcho Island adjustment movement some Yolngu at least had a definite idea as to the role of anthropologists in presenting their culture to outsiders *and more importantly* in upholding its values. Thus Buramura, in a sermon, spoke in Warramiri on the duty of anthropologists as follows (Berndt, 1962:77):

> I am taking this opportunity to explain the duty of anthropologists. They come around in order to find out the meaning of our dances, songs, *mada* and *mala,* our *mareiin* and *rangga,* our kinship and so on—all the tbings we've got and all the things we do . . .

> they stand for this: this is their duty. This means that they are holding the world firm. And they are holding up the Government too . . . And anthropologists can go all over the place, not just to us but to white people too . . .

Over the years Yolngu people have become increasingly aware of the complexity of European Australian society and of the need to direct their message to particular categories of people. At the time of the Gove land rights case, sacred objects were displayed to lawyers (Stanner, 1979:278) and 10 years earlier bark paintings were prepared for the members of the Parliamentary Select Committee investigating the condition of the people of Yirrkala (Wells, 1981:38). In 1975 the Principal and Chairman of the Institute of Aboriginal Studies asked a meeting of Yirrkala clan leaders for their comments on conditions of access to a book of clan paintings that had just been published.[6] One clan leader urged that the book should be sent to every Member of Parliament, all lawyers in contact with Aboriginal people or working on Aboriginal Land Rights and to directors of mining companies. Clearly, people were becoming aware of who it was they had to influence and the way in which the work of anthropologists could be put to better effect.

The giving of paintings to departing missionaries and the holding of ceremonies for visiting or resident Europeans can be seen as part of the same process of asserting the value and by implication the autonomy of Aboriginal culture. At first glance the giving of 'sacred' paintings to missionaries in joint Aboriginal-mission sponsored ceremonies may seem to be a sign of assimilation to European values, reducing the significance of a sacred painting to the level of a birthday present. On further reflection, it is almost a subversive act: an assertion at an introduced ceremony that the most valuable thing you have to offer is something of your own culture, an object of great value that has nothing to do with the coming of Europeans, an item that through your generosity you are prepared to share with them. Aboriginalisation of European ceremonial contexts is clearly a means of asserting Aboriginal identity and culture to outsiders as well as within the community. Whether the recipients understand the significance of the object, the meaning of the painting or even whether they like it is irrelevant to its purpose.[7] They have been made aware that to the givers it remains a thing of value; they have also received the message that the people have retained their cultural identity as Aborigines and that there are things of importance to them in their land which are very different from things that Europeans value.

The bark petition sent to the House of Representatives in 1963 had many of the same objectives as these more local exchanges. The petition consisted of written submissions in Yolngu and an English translation—pasted to two sheets of stringybark, around the borders of which were painted designs belonging to the two clans whose lands were most threatened by mining activities. The petition essentially asked that their rights in land should be respected and that they should be consulted before any land was excised from the then Arnhem Land Reserve. The genius of the bark petition was that it introduced an Aboriginal symbol into Parliamentary discourse, making it harder for Europeans to respond in terms of their own cultural precedents. Petitions framed in parliamentary language can be dealt with through parliamentary procedures. Petitions framed with bark paintings add a new element. The bark petition emphasised the difference between 'Aborigines' and other petitioners, and it did so in such a way that the issue was likely to be taken up by the media.

It is impossible to assess at this stage the significance of the Yirrkala bark petition in the movement towards Aboriginal land rights in the Northern Territory. For the people of Yirrkala it set an important precedent by engaging them in direct negotiations with the Commonwealth Government, a precedent they were to follow consistently over the next decade. The Parliamentary Select Committee set up to look into their grievances failed to prevent the mining from going ahead, and finally they chose to negotiate through the courts in the Gove land rights case (see, e.g., Stanner, 1979 and Morphy, 1978a). Again they lost and failed to gain legal recognition under Australian law of their ownership of their land. However, the publicity gained by their action was instrumental in setting up the Woodward Commission into Land Rights in the Northern Territory, which finally resulted in the *Aboriginal Land Rights (Northern Territory) Act* of 1976.

The bark petition was important in this process, not because it was absolutely the first step but because it was the first step to gain national attention and because it introduced a form of evidence, sacred paintings as title deeds to land, that signified that factors other than those generally considered under Australian Law were relevant to the negotiations. Indeed, as far as the Yolngu were concerned, it was not a first step but a stage in the process of gaining cultural recognition and recognition of their rights by Europeans. The process began with European contact but the issues became more precisely defined as the points of conflict emerged over the years. Earlier transactions had set the scene for the Gove land rights case, not only by enabling Yolngu to discover what the basic issue was and to understand something of where power lay in Australian society, but in setting the preconditions for enabling Yolngu symbols to be used in an effective dialogue with Europeans. Had paintings from Yirrkala not been released over the years, had there been no Elcho Island Memorial, no paintings in the Yirrkala church and no interest by outsiders in Yolngu art and culture, then bark paintings would not have emerged as an appropriate symbol. Had Yolngu art not been released earlier, then it would not have existed as a possible symbol. Art locked away in a secret ceremonial ground might have been replaced by a telegraphed petition to be buried in the National archives. Moreover, the Elcho Island Memorial, and the concern for a wider basis of unity among Yolngu clans that underlay it may well have been effective in enabling the people of north-east Arnhem Land to present a united front in their negotiations with Europeans as well as being a stage in the formulation of their aims and methods of achieving them.

An event such as the Gove land rights case was not a historic inevitability. Although the circumstances that led up to it would doubtless have occurred elsewhere in Australia at another point in time, it may well prove with hindsight that in the history of the colonisation by Europeans of Australia the intersection of time and space left only a small sector in which Aboriginal land rights were a possibility. It was fortunate that the people of Yirrkala were able to seize upon that possibility.

In the remainder of this paper I consider why paintings are an effective means of demonstrating rights of ownership in land, from the Yolngu point of view. Although the main effectiveness of paintings given to Europeans, and of bark petitions sent to Parliament, may lie in their being symbols of Aboriginal identity and of the possession of a unique culture, there is no doubt that Yolngu believe that in their paintings they possess objects that are broadly equivalent to the European concept of title deeds. Before summarising the kind of information that paintings in north-east Arnhem Land provide about land-ownership, I must first discuss briefly the system of land tenure.

YOLNGU LAND-OWNERSHIP

Land in north-east Arnhem Land is owned by named patrilineal clans. In the case of large clans, different lineages may be more closely associated with one area of the clan's land than with others. Should the clan divide into two on the basis of lineage segmentation, then the land with which the lineages were most closely associated will become the respective territories of the new clans. However, while the clan remains a single entity its members will acknowledge, publicly at least, joint ownership of all the clan's lands, although different patrilines may be acknowledged to have primary responsibilities for different areas.

In the western part of the Yolngu region in the area of Milingimbi the land-owning group is not the clan but a single patrilineage or set of patrilineages within the clan (see Keen, 1978:21). However, as relative to other clans all members of the clan own all of its countries, the system of ownership is largely consistent with that in the eastern part of the region. The difference of emphasis may be due to the fact that in the western region there are a number of very large clans and that they are more differentiated within. While both male and female clan members are owners of the land, female members do not pass on rights of ownership to their children. Children of the clan's women do have certain rights in their mothers' clan's country and certain responsibilities towards it. Collectively the *waku* (ZC) of the clan have certain obligations to perform on behalf of their mothers' clan in ceremonies. Senior male ZS are responsible for manufacturing sacred objects and producing body paintings as well as taking a leading role in the dancing. They should be consulted as to the correct performance of a ritual, and they should be consulted before anything is done that affects their mothers' clan territory, for example before a road is built through it or a settlement site selected.

Sister's children cannot in any circumstance take over ownership of their mothers' clan territory. The mothers' country belongs to a clan of the opposite moiety to ego, and land should never change moiety ownership. If the clan dies out, then it should be succeeded by members of a (Z)DC clan, a clan of the same moiety and linked to the extinct clan by descent. There may in fact be a number of clans with a strong claim to take over the land and ceremonies of an extinct clan, with the final outcome depending on political process over many years. (See Morphy, 1977:81ff; Peterson et al., 1977, and Keen, 1978:140.)

PAINTINGS AND LAND

Paintings are part of the corpus of ritual knowledge, which includes the paintings, songs, dances, power names and sacred objects, that can be referred to as *maḏayin* ('sacred law'). Rights in *maḏayin* are distributed on precisely the same basis as rights in land. Paintings are owned by clans. Within the clan, rights in paintings are distributed on the basis of age, status, sex, and in the case of large clans, patrilineage affiliation. Maximum control over paintings is exercised by the senior male clan members. Theoretically, men should be given knowledge of the clan's paintings on the basis of seniority, with eldest sons being taught before second sons and so on. This does not always happen since the transmission of knowledge depends partly on the interest and ability to learn shown by the initiate. Some people never fully exercise their right to learn, although their right to do so is still acknowledged. Men learn first the paintings associated with the land most closely linked to their own patrilineage, though as with land ownership it must be stressed that differential rights at the level of patrilineage is an implicit not an explicit part of the pattern of ownership. Clan members will assert that the paintings are owned by the clan as a whole and that all members can acquire the right to paint them. The most senior clan members may indeed produce paintings associated with all the sublineages, but before doing so they may refer to the senior members of the other patrilines. Women are taught to do some of their clan's paintings, and as they grow older acquire increasing knowledge of the clan's *maḏayin*. They may also produce paintings for sale and for use in ceremonial contexts. Senior female clan members will be consulted about the clan's *maḏayin*, and their advice sought before a ceremony is held. However, publicly women are not acknowledged to have the same level of knowledge as men, nor do they exercise the same control over paintings.[8]

Rights in paintings extend beyond the clan to members of the (Z)DC clans and to the *waku* (ZC) of the clan. In this case the rights are not ones of ownership, although in the case of (Z)DC clans these rights can be used as a basis for making claims of ownership should the MM(B) clan become extinct. In the case of the ZC, they are to a certain extent managers or guardians of the clan's paintings, Senior ZS are said to 'look after' the clan's *maḏayin*. They are expected to produce the paintings for their mothers' clan on ceremonial occasions, when they are requested to do so. As compensation they are allowed to produce their mothers' clan's paintings for sale, so long as they do not exercise this right too often. If they paint their mothers' paintings too frequently then members of the owning clan will start complaining and suggesting that they pay them part of the price obtained. Only senior ZS will exercise the right to paint their mothers' paintings. Others will not unless they are requested to do so or unless they have asked permission to do so first.

Rights in MM(B) clan paintings are acquired after rights in one's own clan's paintings and mother's clan paintings. Although some knowledge of the MM clan's *maḏayin* is passed on to most members of the (Z)DC clan, only senior members of the clan will exercise the right to produce the MM clan painting, and they tend to do so infrequently and with specific permission. They may be called upon to produce the painting in a ceremonial context on behalf of the MM(B) clan, but this is extremely rare. I have argued elsewhere (Morphy 1978b:218) that the extension of rights to (Z)DC is a reflection of the close spiritual tie between MM(B)s and (Z)DCs, and of the strong structural alliance between MM(B) and (Z)DC clans. The rights will only be exercised if the MM(B) clan should become extinct, or if it should consist only of young uninitiated men. In the former case the (Z)DC clan will be able to take over the ritual obligations of the extinct clan, and by fulfilling its ceremonial role 'keep alive' the paintings. In the latter case, senior members of the (Z)DC clan will be able to teach the young members of the MM(B) clan the latters' clan paintings, ensuring that they do not lose their inheritance. Knowledge of MM(B) clan paintings can place members of a (Z)DC clan in a position of power over a MM(B) clan's members, especially if that clan is weak. They may, for example, deny members of the clan access to their own paintings and songs by not producing or performing them (see Keen, 1978:180). Should a clan become extinct then a strong (Z)DC clan can use its knowledge of the paintings to assert its rights to take over the clan's land. It may indeed try to pre-empt that decision by absorbing remaining members of the MM(B) clan within its own body. Perhaps because they can in certain circumstances represent a challenge to the authority of the MM(B) clan, rights in MM(B) clan's paintings are exercised infrequently by (Z)DC (for a detailed discussion see Morphy, 1978b).

CLAN DESIGNS

To the Yolngu their paintings are creations or manifestations of the Ancestral World *(Wangarr)*. Their form was set in the Ancestral past, and produced in ceremonies they become the loci of Ancestral power and a means of establishing contact between Yolngu and the world-creative powers. Yolngu paintings are at the the same time part of a complex system of meaning concerned with the relationship between living Yolngu and the Ancestral determinants of the Yolngu world and way of life. Part of their meaning concerns the relationship between people and the land, a relationship mediated by the Ancestral past. The two main ways in which meanings connected with land ownership are encoded in paintings are through clan designs, which precisely signify the clan ownership of a painting, and through representing features of the topography of the landscape itself in the form of the painting.[9]

One of the main components of Yolngu paintings consists of geometric designs which cover nearly the entire surface of the painting between figurative representation.

Indeed, in sacred paintings the geometric component is predominant.[10] The geometric component varies according to which set of Ancestral Beings the painting is connected with and which clan the painting belongs to. Each major set of Ancestral Beings is associated with a basis design form. The set of Yirritja moiety Ancestral Beings which includes Fire, Wild Honey and Crocodile Ancestors is associated with a linked diamond pattern . The set of Ancestors which includes Mangrove Tree and Kingfish is linked with an open diamond pattern . Other Yirritja moiety sets are associated with triangles , pointed ovals , and parallel meandering lines .

Each area of land is associated mainly with the activities of one set of Ancestors, and although the Ancestral tracks frequently intersect, one of the basic design types only is associated with any given area of land. Thus Madarrpa clan paintings from Gunmurrutjpi on the north of Blue Mud Bay and Gumatj clan paintings from Biranybiranybuy on Caledon Bay both have a variant of the linked diamond design on them, signifying that the places are connected with the actions of the Crocodile and Fire Ancestors (see Plates 1 and 2).

Although a number of clans of the same moiety may be linked to the same set of Ancestral Beings, each clan will own its own version of the design associated with the set, and each may have a different myth explaining the origin of the design. Many Yirritja moiety clans own a variant of the linked diamond pattern each of which differs from those of every other clan. Thus the Gumatj design referred to above consists of sets of elongated diamonds joined at the edges (Plate 1). The Madarrpa design in contrast consists of separated chains of elongated diamonds ending in a shield-shaped figure (Plate 2). Other variants include equilateral diamonds of different dimensions and elongated diamonds of different dimensions to the Gumatj ones. Some clans own more than one version of the diamond design which are associated with different areas of the clan's territory. In such cases the basic diamond shape remains constant, with the design varying in some other detail of its form. The Dhalwangu clan, for example, has a diamond design outlined in dotted lines for swampy country and one without that embellishment for dry country (Fig. 1).

Different parts of a clan's country are most often associated with different Ancestral tracks. Following from this, the paintings from different areas of the clan's territory have different basic geometric design types painted on them. Each design type links the clan with a different set of other clans which share a variant of that design type (for examples of this see Morphy, 1977, chapter 7).

Fig. 1
A Dhalwangu clan design.

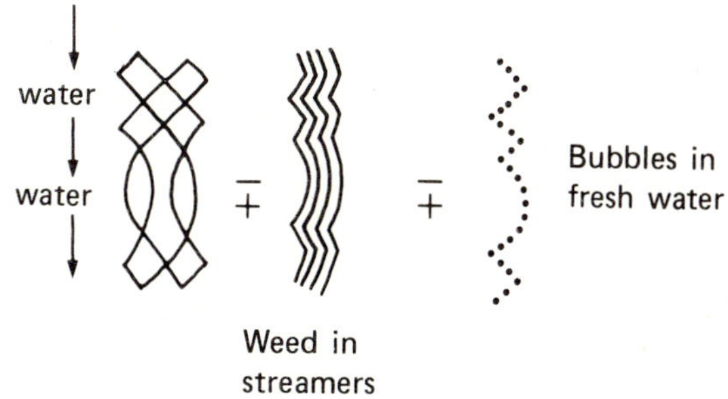

Plate 1
Artist Yama, clan Yarrwidi Gumatj. Painted at Yirrkala in 1974. The painting represents the Ancestral Crocodile off the coast of Caledon Bay. The background pattern represents fire.

Overall, the system of clan designs provides a network of relationships of similarity and difference that extends across Arnhem Land. Each clan owns a set of designs, each of which links it with a set of other clans sharing the basic design type, but each of which differs in some way from every other design in the same set. This means that on the basis of clan design alone a knowledgeable man can tell of a particular painting which clan it belongs to, which set of Ancestral Beings it is connected with and which

Plate 2
Artist Bakulangay Marrawili, Madarrpa clan. Painted at Yirrkala in 1976. The painting shows ancestral hunters harpooning a dugong at Yatikpa in the North of Blue Mud Bay. The cross bars represent sand bars and the ovals rocks beneath the water. The background pattern represents fire.

area of the clan's land it is associated with. Not surprisingly, Yolngu frequently refer to clan designs as marks of ownership or as 'copyright' marks.

MAPS OF THE LAND

Many Yolngu paintings, as well as being closely associated with a particular place through the clan designs on them, are related in a more specific way to details of the topography of the area concerned; they are in a sense maps of the land. Paintings may be approached from two main interpretative perspectives: as accounts of actions that took place on the journeys of the Ancestral Beings through the area of land concerned, and as maps of the topography of the land with reference to its mythological significance. In a sense, as we shall see, these are two sides of the same coin.

The painting in Plate 3 can be interpreted as events on the journey of a set of Ancestral Beings led by the Guwak (Koel Cuckoo). The painting belongs to the Manggalili clan and is associated with the country of Djarrakpi (Cape Shield). It was painted by Narritjin Maymuru, a member of the clan. The painting shows two Guwak (represented by the elongated figures to the right and left of the painting) sitting on top of a native cashew tree, feeding off the nuts. Each night on their journey across Arnhem Land from Donydji in the centre to Djarrakpi in the south-east they rested at the top of the trees and instructed their workers, the Possum Ancestors, to climb up the tree spinning their fur into lengths of string. They gave lengths of the string to members of Aboriginal groups living in the area where they camped that night so that

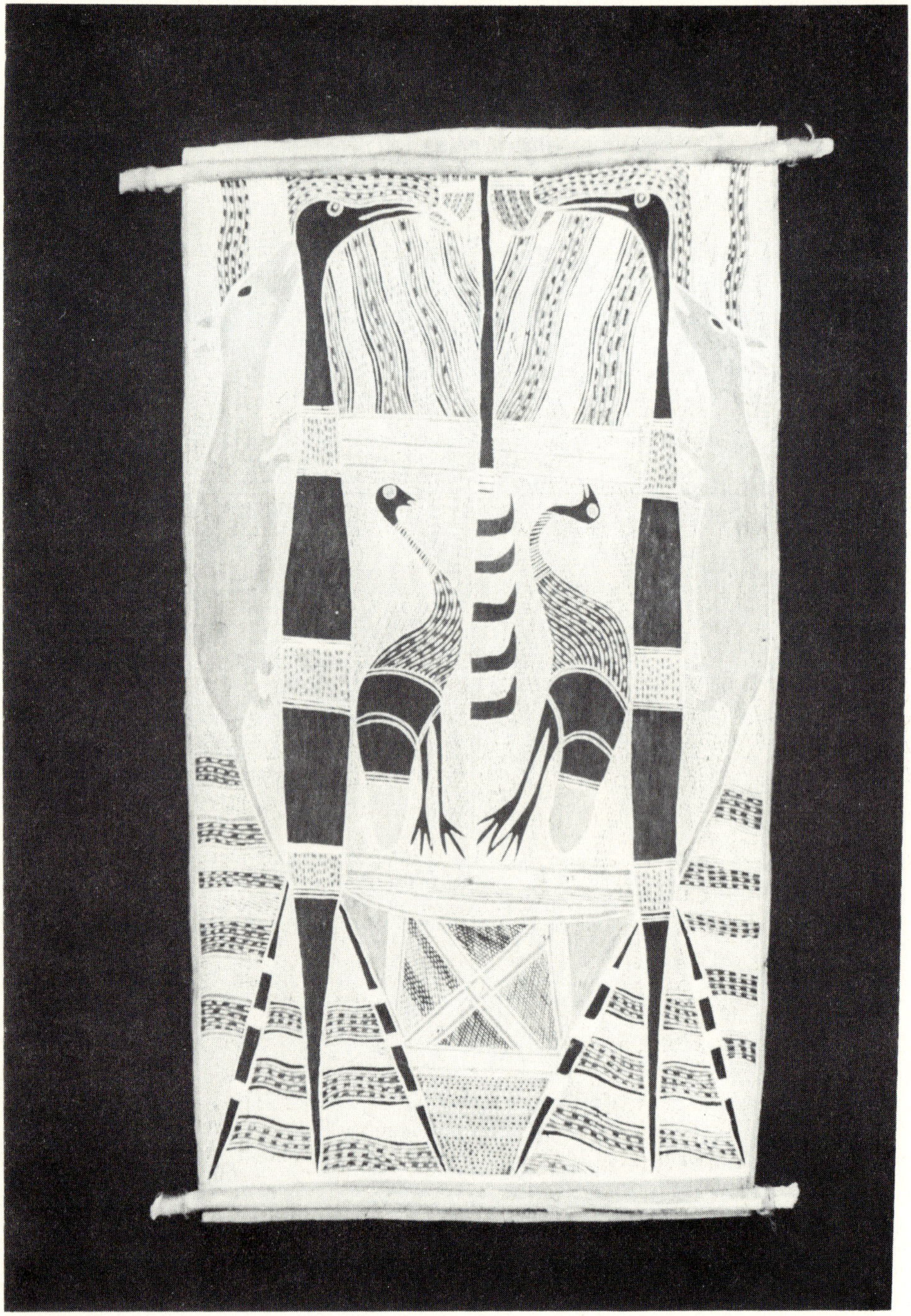

Plate 3
Artist Narritjin Maymuru, Manggalili clan. Yirrkala 1974. A painting of Djarrakpi and of the journey of the Guwak bird, possum and emus to Djarrakpi.

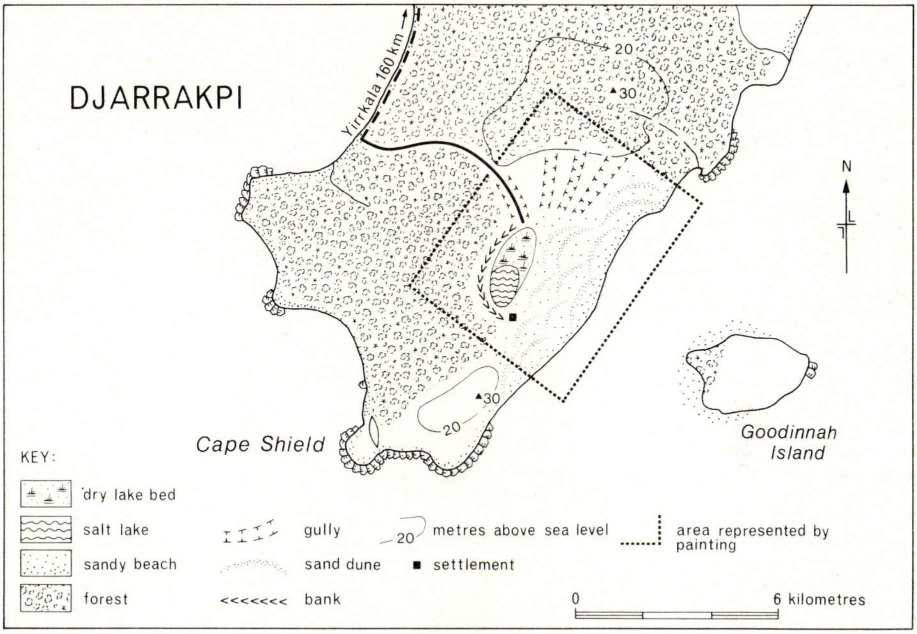

Fig. 2
Map of Djarrakpi, Cape Shield. The area represented in Narritjin's painting (Plate 3) is marked by the broken outline.

they could be used in manufacturing sacred objects to commemorate them. They were accompanied by the Emu Ancestor who scratched the ground looking for water, creating waterholes at the places they visited. At this level the painting can be interpreted as an illustration of those events as they occurred at any of a number of stages along their journey.

However, the painting can also be interpreted at a more specific level as a map of Djarrakpi itself, the destination of this section of the Guwak's journey, by locating events that took place in the context of specific features of the environment that resulted from the Ancestral Beings' actions. Fig. 2 represents a schematic map of the Djarrakpi area. The section of the map relevant to the painting is the area surrounding the lake, bordered on the seaward side by high sand hills and contained on the inland side by a long low sand bank which borders this side of the lake from the sand hills in the north to the settlement at the southern end. The settlement is located at the site of an ancient casuarina tree, the final destination of the Guwak. The painting (Plate 3) can be interpreted as a map in the following way.

The bottom right-hand corner represents the place where the Ancestral Beings first arrived in the area on their journey from Donydji. The lines extending from the base of the elongated figure represents gullies in sandhills that were formed by lengths of possum fur string laid out by the Guwak for gatherings of clans in the region. The Guwak continued his journey along the lake's edge to a grove of wild plum trees, marked by the line across the base of the elongated figure to the right. There the Ancestors rested at night, the Possum feeding off wild plums and continuing to spin possum fur string. In the morning the Guwak flew on to a second grove of trees, this time native cashew trees, further along the lake margin, carrying in his beak the length of string. He laid the string on the ground between the two groves, where it became

Plate 4
Djarrakpi, Cape Shield.

transformed into the low sandbank that today defines the inland margins of the lake (Plate 4 and Fig. 3). The Guwak then flew onto the casuarina tree, signified by the nuts in the top half of the painting. The Emus meanwhile looked for water in the place where the lake now is. On the seaward side of the lake lived two female Ancestral Beings, the Nyapililngu. These two learnt the technique of string-making from observing the Possums at work. They began to make string themselves, which formed the high sandhills that separate the lake from the sea (Plate 4). The painting contains a number of other topographical referents that need not be considered here. I hope that the information given so far enables it to be seen that the painting can be used as a conventionalised topographical map, encoding the major features of the topography and the relationship of the features to one another. However, perhaps most significant is the fact that the painting represents the landscape not as a series of abstract topographical features, but in terms of how the land was made, by selecting out mythologically significant features.[11]

Yolngu paintings such as this, because they can be interpreted as topographical maps, enable people to learn about the mythological significance of their land when separated from it by considerable distances, and to keep in touch with the land when they are away from it. The leader of the Manggalili clan, Narritjin Maymunu, had been away from his country for some 30 years prior to the establishment of his outstation at Djarrakpi. He had, however, learned the details of the land through

Fig. 3
Significant features of the landscape represented in Plate 4. *a*, the low sandbank; *b* the lake; *c*, the sandhills.

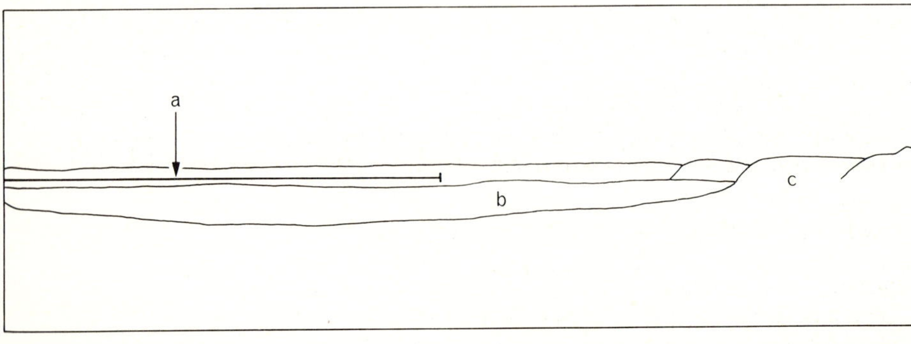

Plate 5

Artist Welwi, Marrakulu clan. Painted at Yirrkala 1974. The painting represents a waterhole at Balmawuy on Blue Mud Bay, shown as the black circle. The surrounding pattern is a Marrakulu clan design representing running water. The two linear forms on either side represent digging sticks of the Djankawu, Ancestral Beings who created the waterhole. Catfish, a symbol of spiritual continuity are represented flowing through the waterhole, in embryonic form below the waterhole, in mature form above it.

Plate 7

Artist Yanggariny Gumana, Dhalwangu clan. Painted at Yirrkala 1974. The painting represents adjoining countries belonging to two clans. The long necked fresh water turtle is associated with Dhalwangu country as is the background pattern. The lower panel represents Madarrpa country and the clan design is a Madarrpa one associated with the Ancestral Snake Mundukul.

◀ **Plate 6**

Artist Dula Ngurruywutun, Munyuku clan. Painted at Yirrkala 1975. A painting of the Yirritja moiety hammerhead shark, *garra ngunung* at Nuparrwuy, inland to the North of Blue Mud Bay. The diamond design represents the freshwater country inland and the zigzag design represents salt water in the flood plain near the estuary of the Maya Wunydji River.

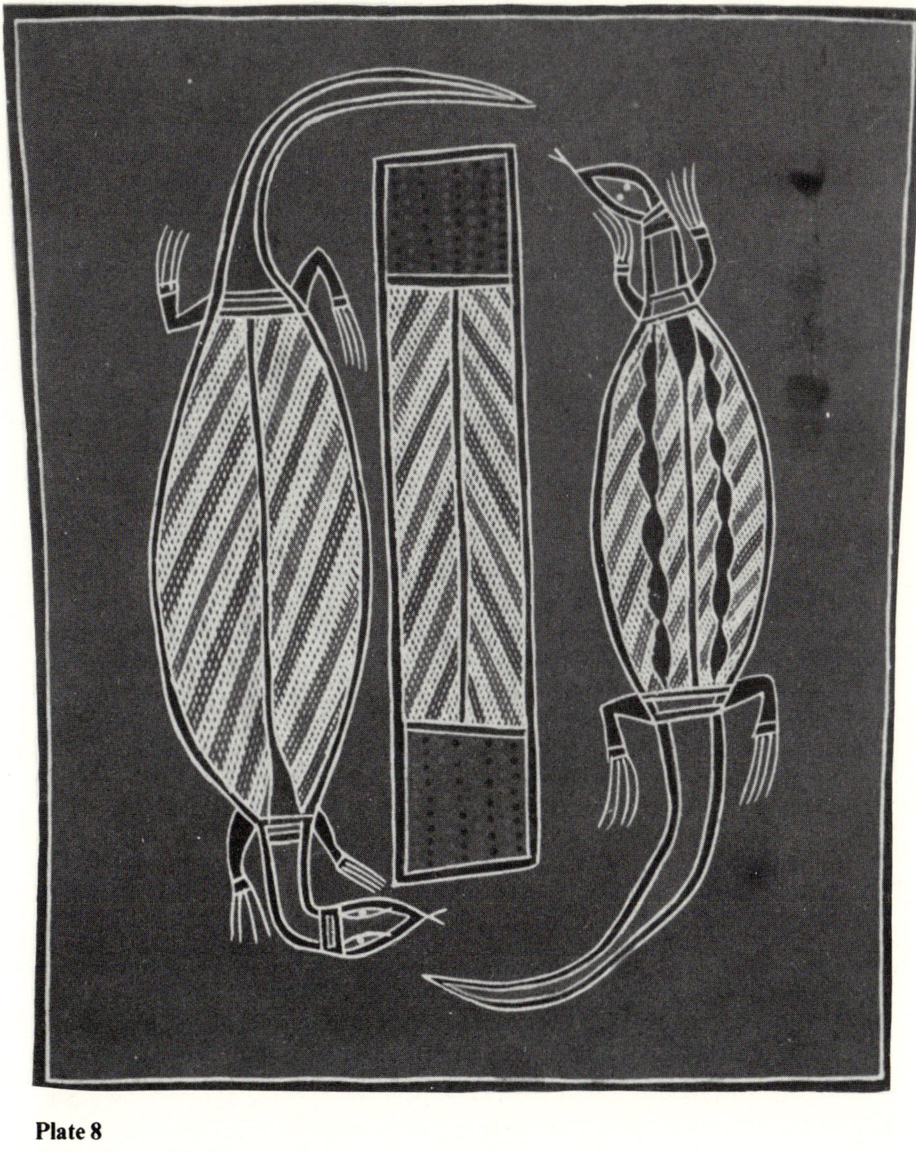

Plate 8

Artist Jimmy Moduk, clan Djinang. Painted at Gadji Creek, June 1974. The painting belongs to the Djinang Maringu clan and is associated with country near Gadji.

◀ **Plate 9**

Paintings by Bukarra Maymuru, painted at Yirrkala 1976. The painting belongs to his mother's clan, the Marrakulu. Bukarra's painting shows two water goannas *(wan'kawu)* moving around a hollow log coffin. The goannas are shown holding in their mouth a shellfish *(djaruwit)*. The background design represents water and rocks, the dots signifying air bubbles coming from the goanna. The goanna travelled from inland to Trial Bay (see Plate 10).

paintings taught him by a classificatory (Z)DC and was immediately able to re-establish himself in his land by identifying the features he had learned about through paintings; by projecting the paintings back onto the land.

Not all Yolngu paintings map areas of land at the level of detail of Banapana's painting of Djarrakpi. Some paintings focus on a single feature of the landscape, such as a particular waterhole (Plate 5), whereas others encode more general features of the relationships between different areas of a clans land (Plate 6) or the relationship between the lands of different clans (Plate 7). All Yolngu paintings, however, are relatable to areas of land and elements of all paintings encode meanings that can be interpreted to refer to specific topographical features.

Plates 8 and 9 represent versions of a design that belongs to a large number of Dhuwa moiety clans over a wide region that extends outside the Yolngu-speaking area. The design is one painted on the chests of leading dancers and/or initiates during phases of the Djungguwan ceremony (see Warner, 1958:274ff., Morphy, 1977:129ff.). At one level the painting represents Ancestral goannas associated with one of the manifestations of the Ancestral Being Yulengurr.[12]

The design varies in detail from owning clan to owning clan and in the case of each clan it can be related to the topographic features of specific sites in the respective clan's territory. The Djinang painting (Plate 8) represents a site, close to Gatji Creek, south of Milingimbi, which consists of two deep holes on either side of a tall stringy-bark tree. The holes represent places where the male and female Ancestral goannas went into and emerged from the ground. The tree is a manifestation of Yulengurr (the

Plate 10

The beach at Trial Bay. The route the goanna took is today a small creek to the right of the mangrove tree in the middle distance *(a)*. He entered the sea and circled the mangrove tree ending up on the beach in the foregound where he is manifested as the line of rocks *(b)*. White discolourations on the rocks represent air bubbles coming from him. The mangrove tree itself *(a)* is a manifestation of the hollow log coffin which in ancestral times carved the path of the Gurka'wuy River, the mouth of which can be seen in the distance *(c)*.

central figure in the painting). The second version belongs to the Marrakulu clan of the Yolngu linguistic group (Plate 9). It is associated with the same set of Ancestral Beings as the first painting and is acknowledged to represent an earlier stage in their journey across Arnhem Land. In this case the background pattern signifies that the painting is associated with the Marrakulu clan and with Marrakulu land. It is not linked to a single place but can be related to topographical features at a number of different places in Marrakulu country. I will consider its relationship to only one of those places here.

The painting shows two water goannas (*wan'kawu*) moving around a hollow log coffin.[13] The goannas are shown holding shellfish (*djaruwit*) in their mouths. The background design represents water flowing through rocks, the dots signifying air bubbles coming from the goanna. The goannas travelled from inland to Trial Bay. Plate 10 is a photograph taken from the beach at Gurka'wuy settlement on Trial Bay. The route the goannas took from the inland is today manifest in a small creek to the right of the mangrove tree in the middle distance (A). The goannas entered the sea and circled the mangrove tree. They ended their journey transformed into rock formations on the beach. One of the goannas is manifest in the line of rocks in the foreground (B). White discolourations on the rocks represent the air bubbles coming from the goanna. The mangrove tree itself (A) is a manifestation of the hollow log coffin which in Ancestral Times carved the path of the Gurka'wuy River, the mouth of which can be seen in the distance (C).

CONCLUSION

Rights in land and rights in paintings (and other manifestations of the Ancestral World) are inextricably interwoven. According to Yolngu ideology it was the Ancestral Beings who handed over the land to particular human groups on condition that those groups continued to perform the ceremonies and produce the paintings and ceremonial objects that commemorate their creative acts. By guarding their rights in paintings people are asserting their rights in land as well as fulfilling their obligation to the Ancestral Beings on whom those rights ultimately depend. The artistic system enables the relationship between people and land to be precisely encoded in paintings and the production of paintings in ceremonies is a defacto assertion of sets of rights held in land, even if the specific purpose varies according to context.

In releasing paintings to Europeans and in displaying paintings in public contexts Yolngu were giving Europeans access to objects and information that from a Yolngu viewpoint demonstrated conclusively their ownership of the land and the way in which ownership was distributed among different clans in accordance with Ancestral Law. Although this did not in itself ensure their recognition as title deeds under European law, it does explain in part why they were appropriate symbols to use in their transactions with Europeans. The significance of their paintings to them is reflected in their commitment to the objective of land rights. To Yolngu continued ownership of their land is not only necessary for cultural survival, it is the fulfilment of a religious obligation.

NOTES

1. This phrase was used by a Yolngu elder to W.E.H. Stanner during proofing stages of the Gove Land Rights case. Stanner and the Aborigines' lawyer Purcell were taken to a secret place where they were shown a sacred object. 'One of the men said to me: 'now you understand'. He meant that I had seen the holy *rangga* which, in a sense are the clan's title deeds to its land, and had heard what they stood for: so I could not but 'understand' ' (Stanner, 1979:278).

2. A speech given by Narritjin Maymuru at the opening of an exhibition of his and his son Banapana's paintings in December 1978. Narritjin and Banapana had nearly completed a three-month period at the Australian National University as Visiting Artistic Fellows to the Faculty of Arts (see Morphy, 1979).

3. This point is well made by Maddock (1972:19): 'Aboriginal culture appears in the struggles discussed now as a condition and now as a symbol: a condition of the life actually led by Aborigines, in terms of which their longing to change their relations with Europeans is naturally formulated; a symbol of their distinctiveness from Europeans, some of the features of which they are engaged in modifying. That their culture is a condition or a symbol or both of struggle does not entail total rejection of European culture, even in the forms in which it is most familiar.'

4. On this last occasion a quite spectacular ceremony was held in honour of police officers who had organised a search for two young children who had been abandoned in the bush. The ceremony consisted of a re-enactment of the event modelled on an initiation ceremony. The boys were concealed in a ceremonial bough shade and were found within it by the policemen who then carried them out on their shoulders. The policemen were then given a number of expensive bark paintings and carvings purchased from the settlement craft store. Songs associated with the Wawilak sisters mythology accompanied the ritual performance (cf. Warner, 1958:250ff.). Many members of the community did not participate in the event as they suspected the motives of the organisers, and as many felt that the police had hindered the search for the lost boys by their methods. Indeed, neither of the boys was in fact found by the police but by groups of Aborigines operating independently of the main search.

5. I have argued elsewhere (Morphy, 1978a) that the idea that Aborigines did not own the land was both legal fiction and ideological mystification and that it did not reflect the state of knowledge of Aboriginal systems of land tenure. Indeed, many early accounts accepted as self evident that Aborigines owned Australia prior to European contact (see, e.g., Lang, 1847:463).

6. Helen Groger Wurm's *Australian Aboriginal Bark Paintings and their Mythological Interpretations*, published by the Australian Institute of Aboriginal Studies in 1973.

7. Of course such ceremonies vary enormously in their form and their significance to the participants. Many are conventional affairs organised by a few councillors, the church and/or the school—they are in many respects typical office farewell parties held in more exotic surroundings with gifts of bark paintings instead of coffee-table books. On other occasions when the recipients are close to the community in their social relations and in their perceived aims, then the affair takes on more of the form of a Yolngu ceremony and less that of a European one. Wells (1981:3a) provides a description of a ceremony held for him in secret on the men's ceremonial ground. In the latter case shared meanings and an understanding of the significance of the content of the ceremony is clearly relevant to the purpose of the ceremony. However, in such cases it must be assumed that the European recipient is already largely committed to the value of Yolngu culture. The ceremony reinforces the bond, it does not create it.

8. For an excellent discussion of the distribution of religious knowledge in Yolngu society, see Keen, 1978:384ff. For a detailed discussion of the way in which 'sacred' paintings are integrated within this system of restricted knowledge see Morphy, 1977 (for a briefer discussion see Morphy & Layton, 1981).

9. For a detailed discussion of the Yolngu artistic system see Morphy, 1977. A more general account is given in Morphy, 1979.

10. For a discussion of the componential structure of Yolngu art see Morphy, 1977. Groger-Wurm (1973), reproduces well documented paintings from many different Yolngu clans, showing something of the variety of different clan designs that occur.

11. Not only painted designs can be structured to represent the relationships between topographical features. Such relationships can be encoded in the organisation of dancers in ceremonial contexts and in the relationships between ceremonial constructions. Berndt (1974, fascicle 2, plates 42–46) demonstrates clearly the way in which a set of ceremonial structures, consisting of sand sculpture, posts and featherstring represents details of the topography of the Riratjingu clan country of Yalangbara (Port Bradshaw). Peterson (1972:18ff. and figures 1–3) shows how different designs and designs in different media encode features of the same landscape in different ways. In Morphy (n.d.) I have shown how the structure of an entire burial ceremony can be organised partly on the basis of spatial relationships between places and hence how from one perspective ceremonies can be seen as representations of the landscape.

12. In some areas this refers to the snake who swallowed the Wawilak sisters (see Warner, 1958:250ff.). It also refers to various manifestations of Yulengurr which include a sacred drone pipe used in the Djungguwan. Details of the mythology associated with painting (Plate 8) are provided in Borsboom, 1978.

13. One of the manifestations of Yulengurr and a public interpretation of the design.

REFERENCES

Berndt, R.M. (1962) *An Adjustment Movement in Arnhem Land.* Paris, Mouton.

Berndt, R.M. (1974) *Australian Aboriginal Religion.* 4 fascicles. Leiden, Brill.

Borsboom, A. (1978) *Maradjiri: A modern ritual complex in Arnhem Land, North Australia.* Nijmegen, Katholieke Universiteit.

Chaseling, W.S. (1956) Yulengor: nomads of Arnhem Land. London, Epworth.

Durkheim, E. (1961) *The Elementary Forms of Religious Life.* New York, Collier Books.

Groger-Wurm, H. (1973) *Australian Aboriginal Bark Paintings and their Mythological Interpretations. Vol. 1. Eastern Arnhem Land.* Canberra, Australian Institute of Aboriginal Studies.

Keen, I. (1978) *One ceremony, one song: An economy of religious knowledge among the Yolngu of North-east Arnhem Land.* Unpublished Ph.D thesis, Australian National University, Canberra.

Lang, J.D. (1847) *Cooksland in North Eastern Australia.* London, Longman, Brown, Green & Longmans.

Maddock, K. (1972) *The Australian Aborigines, a portrait of their society.* London, Allen Lane.

Morphy, H. (1977) *Too many meanings.* Unpublished Ph.D. thesis, Australian National University, Canberra.

Morphy, H. (1978a) Title to their Land. *Quadrant, XXII* (9): 36–43.

Morphy, H. (1978b) Rights in paintings and rights in women: a consideration of some of the basic problems posed by the assymetry of the 'Murngin system'. In J. Specht & P.J. White (eds), Trade and Exchange in Oceania and Australia. *Mankind, II* (3): 208–19.

Morphy, H. (1979) Geology in ochre. *Hemisphere, 23:* 120–27.

Morphy, H. (1980) The effect of commercialisation of art on traditional cultures. In: R. Edwards— (ed.) *The Role of Museums in the Preservation of Indigenous Cultures.* Canberra; Australian Government Publishing Service for UNESCO.

Morphy, H. *Journey to the Crocodile's Nest.* Canberra, Australian Institute of Aboriginal Studies (forthcoming).

Morphy, H. & Layton, R. (1981). Choosing among alternatives: cultural transformation and social change in Aboriginal Australia and French Jura. *Mankind,* 13 (1): 56–73.

Narritjin in Canberra, film directed by Ian Dunlop. Film Australia.

Peterson, N. (n.d.) Culture and articulation: the genesis of landrights in the Northern Territory. Paper presented to the Second International Conference on Hunting and Gathering Societies, Quebec City, 1980.

Peterson, N. (1972) Totemism yesterday. Sentiment and local organisation among the Australian Aborigines. *Man* (n.s.), 7 (1): 12–32.

Peterson, N., Keen I. & Sansom, B. (1977). *Succession to land: primary and secondary rights to Aboriginal estates.* Submission to the Ranger Uranium Environmental Inquiry.

Simmel, G. (1905–1906) The sociology of secrecy and secret societies. *American Journal of Sociology,* vol II.

Stanner, W.E.H. (1979) The Yirrkala Case: dress-rehearsal. In: *White Man Got No Dreaming, essays by W.E.H. Stanner.* Canberra, Australian National University Press.

Warner, W.L. (1958) *A Black Civilisation.* Chicago, Harper & Row.

Wells, A.E. (1971) *This is their dreaming.* St Lucia, University of Queensland Press.

Wells, E. (1981) Some events at Yirrkala during 1962 and 1963. *AIAS Newsletter,* New Series No. 15, pp. 31–40.

6 RIGHTS, RESIDENCE AND PROCESS IN AUSTRALIAN TERRITORIAL ORGANISATION

Nicolas Peterson

The pervasiveness of flexibility in the composition of hunter-gather residential groups throughout the world turned out to be a major theme of the 1966 *Man the Hunter* conference. It received enthusiastic emphasis, not only because it contrasted so markedly with the expectations raised by Steward's ideas on the patrilineal band but also because it articulated the same elements of demography, ecology and social behaviour into a more realistic adaptive model. Flexibility counters demographic inequalities between groups, allows numbers to adjust to resources and reduces the likelihood of conflict turning into combat. Unfortunately the emphasis was then and has since been largely on short term individual adaptive strategies to the neglect of longer term adaptive processes.[1] In consequence, flexibility has come to be identified almost exclusively with movement and the longer term diachronic implications to be ignored, culminating in such extreme views as that reached by Yellen (1977:37) who believes Kung movement is best conceived as random. A more interesting development is the renewed concern (see Lee, 1976:90-91) with the widespread pattern of seasonal aggregation and dispersion first emphasised by Mauss (1904-5 see 1979).

In retrospect, the emphasis on flux appears as much as a reflection of anthropological methodology as of the realities of hunter-gatherer daily life. Until the revival of interest in working with hunter-gatherers during the 1950s thinking about their society was drawn mainly from work that focused on normative behaviours and belief systems. In a context of memory culture and formal interview, behaviour had merged with ideology to give rise to apparent organisational uniformity in conditions of ecological diversity (Steward, 1936). With ideology so strongly in the ascendant, field studies could only raise the star of ecological influences and in the process flexibility, manifested as movement, came to be seen as a crucial mediator between environment and society rather than a characteristic of the mediating processes. The subsequent focus on flexibility has tended to over emphasis non-verbal behaviour to the neglect of ideology and the interplay between the two.

The neglect of the interplay between practice and ideology was originally inhibited by the wide acceptance of Steward's model of the patrilineal band in which they were equated. How rights and residence came to be so firmly confused is partly a matter of speculation but it seems that, among other things, answers to questions about where people lived or should live after marriage were assumed to reflect rules for residence rather than statements about strategies for exercising and maintaining rights. Yet even as Radcliffe-Brown and Steward were refining the patrilineal model, Australian field-workers were reporting that they could find no such groups where they were (see Sharp, 1937; Stanner, 1933:403-405; Hart & Pilling, 1960—reporting 1928-29 fieldwork) but passed over the matter briefly. When in 1962 Hiatt finally established the need to separate land-use from land-ownership, residence and rights became so firmly parted that they have been treated as almost completely independent ever since.

Thus while the emphasis on flexibility is important since it has allowed attention to be focused on the divergence between behaviour and ideology in hunter-gatherer residential patterns, it is now time to recognise that flexibility is really only an entailment of the assumption that, generally speaking, hunter-gatherers are reasonably well attuned to the conditions in which they live. It is, therefore, more appropriate to assume such flexibility in an ecologically based approach since flux in the natural environment and processes is all pervasive, and focus on the impact of such flux on social process. Here I want to consider demographic fluctuation and its relationship to residence and rights, for it raises an interesting paradox most evident in Australia but found wherever there are lineal interests in hunter-gatherer society.

The paradox arises because the land-owning descent groups are of such a size that their existence is constantly under threat from the demographic process. How is it and why is it, then, that the Australians maintain patrilineal descent groups in the face of this recurrent threat of extinction? I shall begin by briefly looking at the demographic aspect and then turn to the questions of how and why.

A RECURRENT PROBLEM

Two lines of evidence point to extinction of land-owning clans[2] being a recurrent problem: there is the theoretical evidence from demography and the ethnographic evidence from 1899 onwards.

Table 1 sets out the little information there is on the *average* size of clans in various parts of Australia. Apart from the Yir-Yoront, among whom Sharp (1934:405) says there had been substantial population decline, the majority of clans have an average size of between 25 and 50 with a range of 15.6-66 where numbers are specified.

Theoretical evidence that groups in this size range are vulnerable to quite small variations in the sex ratio at birth or in the incidence of fertility and mortality, whether occasioned by natural or cultural factors, hardly requires elaborating, but McArthur (1976:55) in a computer simulation of the dynamics of growth and decline in small populations has shown that:

> When 20 populations generated from 3 married couples in which the wives were aged 21,22 and 23 years with monogamy the only restriction on marriage were printed out

Table 1. Average clan size in various regions of Australia

Area	*Year*	*Population*	*No. of clans*	*Average no. in clans*	*Comments*
Cape York: Wik-Munkan	1927–28	1500–2000	*c.*30	50–66(est.)	McConnell (1930:181)
Cape York: Yir-Yoront	1933–35	200+	28	30+ to 1	Sharp (1934a:405; 1934b:20)
Groote Eylandt	1941	300–500	11	27–32	Rose (1960:12,16)
Groote Eylandt	1953	450	12	37	Worsley (1954:66–67, table 15)
NE Arnhem Land: Murngin	1926–29	—	*c.*40	40–50	Warner (1958:39–51,16)
Blyth River: Gidjingali	1958–60	297	19	15.6	Hiatt (1965:19)
Bathurst I.: Tiklauila	1928–29	214	6	35.7	Hart (1930:175; 1954:244)
Port Keats: Murinbata	1950	339	15	26.6	Falkenberg (1962:32)
SE Arnhem Land: Nunggupuyu	–	300+	10	30+	Biernoff (1979:153)
Central desert: Warlpiri	1953	1000–1200	*c.*40	25–35	Meggitt (1962:32,205, 206). Est. of trad. population.

at 5 year intervals in the course of their evolution to a maximum of 300 years, 9 became extinct, 3 were doubtful and 8 were presumed to be successful.

Wobst (1974:174), using different assumptions, calculated that the half-life of a group of 25 people was 180 years and that in a regional population of 19 bands each with 25 members, 5 nuclear families would be discontinued in an average year. Although both these simulations and their assumptions are several steps from actuality, they confirm the vulnerability of small groups. Of course it is important to emphasise that just as some groups decline and die out, others must expand and then split if the whole population is not to disappear.

The ethnographic evidence for extinction of clans is substantial but raises the question of the extent to which it reflects alien impact on Aboriginal society rather than demographic process under pre-colonial conditions. Apart from statements by ethnographers there are three regional censuses of clan membership that indicate the high threat of extinction. All three censuses set out in Tables 2 and 3 come from the tropical woodlands and show the same general range in size but marked differences in the frequency of small clans. This may reflect recent history since the Blyth River and Port Keats areas have had slightly greater protection from destructive contact with aliens than the Cape York populations. Even so, in these two areas the median size of clans is small. Today, however, there are clans with as many as 200 members at places like Milingimbi, although the existence of groups of this size appears to be a function of village life, if the arguments below are valid.[3]

The earliest discussion of the problems posed by small clan sizes provided by Hart on the Tiwi. He noted that while each of the nine Tiwi districts always had enough men to protect its integrity, the clans (*yirt'amini*) that own the several estates[2] that go to make up the district, do not. Indeed he asserts (Hart, 1930:174,175) that clans do not last more than three generations before they lapse for want of sufficient able-bodied men to enforce their title, neglecting that some must have expanded to keep up district numbers. His account also gives the impression that it is residence rather than descent that is the basis of land-ownership but Goodale (1971:97) corrects this. However, she supports (Goodale, 1971:103) his main point that the life history of an estate as a distinct social and geographical entity is only as stable as its owning group.

If this ethnographic evidence is less than satisfactory it is greatly strengthened when seen in the light of the cultural evidence.

Table 2. Size distribution of clans in three areas of Australia

		Numbers in clan													
Area	*Date*	*0-5*	*6-10*	*11-15*	*16-20*	*21-25*	*26-30*	*31-35*	*36-40*	*41-45*	*46-50*	*51-55*	*56-60*	*61-65*	*Totals*
Cape York	1933–35	24	5	8	4	2	—	1	1	—	1	—	—	—	46
Port Keats	1950	—	1	3	3	1	2	1	1	1	—	1	—	1	15
Blyth River	1958–60	3	7	3	1	2	1	1	—	—	—	—	—	1	19

Table 3. Analysis of data in Table 2

Area	*Mean size*	*Median size*	*Range*	*Source*
Cape York	9.8	0–5	1–48	Sharp (1937)
Port Keats	26.6	11–20	6–64	Falkenberg (1962:32)
Blyth River	15.6	6–10	2–61	Hiatt (1965:19)

SUCCESSION TO ESTATES

Fortes (1953:24), in his discussion of the structure of unilineal descent groups, states that they, 'are not of significance among peoples who live in small groups, depend on a rudimentary technology and have little durable property', curiously ignoring that throughout Australia the primary interests in land are almost always inherited patrilineally.[4] Both Berndt (1955) and Meggitt (1962) have taken Fortes up on this point but they neglect to draw attention to the fact that the clan is not a tightly bounded descent group. Membership may be supplemented other than by birth, through the conversion of a number of non-patrilineal interests held by outsiders in a clan's land and through the incorporation of dying clans by those expanding (e.g., see Morphy, 1978:53).

Non-patrilineal interests in land may be divided into three kinds: those mediated by kinship, those by residence, and those by both. Two non-patrilineal interests in land are mediated by kinship: one arises from being the child of a female land-owner and is usually referred to as the managerial interest and the other from a regionally variable range of kinsmen but most generally the MMB. Although Radcliffe-Brown referred to the managerial interest in 1913 (147) and Elkin in 1931 (58) it remained neglected until it was extensively documented among the northern Aranda by Pink in 1936. Recently it has received more attention and has been found to be widely prevalent in northern Australia (see Meggitt (1962) on the Warlpiri; Hiatt (1965) on the Gidjingali Maddock 1972:36, 38) for central Arnhem Land; Radcliffe-Brown, (1913:147) on the Kariera; Myers 1976 on the Pintupi; Avery & McLaughlin (1977) on the Borroloola area).[5] In general, the managerial interest gives a nephew the right and obligation to look after the ritual property of the MB, the sacred places within the estate and to stage-manage the ritual performances held by that clan. Nieces have similar rights in their mothers' ritual property where women's ritual life is well developed. It is unlikely that these interests could lead to succession to the estate of a dying clan if patrilineal moieties are present, since that would mean a change of moiety, but it is a most important and influential interest wherever it exists. Little is known about the significance of interests in the estate of actual kinsmen based on genealogy alone, except in northeastern Arnhem Land. There a man has a right to use the sacred designs related to the MMB estate (see Morphy, 1978a; Berndt, 1955:90), a relative structurally equivalent to elder brother, indicating a strong interest. Only further research will indicate the significance of actual genealogical ties elsewhere.

The interests mediated by residence are better known. They are those arising from conception, birth or burial in an area. At least since the work of Spencer & Gillen (1899:300–303) it has been known that conception in an area frequently conveys important interests. The strength of these interests varies from a high among the desert peoples to a much lower level among most of those living in the tropical woodlands but they are widely reported (e.g., see Tonkinson (1974:75–77) on the Mandjildjara; Myers (1976) on the Pintupi; Elkin (1933:268) on the Forrest River area; Falkenberg (1962:250) on the Murinbata; Sharp (1934a:24) on the Yir-Yoront). Interests mediated by place of birth[6] are found mainly among desert people such as the Pitjantjatjara (Berndt & Berndt, 1943:362–75; Layton & Rowell, 1979:2–3) and Pintupi (see Myers, 1976) and possibly among the peoples of the Forrest River area (see Elkin, 1933:268). Interests mediated by place of burial of an important relative are best documented among the Tiwi (see Hart, 1930:173; Goodale, 1971:99–100) although it is evident that the place of burial is significant in many other areas. This is reflected in communal burial grounds (e.g., in south-east Arnhem Land see Peterson (1976); coastal Queensland see Haglund (1976); South Australia see Pretty (1977)) although little is known about the kind of interests involved. It is also a widespread practice to refer to the deceased by the place at which they are buried with the consequence of at least a strong sentimental attachment to areas often lying outside the patrilineal estate.

The interests mediated by both residence and kinship are associated with ceremonial links between people or localities. Frequently a person may be conceived or born on the track of an ancestral hero who travelled across many estates, or they may be the clan owner of a section of an ancestral track where it crosses their estate. Clans or individuals linked in this way have strong shared ceremonial interests in places along the track (e.g., see Strehlow (1947) on the Aranda; Falkenberg (1962:111–18) on the Murinbata; Thomson (1949:10) and Elkin (1972:92–95) on central Arnhem Land).

Although Radcliffe-Brown stated (1930:35) that, 'There is normally, in the tribes about which we have adequate information, no provision by which a man could leave his own . . . clan and be 'adopted' or 'naturalised' in another' there is considerable evidence that these non-patrilineal interests can be and frequently are converted either directly or over time into patrilineally transmitted interests (e.g., see Hiatt, 1965). From his use of the word 'normally' it would seem that he was aware of such a process, most probably from Spencer & Gillen's account (1899:300–303) of the revival of an Aranda clan through conception. At the time he was writing, however, there was no published evidence indicating that the Aborigines were actually anticipating the problems created by clan depletion. This first became clear from Sharp's work (1934a:24) in Cape York:

> When a woman discovers her pregnancy, the circumstances of the 'finding' of the natural agent, which may have been several months previous, are remembered by the mother or by a father. Since the responsible ancestor sends 'spirit children' only of his own clan to the countries of his own clan in his own tribe, the resultant offspring is affiliated with the clan in whose country the natural agent was 'found'. With the aid of various obvious fictions, the 'spirit child' is usually found in the clan country of the child's real father. But a child is sometimes found in the clan country of a classificatory father, i.e., in the country of a clan which is associated with the real father's clan in a patrilineal descent line of the kinship system. In this event the child is excluded from its real father's clan, but is brought up by its own family, with the result that a family may include several children of the father's clan and several children of different but associated clans. The position of a given man's children is thus fixed as regards the kinship system, but variable as regards the clans. A person belongs to his 'father's clan, but it may be the clan of a real father or the different clan of a classificatory father. The real reasons for this variation from strict patrilineal descent of clans are not obvious, though in some instances it is explicitly stated that the change was made to fill up the depleted membership of an associated clan. In any event, it is clear that the fixed patrilineal kinship group serves as the limiting factor in clan descent, whatever may be the reasons which determine affiliation with a specific clan within this group.

A specific case of anticipation was provided in the Yirrkala land rights case. Well before the case began in 1968 the Lamamirri clan had been reduced to two old women and the country looked after by members of the Gumaitj clan of the same moiety. In discussing the general problem of the extinction of clans before Mr Justice Blackburn, one Yirrkala man commented (Supreme Court of the Northern Territory, 1968:25–60):

> if all the Gumaitj die and nothing left or one left that person him might say: 'Who can I bring with clan to stand for this clan or stand for the land and totem and Malanga (group) and Bunggul (songs). If I leave area without anyone to stand someone will just come and take it. I have to show someone—Gumaitj will show him someone from Wangurri tribe. If no-one appointed someone will certainly come and take it (the land) whether they are European or whether they are Aborigines.

It is significant that Gumaitj and Wangurri are ceremonial allies. A second Yirrkala man remarked (1968:297):

> Before, or after he died the Lamamirri, boss of that country Bululunga; when he died, first he said to Munggurrawuy, this I will—now die: I'll leave this place without any people because we have all died. This country, hold it, look after it after me, when I die. The ceremonies, the songs and the people.

The size of a country or estate may vary considerably from large tracts of hundreds of square kilometres to simply an area of a few hectares. Spencer & Gillen (1899:9) make a most interesting observation in this regard pointing out that in some cases among the Aranda, at least, the size of the clan and of its estate are related:

> at the present time the Witchetty Grub clan is represented by exactly forty individuals (men, women and children), and the area of which they are recognised as proprietors extends over about one hundred square miles. In contrast to this, one particular group of 'plum tree' people is only, at present day, represented by one solitary individual, and he is the proprietor of only a few square miles.

While this correlation certainly does not always hold it is interesting in its implication that an estate can be dismembered and incorporated into a number of other estates on the basis of different ties of outsiders to different parts of the estate. It points to an alternative to supplementing the membership of a dying clan thus enabling it to hold on to its estate intact. Which of these possibilities is realised depends greatly on personality and political process. Because the clans are so small the number of senior men in an average clan will only be four or five. Although they have a collective clan interest in their own estate each man is the focus of a unique set of other interests in land (see Barker, 1976:229-31) and each clan is under the leadership of the senior male. Control over the estate and the assimilation of areas outside to it is thus based on individuals and the political process in which senior men make competing claims to be the holder of ritual property in situations where the holders are losing their control. An influential man may be able to hold together a large estate even if the membership of the clan is severely reduced but the likelihood of him being able to pass it on to the succeeding generation is small.

Much remains to be learnt about the range of interests in land and the processes of transmission, but even from this cursory survey it is evident that succession to the estates of dying clans is a problem that concerns the Aborigines.

WHY DO THE AUSTRALIANS MAINTAIN A PATRILINEAL CLAN IDEOLOGY?

If the clans are constantly dying out and people regularly recruited by means other than birth, why do the Australians maintain a patrilineal clan ideology rather than have larger and more stable groupings or a bilateral approach to inheritance?

One view has been developed by Kroeber (1938:305, 309) dealing expressly with the Australian situation:

> Instead of considering the clan, moiety, totem or formal unilateral group as primary in social structure and function, the present view conceives them as secondary and often unstable embroideries on the primary patterns of group residence and subsistence association . . . much of the formalised social organisation of primitive peoples is in the nature of unconscious experiment and play of fashion rather than the core or substance of their culture. In certain cases, as in Australia, it may well represent the pinnacle of their achievement.

There are several difficulties with this view as far as clanship is concerned. Although it receives apparent support from the general agreement among

Australianists with Hiatt's view that the patrilineal band never existed in Australia (Hiatt, 1962) and the opinion of Helm (1968:124-25) that there is little difference in the band composition of the Dogrib, !Kung, Nambikwara and Arnhem Landers, it ignores the not uncommon prevalence of patrilineal ideology among hunter-gatherers. It also requires acceptance of a remarkably uniform play of fashion across a continent of nearly eight million square kilometres. Further, at the time of writing Kroeber did not know of Hiatt's and Helm's evidence and assumed patrilocal residence, at least, to be the norm in Australia. Thus although he appears to be suggesting that all aspects of formal social organisation are equally arbitrary embroideries on residence and subsistence association, he is in fact suggesting that clanship at least, had its basis in residence: it is only today that the implication can be drawn that the relationship with residence may be arbitrary.

Such a disjunction between residence and rights would pose as many problems as it solves, for the assumption that they are related is of long standing (e.g., see Lowie, 1920:70-74, 157-62), received empirical support from Murdock's correlations (1949:Chapter 8), makes good sense and, I believe, the Australian evidence supports it.

The support is to be found in the fact that, generally speaking, the average numbers in clans and the average numbers in bands are similar, although undoubtably the composition is quite different. The documentation for the numbers in clans is supplied in Table 1. There is no systematic documentation of the numbers in bands so I will simply rely on the commonly accepted assertion that with a few exceptions (see especially Hiatt (1965) on the Gidjingali) most Australian bands appear to fall within the magic number range of 25-50 (e.g., see Birdsell & Stanner in Birdsell, 1970). If this is correct then the number of clans and the number of bands will be similar, although the composition will certainly be different, suggesting an interrelationship between residence and rights.

The reason for this similarity would seem to be that the underlying logic of the pattern of Aboriginal population distribution and numbers is, *in the long run,* the range/resource nexus/life-space (see Stanner, 1965; Silberbauer, 1972)—a set of resources, the spatial distribution of which is defined in terms of efficient exploitation and which will support a band year in year out under most conditions. Through the influence of cost/benefit factors the band and life-space will tend to maintain a more or less constant size, except when there are technological innovations or altered resource distributions, but the clans and estates will expand and contract largely in concert with their demographic fortunes (see Fig.1). As a clan grows above average size even more of its male members than usual will be living on other people's estates for personal, marital, economic and political reasons. Some will be living on estates which belong to ceremonial allies, others will be conceiving children and dying on foreign estates setting up new non-patrilineal residential interests or reinforcing old ones from the previous generation. In some of these areas, the owning clan will be dying out. Where the non-patrilineal interests are of a kind that can be converted and passed on unilineally the demise of the owning clan will provide the opportunity for the members of the growing clan to unify all or part of the estate with their original one. While two life-spaces may be united, at least in terms of ownership, for a while this can only be maintained at a cost. If two distinct bands remain the clan leader will have to be active in maintaining unity by moving between the two, organising and participating in the many rituals. Some, particularly those to do with death, are bound to be held without him and over time the long-term residents likely to assert independence because of closer ties to the area in which they are living. If the two bands became joined in one large band uniting the two life-spaces into one for a while, it can be expected that sooner or later the economic logic underlying the life-spaces would result in the reappearance of the two bands. In both cases the life-spaces would reinforce any potential lines of fission in the enlarged clan. These would be realised relatively quickly given the short genealogical memory and different matrilineally traced ties to other clans among siblings of a common father. With the fissioning, life-space and estate would become more or less congruent. Later this congruence might be threatened by

Fig. 1

A highly schematised model of one possible sequence of relationships between estate *(square boxes)* and range *(sinuous outlines)* over a long period.

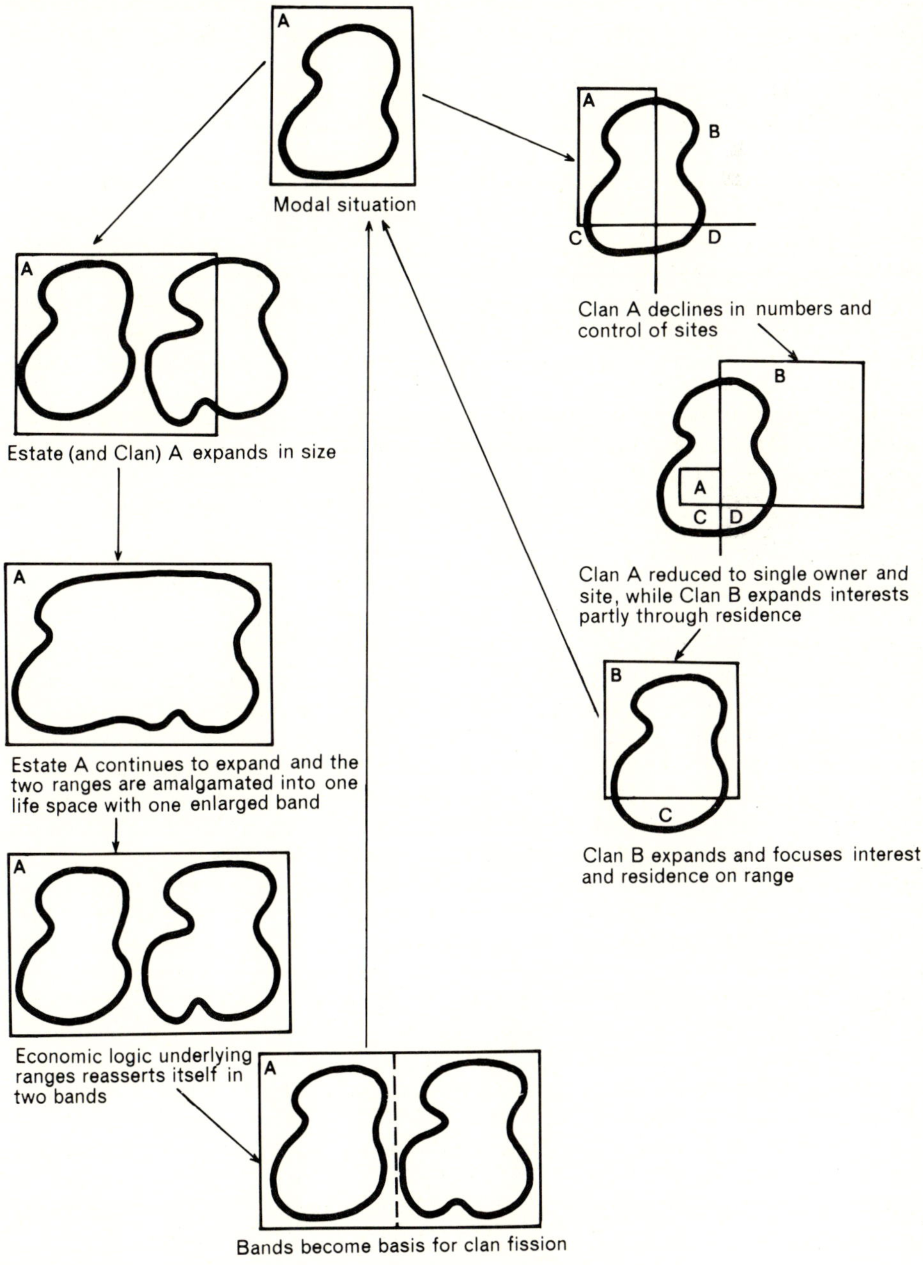

clan extinction and the assimilation of various parts of the estate to neighbouring groups continuing the interplay between demography, residence and rights. It is probable that this process was going on more rapidly in the desert region where clans were smaller than in the tropical woodlands where they were bigger on average (see Berndt 1976).[9]

There has been little discussion of the relationship between the life-space and the estate since Radcliffe-Brown argued that they were identical. Hiatt (1962, 1965) has provided ethnographic evidence showing that they do not coincide in one region and other authors simply assume that they do or do not as suits their views on the patrilineal band itself. The suggestion put forward here has been in terms of the *long-term modal level* about which fluctuations take place in land-ownership and land use. The average size of clans is small because the rights they have in land are only maintainable, in the long-term, through residence by the senior clansmen on their land. Such an argument does not, however, illuminate why clans exist at all or why they are patrilineal.

These two questions would seem to be interrelated about the development of gerontocratic polygyny and its interplay with the objectification of rights in land. The relationship between people and place has been objectified to a remarkable extent in ceremonies, songs, designs and objects of fibre, wood and stone. As heritable property, the legitimate ownership of which is evidence of a persons interests in land, they appear as fundamental in the maintenance of lineality. They are also part of an elaborate hierarchy of knowledge which older men use to control young men's access to wives by making initiation into the clan's cult lodge a precondition for marriage. Given the geographical basis to authority, control over women will be greatest when a man is resident on his own estate. Why there should be such an emphasis on polygyny[10] in Australia in contrast with other hunting and gathering societies remains a question for investigation, but what is evident is that large households arose from a combination in which demographic chance was as essential as political ruthlessness.[11]

CONCLUSION

Because the patrilineal ideology of the Australians has frequently been treated as if it were a set of rules rather than a matter of rights, flexibility in residential group composition seemed important. This confusion of rights with rules arises because the rights have land as their focus so it is easily assumed that they reflect residence rules, particularly when Aborigines may stress that they should live on their own estates. The Aboriginal statements, however, refer to a strategy for exercising rights to the fullest rather than to prescriptive residence rules that never existed. Although the rights do exist independently of residence, they were most effectively held, exercised and transmitted by prolonged residence in the estate in the past. Thus the contradiction between residential flexibility and patrilineal descent is more apparent than real.

ACKNOWLEDGEMENTS

Some of the points discussed here were first presented in a paper written jointly with Ian Keen and Basil Sansom (see Peterson, Keen & Sansom, 1977). I am also indebted to Howard Morphy and Hal Scheffler for their critical comment and interest.

NOTES

1. I take these terms from John Bennett (1969).

2. I use the term clan here because it is more convenient than land-owning group or estate group, neither of which indicate that the ideology of land-ownership throughout Australia is patrilineal, and because in the argument developed here the land-owning group in its *modal form* is accurately described as a clan.

However, for reasons discussed, the actual land-owning group is often reduced to a lineage and may incorporate people other than by birth. Following Stanner (1965) I refer to the area owned by a clan as its estate. Some authors refer to totemic clans and cult lodges, by which they usually mean the adult initiated males of a clan only, although not always.

3. This is according to Ian Keen. There is a problem defining clans, however, because from a Yirrkala perspective the 200-strong Gupapuyngu clan is seen as three separate clans: Birrkili, Daygurrgurr and Guyamirililili.

4. Layton & Rowell (2979:2–3) report ambilineal descent amongst the Pitjantjatjara. Hamilton (1981) argues, however, that once settled an underlying patrilineal emphasis emerges and a patrilineal pattern of inheritance comes to dominate.

5. The list of references provided in this section does not attempt to be comprehensive but simply to indicate the general range of the phenomena from the main sources.

6. It is often unclear whether birth refers to conception in some of the reported cases. Aborigines frequently speak of being born at a place meaning, in our terms, that their spirit entered their mother's womb there. Among the Pitjantjatjara the important place is the locale in which the tied umbilical cord fell off (see Layton & Rowell, 1979).

7. Any clan which is structurally equivalent to the father's clan.

8. This is, generally speaking, any but the managerial interest.

9. Berndt's point is essentially this although he is making it in terms of a rather larger unit in Arnhem Land.

10. In how many hunting and gathering societies are there men who had as many as 23 wives at the one time, as Wongo of Caledon Bay, Arnhem Land, did?

11. I think that Blainey's recent suggestion (1975:105–13) that warfare was probably an important element in the demographic dynamics is correct.

REFERENCES

Avery, J. & McLaughlin, D. (1977) *Submission by Northern Land Council to Aboriginal Land Commissioner on behalf of traditional Aboriginal owners in Borroloola region of the Northern Territory*. Darwin, Northern Land Council.

Barker, G. (1976) The ritual estate and Aboriginal polity. *Mankind, 10:*225–39.

Bennett, J.W. (1969) *Northern Plainsmen: adaptive strategy and agrarian life*. Chicago, Aldine.

Berndt, R.M. (1955) 'Murngin' (Wulamba) social organisation. *American Antrolopologist, 57:*84–106.

Berndt, R.M. & C.H. (1943) A preliminary report of fieldwork in the Ooldea region, western South Australia. *Oceania, 13:*362–75.

Berndt, R.M. (1976) Territoriality and the problem of demarcating sociocultural space. In: N. Peterson (ed.), *Tribes and boundaries in Australia,* Canberra; Australian Institute of Aboriginal Studies, pp. 133–61.

Biernoff, D. (1979) Traditional and contemporary structures and settlement in eastern Arnhem Land with particular reference to the Nunggubuyu. In: M. Heppell (ed.), *A Black Reality,* Canberra; Australian Institute of Aboriginal Studies, pp. 153–79.

Birdsell, J.B. (1970) Local group composition among the Australian Aborigines: a critique of the evidence from fieldwork conducted since 1930. *Current anthropology, 11:*115–42.

Blainey, G. (1975) *Triumph of the Nomads*. Melbourne; Macmillan.

Elkin, A.P. (1931) The social organisation of South Australian tribes. *Oceania, 2:*44–73.

Elkin, A.P. (1933) Totemism in north-western Australia. *Oceania, 3:*257–96.

Elkin, A.P. (1972) Maraian at Mainoru, 1949. In: A.P. Elkin, *Two rituals in south and central Arnhem Land*. University of Sydney (Oceania Monograph 19).

Falkenberg, J. (1962) *Kin and Totem: group relations of Australian Aborigines in the Port Keats district*. Olso University Press (see especially pp. 21–162, 203–41.

Fortes, M. (1953) The strucure of unilineal descent groups. *American anthropologist, 55:*17–41.

Goodale, J.C. (1971) *Tiwi Wives: a study of the women of Melville Island, north Australia*. Seattle, University of Washington Press.

Haglund, L. (1976) *The Broadbeach Aboriginal Burial Ground*. Brisbane, University of Queensland Press.

Hamilton, A. (1981) Descended from father, belonging to country: rights to land in the Australian western desert. In: E.B. Leacock & R.B. Lee (eds.), *Politics and history in bond societies,* Cambridge University Press.

Hart, C.W.M. (1954) The sons of Turimpi. *American anthropologist, 56:*242–61.

Hart, C.W.M. (1930) The Tiwi of Melville and Bathurst Islands. *Oceania, 1:*167–80.

Hart, C.W.M. & Pilling, A.R. (1960) *The Tiwi of North Australia.* New York, Holt, Rinehart & Winston (compare with Goodale, 1971).

Helm, J. (1968) The nature of Dogrib socioterritorial groups. In: R.B. Lee & I. DeVore (eds.), *Man the Hunter,* Chicago, Aildin, pp. 118–25.

Hiatt, L.R. (1962) Local organisation among the Australian Aborigines. *Oceania, 32:*267–86.

Hiatt, L.R. (1965) *Kinship and Conflict. A study of an Aboriginal community in northern Arnhem Land.* Canberra, Australian National University Press.

Kroeber, A. (1938) Basic and secondary patterns of social structure. *Journal of the Royal Anthropological Institute, 68:*299–309.

Layton, R. & Rowell, M. (1979) *Ayers Rock — Mount Olga National Park and Lake Amadeus traditional land claim.* Alice Springs, Central Land Council.

Lee, R.M. (1976)!Kung spatial organisation. In: R.B. Lee & I. DeVore (eds.), *Kalahari hunter-gatherers,* Cambridge, Mass, Harvard University Press, pp. 73–97.

Lowie, R. (1920) *Primitive Society.* New York, Boni and Liveright.

Maddock, K. (1972) *The Australian Aborigines: a portrait of their society.* London, Allen Lane, the Penguin Press.

Mauss, M. (1904–5) *Seasonal Variations of the Eskimo* (translated from the French by J.J. Fox). London, Routledge & Kegan Paul, 1979.

McArthur, N. et al. (1976) Small population isolates: a microsimulation study. *Journal of the Polynesian Society, 85:*307–26.

McConnel, U. (1930) The Wik-Munkan tribe, Pt II. *Oceania, 1:*181–205.

Meggitt, M.J. (1962) *Desert People.* Sydney, Angus & Robertson (in my view, the best account of any Aboriginal group; see especially pp. 1–84. Meggitt introduces a confusion on the nature of the land using group).

Morphy, H. (1978) Too many meanings: an analysis of the artistic system of the Yolngu of north east Arnhem Land. Unpublished Ph.D. thesis, Department of Prehistory and Anthropology, Australian National University, Canberra.

Morphy, H. (1978a) Rights in paintings and rights in women. In: J. Specht & J. White (eds.), *Trade and Exchange in Oceania and Australia* Sydney University Press, pp. 208–19.

Murdock, G.P. (1949) *Social Structure.* New York, Macmillan.

Myers, R. (1976) *To Have And To Hold: a study of persistence and change in Pintupi social life.* Ann Arbor, University Microfilms.

Peterson, N. (1976) Mortuary customs of northeast Arnhem Land: an account compiled from Donald Thomson's field notes. *Memoirs of the National Museum of Victoria, 37:*97–108.

Peterson, N., Keen, I. & Sansom, B. (1977) Succession to land: primary and secondary rights to Aboriginal estates. In *Official Hansard Report of the Joint Select Committee on Aboriginal Land Rights in the Northern Territory.* Canberra, Australian Government Printer, 19 April 1977, pp. 1002–14.

Pink, O. (1936) The landowners in the northern division of the Aranda tribe, Central Australia. *Oceania, 6:* 275–305 (an interesting account of land holding northwest of Alice Springs describes some land as jointly owned, compare with Strehlow, 1965).

Pretty, G. (1977) The cultural chronology of Roonka Flat. In: R.W.S. Wright (ed.), *Stone Tools as Cultural Markers,* Canberra, Australian Institute of Aboriginal Studies, pp. 228–331.

Radcliffe-Brown, A.R. (1913) Three tribes of Western Australia. *Journal of the Royal Anthropological Institute, 43:*143–94. (his account was written shortly after Radcliffe-Brown's first fieldwork in Australia while he was still close to the field experience and depicts a relatively fluid and flexible system).

Radcliffe-Brown, A.R. (1930) The social organisation of Australian tribes. *Oceania, 1:*34–63.

Rose, F.G.G. (1960) *Classification of Kin, Age Structure and Marriage Amongst the Groote Eylandt Aborigines.* Berlin, Akademie-Verlag.

Sharp, L. (1934) Ritual life and economics of the Yir-Yoront of Cape York Peninsula. *Oceania, 5:*19–42.

Sharp, L. (1934a) The social organisation of the Yir-Yoront tribe, Cape York Peninsula. *Oceania, 4:*404–31.

Sharp, L. (1937) The social anthropology of a totemic system of north Queensland. Unpublished Ph.D. thesis, Harvard University.

Silberbauer, G. (1972) The G/wi Bushmen. In: M.G. Bicchieri (ed.), *Hunters and Gatherers Today*. New York, Holt, Rinehart & Winston, pp. 271–326.

Spencer, W.B. & Gillen, F.J. (1899) *The Native Tribes of Central Australia*. London, Macmillan.

Stanner, W.E.H. (1933) The Daly River tribes: a report of fieldwork in north Australia. *Oceania, 3*:377–405.

Stanner, W.E.H. (1965) Aboriginal territorial organisation: estate, range, domain and regime. *Oceania*, 36:1–26.

Steward, J.H. (1936) The economic and social basis of primitive bands. In: *Essays in honor of A.L. Kroeber*. University of California Press, pp. 331–50.

Strehlow, T.G.H. (1947) *Aranda Traditions*. Melbourne University Press.

Supreme Court of the Northern Territory (1968) Transcript of Proceedings of No. 341 of 1968 between Millirripum (sic) plaintiff and Nabalco Pty. Limited etc. Canberra, ANU Law Library.

Thomson, D.F. (1949) *Economic Structure and the Ceremonial Exchange Cycle in Arnhem Land*. London and Melbourne, Macmillan.

Tonkinson, R. (1974) *The Jigalong Mob: Aboriginal victors of the desert crusade*. Menlo Park, Calif., Cummings.

Warner, W.L. (1958) *A Black Civilisation: a social study of an Australian tribe*. Harper Brothers.

Wobst, H.M. (1974) Boundary conditions for Paleolithic social systems: a simulation approach. *American antiquity, 39*:147–78.

Worsley, P.M. (1954) The changing social structure of the Wanindiljaugwa. unpublished Ph.D. thesis, Australian National University.

Yellen, J. (1977) *Archaeological Approaches to the Present: models for reconstructing the past*. New York, Academic Press.

PART TWO

INTERACTIONS AND ADJUSTMENTS: ABORIGINES, LAW AND ANTHROPOLOGY

7

ROOTS AND BRANCHES, OR THE FAR-FLUNG NET OF ABORIGINAL RELATIONSHIPS

Maria Brandl and Michael Walsh

> I [Brandl] asked the woman at the wheel of the car, 'Why has the Prince never married? Do you think he ever will? Who will carry on the *danggalaba* clan name?' I was voicing questions that had long puzzled me, not only in work with the Prince of Wales and other Larrakia and Wagaidj people around Darwin but, even earlier, with the Tiwi of Melville and Bathurst Islands and others in north-east Arnhem Land. My listener was a Chinese Aboriginal born in the Darwin area.
>
> Why didn't the last members worry about their family dying out? Why weren't the men anxious to marry and become fathers so the name and other spiritual and temporal inheritance would go on in the male line?

In this paper we address two separate but related issues: the non-discreteness and interconnectedness of Aboriginal groups, and the puzzle of why in Aboriginal Australia one finds so many distinct languages among so few people. These questions have been raised by other researchers but here we provide recent data from the Darwin area which, though little studied in the past, have special relevance for the consideration of these topics. The first issue, interconnectedness, has been raised by earlier workers such as Berndt & Berndt (1970:212) and Stanner (1966:37), and has been mentioned in passing by many others. The recent work of von Sturmer (1978) and Sutton (1978) faces this issue in the context of Cape York Peninsula, while land claim research recently undertaken by Keen (1980), Layton, Williams (Layton & Williams, 1980), and others confront the same problem in the highly multilingual Darwin area. The second question—why so many languages among so few people—receives particular prominence in the work of Sutton (1978) among the people of Cape York Peninsula. While this is not the first attempt to show that Aboriginal groups are not discrete, we feel it goes further than any other in illuminating the matter of social continuity and the difficulties of wedding concepts like 'tribe', 'social disintegration' and 'cultural collapse' to Aboriginal reality.

The *danggalaba* clan belongs to the so-called Larrakia language group of the Darwin area in the Northern Territory. Linguistically they belong to the two member Larrakian family, the other member being the Wulna, their easterly neighbour (Wurm, 1972:120).

In December 1978 one of us, Maria Brandl, and Adrienne Haritos of the Northern Land Council were recruited to prepare a land claim for an island near Darwin. Four people were listed as claimants, and they all turned out to be members of the *danggalaba* clan. By the time we had located them we found one had died, one had long been severely ill, one was an ageing bachelor and the fourth a shy young woman. We located four more, but in doing so we found ourselves talking and working with people of at least seven other language affiliations—Wadjiginy, Ami, Manda, Tiwi, Kungaragany, Warai and Limilngan.[1]

It quickly became clear to us that the island being claimed could be limited neither to the label Larrakia nor to the area of land bordered by sea and reefs. To understand its place one had to look at its wider social, geographical, ecological and anthropological contexts.

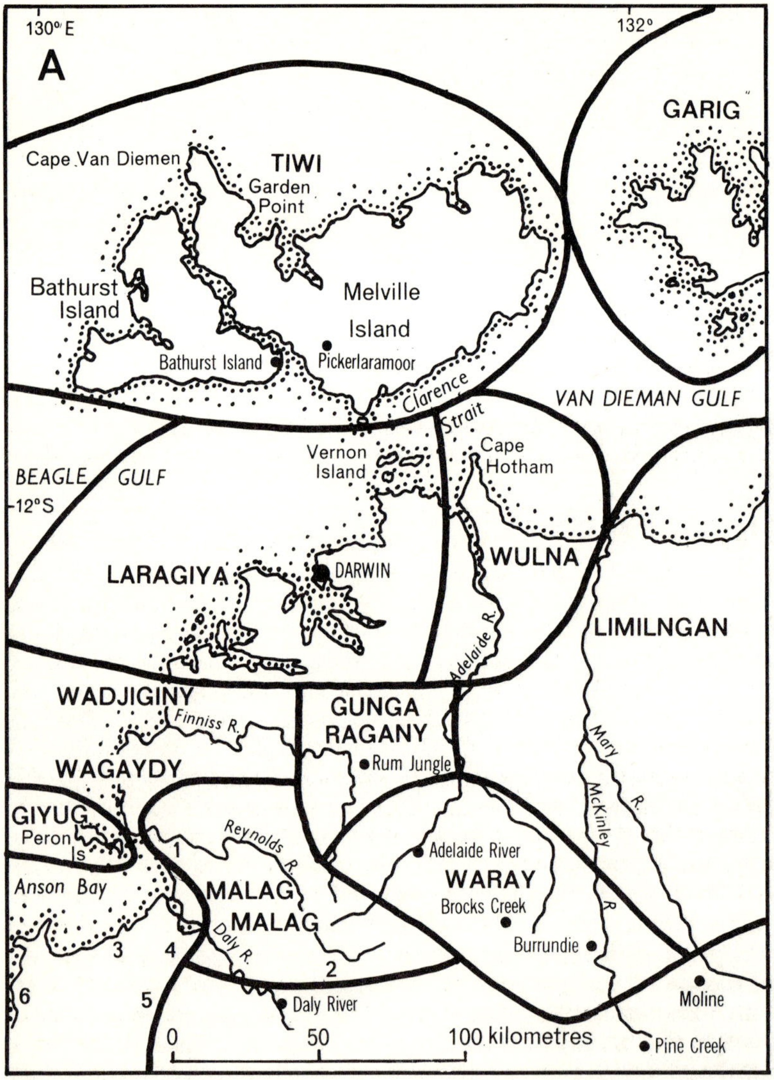

Fig. 1
Some language groups in the Darwin area. 1, Dyeraidy; 2, Malagmalag; 3, Ami; 4, Kuwama; 5, Maranunggu; 6, Manda.

We decided to find out first who were these people on the ground getting in the way of our pursuit of Larrakia people and Larrakia knowledge. What did this irritating and constantly heard term 'mixing' or 'all mixed' mean?[2] Ceremonies were called 'mixed'; languages were 'mixed'; people were 'mixed'.

So we explored how people identify. Any one individual's identity is composed of experiences, both personal and shared, some labelled (such as initiation) and others not. When a person's identity is being asked for the response—the corresponding experience called up—will depend on who is doing the questioning, where and why and when. For individuals in the claim area we might visualise a personal identity as a multifaceted cut stone with each facet representing an experience, personal or shared (for which there may or may not be a cultural label). The responses will result from one or other facet being illuminated by a question.

When a person, say George Munggalu, is asked how he identifies himself, he will look first at the questioner and attribute motives, and then at the circumstances of the question. He then seeks to select those facets of his identity that correspond to these factors. George is a man about 60 years of age. He was born in Darwin; his 'country' is Banagaya south of the Daly River; his principal clan affiliation is *durlg,* or sea-monster or whale or rainbow. His mother's language was Djeraidj, his father's Wadjiginy. He was initiated at Bilurrgwa east of Darwin by men of the *danggalaba* clan of the Larrakia linguistic group, and he is often said to be Larrakia. During the Second World War he served in the Black Watch of the Australian Army, which guarded our northern coast, and has lived now for many years with his friend Roy Edwards, a pastoralist, at Newcastle Waters, many hundreds of kilometres from the Darwin area. He was described to us by many as the person most knowledgeable about the island's area.

Another case is Andrew Henda, a somewhat younger man. In *Bunji* (January 1973) he said, 'My father was Wadjigan Larrakia and my mother she's a Gurindji'. Johnny Fejo, in the same article, said, 'Andrew is part of my father, Nipper Rankin, because his father is my full uncle. My father, Wadjiginy, was married to my mother, full-blood Larrakia. I refer to me as full-blood Larrakia, that's our way . . . If one girl marries to a white bloke and has a baby, it is 'half-caste', but we call it full-blood Larrakia . . . Little boy of mine, Barradimi, he is a Larrakia.' Johnny, now dead, was married to a woman of the Warai linguistic group. Identification is bilateral then and 'full-blood' is taking on a sense equivalent to 'authentic'. Topsy Secretary, a Larrakia woman, says of the part-European daughters of her mother's sister: 'We say Larrakia full-blood'.

Another example of the 'mixing' of social components in a single identity is provided by Maudie Bennett. She is a daughter of a man of the Ragbadjala territory, on North Peron Island, of the Kiuk language group, though she does not speak that language. Her mother spoke Kiuk. She was born at Kahlin Compound in Darwin and she has a conception totem at Talc Head near Darwin. Maudie identifies sometimes as Wagaidj, sometimes as Wadjiginy, or Kiuk, or Ragbadjala. She grew up on the Cox Peninsula and is recorded as being a schoolgirl at Delissaville in 1941 (E. J. Murray, 1942), when she went through her woman's ceremony. She has been married to men of both Tiwi and Larrakia language groups. Her Larrakia-speaking husband, the now dead Tommy Lyons, or Imabulg, a senior man of the *danggalaba* clan, imparted to her safe-keeping knowledge of sites on the Cox Peninsula and the islands. A lot of their married life was spent together on Indian Island and the Cox Peninsula, which she probably knows better than any other living person. George Munggalu has also passed on his knowledge of the area to her, to be handed on as Tommy Lyons wishes to their daughter Olga. Maudie, too, has attended *danggalaba* and other so-called Larrakia-style initiation ceremonies, and shares knowledge of these with others such as George Munggalu and her uncle Norman Harris, or Barral, another man of senior 'Larrakia' status, but not in the *danggalaba* clan.

Cutting across the labels we have used here are her *durlg* and *ngirawad* identities. *Durlg* is her 'dreaming' or local descent group label, and *ngirawad* refers to her namesakes.

Another example is Josephine Rankin, daughter of a now-dead Larrakia-speaking woman of the *inyarany* clan (itchy 'dreaming'). Her mother died soon after she was born and she was raised by a Wadjiginy man with Kiuk affiliations in Darwin and on the Cox Peninsula. Her *genitor* was a Chinese-Aboriginal (who was himself brought up by Aboriginal kinsfolk in the Daly River area). The man married to her mother when Josephine was born was a Larrakia man of the *danggalaba* clan, who also died when Josephine was young. She was often cited to us as an owner of the claim land, although her upbringing, first in Wadjiginy language surroundings and later as a part-Aboriginal segregated from tribal people, makes her reluctant to claim affiliations that others acknowledge to be hers. 'She belongs here, to Kalalak', said Kathleen Secretary. 'But what does she say?', said Bobby Secretary. 'I say better leave it', said Josephine. She has married a man who is a mother's brother to Maudie Bennett and father of Johnny Fejo. She has adopted children from other language groups again and some of her stepchildren had a Larrakia-speaking mother. So, depending on the circumstances of a request to identify herself, she may give any one of a number of responses.

Another woman linked to the *danggalaba* clan through affinal connections is Carol Collins. Her mother's mother, still living, belongs to the *inyarany* clan of the Larrakia language grouping. This woman is deaf and dumb and therefore has not been able to pass on much traditional information to her descendants. We were told that this woman had been promised to Tommy Lyons of the *danggalaba* clan, who later married Maudie Bennett. She, however, married a European and had two daughters, one of whom was Carol's mother. Carol Collins' father was reportedly Tamil, yet Carol has often thought of herself as 'Larrakia', and knows herself to be a relative of the Secretarys. But she has never known the precise genealogical links that Bobby and Topsy Secretary can explain. Her life has been largely in urban Darwin, but she lives now in the township of Batchelor. She, too, depending on where and by whom a question is being asked, will select an appropriate identification.

One final example is Delfin Cubillo, who lives in Darwin with his family. About 60 years of age, he is one of 10 children of a Filipino diver, Juan Cubillo, who came to Darwin around the turn of the century to work on pearling ships. In 1910 Juan Cubillo married Lily McKeddie, daughter of an early Melbourne settler in the Cox Peninsula —George McKeddie—and a Larrakia woman named Annie, who came from the Belyuen area. Lily's brother, Jack, married Victoria Dashwood, sister of George Munggalu, the most knowledgeable man of the area today. Delfin has an active interest in his family history, but never knew his mother's mother. It is, however, part of his family's traditions that his grandmother told his mother of a waterhole, a dreaming place for the rainbow, at Delissaville (now Belyuen). He also knows that Old Man Rock off Casuarina Beach in Darwin is supposed to have travelled before settling there, and that it is a dangerous area.

The Cubillos apparently have connections to the claim area. Delfin's brother, Edward, married Rose, sister of two of the main caretakers in the area, Margaret Rivers and Kitty Moffat, and so his and Rose's children have a strong interest in the area, and this is repeatedly asserted to be so by Margaret and Kitty.

FACTORS AFFECTING IDENTITY

The selection used by these people is neither distorted nor confused. Rather, it is a choice from among authentic identification labels of that most appropriate to a given question. This is a feature of social identification among people anywhere.

So where an Aboriginal person is born and raised and by whom, and what language (or languages) the real or step- or foster-parent speaks, strongly influence how a person identifies. An even more powerful influence is what ceremonies a person has participated in and where and to what extent. Thus Wadjiginy-speakers such as George Munggalu, Roy Madbulg and Johnny Biyanamurrg, and Kiuk men such as Normal Barral and Nipper Rankin, were identified, together with Bobby Secretary, as ceremonial leaders with Larrakia-language titles. In contrast, Prince of Wales, son of the senior *danggalaba* clan ritual leader, King George, and a Wadjiginy-speaking mother, went through a so-called 'Wagaidj' initiation and therefore has no responsibility for ceremonies of his own clan. 'Prince go back to Wadjiginy way, because his mother and his grandfather Wadjiginy . . . that's the way', said one of our informants.

Similar examples of what we have called multifaceted identity could be given by any of the claimants.

NGIRAWAD : A NAMING PROCESS

A custom bearing upon the 'mixing' of people in the claim area has already been briefly referred to. This is the *ngirawad*. Another is *maruy* (or conception totem) which is generally better known in the literature, so we will not go into it here.

Ngirawad can be roughly translated as 'namesake'. A person in the claim area can have a name from another person or from a place, and places can be namesakes for one another, too. This exchange of names, a formal affair, is one of the activities that cuts across people in the social field and links them with people to the east, west and the south. It is reported from the Port Keats area by Stanner (1936:303-308) as extending across a number of linguistic boundaries to the Daly River; by Falkenberg (1962:265) among groups at Port Keats; by Nancy Williams (personal communication to Mabrandl) in the Finniss River area and ourselves in the South and East Alligator rivers region and for the Warai around Humpty Doo; and by Herbert (1873:27), Daly (1887:66), Parkhouse (1859:640), and in some detail by Elkin (1950) in the claim area. Where the *ngirawad* is between people restraints, even taboos, are placed on interaction. Release from them requires a ritual and exchange of gifts. We recorded numerous examples of *ngirawad* among our claimants, some at Belyuen (Delissaville), one with a Wulna-speaking woman at Humpty Doo, one with a Limilngan woman at Humpty Doo, two with women from Daly River, and two with people from Port Keats. The claimant Peggy Wilson was able to describe the ritual of release to us from her own experience. Claimant Lorna Tennant expects to complete her rituals and exchange in the near future.

MANAIDJ: 'GODPARENT'

Another custom which cuts across linguistic and territorial boundaries is *manaidj*, or godparent, where a woman such as Peggy Wilson gives the welfare of her daughter, Christine, to another, in this case to Maudie Bennett. Peggy's *manaidj* is a Kiuk-speaking man, Daly Young, or Mirringga.

Ngirawad, like *manaidj* and *merbok* (Stanner, 1933-34:156), a complex system of 'intertribal' exchange, served to link people with people, and people with land, and land with land, over a wide area. Like kinship links and alliances forged through marriage (Tonkinson, 1978:8), these were devices which expanded the social field of individuals and of groups, particularly with regard to territorial and socioreligious affiliations.

Some of the reasons why the social field required expansion are better understood once the history and history of contact in the area is examined (see Brandl, Haritos & Walsh 1979: chapters 4 and 5). These reasons bear upon the traditional pattern of ownership and use of land in the claim area, and provide a demonstration of the strength of attachment of the traditional owners, the *danggalaba* clan, to their estate.

People with an interest in land in the claim area are identified by others and among themselves through the following principles:

- ceremonial initiation and progression,
- marriage to *danggalaba* local descent group members,

- birth or conception 'dreaming' at a site in the claim area,
- burial site of a relative,
- right of forage,
- *durlg* site in the claim area,
- residence which is additional to the above principles and may be combined with any of them.

The details of how people relate to land are discussed in the claim book. Some names appear on more than one list, but this demonstrates their multiple linkages to land in the area.

At a Belyuen meeting once we were told that singling people out according to their father or mother divides people. Where land is concerned they would prefer as a community to state, with evidence, their relationships to the claim area and their interest in it.

Time and time again people in the claim area have referred to the 'mixing' of Aboriginal people that has taken place there. This refers not only to people but to their actions and beliefs and attitudes — social and cultural features, including rights in land.

'MIXING'

'Mixing' does not mean 'mixed up' or confused. Rather, it describes the intricate interconnections of all the activities of people in the area claimed. It was not the case that specific Aboriginal groups, here or anywhere else in Australia, lived in isolated capsules with languages or ceremonies, for example, that were peculiarly their own. No Aboriginal group, even island communities like the Tiwi and the Groote Eylandt people (see Turner, 1974:197), can be considered a 'unified whole' (Stanner, 1966:36). 'Tribe', however, is a concept implying this and, like others before us elsewhere in recent years, we do not consider it a useful term for people in the claim area.

But we do need to identify the claimants and we have therefore used some of the ways they themselves identify to one another, both as groups and as individuals. Von Sturmer (1973) has pointed out at least five basic dimensions (and we will add more): kinship and marriage, territory, totemism, language and ritual. In brief, no one principle, even language (Sutton, 1978:28) orders the totality of interaction (Stanner, 1966:36).[3] In the claim area is a 'mixing' of principles, plainly manifested in the activities of the claimants. Stanner tells (1966:37) how the Murinbata use sticks and stones to describe the articulation of groups. Their constructions emerge looking a little like a branching tree or a flung fishing net.

In the physical and social environments which provide the opportunity, the mesh becomes tighter. The interconnections increase in range, frequency and degree of strength. Mission, government and pastoral property settlements intensify these even more, as a simple result of even closer proximity. What we are looking at, then, is a social field. Sutton (1978:116) uses this term for coastal groups on Cape York Peninsula. The claim area and its periphery bound the social field we are documenting in this claim book.

The range of activities in which are demonstrated the complex sociocultural links between people in the claim area includes the following:

- marriage and kinship;
- attendance at and participation in ceremonies—death and initiation, for example;
- access to religious knowledge and inheritance of this;

- territorial affiliations;
- hunting and gathering;
- name exchange;
- shared experiences such as resettlement, the war, surviving cyclones, building a settlement, drinking[4], land rights movements;
- multilingualism;
- life crisis situations, birth and death of kin;
- socialisation.

SOCIETY NOT STATIC

Apart from the picture of the social field as it is in the claim area today, it is worth illustrating the concept of 'mixing' by a glance at the past.

A danger ever-present in ethnographic work is to see a society as static, because the researcher views it during a limited period of time. Intentionally of unintentionally 'blueprints' (von Sturmer, 1978:559) may be established. These mirror the 'ideal' models of a society that its members have in their minds at the time of the ethnography. The 'ideals', the 'blueprints' of social action in people's heads, provide the stability and continuity that seem necessary (but not sufficient) conditions for a human group to be called a society (see Williams, n.d.3-23, for a discussion of this with regard to Aboriginal land ownership in north-east Arnhem Land). Blueprints also facilitate the maintenance of a society while change occurs. But they do not account for change.

ALTERNATIVES ARE BUILT IN

Such 'ideal' models for action always have alternatives built in, which one or any or all individuals make use of. All field workers in Aboriginal Australia have felt nonplussed when watching eventually a ceremony they have been hearing about from people for some time. Much does not occur as it 'ought' to do, according to the predictions they have been told. The 'is' rarely, if ever, conforms to the 'ought'. This does not mean that the participants are wrong, or ignorant, or forgetful. It does mean, however, that a blueprint does not always delineate the range of alternatives and choices permitted to the actors. Its purpose is to provide the model for reality, not the blueprint.

These comments on alternatives and choices apply particularly to societies experiencing suddenly—and then persistently—many foreign elements. The Aboriginal people in the Darwin area are such societies. The rubric 'social disintegration' often applied to them is a misnomer because it refers to models from one (or other) point in historical time, often ignoring the contemporary models and certainly the contemporary reality. Further, it denies the members of those groups, as human beings, the ability to adapt and to think their way through the possibilities offered by their culture. It also denies the quite clear assertions by living Aborigines that Larrakia people still live in the Darwin area and are traditional owners of the claim area. With regard to land in the claim area, what we have documented are the living, continuing traditions as they were at the time of our research.

No human tradition is fixed and unchanging. Traditions are social processes which are always undergoing adjustments, manipulations and reappraisal.

CONTINUITY OF TRADITION

When a particular tradition or set of beliefs, attitudes and behaviours is viewed at different points on a time scale, one observes what can be called transformations in that tradition. These transformations in no way impinge on the central themes or imperatives of that tradition. For instance, a Christian church service in Darwin today bears few observable resemblances to one of the first century in, say, Rome, but any Christian would aver that the religious purposes were the same and the sacred themes identical—despite the differences in language and style, despite the differently built environments, despite electric lighting and seating, clothing style of the congregation, time of day of the service, and so on. The Christian tradition is a continuing one.

In an Aboriginal context, Tiwi mortuary and *kulama* rituals today provide a similar example (see Brandl, 1971), where numerous differences are observable in the manner of performing them, their duration, the age of participants, and so on, when compared to Spencer's observations in 1912. Their purpose remains however the same.

The tradition of Aboriginality itself is another example within the wider Australian setting. A sense of identity coupled with distinctive behaviours and attitudes mark out many thousands in this country. This distinctiveness is part of a continuing tradition unbroken by some 200 years of contact with people who identify quite differently.

ADJUSTMENTS TO TRADITIONS

Adjustments within a human tradition are on-going and ever-present, but certainly can be accelerated. A major impetus is a fluctuation in population from whatever cause (for example, massacres as in the case of the Warlpiri; disease and dislocation as in the Larrakia case). But, where people identifying as a distinctive Aboriginal group still live, to that extent so does their distinctive heritage of traditions, albeit transformed from what they must have looked like 100 years ago (see also Turner, 1974:193-35). An Aboriginal tradition may only begin to be considered extinct when the last person identifying with that tradition has died. Neighbours and friends incorporate elements from a nearby group into their own traditions so that it is questionable whether a tradition is indeed ever extinct. People in and adjacent to the claim area provide example of this. Some hundreds of people in Darwin identify as Larrakia and Wagaidj, even though events have worked steadily against the continuity of their traditions.

TRANSMISSION OF TRADITIONS

Traditions are transmitted in a variety of ways. Socialisation—just growing up in a particular human social setting and learning appropriate behaviours—is one way. Socialisation patterns among people in the claim area are distinctively their own and differ in substantial ways from those of other Australians.

Another way of handing on a tradition is via ceremonies and ritual. This means assumes particular emphasis in non-literate societies with a non-complex technology. The symbols and procedures and accompanying language of a ritual act as keys or prompts to knowledge in human minds. Rituals in such societies often perform functions of a library in literate societies. Hunting, foraging and moving through a landscape also provide opportunities to transmit information about a heritage. The natural features and species act as cues to knowledge in the minds of people who know the country, live on it and belong to it.

When literacy is adopted and where technical aids are available, other additional means are used to house and pass on knowledge. People in the claim area, for example, have and frequently use tape recorders and cameras for storing and transmitting their heritage. They have also written down information (see appendices to Brandl et al. (1979) by Olga Singh and the children's stories from 1960).

TRANSFORMATIONS

Given the unceasing pressures on people in the claim area it is not surprising that viewed from 1979 profound and far-reaching transformations have occurred in both the content of their heritage and the ways in which it is transmitted. Walking through the land is not so common today when people have to make the best use of available time away from employment and education commitments at Belyuen. Consequently, fewer opportunities exist to acquire at leisure and in detail information keyed in the landscape.

Leaders of the *gulida, beliya* and *malinya* ceremonies endeavoured to secure their continuity and the heritage of knowledge within them by recruiting successors. Thus Billy Belyuen, father's father to traditional owner Kathy Minyinma, gave to George Munggalu the right and the responsibility to pass on knowledge to young men of the *danggalaba* clan. Given that no males with issue in the direct patrilineal line remain, men like Munggalu face critical decisions where secret-sacred information, a small percentage of the total heritage, is concerned. Men from other clans—the Wadjiginy, Ami and Kiuk language groups in particular—have been given this information to transmit and it has inevitably become interwoven with the rituals of their groups, where it has amplified and transformed the traditions of those people in its turn. There is nothing un-Aboriginal or unprecedented in this. The Warlpiri and Kartangarurru-Kurintji land claim 1978 documented a similar process (Peterson et al., 1978:97), as did the Borroloola claim (Avery & McLaughlin, 1977:4). Migrating Aboriginal groups in Arnhem Land too (Berndt & Berndt, 1970:212; Hiatt, 1965:20), use these and other alternatives to safeguard the sacred heritage keyed in the landscape.[5]

CORE OF TRADITION CONTINUES

The purposes, the themes, the imperatives continue as the core of these traditions: mortuary rituals are still held to ensure the safe passage of the deceased from life to death; they are still believed to protect the bereaved from any malign influences of an unappeased spirit, and they provide opportunities to affirm the status of the survivors. Initiation rituals for both girls and boys are still called to mark the entry of the young into the serious business of adult life and social responsibility and to ensure the welfare of all.

These ceremonies serve to link people into networks which ensure the continuity of the traditions. They mark indelibly moments in the lives of those who participate in and share them.

Where more public knowledge is concerned, it is being handed on in ways such as that employed by the late Tommy Lyons, via his wife to his daughter, traditional owner, Olga. Men like Tommy Barradjab (or Burrinjuck) and Bobby Lane exercise the right to compose songs about places in the claim area. Traditional owner, Bobby Secretary, has permitted others—who live within the claim area—to exercise his and his siblings' spiritual responsibility in these matters. This does not mean in any way that he has ceded that responsibility, nor is he seen to have done so.

The Aborigines of the Darwin area are not unique in using these strategies to link themselves to others and to preserve a heritage. About north-eastern Arnhem Land Williams (1978:6) says:

> I was discussing with Daybalipu Mununggurr, a leader at Yirrkala, principles of Aboriginal land tenure . . . He drew a tree . . . 'The roots of the tree are its foundation. People may be likened to trees. As the trunk of the tree grows and as the branches extend out and leaves grow from them, so groups of people grow. These groups of people, though, remain attached to the original site and founding group; other groups of people also establish relationships with those of the foundation groups . . . They are also attached like the leaves of the tree. Then something may happen to the tree. Part of it may die off, or all of it may die. But the roots, the foundation, always remain, and from them a new tree will grow.'

Our search for the Larrakia took us on a journey through a life-sized kaleidoscope of events depicting social and cultural features of people of diverse linguistic, ceremonial and other labels, before we emerged to view the activities in our social field with some comprehension. Two principles seem plain: the basic issue, physically and spiritually, is survival.

Aborigines, as all human beings, need to be able, for social purposes including survival, to group themselves with one another for some purposes and yet remain separate. The application of so many labels serves both to distinguish, separate and exlude people one from another and to incorporate, include others for particular purposes—such as preserving a human heritage. Social life is often a tension between these two labelling activities.

> The woman at the wheel of the car turned to me, somewhat surprised, and said in reply to my question: 'Aboriginal people don't think like that, my friend, we know there are always others to help—just like we're helping Prince and his people now.'

NOTES

1. The *danggalaba* clan were unanimously asserted to be the owners of the land in the Darwin area.

2. The word 'mixed' is often found in direct reporting of Aboriginal statements of identity (see, for example, Sandy McDonald's statement in Shaw & McDonald, 1978:124).

3. Language, however, has often been invoked as an especially apt criterion for group membership (see Tindale (1974) for instance), but it raises problems when used to label social groups (von Sturmer, 1978:13).

4. Sansom (1977) gives some indications of how the social field is expanded through people drinking together near the claim area.

5. Falkenberg (1962:34) for the Port Keats area gives examples of men from one clan being taken into another through initiation processes.

REFERENCES

Avery, J. & McLaughlin, D, (1977) Submission by the NLC to the Aboriginal Land Commissioner on the Borroloola Region Land Claim. Northern Land Council, Darwin.

Berndt, R. M. & Berndt, C. H., (1970) *Man, Land and Myth.* Sydney, Ure Smith.

Brandl, M. M. (1971) *Pukumani: the social context of bereavement in a north Australian Aboriginal tribe.* PhD thesis, University of Western Australia.

Brandl, M., Haritos, A. & Walsh, M. (1979) *Kenbi land claim to vacant crown land in the Cox Peninsula, Bynoe Harbour and Port Patterson areas of the Northern Territory of Australia.* Darwin, Northern Land Council.

Daly, D. D. (Mrs) (1887) *Digging, Squatting and Pioneering Life in the Northern Territory of South Australia.* London, Low, Marston, Searle & Rivington.

Elkin, A. P. (1950) Ngirawat, or the sharing of names in the Wagaitj tribe, Northern Australia. In: I. Tonnies (ed.), *Beitrage zur Gesellungs-und-Volkerwissenschaft.* Berlin, Gebrüder Mann.

Falkenberg, J. (1962) *Kin and Totem: group relations of Australian Aborigines in the Port Keats district.* Oslo University Press.

Herbert, S. W. (1873) Reminiscences of life in the Northern Territory during the construction of the Overland Telegraph Line. (Ms on microfilm in the AIAS Library, Canberra; original held in South Australian Archives).

Hiatt, L. R. (1965) *Kinship and Conflict*. Canberra, Australian National University Press.

Keen, I. (1980) *The Alligator Rivers Stage II Land Claim*. Darwin, Northern Land Council.

Layton, R. & Williams, N. (1980) *The Finniss River Land Claim*. Darwin, Northern Land Council.

Murray, E. J. (1942) Activities of Native Patrol, Delissaville 1942. (Unaccessioned item, Australian Archives, Darwin).

Parkhouse, T. A. (1895) Native tribes of Port Darwin and its neighbourhood. In: *AAAS Report*, vol.6.

Peterson, N., McConvell, P., Wild, S. & Hagen, R. (1978) *A claim to areas of traditional land by the Walpiri and Kartangarurru-Kurintji*. Alice Springs, Central Land Council.

Sansom, R. (1977) Aborigines and alcohol. *Australian journal of alcohol and drug dependence, 4*(2).

Shaw, B. & McDonald, S. (1978) They did it themselves: reminiscences of seventy years. *Aboriginal history, 2*.

Stanner, W. E. H. (1933–4) Ceremonial economics of the Mulluk-mulluk and Madngella tribes of the Daly River. *Oceania, 4*.

Stanner, W. E. H. (1936) Aboriginal modes of address and reference in the north-west of the Northern Territory. *Oceania, 6*.

Stanner, W. E. H. (1966) *On Aboriginal Religion*. University of Sydney. (*Oceania* Monograph No. 11).

Sutton, P. (1978) Wik: *Aboriginal society, territory and language at Cape Keerweer, Cape York Peninsula, Australia*. PhD thesis, University of Queensland.

Sutton, P. (1980) Language groups and Aboriginal land ownership. Paper prepared for AIAS Biennial Conference in May, 1980.

Tindale, N. B. (1974) *Aboriginal Tribes of Australia: their terrain, environmental controls, distribution, limits and proper names*. ANU Canberra, Australian National University Press.

Tonkinson, R. (1978) The cultural roots of Aboriginal land rights. Seminar paper given in the Research School of Pacific Studies, Australian National University, Canberra 1978.

Turner, D. H. (1974) *Tradition and Transformation: a study of Aborigines in the Groote Eylandt area, north Australia*. Canberra, Australian Institute of Aboriginal Studies.

von Sturmer, J. (1973) Changing Aboriginal identity in Cape York, In: D. Tugby (ed.), *Aboriginal Identity in Contemporary Australian Society*. Milton, Qld, Jacaranda.

von Sturmer, J. (1978) *The* Wik *region: economy, territoriality and totemism in western Cape York Peninsula, North Queensland*. PhD thesis, University of Queensland.

Williams, N. (n.d.) Land tenure: principles of the Yolngu system. (Ms held by the author. Australian Institute of Aboriginal Studies, Canberra.)

Wurm, S. (1972) *Languages of Australia and Tasmania*. The Hague, Mouton.

8 OLD BUSINESS, NEW OWNERS: SUCCESSION AND 'THE LAW' ON THE FRINGE OF THE WESTERN DESERT

John Stanton

This paper is based on material gathered during the fieldwork conducted since 1974 at Mt Margaret, in the North-Eastern Goldfields region of Western Australia. In the process of documenting the sometimes complex processes of serial migration by which the former mission station came to be settled, it has become clear that the more recent inhabitants of the area have assumed the guardianship of sacred sites in the region that they have occupied. These people are currently elaborating on the earlier mythological associations of the area on the basis of their own traditional affiliations. Such a process may have important implications for the future of Aboriginal land rights claims in areas where non-traditional occupiers are able to claim direct or indirect affiliations with the territory that they have come to regard as their own home. The developments discussed in this paper are not unique to the North-Eastern Goldfields; reports from the central Australian reserves and the southern Kimberley indicate that similar processes of adoption and elaboration of mythological sacred sites are taking place elsewhere, and are likely to have accompanied similar demographic movements in the past.

The Aboriginal people at Mt Margaret are asserting their link with the land in a number of different ways: through the realignment of beliefs about conception and birth 'totemism'; through adoptive custodianship of sites and ritual objects derived from the previous inhabitants; through the extension and elaboration of their own primary Dreaming associations on the basis of existing mythological 'Law lines' in the area; and by the recognition and definition of new associations.

The present pattern of life in the North-Eastern Goldfields has been briefly dealt with elsewhere (Stanton, 1979). Mt Margaret is a former mission station situated 1000 km north-east of Perth on the edge of the Great Victoria Desert, 30 km south-west of the town of Laverton. A relatively stable population comprising some 60 adults lives on the settlement. Most of the adults are pensioners, and there is an equal number of schoolchildren. This group identifies itself strongly with Mt Margaret, despite the existence of kin-based and territorial affiliations elsewhere. The settlement is spatially located midway between the Central Aboriginal Reserve (centred on the former Warburton Range Mission, although now including a number of semi-autonomous outstation settlements) and the towns of the Eastern Goldfields. The strategic positioning of the mission station at the time of its establishment has already been noted (R. & C. Berndt, 1970:56–69): this has enabled the settlement to provide a point of convergence for Aboriginal groups moving out of the interior of the Western Desert region over a long period, and has contributed significantly to the successful development of Mt Margaret Mission.

When the mission station was established in 1921 by Mr Roderick Schenk, under the sponsorship of the Melbourne-based fundamentalist Christian organisation later known as the United Aborigines Mission, the small settlement attracted numbers of Aboriginal families from the fringe camps associated with the nearby mining towns of Mt Morgans, Laverton, Leonora and Kookynie. Many of these people were remnants of the *Mankulkatjarra, Nyanganyatjarra,* and other local territorial groupings, suffering severely dislocated social organisation and religious affiliations which were the outcome of massive depopulation through ill-health and hostility engendered by the mining communities of the North-Eastern Goldfields. Even by the 1920s, it would appear, many of the original inhabitants of this area had long since disappeared. The occupation of the region by Europeans, following the discovery of gold near Mt Margaret in 1893, had its effect, and within a year many deserted Aboriginal encampments were noted (Göczel, 1894:27). The relationship of Aboriginal groups with their territory was already changing, and the predominantly *Nyanganyatjarra* newcomers to Mt Margaret some 30 years after Göczel made his observations were faced with similar problems to those which were to emerge yet again in a subsequent generation.

MIGRATION AND SUCCESSION

One of the most fundamental internal differences within the current Mt Margaret community lies in the divergent regional affiliation of the population. There have been three successive waves of migration into the settlement: firstly, the local *Nyananyatjarra*-speaking people in the 1920s, who earlier had been attracted to the fringes of the first mining towns; secondly, the *Mantjintja*-speakers, who came from the north-east of Laverton in the 1930s; and most recently of all, the *Ngaatjatjarra,* who shifted from the southern *Pintupi* area north of Warburton Ranges in the 1950s. Each group has contained people from a number of different territorial units, but each is identifiably discrete in terms of both its social structure and its primary religious affiliations.

The movement of people into the North-Eastern Goldfields from the east and the north-east (see accompanying map) is indicated by the range in variation for the places of birth of different age groups. Of the 52.8% of adults born in the North-Eastern Goldfields now living at Mt Margaret, only 16.4% were born in the immediate locality of the Mission, and all these people are under 30 years of age. Such a feature is, however, more an indication of the influence of European health practices than anything else. The age distribution of the 47.2% of those born in the desert reflects the successive movements of Aboriginal groups out of the area from the early contact period, and this continued through to the 1960s with the final 'clearing' of the Great Victoria and Gibson Deserts for the missile-retrieval programme (Grayden, 1957; R. Berndt, 1959). Most of the people who lived in the desert during their youth came to the settlement in the immediate post-war period, although one family was amongst the last to leave in 1966 (Dunlop, 1966–70). The desert life here has yet to become the 'memory culture' (suggested by R. Berndt (1963:397)) in the minds of those living at Mt Margaret. The 'desert experience', as it may be termed, is immediate and powerful, providing the charter for the pattern of living for most of those now residing at Mt Margaret. Nearly all adults in the community were reared in the desert; since leaving their home countries few have been able to return, even for a visit, and ritual activities relating to particular localities have had to be carried out at a distance.

Only one child at Mt Margaret today was born in the desert in his own country (a member of the above-mentioned group which left its semi-nomadic lifestyle in 1966). All of the other children were born at nursing posts at the more isolated mission stations such as Warburton Ranges or at the district hospitals in the Eastern Goldfields. The influence of contemporary nursing practice is pervasive: the recent tendency to send many pregnant women from the Laverton and Leonora districts to the Kalgoorlie Regional Hospital for the births of their children has meant that children are being born even farther away from the areas of traditional affiliation as well as

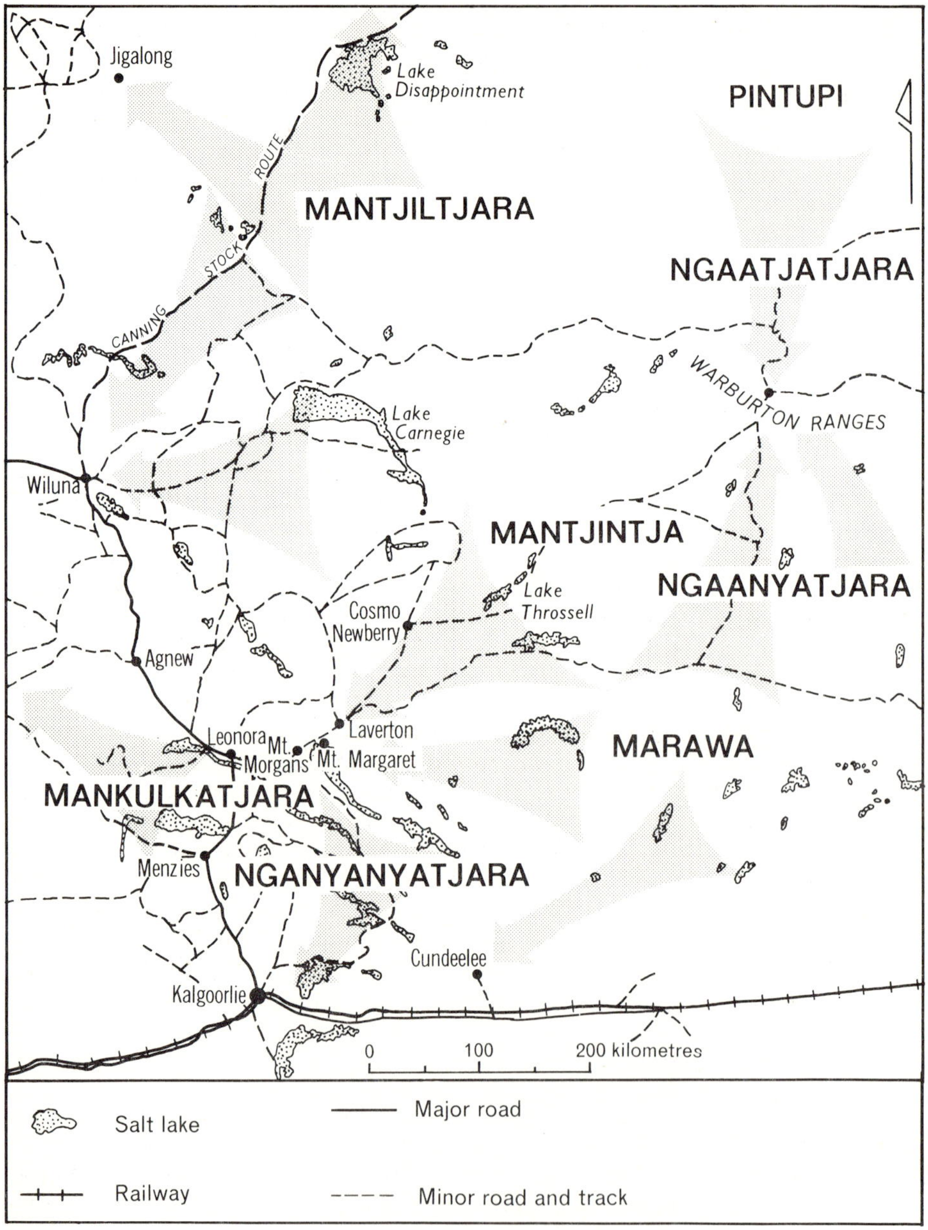

Fig. 1

The Eastern Goldfields and the Western Desert. Settlements and linguistic affiliations of significance to the Mt Margaret people.

from their country of adoption. All these processes have posed problems for the less acculturated members of the community who may wish to maintain the appropriate religious links with the territories from which their kin moved during the early post-contact period.

The pattern of serial migration into Mt Margaret is clearly conceptualised by the members of the community. It finds its material expression in the spatial distribution of housing, and these distinctions are reinforced by linguistic variations and by the different attitudes expressed by the mission staff to the members of each of the groups. At the time of the establishment of the mission station people were attracted from the nearby towns into the locality. The Mt Margaret area had, according to Tindale (1974:258) been originally occupied by a group of people calling themselves *Waljen,* but the land was deserted within a few years of the first gold strikes since many of the inhabitants had succumbed to disease, and to the attractions of life on the fringes of the new townships to the west. Many of those coming to Mt Margaret in the 1920s made claims, of a varying nature, to some right of occupation. These were usually couched in terms of kin-based or religious links. Later, members of groups from the area to the east of Laverton settled at Mt Margaret, and these people were in turn followed by others from the distant north-east. In this manner, then, the Mt Margaret Mission was occupied and reoccupied. As had occurred before, each set of newcomers brought with them their own affiliations: religious, social and linguistic. At the same time, they adopted features of the group into which they moved. Linguistic changes serve as a particularly useful indicator of group migration since they are commonly used as boundary-maintaining devices by many Aboriginal societies. Although the general similarity of languages of the southern Western Desert area is well recognised, dialectal distinctions are maintained. Labelling these is difficult, however, since in many cases different groups will have their own labels for the same dialect. During the early period of the mission station at Mt Margaret a particular dialect of the Western Desert language was spoken there. This has been termed *Nyanganyatjarra* or *Puntjtjarra,* according to the idiosyncracies which appear in it (Douglas, 1964:135-40). However, with the influx of people from the north-east this dialect has steadily fallen out of use as more of its speakers move away or die, and today it is heard only occasionally. It differs little from that of the *Ngaatjatjarra*-speaking *Pintupi* people who at present form the majority of the population at Mt Margaret.

The changes continue: the greater interaction taking place between distant Aboriginal communities on the fringe of the Western Desert and on the Central Reserves, primarily through improved communication and access to the means of effecting such interaction, is acting to diffuse religious and social patterns throughout the entire cultural bloc. Not only does this provide in the short term some new kinds of knowledge for other groups but, looking into the future, it may well serve to minimise the linguistic, social and ritual differences present between Western Desert Aboriginal societies today.

RELIGIOUS AFFILIATIONS

For the people at Mt Margaret 'totemic' affiliations have changing meanings and significance in the post-contact period. A singular degree of diversity within the population of the community has already been noted; the importance and nature of totemic affiliations vary accordingly. The earliest groups to settle at the mission station arrived from the fringe camps of the neighbouring towns. Some groups were remnants, severely depopulated and depressed and lacking any significant degree of social cohesion and group identity. Others, such as the *Mantjintja*, were more fortunate in arriving much later at the sanctuary which the mission station appeared to provide. Members of this later group retained a depth of knowledge of religious matters but it was not always possible for parents to pass this on to their children, who lived in dormitories away from daily participation in life at the camp. Many of these children had a mixed parentage, and to some Aboriginal people appeared to lack in part the essential totemic bonds with their religious heritage since they were denied any spiritual affiliation through their father. Europeans labelled them 'half-castes'.

Although it would have been possible for Aboriginal parents to exercise claims to territorial and group identification on behalf of their offspring, such children were systematically removed from the influence of their non-European parents and relatives in order that they might be given the 'opportunity' to grow up more like their European parents (cf. Tindale, 1940–41). Despite a common heritage, the gap between these 'half-castes' and the 'full-bloods' has widened over the years in the Eastern Goldfields — not because of any inability of the traditional social structure to accommodate the dual nature of such parentage but because of governmental intervention, as delegated to and exercised by the missionary organisation.

The most recent arrivals at the mission station still attach great significance to their 'totemic' religious affiliations, and their active involvement in the religious life overshadows that of the few elderly remnants of the earlier Mt Margaret inhabitants. These individuals are now all very old and are unable to 'look out for' (that is, take care of) their specific ritual obligations: in some instances, guardianship of material objects has been passed over on an individual basis to other more recent arrivals in the community but rarely has full knowledge been transferred. This responsibility has become something of an embarrassment to the active guardians of 'the Law' (as it is called), who must regularly maintain and perform the activities necessitated by their own affiliations. For these reasons discussion of religious matters at Mt Margaret is largely restricted to those pertaining to the 'Easterners' who are today the most active custodians of the Law.[1]

In common with other desert people, the most important 'totemic' affiliation is the cult lodge totem, termed *tjukupi*, although linkages derived through place of conception and birth are also significant. The term *tjukupi* is also used in reference to a specific stretch of country connected by a major Law line, or track, or to an important mythological cycle. The term *kapi*, or water source, is commonly used to identify a group of kin-related people occupying a particular territory, for which the major waterhole is usually the point of reference. In the earlier period an emphasis on patrilocal marriage ensured that children were usually born in the territory of their fathers, but at the same time a woman would retain her own affiliations when moving into the country of her husband, and her children would have rights of affiliation which they could exercise through her as well. In practice, though, this meant that claims *could* be made through any known ancestor, and the shallow depth of genealogical knowledge ensured that the scope for this was relatively restricted. Specific terms for 'mother's country', 'mother's father's country' and the like have been noted. However, as with all rights of territorial affiliation, claims must be activated by occupation and participation through initiation in the religious life of that particular territory. Dual claims could not be held simultaneously, only alternatively, through choice of occupation. These may best be regarded as secondary rights, since it was the father's 'totemic' identity which was held to be more important in the ritual life of the group. Indeed, it was thought desirable that birth and cult totemism should coincide, since this strengthened the claims of an individual to initiation, participation and eventually to some degree of leadership in the ritual activities associated with the land. Similarly, marriage between members 'of the same line' (that is, with the same cult totem) was encouraged, provided that the rule of local descent group exogamy was maintained.

The nature of conception totemism varies between the different groups at Mt Margaret, reflecting their different origins. On the one hand, those from the north believe that spirit children are to be found by the father in the form of an animal or a plant, which is a temporary manifestation of a mythical being with whom the father is associated. When hunted or eaten, this imparts the life essence into the woman. The position of a child's birthmark may give further support to that belief.[2] Groups from the east and north-east, however, emphasise the significance of spirit centres which are often tree-covered hills. These places are the homes of many spirit children, who can travel vast distances in search of potential mothers. Each spirit centre was created by a particular mythical being of the Dreaming, and the spirit children are believed to have a preference for seeking fathers who share in that mythical association. As well, there is an increasing emphasis on the place of birth, rather than on the place of conception: the birth should ideally take place in the territory of the father, where the appropriate *tjukupa* is in evidence. None of these variations though is viewed as being more important than the others: rather, territorial affiliation is regarded as the outcome of a number of factors, some of which can be manipulated for the perceived benefits to be gained in emphasising one kind of mythical affiliation against another.

In the light of these migrations significance must be attached to the phenomenon of disrupted identification: the birthplaces of offspring differ greatly from those of their parents, with consequent dislocation of territorial affiliations. This feature is being progressively masked, however, as younger people are being born and raised primarily in the same place as that in which their parents are now living. Members of this new generation group are coming to identify more readily with their new country than with those places that their primary religious affiliations would suggest. The different groups within the population at Mt Margaret perceive this process within their own perspective, however. Mt Margaret, Laverton, Leonora and the adjacent pastoral stations are well established 'homelands' for those people who came first to live at the mission, and it is only recently that a younger group is emerging from amongst the newcomers; one that is a second generation removed from the traditionally occupied territories located farther inland.

The increasing divergence of actual birthplaces from those desired by parents has made necessary a reinterpretation of certain aspects of the nature of religious affiliations, and a redefinition of some of the principles of territorial identity. These modifications can not be divorced from other changes taking place in the redistribution of the pattern of settlement, nor can they be seen solely as a matter of individual choice as to where putative bonds can be established. Fundamental religious associations provide the particular framework for these linkages. In accordance with traditional practices, those entering a territory as strangers may ultimately, after the passage of sufficient time has permitted the establishment of other bonds, adopt or be given custodial roles within the local religious life which will affirm and strengthen their new position within the community.

Religious affiliations provide the basis for the elaboration and further orientation of social groups on the fringe of the Western Desert. Spatial dislocation from territories of traditional occupation is hardly new (cf. R. & C. Berndt, 1945: 2–3), and indeed it is likely that population movements have been taking place always. Nevertheless, the scale of migration and the influence of alien beliefs and practices has had a unique impact: some bonds between people and their country of origin have been weakened, while others have been strengthened through that very same process. Simultaneously, serial migration over many decades has exposed certain groups to participation in the ritual life of what would otherwise have remained distant and unknown territories. Genealogical and religiously based relationships have been established with these communities, and these links have been maintained and elaborated during subsequent demographic shifts.

Despite their improved access to European forms of transport and communication, few Aborigines have been ever able to return to their own countries since they originally left them. The notable vigour with which the outstation movement has grown on the Central Reserves is indicative of the strong desire of some groups to return to the territories that they formerly occupied. Even with this development many areas have remained uninhabited because of a lack of sufficient supplies of water with which a necessarily larger population could be sustained than would have ranged over the area in pre-contact times. For the 'Easterners' at Mt Margaret, their countries are often too distant, too inaccessible, and too arid to support the contemporary population. They have, either through compulsion or choice, made Mt Margaret their home for now. Religious affiliations have enabled them to do this.

OLD 'BUSINESS'

European settlements on the fringe of the Western Desert have for a long time provided Aboriginal groups with a focus for communication, and even settlement. From the turn of the century, the Laverton–Leonora area was an important point of convergence between the ritual cycles of the Western Desert peoples, and those of the Eastern Goldfields and Murchison regions. The exchange of ritual objects, the trade in artefacts and raw materials such as ochre and pearlshell, together with the periodic exchange of ritual knowledge and the occasional transfer of great ritual complexes such as the *kurangara/dingari* cycle, all added to the significance for Aborigines in the desert areas of these outposts of the European world. Their strategic importance has continued into the present. The depopulation of the neighbouring towns of Laverton and Leonora, and the demise of religious activity in these centres, has resulted in Mt Margaret becoming, largely by default, the key link between the large and ritually important communities of Cundeelee, Wiluna and Warburton Ranges, and communities more distant.[3] Kinship and religious affiliations provide the basis for relationships between these communities.

Mt Margaret is different from these other communities, though, in one important respect: virtually none of the people living on the settlement are held to be the 'countrymen' (that is, the owners) for that locality. The handful who can be so regarded are unable to maintain an active ritual life because of advanced age and small numbers. Their offspring (products of the dormitory system that operated at the mission for so long) are now dispersed throughout the Eastern Goldfields. This duality was not always so peaceful, however. The arrival of visitors from the Central Reserves was not opposed since they brought with them new ceremonies, but their tendency to occupy the mission on an increasingly permanent basis from the 1940s onwards was the source of much discontent and even violence expressed by the earlier inhabitants of Mt Margaret. It was necessary at that time for the newcomers to emphasise the strength of what has already been termed secondary territorial affiliations that were used to provide some justification, albeit a tenuous one, for permanent occupation of the settlement. Only with the passing of the years, and progressive loss of the earlier occupants through migration to other towns and through death, have these 'Easterners' been able to assert their ritual affiliations and social systems over the remaining population without opposition.

During this process of displacement the newcomers introduced amongst other things a different language dialect and different section terms, and brought with them their previous ritual affiliations. All these features helped the 'Easterners' to affirm eventually their position of dominance within the community, with respect to other neighbouring centres of Aboriginal religious practice. Initially, these people had moved with many related groups from their countries to the north and north-west of Warburton Ranges towards the newly established mission station in the late 1930's. The problems of overcrowding and the convergence of greatly differing Aboriginal societies resulted in conflict and disquiet. Most stayed to make Warburton Ranges Mission their new home, but a few families chose increasingly to stay on in the North Eastern Goldfields after the annual round of ceremonial and ritual activities had been carried out there. It is these people and their descendants who today form the majority of the population at Mt Margaret.

It was not a coincidence, though, that these particular groups of *Ngaatjatjarra*-speaking people selected the North Eastern Goldfields as a new home. The shared ritual activities had already established particular links; others were supplied by kin-based bonds. The common religious orientation was based on shared 'totemic' affiliations. In particular, the *Wati Kutjarra* (Two Goanna Men) line travels from west of the Leonora area towards the east just north of the mission station, to cross the *Waanampi* (Water Serpent) track adjacent to Mt Margaret. Further east is the deathplace of *Wati Malu* (Kangaroo Man). All three mythical beings were active in the countries of the 'Easterners'; indeed, *Wati Kutjarra* and *Malu* are their two most important ritual affiliations, and the *tjukupa* (Dreaming) of the two most significant cult lodges at Mt Margaret today.

Given the prior existence of these particular mythological affiliations in the region, it was not too difficult for the newcomers to emphasise the commonality of interest and spiritual origin, and so attempt to avoid the classification of being 'outsiders'. Of course, there was opposition to this process of occupation from some of the people long resident at Mt Margaret, particularly in view of their own weaknesses. They lacked the numbers and the vitality to withstand the pressures from the 'Easterners'. The newcomers had already been initiated into some of the religious cults of the North-Eastern Goldfields, and some of the most sacred objects reserved for the eyes of the oldest and most experienced men have come into the custody of the present ritual leaders at Mt Margaret. In some instances the knowledge that accompanies these objects was passed on during an earlier period, but the memory of this is now fading in the minds of the senior men, as successive years pass without the appropriate rituals and stories being sung. Since 1974 several ritual leaders of the 'old Mob' have died, leaving nobody at Mt Margaret or elsewhere with the authority to sing the old *inma,* or song lines. The artefacts survive in the material form, but the detailed knowledge by and large has not. With the passing of time, it is possible that these objects may come to have a new significance. Meanwhile, though, they are cared for by ritual leaders who no longer can recall much detail of their meanings.

Ritual objects are not the only remnants of an earlier occupation which have come under the guardianship of the new leaders at Mt Margaret. Many sacred sites in the North-Eastern Goldfields are known to the present ritual leaders at Mt Margaret; some of these have particular relevance to contemporary religious affiliations, and are periodically inspected and cleared of vegetation. Sites associated with *Nyanuti* (turkey), *Kalaya* (emu), *Wayuta* (brush-tailed possum), *Piwi* (owl), and *Papa* (dingo) are all identifiable, as well as those associated with the above mentioned *Wati Kutjarra* (Two Goanna Men), *Winba* (Rainmaker) and *Waanampi* (Water Serpent) tracks, although as custodians they hold less detail of ritual knowledge associated with many of these sites than they did in the past.

THE 'NEW' OWNERS

The present occupants of Mt Margaret have been faced with the problem of asserting a valid claim to live in the North-Eastern Goldfields. The way in which they came to occupy part of this region is largely historical: the product of demographic pressures and the pervasive influence of the European explorers, miners and settlers. At the same time, traditional religious affiliations provided the mechanism by which the claim to occupation can be legitimised. They have passively assumed responsibility for the care and protection of certain relics from the earlier occupants—both artefacts and sites.

They have also undertaken in a most active sense to cement their affiliations with this land.

When they were living in their own territories, such associations would have once been regarded as of secondary importance to the 'totemic' relationships they maintained with their own *tjukupa.* Now, the exercise of such secondary rights has provided entré into a distant and somewhat hostile society on the fringe of the Western Desert. Once access had been achieved the status of these people within this regional community had to be entrenched. Rights to occupancy could not be deliberately relinquished: only with the passage of time could the 'Easterners' assume a position of importance in their new country. The 'old Mob' did not migrate away from Mt Margaret and the North-Eastern Goldfields *because* of the occupation of their land by outsiders—they were already on the move at the turn of the century, hesitating for a few decades whilst the mission station could provide some attraction, then continuing their south-west movement in their search for improvements in employment opportunity and living conditions, the same factors which were drawing the 'Easterners' towards Mt Margaret. By progressively occupying the vacuum that was developing at Mt Margaret the newcomers were able by default to impress their interpretation of the Law on the few who stayed behind. In return for their exposure to the 'strength' of the desert Law, the old people passed on some of their own knowledge. This provided the basis through which the 'Easterners' could consolidate their position. This could be achieved in either of two ways: firstly, through the transfer of conception and birth Dreamings to the new setting, and secondly, through the elaboration and definition of these mythological associations.

The beliefs attached to conception and birth are changing in this section of the Western Desert, as elsewhere. The northern tradition of animal and plant manifestation is now uncommon, although reiterated by those who live periodically in Wiluna, and some recent innovations have already been cited (see Note 2). With more people occupying territories different from those with which primary links are held the emphasis has shifted to an elaboration on the manner in which spirit children can travel long distances through the air from a particular place created by a relevant mythical ancestor, seeking out women married to a man with the same *tjukupa,* that is, originating from the same spiritforce. It is said that the spirit children can travel over or under the ground along the track of the very same mythological ancestor; the presence of appropriate 'Law lines' near Mt Margaret ensures that traditional totemic affiliations can be maintained despite the inability of people to occupy their home countries, or even to visit them.

To ensure a continued supply of spirit children the Mt Margaret people must maintain the strength of the Law in the North-Eastern Goldfields, even though some of the relevant tracks lie some distance from the mission. This is achieved through the performance of ritual by both men and women. Four main categories of ritual activity can be distinguished: initiation, commemoration, increase and rain-making. Participation depends on sex, kinship and 'totemic' affiliations, as well as on the expertise of the initiate.

Male initiation ritual comprises two important cycles; the first is associated with *Wati Malu,* the mythical Kangaroo Man who is believed to have performed the first circumcision and subincision rituals near the Warburton Ranges, and this is a very significant association for this particular area. The second important ritual sequence concerns the activities of the two mythical Goanna Men, *Wati Kutjarra,* whose exploits cover much of the Western Desert. Initiation rituals are carried out at Warburton Ranges and at Wiluna since there are now insufficient numbers of people to perform adequately the full ritual cycle at the mission. Preliminary ritual and the associated ceremonies are still performed near Mt Margaret (not *at* Mt Margaret, in deference to the wishes of the Christian community), and this is regarded as being extremely important since many of the 'Easterners' have close territorial affiliations with the *Wati Kutjarra*.

Commemorative rituals involve the re-enactment of episodes from the lives of the mythical beings for the further education and affirmation of the initiated. For the people at Mt Margaret these rituals of commemoration are the most common form of religious activity, helping both to maintain the necessary ties with the sites of mythological significance which they knew in the past and to ensure the perpetuation of the knowledge in the minds of the participants. Each person knows best the set of myths associated with his/her own country: the waterholes and other physiographic features of the landscape provide a charter for the claim to that country, and it is these that are incorporated in myth and expressed in ritual. In the performance of such commemorative rituals, each participant is called upon to contribute a detailed knowledge of specific territory. This may give rise to a number of versions of the one songline, but the main events will be agreed upon by the members of the group. Physiographic features are recognised as being indicative of the past activities of any of a number of mythical beings. By locating familiar mythical associations in their new territory the ritual leaders at Mt Margaret are able to incorporate features of their own mythologies into their current situation, thus confirming the strength of their claim to occupation of this area and their custody of this land. The site-specific mythological stories of the earlier occupants are incorporated within their broader knowledge of the main songline.

Increase ceremonies have been traditionally performed at sites associated with certain ancestral beings to ensure the continued supply of the particular natural species concerned. In this sense, then, 'increase' is a misnomer, but it remains the generally accepted term. Each increase centre is 'owned' by the local group members who share that species as their *tjukupi;* it is the men who direct the annual rites and symbolically 'drive' the as yet unborn young of the species in the directions in which they are required. There is only one such site in the vicinity of Mt Margaret, and this is maintained with the support of the wider community by the *Mantjinta* men who have since settled at Warburton Ranges and at Mt Margaret. For most of the people living on the settlement, though, their most sacred sites are far away in their own countries, and the only means of maintaining contact with the *tjukupa* there is for contemplative commemoration to take place, usually in the presence of very sacred objects associated with that *tjukupa;* and for individual *kuuti* to make dream spirit journeys and to perform the appropriate ordinance *in absentia*.

Rainmaking rituals derived from the Wiluna community are performed annually at one of several important sites of association near Mt Margaret, utilising material objects transported from many more distant places also associated with *Waanampi* (the Water Serpent) and with *Winba,* the mythical Rainmaker of the Creative period (cf Tonkinson, 1974:89-90). Men and women participate in these rituals, both separately and together.

SUCCESSION AND 'THE LAW'

It is clear that Aboriginal communities on the fringe of the Western Desert, at Mt Margaret at least, are endeavouring to consolidate their position as occupiers in the face of opposition from earlier inhabitants. That the 'old Mob' did not take stronger steps to throw off this threat may be attributable to the demographic processes taking place in the 1950s, but the conditions of their own occupation some 30 years earlier may well have acted to subdue their reaction. Whilst the 'Easterners' have introduced a number of cultural elements from their own society, they have freely adopted those aspects of the existing social order which have had relevance to their own religious associations. In the absence of much opposition they have come to consider themselves permanent residents of this country, even though they are the first to admit their origin. For the youths growing up at Mt Margaret and in the neighbouring towns, the desert Law is pervasive and all-powerful. Overtly, nothing remains of the earlier occupants that sets them aside from the newcomers—except for some linguistic variation, which is becoming less and less common. The presence of the 'Easterners', and their custodianship of the land they have come to occupy, is now recognised and accepted within the Eastern Goldfields, since few descendants of the earlier occupants retain any detailed knowledge of their country.[4] The 'Easterners' are viewed as the 'Guardians of the Law', competing through the orthodoxy of their beliefs for a place in the circle of ritual and exchange that spans the Western Desert today.

CONCLUSION

The experience of Aboriginal migrants into the area of the North-Eastern Goldfields poses a number of problems for some of the more general assumptions in land claims.

Most importantly, the concept of the sacred site as an unchanging and immutable portion of the landscape has been emphasised without regard to the processes of change which were probably taking place even before contact was made by Europeans. The activities of the Macassan trepangers on the northern Australian coastline for example have been historically documented, but the impact these aliens had on the Aboriginal societies affected has rarely been evaluated. The demographic and ecological pressures in the interior of the continent suggest that some form of slow-moving migration outward may have been under way, at least in the Eastern Goldfields, from the very earliest period of contact if not before. Such demographic changes, if they have taken place in the past, must have altered the pattern of occupation and mythological affiliation for the Aboriginal groups involved. Since it is likely that contiguous communities were affected in the first instance, it is not unrealistic to assume that processes of succession to the land and subsequent transformation of religious associations have taken place in a manner similar to that outlined here.

If this is the case, one must pose the question: just which individuals are the 'traditional owners' of a particular territory, in a succession of communities of occupation? Which people have rights of control when occupancy has been achieved either by force or, as in the case of the 'Easterners' at Mt Margaret, by default, and when ritual knowledge and the material expressions of some mythological affiliations have been transferred to the custody of the newcomers? Certainly, the post-contact situation is complex, and the large-scale decimation of many Aboriginal societies through disease and violence has been a significant alien influence on the pattern of occupation and succession. The problem remains, however.

Another point of contention is the position of the 'disinherited', that is, those descendants of the earlier occupiers who were removed, often with force, from their parents and relatives to dormitories and hostels, denied their Aboriginality, and yet all the time occupying (in the sense of being present on) the lands of their grandparents. What are their rights to this land, the presence of contemporary Aboriginal occupants notwithstanding? This particular problem is of considerable relevance to those living in the Eastern Goldfields, since Mt Margaret Mission occupied a role at one time integral to this very process of disinheritance.

These problems are faced by European administrators as well as by the contemporary inhabitants of the Eastern Goldfields. They *know* who the land belongs to. They *know* that the 'Easterners' have occupied the region by the exercise of secondary affiliations, reserving at the same time their rights to their own countries to the east and north-east. The tracks made by the travels of the mythical beings of the Dreaming, and the sites they left behind, all chart this country. They provide the focus for claims of affiliation. Whilst on an extended time scale the meaning and the delimitation of sites may change, their nature does not. One (mission-raised) Aboriginal man likened it to the successive versions of the Bible, and the constant drive toward truth and authentication asserted at every period; yet in retrospect constantly changing; only the nature of the message, the spiritual force, remaining constant. It is, perhaps, a useful parallel. To this man, it was, and he knew both worlds.

NOTES

1. In deference to contemporary Aboriginal opinion, no material deemed by the Mt Margaret people to be of a secret-sacred nature is included in this paper.

2. More recently, conception Dreamings involving such European items as aeroplanes and motorcars have been mentioned in some cases, and these alien items are being incorporated into mythological sequences, principally through the use of syncretic elements of the *Winba* rain-making ritual cycle.

3. With the recent (1978) up-grading of the 'Gunbarrel Highway' between Wiluna and Giles, a number of ritual cycles have been conveyed directly to or from the Central Reserves without following the traditional route through the North-Eastern Goldfields. To some degree this is the result of recurrent problems involved in passing through Laverton, but this practice has nevertheless angered many of the Wiluna and Mt Margaret men, who sense increasing domination from Jigalong, Strelley and Warburton Ranges over the ritual activities of this section of the Western Desert.

4. In December 1979 the remaining leader of the 'old Mob' left Mt Margaret for hospital treatment. His absence from the settlement will significantly alter the power balance within the community. Although he was never active in ritual life, his position at the mission has always been respected by the 'Easterners' (to whom he is related through his wife), who recognise him as, in their words, 'Mission boss, the really one'. His permission had always to be sought, albeit nominally, whenever local land was required by the 'Easterners' for use as a ritual ground, and his advice in such matters heeded. Now that he is unlikely to return there is no barrier remaining to hinder the 'Easterners' in their full exercise of occupational rights over the settlement.

REFERENCES

Berndt, R.M. (1959) The concept of 'the Tribe' in the Western Desert of Australia, *Oceania, 30*:82–107.

Berndt, R.M. (1963) Surviving groups with minimal association with Europeans. In: H. Sheils (ed.) *Australian Aboriginal Studies*, Melbourne University Press, pp. 385–408.

Berndt, R.M. & Berndt C.H. (1945) A preliminary report on fieldwork in the Ooldea region, western South Australia. *Oceania Bound Monograph*.

Berndt, R.M. & Berndt, C.H. (1970) Some points of change in Western Australia. In: A.R. Pilling & R.A. Waterman (eds), *Diprotodon to Detribalization*. Michigan State University Press; pp.73–79.

Douglas, W.H. (1964) *An Introduction to the Western Desert Language*, Sydney, Oceania Linguistics Monograph No. 4.

Dunlop, I. (1966–70) *People of the Australian Western Desert*. Canberra, Australia Commonwealth Film Unit for the Australian Institute of Aboriginal Studies. (film series).

Göczel, S. (1894) Report on the interior gold region of Western Australia, Appendix 4. *Mines Department Report 1894*. Perth, Government Printer.

Grayden, W. (1957) *Adam and atoms*, Perth, the author.

Stanton, J.E. (1979) The Mt. Margaret Community. In: R.M. & C.H. Berndt (eds), *Aborigines of the West; their past and their present*, Perth; The University of Western Australia Press; pp. 119–25.

Tindale, N.B. (1940–41) Survey of the Half-caste problem in South Australia, *Proceedings of the Royal Geographical Society, South Australian Branch, 42*:66–161.

Tindale, N.B. (1974) *Aboriginal Tribes of Australia*, Canberra; Australian National University Press.

Tonkinson, R. (1974) *The Jigalong Mob: Aboriginal victors of the desert crusade*. Menlo Park, Calif., Cummings.

9

MIGRATION AND RIGHTS TO LAND IN THE PILBARA

Kingsley Palmer

In this paper I discuss an area of the north-west of Western Australia where there have been significant changes in the Aboriginal population since initial European settlement, particularly during the last 30 years. In such a situation individuals have had to adapt to the new dispensation with respect to their rights in land. Moreover, the nature of the rights themselves may also have been modified. Despite these changes Aborigines in the region have maintained their basic beliefs concerning rights in land, and the fundamental principles by which such rights are derived have remained intact.

In 1946 a number of Aborigines employed as labourers on the pastoral stations in the east of the north-west of Western Australia went on strike for better pay and conditions.[1] Some of the Aborigines who went on strike owned the country in which they worked and which had been settled and appropriated by the European Australian settlers. Others had territorial affiliations with country in the Great Sandy Desert, east of the Nullagine and Oakover rivers and to the east of land settled by European Australians. These Aborigines had formerly migrated west to the new station properties where they settled and worked.

The Aborigines involved in the strike organised their own cooperative enterprises that made them largely independent of the European Australian pastoralists. However, in order to maintain a living the strikers had to move from the east Pilbara region, and for many this meant leaving country with which they had a traditional spiritual affinity. Some of the strikers finally came to settle at Yandeearra, a cattle station which the Aborigines now run. Yandeearra is situated in the central Pilbara, some 120 kilometres south of Port Hedland.

As a result of these movements most of those who presently occupy land at Yandeearra are not the Aboriginal owners of that region. They retain rights to, and spiritual affiliation with, country that may be hundreds of kilometres to the east, but in day-to-day terms, they must live in country that they do not own.

The land-owning situation at Yandeearra is complicated by other circumstances that are also the product of changes that have taken place as a result of European Australian settlement. The local Aboriginal land-owners have become reduced in numbers, local groups have become fragmented, and in some cases have disappeared altogether. The changing status of immigrants and their possible assimilation into the present system of land tenure is closely related to the effectiveness of the claims of local land-owners. It is therefore necessary to examine first the status and condition of the indigenous land owners, and the rights that they now exercise. I then examine how local land-owners relate to the newcomers from the east.

Yandeearra Aborigines state that an individual inherits rights in the clan estates of his matri-kin and his patri-kin. They espounse the ideal that a man should become familiar with spiritual matters relevant to his father's estate as a priority, and consequently there is an emphasis on the inheritance of rights in father's country. However, rights in country are potential and must be realised through ritual induction, during which the novice learns of the religious mysteries which relate to the inherited estate. Moreover, a land-owner is required to demonstrate his interests in his country, as well as an ability to meet his obligations as an owner to ensure the safety and integrity of his estate. A land-owner is also responsible for the conduct of all religious affairs that take place in his country. A land-owner, who is either physically incapable of meeting these obligations, or who has not realised his rights in country through ritual induction, and shows no interest in doing so, is regarded by the Yandeearra Aborigines as an ineffective land-owner.

There are seven discrete territories in the reserve which makes up Yandeearra. Following Stanner (1965:2) I call these territories 'estates'. I call members of the group with rights of ownership in an estate, the 'local group' or 'clan'. Not all estates at Yandeearra share common boundaries, and the interstices are said to belong to defunct local groups and are now the responsibility of the surviving land-owners. I will briefly review each estate and the clan members who have rights within them.

Estate 1. The estate is composed of what was formerly two clan territories. The clan is represented by an old man, 'A', who inherited one area from F. and F.F. He inherited the other area through his M.B. 'A' has no surviving sons, and his grandsons are absent from the community and express no interest at present in traditional matters.

Estate 2 and 3. Four half-brothers, 'B', 'C', 'D' and 'E', inherited estate 2 patrilineally. In addition, brothers 'D' and 'E' inherited estate 3 through M.F. In the face of an ineffective patriline surviving 'A' of estate 1, 'D' and 'E' could claim inheritance of that estate, since their M.F. is brother to the mother of 'A'.

Estate 4. This estate was inherited patrilineally but the owners do not live at Yandeearra, nor do they have any interest in the ritual or social life there.

Estates 5, 6 and 7. The descent line is represented by a man, 'F'. He inherited estate 5 patrilineally from his social father. He inherited estate 7 matrilineally, along with his two brothers, neither of whom lives at Yandeearra or demonstrates any interest in the country. 'F' has told me that he considers that he should inherit estate 6 affinally, for his sister married the land owner and he has no issue. 'F' has no issue either, but he has a nephew, 'G'; more of whom later.

Aborigines at Yandeearra consistently assert that a necessary concomitant of realised rights of ownership in an estate is the expression and demonstration of 'interest' in the estate. This does not necessarily mean a desire to live on the estate, or even close to it. But land-owners should demonstrate that they have a spiritual concern both for the land and for sociocultural community activities such as ritual. In ritual, land-owners can demonstrate their spiritual relationship with land through the purveyance or revelation of esoteric songs or objects which are symbolic of their relationship with their country. Such a relationship would involve obligations to 'look after' the country and ensure that miners or prospectors and other intruders did not destroy or alter the countryside. Being absent from the country and living in a European Australian town with no 'traditional' interests is taken by Yandeearra people as signifying loss of interest. However, even the most extreme cases of such cultural neglect cannot alter the fact, as Aborigines see it, that a man is a land-owner if he inherited the estate as the member of a local group. He may be ineffective but he remains the land-owner, and nothing except death can disqualify him from that status.

What is important then, is that Aborigines differentiate between what can be termed effective and ineffective land-owners. When one land-owner is considered to be ineffective it is possible for another member of the local group, to claim rights of ownership within the estate. For example, 'F' claims to be the sole owner of estate 7 because his two brothers, with whom, strictly speaking, he shares rights in that estate, are ineffective owners. In general, a man who claims to inherit an estate either matrilineally or patrilineally but has shown himself to be uninterested in the country, or has not realised his rights through ritual induction, will not be regarded as the

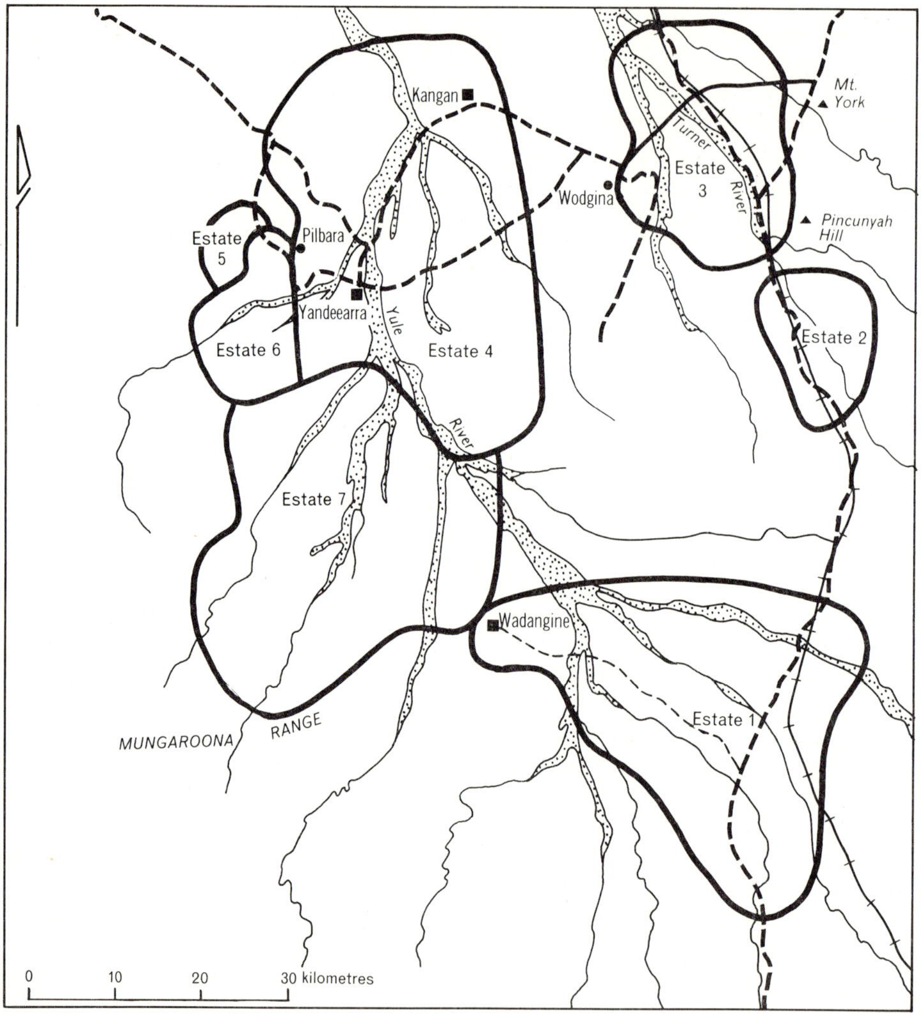

Fig. 1

Estates of local land-owners at Yandeearra.

effective owner of the estate. On the other hand, a man who lives at the community who has realised his rights through ritual induction and who can demonstrate an equally strong claim to rights in the estate through descent is likely to be regarded by the other community members as the effective owner of the estate.

When there is only one ineffective land owner, and no other members of the clan to present rival claims, members of an adjacent estate may claim to have rights to 'look after' that country on behalf of the ineffective land owner. Such is the case in respect of estate 4, since man 'F' claims to have *de facto* control over this territory.

The principle of descent is also the subject of negotiations between rival claimants to rights in an estate. If the principle of unilineal descent is not applicable because inheritance through the male or female line is impossible, other principles must be applied. This has happened in one case. The man identified as 'F' is making a claim on estate 6 on the grounds that his sister married the land-owner, and that he, the land-owner, has no issue to inherit the estate.

In summary, then, the land-owning groups in the area are quite firmly established but have been subject to changes as a result of colonisation which have affected the manner of the inheritance of land. Aborigines at Yandeearra differentiate between effective and ineffective land-owners. Effective land-owners are those with inherited rights in an estate, which rights are realised through ritual induction, and are exercised. An ineffective land-owner, on the other hand, either has not realised his rights in the estate, or does not exercise his rights in practice. Some owners may gain *de facto* control over estates in the absence of rival claimants. Moreover, if the principles of patrilineal or matrilineal descent are inappropriate, owners have traced their acquisition of rights according to different principles.

I now examine the position of the local land-owners in relation to the immigrant members of the community. These immigrants have spiritual affiliations with country some distance to the east of Yandeearra, and are mainly Nyamil and Nyangumada speakers who, as I have previously noted, originated from the eastern Pilbara or from the western areas of the Great Sandy Desert. They acknowledge that they have no rights as land-owners in the Yandeearra region, and state that they are 'strangers'.

Numerically, the strangers are in a majority, forming well over 70% of the population.[2] This means that they can compensate for their non-land-owning status by dominating the control of both ritual and everyday activities.

These migrants have adapted to the physical distances that separate them from their homelands. In a number of ways they are able to assert their rights to territories no longer occupied. These processes can be briefly noted. Men who have special spiritual talents are believed to be able to make visits to their country in the course of natural sleep (Tonkinson, 1970). During the course of these dream spirit journeys, men believe they are able to inspect sites and places of importance in their clan estates and to report back to their fellows on the state of affairs in their distant and now-vacated country. In addition, men who go on dream spirit journeys sometimes are 'given' songs by spirit beings and are shown ritual dances. The traveller rehearses these songs and dances when he awakes, and a whole series of songs and accompanying ritual dances form a 'corroboree'. One man at Yandeearra sings the songs of a corroboree he was given during a dream spirit journey. In the songs his own country is commemorated. So, through its performance, he is able to stress both the existence and the importance of his own country, both to himself and to those who listen to his songs.

The detailed knowledge that a man with realised rights in his clan estates possesses concerning a particular area of land marks him off as a land-owner amongst his peers. Such knowledge may be expressed in a variety of ways. A land-owner may talk about particular places within his country where mythological beings accomplished specific deeds during the Dreaming.

Knowledge of country may also be expressed through mythoritual song cycles which tell of the journeys of beings during the Dreaming. The songs describe the places the mythological beings visited, and the various deeds they performed. In particular, the major mythoritual song cycles that accompany and follow initiation rituals concern particular areas of countryside. Such song cycles extend across the territories of many different land-owners, but each land-owner is responsible for the transmission of detailed information relevant to his own particular stretch of country (R. & C. Berndt, 1977:241). A man is able to assert publicly that he sings and talks for the territory of his clan by the purveyance of ritual or knowledge which is specific to country. Consequently, he can assert his ownership of country through ritual performance and the enunciation of mythology which is a signal of his land owning potentialities. Physically, however, he may be many hundreds of kilometres away from his country, and indeed unable to return there easily.

Some esoteric ritual objects are symbols of land-owning rights. An individual gains command and control of such objects through ritual induction by which he realises his rights to his clan estates. Physical possession of objects is of critical importance to land owners. To have such paraphernalia at hand is to demonstrate land-owning status to other land-owners, for the artefacts are the witness of a man's rights to country. Over the last five years the immigrants at Yandeearra have consistently imported these paraphernalia from their homelands. The importation has been done with great care. Local land-owners have been consulted continually, and their permission sought before any such innovations took place. Special rituals were held to legitimise the introduction of the 'new' material objects. The immigrants acted with deference to the indigenous land-owners, stressing that their own role was one of 'stranger' and that they had no authority in ritual held in estates that were owned by the locals. Yet, the immigrants were able to assert their ownership of distant and now unoccupied territories by their physical possession and ritual revelation of paraphernalia which are symbols of land-ownership.

The importation of ritual paraphernalia was also instrumental in affecting the negotiations that took place between the immigrants and the locals. The paraphernalia under the control of the immigrants soon came to outnumber the artefacts controlled by the local land-owners. Subsequent indoctrination of young men into the mysteries of religious knowledge, whereby they realised their rights in their clan estates, by viewing esoteric objects was consequently under the direct control of the immigrants, for it was they who held a monopoly of the ownership of these objects. At Yandeearra immigrants are able to control the dissemination of knowledge through the revelation of esoteric objects which they direct through rights of ownership. The immigrants therefore have come to have control and authority in ritual matters to the virtual exclusion of local land-owners.

Esoteric ritual paraphernalia utilising materials from the Yandeearra estates may be made only by local land-owners, or under their direction. At Yandeearra some immigrants have entered into negotiations with local land-owners. The land-owner provides the raw material, while the immigrant agrees to supply the labour to make artefacts. The local land-owners retain rights of ownership over the paraphernalia, but the immigrants may claim subsidiary rights by virtue of the labour they have invested in the objects. Such subsidiary rights can be exercised only in accord with the land-owners' rights, and concern how the object is used, revealed or withheld in rituals. On the death of the land-owner the stranger is in a strong position to claim total control of the object he has worked upon, particularly in the absence of rival claims.

In summary, then, Aborigines at Yandeearra have used both belief and ritual practice as a form of religious knowledge. By purveying that knowledge the immigrants have been able to assert and maintain their rights in country which they no longer occupy. However, they have also utilised religious knowledge to solve a second problem; how to occupy land they do not own and come to terms with local land-owners.[3] Immigrants have imported ritual paraphernalia and consequently control the communication of religious knowledge to young men, reducing local land-owners to a status of nominal importance. Moreover, through negotiations with local land-owners, immigrants may obtain rights over paraphernalia which are symbols of local land-owning rights.

There are two additional processes which are important in a consideration of the adaptive strategies of immigrants at Yandeearra. One concerns marriage alliances. The other concerns how some people at Yandeearra have acquired spiritual affiliations with the countryside around Yandeearra, while their parents, as immigrants, have spiritual ties with far distant country.

The leader of the community is an immigrant. His sister's son married the sister of man 'F', who is owner of estates 5, 6 and 7. 'F' has no children but his nephew 'G' would be well placed to inherit these estates since inheritance through M.B. is a principle generally accepted by Yandeearra residents. The leader of the community has also been a 'foster father' to 'G'. Thus the family of the leader of the community is directly connected by marriage to local land owners, and the leader himself through his influence and control of 'G' stands to have a strong political influence over estates 5, 6 and 7.

The immigrants have been at Yandeearra for well over a decade. They also held the station for several years soon after the strike in 1946. Consequently, a great many of the children, and some of the teenagers too, were born while their parents were living at Yandeearra. In common with many other areas of Aboriginal Australia, Aborigines at Yandeearra believe that a man or woman's spiritual essence is derived from a particular place. Initial spiritual quickening is often associated with physical conception, or early signs of pregnancy. Clan members usually expect to have their spiritual conception place, or *yinda,* as it is called at Yandeearra, within their own estate. It is likely that there were occasions in the past when this was not so. At Yandeearra, however, many of the younger generation have been born outside their parents' estates, and it is believed that their spiritual conception sites are at Yandeearra.

There are two seasonal renewal sites[4] for spirit children in the Yandeearra reserve and both are now considered to be the spiritual origin of children who were born while their parents lived at Yandeearra. Consequently, these children and young people are believed to have a special spiritual affinity with the area where their *yinda* or spirit conception site is located. These young people cannot and do not claim to be land-owners, but they do say, 'I belonga Yandeearra'.

I now examine these younger Yandeearra immigrants and consider how they relate to the existing land. Although they do not constitute a local group, they do have restricted rights within the area of their *yinda,* and so are owners in the strict sense.[5] It is helpful in this instance to make a distinction between land-owners with primary rights and those with secondary rights.[6] At Yandeearra people see primary rights as those which accrue through descent and inheritance in the forms outlined above; secondary rights derive from the place of spiritual conception.

Primary rights are inherited, either from matri-kin or patri-kin, but Aborigines at Yandeearra may argue that estates can also be inherited in other ways in certain circumstances. In order to inherit primary rights an individual must be a member of a local group. Rights must be realised through ritual induction and by a land-owner showing himself to be active in religious matters relevant to his country. Rights in an estate concern degrees of spiritual authority in ritual action, or in the revelation of esoteric paraphernalia that are direct representations of a spiritual affinity between land-owner and his land. Consequently, a land-owner has a primary spiritual responsibility for his estate. This means that he controls the use of materials found within the estate for ritual purposes, he must ensure the integrity of all the countryside, and particularly the safety of special places, such as renewal sites, within it.

At Yandeearra a land-owner has the right to forage over his estate, but this right is freely accorded to all others. The same right, however, would not automatically be accorded to the exploitation of minerals, for example, which have potential economic value at Yandeearra. In the past, however, minerals have been exploited by immigrants with the consent and assistance of land-owners.

Secondary rights are not inherited but exist by virtue of the spiritual conception site. They obtain over a limited area surrounding the *yinda* itself. Secondary rights concern spiritual responsibility for the site and the right to authority in any ritual matters that concern that site. However, these rights must be exercised in accord with those in whose clan estate the *yinda* is located.

It seems that in certain circumstances those with secondary rights may acquire primary rights within the whole estate. In the absence of other claims those with a *yinda* in the estate of an extinct clan have a strong claim to exercise rights over the whole of the estate. In doing so, however, they are able to adhere to the principles of Aboriginal belief concerning land-holding. This belief rests on the recognition that there is a spiritual relationship between man and land. I have not noted the progression from secondary rights to primary rights at Yandeearra, but there is an interesting example from the Kimberley region which illustrates the point nicely.

A man I will call Bill explained to me that his father and father's father owned country far to the south of where he now lived. However, owing to the migration of Aborigines from desert regions to the fringes of European Australian settlement, Bill's father travelled north to live in the estate of another patriline; all the members of this patriline had either died or been murdered or deported. Bill said that his *yinda* was in this country for he was born after his parents had migrated. Bill also said that his patriline, that is his son and grandson, were now the land-owners for this estate, with primary rights over it. Moreover he justified the spiritual continuity between his estate and the estate of his father and father's father to which he also claimed rights of ownership. He said that before he was born his spirit 'ran' up across the countryside, many miles from his father's clan estate to the new one. His father 'followed' it, and finally 'found' it in a pool (the *yinda*) in the new estate. However, Bill explained that if there had been surviving members of the new estate he would have had to 'share' rights with them. But he did not suggest that his rights would have then been merely secondary.

It is possible, then, indeed likely, that the rights of clans in estates may change over time. People may acquire influence over estates through marriage alliances or claim *de facto* ownership in the absence of effective owners. There is room for negotiations between those who claim rights in an estate when the principles of patrilineal or matrilineal descent are inappropriate to circumstances. Perhaps most significant of all is the fact that people with secondary rights whose inherited estates may be far distant from their present abode may assert that they have primary rights in an estate formerly owned by someone else. Yet, even where there have been changes of this magnitude, Aborigines have adapted to new circumstances without surrendering traditional values. W.E.H. Stanner (1965:12) has suggested that long-term shifts of estate and range may have been more common than was formerly supposed and political negotiations for land have been noted elsewhere (Sutton, 1978: 78–80).

There is no land rights legislation in Western Australia. Clearly, if there were to be, such changes in ownership would have to be taken into account. For residents at Yandeearra and elsewhere, the major problems are how to occupy land they do not own and how to own land they do not occupy. These are problems which they solve by recourse to their beliefs and through the conduct of their religious affairs. In so doing, however, they may render inappropriate existing concepts of European Australians regarding land rights legislation.

NOTES

1. For an account of the strike see Stuart (1959), Brown (1976), Palmer & McKenna (1978). The strike is also discussed by Rowley (1972:251–61) and Wilson (1979).

2. The total population varies between 150 and 200.

3. This double problem was identified for me by D.H. Turner (1978).

4. Called *dalu* in the vernacular at Yandeearra and elsewhere in the north-west of Western Australia.

5. I call owner anyone who owns a right in a thing.

6. Peterson, Keen & Sansom (1977) discuss the derivation of secondary rights in the Northern Territory. They include place of conception as ground for claiming secondary rights in country, but they also list five

other grounds: place of birth, place of death or burial of important relative, kinship ties through M.M., totemic affiliations, and being the child of a female clan owner (op.cit.:4–5). In addition, Aborigines only appeal to secondary rights when those with primary rights are lacking (op.cit.:1).

REFERENCES

Berndt, R.M. & Berndt, C.H. (1977) *The World of the First Australians.* Sydney, Ure Smith, (first ed. 1964).

Brown, M. (1976) *The Black Eureka.* Sydney, Australian Book Society.

Palmer, K. & McKenna, C. (1978) *Somewhere Between Black and White.* Melbourne, Macmillan.

Petersen, N., Keen, I. & Sansom B.L. (1977). Succession to land, primary and secondary rights to Aboriginal estates. Unpublished submission to Ranger Uranium Environmental Inquiry.

Rowley, C.D. (1972) *The Remote Aborigines.* Sydney, Penguin. (first ed. 1970).

Stanner, W.E.H. (1965) Aboriginal territorial organization: estate, range, domain and regime. *Oceania, 36* (1):1- 26.

Stuart, D. (1959) *Yandy.* Melbourne, Georgian House.

Sutton, P. (1978) Wik: *Aboriginal Society, Territory and Language at Cape Keerweer, Cape York Peninsular, Australia.* Unpublished PhD Thesis, University of Queensland.

Tonkinson, R. (1970) Aboriginal Dream-spirit Beliefs in the Contact Situation: Jigalong, Western Australia. In: R.M. Berndt (ed), *Australian Aboriginal Anthropology,* Perth, University of Western Australia Press, pp. 277- 91.

Turner, D.H. (1978) *Dialectics in Tradition.* London, Royal Anthropological Institute of Great Britain and Ireland. (Occasional Paper No. 36).

Wilson, J. (1979) The Pilbara Aboriginal social movement: an outline of its background and significance. In: R. & C. Berndt (eds), *Aborigines of the West.* Perth, University of Western Australia Press.

10

LAND AND A FRINGE-DWELLING COMMUNITY: A CASE STUDY FROM WESTERN AUSTRALIA

Hans Dagmar

In spite of justifiable and deep-seated pessimism about relations between Aborigines and white Australians (cf. Tatz 1979:1–5), the provision of land rights for Aboriginal groups is a significant event in this conflict-ridden relationship. It reflects a growing recognition in certain circles that Aborigines should be free to choose their own life-style, to retain their own cultural identity, and that in order to do so some form of territorial autonomy is required.

As the relationships of Aboriginal groups to land vary, particularly as a result of the differentiation of Aboriginal society under the impact of colonisation, so do the background and nature of claims to land and the government instrumentalities to deal with them. Thus, for instance, land claims granted under the *Aboriginal Land Rights (Northern Territory) Act* to large traditionally orientated groups differ from the control of land acquired by a fringe-dwelling group through the purchase of land by the Aboriginal Land Fund Commission.

It is against the background of this wide range of different needs for and purposes of control of land that I discuss the problems encountered by fringe-dwelling Aborigines in the Gascoyne district[1] of Western Australia to acquire land of their own.

THE SETTING

In the Gascoyne district approximately one-fifth of the total population of 7500 consists of people of Aboriginal descent. The people with whom I am mainly concerned here—because they have shown interest in acquiring land of their own—are the ones in whose lives the pastoral stations of the region still play a predominant role. Most of them live on the Aboriginal reserve in the town of Carnarvon, while a smaller number reside in fringe camps in other areas of town, and on pastoral stations. During the past four or five years a few have acquired a house in the built-up area of the town. This group consists of approximately 400 people, and when in the course of this paper I speak of Aborigines of the Gascoyne, or fringe-dwellers, I mean those with an orientation to the pastoral state and not to all people of Aboriginal descent in the area.

The relations between Aborigines and pastoral stations date back a long way. Some 20 years after the country along the Gascoyne River was explored by F.T. Gregory in 1858, sheep stations were established in the district. Soon these stations occupied all the available land in the district and fundamentally disturbed the Aboriginal way of life. In 1905 the Roth Royal Commission found that Aborigines were forbidden to camp near waterholes and other sources of freshwater because they disturbed the flocks (Biskup, 1973:61). In the 1920s attempts were made to create an Aboriginal reserve some 160 kilometres from Carnarvon. The reserve did not have the purpose of enabling Aborigines to live in their accustomed manner, but as a place where 'a native can be ordered to go if he should prove an annoyance on any part of a sheep run' (Department of the North-West, file 256/24). Even though the proposed reserve was only to be a small one, there was much opposition to it on the part of pastoralists, and the plan was finally abandoned (Dagmar, 1978a:129).

The history of relations between Aborigines and whites in the Gascoyne shows an almost feudal control of Aborigines by the station owners and managers in the district. Anyone interfering with this control met with fierce opposition. Thus when in the 1880s the missionary Gribble tried to establish a mission in the Gascoyne district and spoke up about the maltreatment of Aborigines by the pastoralists, he was threatened with physical force and eventually had to leave the district (Hunt, 1978).

In understanding the present situation of the fringe-dwelling Aborigines in Carnarvon, it is hard to exaggerate the influence pastoral stations have had on their lives. As I have described more fully elsewhere (Dagmar, 1979b:79–84), Aborigines who grew up on a pastoral station form a distinct group with sociocultural characteristics of their own. As such, they are clearly distinguishable from those who grew up in a town environment, most of whom are of part-Aboriginal descent, live in conventional houses, and have jobs in town.

One important characteristic of the fringe-dwellers is that the majority of male wage-earners still work in the bush on sheep and cattle stations. When in 1972 and 1973 I interviewed men about their job preferences most of them said they preferred work on a station. Asked about the reason for this choice, many had difficulty in pointing out specific causes. It was as though to them their choice needed no explanation, and when pressed for an answer they often replied that they had lived in the bush all their lives and that they had never known any other work but that on the station. When any explanation other than force of habit was given, men said that work in the bush kept them away from drink, and thus out of trouble.

Station work, however, is increasingly difficult to find. On the approximately 60 sheep stations in the Gascoyne only some 40 men have a more or less permanent job, while the majority of the roughly 120 potential station employees can find only temporary work, sometimes for not more than a few months per year. As the pastoralists prefer to employ men they know, young men in particular find it hard to get a job. Most men do not want a job in town, but even if they did they would have great difficulty in finding one. Not only are there many forms of subtle, and sometimes even unconscious, discrimination on the part of employers, but basically the jobs are just not available. There is little likelihood that this situation will change in the foreseeable future, and unemployment will remain high among the fringe-dwelling men. Many now rely on unemployment benefits for part of their income. Also, during the last two or three years a number of men have found temporary work on stations under the National Employment and Training Scheme (NEATS), through which the Commonwealth Government pays part of a worker's wage.

Although the men still work in the bush family life revolves around the town. This typical pattern of men earning a living in the bush while wives, children and age pensioners stay behind in town, is an important background factor in the social problems and disorganisation of the fringe-dwellers' community. I return to this point later.

It is hard to say exactly when the movement of Aboriginal families from the stations into the town started. According to popular notion, introduction of the compulsory payment of award wages to Aboriginal workers in 1967 set off the large-scale movement of Aborigines into town. Station owners in particular give this explanation. They emphasise that the implementation of this rule was detrimental to Aboriginal welfare as it meant that pastoralists could no longer afford to keep the families of Aboriginal workers on the stations. I doubt this explanation. There are indications that the movement into town started well before the late 1960s, and that it was a gradual rather than a sudden change. Already in the 1940s and 1950s the number of men permanently working on stations had dropped considerably. Thus, in 1957 on 34 sheep stations in the Gascoyne district only 91 adults and 31 children were more or less permanent residents. Judging by the total number of Aborigines in the district, at that time a considerable number of men must have been in temporary employment already. Moreover, the concern of pastoralists with Aboriginal welfare gains a strange perspective if we consider that during the 1950s and 1960s 'keep' provided for Aboriginal workers and their families consisted of free meat only.

More important than the time of movement into the town, however, are the social backgrounds and consequences of this movement. Examination of these backgrounds shows that loosening ties with their tribal countries was the price that Aborigines had to pay for becoming less dependent on the station owners. When Aborigines gave up residence on their land it was not only accompanied by disintegration of Aboriginal culture, but created a stronger bargaining position for Aborigines on the labour market, and consequently better working conditions on the stations. If one looks at the total Aboriginal population of Carnarvon today it is clear that those who—for whatever reason—have broken away from the pastoral stations are by and large much more successful in white Australian terms (e.g., income, housing, education) than the ones who are still tied to station life.

Significant also in the fringe-dwelling group, with its strong association with the pastoral stations, is that the influence of traditional Aboriginal culture is still relatively strong. In considering the importance of their land rights claims, this certainly is a factor to be taken into account. Elsewhere (Dagmar, 1978b:61–77) I have dealt extensively with the role of Aboriginal traditional culture in Carnarvon and here I only point out some of the crucial aspects.

Culturally the fringe-dwellers form a very heterogeneous group. As we see in other areas (cf. Kolig, 1973:12–14), the largest group in Carnarvon is one whose home territory is not in the immediate vicinity of Carnarvon. The group concerned are the Wadjari-speaking people whose large country occupies the upper Gascoyne and upper Murchison areas. Another relatively large group are the Ingada speakers, who lived in the country south of the lower part of the Gascoyne River. All in all, the fringe-dwellers comprise representatives of some dozen language groups and the older members of these groups still have a very definite conception of the boundaries of 'their' land.

Although people generally speak English, much of their conversation is interwoven with Aboriginal words and sentences, and old people prefer to converse in their own language. Even young children still use Aboriginal kinship terms. The traditional kinship system of intermarrying sections has almost completely broken down, even though people still remember the names of the sections and a considerable number of adults know what section they belong to. Belief in 'mabarn' (magic) is still widespread and people seek cures from 'mabarn men' and 'bush medicine'.

There is however, an increasing gap between the generations in knowledge of traditional culture and much traditional knowledge and meaning is no longer passed on from the old to the young. In 1980, for instance, no young men were sent away to be initiated, nor did a group of representatives from Carnarvon attend initiation ceremonies in the Ashburton district as they have done during all of the 1970s. A partial explanation for this is that all major manifestations of Aboriginal traditions take place in areas far away from Carnarvon where they only have an impact on the relatively small group of faithful Law followers. Attending a meeting also requires much organisation and preparation (transport, food, etc). This may not present a big obstacle in areas where the Law is strong, but it certainly does in areas where only a small group of people are actively involved in a struggle to keep the Law alive.

Thus, partly the motive behind the request of the Carnarvon people to get back some of their land is a wish to have their own Law ground so that they can carry out their own initiations. This would make it easier for the local people to attend and Carnarvon people could at last 'pay back' the groups in the Pilbara region who during the last decade have been their hosts at ceremonies. It should be emphasised, however, that strengthening of the Law is by no means the sole reason for the fringe-dwellers' interest in getting land. Right from the time when I first learnt of their desire to have land of their own, people were basically interested in getting away from the town, in living without outside interference, in giving a new significance to family and intergenerational relations.

Since the early 1970s, many basic features of the fringe-dwellers life have not changed much: they still suffer high rates of unemployment, have a very low income, live in substandard housing (although in this field some slow progress has been made), and have considerable drinking problems and relatively poor health. What has changed, however, is that the already weak internal cohesion and organisation of the group is increasingly breaking down. This is particularly evident in the reserve community, which can truly be seen as the core of the fringe-dwelling group.

In the early 1970s the reserve community still managed to present a face of community spirit despite the many social problems. At that time, for instance, regular 'courts' were held by the reserve group to discuss and punish transgression of the rules by its members. This included things like 'relations' sleeping together, creating a disturbance when drunk, fighting, etc. Core members of the 'court' were 'the Committee', a group of elderly men and women. They felt responsible for the quality of life on the reserve and were always actively involved in settling disputes and ending fights. From their midst they chose a man of physical strength as 'caretaker' of the reserve, giving him special responsibilities to end fights and keep drunkards in order.

Aboriginal Law played a role in getting people together for a common purpose. All male Committee members were Law men and they organised the men's meetings to discuss which *malulu* (young men to be initiated) they were going to send up to the Pilbara meeting. They also made sure that people had supplies of food ready when it was time to travel up to the initiation meetings; they organised dances and ceremonial mournings, and took care of fund-raising through games of cards. Even though not everybody participated in all of these activities, they still gave life on the reserve a distinct quality and were an influence in the lives of even nonparticipants.

Perhaps one of the most important achievements of the Committee was the establishment of the so-called 'Koorda Club', an organisation which aimed at the promotion of self-help among the reserve group. The club acquired an old truck which was used for such things as rubbish collection, carting of firewood and transporting people to tribal meeting grounds in the Pilbara district.

Now, in 1980, hardly a trace of these activities is left. Partly this is a consequence of the death of a number of leading Committee members, including the truly charismatic leader Bob Williams. More fundamental, in my opinion, has been the constant pressure of government agencies on Aborigines to assimilate, and their failure to understand the separate cultural identity of a section of the Aboriginal community of Carnarvon. Having closely followed the development of the Aboriginal community during the last decade, I have seen clearly that there was absolutely no reward attached to the expression of a separate Aboriginal identity. Government help, both financial and in the field of guidance, has not truly benefited those whom, for lack of a better word, I will call the least assimilated. The State Housing Commission Policy is unequivocally assimilative in Carnarvon interspersing Aboriginal families among those of white Australians. Consequently, those Aboriginal families whom the white officers of the Commission judge to be least offensive to their prospective white neighbours are given houses, and they are expected to live in a house according to white standards. This has meant removal from the reserve of a stable element of the population. Thus most of the former Koorda Committee members have by now left the reserve. Interestingly, among the people who have moved into town from the reserve (or directly from a station) we find many who have expressed an interest in regaining Aboriginal land and living on that land. Some of them are Law men and their movement into town does not really reflect a desire to become like white Australians but merely a dissatisfaction with reserve life.

The Koorda Club, which as I have explained earlier, was initially truly an organisation of the reserve people, has also had to succumb to assimilative pressure. After 1973 a process started in which members of the strongly assimilated town group became increasingly involved in its activities (Gray, 1978:147–57; Dagmar, 1978b:99). In 1974 the Koorda Club became a general local organisation with the purpose of furthering the welfare interests of all people of Aboriginal descent. There is no doubt that government officials have encouraged this development (cf. Gray, 1978:152). Since that time the Koorda Club has had considerable government funds for various projects but has become of peripheral importance in the lives of fringe-dwellers. All the projects which the Club has undertaken were town-based activities in which fringe-dwelling men did not participate, orientated as they are to work in the bush. The influx of government funds, necessitating administrative skills, together with the Club's concentration on projects which did not fit their skills and interests, made it increasingly impossible for the reserve people and others of the fringe-dwelling group to play a significant role in the Club. Moreover, well paid positions, like those of Aboriginal liaison and field officers in the spheres of welfare and legal aid, are also outside their reach as most of them are completely or practically illiterate.

Considering how the fringe-dwellers have fared in a town environment so far, it seems unlikely that their problems will soon be solved. A new policy is necessary, basing itself on Aboriginal skills and affinities and thus strengthening Aboriginal self-confidence. In this respect land rights seems the most promising policy, although the Gascoyne Aborigines have fared poorly in their attempts to secure land.

A RECORD OF UNSUCCESSFUL LAND CLAIMS

With a keen perception of the importance of the land issue, the beloved leader of the Gascoyne Aborigines, Bob Williams, already in 1971 said: 'We want land in the country for meeting places and holidays and working, and showing the young people the old ways.' Aboriginal hopes for a new deal and overdue understanding of their plight were raised by regular visits from officers of various government departments who brought a, till then unheard of, message that the Government was interested to know what the Aborigines wanted. Partly also in an effort to facilitate their work and to raise Aboriginal interest in their visits, these officers impressed upon the people that they could only do their work properly if Aborigines came forward and told them all about their wishes for and ideas about improvement of their present living conditions. In May 1972 a representative from the Office of Aboriginal Affairs said to a meeting of the Koorda Club: 'We want to hear from the Aborigines what they want; for instance, do you want a station, or a place on the coast for holidays, or do you want to live in houses at all?'

Clearly, a sheep station was what people wanted, and there was much talk about it both at informal gatherings and at official Koorda Club meetings. But people did not just talk, they also looked around for suitable properties, and finally settled for Mooloo Downs Station. In September 1972 Bob Williams asked the Federal Office for Aboriginal Affairs to acquire this property for them. Two months later the Minister for Aboriginal Affairs replied that this station had been sold, but he added: 'Should at any time the Koorda Committee locate another property which is on the market and in which the Committee is interested, please do not hesitate to write me again.' Although the people were disappointed, this did not stop them from getting to work again.

Four months later, in May 1973, another application was made out, this time for Minilya Station. Hearing that this property was on the market, the reserve people arranged meetings and many young people attended, which did not happen often. They had become interested in the old people's attempts to get a piece of their own land back, and expressed support. This was really important for the Committee as they felt that the young people were drifting away from them. The young people on their part looked upon the older generation as people whose knowledge had become irrelevant to modern living and who were no longer in control of Aboriginal life.

During those months there was an atmosphere of hope and expectation on the reserve as the people felt that a place which had such a long association with Aborigines in the district might now become theirs. They looked forward to working a station owned by their own company where they could train their young fellows, where old people could live, and where schoolchildren could spend their holidays. As I later wrote about this period: 'Never during my stay did I see such a keen interest in a project aimed at promoting Aboriginal welfare. Certainly this was not based on material considerations, for the financial prospects of this undertaking were not even considered, and if they were, one realised that they would not be great. Instead it was the life in the bush that formed the main attraction: being close to the land, animals and plants that one knew and loved, away from the troubles of the town, hoping for a new meaningful relation between generations and families, making out themselves what was important in life and what not.'

Six months after they had put in their application they were informed by the Director of the Department of Aboriginal Affairs (DAA) that Minilya had been sold. Eighteen months later, in April 1975, after unsuccessful talks with station owners about letting them have a small piece of land to use as a meeting ground for initiation and other ceremonies, the Aborigines of Carnarvon asked for Mount Phillip Station. They put a lot of work into this, as they did with earlier applications, documenting the significance of this land to their Aboriginal traditions, mapping historical/mythological places and setting out their proposed use of the station. In May 1975 they received a reply that no action could be taken until the Aboriginal Land Fund Commission (ALFC) was established. During that same month it was decided at a meeting of the Koorda Club that they should apply for both Mount Phillip and Gifford Creek stations which, as adjoining properties, had more chance of being run on an economically viable basis together. Again they put in a lot of work, gathering the information the DAA required before they would consider buying. In August 1975 the DAA regional officer told them he would prepare a submission and send it off to the ALFC.

In February 1976 the people were informed the DAA would send out an expert to value and advise on Mount Phillip only. A month later they received news that Mount Phillip had been sold. Then, in April 1976, DAA asked the Aboriginal people what they thought of Gifford Creek. That same month Gifford Creek was valued and in September they were informed by DAA that the station was 'badly run down' but that 'a proposal for an alternative, better developed and maintained property will be fully considered' by the Minister. That Gifford Creek was run down was, in fact, well known among the Aborigines. They had notified DAA of this in their application for Mount Phillip and Gifford Creek together.

The interest in getting their own land remained very strong and during the next year another property with which the Gascoyne people had had a long-standing relationship was discussed. At that time the Aboriginal community had gained the services of a DAA community adviser and they asked him to make a submission for

Mount Augustus Station on their behalf to the ALFC. In June 1978 an application for this station was sent out from the regional office of DAA in Geraldton but, for some unknown reason, this application never reached the ALFC. It was not until May 1979 that the DAA community adviser again sent off an application for Mount Augustus to the ALFC with 30 signatures on it. In January 1980 they were informed that Mount Augustus station had probably been sold and that the ALFC was unable to find out whether this sale was definite or not.

A FAILURE OF ABORIGINAL ADMINISTRATION

The long struggle of Aborigines in the Gascoyne area to realise something of an independent position apparently has not met with any success. It is hard to underestimate the effects of this on the people's morale. If the aim of government policy is to 'develop Aboriginal self-sufficiency and help Aboriginals enhance their dignity, self-respect and self-reliance', the case history given above does not stand out as an example of a successful method to achieve this aim.

The basic obstacle to acquisition of land for the Gascoyne people has been the failure to set up an adequate administration of Aboriginal Affairs. In spite of good ideas and promising political programmes conceived by a small group of well informed and dedicated experts, the Federal and State governments have great difficulty in translating these programmes into action or, as in the case of Western Australia, are simply unwilling to follow a promising course of action. Seen from this perspective, it is not without significance, I think, that Western Australia lacks an adequate government organisation to deal with the problems of its Aboriginal population.

In 1972 the Western Australian Government put an end to the existence of a special department dealing with Aboriginal welfare. Presented as a progressive, enlightened piece of legislation, the integration of welfare and other services for Aborigines with those of other Australians did not really serve the cause of all those of Aboriginal descent, denying as it did the separate identity of some Aboriginal groups. The aim of this policy was purely one of assimilation, neglecting the special problems and needs of the Aboriginal people. It presented a false image of a harmony between Aboriginal and white Australian interests where there was more often conflict.

Certainly, it cannot be said that the Western Australian Native Welfare Department, which was dissolved in 1972, was always a champion of Aboriginal interests, but provided it was given a proper charter, a separate 'Aborigines Department' could have been a strong force in the Aboriginal fight for self-determination. The Aboriginal Affairs Planning Authority (AAPA), established in 1972 to promote the economic and social development of the Aboriginal people, was far too centralised and weak to serve its purpose. Carnarvon, for instance, did not have an officer of this organisation but was visited every now and then from a town 500 kilometres to the south.

Thus, socioeconomic and cultural problems of Aborigines in Carnarvon were primarily dealt with by officers of the local branch of the Department for Community Welfare, which invariably meant that these problems were reduced to their individual levels such as intramarital tensions, neglect of children, economic hardship, etc. That these officers were primarily working on the symptoms of Aboriginal problems was borne out by the fact that they spent much of their time working on court cases against Aboriginal children and adults and appearing in the Local Court of Petty Sessions on their behalf. Basically the Community Welfare officers were waiting for clients to turn up and they most certainly did not constitute an active force in working on a solution to Aboriginal problems at a more structural level.

Community projects, such as the acquisition of land, were left to the AAPA officer, and since 1977 to the lone community adviser of the Federal Department of Aboriginal Affairs who was posted in the town. It is unnecessary to discuss their individual roles in Aboriginal attempts to get land. What is important, however, is to stress the absense of a stable and well organised government body that could assist an increasingly disinterested and socially disorganised people in regaining a sense of direction and purpose in life.

Ever since the Aborigines of Carnarvon first expressed an interest in land the various government bodies have left it to the Aborigines themselves to find a suitable pastoral property for sale and to document the background, purposes and ramifications of their claim. This they have always done remarkably well and quickly, but they have never succeeded in beating the fumbling machinery of government. Nearly all their attempts to get land have failed because the sheep station that they had chosen was sold long before government authorities had completed their bureaucratic procedures.

It is important to note here that never during the past eight years was the land claim of the Gascoyne people refuted on substantial grounds: that is, it was never communicated to them that their claim was not a sound one. From as high as ministerial level they were informed that, unfortunately, the land they had asked for could not be made available as it was sold before acquisition procedures could be initiated, but they were encouraged to keep looking for suitable properties. Now, if this was an indication that government authorities were seriously committed to acquiring land for this group—and I fail to see how else one could interpret the messages that were repeatedly conveyed to the Gascoyne people—they also had the moral obligation to make every possible effort to see these people received their land. Yet, looking back at the period concerned, one is struck by a complete lack of initiative in this matter on the part of government bodies. In spite of the fact that in the Gascoyne district dozens of pastoral properties have been on the market, the Department of Aboriginal Affairs has not been able to acquire one bit of land. This is particularly disappointing in view of the fact that both in 1977-78 and in 1978-79 the Aboriginal Land Fund Commission was unable to spend all the money allotted to it for land purchases.

This plea for a strong and influential organisation dealing with Aboriginal welfare seems to be in conflict with the views of those who argue that welfare agencies increase, rather than end, the problems of ethnic minorities. In a recent paper Howard (1979), for instance, points out the role of the Aboriginal Department in the perpetuation of Aboriginal dependency. The oppressive influence on Aborigines' lives of former organisations like the Western Australian Native Welfare Department, or of any contemporary welfare agency, cannot be denied. However, in the social process which led to the subjugated position of Aboriginal groups, welfare agencies were merely instruments, not causes. There is no logical reason why a well organised Department of Aboriginal Affairs cannot be an instrument in helping Aborigines to achieve greater social and economic independence. Indeed, Aboriginal problems can only be alleviated by a radical improvement in their access to economical and political resources. In the Gascoyne district such a redistribution of resources has been precluded by the absence, rather than the presence, of a strong welfare organisation.

Of particular importance in the proper functioning of a useful welfare organisation are the men and women who help to implement the agency's policies in the field. Others have already pointed out the necessity for a well-trained corps of advisers to Aboriginal communities. Berndt (1966:310), for instance, already in 1966 advocated 'the employment of a skilled liaison-welfare officer with anthropological training to be located at each major development centre.[1] Similarly, Rowley (1978:218) emphasises the need for 'field staff of the highest commitment and competence', while Tonkinson (1978:138) points at the value of 'extremely able and dedicated advisers'. The organisation in which these field officers work must have enough flexibility to allow the

Aboriginal communities and their advisers require a great deal of autonomy in selecting goals and procedures to achieve them. On the other hand, it must be committed to a rigid programme of acquisition of resources. It is for this reason that it needs all the support it can get from a government that, in its policy making, is prepared to proceed from a model of fundamental conflict between Aborigines and those white Australians who now control the country's wealth.

THE CASE FOR LAND: SOME PRACTICAL IMPLICATIONS

Giving Aborigines in the Gascoyne district the control of sheep stations is a policy appropriate to their lifestyle or culture. To many Aboriginal men, life in town is mainly a transitional period while waiting for a job in the bush. Mentally, they are adjusted to life on the sheep stations. This is certainly not only true for older people; young men also prefer station work, although they often explain their choice as a means of getting away from the drinking in the town. Aboriginal men are wavering between two ways of life: on the one hand, life on the stations where they are in an environment they know well and which interests them; on the other, life in town where many are subject to heavy drinking and strained social relations. Still, relatives and friends attract station workers to town, and the biggest drawback of pastoral employment to them does not appear to be the poor wages but the necessity of leaving the Aboriginal community which is now established in the town.

The prolonged absence of men from the town contributes to community disorganisation, particularly since it is the more 'mature' men who find work for the longest periods. Teenagers and young adults are often unemployed for the greater part of the year. Adult men have no stake in town life. They are passers-by who come to town for a short visit during which they are only interested in having a good time and a 'booze-up' with friends. It is significant that the Koorda Club, even when it still flourished on the reserve, has drawn hardly any support from the station workers. None of the costly projects initiated under the Koorda Club's auspices were adapted to the interests of this group.

Much of the disorganisation of family life is also a consequence of the absence of the men. Women are left to raise their children by themselves or, when both husband and wife go to a station, school-age children are left behind with relatives or in a mission hostel. Many children grow up without the guidance of adult Aboriginal men. The men they see most often are those who belong to the hard-core unemployable group or those who come to town as an interlude between station work and have no real interest in town life. If Aborigines had their own sheep stations the structure of their community would be strengthened and a new meaningful relation between the generations could be worked out.

Provision of land would also support Aboriginal culture in another way. Having their own territory, the Carnarvon people would at last be able to open up a tribal meeting ground of their own. As the lives of a considerable number of people would focus on the territory, either permanently or temporarily, the Law might be reinforced through the greater number of people having easy access to the meeting ground. As the Gascoyne people have shown, interest in the Law is still alive and new adaptations to Aboriginal traditions can still be made. In a time when funds are made available for teaching urban children an Aboriginal language and instructing them in traditional customs, it would be anomalous to refuse support to people who, under the most adverse conditions, have managed to retain aspects of traditional Aboriginal culture as a regular influence in their lives.

Revival of traditional culture is not, however, the main reason for granting land rights to these people. Nor, for that matter, is it the basis of interest in land of all the

Aboriginal people here concerned. Just as important are the social and economic backgrounds of such a claim, and with these aspects in view, the granting of control of one sheep station to the Gascoyne people can be seen as only the beginning of a new process of social development of this group. Transfer of the fringe-dwelling population of Carnarvon to one sheep station will not mean the end of their problems. No purpose of self-management can be served by this, as not even the best property in the district could support such a large population other than by external government subsidies. Admittedly, at present the majority of fringe-dwellers are wholly or partly dependent on government subsidies for their income, and no quick change in this situation can be expected. Seen from this perspective, the temporary move of a considerable number of Aborigines to a sheep station will not really make their situation worse. From another point of view, accommodation, there would also be little change, for many fringe-dwellers live in substandard housing in the town. It is for these reasons that the present resistance of the Western Australian Government to the establishment of Aboriginal communities on pastoral properties seems so mistaken. The same Government that has failed to create decent living conditions for Aborigines, both in towns and on pastoral stations owned by white Australians, and that carries a heavy responsibility for Aboriginal social and cultural decay, now refuses to transfer pastoral leases to Aboriginal groups because, it claims, the living conditions on Aboriginal stations are inadequate. But, coming back to my earlier argument, the lumping together of some 300–400 people on one sheep station is unwanted because, in this particular instance, it will not enhance Aboriginal independence for just as I think that the fringe-dwellers are not to be regarded as merely economically deprived people, so I think that their community is not based on a self-sufficient Aboriginal culture. Unlike the Jigalong community, for instance, which through its strong and coherent cultural traditions manages to preserve a certain unity and sense of direction (cf. Tonkinson, 1978), the Carnarvon Aborigines probably could not live a meaningful and organised life without sufficient employment opportunities.

Generally speaking, of course, one may ask if the Aboriginal cultural background accords with this living in large sedentary communities. For example, in the Ashburton district north of the Gascoyne the sheep station acquired by the people of that region as a communal asset is in fact very much a family affair. On the other hand, the Aboriginal community living at Strelley Station near Port Hedland seems to be successful in helping a large number of Aborigines of different language groups to live and work harmoniously together. Be this as it may, it seems unlikely that a pastoral station — if it is to be more than just a residential area — can be run along the same organisational lines as, for instance, a large tribal meeting camp. It is necessary to set up comparative studies of ongoing Aboriginal pastoral concerns to see what makes for the success of one and failure of another. From such studies we can learn which organisational structures will have the best chance of leading to successful communal pastoral enterprises under particular sociocultural and economic conditions.[2]

For the Gascoyne area I would advocate the establishment of a number of sheep stations controlled by small Aboriginal groups. Probably such groups will be formed along family lines. Among the Aborigines there are many experienced station workers holding responsible jobs; some are overseers, others take care of part of a station run single-handedly. It is around these people that new station communities can be formed. The Gascoyne, in this respect, can be an interesting experimental area for a Government that is interested in self-management.

Advocating small groups on stations does not necessarily mean that such groups have to run their stations along exactly the same lines as do the white Australian pastoralists, aiming at maximum profits for the smallest possible group of participants. A major argument in favour of Aboriginal-owned pastoral properties is that Aboriginal life is not dominated by a striving for maximum monetary reward at the expense of others. For this reason it may be expected that Aboriginal stations will offer a congenial existence to a far greater number of people than properties owned by white Australians. In a time when lack of employment opportunities presents increasing problems, this aspect is of great importance.

Thus acquisition of one sheep station for the Gascoyne people can be seen as a good start but not a final aim. If the transfer of land to Aborigines is to be beneficial, it must be done on a large scale. A similar policy has been advocated for the American Indians by Jorgensen (1971:70), who pointed out the 'need for massive funds to develop industries agricultural or otherwise — under the ownership and control of Indians'. Of course, such a policy would be bitterly disputed by white Australian pastoralists who now reap benefits from the former Aboriginal territories. Opposition from this side rings through in the refusal of the Western Australian Minister for Lands to transfer pastoral leases to Aboriginal groups. Again, this emphasises the need for bestowal of greater powers on the Department of Aboriginal Affairs so it can truly defend Aboriginal interests when they conflict with those of white Australians. As others have said before, the Commonwealth Government should use the mandate given to it through the 1967 referendum to make sure that its Aboriginal policies are carried out and made effective in all parts of Australia.

If the financial consequences of my proposals seem high, a few things should be given consideration. First, from the point of view of compensation for the loss of Aboriginal lives, resources and independence, the costs are in effect disproportionately low. Second, in the past years considerable amounts of money have been spent on projects which have not, or have only marginally, benefited the people concerned. Koorda Club projects, for example, have used more than \$100 000. In a period of two years the Shire of Carnarvon has been given a subsidy of \$120 000 to employ Aboriginal men but no permanent employment opportunities have resulted from this scheme. A large part of that subsidy, moreover, was spent on materials used for the construction of objects which did not specifically benefit the Aboriginal community at all. Third, by creating large-scale employment on Aboriginal sheep stations the Government could save large sums of money now paid out in the form of unemployment benefits and 'subsidies' to white-owned pastoral stations through payment by the Government of part of the wages of Aboriginal workers under NEATS.

CONCLUSION

In a search for measures to improve the social, economic and cultural position of a fringe-dwelling group, I have expressed support for a policy giving Aborigines control of their own land. Not only will this be a requittal for the large losses Aborigines have suffered in the past; it will also form a new basis for Aborigines' management of their own affairs and give them a measure of economic independence. To a group that is still, as it were, on the brink of two cultural worlds of meaning, it will also present an opportunity to reassess, without the overwhelming assimilative pressures of life in town, their position in relation to Aboriginal Law. A very important aspect of this policy, I have argued, is that it bases itself on the fringe-dwellers' knowledge, skills and aspirations, offering them an area of competition in which they could really hold their own.

The Australian Government (Department of Aboriginal Affairs, 1979) continually reminds us that its policy allows 'for Aboriginal people to be integrated into the wider Australian society, maintaining their cultural heritage, while at the same time enjoying opportunities for economic social and cultural development which are at least equal to those available to other Australians'. In the Gascoyne district, covering 110 000 square kilometres, Aborigines control not one hectare of land (apart from a few suburban building blocks). Yet, the total Aboriginal population directly dependent on the pastoral properties in the area is bigger than that of the white Australians. Surely, this is not what the Government means by 'at least equal opportunities'.

ACKNOWLEDGEMENTS

The field research on which this paper is based was carried out during various periods between 1972 and 1980. I thank the Australian Institute of Aboriginal Studies, the Netherlands Organization for the Advancement of Pure Research (Z.W.O.), and the Niels Stensen Stichting for their support. I would also like to thank Dr E. ten Raa for his stimulating comments on an earlier draft of this paper.

NOTES

1. The area to which I refer in this paper roughly comprises the local government areas of the Shire of Carnarvon and the Shire of Upper Gascoyne.

2. I certainly do not wish to imply here that the provision of pastoral properties to Aboriginal groups should await the outcome of these studies. On the contrary, research must accompany a rigid programme of land acquisition.

REFERENCES

Berndt, R.M. (1966) The effect of area development on Aboriginal Australians. In: I.G. Sharp & C.M. Tatz (eds), *Aborigines in the Economy. Employment, Wages and Training.* Brisbane, Jacaranda, pp. 304–13.

Biskup, P. (1973) *Not Slaves Not Citizens. The Aboriginal problem in Western Australia 1898–1954.* St Lucia, University of Queensland Press.

Dagmar, H. (1978a) Marginal Australians. A Prelude to Political Involvement. In: M.C. Howard (ed.) *Whitefella Business. Aborigines in Australian politics.* Philadelphia, Institute for the Study of Human Issues, pp. 125–46.

Dagmar, H. (1978b) *Aborigines and Poverty. A study of interethnic relations and culture conflict in a Western Australian town.* Nijmegen, Katholicke Universiteit.

Department of Aboriginal Affairs (1979) The History of Aboriginal Affairs Policies, November 1979 (Background Notes No. 7)

Department of the North West (1924) File No. 256/24.

Gray, D. (1970) *Identity Amongst the Carnarvon Reserve Mob.* MA Thesis, University of Western Australia.

Howard, M. (1979) 'The Perpetuation of Dependency Among Australian Aborigines'. Paper prepared for the Eighth Annual Meeting of the Association for Social Anthropology in Oceania. Clearwater, Florida.

Hunt, S.-J. (1978) *The Gribble Affair: a study of Aboriginal–European labour relations in north-west Australia during the 1880s.* BA (Hons.) Thesis, Murdoch University, Western Australia.

Jorgensen, J.G. (1971) Indians and the Metropolis. In: *The American Indian in Urban Society.* Boston, J.O. Waddell & O.M. Watson, pp. 67–113.

Kolig, E. (1973) Tradition and Emancipation: an Australian Aboriginal version of 'Nativism'. *Western Australian Aboriginal Affairs Planning Authority Newsletter* **1** (6), Suppl.

Rowley, C.D. (1978) *A Matter of Justice.* Canberra, Australian National University Press.

Tatz, C.M. (1979) *Race Politics in Australia: Aborigines, politics and law.* Armidale, University of New England Publishing Unit.

Tonkinson, R. (1978) *The Mardudjara Aborigines. Living the Dream in Australia's desert.* New York, Holt, Rinehart & Winston.

11 LAND RIGHTS LEGISLATION IN QUEENSLAND: THE ISSUE OF HISTORICAL ASSOCIATION

David S. Trigger

The land rights legislation in the Northern Territory grants title to land on the basis of 'traditional ownership'. The traditional owners are identified in an Australian court by a white judge applying a statutory definition which stresses traditional knowledge and association with the land. This paper argues that land rights legislation based on such traditional knowledge and association would be inadequate for Queensland since it would prohibit large sections of the Queensland Aboriginal and Torres Strait Islander population from making claims (see Fig. 1).[1] The Queensland situation requires that any land rights legislation give legal recognition to a continuum of historical associations between people and place. At one end of the continuum there are people with traditional (and therefore also historical) associations with land of the kind catered for under the Northern Territory legislation, while at the other there are people without such traditional associations but with substantive, and often long standing, historical associations with land. People at both end of this continuum need to be able to legitimately claim land under any just legislation.

TRADITIONAL CLAIMS

A substantial proportion of the Queensland Aboriginal population is in a position to claim traditional lands on the basis of the kinds of evidence required by the Northern Territory legislation. That is, local descent groups can be identified as having primary spiritual responsibility for estate areas and rights to their resources. The traditional owners association with the land can be described in terms of genealogical inheritance of ownership (and managership) rights, place (or site) names, resource useage, totemism, mythology, kinship, moiety/section/sub-section/semi-moiety affiliations, etc.

Traditional associations to land (and the traditional claims which are based on them) operate in the case of groups resident on some Aboriginal reserves (e.g., Wujal Wujal, population 263; Lockhart River, population 413; Torres Strait Islands, population 6992; Doomadgee, population 1003), Aboriginal local government shires (Aurukun, population 830; Mornington Island, population 850), in other rural town areas, including some country reserves (e.g., Normanton, population 650; Coen, population 130), and in some urban areas (e.g., Cairns, Townsville, Mt Isa). It is important to note that these are references to groups of people, and only in some cases do the places of residence noted above consist of or contain the groups' traditional lands.[2]

Traditional claims usually involve the notion of a historically continuous association between a group of people and an area of land but they also involve historical discontinuities, given increases and decreases in both the area of land and the membership of groups, as a result of traditional political and demographic processes. Within this general context it is possible to describe three specific categories of historical association between people and place: habitual associations,[3] specific event associations,[3] and biographical associations.

- Habitual associations: places used (or not long ago used) habitually for such purposes as resource obtaining, camping (eating, sleeping), fighting, ritual, etc. The regularity of use may vary from daily use at one point in the seasonal cycle to complete lack of use at another point; and factors other than seasonal considerations (such as inter- and intra- group politics) may have resulted in continued (though not necessarily always regular) usage. As well, totemically significant areas may be said to be in a sense used intellectually in an habitual way.
- Specific event associations: places associated with such specific events as a particular resource attainment (e.g., where a particularly distinctive emu was speared), a particular fight or ceremony, a specifically known-of encounter with totemic powers within the landscape, etc.
- Biographical associations: places associated with particular people and/or events in their lives, e.g., birth, initiation, death and/or where they carried out particular behaviours. Clearly, personal biographies are often critical features of habitual and specific event associations.

From the Aboriginal perspective all three kinds of historical association represent a framework within which the more formal systems of traditional knowledge associate people with land. Through rich oral tradition, historical associations of people with place tie individuals (and their groups) to specific places so that their lives are interpreted with strong reference to the areas within their 'country' that they have habitually lived in and visited for some specific memorable purpose(s). Claims to traditional lands are usually couched within, and justified by, such oral history, quite apart from the formal system of rights to land.

HISTORICAL CLAIMS

A major section of the Queensland Aboriginal population is not in command of such systematic traditional knowledge which associates people with land. The situation varies a great deal in various parts of the state, and in many areas *aspects* of traditional knowledge are maintained in various forms. Such forms include:

- Places which have names in local Aboriginal languages —place names often appear to be maintained when most vocabulary and grammar has ceased to be known. In some cases the names have become accepted and are used within the local European population (as well as at times on official European maps of the area).
- The significance of named (in Aboriginal language or English) and unnamed places may be that a certain resource is obtainable there (e.g., fish), and/or that a place has mythological significance.

However, there are two major differences here from a traditional claim: firstly, whatever aspects of traditional knowledge about land are held will lack the systematic formulation maintained in the traditional situation; secondly, the lack of formal and systematic knowledge associating land with people will be most apparent through lack of genealogical connection of individuals and families (lineages, clans) to specific areas or estates. Such connection may well be between a generalised 'mob', perhaps defined by language, and a generalised 'country' or area in which that language was spoken, but this is different from genealogical inheritance of specific sites and tracts. If such

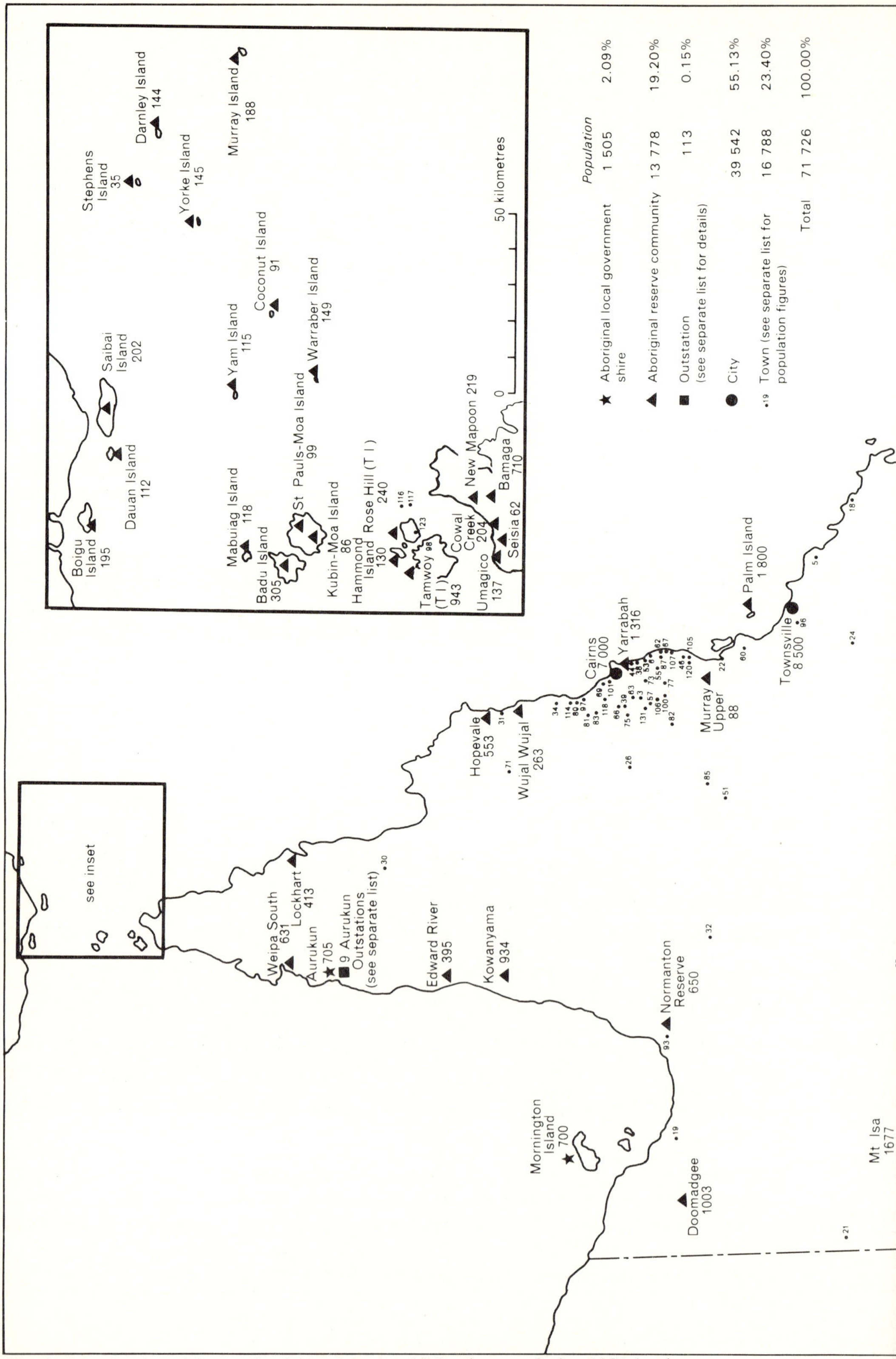

Fig. 1 Distribution of Queensland Aboriginal and Islander population 1981 (major source: DAA *1981 Community Profile Statistical Collection, Newsletter No. 11*).

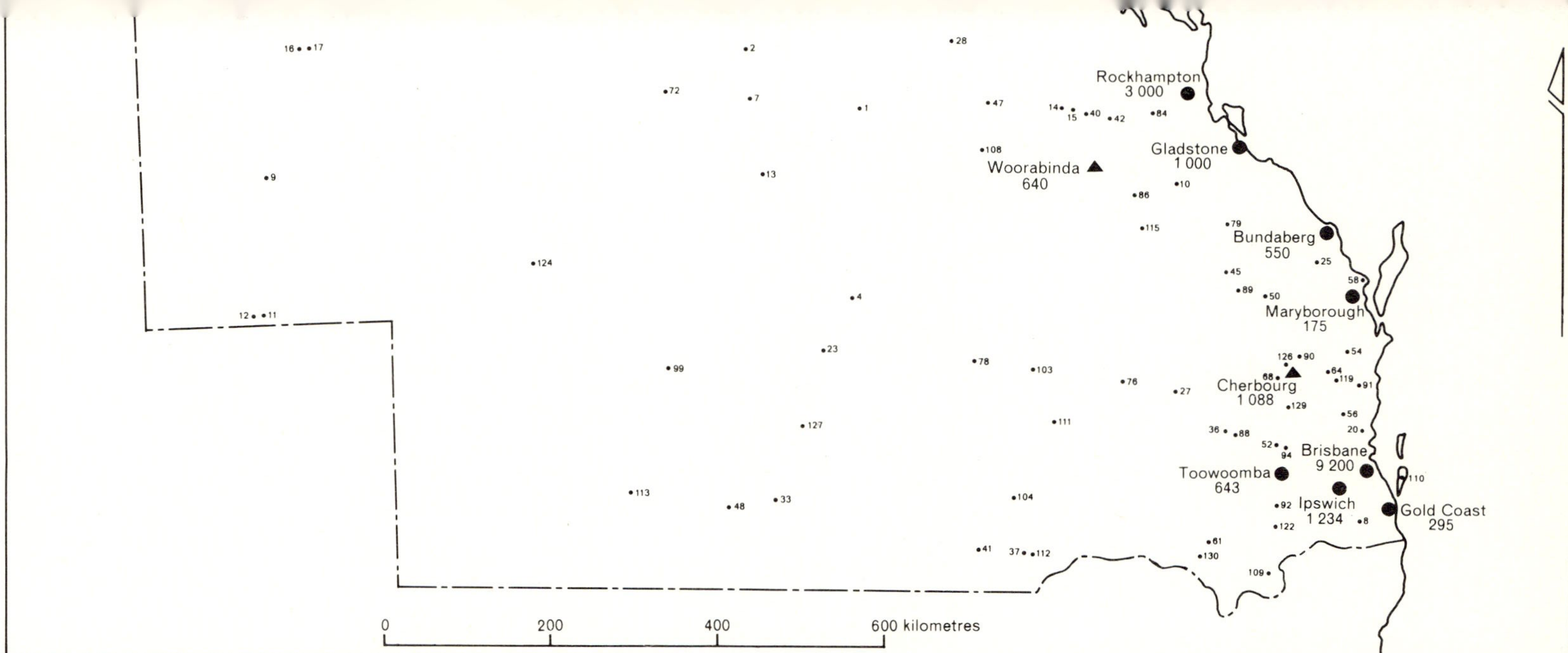

OUTSTATIONS	*Population*
Aurukun-Aayk	14
Aurukun-Dishyard*	
Aurukun-Kencherang	18
Aurukun-Knox River*	
Aurukun-Love River	9
Aurukun-North Kendall	22
Aurukun-South Kendall*	
Aurukun-Ti Tree	25
Aurukun-Wathanin	25

TOWNS

1	Alpha	29
2	Aramac	9
3	Atherton	190
4	Augathella	26
5	Ayr	550
6	Babinda	136
7	Barcaldine	180
8	Beaudesert	
9	Bedourie	12
10	Biloela	68
11	Birdsville	55
12	Birdsville Compound	12
13	Blackall	28
14	Blackwater	36
15	Bluff	37
16	Boulia	157
17	Boulia Reserve	24
18	Bowen	500
19	Burketown	137
20	Caboolture	85
21	Camooweal	153
22	Cardwell	60
23	Charleville	358
24	Charters Towers	500
25	Childers	80
26	Chillagoe	170
27	Chinchilla	53
28	Clermont	32
29	Cloncurry	473
30	Coen	130
31	Cooktown	73
32	Croydon	82
33	Cunnamulla	511
34	Daintree	25
35	Dajarra	175
36	Dalby	107
37	Daymar	33
38	Deeral	200
39	Dimbulah	15
40	Dingo	45
41	Dirranbandi	160
42	Duaringa	74
43	Duchess*	
44	Edmonton	220
45	Eidsvold	280
46	Elarish	38
47	Emerald	60
48	Eulo	25
49	Far Beach Fringe Camps	47
50	Gayndah	87
51	Georgetown	26
52	Goombungee	35
53	Gordonvale	320
54	Gympie	87
55	Happy Valley	15
56	Harlin	4
57	Herberton	70
58	Hervey Bay	200
59	Hughenden	200
60	Ingham	350
61	Inglewood	19
62	Innisfail	1000
63	Innot Hot Springs	22
64	Jimna	14
65	Julia Creek	53
66	Kairi	8
67	Kennedy	95
68	Kingaroy	15
69	Kuranda/Mantaka/Oak Forest/	
70	Kowrowra/Koah	600
71	Laura	66
72	Longreach	91
73	Malanda	52
74	Malbon	32
75	Mareeba	600
76	Miles Incl. Drillham	38
77	Millaa Millaa	8
78	Mitchell	137
79	Monto/Mulgildie	28
80	Mossman	600
81	Mount Carbine/Maryfarms	9
82	Mount Garnet	160
83	Mount Malloy	10
84	Mount Morgan	500
85	Mount Surprise	4
86	Moura	32
87	Mourilyan	40
88	Mount Tyson	31
89	Mundubbera	32
90	Murgon	120
91	Nambour	86
92	Nobby	27
93	Normanton	650
94	Oakey	40
95	Orana Park Reserve	58
96	Pioneer River	18
97	Port Douglas	30
98	Prince of Wales Island	30
99	Quilpie	91
100	Ravenshoe	130
101	Redlynch	50
102	Richmond	80
103	Roma	203
104	Saint George	202
105	Silkwood	80
106	Silver Valley	8
107	South Johnstone	40
108	Springsure	26
109	Stanthorpe	18
110	Stradbroke Island	250
111	Surat	29
112	Thallon	11
113	Thargomindah	33
114	The Gorge (Mossman)	130
115	Theodore	116
116	Thursday Island (East)	580
117	Thursday Island (West)	415
118	Tolga	61
119	Toogoolawah	5
120	Tully	360
121	Urandangi	30
122	Warwick	71
123	Wasaga Township Is.	70
124	Windorah	51
125	Winton	90
126	Wondai	53
127	Wyandra	20
128	Yalambee Reserve* (Mount Isa)	135
129	Yarraman	7
130	Yelarbon	24
131	Yungaburra	30

*Nil population time of survey.

generalised populations represent descent groups they are not 'local' in the sense in which the term has mostly been interpreted for traditional claims.

In fact, the main kind of knowledge associating land and people here may be subsumed under the term 'historical'. So as to impose some order on the vast variability across the state, two major kinds of situation are considered. Current residence is the key used in defining the types. On the one hand, there are populations currently resident within the region traditionally inhabited by earlier generations, and, on the other hand, there are those that are not.

In the case of the former there are substantial Aboriginal populations living within the region of their traditional estates, whose associations with the land consist of historically continuous residence there over generations, and the current living generations' knowledge of that residence. The knowledge invariably includes associations with places marking their distinctiveness, and no doubt major categories of such distinctiveness are the three kinds stated for traditional claims. However, as well as (or in many cases instead of) traditional historical factors, post-European invasion or 'contact' factors are important. For example, habitual associations include occupational-cum-residential involvement with such ongoing European-directed industries and activities as pastoralism, commercial fishing, mining, missionising, etc. Specific event associations include such features of 'contact' as places where violence occurred between Aborigines and Europeans (particularly where deaths resulted on either side), and biographical associations include the biographies of non-Aboriginal individuals as well as Aborigines.

The term *region* is used here because the historical associations are to a generalised region rather than to specific discrete genealogically inherited estates. Certainly, parts of the region may be considered 'home' (or perhaps one's parents' and/or grandparents' and/or great-grandparents' 'home') and it is these areas (or blocks within them) which may well be claimed. This kind of historical association (and claim) with land operates in the case of parts of the large populations on some Aboriginal reserves—that is, in the case of groups of people in whose traditional region the reserve they are now resident on was established (e.g., descendants of Yidinji and Kungkanji speakers at Yarrabah). It may also operate in the case of corporate groups and individual families resident outside reserves in rural town settings (e.g., Mareeba, pop. 700; Dajarra, pop. 175; and the Wide Bay-Burnett Region, not including the Cherbourg Reserve, pop. 1515).

Populations currently resident outside the region traditionally inhabited by their earlier generations were largely created by the Queensland Government's statutory power to forcibly remove Aborigines to reserves. This power existed from the passing of the *Aborigines Protection and Restriction of the Sale of Opium Act* in 1897 until the Act was superseded in 1965 by the *Aborigines' and Torres Strait Islander Affairs Act*. Section 9 of the 1897 Act gave power to the Minister 'to cause Aboriginals within any district to be removed to and kept within the limits of any reserve situated in the same or any other district'. Anderson (1981:61-2) describes in some detail the history of removals and its relationship to the gazettal of reserves. Here, it is sufficient to state that substantial numbers of people were removed from their traditionally inhabited region to other regions. Their descendants are mostly now living on (or near) reserves, (e.g., Palm Island, pop. 2088; Woorabinda, pop. 640; Cherbourg, pop. 1088) and within rural towns (e.g. Cloncurry, pop. 473; Cunnamulla, pop. 576). but also in urban areas (e.g. Rockhampton, Brisbane).

Two kinds of historical association are operating in these cases: associations with the traditional region from which populations were removed (or moved voluntarily), and associations with the region populations are currently resident in:

- Historical associations with the traditional region from which populations were removed (or moved voluntarily): The traditional region is known of, although in many cases it may never have been visited. It is known through information passed on by earlier generations, some of whom were resident for part of their lives in the traditional region prior to relocation. For people who have never visited the traditional region aspects of traditional association may be few indeed, if not non-existent, although some cases may be exceptions, particularly where people can visit the traditional area and meet with relatives (close or otherwise) who may have remained there and maintained certain kinds of traditional knowledge (See, for example, Brady et al. (1980) concerning the Palmer River region). The strength of historical association is subject to the same kind of variability.
- Historical associations with the region of current residence. Having lived all or the large part of their lives in their current place of residence, the people have established strong historical associations to that region. Habitual, specific event, and biographical associations operate there. However, the biographies of previous generations may still be associated with the traditional region, where it is known.

Historical associations with both these kinds of region may of course operate together. Which of them is likely to generate most commitment to a land claim would vary. For some groups the current place of residence is 'home', while for others it may represent a distasteful place which individuals and families would gladly leave, especially if they were able to rely on links with relatives who have remained in the traditional region.

CHANGE AND 'TRADITION'

To discuss a continuum of kinds of relationship to land is another way of examining the differing directions in which Aboriginal groups have changed following the impact of European society. Implicit in the discussion has been the notion that certain groups have remained 'more traditional' than others and are thus more able to make a 'traditional claim' to land. Two important points should be noted here.

Firstly, the 'more traditional' groups have by no means remained static. They have invariably adjusted to the European presence by incorporating a range of European material items and some, though notably fewer, aspects of European social and intellectual life. What they have maintained of their traditions includes knowledge of their relationship to the physical environment — its physical habitation, intellectual conceptions of it and the system of social organisation distributed across it. The local groups now physically occupy their lands for varying lengths of time and with varying degrees of intensity, but all maintain as an integral part of their traditions the knowledge of their families' continued occupation of them until the effects of the European presence displaced that occupancy.

Secondly, it must be made clear that those groups which do not hold such knowledge and hence are not in a position to make a traditional claim, are not without *traditions*. To say as much is to suggest that such a group of people is without culture; at best, this notion is usually expressed by white Australians as 'culturally deprived', at worst as 'deculturated'. It confuses the situation least to speak of *change* in a society's knowledge rather than *loss* of knowledge. For *loss* implies some notion of a cultural vacuum, and this description simply does not fit the facts. Aboriginal groups described above as unable to make a 'traditional claim' to land do not lack cultural traditions about their relationship to land; rather, their traditions provide knowledge of associations between people and place which have *changed* in varying ways over the recent period of their societies' contact with European culture. The change was noted above as from the extremely fine-grained pre-contact association between person, group, and features of place to the more general associaton between 'mob' and region in which that 'mob's' language was spoken. In other cases, the fine-grained quality of the people-place association may have been maintained but it is now expressed and spoken of using Aboriginal-English linguistic and conceptual forms that, for example, include much thinking and speaking of the recent history of European invasion of the 'country', but little knowledge of discretely owned clan or lineage waterholes, ceremonial sites, etc. In all cases, it is the knowledge (often perhaps better described as mythologised knowledge) of prior *Aboriginal* occupancy and custodianship of the region over generations which give the 'historical claims' their moral imperative and, incidentally, distinguish them from often intimately held and intensely expressed European claims of historical association with certain areas.

The discussion has been of culturally defined associations with land. Yet it is the issue of 'race' which is seen as of crucial importance in some circles. How, some would ask, can change and continuity in relationships to land among Aboriginal people across Queensland be discussed, without dealing with the fact that considerable numbers of people are of mixed descent? However, despite its centrality to much popular discussion, the concept of 'mixed' as opposed to 'full' descent bears little relevance to the discussion of relationships to land as they operate in Aboriginal societies. It is the fact of sociocultural knowledge and identity rather than 'race' which is important. It suffices to state that since European colonisation Aborigines have interbred with Europeans, Chinese, Indians, Afghans, Papuans, Pacific Islanders, etc., that is, with people of many cultures and of non-Aboriginal descent.[4] People of mixed descent are thus resident in many areas. However, within the schema proposed above, a working definition is that an Aboriginal person is a person of Aboriginal descent (not necessarily 'full descent'), a person who identifies himself or herself as an Aborigine, and who is accepted as such by other Aboriginal individuals and groups.[5]

A further issue which may be raised in objection to the proposals in this paper involve what are termed 'Aboriginal relics'. It is often claimed that land rights legislation is unnecessary in Queensland as 'Aboriginal relics' are protected and preserved under the State's *Aboriginal Relics Preservation Act* 1967–1976. Elsewhere (Trigger, 1981), I have discussed the Relics Act and focused on inadequacies of the intellectual models in terms of which it is constituted and the social context in which it is administered. Three points only need be made here. Rather than try to make the same statement in different words, the first point is best quoted from my paper on the Relics Act (Trigger, 1981):

> . . . the Act ignores completely sites or areas perceived as significant by Aboriginal people but which do not exhibit physically observable features of man-environment interaction: e.g. named and unnamed places seen as distinctive due to mythological (in some cases secret and/or sacred) associations, historical associations, particular kinds of resources there, etc. In avoiding the way Aboriginal people *themselves* understand their historical relationship to their physical environment, and to so-called Aboriginal relics . . ., the Act avoids completely the broad Land Rights issues.

The second related point is that power to take steps to protect relics, for example through declaration of "Aboriginal sites" in the areas containing the relics, rests solely with the Minister for Aboriginal and Islanders Advancement, and the Minister has not shown himself keen to declare Aboriginal sites. To take the south-east Queensland region as an example, of a minimum of some 500–700 relics officially known of (primarily in the Moreton Bay and Wide Bay–Burnett regions) by the Archaeology Branch of the Department of Aboriginal and Islanders Advancement, three small areas have been declared as Aboriginal sites. In other regions, further sites (including a few larger areas) have been declared, bringing the total for Queensland to nine.

The third point is that under the Relics Act rights of ownership and access with respect to relics is controlled by the state, *not* Aboriginal people whether local to the area where the relic(s) is located or otherwise. The Relics Act is concerned with the meaning which relics have for European society, *not* Aboriginal society.

The final issue which may be raised in objection is that the schema is impractical in the case of the large urban-dwelling populations. Particularly in northern parts of the State, sections of these urban-based populations are in a position to make a traditional claim on the basis of traditional associations with their traditional land located outside of the town; indeed in some cases, their position in the town is more in the nature of temporary dwellers on the periphery of urban society than permanent urban residents. In other cases populations will maintain historical associations with land in one of the ways outlined in the previous section. Urban dwellers do not provide any problems in relation to the schema that has been proposed. However, one further point requires comment.

In some cases, people with primary historical association with a region (usually a reserve earlier generations in their family were removed or moved voluntarily to) have moved away, often to urban areas. Movements from Cherbourg to Brisbane (and other towns on the south-east Queensland coast), from Palm Island to Townsville and from Yarrabah to Cairns are good examples. In a sense, these people are 'twice removed' from the traditional region. Land associations for such populations (and for those which may have moved, or been forcibly moved, any number of times) may still be traced back to the initial area their families were moved to (e.g., Cherbourg in the case of some people currently resident in Brisbane). That place is still 'home'. On the other hand, some may claim primary association to their current urban residence. This raises the more general issue of the areas of land available for claim on the basis of the various kinds of association outlined in this paper.

CLAIMABLE AREAS

The most clear cut areas are the Reserves, including the substantial number of country reserves which are located on the outskirts of towns.[6] While most inhabitants of most of the major northern Reserves are in a position to make traditional claims, claims to some parts of several major northern reserves, most of the major southern reserves, and a majority of the country reserves throughout the State would be on the basis of the several kinds of historical association outlined in this paper. Granting of title to reserves would affect a substantial proportion of the Aboriginal population of Queensland.[7]

However, there are some traditional claims, and many more historical claims, which would be to areas other than reserves. In the Northern Territory such areas are often unalienated Crown Land and hence claimable under the *Aboriginal Land Rights (NT) Act* however in Queensland there is very little unalienated Crown land (see Anderson, 1981). The areas outside of reserves in Queensland are invariably some form of leasehold or freehold blocks, sometimes in an urban setting. While it is unlikely that traditional claims would be made to urban areas, historical claims may be, from the situation of the 'twice (or more) removed' urban dwellers referred to above as well as by families which have lived in urban—often rural town—areas for longer periods of time. A mechanism to deal with claims to such areas exists in the form of the Aboriginal Development Commission (ADC), which is empowered to acquire non-reserve land on behalf of Aboriginal populations on the grounds of traditional association and/or what has been termed 'need' (Woodward, 1974). Using the terms of reference in this paper, grounds for land acquisition by the ADC can be said to include historical association. While the concept of economic and sociocultural need may certainly be subsumed within the broader concept of historical association, it should be clear that historical association to land represents more than a relationship to that land whereby obtaining of legal title to it results in the satisfaction, partial or otherwise, or needs. At least, such claims are made not only because people have needs for firm title to land and for the associated increased potential for corporate and individual economic viability, but also because of the moral imperative stemming from occupation far pre-dating the current European title.

The fact that the attempts by the Commonwealth Government (in the form of the now non-existent Aboriginal Land Fund Commission) to acquire land for Aborigines in Queensland have been severely curtailed by the Queensland Government (see Rigsby, 1980) leads to some concluding remarks.

CONCLUSION

The main point of this paper is to consider Aboriginal historical associations to land as the basis for historical claims to land. The role of historical association in traditional claims has been outlined. The final point is that I have avoided stating any argument as to why Aboriginal people in Queensland should attain land rights at all, while acutely aware that such an argument is necessary in the current political climate. Rather, the paper attempts to establish that the concept of land rights is not solely workable in terms of 'traditionality', and that return of land to Aboriginal populations can be understood in a context that accounts for the dynamic features of Aboriginal societies. As Aboriginal societies have changed over time a land base has continued to be of great importance. In itself, land rights legislation in Queensland will not necessarily lead to the end of problems for Aborigines or to good race-relations, but if it is broad enough in its understanding, legislation can provide good foundations.

NOTES

1. I set aside the question of whether the Northern Territory legislation definition of 'traditional owner' is adequate. Throughout this article the term 'Aboriginal' should be understood to include reference to Torres Strait Islands people as well.

2. Population figures are given here (and below) as a general indication of numbers of people potentially involved in claims in the example areas. The figures come from a range of sources; recent figures are available for some areas only, and all figures should be interpreted as somewhat low.

3. A.K. Chase and J. von Sturmer have previously suggested these two notions as means of recording traditional historical information in their unpublished 'Anthropological site survey field data book'.

4. Contacts with Papuans in the far north of the State involving interbreeding, may have been occurring for very many generations prior to European arrival.

5. This is very close to the definition currently used by the Commonwealth Government.

6. See Anderson (1981) for a list of all Aboriginal and country reserves in the State, with approximate Aboriginal populations associated with them.

7. As the Aurukun and Mornington Island reserves have recently been de-gazetted, they constitute something of a special case. Claims to these areas, now shires, would be on the basis of traditional association.

REFERENCES

Anderson, C. (1981). Queensland. In N. Peterson (ed.), *Aboriginal Land Rights: a handbook*. Canberra, Australian Institute of Aboriginal Studies, pp. 53–114.

Brady, D., Anderson, C., & Rigsby, B. (1980). Some of us are still alive: the Palmer River revisited, *AIAS Newsletter*, NS No. 13: 30–35.

Rigsby, B. (1981). Aboriginal people, land rights and wilderness on Cape York Peninsula. *Proceedings of the Royal Society of Queensland, 92* (April).

Trigger, D.S. (1981). Aborigines, anthropologists and the relics issue in Queensland. *Occasional Papers In Anthropology No. 10, Anthropology Museum, University of Queensland, 10.*

Woodward, A.E. (1974). *Aboriginal Land Rights Commission: second report.* Canberra, Australian Government Publishing Service.

12

OWNERSHIP OF LAND IN THE TORRES STRAIT ISLANDS

Jeremy Beckett

The Torres Strait Islanders have received little consideration in the debate over indigenous land rights in Australia. This is partly because Europeans, Aborigines, and the Islanders themselves have all tended to emphasise their cultural distinctiveness, and partly because the issue has never become critical. Experiencing little in the way of foreign settlement or forcible displacement, the Islanders have become more confident of their continued occupancy than they should be. Fishing and seabed rights have been of greater concern to them, particularly with the negotiation of the border with Papua-New Guinea, and may well prove the more important in the immediate future, but these raise particular legal problems that go well beyond the scope of the present discussion. Meanwhile, the question of territorial ownership deserves consideration, both in traditional and contemporary terms.

Queensland annexed the Torres Strait Islands by stages, early in the second half of the nineteenth century.[1] Its legislation defines them lying to the north of the latitude 11° South, presumably as far as the border, and they are all Crown land.[2] Some 73, by far the majority, are listed as reserves. The exceptions are clustered round the commercial and administrative centre on Thursday Island, including the airport, a Roman Catholic Mission, a pearl culture station, and a private pastoral lease.

Most of the island reserves are uninhabitable for lack of water, or because they are very small. I estimate that no more than 24 were regularly occupied, even seasonally;[3] but just about all of them were used to gather birds eggs or wild plums *(wongai)*, as bases for fishing expeditions, or staging posts along trade routes; and every one was owned.

In recent years only 13 islands have had permanent settlements. But the removal from islands formerly occupied has been a matter of concentration rather than displacement of population. From the beginning, commercial activity has been concerned with marine produce, mainly pearl shell and trepang. Thus it has required indigenous labour but not the resources on which the traditional economy was based; better to have a pool of cheap labour that could support itself by fishing and gardening when not required on the boats than a proletariat that must be continuously maintained. As for land, the marine industry needed no more than a stretch of beach on which to repair the boats and store the catch. Thursday Island, the site of the region's only commercial and administrative settlement, had been only occasionally used by its traditional owners because of its lack of permanent water.

The evacuation of certain smaller communities was a response to the depopulation of the early years of contact, which left some below the level of viability. Mission Christianity and the growing dependence on the commercial economy also favoured village dwelling in place of the former dispersed pattern of settlement. In the last generation emigration to Thursday Island and the mainland has had the same effect as depopulation in bringing certain communities below the level of viability.

The lack of Commercially exploitable resources on the islands has spared Torres Strait the ordeal of displacement. The protective policy of the Queensland

Government has likewise excluded foreign settlement. Thus the possibility that the authorities might resume control over a reserve scarcely impinges on the people's consciousness. The classification, 'Crown land', means little in practical terms, even if it is known. Islanders have competed for land only with one another, and consequently their conception of ownership remains bound up with notions of traditional rights and community politics. If the authorities are called in to decide a dispute, as they occasionally are, it is as impartial referees, not as final owners. With the emigration of more than half the Torres Strait population from the reserves, the component of community politics has increased over traditional rights. Unable to influence local councils from a distance, some emigrants fear that their rights are being overridden by land-hungry stay-at-homes.

TRADITIONAL FORMS OF OWNERSHIP

Claims to ownership couched in traditional forms are best understood against the background of Torres Strait in the proto-colonial stage. Reports coming to us from the first half of the nineteenth century, particularly the 1840s,[4] suggest a constellation of more or less autonomous communities, each linked with certain of its neighbours, including those on the Papuan and Australian mainlands, by ties of kinship and marriage, trade and ritual collaboration, while separated from others by feuds and traditional enmities. Equipped with heavy ocean-going outrigger canoes, the Islanders were able to exploit the diverse resources of the region as a whole rather than being confined to the more limited micro-environments of their home islands.

The life-style of a particular community must nevertheless be understood primarily in terms of its local resources and its ways of exploiting them. In this respect there was a fair range of variation.[5] The relatively sparse population of the islands off Cape York lived mainly by gathering wild vegetable foods, fishing and hunting turtle and dugong. The people of the small, densely populated Eastern Islands got most of their vegetable food from gardening, and probably spent rather less of their time in search of marine foods. On the tiny sandbanks and coral reefs of the Central Islands the people spent much of their time on the move, and lacking the possibility of either cultivating or gathering vegetable foods, they obtained them in exchange for marine foods and trade goods. Elsewhere, energies were more evenly distributed among planting, gathering, fishing and hunting. Clearly, patterns of economic use varied a good deal throughout the Strait, but the cultural means by which man's relations with his world marine as well as terrestrial, were defined, remained basically uniform.

Islanders identified places both as being owned by living persons or groups, and as the scenes of mythological and legendary events. The heroes of these stories might still be present in the form of natural objects such as rocks or of artefacts such as masks which provided the focus for ritual. But they were, to use Haddon's term, culture heroes rather than world creators. Torres Strait had no cosmology: the origins of life were left largely unexplained while the relationship between the social and the natural order was conceived of in terms of historical accident, rather than the working out of a unitary system. The world view was anthropocentric, with man using whatever practical or magical powers he could put his hand to. In the same way, the human ownership of a place was conceived of as existing prior to, or independently of, the hero's advent. In some narratives men gain possession of a sacred person or object, bringing it back to their place and securing it in a shrine.[6] In other instances, ownership of a 'story place' can be explained in terms of its transmission from generation to generation without any connection, stated or unstated, with the hero.[7]

A distinctive feature of Torres Strait land tenure, when compared with that of Aboriginal Australia, is its recognition of individual ownership. In the Eastern Islands

(Murray, Darnley and Stephen), where most vegetable foods were cultivated and population was dense, all land was or could be individually owned. Elsewhere, most of the land was owned collectively. The system is best understood in the context of the social organisation, which was essentially uniform throughout the region. As befitted a beach-dwelling people, the enduring social groups were defined by reference to a stretch of foreshore. As Haddon showed, the coast of Murray, with its satellite islands, Dauar and Waier, were divided into 22 named sections, each the site of a small village or hamlet.[8] The group associated with this section was a patriclan, its members being the children, real or adopted, of a male member. While having the *right* to live in their section, they might live elsewhere for long periods; but this did not affect their participation in the clan's ritual activities or their placing in the regulation of marriage. A number of adjacent clans were grouped into wider units, mainly apparent in ritual, which the Miriam now call by the English word 'tribe'. The twin communities, Mabuiag and Badu, in western Torres Strait, lacked permanent settlements, but the general principle was the same. Perhaps because of the mobility, the 15 clans were identified by reference to two or three natural species, usually animal.[9] They too were grouped into 'tribes'. Saibai differed in being divided into two widely separated villages; however, each of these was divided into sections belonging to the 10 totemic clans.

Just how big clans were is hard to establish, given the rapid population decline during the early years of contact. If one assessment of the Murray population, 800, is accepted, the 22 clans averaged 36.3 members.[10] If Saibai's population was 600, the mean clan size was 60.[11] Harris has computed the population of Mabuiag as 600, with a mean clan size of 43; and that of Badu at 600, with a mean clan size of 56.[12] There is no obvious explanation for these differences, and the question need not be considered further here.

Returning to the case of Murray Island, it seems that the beach sections were divided into individual residential lots. The owners could choose their heirs but could not pass the land to anyone of another clan. If they lacked heirs their lots reverted to the closest agnates. Back from the foreshore lay the gardens, bamboo groves and grasslands. These were divided into individually owned lots, most belonging to clan members, but some to non-agnatic kin. It was the practice to give a daughter a small piece of land as a dowry, which she might then pass on to her heirs. As a result, the interior of the island was something of a patchwork. The persistence of clan blocks, however, suggests that dowry land was often a stray patch, perhaps inherited from a female ancestor who had bought it as a dowry and recirculated.

In Mabuiag and Badu almost all the land was held undivided in clan blocks, but places of particular value such as wild yam beds and perhaps good gardens were individually owned and transmitted to non-agnates.[13] In Saibai, also, the rare spots that escaped flooding during the north-west monsoon, and artificial garden mounds, were privately owned.

The foregoing account is drawn mainly from the *Reports of the Cambridge Anthropological Expedition*. My own researches of 1958–61 clarified certain ambiguities and filled in a few gaps, though the system was no longer in operation, except on Murray and to an extent on Saibai. However, it was already in some disarray by 1898, and bearing in mind the notorious vulnerability of Oceanic descent and land tenure systems, one might argue that individual ownership and non-agnatic inheritance were innovations. There is no final way of meeting this objection, but Barbara Thompson, who lived as a castaway on Prince of Wales Island between 1844 and 1849, also stated that wild yam beds were individually owned.[14] There was no permanent European presence at this time, so that the indigenous economy was fully operative. Thompson stated that the population, a mere 50, had been considerably reduced, presumably by diseases communicated by passing European vessels, but this would have been more likely to precipitate a shift to collective ownership because of the extinction of whole families.

The idea of land ownership in Torres Strait was, in a real sense, about the control of economic resources. But this function was achieved through a structure which related man to land in terms of history, social relations, religion and emotion as well. What Barbara Thompson said about Prince of Wales Island was true for all Torres Strait: every inch of ground, including reefs and rocks, was owned, whether or not it had economic significance.[15] In the case of scarce resources, for example prime garden land on Murray, or cult sites, ownership was a matter of exclusion. But often it was a matter of the right to include. A man might not live on his clan section, but he still exercised his right to a say in who did. The Prince of Wales Islanders annually entertained more than 100 Nagir visitors from their abundant wild yam beds. In the case of isolated reefs and islets, control was nominal, but it was understood that a kinsmen or friend who collected eggs or fruit there would leave a sign, indicating who had been there. In short, ownership related not just to direct use but to exchange: the complex network of economic, social and religious prestations on which physical safety and survival, and general well being depended. To return to the case of the Prince of Wales Islanders, their hospitality was amply repaid with gifts of garden produce and even canoes. Furthermore, the presence of so many visitors provided a needed protection for a small community rendered vulnerable to attack by rapid depopulation. The mix of group and individual ownership is likewise to be understood in terms of the broader scheme, reflecting the social dialectic between aggregation and individuation on which order depended. The patchwork of individual holdings in the interior of each island was the concrete expression of this: the negation of segmentary tendencies through the recognition of non-agnatic ties.

Despite the many differences between the Torres Strait Islanders and the Aborigines of mainland Australia, Stanner's distinction between *estate* and *range*. (Stanner, 1965), which has done much to illuminate the latter, can also be usefully applied to the former. The kind of ownership implied in the notion of estate refers as much to social organisation and to relations with the supernatural as it does to the control of economic resources. Correspondingly, access to these resources was not confined to, though it might be structured by, the definition of estate. Range implies a more flexible response to local and seasonal fluctuations in the availability of food, but also a tendency to create interdependence between groups and communities. In Torres Strait, as in Aboriginal Australia, society was engaged in the endless task of balancing the need for self-sufficiency against the need to extend relations beyond the immediate circle.

LAND OWNERSHIP IN THE MODERN SETTING

Europeans established a permanent presence in Torres Strait during the second half of the nineteenth century. For the Islanders it assumed the form of a 'pincer' movement: pearlers and trepangers disrupted the old patterns of life while missionaries, backed by government, set about radical reconstruction. Mobile populations became sedentary and settlements became nucleated, focused on a church and an anchorage. Their sacred objects destroyed or taken away by collectors, the Islanders forsook the old cults —the most important of which had been concerned with war—and busied themselves with the new religion.

The cash economy now absorbed much of the labour that had previously gone into subsistence production, with a corresponding dependence upon imported foodstuffs, particularly flour and rice. However, as I have shown elsewhere, the subsistence economy survived as part of the support system of the marine industry.[16] 'Bush tucker' and sea foods supplemented low wages and carried the labour force through periods of recession. This arrangement also enabled some individuals to maintain a relative independence from the cash economy and the controls that went with it.

The subsistence economies nevertheless, underwent considerable changes. Inter-island trade virtually ceased, leaving the Central Islanders almost wholly dependent on flour and rice, though still getting fish, turtle and dugong. The Western Islanders likewise ceased gathering wild vegetable foods and showed a readiness to abandon gardening which, at one point, the authorities had to correct. The Eastern Islander, on the other hand, limited their commitment to the industry to the younger men, leaving their elders to maintain the gardens. Turtle and dugong remained major sources of protein, but much of the hunting was now done from pearling boats and geared to the routines of the industry.

These changes inevitably caused some shifts in range. The pearling boats took Islanders further afield than their boats had done, to places whose owners were unknown to them, or which were not owned at all. On the larger islands such as Badu and Saibai there was some curtailment of the amount of overland movement, and in the distances traversed, so that some places were rarely, if ever, visited. Prince of Wales was left deserted, *terra incognita* to its relocated owners. By contrast, horticultural islands like Murray remained very much in use until the heavy emigration of the last 15 years.

The notion of estate remains valid in the contemporary situation, but its significance has altered. The cessation of cult activity and the reorganisation of residence patterns have reduced the importance of traditional groupings, in some places to the point where they have been forgotten.[17] Society is now organised in terms of 'families', which are small descent groups, often bilateral and rarely more than three generations in depth. Such groups may own residential and garden land collectively or individually, in which case some of the holdings having been subdivided will be adjacent. Beyond the immediate control of residential and cultivable land, ownership is deemed to be tangible proof of a family hereditary right to live on a particular island and in a particular community. Immigrants, correspondingly, stay only on suffrance, as the dependants of those whose land they occupy. But if they have married into the community their children will live there by right.

While most Islanders would uphold this principle, it has no legal force since the lands in question are reserves under the control of the Queensland Government. However, the government has generally left the control of land to the local government councils which have existed since 1899, under its direction. Until recently most councils upheld traditional rights, merely adjudicating boundary disputes and contested succession. However, changes are now in train.

In fact, the first radical innovation occurred in Badu during the 1940s as the result of a powerful immigrant family taking control of the council. When native Baduans tried to deny them access to garden land and challenged their right to live on the island, they instituted a by-law abolishing traditional rights and placing all lands under council control. In the years that followed they accommodated numbers of their own kinsmen and protégés from other islands, while Baduans left in disgust. It should be noted that the latter had not been denied access to land, which was plentiful, but simply the rights of ownership.

Murray adhered to tradition until the mid-1960s. Up to this point gardening remained important, symbolically and economically, and disputes were frequent and bitter. Thereafter, emigration to the mainland, which reduced the community by more than half, began to undermine the system. There had always been the provision for absentees to leave their lands in the custody of a 'caretaker'. But if the caretaker died or himself emigrated, the custodial right tended to become ownership, or the unprotected plots fell victim to land-grabbers. Given the decline in both population and the incidence of gardening, these usurpations had more to do with politics and self-aggrandisement than with economics. More seriously, some councillors described long-term emigrants as *ex*-Islanders, meaning that assimilation into the white Australian community entailed not only exemption from the Torres Strait Islanders Act, but forfeiture of land holdings and even of the right to re-enter the reserve. Some who wished to visit Murray were refused on these grounds. Then in 1978, the council took over a tract of garden land for an airstrip, without consulting the absentee landowners.

In this case the owners were indignant, though they could find no way to act in face of a *fait accompli*. However, it may be asked how many long-established emigrants care about their hereditary rights to land they may never use. A survey conducted in 1973 by Fisk and associates came to the conclusion that few thought of returning home, or even cared much what happened there.[18] But one cannot take too seriously conclusions based on questionnaires administered during the day time — and thus mainly to housewives. For my part, I have been impressed by the speed with which news travelled between the islands and the mainland, even before the setting up of direct telecommunications in 1980. In any case, the prosperity of the early 1970s soon gave way to recession and unemployment, and there have been signs that some migrants are considering going home, or would at least like to keep that option open. The considerable sums of money spent on sending the remains of dead migrants home for burial, and erecting monuments to the dead in island cemeteries, must surely be understood in these terms.[19] It is not too fanciful to characterise the island cemeteries as the latter-day sacred sites of Torres Strait, anchoring a far flung people to their homelands.

Murray, through its cancellation of migrants' hereditary rights, was moving towards the point that Badu had reached some years before: council control of land. This was adopted for all Torres Strait at a meeting of elected island representatives in 1979. However, in the absence of any clear formulation other difficulties became apparent: if the council 'owned' the land — or rather administered it on the government's behalf — who owned the houses built on it? Islanders had in fact already encountered a similar problem, trying to get loans to build houses on land for which they did not have the freehold. In 1980 a number of community leaders petitioned the State Premier to grant them freehold ownership. According to a newspaper report, he persuaded them to withdraw it, with the warning:

> Whether you mean it now or not, some of your people would start to sell any island land they had under freehold and it would not be long before your way of life, your community possessions of your islands, would be lost forever . . . You have control of your islands now—I cannot believe you want to relinquish it.[20]

According to the same source, the State Government had amended legislation to clear the way for the Commonwealth to provide housing funds directly to community councils, and could also give special leases to individuals who wanted to build homes.

The principles subsumed under the headings estate and range seem originally to have complemented one another, if the ethnographic record is reliable. While range was primarily a matter of economic use; estate was a matter of social solidarity, one of the means by which the Islanders maintained their ordered anarchy as well as giving social and historical meaning to the physical world. Under colonial conditions, land was used less intensively and for different purposes, while order and—to a degree—meaning were pre-empted by state and church. Estate was now a matter of the micropolitics of communities more isolated and embattled than they had been before contact. With the end of segregation and the move of more than half the population to the mainland, the principles upon which the notion of estate had been based have come into question, not from the emigrants but from those who have stayed at home. Potential use, or actual—as in the case of the Murray airstrip—is now a basis for undermining traditional forms of estate. Somewhat surprisingly, it is the State Government which is upholding the principle of estate, albeit in a modified form that is tied to community rather than clan or individual. However, this same Government finally controls the island reserves, and the island councils which are for the moment in charge of them.

A POSTSCRIPT

Since completion of this paper there have been signs that changes in the status of the Torres Strait reserves are imminent. Early in 1981 the newly re-elected Government of Queensland announced its intention to repeal the *Torres Strait Islanders Act*. Realising the far-reaching implication of such a move, the Torres Strait Islanders Advisory Council, an official State body composed of the three representatives of the Eastern, Western and Central Groups, waited upon the Premier and secured his agreement that no action would be taken until they had tested the feelings of Islanders in the Strait. Consultations conducted during the month of August 1981, revealed 1047 in favour of inalienable freehold, 44 favouring freehold, 10 favouring perpetual leasehold, and 1 favouring leasehold. The Premier had meanwhile expressed a preference for 50 year leasehold against his Minister's preference for perpetual leasehold.

The *Report of the Torres Strait Advisory Council, Submitted to the Honourable the Premier of Queensland* (nd), from which this postscript is drawn, offers the following recommendations:

> 1. That Torres Strait Islanders be given INALIENABLE FREEHOLD TITLE to all land present designated Reserve Land under the Queensland Land Act 1962–1978 and the Torres Strait Islanders Act.
>
> 2. That a LAND TRUST be established for the purpose of transferring title to Reserve Lands from the Queensland Government. Membership of such Land Trust to consist of 3 Elected Group Representatives and all Elected Torres Strait Community Chairman.
>
> 3. That a STATUTORY BODY be established for the purpose of gradually assuming the present role and function of the Department of Aboriginal and Islanders' Advancement and its statutory bodies. Membership of the body to consist of elected Island Representatives.

Early in 1982 The Queensland Premier (Mr Bjelke-Petersen) came forward with a new proposal, that the Queensland Government should issue deeds of grant in trust for existing Aboriginal reserves. Although apparently acceptable to the Federal Minister for Aboriginal Affairs, Senator Baume, other opinion challenged his assertion that the title would, in fact, 'be for ever'.[21] The scheme also proved unacceptable to the Torres Strait Islanders, according to a press report in May, which is worth quoting at length.

> Residents of Thursday Island in Torres Strait had rejected the Queensland Government's new Aboriginal land legislation, the area's National Aboriginal Conference delegate, Mr Billy [presumably Ben] Nona, said yesterday.
>
> Mr Nona said Islanders wanted inalienable freehold title. About 30 Thursday Islanders discussed the new land policy with the State Minister for Aboriginal and Island Affairs, Mr Tomkins, and his senior adviser at the weekend.
>
> The State chairman of the National Aboriginal Conference, Mr Steve Mam [a Brisbane-based Islander], said Government officials were acting like 'used car salesmen' trying to sell legislation Aborigines and Islanders did not want.[22]

NOTES

1. For a discussion of the border problem, the various acts of annexation and the legal issues, seek Fisk et al. (1974b). A group calling itself the Torres Strait United Party has been talking of a High Court challenge to the annexation.

2. See Queensland's *Torres Strait Islanders Act* of 1971, Pt I,5.

3. I base this estimate on my own reading of the historical sources, and that of A. C. Haddon (1935).

4. Macgillivray, 1852; Jukes, 1847; Moore, 1979.

5. For more detailed discussion of the island ecosystems see Beckett, 1972; Harris, 1977, 1979.

6. See, for example, the myth of Malu-Bomai in Haddon (1908).

7. This seems to be true of the numerous myths, both eastern and western, in which the hero turns into a rock: Haddon, 1904; 1908 passim.

8. Haddon (1908) includes a map indicating the clan and 'tribal' groupings.

9. Haddon (1904) indicates the territorial bases of the totemic clans of Mabuiag.

10. Report of A.W. Murray to the London Missionary Society for September–December 1872, p. 34.

11. Moresby (1876: 133) estimated the population of Saibai at 600.

12. Harris, 1979: 98.

13. This seems to be the gist of Anthony Wilkins' account, which is, however, scrappy and unclear at points (Haddon, 1904: 284–92).

14. Moore, 1979: 171–72.

15. Macgillivray, 1852:II: 28.

16. Beckett, 1977.

17. In 1959 I could find no one on Badu who could tell me his totemic affiliation. On Mabuiag there were many who knew, while on Saibai it was a matter of common knowledge.

18. Fisk et al. (1974a).

19. See Beckett (1978).

20. 'A Win for Joh on Badu?' From undated news-clipping *c.* September 1980, probably from *The Townsville Bulletin.*

21. 'Queensland: Aboriginal land tenure "not secure" says lawyer' by Mark Plunkett, *National Times* for 11–17 April 1982.

22. 'Queensland Islanders reject new land legislation', *Sydney Morning Herald* for 25 May 1982.

REFERENCES

Beckett J. (1972). The Torres Strait Islanders. In: D. Walker (ed.), *Bridge and Barrier: the natural and cultural history of Torres Strait.* Canberra, Australian National University Press.

Beckett, J. (1977). The Torres Strait Islanders and the pearling industry: a case of internal colonialism. *Aboriginal History, I.*

Beckett, J. (1978). A tombstone opening. *Australian Natural History, 19* (special issue Torres Strait).

Fisk, E.K. et al. (1974a). *The Torres Strait Islanders,* vol. III. *The Islander Population in the Cairns to Townsville Area.* Canberra, Australian National University Press.

Fisk, E.K. (1974b). *The Torres Strait Islanders.* vol. V. *The Border and Associated Problems.* Canberra, Australian National University Press.

Haddon, A.C. (1904). *Reports of the Cambridge Anthropological Expedition to Torres Straits,* vol. V: *Sociology, magic and religion of the Western Islanders.* Cambridge University Press.

Haddon, A.C. (1908). *Reports of the Cambridge Anthropological Expedition to Torres Straits,* vol VI: *Sociology, magic and religion of the Eastern Islanders.* Cambridge University Press.

Haddon A.C. (1935). *Reports of the Cambridge Anthropological Expedition . . . ,* vol. I. *General ethnography.* Cambridge University Press.

Harris, D.R. (1977). Subsistence strategies across Torres Strait. In: J. Allen, R. Golson & R. Jones (eds.), *Sunda and Sahul: prehistorical studies in Southeast Asia, Melanesia and Australia.* New York, Academic Press.

Harris, D. (1979). Foragers and Farmers in the Western Torres Strait Islands: an historical analysis of economic, demographic and spatial differentiation. In: P.C. Burnham & R. Ellen (eds.), *Social and Ecological Systems.* London, Academic Press.

Jukes, J.B. (1847). *Narrative of the surveying voyages of H.M.S. Fly .... during the years 1842–1846.* London, Boone.

Macgillivray, J. (1852). *Narrative of the voyage of H.M.S. Rattlesnake ... during the years 1842–1846. London, Boone.*

Moore, D. (1979). *Islanders and Aborigines at Cape York: an ethnographic reconstruction based on the 1848–1850 Rattlesnake journals of O.W. Brierly and information he obtained from Barbara Thompson.* Canberra, Australian Institute of Aboriginal Studies.

Stanner, W.E.H. (1965). Aboriginal territorial organisation, estate, range, domain and regime. *Oceania,* 36:1–26.

13

'OWNERS', 'MANAGERS' AND THE CHOICE OF STATUTORY TRADITIONAL OWNERS BY ANTHROPOLOGISTS AND LAWYERS

Kenneth Maddock

The relative standing of 'owners' and 'managers' among Aborigines in the Northern Territory has become a land rights issue. Anthropological and legal questions are mixed up in this, and it is as important to try to disentangle them as it is to arrive at a judgement on the disputed issue.

The dispute arises out of the need to interpret the definition of 'traditional Aboriginal owners' in s. 3 (1) of the *Aboriginal Land Rights (Northern Territory) Act* 1976. According to this definition:

> 'traditional Aboriginal owners', in relation to land, means a local descent group of Aboriginals who—
>
> (a) have common spiritual affiliations to a site on the land, being affiliations that place the group under a primary spiritual responsibility for that site and for the land; and
>
> (b) are entitled by Aboriginal tradition to forage as of right over that land.

The importance of this definition is that the persons who satisfy it enjoy special powers and advantages under the Act. For example, s. 48 (a) gives the traditional owners of a piece of Aboriginal land the power to veto a proposed grant of a mining interest in that land, and s. 68 (2) (a) gives them the power to veto a proposed construction of a road over that land. Even more important at present is the fact that 'traditional land claims' may only be made 'by or on behalf of the traditional Aboriginal owners of the land'—see ss. 3 (1) and 50 (1). It is through such claims that the total area of Aboriginal land can be expanded.

Now a definition, to be applied, has to be interpreted. This jurisprudential commonplace can be illustrated from the land claims which have so far been made. Thus, because a claim may only be made by or on behalf of the traditional owners of the land, and because traditional owners are defined as a local descent group, it is necessary to determine what will be meant by a local descent group, whether generally or in a particular claim.

The determination of this meaning takes place in two phases of a claim. First, the land council, in preparing a claim, chooses some Aborigines as claimants on the basis of an understanding of the traditional owners definition. Sometimes Aborigines will choose themselves. If that happens, and if the land council respects the Aboriginal choice, then the definition will have to be construed in such a way as to give effect to their choice.

Secondly, the Land Commissioner, in hearing a claim, must ascertain whether the claimants or any other Aborigines are the traditional owners of the land. Here, too, the interpretation put upon the definition is crucial.

It is not to be wondered at, therefore, that the need to arrive at an understanding of traditional ownership has been admitted more than once in the short history of land claims. For example, the Ranger Inquiry, after noting that the definition contains 'a number of key concepts, which have to be understood by reference to Aboriginal customs and traditions' (1977: 255), went on to give its understanding of them. In the

Warlpiri claim, the Land Commissioner remarked of these key concepts that they:

> contain words and phrases the meaning of which is not by any means self-evident . . . I did discuss them in the Borroloola Report but in view of the evidence given in the present hearing and because it is early in the life of the statute they will bear further examination. (paras 64–65)

All of the earlier claims (Ranger, Borroloola, Warlpiri, Alyawarra) saw the definition taken narrowly to mean a descent group the members of which are totemically connected in the male line to a site on the land being claimed. The local descent group of the definition was understood, then, to be patrilineal, even though the definition does not specify a line of descent. The effect was to exclude those Aborigines who are maternally connected to a site. There can be no principled objection to this exclusion, for the concept of a local descent group has to be given a meaning both by the land council preparing a claim and by the Land Commissioner hearing it. As soon as the concept is interpreted, then some Aborigines will be included and others excluded, for the point of conceptual thinking is to discriminate.

Some later claims (Ayers Rock, Mudbura, Utopia, Willowra) have seen the land councils interpreting the traditional owners' definition more broadly to include Aborigines who are maternally connected to a site as well as those who are paternally connected. The Land Commissioner accepted this in the Ayers Rock and Willowra claims, rejected it in the Utopia claim, and made no mention of it in his report on the Mudbura claim. This establishes that the definition is open to significant differences of opinion. Not only will these have to be taken into account when future claims are prepared and heard, but our understanding of Aboriginal local organisation will have to change to accommodate the results of these arguments over land rights and land claims (see Maddock, 1978d: 605–607; 1980: 16–74).

I

The Land Rights Act originated in the work of the Aboriginal Land Rights Commission, the second report of which included a draft bill, and it is instructive to consider that the controversy over 'owners' and 'managers' might never have arisen had the Commission kept to its terms of reference. The Letters Patent to Mr Justice Woodward called upon him to inquire into 'appropriate means to recognise and establish the traditional rights and interests of the Aborigines in and in relation to land' (ALRC 1973: 1; 1974: 1).

That 'managers' as well as 'owners' have ideas about and relations to land which belong under the heading of 'traditional rights and interests . . . in and in relation to land' is indisputable. That rights to land could have been granted in those terms is clear from a South Australian bill (no. 131 of 1978), which makes the basis of a claim the existence of a group of Pitjantjatjara having an interest in the land in accordance with Aboriginal tradition (s. 13).[1] Section 4 of the bill stipulates that:

> 'interest', in relation to land, means social, economic and spiritual affiliations with, and responsibilities to, the land.

However, for reasons which it did not explain, the Commission turned from the expression 'traditional rights and interests' to the expression 'traditional Aboriginal owners'. Probably more was behind this than a wish to use words concisely. The Commission must have been convinced that distinctions ought to be drawn among the traditional rights and interests of Aborigines and that the more important powers and advantages to be created by land rights legislation ought to be distributed accordingly.[2]

Whether such discrimination is justifiable is one question before us under the particular form of 'owners' and 'managers'. Another question is the extent to which discrimination can be supported by the wording of the traditional owners definition. But what seems clear is that the Act (like the draft bill) made an unhappy choice when it used the word 'owners', because this could only provoke confusion with the use of the same term by anthropologists and by Aborigines. A more neutral expression, such as 'traditional right-holders', would have escaped this trap.

It will be useful to comment on these prior usages, for not only do they interfere with each other, in the sense of overlapping and conflicting in meaning, but they can create a preconception about how the traditional owners definition should be interpreted.

Many Aborigines use English words to express the complementary dualism in matters of land or of ritual of persons connected to it through their father and persons connected to it through their mother. 'Owner' or 'boss' is commonly used for members of the paternally affiliated group, while 'manager', 'boss', 'worker', 'mailman', 'policeman', 'helper', and 'traditional trustee' have been recorded for members of the maternally affiliated group.[3]

Of course, not all of these words would be in use concurrently in the same area. There are regional preferences, with 'owner', for example, being favoured on the Beswick Reserve but 'boss' around the southern Gulf of Carpentaria for the paternally affiliated. There are changes through time. Elkin, who worked on and around the Beswick Reserve between 1947 and 1953, found 'mailman', 'boss' and 'working boy', but not 'manager', for the maternally affiliated (Elkim, 1971: 114, n. 3). 'Mailman' was in disuse by 1964, when I started to work in the area, but 'manager' had become common and 'worker', 'policeman' and 'boss' were also used. Finally, there can be transpositions from one area to another as 'boss' shows, for it is in opposition to 'manager' around the southern Gulf, but interchangeable with it on the Beswick Reserve.

Whichever the English word, it is nearly always a gloss on a term belonging to the Aboriginal languages of the area, for we find the complementary dualism in land and ritual expressed through such opposed pairs as *gidjan* and *djunggaiji* (Beswick Reserve), *nimaringgi* and *djunggaiji* (southern Gulf), or *kirda* and *kurtungulu* (Warlpiri). An interesting variation on this is to be found with the Alyawarra, who have *kurtingurla* for the maternally affiliated group but lack a word for the paternally affiliated group.

I do not know of any serious attempt to trace the history of the Aboriginal borrowings from English. Because of the state of spoken English among Aborigines, their illiteracy and their ignorance of many of the realities of Australian life—all of which would have been even more pronounced when most of the borrowings were made —it would be absurd to give these terms their usual English meaning. We can only suppose that Aborigines saw analogies of some sort between certain roles in their own society and some of the activities of white men with whom they came into early contact. The analogies can be quite apt—'mailman', for example, captures the message-carrying function of *djunggaiji* on the Beswick Reserve—but Aboriginal English usage cannot be taken without more ado as a guide to standard English usage, let alone to such legal or quasi-legal expressions as 'owner' and 'trustee'.[4]

Unfortunately and unjustifiably, anthropologists have been tempted to accept the relation to land of its so-called 'owners' as amounting to ownership in some English sense of the word. Because the 'managers' of a piece of land cannot, by the logic of complementary dualism, be its 'owners', the false conclusion has been drawn that their relation to that land does not amount to ownership.

No harm would be done by explaining Aboriginal ideas about, and relations to, land in terms of 'owners' and 'managers' if the writer and his readers kept steadily in mind that these are glosses on paired terms of Aboriginal languages. It is all too easy, however, to conflate 'owners' with proprietors and 'managers' (that is, non-'owners') with non-proprietors. I admit to having fallen into this ridiculous trap myself (for example, 1972:27–42; 1974:206–207, 214).

Not all of the anthropological statements about ownership of land would result from a confusion of categories. A greater problem with the statements is their apparently arbitrary identification of owners. Thus we find some writers attributing ownership to a descent-based group (the Berndts, Hiatt, the later Radcliffe-Brown) and others to a residence-based group (Meggitt, the early Radcliffe-Brown, Thomas).

Even when two writers subscribe to the same principle of ownership they will disagree about the group which has ownership. In the descent camp, for example, the later Radcliffe-Brown credits clans with owning land (1956:365), but the Berndts opt for local descent groups, which they expressly distinguish from clans (1964:42–43). In the residence camp, Meggitt's community, to which he attributes title to country (1962:51), is obviously very different from the early Radcliffe-Brown's typical horde, though having some resemblance to his atypical horde (1930:35–37).

Equally confusing is the fact that writers who use the same word may part company when it comes to the word's legal significance. We have seen this in the case of clans, where the Berndts differ from the later Radcliffe-Brown, but it occurs also in the case of communities. Meggitt speaks of them among the Warlpiri and Hiatt among the Gidjingali, but where Meggitt credits them with title to land Hiatt opts for land-owning units, each of which consists of one or more patrilineal descent groups and a number of which are included within each community (1962:279–82; 1965:14–28).

These difficulties are exacerbated by the tendency of anthropologists to identify land-owners without bothering to explain the relationship of their views to those asserted by other writers. Thus you would not guess from Radcliffe-Brown's work on local organisation that he is drawing substantially the same distinctions as Thomas (1906:8), the typical and atypical hordes of the one being the kin and mixed groups of the other.

Had anthropologists been more interested in comparison, then they would have been readier to ask what is meant by the ownership with which clans, communities, local groups, land-owning units, hordes or local descent groups have variously been credited. Even when it is clear what a particular writer means, as when Hiatt reduces the ownership of land to a ritual relationship of one or more patrilineal descent groups to a site (1962:280, 284; 1965:14–20), it is never clear why he takes that, and nothing else, to be ownership—or why he uses this concept at all.

It is instructive that the people whom the Gidjingali call *ngamonbeninga* and *aburamari* (children and daughter's children of the females of a patrilineal descent group) have a ritual relationship to sites which complements that of the descent group members, yet the maternal connection is neither qualified as ownership nor mentioned in Hiatt's paper on local organisation or in the chapter devoted to this subject in his book. It is discussed, instead, in the chapter on 'Kinship and marriage' (1965:53–68). The effect is a double narrowing: first, ownership is treated as a ritual relationship; and secondly, only the ritual relationship traced in the male line is treated as relevant.[5]

If there is an argument in favour of this attenuation, then it has yet to be stated. Hiatt, to do him justice, seems to doubt the propriety of using the concept of ownership, for we find this revealing turn of phrase in his paper: 'The ownership of land (if the term is to be used). . .' (1962:284). Probably the proponents of the narrow view have assumed that an area of land can have only the one owner. Patrilineal descent groups, because of their bounded and 'corporate' nature, have then seemed suitable candidates for this role. Also it has probably been assumed that ownership is exclusive.

The ritual relationship of the members of a patrilineal descent group to the totemic sites associated with their group has seemed to satisfy this requirement.

If these were the unexamined assumptions of the 1960s and early 1970s, then we can appreciate the dogmatic confidence which crept into statements about ownership. For Peterson, there is no disagreement about the ownership of land by Aborigines, and the whole of Australia is divided into estates owned by patrilineal clans (1970:9). For Peterson, Keen & Sansom, primary rights to land 'are normally unambiguously identifiable. Ownership of an estate or territory is determined by patrilineal descent' (1977:1003). For Shapiro, 'Lodge ownership of the core area is unequivocal' (1979:20).

There would be no point in collecting such examples were it not for their value in illustrating an approach to land law which is the antithesis of the approach indicated by Mr Justice Woodward's Letters Patent and by the South Australian bill on Pitjantjatjara land. The difference lies in the use made of the concept of an estate. The usage of many writers makes of this a tract of land (a division of Australia, a territory, an area). But another usage, more in keeping with English than with continental land law, makes an estate a right or interest in land. The practical significance of this difference is that the English view fosters the fragmentation of ownership by allowing rights or interests in land to be multiplied and to be held by different persons, but the continental view—which does not know a doctrine of estates in the technical English sense—discourages this process by favouring what the Romans called *dominium*, the absolute ownership of land itself by one person.

II

Although Mr Justice Woodward was aware of the difficulty of expressing Aboriginal concepts in English terms, it may be doubted that he found the right solution. It would be hard to disagree with these remarks from his section on 'Aborigines and their land':

> On enquiry, it soon becomes clear that the social organization of the Aboriginal people is highly complex. The problem of understanding it is made worse by a number of factors. These include, firstly, the difficulty of expressing many Aboriginal ideas and arrangements in English terms. Even simple words such as 'owner' and 'tribe' can be misleading. Some words used by anthropologists such as 'horde', 'clan' and 'band' have been given more precise meanings in their writings on the subject, but they have not always been used in the same way and so require definition each time they are used.
>
> Further, some Aboriginal concepts related to land-owning have no parallel in European law. The most important and widespread of the rights in land that lie outside European arrangements is the managerial interest of a nephew in the country of his maternal uncle . . .
>
> Yet another difficulty arises from disagreement among anthropologists as to the exact nature of the relationship between Aboriginal organization for landholding and for land usage. (ALRC 1973:11–12; 1974:135–36)

The conclusion to which this passage points is that land rights should be formulated with some generality and with the use of terms as neutral as possible. But the section on 'Aborigines and their land' ends up by maintaining that land is held by patrilineal descent groups, apparently to the exclusion of the managerial and other interests which had earlier been admitted to exist.

There is, then, a tension between broader and narrower conceptions of traditional rights and interests in Mr Justice Woodward's thinking, with the broader coming to the surface from time to time but the narrower winning out in the end, probably because the weight of anthropological opinion at that time was behind it.[6] Thus his observation in the first report, that to vest title in clans would have the disadvantage of leaving managerial rights unrecognised (ALRC 1973:36), was not built upon in the second.

Now that some of the background to the traditional owners definition has been filled in we are better able to draw attention to a curious aspect of the relation between the language of the Act and the language of the Woodward Commission. This is that the technical term 'traditional Aboriginal owners' occurs nowhere in the Commission's reports, except in the draft bill included in the second report, and that Mr Justice Woodward does not, therefore, discuss what it meant to him or in what relation he saw it standing to his various (and sometimes conflicting) observations on Aboriginal local organisation or to his Letters Patent.

But even it his final opinion was that the more important powers and advantages to be created by land rights legislation should be conferred upon a subclass of those Aborigines who have traditional rights and interests, and even if he thought that this subclass should be defined patrilineally, it would not mean that he should be followed when land claims are made or when land councils seek out traditional owners to ascertain their views on mining and other proposed uses of Aboriginal land. The traditional owners definition will have to be independently interpreted on these occasions and it will be essential not to allow interpretation to be determined by the connotations of such words as 'owner' and 'ownership', whether in anthropological or Aboriginal or ordinary English usage.

The prehistory of the Act, then, is one in which conflicting and overlapping conceptions of ownership were at work. This chaos is still a feature of the scene. The danger is that, despite the inadequacy of these conceptions as jurisprudential formulas, one or other of them will colour interpretation, that is, will enter into the choice of Aborigines to claim land or to exercise powers of veto or to enjoy special financial benefits under the Act. I believe that this has already happened.

Perhaps the danger could be lessened by qualifying the main versions of ownership. Thus the 'owners' (or 'bosses') of Aboriginal usage could be described as vernacular owners. The 'traditional Aboriginal owners' of the Act could be described as statutory traditional owners. The 'owners' of anthropological usage would be owners anthropologically conceived. Such expressions are cumbersome, and sometimes the context will make them unnecessary, but used in moderation they would help to prevent confusion. All of these senses would be distinct from ownership as a concept of analytical jurisprudence. The observations made by the Woodward Commission would then be seen to be a mixture of:

(a) vernacular ownership: 'discussion of land ownership seems to them unnecessary. They know which Aborigines own which tract of land by Aboriginal law'. (ALRC 1973:7)

(b) ownership anthropologically conceived (by those anthropologists who ascribe ownership to a patrilineal descent group): 'Such a system has been supported by most anthropologists who have responded to my request for information and opinions' (ALRC 1973: 35)

(c) independent jurisprudential analysis of traditional rights and interests: 'the social organisation ... is highly complex ... the difficulty of expressing many Aboriginal ideas and arrangements in English terms . . . some Aboriginal concepts related to land-owning have no parallel in European law . . . disagreement among anthropologists'. (ALRC 1973: 11-12; 1974: 135-6)

It does not appear from its report that the Commission went thoroughly into any of these. But from its work came statutory traditional ownership.

III

The traditional owners definition was understood in the early claims to mean a patrilineal descent group. 'Managers' were necessarily excluded because their relationship to site and land is traced through a female link. Those of us who thought that their exclusion was an injustice had therefore to argue that the wording of the definition allowed for maternally as well as paternally traced relationships.[7] The case for this has now been accepted.

Thus, in the Ayers Rock claim the descent groups were ambilineal, being composed of persons some of whom were related to the group's 'estate' through their father while others were related to it through their mother. The descent groups of the Mudbura claim were described as patrilineal but as including the uninitiated children of the female members, which gives them a cognatic character.[8] The descent groups of the Utopia and Willowra claims were described as cognatic, being composed of the 'managers' of the land as well as of the persons patrilineally related to it. The Land Commissioner ended up by recommending against the Utopia 'managers', but this was on evidential grounds and not because the wording of the definition necessarily excludes them; he recommended in favour of Willowra 'managers' after hearing legal and anthropological argument and evidence which were substantially the same as in the Utopia claim.

However, although a uniform interpretation is no longer being urged by land councils or applied by the Land Commissioner, it does not follow that 'anything goes'. If claimants are to be accepted as the traditional owners of the land, then they must satisfy the definition, that is to say, they must conform in some way to the conceptual requirements of being a local descent group, of having common spiritual affiliations and so on. Because these key concepts are undefined in the Act they must be given their meaning in each claim as the outcome of an interplay between what the definition seems to suggest (the impression it makes on those of its readers who are involved at each stage of its interpretation) and the customs and traditions of the Aborigines from whose ranks the claimants have been chosen.

Anthropologists are playing a great part in this process: not only do they advise the Land Commissioner or appear as expert witnesses on behalf of the claimants but they are active before the hearing to carry out research and to choose the Aborigines in whose name the claim is made. In choosing claimants or in commenting on the choice of claimants, they are interpreting the definition; in interpreting the definition, they are helping to decide the distribution of rights among Aborigines. This is more than the usual role of an expert witness, for it involves statutory interpretation as well as interpretation of the significance of reports on earlier claims. Normally these responsibilities would rest with the court and with counsel for the parties.

No doubt this reliance on anthropologists has been fostered by the anthropologically evocative definition of traditional owners. Local descent group is a term of anthropology. Common spiritual affiliations and primary spiritual responsibility are not, but they do call to mind the totemic belief and ritual about which anthropologists have written so much.

There are risks in the roles which anthropologists are now playing, but obviously they will stay in the game. Their interest in land rights (the climate of opinion which made the Act possible was partly their work), their studies of Aboriginal societies and their readiness to express themselves on the nature of these societies make it inevitable that they will continue to be deeply involved. Perhaps it would be different if Aborigines themselves were more forthcoming, but a striking feature of the land rights movement has been the virtual silence of Aborigines on the legal formulation of their rights.[9]

IV

The risks which accompany anthropological involvement can, I suggest, be guarded against in three ways. First, by realism about anthropological terminology. Secondly, by an appreciation of the modern and functional character of the more important powers and advantages created by the Act. Thirdly, by sensitivity about the position of anthropologists in relation to the understanding which Aborigines have and to the prospects which lie before them.

As to the first point, anthropology has no authoritative terms and, even if it did, they would not bind a court of law or other tribunal. It may even be questioned whether anthropology has clearly defined terms to which there is general agreement. Take, as an example of these contentions, the concept of a local descent group. Mr Justice Woodward used the term once (1973: 14; 1974: 137) in his account of 'Aborigines and their land'. He treats it as a synonym for clan, which occurs 54 times. The Berndts are among the few writers on Aborigines to have used this term before the Act. They believe that it 'has a specific connotation in the literature on the Australian Aborigines' (1964: 42)—which can scarcely be true, for it was little used—and they also believe that there is an 'important distinction' between it and a clan: local descent groups are patrilineal, but clans may be matrilineal; and 'actual genealogical ties are inferred' (from what?) in local descent groups, but 'need not be' in clans. The local descent group is 'the land-holding group'.

For the Woodward Commission, then, clans (= local descent groups) own land, but for the Berndts local descent groups (≠ clans) do so. When they distinguish clans and local descent groups the Berndts appear to follow Leach, who was apparently the first to use the concept of a local descent group, but they do not mention him, and in other respects they break with his usage: he does not insist on patriliny; and he conceives of such a group as consisting of adult males of three generations (old men or grandfathers, normal adults or fathers, young adults or sons), to the apparent exclusion of women or boys (1961: 56–58).

Here we see a term with three meanings. It is an anthropological concept, and only an anthropologist could speak about it in an informed way, but the content of the concept is exceptionally variable. None of the meanings could be treated as binding upon anthropologists. This fact is to be welcomed, not deplored, for the flexibility which it gives to interpretation. As soon as the anthropologists and lawyers engaged in the application of the Act realise that the traditional owners definition does not lock them into a cast-iron framework, then they will have freed themselves to interpret the definition in the light of the special circumstances of each claim and of the broad aims thought to underlie the legislation. That is why is has been so important to insist on Leach's original conception of a local descent group. Hence my position is opposed to that of Keen, for whom 'There seems to be no reason why Leach's use of the phrase should have any bearing on the interpretation of the Act' (1977: 2).[10]

Of course, it does not follow that any sort of group could be put forward as a local descent group. A residence-based group of the kind identified by Meggitt or Thomas or the early Radcliffe-Brown as owning land does not seem to meet the descent requirements of the definition. This constraint could be seen as justifying the Warlpiri claim book's assertion that 'the main land-owning group is based on the patrilineal clan' (Peterson, McConvell, Wild & Hagen, 1978: 2) and its silence about Meggitt's attribution of title to communities. A proper jurisprudential analysis might favour the community above the clan, but the Act calls for interpretation of its definition of ownership and not for the kind of exercise in comparative law which occurred during the Gove Land Rights Case.[11]

But it could be said against this consideration that the writers of a claim book should draw attention to any attributions of ownership which have been made in the literature, even if they disagree with them or suppose them to fall outside the scope of the Act. Thus the Warlpiri claim book is open to criticism for failing to mention Meggitt's contrary opinion when asserting that 'communities are not land-owning units' (Peterson, McConvell, Wild & Hagen, 1978: 1). It is not so much that an artful lawyer or anthropologist might be able to represent these communities as local descent groups, but that an awareness of different attributions of ownership helps to open one's mind to the arbitrariness which can enter such attributions and so helps to make one more adventurous in handling the statutory definition.

As to my second point, that the more important powers and advantages created by the Act have a modern and functional character, we are dealing with rights which did not exist traditionally because the circumstances which call for them did not arise in pre-European times. For example, when the Act provides for the traditional owners of a piece of Aboriginal land to veto mining on it, or the construction of a road over it, or when it provides for Aborigines to claim land because they are its traditional owners, then it is making provisions the sense of which presupposes recent history, with its dispossession of Aborigines and the rapid appearance of large numbers of immigrants. Such provisions would make no sense at all were it not for those events.

I see statutory traditional ownership as relevant to the unprecedented powers and advantages which the Act has created to meet unprecedented circumstances. I do not see it as regulating or re-forming the right of Aborigines to engage in activities of a traditional kind, for example, as enabling the *gidjan* of a place to act as though they were its *djunggaiji* or the *djunggaiji* to act as though they were the *gidjan.*

Our task is accordingly to ask, in the light of our understanding of traditional ideas about and relations to land, to whom the new powers and advantages should go. The case for 'managers' as statutory traditional owners rests on that understanding (see, for example, Hiatt, 1965:54–57; Maddock, 1974), as may be seen from the Utopia claim book, which asserts that:

> We have found that in the course of the Central Land Council's operations as a body involved in the management of Aboriginal Land, those who are spoken of in Aboriginal English as 'owners' invariably require the presence of *kurtingurla* when making important decisions relating to that land. In such situations *kurtingurla* frequently take an active, and sometimes a dominant, part. (Hagen & Rowell, 1979:3).

The importance of this point is that some anthropologists and lawyers have acted as though statutory traditional ownership should be conflated with vernacular ownership or with ownership anthropologically conceived. I would not wish to reject, out of hand, the possibility that such a conflation might sometimes be valid, but it must be kept in mind, first, that anthropological opinion about ownership is in a chaotic state, and secondly, that vernacular opinion applies the notion of ownership with varying degrees of breadth, so that the 'owners' of a place are now the members of the moiety with which that place is classed and now a mere handful of people with genealogical links to it and now a grouping which falls between these extremes. The anthropologist or lawyer who decides to rely on a vernacular or anthropological conception must take the further step of deciding upon which vernacular or anthropological conception to rely. And, if he has any awareness of the problems of statutory interpretation, he will then have to argue for his choice as a reasonable construction of the traditional owners definition.

My third point concerns the role of anthropologists. We do not decide land claims but we appear as expert witnesses in them, and our conception of the meaning of the traditional owners definition has a powerful effect on the selection of claimants and on their fortunes during the hearing of a claim. Few if any Aborigines in the Northern

Territory would be able to read the Act with understanding or to construe its definitions. A consequence of this is that we should go out of our way to try to prevent confusion and misunderstanding arising.

It would be a pity if Aborigines were to suppose, without more ado, that the traditional owners of the Act are the 'owners' of Aboriginal English. This danger would not have arisen had the Act spoken of traditional-right-holders.

Connected with this is the importance of anthropologists setting out in their written or oral evidence whatever conceptions of ownership have earlier been advanced about the land now under claim. These should not be treated as anticipations of what the Act is after but as indications of the fluidity and arbitrariness with which English legal ideas are applied to such utterly different societies as the Aboriginal.

Anthropologists should, of course, take care to get their ethnography straight. This is easier said than done, if only because we work at particular times and places, we bring preconceived ideas with us in the light of which we ask questions and observe events, and Aborigines themselves respond to their perceptions of our interests and character. Anthropological research, unlike an experiment in chemistry, can never be repeated. For that reason we should be scrupulous in drawing attention to discrepancies between our findings and those of earlier fieldworkers and in avoiding the assumption that the later disqualifies the earlier.

An interesting example of apparent failure to observe this precaution is to be seen in the assessment of common spiritual affiliations which was made by the Land Commissioner's consultant in the Warlpiri claim. He took it to refer:

> to the belief that every member of a patriline is in some sense animated by the 'patri-spirit' of his clan, to which he is affiliated. (Warlpiri Report, para. 67)

This statement is hard to reconcile with passages in Meggitt's *Desert People,* (1962:206-208, 210) which suggest that a woman does not share a 'patri-spirit' with her father and brothers. Notice that if animation by such a spirit is taken as essential, and if men alone are so animated, then the local descent group of the Act becomes the local descent group of Leach's original formulation! Notice also that if animation by a 'patri-spirit' is treated as essential, then the local descent group will necessarily be patrilineal, and land councils will have an uphill struggle to have an ambilineal or cognatic group accepted should they put it forward (as in the Ayers Rock, Utopia and Willowra claims, for example).

Meggitt might have been wrong about this, and the consultant right, but as it is it looks as though a questionable ethnographic interpretation has entered into the interpretation of a statutory definition, and in fact it was followed in the next of the Central Land Council's claims, in which the Land Commissioner had a different consultant (see Alyawarra Report, para. 47).

Finally, anthropologists should take care to understand the Act, for otherwise their choice of Aborigines as claimants, their advice to Aborigines, or their arguments at hearings of land claims may be distorted by their failure to grasp what the rights and opportunities of Aborigines truly are. An anthropologist will be on the wrong track if he assumes that the Act provides a fee simple for traditional owners or that the Act creates a register of beneficiaries of a land trust (on which 'managers' belong) as distinct from a register of traditional owners (on which 'owners' belong and from which 'managers' should be struck) or that the Act provides for the Minister of Aboriginal Affairs in Canberra to mediate in disputes between rivals to traditional ownership or between them and a land council, yet all of these blunders have been made by anthropologists in responsible positions.

The incapacity of most Aborigines to follow the Act without expert guidance makes these errors all the more deplorable, for they might well take policy decisions in reliance on such mistaken advice. The fact that anthropologists are expressing themselves on what appear to be straightforwardly legal questions nicely illustrates my earlier point that their role under the Land Rights Act goes beyond what is usual of expert witnesses.

V

It may be asked whether steps could not be taken to reduce the likelihood of an unduly narrow distribution of rights or to correct such a distribution after the event.

At the time when anthropologists and lawyers were assuming that the traditional owners definition meant a patrilineal descent group, then a solution would have been to provide independent advice for 'managers'. The justification would have been that their interests appeared to conflict with those of 'owners' and that, in accordance with usual legal practice, they should not be advised by the same person. A drawback to this would have been that the adversary nature of our legal system has not been designed to do justice to relationships in which complementarity and interdependence are of the essence. As it is, the running debate of 1977–80 over 'owners', 'managers' and the choice of statutory traditional owners has probably created enough awareness of the issues to make a resort of adversary methods undesirable.

This does not mean that action by Aborigines against Aborigines will never be called for. Take, for example, the distribution of royalties and compensation for uranium mining in the Alligator Rivers area. According to Keen, 'If Pancontinental goes ahead then one land-owning group with about twenty members . . . will stand to receive very large sums indeed' (1980:184). Payments are determined by traditional relationship to the land affected, the relevant relationship apparently being the one glossed as 'ownership'. But we have seen that a question mark hangs over the value of this concept for the understanding of Aboriginal ideas about and relations to land. The possibility remains, then, that a broader view of Aboriginal land law would result in royalties and compensation being much more widely distributed.

There is, of course, a danger in this line of reasoning. We might be so concerned about recognising the diverse relationships which Aborigines have to land that we overlook the relatively greater weight of some of them. As the Act aims to grant rights on a traditional basis it is proper to act accordingly, even if the result is to consolidate traditional disparities. I have indicated that 'managers' and 'owners' should be on an equal footing, but the effect of this is to enlarge the most advantaged group and not to bring about a levelling of fortunes among Aborigines generally.

Another solution which has been suggested is addressed to the problem raised by the sexual division of labour and knowledge in Aboriginal societies. Women, it is said, are disadvantaged by the land claims procedure because they dislike talking about spiritual affiliations and responsibilities in front of men. That men dislike talking on these subjects when women are present is less important because most of the anthropologists and all of the lawyers involved in claims have been men. The solution is to have more women lawyers and anthropologists involved, even to the point of duplicating every position from Land Commissioner down.

To assess this proposal requires a knowledge of the detriment which flows from the relatively greater reliance on men's evidence. Had a claim been lost for want of the kind of evidence which could only be given by women, and had the women's failure to give it resulted from the masculinity of anthropologists and lawyers, then there would be a strong case for searching out more professional women. However, there does not seem ever to have been such a loss.

The detriment which comes closest to it would be the omission of 'managers' from lists of claimants. It is not, of course, that 'managers' are women and 'owners' men, since people of each sex are included in each category, but that the one relationship is traced through female and the other through male members of a patrilineal descent group. A reliance on men informants might seem to lead to over-emphasising the importance of relationships traced through male links.

But this seems unlikely to have happened, if only because the managerial relationship is of great significance to men. The rights a man acquires through his father do not conflict with those he acquires through his mother, so there is no reason why he should play up the one and play down the other. If patrilineal descent groups were stressed in the earlier claims, the cause is likelier to have been the conflation by anthropologists, lawyers and Aborigines of vernacular and statutory traditional ownership.[12] Recent land claims show that this danger has become quite small, even if it has not altogether disappeared.

Thus a duplication of anthropological and legal roles is no more called for than is the introduction of the adversary method. There is no real evidence of a detriment which could justify such a costly and time-consuming solution. The purpose of the Act is to provide Aborigines with rights to land, not professional men and women with jobs, and neither anthropologists nor lawyers should create a need for their services.

Finally, we may raise the possibility of correcting decisions which, at a later date, come to be viewed as unduly narrow. A mechanism for this seems to be provided by s.24, which requires a land council to keep a register of traditional owners. No doubt the persons whose names are entered in the register will be chosen in accordance with an interpretation of the traditional owners definition. It is inevitable that the recommendations of the Land Commissioner will give the land councils a model understanding of the definition.

In his Utopia Report, the Land Commissioner commented on this section that:

> A Land Council is not bound by my views as to the traditional owners although the work done and enquiries made in connection with a land claim should ensure considerable accuracy in the identification of people and relationships. (para. 84)

Although this has yet to be tested, there appears to be no bar to a land council taking a broader view of the definition when compiling a register than when drawing up a list of claimants. For example, 'managers' were not included as claimants in the Warlpiri claim, but they were in the Willowra claim, which similarly involved Warlpiri-speaking Aborigines. Now that the case for Willowra 'managers' has been accepted (Willowra Report, para. 108), it would be proper for the Central Land Council to give serious consideration to entering 'managers' as well as 'owners' in the register for the land covered by the Warlpiri claim.

But although this step, if taken, would be principled and not arbitrary, one could imagine disputes resulting from it. Thus if a land council sought the views of the traditional owners of an area about a mining proposal, it might turn out that 'owners' supported and 'managers' opposed the mine. If 'managers' had been put on the register because of the land council's reinterpretation of the traditional owners definition, then the 'owners' might try to get around the managerial veto by insisting upon the earlier narrow construction. The matter could end up in the Supreme Court. But if 'managers' had not been put on the register, then they might take action to obtain recognition as statutory traditional owners should 'owners' endorse a proposal objected to by 'managers' or veto a proposal favoured by them.

It may be tempting to deplore these uncertainties of interpretation. The call may go up for a mechanical jurisprudence on which anthropologists, lawyers and Aborigines could rely. But neither from a social nor from a scientific perspective is there anything to commend the abolition of the possibility of reconsideration and revision. Conflicts of interpretation are only to be expected when important material interests turn on the precise way in which Aboriginal ideas and relations are conceived in English legal terms.

NOTES

1. The ups and downs of this legislation as a result of the change of government in South Australia have not affected the substance of its conceptualisation of Aboriginal relations to land, though there are changes in wording. In particular, the concept of 'interest' has been dropped from s.4, and the concept of 'traditional owner' introduced (in imitation, no doubt, of the Land Rights Act applying in the Northern Territory). This is defined to mean, in relation to land, 'an Aboriginal person who has, in accordance with Aboriginal tradition, social, economic and spiritual affiliations with, and responsibilities for, the lands or any part of them' (bill of 9 October 1980).

2. From Mr Justice Woodward's remarks at the AIAS conference in May 1980, and from Nicolas Peterson's correspondence with me, it appears that a motive for this narrowing was provided by the political calculation that a definite assertion of Aboriginal ownership was needed if land rights were to be accepted in the wider community. But this would not, by itself, account for the precise definition or for the precise constellation of powers and advantages created for traditional owners.

3. 'Traditional trustee', which is the only one of these terms not to have been recorded in the literature (so far as my knowledge of it goes), has been used by an Aboriginal consultant to the Australian Law Reform Commission on its inquiry into the recognition of Aboriginal customary law.

4. Under the English law of property a trustee is the legal owner of things which he holds for the benefit of another, who is their beneficial owner. The Land Rights Act has taken advantage of this mechanism by creating land trusts which hold title to Aboriginal land for the benefit of the people who are traditionally associated with the land. The trustee analogy is inaccurate for 'managers', because they traditionally enjoy benefits from the land of which they are 'managers', but if the analogy were to be accepted it would imply that 'managers' are the legal owners of land.

5. Dr L. R. Hiatt has told me that in 1973 he recommended to the Woodward Commission that, for economic purposes, land rights should be vested in communities, not descent groups, since it is the former that held customary rights to resources. He would accept that the veto powers created by the Act are as appropriately exercised by 'managers' as by 'owners'.

6. In view of what I have had to say about the traditional owners definition and its interpretation I should make it clear that until 1977 I was attributing the ownership of land to patrilineal clans. I gather from Peterson that there was a disappointing response by anthropologists to the Woodwood Commission's call for advice, and I am sure that my own submission was of little value. In retrospect, I am puzzled by my failure to treat 'managers' as having as good a proprietorial claim as 'owners', for my publications on ritual and social structure have always stressed the importance of the managerial relationship.

7. As far as I know, the possibility that 'managers' might satisfy the traditional owners definition was first raised by me (1977:13–14), only to be denied by Keen (1977:6). In several later papers I urged their case or explored the reasons given in land claims for leaving them out of the class of traditional owners (1978a:2–3; 1978b:6; 1978c:10–11; 1978d:606; 1979a:19; 1979b). The issue was debated at the AIAS workshop on land claims in May 1979. The Utopia claim book (Hagen & Rowell, 1979) took the bull by the horns and argued expressly for the inclusion of 'managers' as traditional owners.

8. This composition of Mudbura descent groups is mentioned only in passing in the claim book (McConvell & Palmer 1979:38), and it was not commented upon in the Land Commissioner's report or by his consultant.

9. Mr Justice Woodward commented on the poor response by Aborigines to his call for submissions (ALRC, 1973:6–7). At the AIAS conference in May 1980, Aborigines absented themselves from the third session of the land rights symposium in order to hold a political meeting of their own, even though the third session was the one devoted to discussion of traditional rights and their present-day formulation and recognition. That the nature of rights depends on their formulation as interpreted seemed not to be grasped, unless we assume that the absentees had full confidence in the anthropologists and lawyers from whom they parted.

10. It is noteworthy that Shapiro attributes ownership to what he calls 'ritual lodges' (1979:16–20). Now this term appears to have been adapted from Elkin (1954) or Meggitt (1962), who use it to refer to the little group of initiated men who are connected in the male line with a totem. The composition of such a lodge would resemble that of a local descent group in Leach's sense. Shapiro is fudging the distinction between a descent group and its adult male members.

11. *Milirrpum v. Nabalco Pty. Ltd. and The Commonwealth of Australia* (1971) 17 Federal Law Reports 141.

12. That the sex of the anthropologists involved in land claims is entirely irrelevant is shown by the fact that women anthropologists occupied key consultancy positions in three of the first four claims: Catherine (as

well as Ronald) Berndt in the Ranger claim, Marie Reay in the Borroloola, and Diane Bell in the Alyawarra. W.E.H. Stanner was the Commissioner's consultant in the Warlpiri claim. None of the women consultants questioned the patrilineal interpretation of the traditional owners definition, notwithstanding that they had all carried out extensive research beforehand. Nor did Francesca Merlan, the consultant in the Mudbura claim, express any doubts about a patrilineal interpretation.

REFERENCES

Aboriginal Land Rights Commission (1973) *First report*. Melbourne, ALRC.

Aboriginal Land Rights Commission (1974) *Second report*. Canberra, Australian Government Publishing Service.

Berndt, R.M. & Berndt, C.H. (1964) *The World of the First Australians*. Sydney, Ure Smith.

Elkin, A.P. (1954) *The Australian Aborigines: how to understand them*, 3rd ed. Sydney, Angus & Robertson.

Elkin, A.P. (1971) Yabuduruwa at Roper River Mission, 1965. *Oceania*, 42:110–64.

Hagen, R. & Rowell, M. (1979) *The Anmatjirra and Alyawarra land claim to Utopia pastoral lease*. Alice Springs, Central Land Council.

Hiatt, L.R. (1962) Local organization among the Australian Aborigines. *Oceania*, 32:267–86.

Hiatt, L.R. (1965) *Kinship and Conflict: a study of an Aboriginal community in northern Arnhem Land*. Canberra, Australian National University Press.

Keen, I. (1977) Comments on 'Anthropology in the Aboriginal Land Rights Act: a critical comment' by Kenneth Maddock. Unpublished manuscript, 9 pp.

Keen, I. (1980) The Alligator Rivers Aborigines—restrospect and prospect. In: R. Jones (ed.), *Northern Australia: options and implications*. Canberra, Australian National University, Research School of Pacific Studies.

Leach, E.R. (1961) *Rethinking Anthropology*. London, Athlone Press.

McConvell, P. & Palmer, A.B. (1979) *A claim to an area of traditional land by the Mudbura traditional owners*. Darwin, Northern Land Council.

Maddock, K. (1972) *The Australian Aborigines: a portrait of their society*. London, Allen Lane The Penguin Press.

Maddock, K. (1974) Dangerous proximities and their analogues. *Mankind*, 9:206–17.

Maddock, K. (1977) Anthropology in the Aboriginal Land Rights Act: a critical comment. Unpublished manuscript, 23 pp.

Maddock, K. (1978a) Notes on defining descent groups and obtaining genealogical data for use in traditional land claims. Unpublished manuscript, 8 pp.

Maddock, K. (1978b) Comments on the Borroloola and Walbiri 'traditional land claims'. Unpublished manuscript, 7 pp.

Maddock, K. (1978c) Comments on the Aboriginal Land Commissioner's report in the Borroloola land claim. Customary Law Group of Australia's *AIAS Newsletter* n.s. No. 2:5–13.

Maddock, K. (1978d) Einige ungelöste Fragen der Ökonomie und der lokalen Organisation der australischen Ureinwohner. *Ethnographisch-Archäologische Zeitschrift*, 19:601–11.

Maddock, K. (1979a) Comments on the Aboriginal Land Commissioner's report in the Walbiri land claim. Customary Law Group of Australia's *AIAS Newsletter* n.s. No. 3:16–19.

Maddock, K. (1979b) Comments on the AIAS workshop on land claims. Unpublished manuscript, 8 pp.

Maddock, K. (1980) *Anthropology, Law and the Definition of Australian Aboriginal Rights to Land*. Nijmegen, Instituut voor Volksrecht, Katholieke Universiteit.

Meggitt, M.J. (1962) *Desert People*. Sydney, Angus & Robertson.

Peterson, N. (1970) The importance of women in determining the composition of residential groups in Aboriginal Australia. In: F. Gale (ed.) *Woman's role in Aboriginal society*. Canberra, Australian Institute of Aboriginal Studies.

Peterson, N., Keen, I. & Sansom, B. (1977) Succession to land: primary and secondary rights to Aboriginal estates. In: *Hansard of the Joint Select Committee on Aboriginal land rights in the Northern Territory*. Canberra, Government Printer.

Peterson, N., McConvell, P., Wild, S. & Hagen, R. (1978) *A claim to areas of traditional land by Warlpiri and Kartangarurru-Kurintji*. Alice Springs, Central Land Council.

Radcliffe-Brown, A.R. (1930) The social organization of Australian tribes. *Oceania*, 1:34–63.

Radcliffe-Brown, A.R. (1956) On Australian local organization. *American anthropologist*, 58:363–67.

Ranger Uranium Environmental Inquiry (1977) *Second report*. Canberra, Australian Government Publishing Service.

Shapiro, W. (1979) *Social organization in Aboriginal Australia*. Canberra, Australian National University Press.

Thomas, N.W. (1906) *Kinship Organisations and Group Marriage in Australia*. Cambridge University Press.

14

PITJANTJATJARA PROCESSES AND THE STRUCTURE OF THE LAND RIGHTS ACT

Robert Layton

In his report on the Uluru National Park and Lake Amadeus Land Claim[1] the Land Commissioner commented (Toohey, 1979:8): 'The claim has to be looked at not so much as an exercise in Anthropology as an application of the Land Rights Act.' While there are anthropological issues raised by a study of the local traditional culture which are not directly relevant to a land claim, the purpose of this paper is to illustrate some of the common problems which anthropology and the law face in dealing with the culture: each discipline uses concepts not exactly matched in local thought and each uses methods for validating these concepts which are foreign to local behaviour. Moreover, I found the hearings considerably more demanding, as an exercise in anthropology than either an academic seminar or the examination of a thesis. This was most emphatically the case when it came to comparing my own evidence with that of the Aboriginal witnesses who followed; no writer of a thesis or seminar paper is expected to produce his informants and require them to corroborate every aspect of his data and analysis. The *Aboriginal Land Rights (Northern Territory) Act* 1976 is an attempt by the legal system of a bureaucratic State to match concepts expressed in writing with the processes of traditionally non-literate cultures (cultures which vary among themselves as one passes from rich coastal environments to inland desert), and it asks for a demonstration of principles which lie at the heart of those cultures' unwritten assumptions. The question, how is membership of a land-owning group acquired, is by no means of the same order as asking where a person was on the night of a murder, nor is a land-owning group an object of the same type as a fingerprint. One comment which particularly demands reflection is the remark:

> The process of extracting information in order to piece together the responsibility of a land owning group can be a difficult one . . . even so I got the impression . . . that some witnesses were being asked to think for the first time, so far as the hearing was concerned, about matters bearing upon the claim. (Toohey, op.cit.:12).

If it is the Commissioner's view (as it appears to be) that all anthropological evidence should be demonstrated through the statements of Aboriginal witnesses, then a fundamental error was committed in not establishing at the outset which aspects of the anthropological evidence were in fact inferences based on observations or records of Aboriginal behaviour rather than principles which the Aboriginal people habitually state.

The authors of the Warlpiri Claim Book made a rash statement:

> The best test of the accuracy and reliability of the evidence set out here for traditional ownership of the claimed areas is its reproduceability. We are confident that the evidence set out here is highly reproduceable. (Peterson et al., 1978:2).

If everything the anthropologist says were replicated in the Aboriginal evidence then the anthropologist would be superfluous. The anthropologist's role should surely rather be presented as one which will show how Aboriginal witnesses' statements are partial expressions of an underlying pattern of relevance to the Land Rights Act's

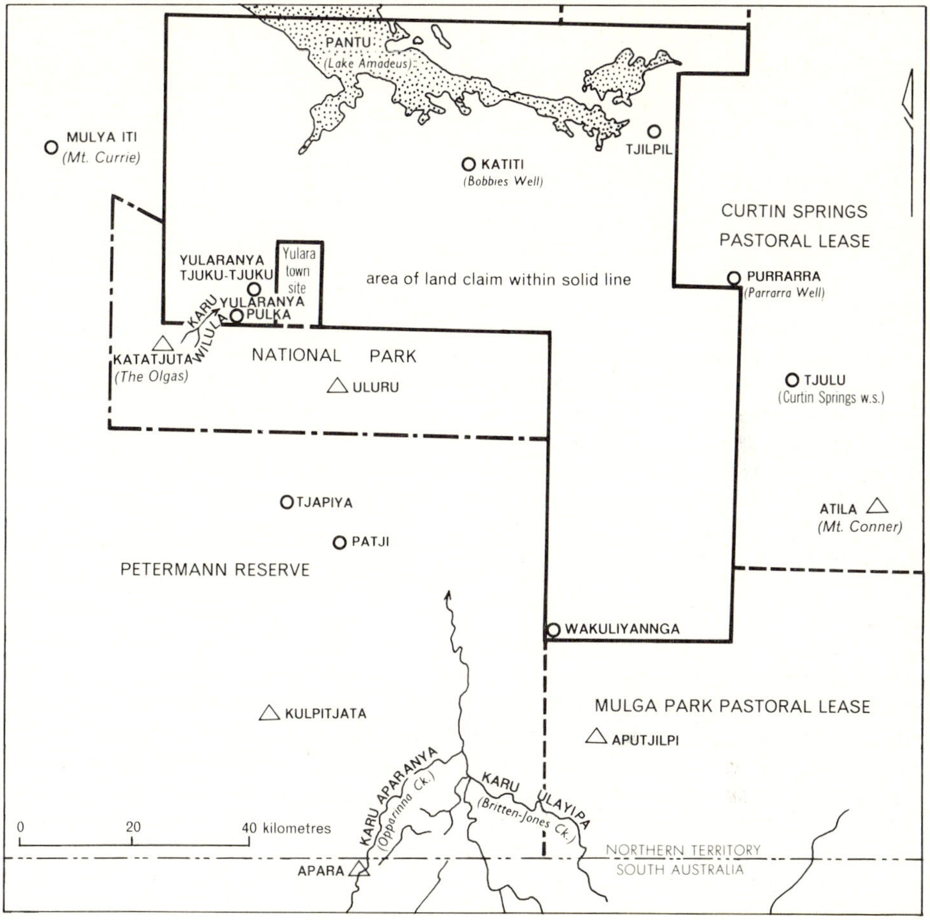

Fig. 1
Location of claim area.

requirements, and one which can provide historical and observational material not accessible to the Aboriginal witnesses. Support for this view can be found in the Commissioner's Borroloola report, where he wrote of the anthropological evidence:

> Mr Withnall categorised Mr Avery's (evidence) as hearsay . . . (but) when Mr Avery described the *nature* of the land owning group, the *concept* of clans and territories, the *attributes* of ownership of the land and the *nature* of semi-moieties and sub-sections, he was speaking as an expert dealing with *general anthropological propositions*. The fact that his opinions were to some, perhaps to a large extent based upon what he had been told by Aboriginals did not make that evidence hearsay any more than it would be right to describe as such the opinion of a physician based in part upon what he had been told by patients over a number of years. (Toohey, 1978:25; my emphasis).

The intention of the paper is not, however, to excuse unsatisfactory aspects of evidence given in the Ayers Rock claim, but instead to learn from that claim how things might have been presented better. Certain of the problems encountered were caused simply by the claim being lodged on behalf of members of a traditionally non-literate culture. Others derived from the more basic problem of obtaining verbal statements about the implicit principles on which behaviour is based, or on the general workings of a social system which may be more apparent to an observer than to a participant. Yet others were created by the etiquette and rules of what can be said in what context by members of that culture. All are issues which I feel should have been more carefully considered than they were in the anthropological evidence.

ELICITATION OF EVIDENCE

Many Aboriginal witnesses were unwilling to talk about sacred aspects of sites on or near the claim area. This led to denials that one site existed or that there were *inma* (song) verses for another:

> *The Interpreter:* If he says it is a secret, then there is something there—it is not a secret any longer. (Transcript of evidence, p. 740; see also Toohey, 1979:12, 17–18; and transcript of evidence, pp. 482, 700–701)

A more general problem was created by different understandings among ourselves and the Aboriginal witnesses about 'proofing'. While we saw it as a way of giving future witnesses some idea of what to expect in court, and of discovering what the answers to particular questions would be when they were asked in court, it became clear that the witnesses saw proofing in terms of traditional modes of instruction. When they had explained certain points to a lawyer during proofing it did not seem appropriate to repeat these points when the lawyer later asked the same question in court.

> *The Interpreter:* They are just saying they have got all that, why do we have to go through it again. (transcript, p. 481)
> *Mr Eames:* All I can say your Honour is that questions have been asked outside the hearing. Unfortunately, it does not seem to follow, having discussed it outside, that it goes smoothly inside. I wish there was another way of doing it. (transcript p. 681)

Although we tried to explain the purpose of proofing to witnesses, such an explanation is not likely to change well-established modes of conduct. Perhaps we should have taken more care to make the proofing look like the court hearing and less like an indigenous discussion.

IDENTIFICATION OF TRADITIONAL OWNERS

It is difficult for members of a culture lacking written history to prove claims based on tradition. Evidence that the claimants' rights and duties have a basis in regular past behaviour, other than witnesses' statements that this is the case, must come from written records compiled by observers. In Aboriginal evidence concerning past events, the only demonstration of the 'truth' is a present consensus among witnesses about what happened. Problems arise where there is no such consensus.

One instance in which this affected the Ayers Rock claim was the question of whether a particular claimant had been born at Ayers Rock, or at Wintawata in the Aparanya estate of the northern Musgraves. Throughout my fieldwork the man in question insisted that he had been born at Pularinya on the south side of the Rock, while others claimed 'never to have seen him around Uluru' when he was young and said he had been born at Wintawata. Issues like this, which may lie dormant during daily life, are brought into the open by a claim. For the Aboriginal community the man's birthplace is of social significance only as far as it helps determine the present status of he and his descendants as members of the Ayers Rock clan. If no one accepted him as a member of the group then the historical fact of his birth there would be unimportant. It should perhaps have been sufficient to ask witnesses whether they accepted him as a member and not enquire about the historical basis for his membership. Unfortunately, Aboriginal practice in the area considers place of birth and upbringing an index of attachment to a land-owning group. It was therefore tempting to look for historical evidence from external sources to test this claim. Nothing definite could be found. Groom's account of a journey made to Uluru and Katatjuta during the 1930s in this man's company (Groom, 1950:140; see also p. 172) shows that his attachment to the area existed long before the land claim or the advent of tourism:

> '*my* country', Tjalkalyiri is quoted as saying, 'go all the way across Lake Amadeus and Oolra and Kuttatutu (i.e., Uluru and Kakatjuta)'.

Susan Woenne, on the other hand, located a reference in census records compiled by Strehlow which gives the man's birthplace as Wintawata (see transcript of evidence p. 918). Circumstantial though this is, Strehlow did not record from whom his information was obtained.

While reliance on written records may seem convincing evidence to us, it is surely important not to overrate its relevance to Aboriginal custom. On the contrary, it is inimical to the resolution of disputes by customary means. This is particularly true of land claims themselves. Once such a point has been brought into issue a finding for or against the man's case becomes part of the bureaucratic record and can in future be consulted. The processes of non-literate society no longer operate freely.

IDENTIFICATION OF ESTATES

The Pitjantjatjara-Yangkuntjatjara approach to many of the items which the Act requires to be identified is existential rather than ideal. General statements are made by extrapolating from the speaker's personal experience according to shared rules, but they are not simply the expression of a shared construct. Members of the culture share ideas about the properties of the units of land held by a land-owning group and about how membership of such a group is conferred; they do not necessarily agree on the exact extent of particular estates or the exact composition of particular local descent groups. The court hearings demanded a consistency in evidence which under less rigorous conditions one might have considered unrealistic, but until the hearings began I probably attributed too great an independent reality to the constructs people had told me about. When collecting lists of sites attributed to the claim area, I was forced to recognise that, despite the consistency between these lists earlier found (see paper on Ambilineal Descent, Chapter 1 in this volume), the people I spoke to were not necessarily repeating a list they had learnt through instruction, but reflecting on their personal experience. From comments made while providing such lists, the premise was evidently that a country (estate) was an area focused on a permanent water source but including peripheral waters up to the zone of access from adjacent permanent waters. This led to remarks like 'Puntitjata belongs to Aputjilpinya because we used to go there from Aputjilipi', or 'Yularanya belongs to Katatjuta because we always went there from Katatjuta'. Consistent with the concept of *ngura inmanguru* (explained in the paper on Ambilineal Descent), however, another criterion was sometimes also used by witnesses to establish the status of peripheral sites: if they lay on a Dreaming track running to or from one of the several adjacent reference places, then they belonged to the estate focused on that reference place.

One result of these mental procedures was that members of adjacent clans sometimes both claimed ownership of certain peripheral sites, and that there were inconsistencies of detail between different lists. In the list of sites Aboriginal witnesses attributed to the estate centred on Katatjuta there are five (out of a total 19) which also appear in the list of places later attributed to the Uluru estate. Another one site was said to be shared by the two estates (transcript of evidence pp. 481-92, 570-73; and see also p. 632). The fact that the land claimed contained only peripheral soaks and rock holes focused attention on these discrepancies. Whether or not sites were said to be shared depended to some extent on the form of the question. To answer the question, 'Which places belong to Ulurunya?', it would not necessarily be relevant to say that some such places also belonged to another estate. The broader question, 'Who sings the songs for Wakuliyannga?'—a peripheral site on the Mala track between Uluru and Aputjilpi, is likely to evoke a general answer such as 'everyone' or 'we all do', because this kind of question seems to suppose premises about shared ritual responsibility (see the discussion of Wakuliyannga on p. 728 of the transcript of evidence). The problem is exemplified by various statements made about two sites in the part of the claim between Uluru and Katatjuta, Kapi Yularanya Pulka and Kapi Yularanya Tjukutjuku. (The names mean, respectively, the big and little waters at Yulara. Yulara is the area after which the new tourist village takes its name, but neither water source lies in the block excised for the village.)

(1) *Mr Eames:* Kapi Yularanya Tjukutjuku and Kapi Yularanya Pulka—are they countries for Ayers Rock as well as Katatjuta, or just Katatjuta?
Peter Bulla (Katatjuta claimant): Katatjuta (transcript of evidence p. 492).

(2) *Mr Eames:* That place Yularanya Tjukutjuku, your mob belongs to it, and Ayers Rock mob belongs to it?
Mr Bulla: Yes.
Mr Eames: Which mob starts singing the songs for that place, is it your mob or is it the Ayers Rock mob, or is it both?
Peter Bulla: Ayers Rock, Katatjuta, both (transcript p.531).

(3) *Mr Eames:* Can you tell us the names of places for Uluru on the empty land?
Toby Nangina (Uluru/Atila claimant): Kapi Yularanya Tjukutjuku, Kapi Yularanya Pulka . . . (transcript p. 570).

(4) At Kapi Yularanya Tjukutjuku, Nipper Winmati (Uluru claimant) explained that men from Uluru used to go to Yulara to camp after rain, but that the principal Dreaming track is one coming from the Olgas, so that Katatjuta holds the dominant interest (transcript p. 649).

(5) *Mr Eames:* Kapi Yularanya Pulka; I just want to know what mob's country that one is?
Nipper Winmati: Katatjuta (transcript p. 740).

There are similar examples in the evidence concerning Purrarra on pp. 570 and 729 of the transcript of evidence, and concerning Katiti on pp. 732A and 732B.)

On the evidence for traditional ownership of Kapi Yularanya Tjuku Tjuku, the Commissioner commented (Toohey, 1979:13):

> the evidence did not establish with any precision which of those estates (Uluru and Katatjuta) had primary responsibility for it. What is clear is that one or other or both have that responsibility . . . Precisely the same comments may be made about Kapi Yularanya Pulka.

Although this seems to offer an excuse for not establishing exclusive ownership of a site through the Aboriginal evidence, it should be noted that both estates were proved to have primary responsibility over other sites within the claim area. Had this not been the case, their ownership of the two soaks at Yularanya would have been critical to their members' status as traditional owners (see the Commissioner's comments on the position of the Atila estate re Purrarra, op. cit.: 16, the Aputjilpi estate re Wakuliyannga and the Apara estate re Katiti, 15).

JOINT ESTATES

The premise that an estate consists of a permanent water source surrounded by impermanent ones also led to differing statements as to how many estates were involved in the claim. The central waters at Katatjuta, Kulpitjata and Aputjilpi are known to be less reliable than those at Uluru, Apara and Atila. Within living memory there have been years when those owning the former estates were forced by drought to move to the latter during the driest months. The three pairs of estates (see paper on Ambilineal Descent) were sometimes spoken of as being single entities. Whereas Peter Bulla identified Katatjuta as the country belonging to one group of witnesses, Tjalkalyiri referred to Katatjuta and Uluru as one place (pp. 467–68). Elsewhere, Uluru and Katatjuta were described as *watjira*, cousins (transcript of evidence, pp. 445, 470, 512). This is noted by the Commissioner in his report (op. cit.:9):

> There are examples of joint ownership, particularly where water is to be found. This was most evident in the case of Uluru and Katatjuta. Some witnesses tended to speak of their country as one or other of those places; some drew no particular distinction between the two.

RECRUITMENT TO THE LOCAL DESCENT GROUP

Although the Commissioner found (Toohey, 1979:5) that 'the notion of estates was familiar to the claimants', the questions of recruitment to and responsibilities of the land-owning group presented the most difficult qualities to demonstrate through Aboriginal evidence.

The Commissioner reported (Toohey, 1979:8) that the principle of ambilineal descent did not emerge with complete clarity from the evidence, but he did find 'it is quite clear that the claimants recognized that country need not be acquired patrilineally'. Leo Williams' country is Katatjuta, his mother's country. His father's was Piltati, in the Petermanns, but Leo transmitted membership of Katatjuta to his children. Some witnesses claimed membership of the Ayers Rock group through their father, but Napala Jack took membership from his mother. Pompey Whistler took membership of the Apara group through his mother (cited from transcript of evidence pp. 524, 540, 703). There are others the Commissioner does not mention. Pompey Douglas and Billy Kaiyipipi, for instance, inherited membership of the Aparanya land-owning group from their mothers, but transmitted this membership to their own sons (transcript of evidence pp. 703–704; Pompey and Kaiyipipi are sons of men who participated in what Tindale called the 'Pitjantjatjara Invasion')[2] Peggy Branston claimed membership of the Ulurunya land-owning group through her grandmother and her father (transcript p. 561).

Peter Bulla stated that he had not learnt about his father's country, Mintulnga, and therefore did not claim it (transcript p. 454). Other witnesses suggested that if a person did not learn the songs of a parent's country he would lose that country, although they were reluctant to envisage this (transcript p. 741).[3]

It appears therefore that despite the failure of the *principle* of ambilineal descent to emerge, the *practice* of what anthropologists have called ambilineal descent was established. What could have been done to improve this position?

The Pitjantjatjara do not have a generic term corresponding to 'clan' (cf. *gunmugugur*, cited in Fox et al., 1977:255), nor do the groups holding particular estates have proper names. Certainly there is no Pitjantjatjara word equivalent to 'ambilineal'. It seems difficult to escape the view that Aboriginal evidence for ambilineality must be indirect. It might have helped if we had asked some or all Aboriginal witnesses to spell out the basis of their own claims in terms which referred directly to ambilineality (e.g., What is your father's country? What is your mother's country? Which country do your children take from you? Why do they take that one?) although the examples cited above show that information of this order was established through the evidence. It was possible to talk about choosing a country; Peter Bulla spoke of his children 'picking out' a country while Tjalkalyiri also spoke of his children 'choosing' and Vachon supplied the Pitjantjatjara phrase *ngura kantjankuku* for 'choosing a country' (transcript pp. 454, 468, 472). Nonetheless, the procedural correctness of asking witnesses this kind of question was several times raised during the Aboriginal evidence (transcript pp. 455–57, 515–21), particularly with respect to whether it constituted a leading, and therefore inadmissable, question during the witnesses' evidence in chief (transcript p. 474). Paul Ekert, during his period as interpreter, pointed out that a man does not 'keep' (i.e., perform senior ritual duties in) his father's country while his father is still alive (transcript p. 671), and this further complicated the questioning.

The root of the problem lay partly, I think, in the fact that my own ideas of 'how the system really worked' were developing throughout the period of fieldwork and preparation for the case. Although the Claim Book discusses the question of selection between mother's and father's countries, and notes that the system is not exclusively patrilineal (Layton & Rowell, 1979:2), it does not use the term *ambilineal*. The term was not introduced until evidence was given in court. Since this evidence was found by the Commissioner to be confusing and lacking in preparation (Toohey, 1979:5) it would have been better to have supplied the additional explanation in the form of a written submission that could have been spoken to in evidence. The extended quotation from verbal evidence which the Commissioner provides in his report would have been clearer if it had included the preceding sentence, 'We could take a hypothetical situation in which both men and women transmit the rights or responsibilities of membership in their group' (Toohey, op. cit.:6,8 and transcript of evidence p. 178). This kind of misunderstanding could better be overcome in a written statement, and the diagram partially reproduced on p. 7 of the Commissioner's report could have been more neatly prepared.

A further consequence of my developing understanding was that the Aboriginal evidence presented a more complex picture than I had done when the hearings opened. I think that I supposed my account of ambilineality provided a complete description of how rights to the land-owning group were transmitted, but it became clear as the hearings progressed that it was simply a model which lacked some of the complications revealed in Aboriginal evidence. There would be nothing wrong in the anthropologist providing such a model, but unless the status of the anthropological evidence as a form of analysis is established it is misleading. The major complication concerns the continued significance of grandparent's countries. In the Claim Book it was stated that 'only in cases where a special effort had been made (or where the grandchild has the same estate as a grandparent) will the body of knowledge about an estate be transmitted to a third generation' (Layton & Rowell, 1979:3). When asked during cross-examination to explain why genealogies showed certain people taking membership of an estate other than that of either parent, I suggested that the most economical explanation might be adoption rather than inheritance (transcript p. 268)! When asked in court to explain how they had inherited membership of a land-owning group, a number of Aboriginal witnesses traced ownership from a grandparent even though in many cases the intervening parent was also a member of the group. Tjalkalyiri, Bill Okai and Cassidy Uluru did this when speaking of their children (transcript pp. 472, 523, 548, 549). Malcolm Winima and Ronny Russell did so when speaking of their own membership of a group, as did Toby Nangina, who cited his uncles, cousins and grandmother as the basis for his membership of his mother's group (transcript pp. 676, 709, 607)

Such instances make it easier to understand the value of claims to belong to a grandparent's group even where the intervening parent belong to another. This was the case with James Severn's claim to belong to Uluru, Leo Williams' claim that his children had inherited membership of Uluru from their 'grandfather' (FMB) and Stanley Kumintjara's statement that his brother and sister's children took membership of the group owning Aputjilpi from their grandmother (transcript pp. 510, 548, 691). It also helps to explain why Bill Okai felt able to say that his children had inherited membership of both their father's father's and father's mother's countries (transcript p. 523).[4]

To account for the entire body of evidence, the model of ambilineal descent should perhaps have stated that choice was exercised between the four estates of the person's grandparents. However, table 4 in the paper on ambilineal descent among the Pitjantjatjara shows that 89% of individuals recorded joined the land-owning group of one or other of their parents. Provided its status as a model is made explicit, there is surely something to be said for keeping the anthropologist's account as simple as possible. If the aim is to explain the difference between unilineal and ambilineal descent, then perhaps it is sufficient to talk about choice between the parents' estates. Listening to the Aboriginal evidence, I remembered a comment made by Edmund Leach at a conference on the use of models in understanding prehistory (in Renfrew, 1973:765):

> If you go into a toy shop and ask for a 'model aeroplane' you are liable to be offered one of two quite different things: one is an object that looks like an aeroplane but does not fly; the other does *not* look like a 'real' aeroplane but will fly.

A useful model should aim to isolate and describe the underlying processes of Aboriginal custom which are of relevance to the Land Rights Act. If, as a result, it does not look like the real thing, the differences should be noted and explained.

PRIMARY SPIRITUAL RESPONSIBILITIES

The fact that the Pitjantjatjara do not have a generic term for 'local descent group' or proper names for individual local descent groups makes it almost impossible to identify the group exercising primary spiritual responsibility for the sites and land comprising an estate except through the group's manifestation in behaviour. I would go so far as to say that among the Pitjantjatjara local descent groups are an epiphenomenon generated by the procedures to which the Pitjantjatjara attach greatest importance: growing up to know a country, taking a leading role in its ceremonies, and having custodianship of the sacred aspects of the estate. This again means that informants or witnesses will identify a group by applying such criteria to their experience of people's accepted roles rather than indicating some body with an external existence. I suspect that one of the sociological functions of Pitjantjatjara totemic ritual may be to express and ratify individuals' allegiances to land-holding groups. These problems are not unique to the Ayers Rock claim, and were encountered as early as the Borroloola case. In that claim book Avery drew attention to a crucial difference between the situation dealt with by the Ranger enquiry and that found at Borroloola; at Borroloola (as at Uluru) there is neither a generic term nor are there proper names for clans (Avery & McLaughlin, 1977: 26). He also reported that, (op. cit.: 28–29) 'No single word in any of the languages of the McArthur River area is sufficient to convey the sense of the unique relationship which exists between a clan and its territory'. The Commissioner rightly pointed out (Toohey, 1978:8) in his report that,

> The real question of course is whether particular claimants constitute in respect of

> each area of land claimed a local descent group meeting the requirements of the (Act's) definition of traditional Aboriginal owners.

The Act's definition is expressed in terms of rights and responsibilities.

At Ayers Rock the situation was slightly simplified by the existence of generally recognised, named estates: the problem was to identify the unique rights and duties of the group holding the estate. Throughout the Gulf country this procedure is made more difficult by the association of both people and blocs of country with semimoieties. Like subsections, semimoieties are categorical terms. They define relationships between members of different categories but do not in themselves constitute corporate groups (cf. Avery's comments on the relevance of semimoieties to behaviour, op. cit.: 36). While one thus plays the role of *djungayi* in the ceremonies of one mother's brothers' semimoiety and sometimes one's father's mother's brothers' semimoiety, there is no sense in which this responsibility is corporately performed by all members of a semimoiety throughout the Gulf country. Avery makes the same point about the role of *nimaringki* (Avery & McLaughlin, op. cit.: 29, 29 n):

> Clan members are Nimaringki to their own territory but are also Nimaringki to the territory of clans in the same patrilineal moiety . . . Nimaringki is a classificatory term (. . . denoting a class of relationships).

I would add that my understanding, from fieldwork for the Cox River land claim, is that both Nimaringki and Djungayi are terms describing ritual offices and therefore applicable not to whole descent groups but only to their senior members.

The Warlpiri claim book discusses similar problems raised by the meaning of the term *kirda,* or 'owner' (Peterson et al., 1978: iii).

The Commissioner reports that Marie Reay, in her comments on the anthropological evidence for the Borroloola claim, took the view that within the language-defined group, all members of a semimoiety constituted a local descent group according to the terms of the Act: 'It seems evident that on anthropological grounds the Anula semimoiety is as much a clan as the unnamed, less inclusive group Mr. Avery identifies as such' (Exhibit 80, p. 10, cited in Toohey, 1978:20), but she accepted that within the semimoiety 'there is a smaller group of people who are more closely associated with particular parts of the territory attributed to their semimoiety than other members are'. Later this exclusive sub-group was defined in terms of 'a common relationship with a particular territory through dreamings'. (loc. cit.)

Avery pointed out in the Claim Book (1977:29) that while men claim the status of *Nimaringki* over all land belonging to their semimoiety, 'people tend not to press their claim to be *nimaringki* to land before the foremost *nimaringki* of the land'. While this kind of criterion is a useful one for anthropologists who work over a period of months in an area and cross-check their data by observing unelicited behaviour and questioning numerous informants, it is not one to rely on in a court hearing. There is no guarantee that different witnesses will not give contradictory evidence. People with whom I worked at Cox River spoke of the design one 'puts on' when being painted for ceremony as being the critical determinant of local group membership. Different local groups within the same semimoiety put on different designs. The only satisfactory way to establish membership of a descent group holding primary reponsibilities for a bloc of land seems to be the drawing up of a *list* of criteria, *all* of which may be discussed in court. Avery (op. cit.: 33-34) does this when he writes of the corporate properties of the local descent group:

> The use of body marks, ceremonial dances, songs and ceremonies which derive from the power, are signs of the power and his ownership of the associated territory. Owners also have control of a stock of personal names.

He does, however, note that both names and body decorations may be conferred (on classificatory) *nimaringki* outside the local descent group, so the full definition should perhaps include the phrase 'the right to use and confer on others'.

The fact that the Act takes primary ritual responsibilities as the first index of membership of the local descent group makes proof difficult where witnesses are reluctant to speak of what their ritual responsibilities include. This is something for the anthropologist to remember when he or she is outlining criteria of membership that the judge and lawyers will then apply to Aboriginal evidence. The Ayers Rock case also suggested that it would be dangerous to rely on a single responsibility as the major index of group membership, since even if valid as a generalisation, any such responsibility may be affected in practice by matters such as death or adoption. While giving preliminary evidence I rashly stated that the responsibility for opening the performance of each *inma* verse during ceremony was the major responsibility of traditional owners of the country to which the verse referred (transcript p. 170). The first problem this raised was that, since uninitiated children could not play this role, they might not be members of the local descent group (see transcript of evidence p. 261). The second problem arose from the death of Paddy Uluru, who had been the most knowledgeable man about the *Mala* songs in his own country. During the hearings it proved that Toby Nangina, whose primary association was with the adjacent estate of Atila, had taken over responsibility for initiating the *Mala* songs until Paddy's sons grew old enough and sufficiently knowledgeable to play this role themselves. Throughout the hearing Toby insisted that because the Kuniya track ran directly from Atila to Uluru, he held considerable rights at Uluru (on p. 541 of the transcript of evidence he states that this makes Uluru his country), and the Commissioner accepted that on the evidence, Toby Nangina was a 'traditional owner' of the Uluru estate within the terms of the Act. A third problem created by relying on a single criterion of primary responsibility was the difficulty of proving that any group held primary spiritual ties to those sites whose songs were too sacred to be mentioned in public. This was particularly the case for one site, Katiti, which lay in the claim area (see transcript of evidence pp. 732A, 732B).

Eventually we attempted to broaden the definition of primary spiritual responsibility by citing other indices: a responsibility for members of the local descent group to transmit knowledge of the *inma* associated with its estate to their children and of the children to learn, a responsibility to perform these *inma,* and a right to live and forage in the estate (transcript pp. 990–91). A fourth criterion mentioned but, because of its sensitive nature, not used during the evidence of Aboriginal witnesses, was the custodianship of sacred objects associated with the estate (transcript p. 261).

There may be claims where groups can be identified at several levels of inclusiveness, who satisfy in their behaviour the requirement of performing a primary spiritual responsibility toward sites and the land. If this is the case, I would recommend identifying in the anthropological evidence that level which is most likely to be described by Aboriginal witnesses in court rather than any other level which might be suggested from comparative anthropological evidence.

RIGHTS TO FORAGE

The second behavioural index of traditional ownership specified by the Act is the right to forage over the estate. This created no problem in Aboriginal evidence since people frequently spoke of foraging in their own country. The fact that this right extended beyond one's own estate did, however, make some difficulties. Witnesses were reluctant to suggest that anyone could be excluded from foraging in a particular area.

Mr. Eames: What people are allowed to hunt in that country around Wakuliyannga?

> *Toby Nangina:* My mother hunted and foraged there. Anyone. (transcript of evidence p. 729; see also pp. 732B, 733).

Any comment that 'everyone' can forage at a site clearly means everyone within a circumscribed range. No one would suppose that Yolngu or Worora, or even Warlpiri, would be able to enter the area and forage as of right. In my evidence I stated that before people could enter an estate other than their own they must first know the songs and they must have seen or been shown the location of the sites in that estate. The Commissioner finds a contradiction between that statement and evidence 'of an entitlement to forage extending beyond one's estate' (Toohey, 1979:17). It appears to me not so much a contradiction as a case of people as a matter of course acquiring the requisite knowledge. Many witnesses did not refer to a prior need to know the country but where such an assumption was not automatic, witnesses did refer to teaching visitors local knowledge. When attempting to establish the limits on 'everyone's' knowledge of songs belonging to the Uluru estate, Geoff Eames asked one witness whether a man from Indulkana could be taught them:

> *The Interpreter:* I asked if a man from Indulkana came here and sat here, not your relation, your friend—and he (Toby Nangina) said, yes, it would be my friend—and he came and sat here, could he teach him that Kuniya dreaming, and Toby said he would be embarrassed, and because he would be embarrassed he would teach him the dreaming.
> *His Honour:* There is a whole new world of local descent groups opening up, Mr Eames (transcript of evidence, p. 612).

Elsewhere, witnesses from Kikingkura (the Docker River area) said that they could not forage at Uluru except in the company of the local traditional owners (transcript pp. 713–14).

Several witnesses spoke of being shown neighbouring estates by their fathers when they were children and of neighbouring groups singing songs together (see Stanley Kumintjara, transcript of evidence p. 696; Pompey Douglas, p. 708; Nyinnga Stewart, p. 719). Nyinnga stated that his father showed him places in surrounding estates when Nyinnga was a boy and later, when he was a man, taught him the songs (loc. sit.). Although the point about prior knowledge was not essential to the success of the claim, it appears that we did not give sufficient thought to drawing out through witnesses' statements the assumptions that they made in first answering questions about the right to forage (see the Commissioner's summary of the evidence on pp. 36–38 of his report).

CONCLUSION

Land claims do require an exercise in anthropology, but not an exercise in anthropological speculation. The anthropologist's evidence should be concerned as far as possible with generalising about points that can be substantiated from Aboriginal evidence given in court. Where this is not the case the anthropologist should state the reasons why he or she is making deductions or proposing models, and such efforts should be clearly related to the terms of the Land Rights Act. Wherever generalisations are based on informants' statements the anthropologist should explain how he or she went about reconciling any inconsistencies found between such statements.

NOTES

1. Here referred to for convenience as the 'Ayers Rock claim', even though the land council was unable to pursue a claim on the national park.
2. Noel Wallace (pers. comm.) and I both concluded that there was no sudden invasion but, rather, a gradual

flow of men from the Mann and Petermann ranges into the Musgraves. Far from displacing the Yangkuntjatjara, the children of these men were, through the operation of ambilineal descent, incorporated into Yangkuntjatjara society.

3. There is, however, one item of counter-evidence on this point; Nyinnga Stewart claimed not to know the songs of his country of birth, Atila, but other witnesses stated that Atilanya was Nyinnga's country (transcript pp. 627, 748–49).

4. Peterson has suggested (pers. comm.) that, given the importance of residence for the transmission of rights to land in this area, membership may be traced to the grandparental generation to underline the strength of one's rights.

REFERENCES

Avery, J. & McLaughlin, D. (1977) *Submission . . . to the Aboriginal Land Commissioner on behalf of traditional Aboriginal owners in the Borroloola region of the Northern Territory* (second edition). Darwin, Northern Land Council.

Fox, R. et al. (1977) *Ranger Uranium Environmental Enquiry: second report.* Canberra, Australian Government Printer.

Groom, A. (1950) *I Saw a Strange Land.* Sydney, Angus & Robertson.

Layton, R. & Rowell, M. (1979) *Ayers Rock—Mount Olga National Park and Lake Amadeus Traditional Land Claim: claim book.* Alice Springs, Central Land Council.

Peterson, N., McConvell, P., Wild, S. & Hagen, R. (1978) *A Claim to Areas of Traditional Land by the Warlpiri and Kartangarurru–Kurintji. Revised version.* Alice Springs, Central Land Council.

Renfrew, C. (ed.) (1973) *The Explanation of Culture Change.* London, Duckworth.

Toohey, J. (1978) *Borroloola Land Claim: report to the Minister for Aboriginal Affairs and to the Minister for the Northern Territory.* Published in 1979. Canberra, AGPS.

Toohey, J. (1979) *Uluru (Ayers Rock) National Park and Lake Amadeus/Luritja land claim: report by the Aboriginal Land Commissioner.* Published in 1980. Canberra, AGPS.

PART THREE

MODERN STRUCTURES

15 THE VICTORIAN ABORIGINAL LAND COUNCIL 1975–77

Bette Moore

The Victorian Aboriginal Land Council (VALC) was formed as a consequence of Federal/State discussions about implementing the Woodward recommendations in the State of Victoria. It existed for only 32 months and failed to fulfil its charter.[1] The experience of this Council's attempts to do so bring to light the specific problems relating to land rights in this State, and other variables upon which land rights are dependent.

The difficulties expressed by members of the VALC indicate two general conclusions: that land rights in the State of Victoria can only be achieved if the machinery for its implementation takes into account issues of relative independence and autonomy of decision-making, and that the existing framework adopted from the Woodward Commission's Report for the implementation of land rights is not adequate. In short, there is a gap between Aboriginal awareness, needs and demands in this State, and the framework adopted from the Woodward Commission's recommendations which supported the setting up of land councils to advise the governments in States outside the Northern Territory. Unlike the land councils in the Northern Territory, which have the backing of legislation that also grants reserve land and allows for claims to traditional land (providing it is in areas which are unalienated Crown land) the Victorian Land Council was without legislative backing.

BACKGROUND

The background context from 1974-79 is important for understanding the confusion, ambiguities and expectations of the VALC, its consequent conflict in its relationship with the Department of Aboriginal Affairs, and its ultimate demise in 1977.

The VALC was created as a consequence of two related events in a specific political context. The first was the passing of the *Aboriginal Affairs (Transfer of Functions) Act* 1974, which superseded the *Aboriginal Affairs Act* 1967 and abolished the Victorian Ministry of Aboriginal Affairs. The important aspect of this Act was that the Commonwealth Government became directly involved in policy, planning and coordination with the endorsement of the Government of Victoria.

The other event was the publication of the Second Report of the Aboriginal Land Rights Commission, or the *Woodward Report*, in April 1974. This Report espoused two general principles: that Aboriginal people must be fully consulted in the implementation of land rights, and that any schemes for granting of land must be sufficiently flexible to meet changing needs and ideas. This Report was limited to procedures for the granting of land to Aborigines in the Northern Territory and did not attempt to examine or investigate the position of Aborigines outside the Territory. However, it was regarded as a model for State governments to follow. In terms of the Victorian situation, the relevant passages of this Report (p. 135) are as follows (my emphasis):

> 744. I must stress, however, *that I have not attempted to investigate the present position of Aborigines outside the Territory and I do not know their wishes or expectations so far as land rights are concerned. What I have said elesewhere, about the importance of finding out what Aborigines want,* is *relevant again in this context.* The Aborigines of Walgett, Redfern or Cape York may have quite different ideas from those of Alice Springs or Arnhem Land.
>
> 745. What I do recommend is that the *approach be followed in the States as has been followed in the Territory.* By this I mean that *regional councils of Aborigines, if not already in existence, should be encouraged to establish themselves. It may be that each State could constitute a region for this purpose or it may be that, in some States Aborigines would find it more convenient to adopt two or three regions.*
>
> 746. Whatever is decided, *each regional council should be provided with independent legal assistance, and whatever administrative help is needed to enable it to formulate its ideas and claims.* I anticipate that the Aboriginal legal aid services could arrange the legal aid in most cases, but stress that *the aid must come from experienced lawyers* who are fully qualified to give it.
>
> 747. Before any claims are finally decided upon, it is important that there should be consultation between the regions, because it is obviously desirable that the basic approaches should be as similar as possible. On the other hand it is probably inevitable that differing problems and ideas will produce some differences between regions—at least on matters of detail. Inter-regional conferences could presumably be held under the guidance of the *National Aboriginal Consultative Committee. No doubt that Committee will also want to express its own views, both to the regional councils and to the government.*
>
> 748. I suggest that the recommendations in this report could represent a starting point for discussions within each state or regional council. When it has arrived at its decisions in the light of its legal advice, its discussions with other councils, and its own deliberations, *those views and claims should be sent to the government.* No doubt the government will indicate whether it intends to establish some authority to collect, co-ordinate and advise on such claims or *whether it prefers to deal directly with the various councils.*

Following the Woodward Commission's proposals, discussions were held between the Federal Minister for Aboriginal Affairs (Senator J. Cavanagh) and the then Victorian Chief Secretary, Mr Vance Dickie, in September 1974. At this meeting it was resolved that an Aboriginal land council be formed to consider the Woodward Commission's Report and develop proposals regarding claims to land after consultation with Aborigines in Victoria.

It is important to note that this land council was the first of its type to be formed outside the Northern Territory, and hence had no guidelines to follow from precedents established elsewhere.[2] The Northern Land Council and Central Land Council models set out in the Woodward Commission's Report, and later incorporated in the *Aboriginal Land Rights (Northern Territory) Act* 1976, were established as the administrative machinery to formulate claims to traditional land in the Northern Territory. These council functions were to directly represent traditional owners and other Aborigines with traditional interests in negotiations over land use and mineral development and to assist Aborigines in the preparation and conduct of claims for land based on traditional use and occupancy. They also nominated members of land trusts, which are title-holding bodies representing communities and traditional owners, appointed in consultation with the parties concerned. Both members of the land councils and the land trusts are local Aborigines chosen by their communities to consult with traditional owners and act in accordance with their wishes.

This structure is democratic in its representative and consultative forms and was linked to Commonwealth legislation granting title to existing reserve land and enabling

Aborigines in the Northern Territory to claim unalienated Crown land where traditional association with land could be established.

The Victorian 'model' was in marked contrast to the Central and Northern land councils outlined in the Woodward Report, as a consequence of the different situation. Firstly, its membership was not elected directly by Victorian Aborigines as members of a land council, and secondly there was no Victorian legislation providing for such a Council to establish land trusts or work on behalf of 'traditional owners'.[3] The membership of the VALC had been discussed by Departmental Ministers and directors, who had independently agreed that the Land Council should include former members of the Victorian Aboriginal Affairs Advisory Council,[4] NACC members for Victoria,[5] and those Aborigines who had been active in land rights. [6] The Lake Tyers and Framlingham Trusts were also invited to nominate their representatives.

The difference between the Victorian situation and that in the Northern Territory was noted by Senator Cavanagh in his opening address to the inaugural meeting of the VALC on 4 April 1975:[7]

> The situation in Victoria is far removed from that applying in the Northern Territory and many of Mr Justice Woodward's recommendations may therefore not be applicable . . . The associations which Victorian Aborigines hold for land are of a different nature to the traditional and religious ties held by many Aboriginal people in other areas of Australia . . . I believe that your Council's best approach will be to seek to identify the *land needs* of the Victorian Aboriginal Community as it *now exists*.[8] Broadly, I imagine that these needs will be:-
> —land for housing, principally in urban areas,
> —land for community purposes, and
> —land for economic development.

Senator Cavanagh then outlined the various government authorities which could provide funding for land and development purposes, and re-iterated Mr Justice Woodward's directive that 'views and claims of the Council should be sent to the Government . . . to determine the most appropriate way of dealing with them'. He also advised that the services of Mr Renkin, the then Director of the South-East Region Department of Aboriginal Affairs, and his staff should be used for any secretarial services, and that the facilities of the Victorian Legal Aid Service be used for legal advige.

The political context was extremely confusing in the period between 1974 and 1977: the admynistrati e, fiscal and procedural machinery of Aboriginal Affairs fluctuated and a policy change occurred when the Federal Liberal Party came to power in 1975.

At the beginning of 1975 administration changed from a State Ministry to the Commonwealth Department (with the exception of housing left under the auspices of the Victorian Housing Commission). Ministers responsible for Aboriginal Affairs changed from Senator Cavanagh and Mr Les Johnson (ALP) in 1974 to Senator Drake Brockman during the caretaker ministry established in 1975 and Mr Viner (Lib.) in 1976. In this period, policy changed from Labor's self-determination to the Liberal Party's self-management.

The principal Act relating to land rights in the Northern Territory was passed in 1976 (after amendments to the original Bill proposed by the Labor Party) and budget allocations of August 1975-76 and 1976-77 reduced expenditure on Aboriginal Affairs substantially. This figure was justified by the Treasurer, Mr Lynch, as a matter of effective priority allocation when he made the point that the promotion of Aboriginal welfare is not 'simply a matter of injecting ever-increasing amounts of money into an ever-increasing complexity of . . . programmes'[9] and by Mr Viner on the basis of a 're-assessment of job-assistance programmes'.[10]

The advent of land rights legislation was in part due to the extra-parliamentary activities and lobbying of Aboriginal organisations, which had expressed their grievances in different forms in the 1960s, creating a greater awareness of the Aboriginal question in the general community. The central issues uniting these various groups were 'land rights' and 'self-determination'.

In Victoria, the issue of self-determination led to the creation of an elected Aboriginal Advisory Council as part of the Victorian Ministry of Aboriginal Affairs, and the issue of land rights evolved around the question of Lake Tyers and the announcement of its closure. The granting of freehold title to Lake Tyers and Framlingham residents was a consequence of this demand. However, these measures were perceived as tokens—only partial and unsatisfactory applications of the expressed principles. The VALC attempted to act as a body to implement them effectively.

HISTORY OF THE COUNCIL

The history of the VALC reveals a central conflict in the different perceptions of the role and function held by its members and that of the Department of Aboriginal Affairs. These were all concerned ultimately with its struggle for autonomy and decision-making powers in a structured situation of fiscal and legal dependency and powerlessness. A sense of futility was expressed at the outset by Sir Douglas Nicholls after a direct application for land needs by the VALC in June was not followed up. He pointed out to the July meeting that the VALC 'could only make recommendations to the Minister for Aboriginal Affairs with regard to submissions for land, houses and compensation for land . . . what then was the point of the Land Council being set up if this is all it could do?'[11]

The short history of the VALC can be seen as a struggle to obtain independence and autonomy from restrictive bureaucratic structures. In its perception of its function, these were the prerequisites for real effectiveness and the fulfilment of its function as a land council. Differences were expressed in numerous ways over several related issues but particularly over the structure and powers of the VALC and its funding and administration.

The procedure suggested by Senator Cavanagh at the inaugural meeting of electing a Chairman and Deputy Chairman was rejected by the VALC in favour of the appointment of a 'senior member' with the responsibility to call meetings and the power to co-opt assistance from other members. This decision, though seemingly trivial, represents a trend towards a democratic structure and was consistent with the VALC's decision to send minutes of Council meetings to all Aboriginal organisations. Problems with the relationship between the VALC and the Department of Aboriginal Affairs were highlighted in late 1975 when it independently elected its own Honorary Secretary (Mrs E. Koumalatsos), and was subsequently informed that it was not empowered to independently elect appointees. If it wished to do so, the Department would have to be notified and give its approval. In response to this, the VALC members decided that the Honorary Secretary would remain 'regardless of Departmental attitudes', voiced the opinion that all Aborigines should be able to attend VALC meetings, and complained that the 'Land Council was not getting due recognition as a body'.[12] It was then agreed that support was needed and should be sought from land councils and land trusts in other States to gain greater recognition of the VALC.

On the question of its lack of power to fulfil Aboriginal land needs as an honorary and advisory committee, the VALC wrote to the Minister requesting that its status be changed to that of a statutory body with funding to buy land and property. The VALC then moved beyond its own status and position to call for a wider structural change in

Commonwealth legislation. This was encompassed in a 'Statement by Acting Senior Member, VALC and members of the Council' sent to all Aboriginal organisations in Australia and to the press.[13] This statement supported Senator Bonner's motion in the Senate about compensation for the dispossession of Aboriginal land, and called for 'legislation to create a National Aboriginal Claims Commission to be established similar to the North American Indian Claims experience'.[14] It also stated that 'Council agreed that the Aboriginal land trusts in New South Wales, South Australia and Western Australia, and the Aboriginal Land Councils in the Northern Territory and Victoria be incorporated in Federal legislation to create the National Aboriginal Claims Commission' and 'on Victorian matters Council agreed that in future all housing funds for Victoria be directed to the Victorian Aboriginal Land Council which will also be part of the National Aboriginal Claims Commission'.[15] The press statement perceived the Commission as a recipient of compensation awarded for the dispossession of land which it would use to research ownership claims and grant land according to traditional ownership criteria.

The issue of funding was the subject of much confusion, delay and frustration at many levels. The initial position of the VALC, as perceived by the Department of Aboriginal Affairs, meant that funding was based on the fact that it was an advisory body responsible to the Minister. At the inaugural meeting, Mr Renkin (then Director of the South-East Region, Department of Aboriginal Affairs) stated that 'members would be reimbursed by cheque for any overnight accommodation and travelling expenses' and secretarial services made available at the Department'. This was clarified by Mr Viner in April, when he stated that 'the Department provides administrative support to the Council through the services of the South-East Regional Office and reimburses costs incurred by the Council and its members in attending meetings, seeking legal advice and secretarial services . . .'

However, the VALC believed and acted upon the belief that it should, and could, buy or sell houses and land for Aboriginal people in this State, until it was informed that it had neither the funds nor the power to do so. At its meeting of 6 June 1975, the VALC moved that a letter be sent to Mr Johnson listing the recommendations for land and housing and including a request for an allocation of $2 million for the 'setting up of a permanent office and associated running costs of the Council in Victoria as claims for land would go on for many years'.[16]

Funding was dependent on a budget to be approved by the Department but, because of the confusion of roles, the conditions for approval became more complex. A letter was circulated by the VALC on 4 December 1975, drawing attention to the difficulty of acquiring the funds set aside for its operation in the 1974/75 budget ($3000) from the DAA Regional Office in Victoria. It stated:

> On different occasions the Victorian Director has said that the VALC would be funded if it nominated an official spokesman with whom he could communicate, when the Land Council's Constitution had been viewed by him funds would be available. Both these terms have been met and the Land Council has not yet been funded.
>
> The latest condition stipulated by the Victorian Director is that the Land Council Constitution be discussed and accepted by the Aboriginal people and other organisations. While the Land Council is made up of members of organisations representing different areas of Victoria I am not aware that the Constitution of one body must be approved by outside organisations . . .[17]
>
> The VLC would also . . . like to point out that the formation of the Land Council was at the discretion of the former Minister and former Director without any consultation at all with the Victorian people. It is our intention when the Land Council is financial to undertake a programme whereby contact will be made with the Aboriginal community throughout the State of Victoria . . .

The question of funding was directly related to the problem of the VALC's function. It wanted to operate along the same lines as the New South Wales Lands Trust, and to this end sought legal advice and prepared a constitution to become a statutory body.[18] After a meeting on 22 August 1975, when Mr Renkin (the Director, South-East Region, Department of Aboriginal Affairs) clarified the Council's position, it was decided to meet on 10 October to prepare a submission for funding from the Aboriginal Lands Commission. This submission requested a total sum of $91 000 to provide salaries for a research officer, an adult secretary, a legal adviser and an auditor and to buy a vehicle, office furniture, and a house in the inner Melbourne area to serve as an office and provide accommodation for VALC members when in the city. Previous requests to the Department of Aboriginal Affairs on 2 December 1975 for funding to buy furniture, appoint a secretary, and set up a library were rejected due to the fact that these facilities were said to be available at the South-East Region office in Box Hill. The letter enclosing the submission stated: 'this submission is for funds to set up facilities for our Council to commence operation along the lines of the Aboriginal Lands Trust of New South Wales. We believe the purchase of a property and our own facilities imperative to our independence'.

In January 1976, letters were again sent to the Land Commission and the new Minister for Aboriginal Affairs, Mr Viner, requesting finance to establish premises and staff.

The limited funds promised earlier upon review of the Constitution were made available for the continual meeting of the VALC. In an article about the VALC, written for *Identity* by Council member Mrs Brabham and approved by the Council, it was noted that the Department of Aboriginal Affairs had refused to fund a secretariat and 'Mr Dexter as much as indicated it was an impertinence on our part to even suggest it'.

Notification was received from the Land Commission in April 1976 that they could not fund the Council, and another budget was then submitted to Mr Viner together with a letter re-stating the need for a research officer and a secretary. At the meeting on 8 April it was noted by the legal adviser that 'the Department's attitude had been to fob off or refer any previous submissions made by the Land Council'.

Mr Viner had earlier conveyed a warning to the Council that 'in the current economic circumstances and in view of the Prime Minister's direction that Ministers should review the need for all advisory bodies I am not able to give any undertaking that your Council will be continued, but this is a matter which I shall be able to consider in the light of the Council's submission'.[19] He requested a report from the VALC by 30 June 1976. The Council wrote to him on 25 May 1976, requesting a meeting 'to inform the Land Council of its present status and future under your Government. In view of the very significant cuts in spending we are very concerned . . .' and further noted that 'because of the Department's somewhat paternalistic attitude we have not been allowed to administer our own affairs properly. For example, because we have no typewriter it is very difficult for correspondence to be dealt with.'

In July 1976 the Council's request for funds was partially met with an appropriation of $25 000 to cover the employment of a full-time research officer and to buy a vehicle. (The Council's submission was for $115 700). Because it was the Supply period, the appropriation could not be finalised until the Budget was approved. A sum of $5000 was granted until August, when approval was given.

A full-time research officer was employed by the Council on 29 November 1976. This was a one-year appointment with the task of preparing a report on Victorian land needs for the Minister. Initially, the research officer was given the use of office space in the DAA office at Box Hill. However, this location was not accepted as suitable by some members of the VALC, who felt it needed to be situated in the inner-suburban area where a considerable number of Aborigines lived. A separate office was then established in Fitzroy in April 1977, and the report was expected to be finalised by November of that year. However, this report was not completed, and hence funding for the VALC ceased because the conditions of its charter had not been fulfilled.

In a letter to the VALC secretary on 10 November, 1977, Mr R. Worthy, the Regional Director; wrote, 'In my opinion history alone will be able to gauge the magnitude of what has been missed in providing, at Government request, a statement of land needs in Victoria'.

CONCLUSION

In the introduction to this paper it is stated that two general conclusions can be reached as a consequence of the Victorian Aboriginal Land Council's experience. This is not to deny the fact that uncertainties and changes in the national political arena were not significant forces operating against the effectiveness of such a Council but to indicate that these were not the fundamental problems.

The first conclusion was 'that land rights in the State of Victoria can only be achieved if the machinery for its implementation takes into account issues of relative independence and autonomy of decision-making'.

This conclusion is based on the history of experience of Aboriginal communities in this State who had lived under a system of changing policies 'from above' involving complex and often confusing regulations and public service procedures outside their control. In the 1960s Aboriginal organisations in Victoria laid great stress on the need to run their own affairs. The expression of this need was followed through by the establishment of the Ministry for Aboriginal Affairs and the particular policy orientation of Mr Worthy, its Director. The Ministry incorporated an advisory council with elected Aboriginal members as a response to this demand. Members of the advisory council had felt a great deal of frustration by its advisory position, and by 1974 expectations of 'self-determination' were strengthened after the Labor Party gained office in 1972 proclaiming 'Self-Determination' as its policy for Aboriginal Affairs.

The VALC was initially formed under the Labor policy of 'self-determination' and it was in this spirit that it attempted to operate. The restrictions and powerlessness of an honorary advisory council did not conform to this policy principle. In this sense, the problem of funding was crucial and linked to the need to be self-determining in its role as a land council.

Related to this was the credibility of the VALC in the eyes of Victorian Aboriginal communities. Because VALC members were responsible to the Minister for Aboriginal Affairs, and were nominated by the Minister in consultation with the Victorian Chief Secretary and departmental heads, it was placed in an invidious position relative to the Aboriginal communities in Victoria. The Council's integrity and the cooperation it needed from Aboriginal organisations and individuals ultimately depended on its ability to actually do something and to be recognised as an autonomous body with some effectiveness.

This position was expressed by a circular sent to all Victorian Aboriginal groups by the VALC's research officer in late 1977:

> Recommendations have been made to Mr I. Viner the Minister for Aboriginal Affairs with regard to the setting up and funding of a Land Council elected and controlled by Aboriginal communities. The present Land Council which was formed in April 1975 comprised of 19 members who were all appointed by the Minister for Aboriginal Affairs or the Department of Aboriginal Affairs. This situation is totally against the policy of Self-Determination.

> Mr R. Henger of the Department of Aboriginal Affairs informed the existing Land Council that any Land Council in Victoria which was community controlled and elected would not be funded . . .
>
> A Land Council fully controlled and supported by the Aboriginal communities is essential if meaningful land-rights and compensation are to eventuate. All Aboriginal Communities must let DAA and the present Land Council know that only a community elected and controlled Land Council can represent Aboriginal communities and any Government controlled groups will not be acceptable.

The second conclusion stated 'that the existing framework adopted from the Woodward Commission's Report for the implementation of land rights is not adequate'.

The Woodward enquiry's frame of reference was to report on the appropriate means to recognise and establish traditional land rights in the Northern Territory. Constitutionally, it could not recommend procedures to be adopted in the States, except for general principles it was hoped would be applied at the discretion of State governments.

The VALC was frustrated by these guidelines because they allowed no real power or recognition of traditional ownership. To this end, it pressed for a change of status to a statutory body, and then referred to the need for the Council to be part of a National Aboriginal Land Fund Commission which would require new State and Federal legislation.

Many references to the issue of compensation for land lost are to be found in VALC minutes. The Woodward Commission stated that cash compensation for the loss of traditional land rights was not an appropriate method of dealing with land rights (para. 53). The Council members perceived compensation as more than a moral claim based on justice, it was a response to a 'hand out' system based on paternalistic welfare. As an advisory body dependent on funding from the Department of Aboriginal Affairs, the Council members were placed in a relationship of dependency and were made to feel like recipients of welfare and the victims of budget allocations.

In his statement to the Senate in July 1974, Mr Cavanagh separated the issues of cash compensation and action to meet land needs. The experience of the VALC seems to indicate that this is a false dichotomy and that the two are very much related and interdependent.

The history of the Victorian Aboriginal Land Council illustrates other more general problems which are not unique to the Victorian situation. State expenditure requires public accountability through the Minister involved, and this in turn requires strict budgeting and accounting procedures, and very often hierarchical bureaucratic supervision. Hence, Aboriginal affairs expenditure can involve a lack of flexibility in the way in which it is managed and used.

Expenditure on Aboriginal affairs, is, like so many other areas of government expenditure, a victim of political pragmatism. The fact that it is a low priority in the minds of voters makes it most vulnerable to cut-backs. Also, governments do not want to put themselves in a position of making long-term commitments, and need flexibility in their budgeting to account for the vagaries of the general economic and political climate.

NOTES

1. The Council was established to prepare a report of what land claims the Aboriginal people in Victoria wished to make and submit this to the Minister for Aboriginal Affairs for consideration.

2. When the Victorian Aboriginal Land Council held its inaugural meeting in April 1975, all mainland States except Queensland had established Aboriginal land trusts to hold title to existing reserve lands. In Victoria, the inhabitants of the only two existing reserves (Lake Tyers and Framlingham) had been granted freehold title in 1970 after the passing of the *Aboriginal Lands Act*.

3. The Commonwealth does not own the land in the States and could not legislate for areas outside its jurisdiction. According to the Constitution, land can only be acquired by the Commonwealth on 'just' terms, and to this end the Woodward Report recommended the establishment of the Aboriginal Lands Commission to buy land for Aboriginal land trusts and corporations in the States.

4. This Council was formed to advise the Victorian Ministry for Aboriginal Affairs and disbanded when that Ministry handed over responsibility for Aboriginal Affairs to the Commonwealth Government. Its members were: Mrs M. Tucker (Melb.), Ms Margaret Briggs (Melb.), Ms M. Jackomas (Melb.), Sir Douglas Nicholls (Melb.), Mr E.A. Cooper (Shepparton), Mr I. Couzens (Corio), Mr Phillip Pepper (Bairnsdale), Ms E.D. Thompson (Bairnsdale).

5. Mrs Nessie Skuta, Mr B. McGuinness, Mr D. Anderson, Mr J. Stanley (President).

6. Mr Stewart Murray and Mr F. Stewart (Swan Hill), Mrs G. Briggs (North Melbourne), Mrs M. Clarke and Mr B. Edwards (Purnim).

7. Mimeographed copies of the speech distributed to members of the Council, recorded in the minutes for 4 April 1975.

8. Emphasis added.

9. Extract from the budget speech by the Treasurer, the Hon. Phillip Lynch, MP, delivered on 17 August 1976.

10. Minute to DAA staff, 21 May 1976.

11. *Minutes*, 4 July 1975. At this meeting the Director of the South-East Region, DAA, Mr Peter Renkin, was invited to attend and explain the functions of the Council as seen by the Department. He said that the Council had no power to buy or sell land or houses and that it did not have the funds to do this . . . it is the Council's job to find out and write down all the different ways in which the descendants of tribal Aborigines in Victoria want land or compensation and then send this to the Minister in Canberra so that he can work out what rules are to be set down to follow in the future. Until this is done, all submissions and applications for land or houses or to set up business enterprises should be sent to the Land Fund Commission in Canberra seeking funds, *not by the Land Council*, but by existing other Aboriginal organisations. (my italics)

12. *Minutes* of meeting, August 1975.

13. This statement was issued on Friday, 8 August 1975 but not published. This was thought to be due to a newspaper printers strike.

14. This statement included its support of the NACC resolution of October 1974: 'that the Australian Government prepare legislation to provide for land rights compensation to be introduced into Parliament as soon as possible, to establish an Aboriginal Claims Commission with similar functions to the American Indian Claims Commission Act 1946 and the Alaska Native Claims Settlement Act 1971'. Moved D. Anderson and W. Skuta (Victoria).

15. These recommendations were incorporated in a letter to Mr Les Johnson, then Minister for Aboriginal Affairs, who replied on 5 November 1975: 'At this stage the Government does not intend to create any Commission to deal with Aboriginal land claims outside the Northern Territory. . .'

16. This letter (dated 17 June 1975) recommended submissions covering the following: a grant to the Echuca Aboriginal Co-operative Ltd. to establish a rehabilitation centre; properties at Orbost to be handed over to the Council; houses handed over to the Housing Commission be given to their tenants and money allocated to the Housing Commission to be handed over to the Council to purchase homes; a grant to the Mid-Murray Aboriginal Co-operative Ltd. to purchase Piambie Farm, and funding granted to the Council to purchase land in the Hallam district.

17. At an earlier meeting in August 1975 called to discuss the Council's position, Mr Renkin said that 'the Council could become a Statutory body and write up a constitution'. He also stated that the Council must document information relating to land and compensation and submit an itemised budget on the costs incurred for this.

18. The Council was informed formally by letter from Mr Renkin, Department of Aboriginal Affairs that 'the legal position of the Victorian Aboriginal Lands Council is quite different from that of the Aboriginal Lands Trust of New South Wales . . . namely, that the NSW Trust was established under provisions of an Act of Parliament and is therefore a statutory body, whereas the VLC is a non-incorporated non-statutory body. The NSW Land Trust has a prime function of holding title to land.' He also wrote: 'I do appreciate the desire of the Council to be autonomous and to get going as soon as possible.' (3 December 1975)

19. 24 March 1976.

16

LAND RIGHTS: A VICTORIAN PERSPECTIVE

Colin Bourke

Land rights in the Victorian context present a number of conceptual and political difficulties for non-Aborigines on account of the issue usually being perceived in terms of the so-called 'traditional' Aboriginal culture and situation in places such as the Northern Territory. It is a concept which brings to mind the traditional meaning of the land, and its importance is stressed within the framework of a traditional culture in danger of being destroyed. Politically it refers to the framework established by the Woodward Commission where 'land rights' entail the granting of freehold title to Aboriginal communities for the land with which they are associated and belong, i.e., reserve land or unalienated Crown land where traditional ownership can be established.

The Victorian situation is different in several respects. On one level Aborigines in Victoria have not been acknowledged in the light of the focus on the Northern Territory and other States where mining companies have created a conflict of interests, and where recalcitrant State Premiers have been unwilling to cooperate with Federal agencies. In this sense the prevalent Victorian Government view has consistently been one of self-congratulation in its handling of Aboriginal Affairs, and it is often popularly presumed that there are no 'real' Aborigines in this State.[1]

It is also distinctive in terms of the rate of assumed 'assimilation' and development in Victoria. The former relating to the dispersal of Aboriginal communities and tribes, and the latter to the fact that original tribal land was taken for pastoral purposes in the early life of the colony and further development of towns and industries was accelerated in the gold-rush period. Europeans assumed that Aborigines felt the same about land as they did themselves, and that one tract of land was as good as another. Aborigines were thus forced to rely on the white population and its officials for their survival. Initially this meant living on those reserves set aside for them, and after they were closed it meant unskilled, itinerant work in country areas. The advent of European immigration and technological innovation brought a strong drift to the cities to find employment opportunities.

There is, in fact, a significant number of Aborigines in this State, totalling 14 745 (from the 1976 Census), and this number is growing at a rapid rate. The majority of the Aborigines (9282) live in the Melbourne city areas and the remainder (5463) in rural districts. The nature of the distribution of the Victorian Aboriginal population, which can be traced back to tribal origins, has been documented by Dianne Barwick who has stated that 'although official policy has long encouraged dispersal and individual assimilation into Australian society, informal discrimination from whites and strong pressures for allegiance to one's membership group still encourage the persistence of Aboriginal enclaves'.[2]

In order to understand the contemporary situation of Aboriginal people in Victoria, it is necessary to review government policy from the late nineteenth century, and its effects. As summarised by Michael Christie in his work on race relations in colonial Victoria:[3]

> Colonisation . . . worked in a vicious circle. The colonisers took the land and debased the Aboriginal people because they claimed they were scarcely human. Having, through a process of terror and exploitation dehumanised those people, the colonisers then said, 'see, we told you they were barely human' and used the Aboriginal condition as an excuse to exploit them further.

Attempts to 'civilise' and assimilate the Aboriginal remnants in Victoria on government and mission reserves were not successful. Success was perceived in terms of the complete breakdown of traditional life-styles.

The situation of unrest and difficulties in achieving assimilationist aims, became the background to the passing of the *Aborigines Protection Act 1886*. This initiated a policy of segregation in the light of the failure of old policies. The Act was significant in that it now defined Aborigines as 'full bloods' only, requiring those people to have special permits to live on the reserves. All the so-called 'part' or 'mixed-blood' Aborigines were forced to leave the reserve areas with the idea that they would be absorbed into the white community. It is no coincidence that this group was the most outspoken and articulate about reserve conditions and treatment by white officialdom. When it became evident that the policy was too harsh, and prejudice too great, to allow for successful integration or absorption, the *Aborigines Act* 1910 was introduced to extend the definition set in the previous Act and thus facilitate welfare assistance to those in need.

The population of the reserves had progressively decreased due to the policy of segregation or 'protection' and the decision made by the Board for the Protection of Aborigines to concentrate all its activities on Lake Tyers—all other reserves were closed down over a period to 1922.[4] Hence the sole focus of Aboriginal policy was directed to the inhabitants of this reserve. Aboriginal mortality was high and the logical assumption made that the race would 'naturally' die out.

In 1957 the McLean Report[5] on the *Aborigines Act* 1910–1928 and its regulations suggested a major policy change; a reversion to the concept of assimilation. It noted that, 'the number of half-castes who are living in primitive conditions is steadily increasing' and stated that 'the terms of reference imply, and it cannot be doubted, that the only ultimate solution of the 'Aboriginal problem' as it now exists in this State, lies in the social, cultural, and economic integration of the remainder of the race into the general community'. It further recommended that the reserve at Lake Tyers should be retained but should be used to train those residents who can be absorbed into the white community and be used to house those who were aged, sick and infirm and thus unfit to fend for themselves in the outside world.

These recommendations were implemented in the *Aborigines Act* 1957. The former Board for the Protection of Aborigines became the Aborigines Welfare Board. Its aim was to encourage assimilation of all persons having (an admixture of) Aboriginal blood by concentrating on areas of housing, education and employment as priority issues in rehabilitation.

In short, the end of the 1950s did acknowledge an 'Aboriginal problem' and by the concept of assimilation perceived that 'problem' in terms of the methods necessary to encourage the Aboriginal people to subscribe to the same values as the dominant society; to conform to its requirements and ultimately to become a part of it on its terms.

The 'problem' area of Lake Tyers became the main focus of the 1960s, particularly highlighting the inadequacy of the Aborigines Welfare Board. Attempts to close Lake Tyers and Framlingham in the 1950s resulted in publicity and drew attention to the plight of Victorian Aborigines. The Welfare Board had pursued its policy objective of assimilation literally by letting the reserve run down and acting in an authoritarian and unresponsive manner to the residents' needs and initiatives. It had housed residents of the reserve in nearby towns without adequate training or preparation and would not allow them to return to the reserve.

The Board's policy and lack of management as well as its overall attitude attracted a great deal of publicity. This covered the consequent racial conflict in country towns and bitter recriminations by the public, a minority of the Board members and outside organisations concerned with Aboriginal affairs and welfare. This situation led to a 'Report on the Rehabilitation and Training for Aborigines at the Lake Tyers Reserve' by the Lake Tyers Planning and Action Committee convened by Dr C. M. Tatz. It recommended development of the reserve and its use as a resource and training centre.

The confusion and abysmal conditions of Lake Tyers and its inhabitants together with a political climate which brought Aboriginal Affairs into the public limelight created the scene for a revision of the policy of assimilation as practiced by the Aborigines Welfare Board.

This revision included both new machinery and administration and new policy directives. The *Aboriginal Affairs Act* of 1967 created a Ministry of Aboriginal Affairs and incorporated an Aboriginal Affairs Advisory Council, which was to include at least six Aboriginal members elected by Aborigines resident in Victoria. Representation included in this legislation was a direct response to the Aboriginal organisation's call for a say in their own affairs.

The end of the 1960s saw a radical departure from former policies of protection and welfare, heralding a new element of representation and stimulating discussion of concepts of 'opportunity', 'compensation for disadvantage', and 'basic rights in conjunction with responsible citizenship'.

The Victorian Ministry of Aboriginal Affairs had specific functional responsibility in areas of education, employment, welfare, health and housing. According to a speech by Mr Vance Dickie, it had its problems. Speaking retrospectively about his Ministry, he said:[6]

> It soon became evident that if the Ministry were to perform its primary task of creating opportunities for Aborigines to participate meaningfully in their own affairs, leading to a reversal of the dependency situation which had been imposed on them since settlement of the colony, then its major role should be advisory. Attempts to be landlord and counsellor clearly highlighted this conflict of roles.[6]

However, it was during the period of the Victorian Ministry (1968–74) that the issue of 'meaningful' representation and land rights was expressed through Aboriginal organisations. The response of the Victorian Government was to pass the *Aboriginal Lands Act* in 1970, which gave full title of the Lake Tyers and Framlingham reserves to their residents in Trusts. This Act encompassed 988 acres at Lake Tyers owned by 70 trustees, and 235 hectares at Framlingham owned by 17 trustees. It was stated that 'this Bill is designed to rectify many of the omissions and commissions of the past with regard to land rights'.[7]

One may well ask: What about the other Aboriginal people living in this State? Were land rights of no concern or relevance to them and their lives? It is here that the crucial issue of what one means by land rights lies and it is here that the former policies of 'assimilation and absorption' come to the foreground once again.

Firstly, from the Aboriginal point of view, land rights in this State are not simply a matter solved by the granting of land to residents of Lake Tyers and Framlingham. They have a much wider and more subtle significance, being an issue relating to Aboriginal identity and Aboriginal knowledge of the past and its consequences. Arising from this knowledge and awareness, land rights are perceived as central to the means whereby Aborigines can make their own special contribution to this country.

Relating to this is the subjective situation of Aborigines in Victoria. Mitchell, in his study of New South Wales, summarises the situation of the displaced Aborigines in his reference to the problem of the 'Marginal Man':

> The central conflict for Aborigines today is how to choose between 'the need to modernise' and the 'desire, or need, to also remain Aboriginal'. Government policies . . . have been based on the premise of white supremacy. They were unrealistic in that their only chance of success depended on a full Aboriginal acceptance of the white view. Such acceptance has not been evident . . . As if in defiance of the dominant culture's attempts to absorb them . . . They continue to perpetuate a distinction between themselves and alien whites, and they continue to strive for autonomy.

Mitchell also notes that 'people move to improve their material welfare, but the improvement is often illusory. They still usually find themselves within the cycle of poverty and remain dependent on Europeans; they remain "marginal" people . . .'[8]

The suggestion is that the psychological level of awareness of 'identity' is a strong motivating force behind land rights claims in this State with the added proviso that it is also relevant to economic and social needs. With few exceptions, Aborigines have not been successfully assimilated and also remain on the bottom level of the socioeconomic ladder. Cooperatives and other organisations have been formed to create the necessary foundation for dealing with their own problems. Land and compensation are vital to the ability of Victorian Aborigines to generate real assistance and real self-help in order to eradicate the damage done by history.

In the period of the Victorian Ministry of Aboriginal Affairs another perspective on land rights emerged.

In 1968 Mr Meagher, the then Minister for Aboriginal Affairs in Victoria, stated that the State Government did not believe that Aboriginal people should be given ownership of the settlements of Lake Tyers and Framlingham and that the Ministry was implementing the principle of land ownership for Aborigines through assisting them to own homes'.[10] In the following year this policy was followed up by an offer of $9000 to any Aboriginal family undertaking to leave a government reserve and buy a house in a town or city where facilities for education and employment existed. Those Aborigines already living in towns were offered grants of $1500 toward the cost of a home. According to Mr Meagher, 'the Government's generous scheme was a realistic attempt to give Aborigines a sense of proprietorship in the community, and *represented a remarkable advance for Aboriginal land rights*'.[11]

In terms of the two existing reserves, Mr Meagher's initial intention was to phase them out on the condition that residents agreed to move. He stated that 'What we want is to encourage every Aborigine to own his own piece of Australia'.[12]

The response from the Aborigines Advancement League revealed another perspective: they agreed that it was an admirable plan for those who wanted to be absorbed, but added that 'this policy of assimilation assumes that the only desirable style of life is the competitive individualistic style which dominates Western life. Is the Government desperately trying to solve the problem by destroying their identity'.[13] These sentiments were reinforced by Pastor Doug Nicholls on National Aborigines Day in 1969: 'Let us enter your society on our terms, living side by side with you but remaining at all times . . . a race of people with an identity'.[14]

This statement followed a reiteration of the Government's understanding of the issue when Mr Meagher said that 'Home ownership . . . is the fundamental land rights issue for Aborigines in Victoria' and added that 'an equity in the purchase of a home selected by the Aboriginal family is provided as a form of compensation for past alienation of land'.[15]

This form of land rights policy conformed to the Ministry's perception of 'equality' and the ending of paternalistic policies. Sharing equally in opportunity and responsibility was translated into policies placing Aborigines in a position where they had to take responsibility for themselves. Measures such as encouraging them to join health insurance organisations and stopping automatic legal aid before the Courts were means to this end.

This particular philosophy of equality places total responsibility on to the individual and treats the causes of any of their problems as personal. It also assumes that the Aboriginal people are no different (that is, they have no distinctive cultural characteristics), and by giving them the opportunity to behave like us, they will prove that they deserve 'equality' and respect.

One cannot deny the necessity for Aboriginal people to have education, health, employment and housing facilities to enable them to attain equality in a material sense, but this policy ignores and denies any sense of cultural identity. The assumption being that the 'assimilation process' has proceeded to such an extent that any talk of Aboriginal culture relating to land is meaningless in the Victorian context. One consequence of this approach was to disregard the calls for Aboriginal autonomy as outside radical influences bearing no relationship to reality.

It is not surprising, then, that the eventful change of policy relating to the transfer of lands to the residents of Lake Tyers and Framlingham was perceived by the Victorian Government as yet another example of their 'progressive' policies. On 6 February 1971 Mr Worthy, Director, Ministry of Aboriginal Affairs, stated proudly that 'we are the only State which has accepted the principle of unconditional land rights'. The reality of this can be seen by the fact that for a population of some 14 000 people of Aboriginal descent, they have title to less than 2000 hectares of land, which is less than one-sixth of a hectare per head.

The current situation is no better—the *Aboriginal Affairs (Transfer of Functions) Act* 1974 passed the responsibility of Aboriginal Affairs to the Federal Minister. Discussions between Senator Cavanagh and Mr Vance Dickie, then the Victorian Minister for Aboriginal Affairs, relating to the Woodward Report recommendations on 9 September 1974, showed a self-congratulatory attitude. 'It was recognised that Victoria had moved beyond the terms of the Woodward Report with regard to compensation. It had introduced a Housing Grants Scheme amounting to $1500 per Aboriginal family to enable them to place a deposit on a home' and 'in line with Victoria's progressive attitude towards Aboriginal Affairs it would co-operate in any investigation relating to claims on the Land Rights issue.' Furthermore, the Ministers agreed that the processes introduced in Victoria in recent years aimed at self-determination and self-help were exemplary.[16]

After this transfer and the passing of the *Aboriginal Land Rights (Northern Territory) Act* 1976, the only avenue left open for land rights in Victoria was through the Aboriginal Land Fund Commission. This Commission operated in Victoria but had general directives under the Act which precluded buying land in metropolitan areas, nor for groups which already had land available to them. Furthermore, it had to assess priorities in terms of the number of applications received and the limited funds available. Of the 10 requests received from Victoria only two were granted.[17] In its 1978/79 Report the Land Fund Commission stated that "the purchase or transfer of property must be the basis of any plan for Aboriginal development". In this sense, Victoria has been a low priority, but with the taking over of the Land Fund Commission's functions by the Aboriginal Development Commission in 1980 this may change.

NOTES

1. This belief has been a consequence of policies directed towards Assimilation and was reflected in the official view that the 'Aboriginal problem' in Victoria was virtually solved. At the initial Conference of Commonwealth and State authorities concerned with Aboriginal Affairs in 1937, Mr A.S. Bailey, Chairman of the Victorian Board for the Protection of Aborigines, said that he had come 'principally as an onlooker. Questions relating to the Aborigines affect States like Queensland, South Australia and West Australia more than Victoria, and probably New South Wales'. Victoria was not represented at the next Conference in 1948, and the Premier declined the invitation to that of 1951 on the ground that in his State 'The problem of the Aborigines had virtually disappeared'. (C.D. Rowley. *Outcasts in White Australia.* Melbourne, Penguin Books, 1973, p.89).

2. *A Little More than Kin,* unpublished PhD thesis, Australian National University, 1971, p.2. [There are some problems with the exact figure because a number of people have indicated on the census forms that their place of birth was outside Australia, suggesting that a number of non-English-speaking Europeans have been included in the total—Editions.]

3. Article entitled 'The unreported war' in the Education Supplement of *The Age* for 20 February 1979, p.28.

4. By 1874, 24 692 acres had been reserved in 13 localities as well as 17 depots to distribute stores and rations. Between 1887 and 1902 12 543 acres of this land was returned to the Crown and most supply depots closed. Framlingham was on the site of a former government Aboriginal station which was closed in 1917 but allowed to remain as a 'reserve for Aboriginal purposes'. The last to close was Coranderrk Reserve near Healesville (revoked on 14 July 1948). In 1886 it consisted of 4850 acres. Today only the cemetery and a memorial plaque remain.

5. Victoria, Parliament. *Report upon the operation of the Aborigines Act 1928 and the regulations and orders made thereunder.* Melbourne, Government Printer, 1957.

6. Second Reading Notes for *The Aboriginal Affairs (Transfer of Functions) Act 1974,* p.3, in which the direct involvement by the Government in Canberra was endorsed by the Government in Victoria.

7. Stated by the Hon. Murray Byrne, Minister for Public Works in the debate on this Bill in the Legislative Council. *Hansard,* p.2402.

8. I.S. Mitchell, *'Aborigines on the move. Personal adjustment in the resettlement of Aboriginal families; a psychosocial study',* unpublished PhD dissertation, University of New South Wales, 1978, pp.531 & xi.

9. For example, housing cooperatives, legal service, health service, Aborigines Advancement League, women's councils, etc.

10. Cited in *The Age* for 25 September 1968.

11. *Ibid* (my italics).

12. Cited in *The Age* for 23 April 1969.

13. *Ibid.*

14. Cited in *The Age* for 12 July 1969.

15. *Ibid.,* 11 July 1969.

16. *Australian Government Digest,* 1974, pp.605–06.

17. 'Baroona', a 128-ha property near Echuca purchased for the Echuca Aboriginal Co-Operative Society in 1977, and New Norfolk, Gippsland, a 12.7-ha property to be used for alcoholic rehabilitation purposes (see *Aboriginal Land Fund Commission Annual Report 1979–1980).*

17

WOMEN AND LAND CLAIMS IN THE NORTHERN TERRITORY

Meredith Rowell

In 1980, four years after the *Aboriginal Land Rights (Northern Territory) Act* was passed, an Aboriginal women's symposium was held in Adelaide as a part of the ANZAAS Conference. A large number of Aboriginal women attended from all over Australia, including several groups from the Northern Territory whose country had been claimed, or was subject to land claim, under the Act. The key sources of discussion amongst these traditional women were, firstly, the importance of land ownership in their own identity and security; and secondly, the neglect of Aboriginal women's status and authority in dealings relating to land and land rights (see Gale, 1983).

In my three years' work with Aboriginal women on land claims as an employee of the Central Land Council, I have seen both the importance of women's status in Aboriginal society in relation to land ownership and issues concerning land, and the neglect of this status in the process of acquiring land rights under European law. I have witnessed also the increasing confidence of Aboriginal women in politely refusing to be ignored by white researchers, lawyers and courts, and in demanding to be heard on one of the matters which concerns them most—namely, land.

THE LAND CLAIMS

From analysing their participation in the land claims, one would hardly think that Aboriginal women comprise 50% of the claimants. In most cases, land claims have been structured in such a way that it would have been impossible for women to play a part equal to that of the men. Claim books, for example, have been prepared usually from information collected by male researchers from Aboriginal men, as if the women had no important knowledge to contribute. Also, in the preparation of evidence, that of men has been treated and presented as if it were of primary importance, while evidence from women has been ignored or left until last, as if it could only be secondary or supportive in nature. Aboriginal women, in short, have been treated as a special interest group rather than as one half of the claimant population, and their knowledge has consequently been ignored or trivialised.[1]

Despite this situation, Aboriginal women have made increasingly large and important contributions to land claims. I briefly show this development through those claims in which I have been involved directly, either through the Central Land Council or as a consultant to the Northern Land Council. I then examine the reasons for both the initially male-dominated form of the land claims, and the growing role of women claimants. Finally, I discuss some of the implications of the land claims for the position and status of Aboriginal women in both their own societies and a broader context.

WARLPIRI AND KARTANGARURRU-KURINTJI LAND CLAIM

In this land claim, the first to be presented by the Central Land Council, the claim book was prepared by four male anthropologists and linguists, over almost two years based mainly on previous field work with Aboriginal men. In the first versions of the claim book only male traditional owners could be listed owing to lack of accurate information about the women. Genealogical and other details were collected from Warlpiri women mainly at the proofing stage, when the hearing was almost under way.

Aboriginal evidence was taken at Lajamanu (Hooker Creek) and Yuendumu in early 1978. Through the presence of a female linguist from Yuendumu, who acted as interpreter and was also used by women claimants as a channel of communication to the Central Land Council lawyers, some Warlpiri women were called to give evidence. While the men were called first and asked to give evidence in individual clan groupings about sites, Dreamings, and matters of religious importance, the women were called to give evidence in two large groups and were questioned mainly about family affairs.

Hence, the evidence of the women was considered as supportive rather than primary by those presenting the case on behalf of the claimants, and their questions were shaped accordingly. The most important aspect of the answers was in showing the Warlpiri strength of attachment to their traditional country. Dora Napurru for example, spoke at Lajamanu of the Warlpiri's dissatisfaction with their contemporary living conditions and of their desire to return to their traditional country (Warlpiri and Kartangarurru-Kurintji transcript, 1978, p.786):

> We are worried about our country. . . my father's country. What we are worrying about and thinking about is fighting or disagreement here both with the Aboriginal people and the white people. . . We didn't like this country. . . It is Kurintji country. . . I would like to be able to visit my country, visit my family.

Dora and other witnesses explained that the solution to the problems of the Warlpiri living at Lajamanu lay in setting up bush camps back on their own country, where their children could be brought up and disciplined according to the Law of their parents and grandparents (transcript, pp.786-87). In addition to this evidence of continuing concern and attachment, the women gave a brief but tantalising glimpse of their own ceremonial responsibilities. They told the Commissioner that they had their own business for Warlpiri country, which includes songs, paintings and dances (transcript, pp.784-85). This was not elaborated further during formal evidence.

Therefore, while women were largely left out of the preliminary discussions and research for the Warlpiri and Kartangarurru-Kurintji claim, their contribution to the hearings provided valuable supportive evidence of the strength of the claim. This can be seen in the Commissioner's Report (Toohey, 1978:45), where he notes that:

> At Lajamanu a number of women . . . spoke of their country using the expression that they were 'worried' for it, meaning that they were concerned because they were living away from their traditional land.

ALYAWARRA AND KAITITJA LAND CLAIM

For the Alyawarra and Kaititja land claim more effort was made by the Central Land Council to contact the women claimants prior to the hearing. Meetings with women yielded nearly all of the genealogical information, which appeared in the claim book as lists of owners, and women's opinions and knowledge were ascertained to an extent before the claim book was finalised.

For the hearing of the evidence at Warrabri, however, it was impossible to assemble and proof all the appropriate women claimants, as they were scattered over a broader area than the male claimants and the Land Council was, as ever, short of female field staff. While evidence was taken first from the men in individual clan groupings, women were called in one composite group. They were asked for information about genealogies and domestic matters and given very little opportunity to express opinions or knowledge about anything else.[2]

This time the women showed their dissatisfaction with the secondary part which had been assigned to them, and they prepared a ceremony for the Commissioner which celebrated their knowledge of and ties to the area under claim. They drew his attention to this ceremony through the anthropologist assisting the Commissioner, a woman, and were thus able to make a visual statement of their attachment to the claim area which had been difficult to express adequately in the formal court situation.[3] Judge Toohey accepted this display as a form of evidence, and wrote in his report (Toohey, 1979:42):

> Much is said at times about the male dominance of Aboriginal society. It is not my intention to enter that debate except to say that it can overlook the very vital role of women in ceremonial life. From what I saw, they had their own ceremonies, and secrets, as had the men, each complementing the other.

In this way, Alyawarra and Kaititja women assumed and asserted what they deemed to be a more appropriate role in their land claim than the small role initially assigned to them.

ULURU (AYERS ROCK) NATIONAL PARK AND LAKE AMADEUS/ LURITJA LAND CLAIMS

For the Uluru claim, the claim book was based mainly on information collected from Aboriginal men by a male anthropologist who had been doing research in the area for some time. Although women claimants were scattered over a broader area than were the men, the Central Land Council allocated less time and resources to contacting the women. While there were four, and later six, male anthropologists and lawyers involved in research, consultation and proofing with the male claimants, I was the only person employed to consult with the women. Hence, the information supplied by the women claimants played only a small part in the preparation of the claim, and the women were given a correspondingly small part in the hearings.

At Ayers Rock a group of men was called to give evidence for each 'country' in the claim area, while women were called together in a single large group. They experienced obvious embarrassment at having to give evidence in front of a considerable number of men and through a male interpreter. The Commissioner showed concern at one stage with the slowness of the women's answers, and suggested that the witnesses there were either not the people with the best knowledge or that they had been inadequately proofed. Counsel replied (transcript p.681):

> All I can say, Your Honour, is that questions have been asked outside the hearing. Unfortunately, it does not seem to follow, having discussed it outside, that it goes smoothly inside.

In this case, to supplement their verbal evidence, which had been delivered with difficulty, the women claimants were particularly keen to guide the anthropologist assisting the Commission, a woman, on a trip around the Rock in order to show her their knowledge and to convey it, through her, to the Commissioner. Thus, as in the Alyawarra and Kaititja claim, the Ayers Rock women drew the Commissioner's attention to their knowledge about their country by choosing to make a visual statement outside the formal court situation.

YINGAWUNARRI (OLD TOP SPRINGS) MUDBARA LAND CLAIM

The Northern Land Council made no attempt in this land claim to contact women claimants until shortly before the hearing. The draft claim book, written by two male researchers, stated simply that women in this area had no ceremonies for their country.

When the hearing was approaching, and it was noted that information was lacking in some areas of the case, two women anthropologists were flown to Yarralin for three days to consult with the women claimants. In these circumstances, it was impossible to contact all the women involved, but these short discussions showed clearly that the women celebrated *Yawalyu* ceremonies in order to nurture and replenish the country. They were eager to show some of their dances to us, but the time was too limited.

Here, then, was evidence of spiritual responsibility for the claim area, an important requirement of the Land Rights Act, which could be seen in the rights of certain women to paint and wear particular body designs, to dance particular dances for the well being of the claim area, and to pass these rights on to younger women. As a result of having this brought to their attention, the authors of the claim book included a statement that Mudbara women did possess ceremonies for the claim area, but owing to the shortage of time there was no opportunity to explore this matter or to present an adequate account of it to the Commissioner. On transcript, spiritual responsibility was explained solely in terms of the 'cult lodge', an 'association of initiated men of the clan who have the right and duty to perform sacred and secret rituals and songs' (Toohey, 1980a:5). I was not present at the hearing of evidence for this land claim, so I cannot comment on the formal evidence of the women claimants.

ANMATJIRRA AND ALYAWARRA CLAIM TO THE UTOPIA PASTORAL LEASE

Women claimants were better prepared and represented in this claim. This was because many of the claimants had also been involved in the hearings for the Alyawarra and Kaititja land claim and were therefore familiar with the proceedings. Also, the Central Land Council had employed a second female field worker, an Aboriginal woman, which made it possible to consult in a more thorough way with the women claimants in the limited time available. Information provided by Aboriginal women played a more significant part in the claim book. Also, the women at Utopia decided to show chosen selections of their rich ceremonial life to Central Land Council staff, both male and female, before the hearings, in order that the people organising their case would be familiar with their formidable knowledge and religious responsibilities. These displays were always an object of pride to male claimants, who would speak about women's business as contributing to the well being or 'happiness' of the country.

For these reasons it became clear to the Central Land Council lawyers and researchers that the women's knowledge of their country was profound and strong, and not to be ignored. Hence, unlike the organisation of previous hearings, women were called to give evidence in a number of land-holding groups rather than in one large conglomerate group. In four out of the five groups the men gave evidence first, and since they dealt with many of the major issues, the women were left to give supportive evidence. But in the case of the Arlparra group, when the women were called to give evidence first, what they said stood in its own right as a description of Alyawarra and Anmatjirra land tenure, of responsibility for dreamings and for sites, of spiritual affiliations to the land, of rights to forage, and of the identity of the claimants for that country (see Bell, 1979b).

In addition to their verbal evidence, which was adversely affected by the court situation, the women prepared elaborate ceremonies, involving body designs, ceremonial objects, and dances for the claim area. Women from all over Utopia and from surrounding areas came to each of these ceremonies to give their support. Due to a general awareness of the small part played by women in previous land claims, there was a conscious effort by the women present to show the Commissioner that women's knowledge of and responsibilities for land are important (see Rowell, 1979). In his report, the Commissioner devoted a separate section to the role of women in the ceremonial life of the Alyawarra and Anmatjirra (Toohey, 1980b:28), observing that:

> The painting and dancing of the women was a vivid demonstration of the importance of ceremonial life and of the significance their country held for them.

Thus, in the Utopia claim the women claimants made a strong statement of their attachment and affiliations to, and responsibility for, the claim area, which was assisted by the involvement of two female researchers and a female anthropologist assisting the Commission, but which they conceived of and accomplished themselves. At least part of this evidence was primary and essential to the case rather than simply supportive.

LANDER WARLPIRI AND ANMATJIRRA CLAIM TO WILLOWRA PASTORAL LEASE

For the Willowra land claim, the claim book was prepared by both a female and a male researcher after several years of contact with the community, and intensive consultations with both female and male claimants prior to the hearing. This claim book explains the subsection system, the composition of the land-owing group, and the inheritance of rights to land in terms of both female and male members of the society, whereas previous claim books had either relegated women to a separate section or assumed that an explanation of the men's relationship with the country covered that of the women (see Wafer & Wafer, 1980).

During the hearing both men and women gave evidence for most land-holding groups, while women claimants gave sole evidence in one case when their male counterparts were unavailable. Women spoke of their society's system of land tenure, of their own spiritual responsibility for and affiliations to sites and to the area under claim, of rights to forage, of the historical events which accounted for the geographical distribution of the claimants, and of the Willowra community's plans for the future. At the request of the women, through Ms Wafer and the anthropologist assisting the Commissioner, Ms Bell, the court was cleared of all but the essential male participants. Speaking thus to a largely female audience, the women claimants showed great confidence in giving their evidence. In addition, they prepared a *yawalyu* as further evidence of their ties to and responsibilities for the claim area.

The women's evidence, as outlined above, was clearly complete and not in any sense secondary to the men's. It is apparent from reading the transcript, and both counsel for the claimants agreed, that the land claim could have been presented successfully on the women's evidence alone; that is to say, they provided sufficient evidence to satisfy all the requirements of the Act with respect to traditional ownership. It should also be noted that this evidence was given with the full support of the male claimants, who stressed often in proofing sessions and in court the importance of the women's knowledge and spiritual responsibiltities, directing questions on some occasions to those women who were recognised by all as experts.

In his report, the Commissioner (Toohey, 1980c:31) draws upon many aspects of the Willowra women's evidence. He notes, for example, 'a strong flame of traditional life kept burning by the relative isolation of the land and . . . portrayed dramatically in the gestures of the women speaking of their responsibility to hold up the country'. Thus, women at Willowra used the resources and channels open to them to prepare and present a contribution which expressed their knowledge of and concern with an important issue of land and law.

It can be seen, therefore, through these land claims that Aboriginal women have been taking an increasingly important part—a part which they have assumed and asserted themselves, in mutual support and approval with their menfolk.

Two questions arise from this development. Firstly, why have land claims been dominated until recently by contributions from men? And secondly, why have Aboriginal women been taking a greater part? I will answer these questions in turn.

WHY HAVE LAND CLAIMS BEEN DOMINATED BY MEN?

I see the reason for this as lying in the interplay between white Australian society, in which social and political structures are male-centred and male-dominated, and traditional Aboriginal society, in which women have a large measure of independent responsibility and authority (Bell & Ditton, 1980:14).[4] There is ample and increasing evidence that the traditional role of Aboriginal women involved much autonomy and independence, not only in the economic sphere but in decision-making and religious matters as well.[5] In the Aboriginal communities in which I have worked, especially those which are situated on their traditional country such as Utopia and Willowra, women live a life which is largely separate from and independent of that of the men. In these places women generally camp with other women, and spend their time gathering and preparing bush foods, caring for children, making ceremonial objects such as hair strings, engaging in ceremonies, visiting relations on nearby stations, and generally engaging in activities in the company of other women. These women talk about their role as that of the provider and the caretaker. They stress the importance of their role in nurturing the adults of the future, and especially in imparting to both boys and girls a basic knowledge of the country and of their people's relationship to it. Babes in arms are taken on foraging trips, and are encouraged to stay awake during ceremonies and clap their hands in time to songs about the Dreamtime figures who created the country. These ceremonies are performed in order to ensure the well being of the community, of species of bush food, and of the country itself. Women see themselves as responsible for 'the whole lot' (Green, 1979:9), and men, although they are not involved in such performances, often declare proudly upon seeing a particularly fat kangaroo or an abundant vegetable patch that 'my wife/sister/mother made that one'.

Clearly, the role of Aboriginal women is seen by both men and women as important and it is a source of pride to both. Diane Bell (1980b:7) makes similar observations about desert women's role:

> Women's role of nurturer is that of an independent operator within a self-contained world. Women's claims to status in these terms are not empty ones for they are legitimated by their direct access to the *jukurrpa,* by their separate and economically independent residential base in the *jilimi* (the single women's camp), and by their exclusively female rituals which are closed to men but which nonetheless affect men. In all these ways women demonstrate their independence, autonomy, solidarity with other women and their importance as members of their society.

With white contact, the roles of Aboriginal women and men have been affected differently. Some have argued that Aboriginal women's status was enhanced by their access to white settlers' homes as cleaners, cooks, and childminders (e.g., Berndt & Berndt, 1964:442-43). While this may have been the case initially, it is clear that the subsequent creation of institutions and bureaucracies, which consulted only with Aboriginal men, undermined the traditional role of Aboriginal women in decision-making. Diane Bell observes that the separateness of Aboriginal women, which was traditionally the source of their independent status, came to mean that they were excluded from white male-dominated domains because they were classified by whites as peripheral to the political process (Bell, 1980b:9).

Let us look, for example, at the structure of the two land councils, institutions set up to carry out the requirements of the Aboriginal Land Rights Act. The Central Land Council employed no female field staff for the first two years of its operation. Consultations regarding mining, land claims, the protection of sacred sites, and other land-related issues were carried out only with Aboriginal men, by a male chairman, male delegates, four to six male field officers, and one male anthropologist. Thus this Land Council came to be regarded by women as a male domain,[6] and women would rarely attend meetings, even when invited, for fear of hearing information restricted to men. In 1978 a female anthropologist was appointed, and in 1979 a female field officer, but it was impossible for these people alone to consult adequately with all the Aboriginal women involved in each issue. This remains the case today, although additional female field staff are high on the list of priorities for future budgets.

The Northern Land Council has had only one female field officer employed on a semi-permanent basis, and that was only for a single year. Permanent staff now include only male anthropologists and field officers, although women are sometimes employed on a consultancy basis for individual claims. Therefore, the structure of the land councils is geared towards consulting Aboriginal men, and there is no comparable or adequate structure for consulting the women. For this reason alone, it has been impossible for Aboriginal women to play a part in the land claims comparable to that of Aboriginal men.

In addition, the nature of the court situation through which evidence is taken makes it very difficult for Aboriginal women to give clear and complete evidence. In each hearing that I have attended, there have been a substantial number of white men present throughout the proceedings. The Land Commissioner is a man; the counsel assisting the Commissioner and those representing the claimants and the other parties have always been men; the Judge's Associate has been a man for all claims except Utopia; and the sound-recorder for the bush evidence has been a man for all claims except the most recent claim presented by the Central Land Council.[7] When giving their evidence the women are always painfully conscious that they are talking in front of a mainly male audience. In this situation, which has no traditional counterpart, women experience a special difficulty beyond ordinary nervousness, especially in answering questions pertaining to Dreamings, to matters of spiritual importance, and to ceremonies.

'Women's business' is just that. It is something which is traditionally discussed amongst women and which does not directly involve men, although it is believed that both men and women derive benefit from the results of these ceremonies.

When asked in a court situation, 'What places does that Dreaming go through?', women witnesses generally discuss the question at length in their own language first before providing any answers. This discussion involves not so much the identity of the sites but, rather, whether the names should be spoken in the immediate company. Generally, women produce fewer site names for the court than the male witnesses. This does not mean that they know of fewer sites than the men; in fact they know of all the men's sites, even the most secret, as they need this knowledge to be able to avoid those places; in addition, they have sites which are significant and secret for women. What their hesitance means is that the situation prevents them from sharing their knowledge openly. In the reverse situation, if there were a group of white female officials appointed to hear evidence from Aboriginal people about their country, the men would find themselves in a similar dilemma. It is significant to note that during the Willowra claim, when there were fewer than usual white men present (Aboriginal men of course voluntarily abstained from attending), the women's evidence was clear, confident and complete, and they produced as many site names as the men.

Further, the part played by Aboriginal women in the claims has been limited by the close relationship between anthropological evidence and the land claims. The Land Rights Act was written in conjunction with anthropological advisers, and the precedents set in the first claims mean that evidence from anthropologists is now required to explain and validate the evidence of the claimants. Hence, the land claims have reflected and highlighted some of the problems and inadequacies within Aboriginal anthropology, one of which is the neglect of women.

As long ago as 1939, Elkin (introduction to Kaberry, 1939: xix–xx) found it necessary to make excuses for the invisibility of Aboriginal women in anthropology:

> There is some excuse for the dearth of information regarding women in Aboriginal life. Almost all the writers and observers, trained or not, have been males, and have somewhat naturally sought their information from and studied native life through, the men. Further, the rigid dichotomy which exists between the sexes in the ceremonial life and to a lesser degree in social and economic life, causes the male anthropologist to become identified with the men . . . and therefore . . . taboo with regard to many matters which belong to the life of the women. To question men concerning such things brings the reply: 'that women's business, you ask along woman'.

I do not have the space to describe here the history of the neglect of Aboriginal women in anthropology. It has been well documented recently in feminist anthroplogical works, as for example in the detailed and enlightening account which appears in Diane Bell's 'Daughters of the Dreaming' (Bell, 1980b:23–65). Suffice it here to say that, because there has been a large record of the complexities of men's role in the literature and only a superficial record of the women's role, most anthropologists have assumed that the former is somehow primary in importance while the latter is by nature superficial or secondary, without considering the reasons for these things appearing to be so.

This assumption has made it seem justifiable for lawyers, who imagine that anthropologists know what they are talking about, to present the evidence of Aboriginal men as primary and that of women as secondary or supportive. It has been seen as acceptable to run land claims primarily on evidence elicited from men, while the reverse (i.e., running a claim solely on women's evidence) has been unthinkable.

This can be seen specifically in relation to the requirements of 'primary spiritual responsibility' and 'common spiritual affiliation' which must be satisfied by the evidence under the Land Rights Act. The spiritual and ceremonial life of Aboriginal men has been characterised by anthropologists as concerned with the sacred and with matters of cosmic importance, while women's ceremonial life has been portrayed as secular and concerned with domestic matters (e.g., Warner, 1937). Hence, lawyers have sought evidence from men to satisfy the requirements of the Act concerned with spiritual matters, while they have called on evidence from women to provide supportive information about foraging and local descent group membership when it was felt that such support was necessary. It has been thought that because women supposedly could only give evidence about domestic matters they were incapable of satisfying the requirements of 'primary spiritual responsibility' and 'common spiritual affiliations'.

In the Warlpiri claim, for example, 'common spiritual affiliations' were explained in terms of 'the belief that every member of a patriline is in some sense animated by the patri-spirit of his clan, to which he is affiliated' (Toohey, 1978:25). Meggitt defines patri-spirit as an essential part of Aboriginal men's personalities not present in the personalities of women (Meggitt, 1962:10). Hence it was implied that men hold spiritual affiliations to country on behalf of women. Naturally, then, questions aimed at ascertaining 'common spiritual affiliations' were directed towards men. It is hardly surprising, therefore, that the women's evidence in this case did not provide complete evidence of 'common spiritual affiliations'. The nature of their evidence simply reflects the questions asked of them.

The same definition of 'common spiritual affiliations' was put forward in the Alyawarra Kaititja claim. The notion that spiritual affiliations were held on behalf of women by the men was apparently supported by evidence from a male witness that women's ceremonies were 'secular events' which 'concern themselves with secular topics' (Alyawarra Kaititja transcript, 1978:263). And yet the *awulya* staged by the women claimants during the hearing provided clear evidence that women's ceremonies are held to be sacred and spiritual; that they are concerned with precedents set down by the Dreaming and with the maintenance of the country, just like men's ceremonies. This was supported by the evidence of the anthropologist assisting the Commissioner. In later claims, as the women gave evidence more confidently, these factors emerged more clearly. In the Willowra claim, for example, women witnesses explained that their dancing 'holds up' the country (Molly Nungarrayi and Lucy Nampijinpa, Willowra transcript, 1980:263-64); that it sustains the country and follows the Dreaming in the correct way. 'We go by virtue of the law and we sustain the law' (Topsy Nangala, transcript, 1980: 297). These statements are cited in the Commissioner's report as evidence of 'common spiritual affiliations' (Toohey, 1980:17).

As the spiritual life of Aboriginal women became more obvious during the claims through their own evidence, the evidence of women anthropologists, and the ceremonies performed for the Commissioner, a broader definition of 'common spiritual affiliations' became necessary: a definition which did not exclude women. (A broader definition was also necessary because the notion of 'local descent group' was extended in the Utopia and Willowra claims to include people outside the patriclan.) In the Utopia and Willowra reports, after strong evidence had been given by women claimants of their spiritual ties to country, 'common spiritual affiliations' were taken to mean 'that the members of the group possess associations of a spiritual nature with sites on the land in question' (Toohey, 1980b:18; 1980c:15). This definition includes no implication that men hold spiritual affiliations on behalf of the women, it allows both to express their respective ties to the country in their own ways.

Thus, the participation of Aboriginal women in land claims has been limited by popular misconceptions about their role and status in Aboriginal society, which were passed from the white European tradition to the anthropological tradition, and from the anthropological tradition to the legal tradition. Somehow, Aboriginal tradition was overlooked.

WHY HAVE ABORIGINAL WOMEN BEEN TAKING A GREATER PART IN THE LAND CLAIMS?

The contribution made by Aboriginal women to the land claims has been influenced by a large number of factors, and by the interplay of these factors over time. Judge Toohey addressed himself to this question in his Utopia report (1980b:27):

> As hearings under the Land Rights Act have taken place, the role women have played has increased. No doubt there is more than one reason for this. People gain confidence through contact with other hearings. The northern boundary for the Utopia claim is the southern boundary of the Alyawarra claim. Some of those present during this hearing were at the Alyawarra hearing. And the presence of female anthropologists in the Land Council and as consultants has encouraged Aboriginal women to speak more freely. Nevertheless, it has been said that many do feel inhibitions about speaking in the presence of a large number of men; that is something to be considered in future hearings.

As Toohey observes, Aboriginal women have become more familiar with the process of claiming land under the Act. As women in each claim learned about the contributions of women in previous claims, they became aware of what was expected of them and also what was possible in terms of giving evidence. As I have shown, groups of women in several cases resorted, of their own volition, to expressing their knowledge through ritual displays when they felt dissatisfied with the court situation. Also, the presence of female researchers has provided a formal channel for the expression of women's knowledge. Where, in the early claims, female researchers were only included by chance, the land councils are now attempting to involve them as a matter of course in each claim. This is because the important contributions made by Aboriginal women to the claims have altered the expectations of the solicitors representing the claimants, who now for the most part regard women's evidence as useful and necessary in the success of the claims.

The Commissioner has also shown a growing recognition of the importance of evidence from women in satisfying the requirements of the Act. This can be seen in his reports and also in his choice of female anthropologists to assist him. By having a woman present in this capacity, women claimants are able to discuss with her matters which they would like the Commissioner to consider but which they feel unable to air openly in a court situation. For example, they have been able to reduce the numbers of men present while giving evidence so that the situation is more appropriate to discussing the business of women. In turn, the expectations of the Commissioner in relation to women's evidence have influenced the presentation of the claims, and have helped about the inclusion of women's evidence as a matter of course.

Therefore, the increasing contribution of Aboriginal women to land claims has been brought about by changes in the attitudes and expectations of those representing the claimants and of the Commissioner, and by changes in the consultative structures available to women. Both these changes grew out of the consistent demand of Aboriginal women to be heard.

SOME IMPLICATIONS OF LAND CLAIMS

Finally, I would like to look at some of the implications of the land claims for the women claimants, both in their own societies and in a broader social context. Through land claims certain information is written down and made available in public documents, and hence forward can be used for a multitude of purposes. Much of this information has never existed in written form before, and in this form it may affect and change the claimants lives.

Lists of claimants, for example, which are published in claim books and in the judge's reports, may subsequently be referred to by organisations such as government departments and mining companies wishing to consult traditional owners about particular matters that affect their lives. They may also be used by one group of traditional owners who wish to strengthen their position in relation to a piece of land vis-à-vis another group of Aboriginal people. Therefore, the accuracy of these lists may have implications beyond the land claim hearings, both within the claimant group and in broader legal terms. If any traditional owners were omitted, for example, then they would be disadvantaged in terms of future consultations and negotiations. While it has been argued that any mistakes made in the lists during land claims could be rectified in the register of traditional owners, which the Land Rights Act requires the land councils to draw up, this ignores the fact that the incorrect lists would remain in existence in published form.

It has also been argued on the basis of political expediency, that land rights be contested on the men's evidence alone and that women's rights be taken into account later.[8] This argument is similarly naive in its failure to consider the implications of the written word. As Diane Bell (1979a:27–28) observes.

> Unfortunately, once names, evidence, clans, etc are written down, the data achieves a new importance and women are further disadvantaged . . . Women have been overlooked and under-estimated in many contexts. It would be a further tragedy if their rights in land were not recognised and their status in white eyes further reduced or denied.

Lastly, it has been said that the mere fact that Aboriginal women comprise 50% of the claimant population should not necessarily imply that they ought to give 50% of the evidence. Children, it has been said, comprise a certain proportion of the claimant population but we do not expect them to give a corresponding proportion of the evidence. It has, however, too often been assumed that Aboriginal women need not be heard in a way comparable to the men, without even asking the claimants for their views on this. If we lay all such assumptions aside and listen to the claimants, we find that women are asking to be heard and that the men are supporting the women in this demand. As long ago as 1939, Elkin (op.cit) pointed out that Aboriginal men would direct certain questions to women; and more recently Diane Bell (1979a:28–29) records that men have commented on the need for women to be consulted and have shown on occasions considerable embarrassment at being asked questions which should rightly be put to a woman. In each land claim that I have seen, the male claimants have taken great pride in the formal evidence and ritual displays presented by their sisters and mothers to the Commissioner, from a respectful distance, and have often directed the questions of counsel to particular women.

Hence, to assume that the evidence of Aboriginal women should be less important than the men's, ignores both the implications of evidence appearing in written form, as explained above, and the demands of both female and male claimants.

CONCLUSION

It can be seen that the form taken by land claims in the Northern Territory has reflected certain assumptions and preconceptions by white Australians about the status of Aboriginal women in relation to land and law. However, the role which has been taken with increasing confidence by the women and reinforced by the men has forced anthropologists and lawyers to rethink their initial assumptions. Clearly, Aboriginal women have an important contribution to make in the hearing and settling of these issues, which ought not to be ignored. As Judge Toohey writes (in Bell and Ditton, 1980:1) of the need for a rapprochement between the customary law of Aboriginal people and the law administered in the courts:

> That understanding will not come unless all concerned listen to the people themselves, not least to Aboriginal women whose voices have too often been still when they should have been heard.

NOTES

1. Jan Larbalestier makes the same observation in her unpublished paper 'Women and land rights: a commentary' (1980).

2. Jennie Green, an adult educator at Utopia, who was present at, and contributed to, the hearings, observed that the women's evidence was elicited as if they had 'no more profound knowledge of their country than that of immediate family structures' (Green, 1979: 12).

3. Diane Bell, the anthropologist assisting the Commissioner, discusses this display further in her article 'Women and the land' (Bell, 1979a: 26).

4. A detailed account from Aboriginal women of their position can be found in the report of Diane Bell and Pam Ditton to the Law Reform Commission (1980).

5. See, for example, Kaberry (1935, 1939), Hamilton (1978), Brandl (1979), Bell & Ditton (1980), Bell (1979a, 1980a, 1980b).

6. The reasons for this image are also discussed by Diane Bell in her article 'Women and the land' (Bell, 1979a).

7. That is the Warlpiri Walmanpa Mudbara Warramungu claim, which I do not describe because the results are not yet available [in 1980].

8. Jan Larbalestier (1980:6) also documents this argument.

REFERENCES

Bell, D. (1979a) Women and the Land. *Identity*, **3**(11).

Bell, D. (1979b) Statement to the Utopia Land Claim Hearing. Exhibit 57 to the Anmatjirra Alyawarra Land Claim to the Utopia Pastoral Lease.

Bell, D. (1980a) Women's business is hard work: Central Australian Aboriginal women's love rituals. Paper prepared for the Burg Wartenstein Symposium No. 85.

Bell, D. (1980b) *Daughters of the Dreaming*. Unpublished PhD thesis, Department of Prehistory and Anthropology Australian National University, Canberra.

Bell, D., Ditton, P. (1980) *Law: The Old and the New. Aboriginal women in central Australia speak out*. Canberra, *Aboriginal History*, for the Central Australian Aboriginal Legal Aid Service.

Berndt, R. M., Berndt, C. H. (1964) *The World of the First Australians*. Sydney, Ure Smith.

Brandl, M. (1979) A fair go for Aboriginal women in Australia. In: *Women and Human Rights*. Geneva.

Gale, F. (ed.) (1983) *We Are Bosses Ourselves. The status and role of Aboriginal women today*. Canberra, Australian Institute of Aboriginal Studies.

Green, J. (1979) Utopian women. Unpublished paper.

Hamilton, A. (1978) Dual social systems: technology, labour and women's secret rites in the eastern Western Desert of Australia. Paper presented to the International Conference on Hunters and Gatherers, Paris, June 1978.

Kaberry, P. (1935) The Forrest River and Lyne River Tribes of North-West Australia. *Oceania*, **15**(4).

Kaberry, P. (1939) *Aboriginal Woman: Sacred and profane*. London, Routledge.

Larbalestier, J. (1980) *Women and land rights: a commentary*. Unpublished paper, Macquarie University.

Meggitt, M. (1962) *Desert People: a study of the Walbiri Aborigines of central Australia*. Sydney, Angus & Robertson.

Rowell, M. Notes on Awulya performed by women during Utopia Land Claim hearing. Exhibit 40 to the Anmatjirra and Alyawarra Land Claim to the Utopia Pastoral Lease.

Toohey, J. (1978) *Report to the Minister of Aboriginal Affairs of the Land Claim by the Warlpiri and Kartangarurru–Kurintji*. Canberra.

Toohey, J. (1979) *Report to the Minister for Aboriginal Affairs of the Land Claims by the Alyawarra and Kaititja*. Canberra.

Toohey, J. (1980a) *Report to the Minister for Aboriginal Affairs of the Yingawunarri (Old Top Springs) Mudbara Land Claim*. Canberra.

Toohey, J. (1980b) *Report to the Minister for Aboriginal Affairs of the Land Claim by the Anmatjirra and Alyawarra to the Utopia Pastoral Lease*. Canberra.

Toohey, J. (1980c) *Report to the Minister for Aboriginal Affairs of the Lander Warlpiri and Anmatjirra Land Claim to the Willowra Pastoral Lease*. Canberra.

Transcript of the Proceedings of the Warlpiri and Kartangarurru–Kurintji Land Claim Hearing, 1977–78.

Transcript of the Proceedings of the Alyawarra and Kaititja Land Claim Hearings, 1978.

Transcript of the Proceedings of the Uluru (Ayers Rock) National Park and Lake Amadeus/Luritja Land Claim Hearing, 1979.

Transcript of the Proceedings of the Utopia Land Claim Hearing, 1979–80.

Transcript of the Proceedings of the Willowra Land Claim Hearing, 1980.

Wafer, J. & Wafer, P. (1980) *The Lander Warlpiri and Anmatjirra Land Claim to the Willowra Pastoral Lease*. Alice Springs, Central Land Council.

Warner, L. (1937) *A Black Civilization*. New York, Harper.

18 THE CENTRAL LAND COUNCIL: THE POLITICS OF CHANGE

Geoff Eames

The establishment of the Central Land Council (CLC) in Alice Springs owed less to the investigation of Mr Justice Woodward into Aboriginal land rights than it did to the walk-off of Gurindji Aboriginals from Wave Hill Station in 1967.[1] In the CLC's early days, the membership showed a keen awareness of the politics of land rights and resisted the efforts of every significant pressure group to stunt its growth and crush its independence.

In late 1975 the CLC was a concept without a reality. One officer of the Department of Aboriginal Affairs liaised with lawyers based in Melbourne and Adelaide. To the Aborigines of central Australia, anxious to take steps to win back their traditional land, the obvious organisation to approach was the Central Australian Aboriginal Legal Aid Service (CAALAS), a spirited body with a well established community controlled office and with credibility amongst Aborigines.

Inevitably, CAALAS was filling the vacuum. The Aboriginal councillors and staff of CAALAS were constantly feeding land rights information to the white lawyers whose knowledge of traditional land ownership theory and practice was marginal at best.

The Aboriginal Land Commissioner, the late Mr Justice Ward, was encouraged by the Federal (Labor) Government to commence his work, despite the fact that the ALP land right legislation had not yet been passed in Parliament. Ward commenced with an urgent hearing of the Supplejack Land Claim. David Parsons and I, both of us lawyers employed by CAALAS, suddenly found that we were the only ones available to appear for the claimants. Armed with copies of Meggitt's *Desert People* (1962) and the Woodward Reports, and with almost no preparation, we attended a hearing at Hooker Creek in a bid to delay the leasing of the land by the Department of the Northern Territory, which was strongly supporting the white licence holder by attempting to alienate the land and thereby ending its availability to land claims.

Shortly after the completion of that hearing the council at CAALAS, at a mass meeting, decided to re-establish the Central Land Council, and in October 1975 I found myself directed to become the lawyer for CLC. I was unhappy to leave CAALAS. I had little appreciation of the plans Aborigines already had for this new body.

At its foundation meeting, Charles Perkins was elected Chairman, and a man whom I barely knew, Wenten Rubuntja became Vice-Chairman and CLC's first full-time Aboriginal employee. My desk was in the DAA building, and independence was clearly needed. Perkins and Rubuntja were well aware of that need. Many of the newly elected councillors of CLC had held similar positions with CAALAS and were very conscious of the intense battles for independence from DAA waged by that organisation.

CLC's determination to be independent was obvious from the start. The Australian Institute of Aboriginal Studies offered the services of an anthropologist, the terms being that he would be employed by and under the direction of the Institute. The members of the Central Land Council stated very strongly that this would not be acceptable, and Milton Liddle, later to become Vice-Chairman of the Council and at the time the President of CAALAS, agreed with this view. Thus Rod Hagen, who was to perform such magnificent work for the Council, became our first anthropologist employee, and in so doing brought into the open an issue that would vex anthropologists thereafter.

The Institute saw the debate in terms of the 'independent science'of anthropology. To central Australian Aborigines the issue was one of control. In reflecting on the success of the CLC, it is clear to me that this first battle, the fight for independence, was the most important one waged in its early years.

Every new community organisation needs a clear victory to maintain the enthusiasm of its membership and to allow assessment of its tactics and performance. The Alice Springs Town claims gave the fledgling CLC an opportunity to seek that victory. In November 1975, when Mr Justice Ward commenced hearing those claims, the most visible sign of lack of interest shown by successive Federal and Northern Territory administrations in the Aborigines was the plight of the 'fringe dwellers' of Alice Springs. Nearly 1000 people lived in creek beds and camps in the most appalling conditions. For the 17 permanent or semi-permanent camps there were only two water taps. Deaths during cold spells were common, and people were literally starving, despite white Australian myths about $200 a week welfare cheques for every Aborigine. There were massive and inevitable problems of malnutrition, alcoholism and violence. There was also a sense of despair in most of the camps. The people were sick of fighting the bureaucrats who denied them title to the land. DAA would fund no improvements without title and the people were caught in a trap.

In the Land Rights Bill provision was made for Mr Justice Ward to hear 'needs' claims and to recommend the grant of leases in perpetuity. I was amazed, in reading the files of government departments, to learn how many times attempts by Aborigines to gain title to land were shelved either on the basis that future white Australian needs for land would come first or because, it was claimed, the camps contained so many different tribal groups that it was impossible to do anything since the Aborigines would never reach agreement among themselves as to what should be done.

Mr Justice Ward's hearings gave real hope for change. He indicated privately how impressed he was with the strong words of Woodward about 'needs' claims of Aborigines not being delayed until supposed white Australian needs were met. Wenten Rubuntja, realising that Mr Justice Ward would probably be unsympathetic to the bureaucrats, set to work.

In 1975 Wenten Rubuntja had not been prominent in CAALAS but had won massive support for the position as Vice-Chairman of CLC. His particular talents for trouble making were exactly what the CLC membership wanted. To belong to a land rights organisation was very difficult for most Aborigines—cattle station workers knew the pastoralists' attitude to land rights. To have a reputation as a 'good boy' with an employer meant not only that you and your family were fed, but also that your relatives could freely visit you. The Gurindji had been seen as trouble makers, and no central Australian pastoralist would allow such notions to effect their own 'boys'. Similarly, to be regarded a 'good Christian' on a mission made life rather more bearable. In short, trouble makers could expect a hard time from every white institution.

Yet the CLC members intended to make 'trouble'. They did, after all, want land rights. No more revolutionary notion could be expressed. With the shield of a large organisation, these revolutionary demands could be pressed. But it was necessary that the administration of the CLC should be headed by people who would not be deterred by bureaucratic processes and political manoeuvrings. Charles Perkins was their choice for a strong, articulate chairman, but the organisation also needed an effective campaign organiser: this was Rubuntja. When, on 7 June 1976, Charles Perkins resigned as chairman, Wenten Rubuntja was elected unopposed to replace him.

In two weeks of creek-bed meetings, Wenten Rubuntja organised the town land claims. He first brought together all the senior Aboriginal men with traditional claims to the Alice Springs area. They discussed the land needs of all the groups living in Alice Springs, then went from camp to camp negotiating, compromising, and suggesting ways to overcome tensions between the neighbouring groups. The town campers, especially those at Mt Nancy led by Geoff Shaw, enthusiastically participated. Rather than present a series of 'needs' claims, the people organised one claim with twelve sections of land involved. It was a brilliant strategy and Mr Justice Ward was obviously impressed; with one witness yet to be called he announced publicly that he was likely to recommend that all the land sought be granted and stated that he rejected the objections of town planners and others.

Then on 11 November 1975 the Governor-General, Sir John Kerr, dismissed the Federal Government headed by Mr Whitlam, and Mr Justice Ward was ordered to stop the hearings. But the victory was there. The bureaucrats for the first time had been forced to publicly state their objections to Aboriginal land rights and to explain their delays in granting titles. They had failed to impress, and their humiliation was both public and final.

The change of government completely altered the situation. Whereas we had all been proceeding with our research on the basis of the ALP draft legislation, the question suddenly arose about Liberal Party plans, if any, for land rights. The election campaign in December 1975 had been as bitterly fought in the Northern Territory as it had been elsewhere. Aborigines had strongly supported the ALP but the opponents of land rights had claimed the victory at the polls. During the election Charles Perkins had stood as an independent Senate candidate. I acted as his campaign manager, and we toured the Northern Territory arguing for Aboriginal land rights.

Before the election the Liberal Party spokesman on Aboriginal Affairs, Mr Ellicott, had sent hundreds of telegrams to Aboriginal communities announcing that 'there will be no change in policy or funding' if the Liberals defeated the ALP. Since the telegram referred specifically to land rights there were grounds for continued optimism that the LCP would adopt the ALP legislation which they had supported when in opposition. Within a month of the election, however, we were advised that major changes would be made to the legislation. A campaign of opposition led by the Australian Mining Industry Council and supported by pastoralists and the Northern Territory Government was bearing fruit.

One of the first signs of change was the very strong rumour that Mr Justice Ward would not be re-appointed as Aboriginal Land Commissioner on the grounds of his ill health. Mr Justice Ward had an unequalled reputation in the Northern Territory for his commitment to Aborigines and for his progressive views. As Interim Land Commissioner he had also brought to the post an acute political consciousness and prior to the 1974 Legislative Assembly election he had been the leader of the ALP in the Northern Territory Parliament. However, the rumour proved to be true. In August 1976 the Government appointed a Western Australian QC, Mr John Toohey. Happily, he had impressive qualifications both as a lawyer and through his involvement with Aboriginal people, and his appointment proved a success.

A major change to the land rights legislation was to be the virtual abolition of the land councils. Their role in making land claims was to be abolished and they were to assume little more than administrative tasks under the control of DAA. Mr Justice Woodward had always regarded the independent land council as central to his whole concept of land rights. For such a dramatic change to be suggested, it was obvious that the strident opposition to the land council voiced by Northern Territory politicians had gained support in Canberra.

This clear failure to honour the promises given by Mr Ellicott incensed the Aboriginal people in central Australia. As if that was not bad enough, the Government, which had in the same telegram promised no cut backs in expenditure for Aboriginal affairs, suddenly launched into an austerity programme which caused the closure of kitchens on many settlements and the dismissal of staff. Thus the Government united every Aboriginal group in a major confrontation with it. On 18 March 1976 an amazing demonstration took place in the streets of Alice Springs. From hundreds of kilometres people arrived in town to stage the biggest march ever witnessed in the Centre. Even the local newspaper, which was opposed to Aboriginal interests, estimated the crowd as not less than 300, but police estimates were 1000. In a town with a population of 13 000 at that time, this was an impressive show of strength.

After the march a rally was held, and a deputation was chosen to take the issue to the southern states. Wenten Rubuntja led the deputation with support from Johnny Lynch, Wilton Foster, Simon Enalanga, Neville Perkins, and myself. This was the start of a major interstate campaign. Land rights were an issue that troubled white people of good will everywhere. Many Liberal Party members were outraged at the reversal of land rights policy and we chose to enlist that support in our campaign. Strong backing came from Aboriginal groups, churches, unions and student bodies.

On this first interstate trip we visited Melbourne, Adelaide, Sydney and Canberra. Once again Wenten Rubuntja's great skills as a negotiator and ambassador were obvious. We raised much money and gained wide publicity for the campaign. The trip culminated in a meeting with the Prime Minister, Malcolm Fraser. There is a story in itself about attempts to prevent that meeting taking place; but the delegation had been told to see the Prime Minister, and as a tangible message of authority Wenten Rubuntja was carrying a rare sacred stone object. Mr Fraser was pressed. Was it true, we asked, that the land rights legislation was going to be handed over to the Northern Territory Government to draft and pass? Mr Fraser denied categorically that the Northern Territory Government would be given any responsibility for the legislation. That night a Darwin newspaper, *The News*, in a typical Murdoch shock/horror headline, screamed 'Aboriginals win on land rights'.

It was a short-lived victory; 14 of the 17 members of the Legislative Assembly (the ALP did not hold a single seat) immediately flew to Canberra and forced Mr Fraser to reconsider. Two days later the new headline was 'Assembly wins on land rights'. Mr Fraser had promised the Northern Territory politicians that they could pass 'complementary' legislation. The battle lines were drawn.

With our private funds we started the 'Land Rights News', appropriately described as an occasional publication. In the first edition in April 1976 I wrote:

> This is the year of Land Rights in the Northern Territory. Victories won now will establish the pattern for the next fifty years of development in Aboriginal Affairs.

My own assessment was shared by the opponents of land rights. For 10 months an exhausting, at times vicious, debate raged around Australia. In May 1976 the Minister for Aboriginal Affairs, Mr Ian Viner, produced the draft of the LCP land rights legislation. If that Bill had become law the land rights campaign would have suffered a severe setback. It was apparent that we would waste our time trying to sway white Australian opinion in the Northern Territory. We concentrated instead on interstate support. Liberal members of Parliament were bombarded with petitions, letters and delegations. One MP told me that it got to the stage that everytime he opened his door he expected to see a minister of religion waiting for him with a new petition.

The Northern Territory opponents of the legislation initially made a tactical error when they assumed that the massive support they were gaining in the Northern Territory was evidence that the campaign was won. However, we knew that most white Australians in the southern States suspected that Northern Territory politicians were racist, and so we staged as many national radio broadcasts, television programmes and press debates as we could, knowing that every appearance by Northern Territory politicians cost them support in the States where the majority of politicians who would vote on the Bill resided. We kept a daily tally of numbers and knew that we were winning. We had enough firm commitments by Liberal politicians to 'cross the floor' to ensure success if only we could keep up the pressure.

To maintain the support we had to work hard simplifying what had become a complex debate for those unfamiliar with the various drafts of legislation. I had been writing analyses and sending these to politicians and key interstate supporters, and 'Land Rights News' was filling a gap. To further help in this communication process I wrote *Land Rights or a Sell Out* (1976), which argued for five major amendments to the Liberal Party Bill:

- The restoration of the role of land councils and the Land Commissioner
- Removal of the distinction between 'needs' and 'traditional' claims
- Reintroduction of the 1975 Bill's mining provisions
- Withdrawal from the Northern Territory Assembly of power to make laws over sacred sites, permits, and entry to pastoral properties
- Control over all roads through Aboriginal land to be held by the Aborigines (1976:18).

A significant section of the interstate Aboriginal community initially rejected the idea of amendments to the legislation until a Bill granting simultaneous land rights in all States was presented, or alternatively argued that the ALP Bill had to be accepted *in toto* by the Government. The instructions of the CLC membership were clear, however. They wanted the Northern Territory Bill amended, then passed without further delay. Wenten Rubuntja and I made many interstate trips to explain this situation, and with the assistance of people such as Wesley Lanhupuy from the Northern Land Council, Leo Finlay from Borroloola, and Pincher Numiari from Wattie Creek that position was finally endorsed at a historic meeting in Sydney in August 1976 at a national seminar staged by the Quakers.

My own position became increasingly difficult in this period. The debate was a complex one, and because Rubuntja's English could not be understood by most white Australians initially, I often found myself spokesman for the campaign. This role had its dangers in the suspicion and resentment that could be provoked. Rubuntja was also upset by implied criticism over his permitting me such a role, and he became increasingly reluctant to attend meetings where he knew that I was likely to be attacked for my part in the campaign. Rubuntja and I had worked together for so long and so closely that neither one of us had any difficulty in limiting or emphasising our own individual roles according to the context of a meeting; but this was not always understood. Yet Wenten Rubuntja had a clear view of the need for a united front across Australia. He believed that all Aboriginal people were linked by the Dreaming tracks of central Australia, and where some tribal people occasionally and unwittingly upset urban Aborigines by their comments, he strongly felt his bond to all Aboriginal people. This empathy was vital in overcoming some of the unintended tensions that occasionally threatened the united front.

Suddenly we found that the debate in the Northern Territory had entered a significant new phase. The opponents of the legislation were delighted to find new support coming from the Finke River Mission of Hermannsberg led by Pastor Paul Albrecht and supported by one of the great names of Australian anthropology, Professor Strehlow. The Finke River Mission (FRM) argument, which opposed the legislation on the grounds that it was contrary to 'the Aboriginal reality', was a perfect one for the miners and Country Party politicians to endorse. To confirm the argument that Aborigines did not want the legislation and, particularly, did not want the land councils, the FRM produced a massive document purporting to be the unedited and spontaneous views of Aborigines throughout central Australia who rejected all of the arguments that we had been advancing for passage of an amended Bill. This twist led to months of acrimonious arguments, threats of defamation actions and, ultimately, in a perverse way, to the long term strength of the Central Land Council.

Paul Albrecht had considerable credibility in central Australia. He and his father before him had spent their lives working with Aborigines on the missions. He spoke Aranda fluently and had grown up with many people who had been prominent in the land rights debate. Many influential Aborigines were pastors in the Lutheran Church. Albrecht's views carried great weight throughout Australia and few people doubted him when he said that he was reporting what Aboriginal people had told him to say. We were all concerned that such a difference in viewpoint appeared to exist. But throughout the year we had held frequent mass meetings where the opinions seemed very clear. Our office in Alice Springs was always crowded by people from the bush and the staff were constantly engaged in field trips where the views of traditional owners were sounded out. Wenten Rubuntja, Rod Hagen and I each travelled nearly 1600 kilometres a week and we had been getting quite different responses to those reported by the FRM staff.

We discovered during a field trip in the FRM area that FRM staff had recently visited camps to 'explain' the Bill. Their explanations had left people with the clear impression that under the legislation their traditional land titles would be held by the CLC staff, and that the staff would decide who could enter the land and how profits from the land would be disbursed. The royalty payments for mining would go to the CLC. We were also told that the reason why people had been unable to purchase cattle stations was because government money allocated for that purpose had been kept by Wenten Rubuntja and myself.

In denying these suggestions we pointed out that section 23 of the Bill gave all the power to the traditional owners. People had not heard that section read before. We also explained that the money to purchase cattle stations was given to the Aboriginal Land Fund Commission and that body had to account for every cent and none of that money was paid to the CLC. We realised that we could not have adequately explained the Bill at Council meetings. The concept of the land trust was being widely misinterpreted and misunderstood.

We finally obtained a copy of the transcripts of the discussions convened by the FRM at cattle stations and mission out-stations. The tapes showed that people were being misled but they also warned us that we had a lot of groundwork to do. The attack on the CLC staff indicated that two quite different interpretations of the legislation were being presented to many Aboriginal people. As the interpreters on both sides had credibility, it was inevitable that the Aboriginal people would have to choose who to believe, thus injecting real tension into the debate.

The arguments against the CLC staff as stated by FRM were echoed in the Legislative Assembly and in Federal Parliament. Typical of the weekly offerings were these words from Rupert Kentish, then Member for Arnhem, who told the Assembly on 19 August 1976:

> . . . but it becomes increasingly evident that the secondary battle [i.e., after the battle over the legislation — GE] under the surface is the battle for who is to control the

> Aboriginal Land Councils and the Aboriginal Trusts and the Aboriginal people when the land rights are achieved. This is the battle of which the public are unaware . . . that is the main battle, it is the big one, that is the big fish . . . They [i.e., 'the controllers' — GE] want to control the whole of the land of the Northern Territory they want to control all the minerals of the Territory, all the water. They want the lot . . . [they] would become the unelected rulers of the Territory if their plans were successful. The Minister would not dare to ignore their advice. Some of these people have already displayed considerable skill in the manipulation of their subjects.

The FRM argument was beginning to have some effect on the numbers of our supporters in Federal Parliament. Fortunately, we were not alone in being disturbed about the role of FRM. Both sides were gaining support. Professor Strehlow entered the debate with an anthropological argument against the legislation. It was difficult for us to counter the FRM position by alleging bias since that was the very complaint made by the FRM against the CLC.

Central to the FRM position was the argument that the 'Aboriginal reality' meant that Aborigines would not take part in any central organisation, be it related to legal aid, land rights or, in the case of the Central Australian Aboriginal Congress, more general political and social development. Each individual clan would by itself negotiate with any mining company which wanted to dig up its traditional land. Albrecht had argued before Woodward that Aboriginal people would be quite satisfied with leases from the Northern Territory Administration. He had, he said, a 'hang up' about land rights because he thought Aborigines should have the same rights and none greater, than white Australians.

Forcing people to meet in a group with different clans or, worse still, different tribes, and even with part-Aboriginal people or women present, was an outrage that they would not tolerate, not even to create a general united front for broad policy change. The land council was perceived, it was said, as a body which would dictate to people about the uses of their own land.

Many people had come to the support of the land council, and the defects disclosed in the transcripts of the FRM meetings were widely noted. Typical of such a reaction was that expressed by the well respected Institute for Aboriginal Development (IAD) in Alice Springs, a body which had good relations with the FRM. In a published statement the IAD made such comments as these:

> Misleading concepts were presented which led to critical misunderstanding of key provisions of the Land Rights Bill 1976 . . . In several cases no adequate translation of the Bill was given . . . Presentation of material on the Land Bill seems to have been biased and selective . . . We express our deep concern that no attempts whatsoever were made to correct misconceptions and misinformation that many Aboriginals obviously have.

During much of this time the Aboriginal Affairs Committee of the House of Representatives was taking evidence about the proposed legislation. The argument with the FRM spilled over into that. The Committee ultimately reported favourably on Aboriginal acceptance of the views which we were arguing.

It seemed that each week could guarantee a new and more bitter exchange. *The Centralian Advocate* published a letter from Strehlow under the headline 'Land Rights Leader a Fraud', which was Strehlow's assessment of Rubuntja. His remarks about me were no more flattering. Strehlow proved to be of limited benefit to the FRM campaign. Attempts made by me to see him were rebuffed. His contributions to the debate were so bitter that little intellectual force was involved in them. I considered that his resentment against Woodward for failing, in his opinion, to acknowledge his eminence in the field of Aboriginal law of central Australia had made him an implacable opponent of the legislation.

The exhausting debate finally came to an end in about November 1976. A large meeting had been convened by the FRM in Alice Springs. Wenten Rubuntja attended and argued for days against the misinterpretation of the Bill which was still being repeated by a number of Aboriginal people. A statement denouncing the legislation was released to the press and Wenten Rubuntja's name was on it. It transpired that Rubuntja (who is unable to read or write) and many others thought it was an attendance list. Bob Huey, the Regional Director of the Department of Aboriginal Affairs, and I both issued press statements in response to the reports that emanated from the meeting. Huey had been present during the meeting.

In my press release I claimed that the meeting had not been a genuine attempt by FRM to discuss the Bill with Aborigines but had been staged in such a way that the alternative interpretation was not fairly presented. I said that when people had come to the CLC office asking where 'our' land rights meeting was being held we discovered then that they had in fact been invited to the FRM meeting. On enquiring from the FRM we were told that only an evangelical meeting was being held and that there was no need for anyone from the CLC to attend, including Wenten Rubuntja, although he attended anyway. I noted that:

> One of the central themes of Pastor Albrecht's opposition to land rights has been the insistence that centralised meetings involving different tribes and clans cannot accurately reflect Aboriginal opinion.
>
> He now argues that just such a meeting is both representative and authoritative as an expression of Aboriginal opposition to the land rights legislation.

I pointed out that as a result of all the debate some Aboriginal people had doubts about the concept of land trusts as embodied in the Bill, and went on to say:

> Even though we believe that those doubts were fostered by the inaccurate explanations of the Bill given to them by Albrecht and others, we accommodated those people by recommending that the Bill be amended to permit clan trusts to be formed.
>
> Albrecht chose never to discuss such an amendment with the people although it would certainly have met the doubts that those Aboriginal people had.

Bob Huey's trenchant press statement suggested that the 'Aboriginal Statement' had been prepared by FRM staff and people were simply invited to sign without its terms being clearly explained. He also spoke of the FRM having actively fostered doubts in people's minds and noted that 'other Aboriginal groups who have had the Bill's provisions explained to them have very clearly and strongly opted in favour of Land Trusts encompassing more than one clan'. Huey then referred to hints from Strehlow that people like Wenten Rubuntja could be killed by angry Aborigines because of their advocacy of the Bill:

> If Aboriginals like Wenten Rubuntja who has the courage to stand up in front of his own people and argue both Aboriginal and European law came to some harm because of white-inspired arguments those white people responsible will have much more on their conscience than they do at present.

After I had issued my press statement I was called down to the meeting to give my interpretation of the legislation and to refute certain accusations that had been made against me. The meeting clearly found my explanations sufficiently convincing to call upon Pastor Albrecht, who was in the same building, to attend the meeting and also explain his position. This he refused to do. Thus the mood of the meeting finally swung in favour of the Bill and the CLC gained much support.

When the *Aboriginal Land Rights (Northern Territory) Act* 1976 became law on Australia Day, January 1977 we had won most of the amendments we sought. The

Central Land Council now had the task of preparing the land claims and meeting the tremendous challenge that passage of the Act entailed.

In retrospect, the debate with the FRM was of great importance for the survival of the CLC. It generated debate on the legislation, which certainly produced a real awareness of the terms of the legislation and provided a model for future processes of consultation, and the CLC staff became aware of the need to maintain 'grass roots' contacts with Aboriginal Communities.

It was interesting that the Gurindji and their neighbours, the Warlpiri, were the most consistent advocates of political action and the least sympathetic to the FRM arguments about negotiating in small clan groups. The Pitjantjatjara seemed to me to have taken their cue from the Gurindji-Warlpiri position and their own battle for land rights owed much to the experience gained over several years' attendance at CLC meetings and participation in its demonstrations and interstate deputations.

With the passage of the legislation the CLC entered a new phase. Debate continued over the contents of the complementary legislation. The Legislative Assembly introduced a set of Bills which were totally unacceptable to Aborigines and a new political campaign developed. The complementary legislation had many easily explained flaws. Aborigines were incensed by the introduction of a concept called 'the authorised Aboriginal' which appeared throughout the Bills. It was a clumsy attempt to use the complementary legislation as a means of destroying the effectiveness of the Federal legislation. Proposals to limit hunting and camping on cattle stations (except by 'traditional' methods) were rejected outright.

The issue dominated CLC meetings throughout 1977. Finally, in about October 1977, Northern Territory Government went to the polls over the issue. There was a massive swing to the ALP, which cost the CLP leader, Dr Goff Letts, his seat in the Legislative Assembly. Neville Perkins and five other ALP candidates were elected. After the election a Joint Federal Parliamentary Committee was established to examine new proposals for complementary legislation, which proved to be a major improvement on the original Letts Bills.

With all this political activity the CLC was constantly being attacked for alleged bias towards the ALP, but the Aborigines showed that they were no one's puppets when the Federal election was held later in 1977. With the massive Aboriginal vote for the ALP in the Assembly elections only a few months before, some people within the ALP argued that the black vote was secure and that land rights policy should not be a prominent issue in the campaign. Aborigines were unimpressed by the reticence of the ALP and, faced with two parties apparently weakening on land rights, simply did not bother to vote, with the result that the ALP candidate lost the election. The message was clear: if politicians wanted the Aboriginal vote then it could be bought only by definite policy commitments.

In 1977 the hearings of the Borroloola and Warlipiri land claims were due to commence. In August Mr Justice Ward had still not been replaced, and to bring matters to a head he listed the Borroloola claim for hearing. The Prime Minister, on an American trip, moved swiftly to stop the hearings, and Mr Justice Toohey was appointed Commissioner. The Borroloola hearings finally commenced in November 1977 and the first week of the Warlpiri evidence was taken in that month also.

The extraordinary effort involved in the preparation of land claims need not be detailed here, but the exercise took its toll on the CLC staff. The anthropologists, Rod Hagen, Meredith Rowell and others, and field officers Duncan Rubuntja, Robin Japanangka and Stanley Scrutton performed magnificent work. It cost the lives of a field officer whom I will simply call Jakamarra, who at 32 years died of a heart attack after one particularly gruelling field trip, and of another worker, Japanangka, who died in a motor vehicle accident.

With the multiplicity of issues demanding the attention of the CLC, it was becoming clear that administrative restructuring was called for. The office simply could not cope with all the work. In June 1978 I resigned my position and moved to Darwin. From my point of view it was a wise move. The pressures did not relent in the following years but the roots of the CLC were, by then, firmly established.

NOTE

1. The Central and Northern land councils were established as a result of the first report of the Aboriginal Land Rights Commission (see Woodward, 1973:41–44) in 1973. The initial purpose was to make submissions on the various points raised in the first report and on any other matters they wished to bring forward. The councils were supplied with independent legal advice. For an account of the Gurindji strike and walk-off, see Hardy (1968).

REFERENCES

Australia, Parliament (1977) *Report of the Joint Select Committee on Aboriginal Land Rights in the Northern Territory.* Canberra, Australian Government Publishing Service.

Eames, G. (1976) *Land rights or a sell out? An analysis of the Aboriginal Land Rights (Northern Territory) Bill. 1976.* Alice Springs, Central Land Council.

Hardy, F. (1968) *The Unlucky Australians.* Melbourne; Nelson.

Meggitt, M. (1962) *Desert People.* Sydney; Angus & Robertson.

Woodward, A.E. (1973) *Aboriginal Land Rights Commission: first report July 1973.* Canberra, Australian Government Publishing Service.

19

SACRED SITES: THE POLITICS OF PROTECTION[1]

Diane Bell

INTRODUCTION

Aboriginal sacred sites and the means by which they may best be protected are emotive issues for many Australians. In late 1980 Noonkanbah (Western Australia) filled the news; in early 1981 the spotlight shifted to Alcoa at Portland (Victoria); more recently sites in the Alice Springs area (Northern Territory) have prompted numerous press reports. However, while in these and other cases the nature of the 'sacred site' has been extensively canvassed by media, courts, parliaments, Aborigines and their representatives, it remains elusive, contentious and open to diverse interpretation.

In this article I focus on sacred sites in the Northern Territory to develop the argument that a potential for conflict exists between the expectations of the competence of Legislation to protect sites and the Aboriginal mode of site protection. To do so I explore three separate but interrelated facets of sacred sites and their protection. Firstly, I look at the genesis and provisions of the *Aboriginal Sacred Sites Act* 1978 and the functions of the authority charged with site protection under that legislation. Next, I turn to an examination of Aboriginal perceptions of sacred sites within the Aranda system of land tenure. Finally, within the context of these legislative and ethnographic considerations I discuss a specific case of 'sacred site' protection in the Alice Springs area which has transformed the registration of sacred sites within town areas into a bitter political issue.

THE LEGISLATIVE CONTEXT

The *Aboriginal Sacred Sites Act* of the Northern Territory differs from other Australian state legislation concerned with site protection in that it focuses exclusively upon Aboriginal sacred sites. To understand why this should be so it is helpful to consider the Northern Territory legislation in conjunction with the Federal *Aboriginal Land Rights (Northern Territory) Act* 1976 to which it is complementary.

The Woodward Commission

Mr Justice Woodward in the Aboriginal Land Rights Commission's Second Report (April 1974:96–98) sought to elucidate the nature of the Aboriginal relationship to land and to define sacred sites. Woodward (1974:para 518) stated that:

> Land generally has spiritual significance for Aborigines but because of the form and content of myths relating to it, some land is more important than other land. Certain places are particularly important, usually because of their mythological significance, but sometimes because of their use as a burial ground or important meeting place for ceremonies.

In using the term 'sacred site' Woodward (1974:para 520) sought to encompass the many nuances of sites of significance to Aborigines. The term sacred sites' is, he stated, 'the simplest and most convenient for my purpose'. Unlike many other aspects of the

Land Rights Act the protection is not confined to land which is Aboriginal land or subject to claim, but rather applies to the entire Northern Territory.

Reciprocal legislation

In accordance with S.73(1) of the Land Rights Act, the Northern Territory Government is empowered to make reciprocal legislation. With regard to sacred site protection s.73(1)(a) extends the power of the Legislative Assembly to the making of:

> Laws providing for the protection of, and the prevention of desecration, of sacred sites in the Northern Territory, including sacred sites on Aboriginal land, and, in particular, laws regulating or authorising the entry of persons on those sites, but so that any such laws shall provide for the rights of Aboriginals to have access to those sites in accordance with Aboriginal tradition and shall take into account the wishes of Aboriginals relating to the extent to which those sites should be protected.

It is evident from Woodward's recommendations and ss.69(1) and 73(1)(a) of the Land Rights Act that there are various ways in which legislation could have been drafted and a body established to provide for the protection of sites in the Northern Territory. It is in the debates of the Northern Territory Legislative Assembly (see Northern Territory Parliamentary Record 28/2/1978-9/3/1978, No 3, Parts 1 and 2, pp. 532-36) that the form of the reciprocal legislation was clarified and refined. Finally, on 14 September 1979 the *Aboriginal Sacred Sites Act* was proclaimed.

On 3 March 1977 the *Aboriginal Lands and Sacred Sites Bill* was introduced into the first Legislative Assembly of the Northern Territory. Because in Mr Everingham's (then majority leader) opinion it was seen to be breaking new ground, and because the issue was controversial (ibid:533), the Bill was left to lie on the table so that interested parties would have time to comment. The Bill was not proceeded with in the life of that Assembly, and the election for a new Legislative Assembly took place on 13 August 1977. In the meantime, the Federal Parliament had set up a Joint Select Committee, one responsibility of which was to examine and report upon the adequacy of provisions of the laws of the Northern Territory relating to the entry to Aboriginal land, the protection of sites of significance, wild life conservation and entry to seas adjoining Aboriginal land (see Report of the Joint Select Committee on Aboriginal Land Rights in the Northern Territory, 1977:iv).

The Joint Select Committee (ibid:44-47; see also pp.25-26) discussed the inadequacies of the *Native and Historical Objects and Areas Preservation Ordinance* (the only legislation at that time under which Northern Territory sites could be protected) and then turned to a critical examination of the Aboriginal Land and Sacred Sites Bill which also it found to be inadequate. While endorsing the principle that the initiative for site protection should rest with Aborigines (ibid:47; see also p.96) the Committee recommended adoption where appropriate of the provisions of the *Western Australian Heritage Act* 1972. Of particular interest here is the recommendation (ibid: para 102(6)) that:

> A Statutory Authority should be established and be responsible for coordination of requests for protection, the initiation of prosecutions and the most appropriate method of protection in each circumstance. The Land Councils should be represented on the Statutory Authority.

On 2 March 1978 the Aboriginal Sacred Sites Bill was introduced as a separate piece of legislation and its divergence from the Western Australian legislation noted. Originally, Ordinance No. 115 of 1978 and then amended by Ordinance No. 116 of 1978, the *Aboriginal Sacred Sites Act* received formal assent on 9 November 1979. The delay was caused by negotiations between the Northern Territory Government and the Commonwealth concerning funding and the finalisation of arrangements for the appointment of members of the Aboriginal Sacred Sites Protection Authority, a body which was in substantial accord with the recommendations of the Select Committee. That sites should only be registered at the request of Aboriginal owners was again emphasised (see Northern Territory Parliament Records, op.cit.:532–36).

The definition of sacred site in the *Aboriginal Sacred Sites Act* preserves the inclusive nature of Woodward's concept and follows s.3 of the Land Rights Act which reads:

> 'Sacred site' means a site that is sacred to Aboriginals or is otherwise of significance according to Aboriginal tradition, and includes any land that, under a law of the Northern Territory, is declared to be sacred to Aborigines or of significance according to Aboriginal tradition.[2]

One difference worthy of comment in the definition section is that the Sacred Sites Act speaks of 'custodians' as the 'traditional Aboriginal owners or other Aboriginals to whom the protection of a sacred site is entrusted by and in accordance with Aboriginal tradition', whereas The Land Rights Act specifies the criteria for traditional ownership in rather more detail. As various land claims have demonstrated, these criteria may serve to place restrictions on the category of persons who may be found to be traditional owners (see Toohey, 1980a, 1980b, 1981). The concept of custodianship embodied in the Sacred Sites Act has ramifications for the registration of sacred sites and the consultative process. It is also, as we shall see in the discussion of Aranda land tenure, one which takes account of the complex web of rights and responsibilities to land and sites.

The Aboriginal Sacred Sites Protection Authority

Under s.13 of the Sacred Sites Act the functions and powers of the Aboriginal Sacred Sites Protection Authority are:

(a) to establish and maintain a register of sacred sites;

(b) to examine and evaluate all claims for sacred sites made to it by Aboriginals;

(c) to record sacred sites, with full details of the significance to traditional Aboriginals, including any story of each sacred site and any relevant factors including custodianship of the sacred site;

(d) to recommend to the Administrator that particular sacred sites be declared protected sites under this Act.

(e) to enforce the provisions of this Act; and

(f) to carry out other such functions relating to the protection of sacred sites as the Administrator may, by notice in the *Gazette,* authorize the Authority to carry out.

The composition of the 12 person Authority, which is a body corporate with perpetual succession and common seal, is stipulated in s.5(2):

(a) not less than 7 positions shall be for Aboriginals chosen by the Administrator from nominations received from the Land Councils; and

(b) the other positions shall be for the Director of the Authority and persons who are experienced in anthropology, land use and survey, Aboriginal studies, site conservation or such other fields as the Administrator thinks fit.

The seven Aboriginal members were appointed by the Administrator from nominations received from the three land councils: Central Land Council, Northern Land Council and Tiwi Land Council. A further four members of the Authority were appointed from applications received after public advertising and interviews by the Senior Executive Officer of the Office of Aboriginal Liaison, Chief Minister's Department. Once established, the Authority advertised widely for a director, and an appointment was made in March 1980, thus completing the 12-member Authority.

Further appointments of an anthropologist and technical and administrative officers were not made until early 1981. Thus the Authority, which is charged with the implementation of the Sacred Sites Act, is small and has only been operational for a relatively short time. Its responsibilities and functions, however, are vast.

In keeping with s.69(1) of the Land Rights Act, the Authority responds to requests for site protection across the whole of the Northern Territory. The scope of its work gives rise to misconceptions that its register[3] should contain all sacred sites in the Northern Territory. However, the register is necessarily incomplete and uneven. The non-comprehensive nature of the register, coupled with the reluctance of Aborigines to consider sites as public property, are important factors in considering the media response to registration of 'new sites' in areas subject to development and government response to site registration in areas required for alternate land use. That sites are 'discovered' in the path of development is often cited as a reason for ignoring Aboriginal requests for site protection or for limiting the work of the Authority (see Harris, 1980). However, as Hagen (1981a:23-28) has demonstrated, where earlier records of sites and their significance exist, as is the case for Alice Springs with Spencer & Gillen (1927) and Strehlow (1971), a remarkable consistency and coherency through time is evident.

The male orientation of the Authority and other bodies in the field has further complicated the process of identification and registration of sites of significance to Aboriginal women (see below p. 283). My appointment as anthropologist to the Authority in some way offset that imbalance, but without parallel structures at the administrative level the rights of women to seek site protection may be frustrated.

The life of a statutory authority working in a politically sensitive area is often limited and its continued existence fragile, for legislation can always be amended to limit its powers when other interest groups are threatened. To understand the parameters of disputes concerning sacred sites in the Northern Territory, it is necessary to bear in mind the composition of the Aboriginal Sacred Sites Protection Authority and its functions. While the breadth of its operations and the Aboriginal participation in decision-making are essential and consistent with the spirit of the Woodward Commission, the Land Rights Act and the findings of the Joint Select Committee, they provide the bases for charges that Aborigines are thwarting development.

THE ETHNOGRAPHIC CONTEXT

The Arandic[4] people of central Australia have been studied widely and a good deal written concerning their relationship to land (see Spencer & Gillen, 1927; Pink, 1936; Strehlow, 1947, 1970). However, in the process of preparing and hearing Aboriginal land claims new data concerning Aboriginal perceptions of sacred sites, the relationship of people to land and its sites, and land tenure systems in general are forthcoming. Here I outline aspects of the Arandic complex of beliefs and relationships to provide the ethnographic context for a dispute concerning sites in the Alice Springs area.

For more detailed data one should refer to the actual transcripts, exhibits and claim books of the relevant land claims (see in particular the Alyawarra-Kaititja claim, 1978; the Alyawarra and Anmatjirra claim to Utopia pastoral lease, 1979; the Lander Warlpiri and Anmatjirra claim to Willowra pastoral lease, 1980, the Warlmanpa, Warlpiri, Mudbara and Warumungu claim, 1980, and the Kaititj-Warlpiri Warlmanpa claim, 1982; Bell, 1979, 1980-88: 204; Hagen, 1980a + b).

Land and law

The Aranda look to the *aljirra,* the creative era, sometimes referred to in English as the

Dreamtime, when the land was given form, shape and meaning by the activities of the ancestors. Aboriginal mythology records the travels of the pioneering ancestors whose tracks cross cut the country; some traversed hundreds of kilometres and in crossing the territory of others provided links between distant groups; others travelled relatively short distances; yet others remained at one place. At significant places where the ancestors paused, camped, performed certain rituals and explained various social institutions and practices, they left behind reminders of their presence. Here, a rock recalls the place where a dingo gave birth to its pups; there a small soakage stands as testimony to the thoughtfulness of the ancestors; elsewhere a tree marks the passage of the caterpillar along a sandy creek bed; and a quartz outcrop represents the eggs of the ancestral caterpillar. Of particular importance are sites which mark the beginnings and endings of the travels of the pioneering ancestors.

The responsibility for the maintenance of land and its sites in accordance with the dictates of the law established by the ancestral pioneers, falls to the descendants of that era. In living in and using the land through thousands of years, the Arandic people continually reaffirm and reassert the relevance of the law to present and future generations. The significance of sites is both enhanced and reinforced through use, and as knowledge is passed from generation to generation. Burial sites, ceremonial grounds and other sites of historical importance stand as testimony to the Aboriginal presence and their relationship to land.

Sites may be located at the intersection of two tracks and provide a meeting point which establishes a relationship between two countries and the persons responsible for that land. Through use and access to sites, and in the acting out of rituals for the maintenance of sites, knowledge is spread through groups and across country. Sites may also be hand-over points where one group terminates its responsibility for a territory or track and passes it onto another. Such sites tend to delineate boundaries but not in any rigid fashion (see Hagen & Rowell, 1978:4). In some areas sites are clearly territorial markers which provide a means of controlling scarce resources.[5] Where water is a critical resource the need to gain permission before drawing water from the territory of another is an obvious management strategy.

Because the Arandic people trace their very identity to the land bequeathed by their ancestors it is not merely an economic resource, it is life itself. Any threat or challenge to relationships to land becomes a threat to social existence and to the well-being of the custodians. While sites and land are being properly maintained health and happiness are assured. But a violation of the law in the desecration of a site indicates that the custodians of that site are not fulfilling their responsibilities. The frequent violation of sites by non-Aboriginal persons in areas such as Alice Springs undermines Aranda confidence in their ability to maintain their land and themselves—sacred trees are felled in the Todd River to make way for a crossing to the new casion; a road scars the crest of a hill of mythological significance; the drainage system of a new subdivision destroys a soakage of ceremonial importance. In the past the sanctions applied to those who transgressed or allowed a transgression, whether wittingly or unwittingly, were severe (see Strehlow, 1970:117). Today, these sanctions are weakened for Aborigines fear retribution from Australian law if they administer violent punishment to a member of their society who has broken, or failed to adhere to, their ancient law.[6]

Arandic land tenure

Arandic country, at one level, is thought of as comprising discrete named blocks of land within which sites tend to cluster in areas of key resources (see Hagen & Rowell, 1978:4). Rights and responsibilities in the countries and to sites are spoken of in several different ways. Relationships may be traced through two distinct lines of descent, through affinal ties, through conception rights, through tracks and site ownership, through ritual expertise and occupancy. While the rights and responsibilities arising out of these relationships to land and its sites are qualitatively different, they are all important to an understanding of site management and control and of those who may correctly be considered to be 'custodians' according to Aboriginal tradition. In this respect the definition of the Sacred Sites Act of 'custodian' as the responsible person is one more in harmony with the inclusiveness of the Arandic system than the exclusivity of the traditional ownership of the Land Rights Act.

As well as the cross-cutting levels of relationships between persons and groups, there is also an important division of labour between the sexes in site management. Restrictions placed on women visiting sites are often cited as evidence of women's secondary status. However, there are women's sites which men may not approach, sites for which men and women share the responsibility, and sites which, although spoken of as 'men's', include areas for which women are responsible. The internal configuration of a site cannot be determined by reference to the gloss 'men's' or 'women's'. There are also, of course, sites which are exclusively the province of men. An appreciation of women's relationship to sites is important as it elucidates the present controversy over the *welatje-terre* site in Alice Springs. The comments offered here are merely to illustrate the complexities of site management and usage and the implications for consultations (see below; also Rowell, p. 256).

Because the bias of anthropology has been male—both in research orientation and the sex of the fieldworker—women's relationship to land has been hazily understood and given little attention. My own research findings concerning the importance of women in the ritual maintenance of country and sites are supported by women's evidence in land claim hearings in central Australia. When asked, 'How do women look after land?', one senior Warlpiri woman at Willowra replied with pride, 'Women lift up the country'. She held her cupped hands before her and gestured upwards. This concept of lifting up country is also apparent during ritual performance, when women lift up the sacred boards which are symbolic representations of the land and its dreamings.

In the 'lifting up of country' women are nurturing, or 'growing up' the land. Elsewhere I have explained this nurturance motif (Bell, 1980:4) in terms of women 'growing up' country just as they 'grow up' children. Their nurturance of the land and the living ensures harmonious relations continue to exist between people and place. In the maintenance of this complex of relationships, women focus on certain places or sites, which are spoken of and to as close kin, as mother and father, as landmarks, and as the ancestors themselves.

In discussions men and women often refer to 'sides' of sites and the associated 'business'. Frequently I have been told, 'that is the woman's side' or 'that is the man's side'. The rich complexity of the 'women's side is cherished and guarded by senior women while its existence is respectfully acknowledged by senior men. Similarly, women acknowledge the existence of men's sites and ritual responsibilities. It is the male orientation of the white Australian consultative and advisory structures which has obscured Aboriginal woman's role in the maintenance of land and contributed to the diminution of her status in the emerging political order of northern Australia. Where the sides were once the more or less evenly balanced halves of a living pulsating whole, now they are ranked. Men with their greater access to white political practice and concomitant scope to develop facility in negotiating have achieved a status as politicians. Such opportunities have been denied to women who have been cast as the down-trodden, neglected and less authoritative half of society. Marked regional variations occur and in each case is necessary to examine the context and the nature of the changes wrought by dispossession and dislocation.

But when decisions regarding women's sites are taken without proper consultation, the responsible women demonstrate that their opinions must be sought and heeded. When the site is one which embraces areas of male and female responsibility both must be involved. In the research associated with the proposal to build a recreational dam in Alice Springs, a site on the Todd River was investigated (1979–80). *Welatje-terre,* a sacred site complex of significance to Aranda, was noted as a possible obstacle to the dam proposal, and consultation began between the traditional owners and various interested parties. After examining and evaluating the requests from custodians for protection, the Authority registered the site and a list of custodians, including women, was recorded (May 1980). In the negotiations it was soon evident that although men would discuss the site, the decision regarding the possible flooding of the site was properly that of the women. The site is predominantly a women's site and, although other facets of the complex are the responsibility of men, women must be heeded. Because consultations have been by men with men, the separate interests of women have been overlooked.

The frustration and embarrassment caused by the male bias of the *Welatje-terre* consultations in 1980 in a sense paved the way for my appointment to the Authority in 1981. Some changes in administrative structures are apparent; however, the myth that only men have sites and only men need to be consulted persists in many areas (see Rowell, pp. 258–59).

Patriclan and Kurtingurla

One is bound by certain rights and responsibilities to and in the country of one's father and father's father. A qualitatively different set of rights and responsibilities applies in the country of one's mother and mother's father. In the maintenance of land and care of sacred sites there is a ritual division of labour based on the interdependence of these two lines of descent. For any given site the associated rituals will be performed by those who call the country 'father' and 'mother'. Both parties must be present and it is a gross breach of the Law to discuss or attend to ritual matters unless both the agnates and children of the senior women, i.e., the mother's people or *kurtingurla* are present. In summary, the roles of these two groups of persons are complementary and interdependent (see Bell, 1980:188–203).

The actual persons who assume the responsibility of site management comprise a smaller (and ideally a subset) of those who can establish the genealogically based relationships of patriclan members and *kurtingurla.* However, pragmatics often cut across prescriptions at this point in such a way that a person who has the requisite knowledge, age and status assumes the role of patriclan member or *kurtingurla.* Such a person may claim rights by virtue of a classificatory relationship but it is likely to be more tenuous. Persons who are resident in a country are far more likely to acquire the necessary knowledge and thus be able to exercise the responsibility for maintenance of sites than those who live in a far off country. We therefore often find a person who is on the spot amassing knowledge and concomitant rights in an area through the exercise of responsibility for the land and its sites (see Toohey, 1981:44–52). Persons who trace direct relationships to land, but are absent, retain rights to the sites but will need to acquire the necessary knowledge before they are accepted as authoritative owners or managers (see Bell, 1979:15). Once again, the notion of 'custodian' accommodates these variations more readily than does the category of statutory owner.

Underlying the division of labour between patriclan member and *kurtingurla* is the notion of ritual reciprocity wherein one may say, 'Today I am "owner" and tomorrow we turn around and I am "manager".' This reciprocity is emphasised at the level of patrimoiety and is underwritten by marriage alliances established between countries (see Bell, 1980:198ff).

In the anthropological literature the rights of patriclan members (often termed 'owners' in Aboriginal English) have been documented in such a way as to overshadow the spiritual role of the *kurtingurla* ('managers') in site management. Although their importance is noted, they appear as a secondary category of persons (see Peterson et al., 1977; Pink, 1936). However, the evidence of witnesses in land claims indicates that regional differences exist and that in parts of central Australia the lines of responsibility are thought of as 'level'. Indeed, the grave spiritual responsibility of the *kurtingurla* was emphasised in various ways in the Utopia, Willowra and Warlmanpa claims (see Bell, 1979:10–18; Hale, 1980; Nash, 1980; Wafer, 1980).

While patriclan members are responsible for many of the important aspects of site management in that they are the actors for ritual celebrations, they hold knowledge of certain sites and they initiate certain ritual segments (see Hagen, 1981b:7), they are under the constant surveillance of the *kurtingurla*. The latter are responsible for ensuring that rituals are correctly staged, that 'owners' follow the Dreamings 'straight' and do not stray into the territory of others, that sacred objects are properly painted and maintained, and that knowledge is transmitted to successive generations. On site visits it is the *kurtingurla* who first approach the site and call out; their presence or permission to visit is essential. With regard to site maintenance it is the *kurtingurla* who ensure that areas are kept clean and safe and who report back to others after a visit. *Kurtingurla* amass considerable knowledge of site and, in the absence of patriclan members of a suitable age and status, they hold the knowledge and may even pass it onto their own children. (In this case the line of descent appears to be through father's mother's father.) Overall, *kurtingurla* must bear witness, ensure that the law is strictly followed, and administer punishments if a violation occurs (see Bell, 1979:9–18; Peterson, 1975:74).

Other rights in land

In addition to the rights and responsibilities of patriclan and *kurtingurla* are those of persons conceived in a particular country. Ideally, one should be conceived within one's father's country, but if this is not so then a person retains rights in the father's country and has a more limited set through conception affiliation in the sites of another's country. Conception confers certain non-inheritable rights in sites and the ritual objects for that site rather than in the territory as a whole. However, given the present day population concentration of Alice Springs and the basically sedentary life-style of the Aboriginal residents, many Aranda today have conception rights in the countries of the Alice Springs region than would have been the case a century ago. (The same applies to other centres of population concentration.)

There are other ways in which persons may attain rights to sites. When one group finds that its territory is too vast to be managed by the available responsible persons a portion may be placed in the custodianship of another. The future status of such transactions depends on demographic factors and the like (see Bell, 1980:203).

THE POLITICS OF PROTECTION: THE SADADEEN DEVELOPMENT

The sacred trust of the Aranda to protect sites asso ciated with several species of caterpillars and the town planners' imperative to locate and develop suitable areas for the future expansion of Alice Springs, raise questions concerning planning, site protection and consultation with Aboriginal people. Within the Sadadeen development in the Eastside area of Alice Springs several site complexes have been identified; some are now protected, some remain unprotected, others have been destroyed by development.

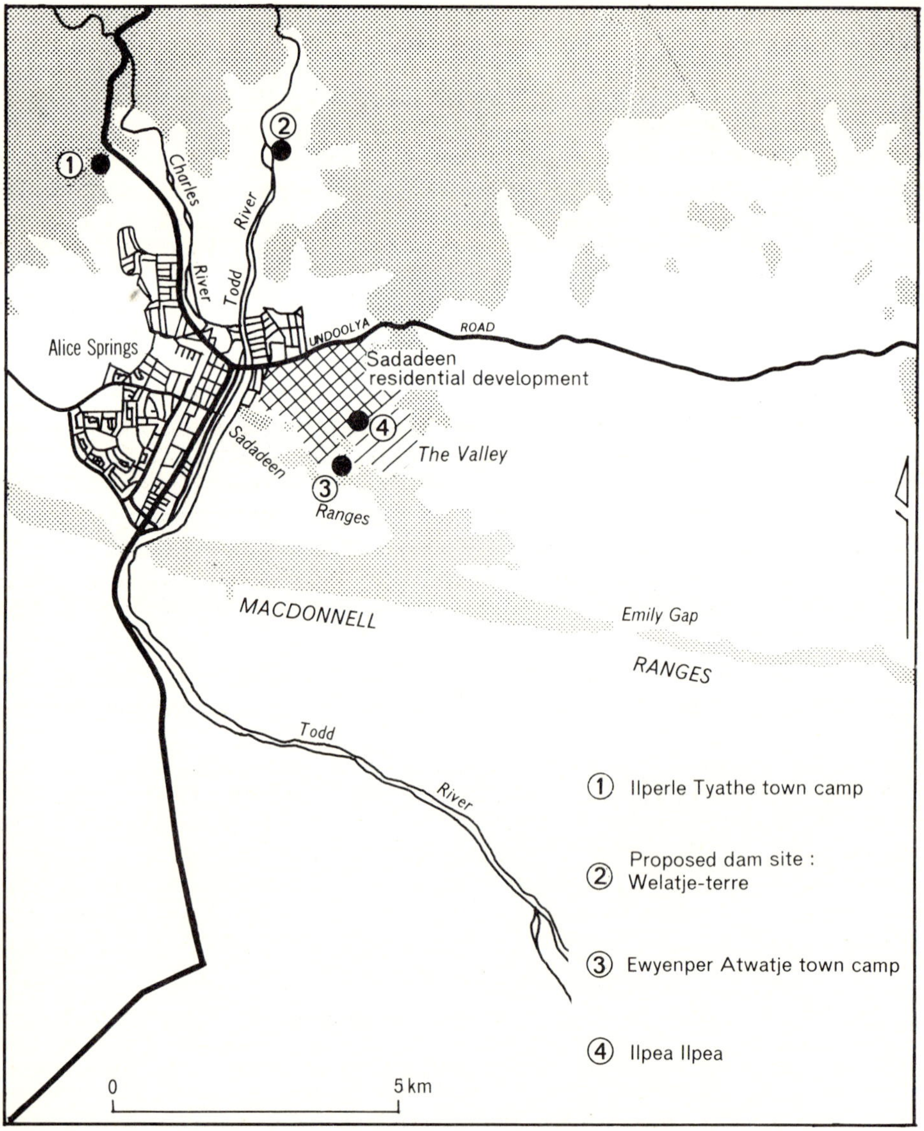

Fig. 1
Alice Springs including the Sadadeen residential development and sacred sites.

The significance of the Eastside area derives from the exploits of the ancestral caterpillars who entered Alice Springs from the north, passed through the Warlpiri camp, Ilpere-tyathe, past the Community College, through the Verdi Club (which is built on a soakage), into the Sadadeen residential and industrial development area and on to Emily Gap, Inturrka, an extremely powerful and dangerous site (see Bell, 1981:3). As can be seen, significant sites have already been desecrated and the closer the development comes to Emily Gap, the more fearful the custodians become.

The distribution and form of sacred sites in the Eastside area illustrates, on the one hand, several of the problems associated with site identification and protection and, on the other, confirms Mr Justice Woodward's observations that the entire landscape is infused with significance. The features which are of heightened significance and may be termed 'sacred sites' are inter-related in a way which reflects Aboriginal land use patterns, ceremonial practice and the function of sites as territorial markers. The Sadadeen residential development (bounded by Undoolya Road and the stormwater drain) and the industrial development planned for the valley to the east of the drain, creates a pattern of land use that impinges on a series of sacred sites: a soakage of mythological and ceremonial significance, a ceremonial ground, and a number of other distinct features in the landscape.

One major soakage located within the Aboriginal town lease of Ewyenper-atwatye (adjacent to the valley zoned for industrial development) is considered 'protected' as it is under the constant surveillance of those custodians who reside on the lease. The Sadadeen Range which bounds the lease (and is another manifestation of the caterpillar) and a cave storehouse for ritual objects in the vicinity, are not as secure, and the custodians would like the lease extended to include these features. For, as the Ilpeye Ilpeye Association (1979: para 4) stated in their original application for the Ewyenper-atwatye lease:

> The importance of sacred sites and the necessary protective zones around them must be regarded as an integral part of the land application since the lifestyle of the Aboriginal groups incorporates both the physical and spiritual needs as well as close affinity with the land.

Which sites were to be identified and which remain secret was a deliberate decision of the custodians at the time of the lease application and one which was in accord with the Sacred Sites Act.

For those participating in ceremonies in the adjacent valley, which is now threatened by industrial development, the soakage at Ewyenper-atwatye provided the only reliable source of water (see Hagen, 1981b: 18). Aranda refer to this valley (and other similar valleys) as 'pockets' in the hills for they provide secure areas where ceremonies may be staged away from the gaze of non-participants. The valley of Ewyenper-atwatye is still being used by the Aranda to stage their ceremonies. The importance of this remaining 'pocket' in the hills was explained by one of the custodians thus:

> We need this valley so we can educate the young fellows. This place is used for initiation still and for generations; it is very important . . . If they use that valley they'll destroy our ground for making our generations. All the places around here, these three cleared areas, that's where the women dance, where the men sing and where the initiation is. If we have a ceremony one night, we might let a young one walk into a house. That's wrong. It must be secret. It's too dangerous for people to see. We've been using it right through . . . It's our private life . . . We can't do it elsewhere . . . We want to keep the generations going. (Transcribed from my notes of a meeting with the custodians at Central Land Council 22/1/81).

The Ewyenper-atwatye soakage and valley do not exist in isolation from other sacred sites in the area; indeed their significance lies partly in the web of interrelations with other sites and the way in which men, women and children are drawn together in their use and maintenance. For instance, the soakage Ilpeye Ilpeye, which lies to the north of the valley (and is within the residential development area) was where the women waited for the return of the initiates and where the ceremonial paint was removed. Thus, within an area concerned primarily with male ceremonial activity we find an area for which women are primarily responsible. All around the soakage grew *ilpeye ilpeye (Hakea leucoptera),* a tree which provided food for the ancestral caterpillar. When I visited this site in January 1981 it was children who enthusiastically called out the name of the tree and impressed upon me the abundance of *ilpeye ilpeye* in the area. Similarly, at Ewyenper-atwatye soakage, the leaves of the *ewyenper* bush, which is also a food for the ancestral caterpillars, were culled for my inspection.

Beyond the valley and the town lease, beyond the physical obstacle of the range, lies one of the most dangerous sites of the area. The intervening sites, the ceremonial ground itself, and the natural barrier provided by the hills are in a sense a buffer zone, a marker recognised by all those schooled in the Law, that to proceed further without observing the strict codes of ritual etiquette will wreak havoc. In trying to explain their concern, 24 custodians of the Ewyenper-atwatye Association wrote to the Acting Chief Minister of the Northern Territory (3 March 1981) and stated:

> We still want the valley. We don't want a road going through, so stop planning that. We've been pushed back too far by governments already on our own country. We're sick of that.

The signatories include patriclan members, *kurtingurla* and those whose rights are based on other interest in land and its sites (as outlined above).

However, the Government regards the claim that the whole valley is a sacred site as unreasonable. In the *Centralian Advocate* (24.6.81) Mr Robertson, Minister for Land, was reported as saying:

> The town of Alice Springs had been 'ring barked' with land claims and claims of sacred sites . . . We can't build the planned light industrial sub-division on the east side because of some supposed more sacred sites . . . The town is sick of the strategy by the Aboriginal organizations — and so am I . . . The Government will not buckle.

Alice Springs is an area of intense ancestral activity, as a glance at the works of Spencer & Gillen (1927: 88–98), Strehlow (1971: map) and Hagen (1981a, 1981b) amply demonstrates. Further, the same factors which prompted town planners to locate industrial development in the Eastside valley underlies the Aboriginal use of the pocket in the hills, i.e., it is a bounded area away from the gaze of other users of the Eastside.

One suggestion has been for a road to be put through the valley in such a way as to leave the cleared areas of the ceremonial grounds undisturbed. But, as the custodians have stated, for the site to be protected it is necessary to maintain the privacy of the valley. Also, as they have said on numerous occasions, a road which goes beyond the valley emperils the Emily Gap site.

The way in which the custodians have attempted to signal their concern for the sanctity of the valley and sites beyond supports one of the major assumptions which underlies the Sacred Sites Act. Aborigines prefer to protect sites themselves and the granting of town leases, such as Ewyenper-atwatye, helps. Aborigines have been prepared to notify town planners of the existence of sites, but only in so far as they have perceived it to be essential to do so; in other words, they have made public marker sites within a buffer zone. The sacred sites which the Eastside custodians compromised by making public 'protected' the sites beyond. As early as May 1975 the custodians attempted to alert planners to the sensitivity of the area. Members of the Eastern Aranda wrote to the then Department of Planning & Urban Development asking for protection of a soakage *ilpurra,* which was associated with the performance of 'sacred ceremonies'.

In the files of the Aboriginal and Torres Strait Islander Housing Panel, Central Land Council, Department of Aboriginal Affairs, Department of Lands, Tangentyere and the Sites Authority we find a steady stream of statements concerning the existence of sacred sites on the Eastside. However, the custodians of sites only divulged as much as they thought necessary to impress the outsider with the importance of the area. That this information was incomplete and that a comprehensive study of sites should be undertaken was repeated by all those involved in site identification and protection (see Lewis, 1975, Smith, 1977). This was not done, and research continued to be undertaken on an *ad hoc* basis. Once the threat became apparent to the custodians they did move to protect the sites under the Sacred Sites Act and they did request that a site survey be undertaken. The latter provided both an overview of ancestral activity in the Alice Springs area and a specific study of the Sadadeen area (see Hagen, 1981b). It was not that they had set out to thwart development by withholding information in a capricious fashion but rather that, in accordance with their law, they were protecting sites by not disclosing their whereabouts because no direct threat was perceived. The nature of the threat to the valley only became obvious in late January 1981 when at a joint meeting of Central Lands Council, Tangentyere, the custodians and the Department of Lands the latter displayed a map indicating the proposed alignment of the road through the valley. They asked that sites be identified within three days so that work could proceed according to schedule and so that sites could be protected (see Bell, 1981:9). However, the answer by the custodians that the valley was a sacred site was not acceptable and in the press was referred to as a 'supposed sacred site'.

In explaining the situation to the Sites Authority, the Ewyenper-atwatye Association wrote:

> We didn't know they were going to build a town around Ilpeye Ilpeye on west side of drain. The Government didn't let us know what they were planning to do. All we seen is bulldozers and earth movers digging up the ground. That sacred soakage Ilpeye Ilpeye used to be the main soakage for women dancing nights to morning. Now it's covered up. That little hill, caterpillar cocoon, near where they're building the drain near the trees, they're damaging that too, they supposed to fence that in.
>
> But just behind there at the top of the little ridge in the entrance to valley, that's where the secret place for Ewyenper-atwatye starts. It goes back east to the hill near where the fence is, and up to the top of the hills right around the valley.

The dilemma facing both Aborigines and town planners as perceived by government was explored in reply to a question in the Legislative Assembly. Mr D. W. Collins asked what efforts the Department of Lands had made to ensure that it was aware of any sites of significance in the area prior to the drawing up of plans. The Minister for Lands and Housing (*Northern Territory Parliamentary Record,* 6 June 1981:8) stated that nothing had come up in the study undertaken in 1975 and that in 1978:

> . . . the Department of Lands specifically requested the Central Land Council and, I understand, our Central Australian Aboriginal Congress to identify specifically any sites of significance in the eastern section of town. They were able to identify 2 which were widely known as sites of significance. My Department was not satisfied that the information was not necessarily all there was to the story and subsequently involved the Department of Aboriginal Affairs and the Sacred Sites Authority. Another 2 sites were then identified, and nothing further. Since work has started in the area, particularly in the industrial subdivision, the entire valley is claimed to be a site of significance.
>
> In fairness to the Central Land Council, it said at the time that these were the only known sites and further research was needed. However, the problem is that the Central Land Council, and indeed Aboriginal people in the area, quite freely admit to the Department of Lands that it will not disclose the sites until such time as all the work is done and—to use its terms—the sites are threatened. Of course this places the government in an absolutely impossible position. We cannot plan around the sites of significance because we do not know they are there and they will not tell us until we

> start with the bulldozers. This involves enormous delays and tremendous cost to the taxpayer. I do not know what the answer is. It certainly seems as if there is a great deal of reluctance on the part of the Central Land Council to co-operate with the Department of Lands in the interests of all.

Indeed, the negotiations between the various bodies did ensure that the sites identified within the Sadadeen residential development were protected. One additional site, the soakage, Ilpeye Ilpeye, was however identified too late to be protected. In March 1981 the soakage was bulldozed (see *Centralian Advocate* for 12 March 1981). The custodians, aware that the drainage system of the residential development would render the soakage dry and that the proximity of houses to the soakage would inhibit ceremonial use of the site, agreed to the development of the area. To commemorate the importance of the soakage to the Aranda, the Department of Lands agreed to erect a cairn and plaque on the site. For the custodians it was a compromise and one which saddened them greatly. Little was made of this compromise but much has been made of their insistence that the development should not enter the valley. Suitable land in Alice Springs is at a premium, a fact which the custodians recognise and they have indicated other areas where development is acceptable. These at present are zoned residential or considered too costly to develop.

What then of the charge that Aborigines identify sites too late for protection to be offered and that developers are placed in an impossible position? The answer lies, in part, in the form that consultation takes and partly in the non-Aboriginal expectation of the competence of legislation to protect the sites.

In the area of the Sadadeen residential development all but one site has been protected. Unfortunately, the persons who, in the first instance, were approached to identify sites, were neither in a position to make such a decision nor given the opportunity to liaise with the custodians over a sufficient period of time for the nature of the threat to the entire area to be apparent to all those with an interest in the area. Indeed, it is questionable if data at this level were available in a form which could have informed a decision regarding development throughout the Sadadeen area. The proposed Alice Springs Town Plan was exhibited on 27 March 1980, and because no objections were lodged within the 3 months available for that purpose the matter was deemed closed. Expenditure was then committed and planning began. However, some sites had been identified, the significance of the area had been noted,and the need for an in-depth study recorded in official files. That the consultations had not been sufficient or undertaken with the correct persons and that the extent of the development had not been made clear until the pegs were driven into the ground and the bulldozers began to roll are important issues. There is, I believe, a need to consider Aboriginal interests in land and its sites as more than an objection which may be raised once a plan is exhibited. If Aboriginal relationships to land were considered as a serious component in the preplanning stage, then a different context within which sites are identified would exist and it would alleviate 'the impossible situation' which the town planners perceive. There is an urgent need for bodies like Tangentyere to develop coordinated land management plans. Too often, Aborigines are caught in crisis management situations.

In areas of intense ancestral activity, such as Alice Springs, site protection is difficult. To pinpoint sites, to erect fences and plaques, is not a form of protection in accord with Aboriginal use of sites. Sacred sites are not monuments to a bygone era, they are an integral part of life in the 1980s. It is not sufficient to locate sites along a track, engage in a consultation with one or two persons, no matter how good their English is or how high their status in an organisation, and declare the resultant decision regarding site protection and identification to be authoritative. The process of achieving consensus amongst those responsible for a site is slow and requires that a number of people be involved. In view of the requirements of town planners, it also needs to be early enough in the process for alternatives to be explored. Finally, for consultations to achieve binding decisions there must be cooperation from all parties. The Aranda have shown they can cooperate and that they will compromise. Their request for site protection in the valley is extremely modest in terms of the land they have lost.

On 2 December 1981 the nature and form of the debate concerning the mode of protecting the valley changed. The Northern Territory Government introduced amendments to the Sacred Sites Act which would render any site registration within town or planning areas a matter for the prior assessment and classification of Cabinet. Mr Everingham, in introducing the Bill for the Aboriginal Heritage Act Serial 171 (which was designed to replace the Sacred Sites Act and incorporate the relevant sections of the Historic Objects and Areas Preservation Act) stated in his second reading speech that there was a need to 'clean up the mess' created by the controversy surrounding the registration of the valley as a sacred site (see *Northern Territory Parliamentary Record,* 2 Dec 1981: 1803–13). In the opinion of the Chief Minister, the definition of sacred sites was so broad, so all-encompassing, that it would lead to the ridiculous situation wherein the entire Northern Territory became a sacred site. He therefore proposed that sites be ranked according to degrees of importance (ibid:1803–4). The unilateral action of the Authority in registering sacred sites was to be curbed and henceforth under the Aboriginal Heritage Act the recognition, registration and/or proclamation of sites, wholly or partly within a town or planning area, would be determined by the Administrator only upon the recommendation of the Executive Council (ibid:1812). In giving his reasons for proposing this mechanism, Mr Everingham expressed dissatisfaction with the way in which the Commonwealth Government had responded to his request for financial assistance to relocate the industrial subdivision. He tabled a letter to the Prime Minister dated 24 March 1981 (ibid) and spoke of a reply on 11 May 1981 (ibid:1811-2). Clearly, then, the Northern Territory Government acted promptly in seeking options after the valley was identified as a sacred site to the Authority in January 1981. It is also evident that the valley has become a test case in the Northern Territory Government's attempts to free itself of Federal constraints.

The amendments have been discussed extensively by the media in the Northern Territory, but whether or not the Act will be amended so as to restrict the activities of the Authority within town boundaries was not known at the time of writing. However, the Government does appear determined that the issue will be resolved in a way which permits the development to proceed. On 6 April, 1982 the Acting Chief Minister, Marshall Perron, wrote to Central Land Council, Tangentyere and the Ewyenper-atwatye Association advising them that the industrial development would go ahead and that the Government 'was prepared to consider adjusting plans to take reasonable account of actual sacred sites in the area provided these are disclosed and justified by 23 April' (*Centralian Advocate* for 6 April 1982). Central Land Council responded with an appeal to Alice Springs residents to preserve and value the beauty of the local landscape and a challenge to the Government's assertion that negotiations with Aboriginal organisations regarding site identification had occurred over the past 12 months (CLC press release, 8 April). The strands of the fabric woven by the moves and countermoves of government, Aboriginal organisations, and the traditional owners themselves form an intricate pattern. In this article I have teased out only a few of the strands to demonstrate the way in which the conflict between the Aboriginal mode of protecting sites and expectations of the competence of an Act of Parliament to protect sites has soured the politics of protection.

NOTES

1. This article is based on my fieldwork in central Australia over the past six years and more specifically on my work experience with the Aboriginal Sacred Sites Protection Authority (Darwin) between January 1981 and January 1982. Many people have contributed to my understanding of issues raised here, and I thank Bob Durnan, Bob Ellis, Rod Hagen, Jane Lloyd, Meredith Rowell, Jeff Stead, John von Sturmer, and specifically the Aranda of central Australia. Needless to say, the views expressed are my own.

2. One terminological difference is that 'under this Act' is substituted for 'under a law of the Northern Territory'. This simply reflects the legislative authority—in one case Commonwealth, and in the other Territory.

3. The Museums and Art Gallery of the Northern Territory maintains a register of sites. In addition, the Australian Institute of Aboriginal Studies has begun rationalising the registration of sites Australia-wide, and is developing computer programmes which will ultimately permit the preparation of a national register.

4. Under Arandic people I include Alyawarra, Anmatjirra and Kaititj speakers for, although there are variations, the underlying model is basically the same. I use 'Aranda' to refer to the Eastern Aranda, who are the traditional owners of Alice Springs.

5. This is particularly evident for coastal peoples where sites are located in estuaries. Permission must be sought to enter the waters and thus the resources of this important environ are protected (see Davis, 1981).

6. Some consideration of these problems is recorded in the discussion paper of the Law Reform Commission, 'Aboriginal Customary Law: Recognition?' (1980:20–22).

REFERENCES

Australia, Parliament (1977) *Report of the Joint Select Committee on Aboriginal Land Rights in the Northern Territory,* Canberra, Australian Government Publishing Service.

Bell. D. (1979) 'Statement to the Utopia Land Claim Hearing.' Exhibit 57 to the Anmatjirra and Alyawarra Land Claim to Utopia Pastoral Lease 37 1. (Manuscript, copy with AIAS).

Bell, D. (1980) *Daughters of the Dreaming.* Unpublished PhD Thesis, Australian National University.

Bell, D. (1981) 'Sadadeen: planning, protection and consultation', a report to the Aboriginal Sacred Sites Protection Authority, 30 January 1981, 13 1 (manuscript, copy with AIAS).

Bell, D. & Ditton, P. (1980) *Law: the old and the new: Aboriginal women in central Australia speak out,* Canberra, Aboriginal History for central Australian Aboriginal Legal Aid Service.

Davis, S. (1981) 'A Report on Aboriginal Sites of Significance in North Eastern Arnhemland, Section 1, Land Tenure among Yolnu', Darwin, Aboriginal Sacred Sites Protection Authority, May 1981.

Hagen, R. (1981a) 'Sacred Sites in the Alice Springs area: the proposed Alice Springs-Darwin Railway', report to the Aboriginal Sacred Sites Protection Authority, July 1981.

Hagen, R. (1981b) 'Sacred Sites in Alice Springs: A preliminary survey', report to Aboriginal Sacred Sites Protection Authority, February 1981.

Hagen, R. & Rowell, M. (1978) 'A claim to areas of traditional land by the Alyawarra and Kaititja', Alice Springs, Central Land Council, 41 1 (manuscript, copy with AIAS).

In *Official Hansard Report of the Joint Select Committee on Aboriginal Land Rights in the Northern Territory, Canberra: Government Printer, pp.1002–1014.*

Hale, K. (1980) *'Remarks on the joint land maintenance responsibility of Kirda* and *Kurdungurlu',* Exhibit 47 to the Lander Warlipiri/Anmatjirra land claim to Willowra pastoral lease, 4 1.

Harris, M. (1980) Selling suckers sacred sites. *Bulletin,* 16 Sept., pp.31–32.

Ilpea-ilpea Association (1979) 'Lease application Sadadeen area, Alice Springs, prepared for the Association by Lester, Firth & Mutton.

Law Reform Commission (1980) 'Aboriginal Customary Law—recognition?' Discussion paper No. 17, November 1980.

Lewis, D. (1975) 'A report to Central Land Council on Alice Springs sites' (restricted).

Nash, D. (1980) 'A note on *Kurdungurlu'* prepared for AIAS Biennial Meeting, Canberra.

Peterson, N. (1975) The ownership of sacred sites. In: Robert Edwards (ed.), *The Preservation of Australia's Aboriginal Heritage.* Canberra, Australian Institute of Aboriginal Studies.

Peterson, N., Keen, I. & Sansom, B. (1977) Succession to Land, Primary and Secondary Rights to Aboriginal Estates. Official *Hansard* Report of the Joint Select Committee on Aboriginal Land Rights in the Northern Territory. Canberra, Government Printer, pp.1002–1014.

Pink, O. (1930) The land owners in the Northern Division of the Aranda tribe, Central Australia. *Oceania,* 6(3), 275–306.

Smith, K. (1977) Correspondence on Department of Aboriginal Affairs file.

Spencer, B. & Gillen, F.J. (1927) *The Arunta.* London, Macmillan.

Strehlow, T.G.H. (1947) *Aranda Traditions,* Melbourne University Press.

Strehlow, T.G.H. (1970) Geography and the totemic landscape in central Australia. In: R. & M. Berndt, (ed.), *Australian Aboriginal Anthropology.* University of Western Australia Press, pp.92–140.

Strehlow, T.G.H. (1971) *Songs of Central Australia,* Sydney, Angus & Robertson.

Toohey, J. (1980a) 'Alyawarra and Anmatjirra land claim to Utopia Pastoral Lease', report by the Aboriginal Land Commissioner. Canberra, Australian Government Publishing Service.

Toohey, J. (1980b) 'Lander Warlpiri Anmatjirra land claim to Willowra Pastoral Lease', report by the Aboriginal Land Commissioner. Canberra, Australian Government Publishing Service.

Toohey, J. (1981) 'Finniss River Land Claim', report by the Aboriginal Land Commissioner, Canberra.

Wafer, J. (1980) 'Various arguments against the inclusion of *Kurdungurlu* in the Willowra claim refuted', Exhibit 50 to the Lander Warlpiri Anmatjirra Land Claim to Willowra Pastoral Lease.

Woodward, E. (1974) Aboriginal Land Rights Commission. Second Report, April 1974. Canberra, Australian Government Publishing Service.

20

PITJANTJATJARA LAND RIGHTS

Bill Edwards

During the last few years negotiations have taken place between the Government of South Australia and the Pitjantjatjara Aboriginal people, leading to the passing of the *Pitjantjatjara Land Rights Act* early in 1981. In this paper I outline briefly the earlier history and policies relating to the Pitjantjatjara people and their land and record the story of the recent negotiations. As Superintendent of Ernabella Mission from 1958 to 1972, I was in contact with the Pitjantjatjara people during a period when little attention was given to land rights. As an Area Chaplain based at Fregon in 1973, and at Amata since 1976, I have been involved in the recent negotiations as an interpreter and as minute secretary for the Pitjantjatjara Council since its inception in July 1976.

The names given to Aboriginal language groups had a relative rather than an absolute reference, and in the area under consideration where the suffix *-tjara* denotes possession, the various dialect groups referred to other groups by a word used in the other dialect with this suffix added to the word. Thus, the Pitjantjatjara are the people who have the word *pitjantja,* meaning 'coming'. Other groups were known as Yankuntjatjara, the Matutjara, the Ngatjatjara, etc. With the use of Pitjantjatjara in literature, education, language teaching, etc., there has been a tendency to use this term to cover all of the people who spoke several dialects and who, for untold milleniums, had enjoyed occupancy and use of a large tract of land adjacent to the junction of the borders of South Australia, Western Australia and the Northern Territory.

We may assume that because of limited interaction with other groups, these people had experienced little challenge to the enjoyment of those land rights. They were unaware in 1770 that Captain James Cook had annexed the eastern part of Australia to the British overseas possessions, nor that later divisions of the land into states and a territory would lead to the problems of negotiating with three (and now four) governments when asserting their claims to land. Cook and the administrators who divided the land were also unaware of the existence of the Pitjantjatjara people and of their sentiments regarding the land they occupied.

During these milleniums there had evolved amongst the Pitjantjatjara people a belief system which provided a pattern for daily living and social relationships. They believed that they were descended from ancestral beings—*Wati Malu,* kangaroo-man; *Wati Kalaya,* emu-man; *Minyma Ikarka,* bowerbird-woman; etc.—whose actions as they moved over the surface of the land during the *Tjukurpa* or Dreaming period had shaped the hills, waterholes, trees, sandhills and other physical features and given them the form we see today. The same *Kurunpa,* or spirit which inhabits humans, also resides in these natural features and in the animals which are also descended from the ancestral beings. Thus the Pitjantjatjara person believes that he or she exists in a special relationship with the land, a relationship of mutual interdependence.

THE ROLE OF INTERPRETATION

As indicated above, my main role in the recent negotiations on Pitjantjatjara land rights has been as an interpreter. An interpreter interacts with two other parties, and in this case, because of the great difference between the understandings about land of the parties involved, the task of interpretation goes well beyond the translation of words, to giving each of the parties some understanding of the other parties' concepts relating to land. Thus the role had involved on the one hand, assisting the Pitjantjatjara people to explain to other white Australians the concepts formulated from their unique relationship to the land, and on the other hand, attempting to make clear to them the need to have titles to the land that are recognised by the parliaments and courts, and explaining the concepts underlying such titles. The role is a difficult one as there are frequently no words in one of the languages having a near-equivalent meaning to words used in the other language. For example, words used by English speakers in these negotiations such as title, lease, freehold, and incorporation have no corresponding terms in Pitjantjatjara. Through this role the interpreter seeks to assist others involved in the negotiations to arrive at legislation enshrining the best possible reconciliation between the varying concepts related to land, between the concepts of ownership as against relationship, and between the concepts passed down from generation to generation by oral tradition and expressed as being 'in the head' and those recorded on paper through bureaucratic processes.

EARLIER HISTORY

The first European intruders, the explorers Gosse and Giles, and their respective parties, entered Pitjantjatjara territory in 1873. The comments of Ernest Giles (1889: 173) indicate that this was a year of above average rainfall:

> This was really a delightful discovery. Everything was of the best here—timber, water, grass, and mountains. In all my wanderings over thousands of miles in Australia, I never saw a more delightful and fanciful region than this, and one indeed where a white man might live and be happy.

The last comment typified the attitude of Europeans towards the original inhabitants and their land for many decades to come. In a later comment, Giles was quite explicit about the fate of the original inhabitants (Giles, 1889: 184):

> The great Designer of the universe, in the long past periods of creation, permitted a fiat to be recorded, that the beings whom it was His pleasure in the first instance to place amidst these lovely scenes, must eventually be swept from the face of the earth by others more intellectual, more dearly beloved and gifted than they.

During the next 50 years there was increasing penetration of the area by surveyors, prospectors, 'doggers', and other adventurers (Hilliard, 1976, chapters 4-6: 55-88). In an attempt to protect the Pitjantjatjara people from the fate of other Aboriginal groups in the southern parts of South Australia, demands were made for the setting aside of reserves and an area of 56 721 km^2 in the north-west of the State was gazetted in 1921 as a reserve for the use and benefit of the Aborigines. The Government reserved the right to resume the land if the occasion demanded it. Adjacent areas in Western Australia and the Northern Territory had been set aside as reserves for Aborigines in 1918 and 1920 respectively. Additions to the north-west reserve in South Australia were made in 1938 and 1974.

The first provision of training, employment, health and educational services in the area was made with the establishment of Ernabella Mission by the Presbyterian Church in 1937. An Adelaide surgeon, Dr Charles Duguid, having visited the area, and observing the dignity and self-confidence of the people, advocated the establishment of the mission. 'Unless some action was taken, these tribespeople would also be driven out of their territory' (Duguid, 1972: 120). The mission was to act as a buffer between the

Aborigines and the encroaching white man and 'there was to be no compulsion nor imposition of our way of life on the Aborigines nor deliberate interference with tribal custom' (Duguid, 1972: 115).

As the criticism is often made that missions sought to uproot people from their traditional areas and coerce them to the patterns of settlement life, it should be noted that the Ernabella staff encouraged the Pitjantjatjara people to maintain links with their land by taking out supplies to trade with them for dingo scalps during summer and spring holidays each year. During the 1950s and 1960s nickel exploration in the Mt Davies and Wingelinna areas encouraged some of the people to congregate near the mining camps because of the availability of food there. However, the presence of these camps, the lack of consultation with the people, and the failure to provide for the recording and protection of significant sites revealed the weakness of the reserve system. Following a visit to the area in 1957, Dr Duguid commented as follows (Duguid, 1963: 107).

> For the reserve had now been radically altered by the establishment of the rocket range and the leasing of certain areas to mining interests. Traversing the Musgraves and the Mann Ranges we visited the mining camp at Mt Davies in the Tomkinson Ranges and went on to the Blackstone Range in Western Australia. Here was situated the headquarters of the West Mining Company . . . This was the Great Central Reserve for Aborigines in 1957.

Ernabella was not situated on the reserve but on a pastoral lease bordering the reserve after the 1938 additions to the latter. During the 1950s there was pressure on the Government of South Australia to open up parts of the reserve for pastoral development by white Australians. Partly to forestall this, and partly to provide increased opportunities for the growing population at Ernabella, the mission established a cattle outstation at Fregon and the Government established Musgrave Park (now Amata) settlement on the reserve in 1961.

During this period the emphasis was on reserving areas of land to provide protection and for the establishment of institutions for training and adjustment rather than on the granting of land rights as such. It was the era of assimilation policy and it was assumed that the people, once assimilated, would be able to obtain land titles in the same way as white Australians. With the emphasis on the need for an economic basis for permanent settlement and the problems of developing viable industries in the area, it was assumed that the people would eventually move from the area to places where work was available.

One of the first clear espousals of land rights in this period was contained in a pamphlet by Frank Engel, *The land rights of Australian Aborigines*, issued by the Australian Council of Churches in 1965. The first official recognition of this right came with the passing of the South Australian *Aboriginal Lands Trust Act* in 1966, under which reserves could be vested in an Aboriginal lands trust at the request of the councils, and the land leased back to the local people on a 99 years lease.

In the Pitjantjatjara area there was little reaction to the passing of this Act, and when members of the land trust, who were part-Aboriginal people from the southern parts of the state, visited the area the Pitjantjatjara people did not identify with them. At this time the Pitjantjatjara people were unaware of the existence of the assimilation policy. They enjoyed occupancy of their tribal land and had adapted to alien intrusions into this land to gain what benefits they could from the intruders. They would have been surprised at any suggestions that in fact the land was not their own.

Mining developments served to raise amongst Aboriginal people and their advisers, a consciousness of the need for land rights legislation and of the shortcomings of the reserve system. Church and government had failed the people of Weipa by acceding to the provisions for the development of bauxite mining on the site of the mission. However, lessons learned from this experience encouraged the Church and others to take up the cause of the Yirrkala people when similar development was planned there. The ABC's Guest of Honour on 5 January 1969, Dr H.C. Coombs, emphasised the disadvantages the lack of adequate interpretation imposed on the Aboriginal people there.

During my last full year as Superintendent of Ernabella Mission (1971), two meetings there served to make the men aware of the challenge to their accepted ownership of the land. In the course of a regular series of meetings to discuss current issues, I mentioned the problems likely to be associated with the possible development of mining at Wingelinna, just across the border in Western Australia. After I had drawn a map on the blackboard a man took the chalk and outlined the track of the *Malu* or kangaroo Dreaming story and declared that the land encompassed by that line belonged to his people. This illustrated the relationship in the Pitjantjatjara mind between mythology and land.

This relationship was emphasised by the late Paddy Uluru when Ayers Rock *(Uluru)* was discussed at a meeting of men at Ernabella in November 1971. 'Uluru is my camp', Paddy said (quoted in Wallace, 1977: 60), 'This is mine, this holy cave; my fathers and grandfathers entrusted me with this cave.' He related that he had been chased from Ayers Rock many years ago and had not passed on this trust to his sons. However, following support given to his claim by other men at this meeting, he returned to live at the Rock until his death in January 1979. His return symbolised a change in Pitjantjatjara attitudes and aspirations.

Further impetus to the land rights movement was given by the appointment by Prime Minister Whitlam of Mr Justice A.E. Woodward in 1973 to report on the establishing of the traditional rights of the Aborigines to land in the Northern Territory. As Pitjantjatjara and Yankuntjatjara people residing in South Australia had traditional interests in land in the Northern Territory, a solicitor assisting the Commissioner visited Amata in 1973 to meet with some of the men. Having interpreted at that meeting on the 16 November 1973, my main impression of the reaction of the men, following the solicitor's outlining of the proposal to give titles to land and her request for information on boundaries, was one of incredulity: 'What are you white people talking about? This *is* our land.'

Until this time approaches to governments or other authorities by Pitjantjatjara people were mediated through government departments and Church bodies. They lacked a forum through which they could voice united political aspirations. They were beginning to assume authority through local community councils (see Edwards, 1973: 70–80), but there was no structure through which they could be educated about the need for asserting their claim to title of all Pitjantjatjara land and through which they could convey this assertion. The incorporation of The Pitjantjatjara Council in 1976 provided this structure.

THE PITJANTJATJARA COUNCIL

Following a sports weekend at Amata in July 1976, representatives from other communities were invited by the Amata Community Council to remain for a meeting to discuss matters of mutual interest. Over 50 men from Indulkana, Mimili, Fregon, Ernabella, Amata, Pipalyatjara (SA), Blackstone, Wingelinna (WA), and Docker River (NT) with some advisers, met at Amata on the 13 July and decided to establish the Pitjantjatjara Council and seek incorporation of that body. Land was one of the main topics discussed at the meeting and it was recorded that 'The Pitjantjatjara people claim all of the land from Indulkana to Docker River' (minutes of the

Pitjantjatjara Council, 13 July 1976, p.4). Since then, the desire to establish this claim has been one of the major factors in motivating the development and continued existence of the Council. At this first meeting there was further discussion about the boundaries and an assertion that the whole area should be regarded as a unit and should not be divided up. There was a feeling that research on the relationship of families to particular areas had been carried out with the intention of dividing and weakening them. The matter of granting permits for entry to the reserve was discussed, and through this the men became aware that control of the reserve was vested in the hands of the Minister for Community Welfare. They asserted that control should be transferred to the Pitjantjatjara people.

Meetings of the Council have continued bi-monthly since the first meeting, and the attendance and number of communities represented have increased. Minutes of the meetings are available for perusal in the library of The Australian Institute of Aboriginal Studies. Here, I summarise the main points made about land at those meetings and comment on interaction with other bodies involved in the negotiations.

At the second meeting held at Docker River on 7 September 1976 the problems related to State boundaries were discussed and legal aid advisers were requested to seek the setting up of a Pitjantjatjara lands trust for all Pitjantjatjara land. It was asserted that as the traditions emanating from the *Tjukurpa* or Dreaming united all of this land, this Dreaming should override the lines drawn much later by white Australians on their maps.

A week later, on 15 September, representatives of South Australian communities met at Ernabella for a Department of Aboriginal Affairs area budget conference. Although this was not a Pitjantjatjara Council meeting, the confidence gained at the two Council meetings enabled the people to express their demands relating to land in the presence of government officials and other white Australians. The interaction at this meeting sharpened the focus on some relevant issues and the Pitjantjatjaras here first expressed in such a forum some of the points which were to be reiterated strongly in later negotiations. A representative from the South Australian Aboriginal Lands Trust presented a paper on the Trust and sought to assure the Pitjantjatjara people that their land could be vested securely in that Trust. Lengthy discussion ensued. When questioned about entry permits for the reserve, the representative held up a copy of the *Community Welfare Act* and stated that this Act gave the Minister control over permits. This produced an immediate indignant response from the men who saw a piece of paper as weak in comparison with the Dreamtime Law. 'We owned the land before white men came. Our relationship stems from the Dreaming and not from a scrap of paper, nor from the thinking of men.' The men stressed that their interest in the *pana* or earth was not restricted to the covering *tjanpi* or spinifex, nor the *ulpuru* or surface dust, but extended to the *puli* or rock. The rocks in many places are regarded as *milmilpa* or holy and fear was expressed that mining operations could destroy sacred rocks unless the titles of land covered the rocks under the surface.

At the meeting of the Council at Indulkana on 1 December 1976, the lawyers reported that it might be impossible to have one Pitjantjatjara land trust to cover land in South Australia, Western Australia and the Northern Territory, but pressure should be applied to have the laws in the three areas similar to each other. The people again insisted that they wanted a Pitjantjatjara land trust as distinct from vesting the land in the South Australian Aboriginal Lands Trust, and when the Secretary of the Aboriginal Lands Trust asked what advantages this would have, they replied that the latter was administered mainly by part-Aboriginals who had lost their traditional law whereas Pitjantjatjara Law was still alive and related to the care of the land. At this meeting it was intimated that Mr Don Dunstan, then Premier of South Australia, who as Minister for Aboriginal Affairs had introduced the Lands Trust Act in 1966, still felt a commitment to the provisions of that legislation. He had also expressed concern that if freehold title was granted to a Pitjantjatjara land trust later generations might sell the land as had happened in the United States of America with Indian land and in New Zealand with Maori land. He had also been advised that people now living at Yalata but having an interest in southern Pitjantjatjara land were happy with the Aboriginal Lands Trust.

Representatives of South Australian Pitjantjatjara communities met at Amata in January 1977 to prepare a submission and elected delegates to meet with Mr Dunstan in Adelaide. It was agreed that a request be made for an inalienable freehold title to be granted to a Pitjantjatjara land trust. Following the meeting with Mr Dunstan in February the delegates reported back to a meeting of the Council at Blackstone on 22 February. They reported that Mr Dunstan had given general approval to the concept of a Pitjantjatjara land trust but that he required assurances that this was a genuine request from the Pitjantjatjara people. He was no doubt aware that, as has since happened, opponents of such a proposal would accuse white advisers and agitators of initiating the proposal. Community advisers, Aboriginal legal aid lawyers and other white Australians had attended Council meetings, but the people had made it clear at the first meeting that white people should attend by invitation only, they should be there to assist them to understand the issues involved and to give advice and assistance with legal and administrative matters, but not to dominate the meetings. Mr Dunstan visited the area in May 1977 and was convinced of the people's genuine desire for the Pitjantjatjara land trust, and that although assisted and advised they were not being manipulated.

PITJANTJATJARA LAND RIGHTS WORKING PARTY

On 24 March 1977, Mr Dunstan appointed a Pitjantjatjara Land Rights Working Party, chaired by Mr C.H. Cocks, SM, 'to examine the feasibility of establishing by legislation a separate Pitjantjatjara Lands Trust . . .' (Report of the Pitjantjatjara Lands Rights Working Party of South Australia 1978:2). The members of the Working Party visited the area in July 1977 for discussions with people of the Pitjantjatjara communities. The people were somewhat resentful of having, after convincing Mr Dunstan, to go through the exercise again and repeat their demands to others. They experienced difficulty in understanding some of the concepts introduced by members of the Working Party. For example, the Working Party suggested that a trust composed of a few old men could have title vested in it on behalf of all the Pitjantjara people.

There was talk of separate entities for the title-holding and managerial roles. This confused the people and some felt that it was going back on points they had stressed in their earlier demands. One man expressed it as follows: 'The Pitjantjatjara Council has fought for the land rights. Why cannot it hold the papers?' The people were unable to conceive of the role of the Trust as expounded by the Working Party and confused it with managerial functions, and said that the old men could not manage this work. The Council had a Secretary and an office and should handle these matters. People who had stressed the mythical basis of their relationship and right to the land were beginning to grapple with the need for a bureaucratic model which fitted their traditional structure.

The first round of meetings with the Working Party left a feeling of suspicion and hostility as the people found it difficult to grasp the concepts presented to them and which were based on European concepts of land ownership rather than deriving from their own concepts of relationship. They stressed the ownership of all the land by all the people and rejected the concept of recognising groups of traditional owners of discrete areas as accepted in the Northern Territory legislation. Although the tension following the initial meetings was traumatic at the time, it served a good purpose in motivating the members of the Working Party to seek deeper understanding of the Pitjantjatjara concepts, and this resulted eventually in a report acceptable to the Pitjantjatjara people.

The Working Party members met with the people at Amata on 3 August 1977 and presented a plan to put the Pitjantjatjara land in a trust in the name of all Pitjantjatjara people. The legacy of suspicion from the previous meeting led to further confusion at the Amata meeting. One of the accusations made by the Pitjantjatjara people was that the white men were trying to change their Law, referring to the Pitjantjatjara traditions by this English term. They asserted firmly that while white laws written on paper can be altered, the Law stemming from the Dreaming cannot be changed. Aware of the frustrations amongst the people because of slow progress and problems of discussing the finer points at issue with large groups, and yet requiring further clarification of the people's ideas and their consent to the recommendations which were being formulated, the Working Party met with a selected group of representatives, advisers and consultants in Alice Springs on 3, 4, and 5 October 1977 and again in April 1978. As a result of these meetings progress was made towards the finalisation of the report.

At the July 1978 meeting of the Pitjantjatjara Council at Pipalyatjara it was reported that the Working Party's report had been approved by Mr Dunstan and would be discussed with his Cabinet and introduced into Parliament. At the Mimili meeting in October it was reported that the legislation had been prepared and would be presented in Parliament the following month. The legislation incorporated the Working Party's recommendations that the reserve land and nearby areas now occupied by Pitjantjatjara people should be vested under an inalienable freehold title in a body to be known as the Pitjantjatjara Peoples or *Anangu Pitjantjatjaraku*. These lands would be known as nucleus land. Membership of the land holding body would comprise Aborigines with a traditional interest in the nucleus lands. A tribunal would be established to hear claims for the addition of adjoining land, which would be known as non-nucleus lands. The Pitjantjatjara peoples would have the power to control the exploration for, and exploitation of, minerals on their land.

At first the Working Party had sought to confine their recommendations to matters strictly related to such matters as land but the people expressed concern that the new legislation would not give any controls over the introduction of liquor to the area. The existing Community Welfare Act provided for such controls and permits for possession of liquor but this would lapse with the introduction of new legislation. Following pressure from the people the Working Party recommended that the new legislation should include a provision for such controls.

The Pitjantjatjara people, having now battled for over two years through their Council to achieve this objective, and assured that the legislation incorporated their demands, waited hopefully for the fulfilment of the promises that the Act would be passed. However, there was a lingering suspicion that whites do not keep their word.

POLITICAL CHANGES IN SOUTH AUSTRALIA

The Liberal Country Party majority in the Legislative Council referred the proposed legislation to a Select Committee as they were concerned about the provisions relating to non-nucleus lands and mining. Representatives of the Pitjantjatjara people met with members of the Select Committee in Adelaide on 9 March 1979. In the meantime, Mr Dunstan, had resigned on 15 February because of ill-health. That the negotiations had proceeded thus far was due largely to his commitment to the principles of land rights and his long-term interest in Aboriginal affairs.

Over the previous year or so there was growing concern amongst the Yankuntjatjara people living towards the eastern end of the area covered by the proposed legislation at Indulkana and Mimili about increased opal mining activity at Mintubie *(Mintupai)*. Mintubie is on the Granite Downs pastoral lease in the area designated as non-nucleus lands by the Working Party. Fears were expressed on two grounds. Firstly, the opal field was close to sacred sites and it was feared that these could be touched and that the search for opals might extend to other sacred areas. At a meeting with Uniting Church officials at Fregon in November 1979, men associated with the area said that if these rocks were disturbed they and their Law would be broken. Secondly, the availability of liquor at Mintubie was causing considerable social disruption at communities in the area.

At the Pitjantjatjara Council meeting at Amata on 3 April 1979 the men from Indulkana repeated their claim to land on Granite Downs station which was outside the area defined as nucleus lands. It was reported that the Government had placed some controls on expansion of the search for gem stones on Granite Downs. It was also reported that while all political parties in the South Australian Parliament agreed with the concept of granting freehold title to nucleus lands, the Liberal Country Party was concerned about control over mining and the possibility of claims being made for non-nucleus lands now under pastoral leases. The Select Committee had asked for some changes to be approved by the Council, but as some were of a technical nature it was difficult to interpret them. For example, it was requested that the period for leasing back blocks of land to government or other bodies for the erection of schools, hospitals, etc, be extended from 5 to 50 years. Role-play was employed in an attempt to communicate the meaning of these changes. It was advised that the legislation would be introduced in the June 1979 session of Parliament.

The meeting of the Council held at Nyapari on 15 October 1979 was told that the Labor Government of South Australia had resigned and that a Liberal Country Party government under Dr David Tonkin had been elected at the subsequent election on 15 September. Representatives of the people went to Adelaide to see the new Premier. The Assembly member for Eyre, Mr Graham Gunn, and other Liberal Country Party members of the Assembly attended the next Pitjantjatjara Council meeting at Indulkana on 10 December. Mr Gunn reported that Dr Tonkin had asked him to give an assurance that an inalienable freehold title would be given over the nucleus lands. There were problems associated with other provisions of the Bill as prepared by the previous government and he and the others had come to hear what the people thought about these matters. The Pitjantjatjara people were exasperated at the need to repeat the same points which they had been asserting for the past three and a half years.

On 3 February 1980 the Premier announced that mineral exploration would be permitted on sections of the non-nucleus lands and that a Committee of three persons would be given three months to identify sacred sites so that they could be protected. The Pitjantjatjara people, indignant that they had not been consulted about this decision and the membership of the Committee, responded by arranging to hold a meeting of the Pitjantjatjara Council in Adelaide. Over 120 Pitjantjatjara men, women and children, with a few advisers, travelled by road to Adelaide to camp at a site prepared by an Adelaide-based Lands Rights Support Group on the Victoria Park Racecourse. The meeting was held on 13 and 14 February. After meeting to identify the issues they wished to raise the Pitjantjatjara were addressed by the Leader of the Opposition in the South Australian Parliament, the Premier, and other members of Parliament. On the afternoon of 14 February members of the Council Executive and their lawyer and interpreter met with the Premier and other Ministers to identify points of agreement and points still requiring further negotiation.

This historic Adelaide meeting received widespread sympathetic coverage by the press and television, and the dignified and polite manner in which the Pitjantjatjara people affirmed their demands served to advance their cause before the public. They consistently affirmed their claim to areas of the non-nucleus lands. The demarcation between nucleus and non-nucleus lands had been made by white Australians and as traditional story-lines crossed the boundaries there was no difference between these areas in the mind of the people. They affirmed the need for controls over mining which would provide adequate protection for their traditions and associated sites. They expressed a determination not to co-operate with the Sites Committee, which had been selected without prior consultation with them and which contained no Pitjantjatjara person or their nominated advisers. Speaker after speaker insisted that the legislation as recommended by the Working Party, drafted by the Labor Government, and approved with some modifications by the all-party Select Committee, should be introduced into Parliament without further alteration or delay.

OPPOSITION

While the proposed legislation has received widespread support from churches and other bodies, it was opposed by mining and pastoral organisations which saw its provisions as inimical to their interests and stressed the importance of mineral and pastoral development for the economic and social welfare of South Australia. Opponents have misrepresented the demands of the Pitjantjatjara people. The Deputy President of the United Farmers and Stockowners of South Australia at the time of the Adelaide meeting, quoted in *The Advertiser* on 14 February 1980, expressed fears about the Pitjantjatjara people being segregated and isolated, and warned of the possibility of the Pitjantjatjara acquiring land over the whole of the State. The Chairman of the Coober Pedy Progress and Miners Association Mining subcommittee raised the irrelevant issue of apartheid policies and also stated that other tribal groups had a claim to areas being claimed by the Pitjantjatjara *(Opal Chips,* Coober Pedy, vol. 4. No. 5, July 1979). Among the tribes he listed were the Yankuntjatjara, who have participated in Pitjantjatjara council meetings and who would be members of the land-holding body. Critics of the proposed legislation ignored the definitions and restrictions clearly set out in the Working Party report. The Australian Mining Industry Council issued a statement on 13 March 1979 criticising the proposed legislation and making some dubious assumptions about Australian society and priorities of values in that society, ignoring any consideration of the Aboriginal viewpoint on their relationship to the land.

The Professor of Economic Geology at the University of Adelaide, Professor Ypma, underestimated the part played by the Aboriginal people themselves in asserting their claims, and the widespread support given by people of varying age groups and political sympathies, when in a letter to *The Advertiser* (8 February 1980) he referred to the role played by inexperienced white people in their early 20s in the land rights movement. Observing the meeting of the Pitjantjatjara Council with the Premier was 95 years old Dr Charles Duguid of Adelaide, who has retained a close link with the Pitjantjatjara people since advocating the establishment of Ernabella Mission in 1936. He was quoted in *The Advertiser* for 15 February 1980 as saying, in reply to a question as to whether he supported the proposed legislation, 'I have been of this opinion for 50 bloody years'.

CONCLUSION

As I have outlined above, the Pitjantjatjara people have been more fortunate than many Aboriginal groups in that they have retained close ties to their land and maintained many of the traditions associated with it. Despite the intrusion of white Australians into the area, they have felt little challenge to their assumption that the land is their own. Thus one of the tasks of white advisers has been to warn them of the dangers which could ensue if they did not hold title to the land recognisable under Australian legal and political systems. The formation of the Pitjantjatjara Council provided a structure through which they could be educated about the dangers, the concepts of land ownership under Australian law, and the possible courses of action which could be undertaken. It also provided a structure through which they could voice their demands as their consciousness of the issues was raised.

Their own understanding about land has been interpreted in turn to legal and other advisers, to Mr Dunstan and other Government Ministers, to the land rights Working Party, and to other politicians and the public. In their interaction with these parties they have moved between the poles of hope and despair, and have become bitterly frustrated when promises to pass the legislation within defined time limits have been unfulfilled. English words absorbed into Pitjantjatjara grammatical forms have been used to express their feelings. They have returned from meeting to report *'Nganana winaringu'*—'We have won', or *'Tjana rapamilanu'*—'They have robbed us', or *'Tjana ngananaanya tarikamilanu'*—'They have tricked us'. Those involved in the negotiations and preparation of new legislation should be aware of the frustration caused by the long delay in bringing this matter to fruition.

The Pitjantjatjara Council has gained strength over the past four years as it has spearheaded this struggle. In the past, Aboriginal groups have suffered because viable political structures have lacked visibility. Grappling with this issue has enabled the Pitjantjatjara people to evolve a structure in which traditional authority has been respected and through which they have been able to interact authoritatively with modern political and bureaucratic bodies. Whereas in the Northern Territory the Aboriginal Land Rights Commission instigated the setting up of the first land councils, the Pitjantjatjara Council was formed by the people with minimal outside help and has initiated the Pitjantjatjara land rights movement.

Over the past four years the Pitjantjatjara people have consistently claimed the right to ownership of the land on the basis of their relationship to it, their long occupancy of it, and their inherited responsibility to care for it and to perform the ceremonies associated with it. They have buried their dead in this land, they have been born on it and had their umbilical cords placed in it. They have consistently emphasised the unity of the area and the traditions and that the total area should be vested in the total Pitjantjatjara population. They have repeatedly emphasised that their responsibility pertains to the total substance of the land, not just to the surface dust but also to the rocks. That substance enshrines their traditions and Law, and the fracturing of that substance will shatter their society and individual lives, for the land, the traditions and the people possess the same spirit.

I closed the previous section with a quotation of an old white man. I end with a quotation of the interpreted remarks of an old Pitjantjatjara man, Billy Kayipipi, as he addressed the Select Committee in Adelaide, which sum up the Pitjantjatjara perspective (Minutes of Evidence, Select Committee on Pitjantjatjara Land Rights Bill, 1978, p.95):

> The laws came from our grandparents. It is a strong law and we want to keep it strong. We want to keep the land, hold the land, that is our strongest desire. It is our land, it cannot be changed. We have been holding it forever. We wish to do so. It comes down through the generations to be passed on from one generation to the other. We cannot change the law every year; it is one law and it is there forever. We hold the law and our beliefs in our head, not on pieces of paper. How will we stay there in the future? We

want to live happily on the land. We do not want to be sad. Our laws lie in the land, and the law is part of the land. We want to get and keep the land. I ask the Government for the rights to keep our land.

REFERENCES

Duguid, C. (1963) *No Dying Race.* Adelaide, Rigby.

Duguid, C. (1972) *Doctor and the Aborigines.* Adelaide, Rigby.

Edwards, W.H . (1973) The changing climate of Aboriginal development. *Interchange (Sydney),* No. 14.

Engel, F. (1965) *The Land Rights of Australian Aborigines.* Sydney, Australian Council of Churches.

Giles, E. (1889) *Australia Twice Traversed.* London, Sampson Low, Marston, Searle & Rivington.

Hilliard, W. (1976) *People in Between.* Adelaide, Rigby, Seal Books.

South Australia (1978) *Report of the Pitjantjatjara Land Rights Working Party of South Australia* Adelaide, Government Printer.

South Australia, Parliament (1978) *Minutes of Evidence. Select Committee on Pitjantjatjara Land Rights Bill.* Adelaide, Government Printer.

Wallace, P. & Wallace, N. (1977) *Killing me Softly.* Melbourne, Nelson.

PART FOUR

MINING

21

MINING AND THE CHALLENGE OF LAND RIGHTS

Daniel Vachon and Phillip Toyne

How can Mr Court say that his Government owns this country? It belongs to the Dreaming and not to him. Does Mr Court also say that he owns the moon, and the sun and the sky?

Fred Forbes
Chairman, Ngaanyatjara Council
Jamieson, WA, 26 August 1980

Ever since the Gove case[1], Aboriginal land rights have been inexorably linked to the question of mining. Today, overshadowing the influence of missions, pastoralists, and government agencies, mineral exploration and extraction have emerged as the major contact point between Aboriginal and European societies in remote Australia. Mining is a fact of life and, though opinions on the subject may vary, resource development will be part of the Australian scene for many years to come.

In respect of the relationships of miners and Aborigines, especially those people who continue to make their living and practice their religion on land potentially rich in oil and minerals, two contrasting developments in the issue stand out: the political confrontation at Noonkanbah and the process of direct negotiation devised by the Pitjantjatjara Council. The significance of Noonkanbah for the major actors involved —Government, Aborigines and miners—will be discussed, following a very brief introduction to the various positions held in respect to resource exploration and development in Australia. Closely related to the events at Noonkanbah are the changes taking place in Western Australia and elsewhere as Aboriginal groups and organisations (and, interestingly, miners as well) develop strategies to avoid the possibility of further confrontation. It is in the context of emerging alternatives that we describe the so-called Pitjantjatjara model; the process whereby the Pitjantjatjara Council (which represents all Aboriginal people in the north-west of South Australia, Western Australia from the border west to Warburton, and the Northern Territory north to Ayers Rock and the Docker River), negotiates directly with mining companies interested in conducting exploration activities on land which has traditional significance to its members *regardless of the legal status of the land in question.* The lessons of Noonkanbah for Amax, the American-controlled company which remained silent throughout most of the debate, is considered vicariously in respect of the positions expressed by other transnational companies in their direct negotiations with the Pitjantjatjara Council, even though the essential interests of miners—uninterrupted production and maximum profit—remain unchanged. Finally, a closer assessment is made of the risks and benefits of direct negotiation for Aboriginal groups and corporations.

MINING: INTERESTS AND PERSPECTIVES

Today in Australia, nearly every State and Territory government is organising and reorganising its economy to meet the resources boom; central to the programme of all political parties is their position on mining. The owners and managers of (mostly foreign) capital are being wooed by competing State administrations to invest in political and financial climates assured to be safe and favourable for long-term production and profit. Cheap power for processing raw materials is being offered; payment of royalties is deferred and tax concessions are provided; anti-labour legislation is passed.[2] Drawn by the high rate of profit, enormous amounts of capital are shifting from the manufacturing sector to resource development. There is little doubt that the results of these changes will affect not only Aboriginal people but all Australians as well.

The risks and benefits entailed in transnational mining are matched by a considerable range of opinion on the issue. From the 'man must mine, dig or die' side, it is argued that mining, and indeed all forms of resource extraction in Australia, will 'get us moving again'. Mining will overcome inflation, produce more jobs, stimulate 'development' and maintain a healthy balance of trade. All Australians must give mining companies a mandate for the 1980s. Then, anything will be possible and everyone will gain in a land so rich in natural resources.

For many people opinions on mining are not so clear-cut and consistent. Certainly, many do not question that their interests are being served by transnational corporations. Whereas for some the lure is shared success in the stock market, for others the choice is between mining and the increased risk of unemployment and falling living standards. But there is an overlapping section of the Australian population that is not convinced of the good intentions of miners and governments which support them. Crucial questions are asked. Are there sufficient environmental and safety standards? Are transnationals truly motivated by the interests of the 'public'? Will miners leave behind a country of half-worked quarries when their profits fall? What of the future in the mad rush by governments to sell out non renewable resources which, apparently, 'belong to all the people'?

Somewhere in all the digging, discussion and debate, is the matter of Aboriginal interest in mining. Here, again, the position not without contradiction; even Aboriginal people with a regular involvement with their land do not agree necessarily on the mining issue. Under the *Aboriginal Land Rights (Northern Territory) Act* 1976, for example, Aborigines who have won their land back through the legislation and land claims will be caught in a potentially divisive situation; whereas some 'traditional owners' may wish no mining and, instead, will choose to develop their land on their own terms, others will be pulled toward the promise of bounty through mining royalties. But this is the obvious focus of potential conflict. At present, the three statutory Northern Territory land councils, which represent all traditional owners, are funded by mining royalties through the Aboriginal Benefit Trust Account and Department of Aboriginal Affairs loans (repayable with future royalties). In other words, the very existence of land councils depends on the development of interests which are likely to be contrary to the interests of many of the people that the land councils represent.

Indeed, for all Aboriginal groups the pull towards making 'deals' with companies wishing to mine on Aboriginal land can only become greater as cutbacks in Aboriginal funding and government policies frustrating Aboriginal aspirations continue. Whatever the case, given 200 years of Aboriginal involvement in the wider Australian economy, it should come as no surprise that Aboriginal people are realising both the value of their land in acquiring goods and services and the land's value to others, whose use of it could have disastrous effects on Aboriginal interests.

It is not possible in this article to present an economic analysis of the potential benefits and risks of allowing transnational corporations to mine in Australia. The purpose here is more specific and focuses on the ways Aboriginal groups and organisations can attain a measure of effective control over miners on their land. But the question, must be asked: Mining and development for whom? For those working for Aboriginal organisations the conclusion that mining is not in the interests of Aborigines comes easily; they seem to be affected by all the negative aspects of mining. Seen in a wider perspective, this may not be so. The disastrous effects of resource extraction by transnationals in underdeveloped countries, for example, are well known and, rather than being the problem of 'special interest groups', it is the majority of the populations of many countries in Latin America and Africa which suffer from the policies and practices of corporate miners.[3]

While Australia could not be considered an underdeveloped country (although certain sections of the population such as the Aborigines display most of the impoverished characteristics of third-world peoples), the negative effects of mining may not be as much restricted as they are hidden. In a rare undertaking, commissioned by the Federal Minister for Minerals and Energy to examine the effect of mining on the general welfare of Australians, the author concluded in his report:[4]

> . . . that some of the vaunted benefits from the mineral industry's spectacular growth rate in capital formation are illusory. The Australian people have been financing a large part of the growth through the Byzantine passage of 'deferred tax' accountancy, and a substantial part of their contributions will add nothing to the national income of this country, whatever it will do for other countries.

That is, mining, not in principle but as it is now being conducted in Australia, may be more than a 'Black problem'; public welfare is possibly being weakened by investment which shows little public return.

If land rights anywhere in Australia were ever a simple moral issue this is no longer the case. The economic dimension to the arguments cannot be ignored. Where people, particularly urban Australians, may have felt that the issue of land rights did not concern them, except as an abstract matter of justice, there is now a need to come to terms with the linked questions of land rights, sacred sites and mining, and of the costs and benefits of mining to the whole community. Whatever the outcome of the debate, mining is a fact in Australia, and though opinions may vary according to real or anticipated effects on economic interests, Aboriginal organisations will need to devise ways of meeting this new intrusion on their lands. There is no choice; to make no response is to deny the importance of the land and land rights. But the range of response is great and will be set in a complex and confusing mix of competing interests, relative strengths, truth and half-truth, confrontation and compromise. There is no time for sterile, academic debate for those Aboriginal people who need to find ways to defend their way of life and religion on land potentially rich in oil and minerals.

NOONKANBAH AND CONFRONTATION

During the months that the Noonkanbah dispute raged over the 400 km^2 Aboriginal-held pastoral lease in the Kimberleys, Australians witnessed one of the most publicised accounts of conflict between the mining industry, Aborigines and government. Perhaps to some observers it appeared as if Amax (the managing partner of the mining consortium involved), the Noonkanbah Aborigines and the Western Australian Government were all acting in an incomprehensible, irrational and suicidal manner. To others, Noonkanbah represented another classic case of confrontation politics between two cultures barely understanding what the other had become so excited about.[5]

If the newspaper editorials at the time can be used as any indication,[6] the Noonkanbah people were not isolated in their plight but, instead, received considerable public support. The banner was taken up by churches, student groups, Aboriginal organisations and support groups both within and outside Australia. Not a single trade unionist could be found to drive the State Government's trucks or operate its drilling rig, as member unions of Western Australia's Trades and Labour Council closed ranks against the strong-arm tactics at Noonkanbah. It may be that Noonkanbah's wide appeal went beyond public support for Aboriginal rights and the protection of sacred sites. Here, too, was an example of a small group of people taking on 'Big Government', single-mindedly furthering the interests of 'Big Business'. As such, Noonkanbah had a pre-existent following which easily identified with the issues involved. Ironically, it was independent truck drivers and non-union workers, small businessmen and entrepreneurs, who traditionally have fallen before the interests and expansion of large capital, who tacitly approved the Government's position and agreed to set up the oil rig near Pea Hill—the Goanna Dreaming site.

In 1979 the American-based Amax Iron Ore Corporation was granted a permit by the Western Australian Government to test-drill for oil on Noonkanbah. Anxious that the company might damage culturally sensitive areas, the Yungngora Community, with the assistance of the Aboriginal Legal Service, demanded that the Government send site recorders from the Western Australian Museum to Noonkanbah. The people willingly cooperated with museum staff; and in the museum's assessment Amax's planned drill holes were located within the 'sphere of influence' of traditional sacred sites. The Government refused to release the report.

The exact definition of Pea Hill appeared to be the original point of contention between the Government and the Noonkanbah people. According to the Government, the anthropologist who reported on Noonkanbah took an excessively broad view of the 'sphere of influence' of Pea Hill—one which would preclude mineral exploration. In order to overcome the difficulties the museum might create for mining companies, the Government previously had amended the Aboriginal Heritage Act.[7] The Minister could reverse any recommendation by the Museum trustees for the protection of a sacred site; a site would be considered 'genuine' only if the Government did not object; this was the response to the 'genuine status' of Pea Hill.

As the confrontation escalated, major viewpoints on the issue became both crystallised and polarised. Gradually, the public began to wonder if the central issue at Noonkanbah *was* simply a matter of who was running the State. With the Western Australian Government noisily crying for law and order on the land, the question of protecting Goanna Dreamings was being transformed into demands for 'land rights'. When the first act of the drama closed, the Government's drilling rig securely fenced and guarded at Noonkanbah, few imagined that oil was the prize for all the effort or that Sir Charles Court had suddenly embraced socialist ideals and had taken the first step toward nationalisation of mineral production in his State. The rig stood tall as a clear symbol to everyone that control over the land was resting where it had been before all the fuss began.

In the official interpretation of events, contained in the pamphlet *Noonkanbah: the facts*,[8] the Western Australian Government begins by presenting the position which carried it through the Noonkanbah debate. The essential issue is control. In its view, the acceptability of mining proposals and the benefits which will flow to the community from mining, the nature of the relationship between miners and Aborigines and the type of protection the community will receive, the status of 'genuine' sacred sites—in all, the control the Noonkanbah people will have over their land will be determined, unilaterally, by the Government. The Government will act as mining consultant, policeman and anthropologist. Aborigines 'need the sort of assistance they are getting now' and will have the same rights over mining as other citizens in Western Australia.

On the question of land rights, the position in the pamphlet is clear: 'The Aboriginal citizens of this state do not need land rights' (p. 10) as an added measure, we are given a glimpse of the anarchy which would prevail should control slip away from government authority and into the hands of 'white advisors', 'union leaders' and 'propagandists' (p. 10).

> Slogans about Aboriginal 'land rights' are frequently used but seldom explained. If Aboriginal access to land was based on 'traditional ownership' very few of the Yungngora Community would have any right to the land at Noonkanbah (see Anthropology).
>
> In reality, the slogan is a cruel deception because it creates an expectation that cannot be met. It has led some Aborigines to believe that they can take complete control of parts of Australia without reference to the laws of the total community. This is an impossible proposition which would now and in the future create serious conflict not only between Aboriginal and European citizens, but also among Aborigines.

That all Aboriginal land rights have been granted through *legislation* and thus, by definition, are in 'reference to the laws of the total community', is not mentioned. Crudely put, what the Government is saying is that land rights are bad: bad for Aborigines, bad for European citizens bad for the total community. This is the critical message. Otherwise, if land rights—the control over development on the land—were presented as good for Aborigines, non-Aboriginal people in the State might demand similar control over the development of the State's resources. At the very least, the rational basis for objections to Aboriginal land rights might begin to be questioned.

Therefore, the Government has no choice but to monitor and maintain conflict between black and white on the issue of land rights by stressing that Aboriginal demands are unreasonable, dangerous and contrary to the wider good. In the Government's insistence that it will act as sole arbiter and judge in matters relating to miners and Aborigines, it has done nothing to reduce the possibilities of future conflict. The barricades on all sides are as firmly in place as ever and a climate of uncertainty and tension remains.

The Western Australian Government succeeded in wrestling its drilling rig to Noonkanbah. But in attempting to bulldoze the Noonkanbah people into submission, the Government has inadvertently propelled them, along with other Aborigines, into a political arena where land rights, and not only the protection of sites, may just be possible. The threat to Aboriginal interests was so real that an alliance of concern with the Noonkanbah people inevitably was formed. Noonkanbah received support from a variety of non-Aboriginal organisations and individuals as well as Aboriginal groups elsewhere in the State. The latter, prior to these events, passively accepted Government and mining interference but have now been galvanised into action. They identify closely with the Noonkanbah people but more significantly they are communicating with them. Contrary to everything the Government may have intended, a pan-Aboriginal unity has begun to emerge in Western Australia.

A clear example is the Ngaanyatjara Council. On 26 August 1980 at the tiny community of Jameson, Aboriginal representatives of all communities in the Central and Warburton reserves met to discuss their land, their law and Noonkanbah. Telegrams of protest were sent to the Premier and telegrams of support went to Noonkanbah. Plans were made to visit Noonkanbah to discuss a joint strategy for survival. No previous issue has had the force to make this happen. Attempts to suppress Aboriginal rights have produced the determination to fight for them and assert them.

For the Ngaanyatjara people, this has been even more forcefully brought home by the very different series of events in the South Australian lands of the Pitjantjatjara Council. Ngaanyatjara communities in Western Australia are members of the Council and share a common social and religious tradition but enjoy none of the protection their kinsmen do across the border. Through protracted negotiations the Pitjantjatjara

Council has reached a land rights settlement with the South Australian Government,[9] as well as gaining significant protection from mining of sacred sites *outside* the lands held by the Council in freehold. Such success in South Australia is being regarded by Aboriginal groups as possible elsewhere through united action. Support by the Pitjantjatjara Council for the Ngaanyatjara Council is being extended by the latter to the Kimberley Land Council, and thus to Noonkanbah and so on.

The single-minded promotion of oil and mineral exploration or other culturally aggressive activities on Aboriginal land is becoming less and less possible throughout Australia. In Western Australia and also in Queensland, opposition to uncontrolled mining is increasing. Even if governments hold firm to obsolete principles, the mining industry is likely to duck out of uncomfortable alliances, not for ideological reasons but for pragmatic ones. Mining companies are in the business of furthering their own interests; they are not becoming champions of ethnic rights or critics of right-wing government policies. There is little doubt that if Noonkanbah had 'worked', if the Aboriginal people had not resisted, and if the Western Australian Government had inspired confidence that Aboriginal demands would be effectively silenced, the strategy would have the support of the mining industry. But public confrontation is not an efficient or viable way of doing business if uncertainty is the result. Amax only attempted to withdraw completely from Noonkanbah when the Aboriginal people there became a 'problem' and legal solutions failed to work. It is hard to believe that the company, or any other transnational would willingly engage in such a self-destructive public-relations campaign. More importantly, Noonkanbah made land rights a public issue in Western Australia; a situation mining companies would be keen to avoid.

The final irony of Noonkanbah is that no mining company will follow the Western Australian Government's lead, or its bluff, as Amax has done. If state-sanctioned force is to be replaced by other strategies at this time mining companies will devise them, if necessary, outside of government involvement or accept conditions placed upon their activities by Aboriginal groups. As long as transnational corporations see accommodation as a rational alternative to confrontation, they will choose to further interests through direct negotiations with the Aboriginal people involved. It remains to be seen if Aborigines can use this new situation to their long-term advantage.

THE PROCESS OF NEGOTIATION

When the Pitjantjatjara Land Rights Bill became law, the Aboriginal people in the north-west of South Australia gained freehold title to an area of land over which they exert unique control. But the freehold lands were secured, in part, as a result of assessments of what was politically possible at the time and not in reference to the economic and religious interests of all Pitjantjatjara. The fact that these interests extend beyond the lands was recognised by the Land Rights Working Party[10] and the South Australian (Dunstan) Government as well. Thus, in Labor legislation, provision was made for land claims outside the 89 000 km^2 'nucleus lands'.

It became obvious in the early stages of negotiation with the Liberal Government that the new administration would not accept legislation which enabled the Pitjantjatjara to extend their land-holding either by claim or purchase. Notwithstanding the Government's position, the Pitjantjatjara Council still regarded the protection of areas of cultural significance outside the nucleus lands as necessary. In the face of rapidly expanding mineral exploration in the north-west, the matter became urgent. In the Council's view, the issues were identical to those which had given rise to the demands for land rights in the first place. In this case however, extra-statutory solutions were required.

When Afmeco, a French-owned company, was granted an exploration lease for uranium on a pastoral property near the eastern border of the nucleus lands, the Pitjantjatjara Council decided to contact the company and request a meeting. The Council told Afmeco's representatives that the land over which they intended to explore contained sites of religious significance to its members and, if they desired to maintain good relations with the Council and avoid confrontation, certain arrangements would have to be made. The company agreed to re-imburse the Council for an anthropological survey of the area and agreed to work only in those areas defined as 'safe' by the Council. Since that time, a number of successful negotiations between the Pitjantjatjara Council and mining companies, as well as other interests have been completed.

The Council has negotiated with, and approved to the satisfaction of the traditional land-owners and miners, the exploration programmes of Comalco, Layton Geophysics, Shell and Getty Oil, as well as Afmeco. In every case, agreements involved activities on land for which the Council has no title and about which the companies concerned had little or no geological information. The proposed re-routing of the Port Augusta–Alice Springs road was also approved, and a satisfactory agreement was reached in four days of fieldwork with the traditional owners. Although the South Australian Department of Mines and Energy saw these developments as weakening their control and made attempts to frustrate negotiations such as the exploration programmes on the 'Maralinga Lands', its arguments could not be easily sustained: Comalco had accomplished through direct negotiations in two months, without so much as a political ripple, what Amax at Noonkanbah failed to accomplish in over a year.

Outside South Australia, the Central Land Council has been engaged in approving an enormous seismic survey conducted by Pan-Continental and the programmes of Weekes Petroleum, Dampier Mining and Sion Resources, all of which are operating on land that is not held in Aboriginal freehold or leasehold. In Western Australia itself, and on Noonkanbah, Aborigines have entered into direct negotiations with CRA and Mobil Oil.

Except for the powers granted under legislation to the Pitjantjatjara and some Aboriginal groups in the Northern Territory (and these only apply to lands legally, not culturally, defined), the majority of Aboriginal people have no legal basis to demand that companies so much as talk to them or their advisors. Political and, ultimately, economic reasons have led to re-assessments in dealing with Aboriginal interests. For the first time in the history of resource exploration (and extraction) in Australia, Aboriginal people are being given the opportunity to negotiate, regardless of their legal rights.

If transnational mining companies are more willing than ever before to seek accommodation with Aboriginal groups who have a historical and cultural relationship to the land, the way that accommodation is reached clearly becomes a critical consideration. It must be taken for granted that companies will use their considerable economic and organisational strength, political ties and legal advantage to structure their dealings with Aborigines so as to achieve maximum benefits to themselves. On the other hand, if some Aboriginal people consider mining agreements to be a means of protecting and furthering their interests, then they must strive to gain consensus on basic negotiating principles consistent with Aboriginal aims.

The rules are simple. Firstly, it must be accepted and recognised that *Aboriginal people* are *the experts* in matters relating to the religious significance of their land. Furthermore, the knowledge is theirs by right and therefore, must be *controlled* by the people whose ancestors have responsibly held such knowledge for ages. Should information on sites and Dreamings be made freely available to mines departments and mining companies control is lost. The inevitable result is that consultation with traditional owners about matters relating to activities on their land is no longer felt to be necessary, no matter how inaccurate the information may be which is used as a substitute. It is difficult to guess the form that land rights might have taken in Australia if 'sacred sites' were not a feature of Aboriginal social organisation. But given the social reality of sites for Aborigines or, rather, focuses of significance, the anthropological position in respect to these areas will, to a great extent, identify political interests and determine political strategy and hence the form the land rights debate will take. As is often the case, opinions and pronouncements in respect to just what Aborigines themselves think about the land tell us a great deal about who said them and practically nothing at all about Aboriginal people.

For members of the Western Australian Government, their interest is a law and order one: the Government, not Aborigines, shall control access to the land. The Government, through its Museum, provides the service for classifying (and declassifying) 'genuine' sacred sites: when Aboriginal people express their own views on the land as they see it, they are told that they are not playing the game as others define it and the public is led to believe that they are 'inventing sacred sites'.

In the Government's Noonkanbah pamphlet, Aboriginal people in Western Australia are informed from page three to page seven that the Government does not belittle their religious beliefs. Indeed, the protection of 'genuine, identified sacred sites' is guaranteed; 'the Government has not betrayed its word on sacred sites'. Then, on page 10, Aborigines are told that they do not want land rights. White stirrers want land rights whereas Aborigines want sacred sites and not the land. Sites are as significant to such governments as they are to Aborigines but for very different reasons: so long as sacred sites are defined as the prime interest of Aborigines then land rights, effective Aboriginal control over the *land* need not be considered. Furthermore, governments encourage Aboriginal people to disclose information on sacred sites *in order* to 'matchbox' them thereby satisfying (and defining) Aboriginal interest. 'Free land' is, therefore, rendered unimportant to Aboriginal people and open to resource exploration and development. A one-sided emphasis on sacred sites is consistent with the political goal of assuring that control over the land stays firmly in the hands of the government with conditions of access varying from time to time and place to place.

Interestingly, exploration companies take a slightly different view. In many cases their interest is in areas, often vaguely defined, where they can proceed with various geological surveys without interruption. Initially, control over the land is not a long-term interest; the miners will move on when their work is done or if they find nothing. It has been the experience of the Pitjantjatjara Council that companies do not want to know the locations, size and significance of sacred sites; miners want to know where they can operate with confidence. As a result, exploration companies have seen it as the business of the Pitjantjatjara to define areas of work and access to the land and, just as with other specialist consultants to companies, the Council charges for its services.

For Aboriginal people, it is the control over the *land* which is of central importance —there is no larger issue. Secret/sacred sites make living on the land *as Aborigines* possible, but people do not live only on the sites. People *make their living* on the land, whether it be hunting kangaroo or raising cattle. These two cultural geographical entities—sites and the 'land between'—cannot be and never were separated; the one derives its existence from the other. Thus, it is no surprise that Aborigines do not separate, politically the issue of site protection from land rights. No Aboriginal group would accept a situation where islands of '100 square metres of sacredness' are surrounded by open-cut mines, access roads, mining camps and drilling rigs, in short, *uncontrolled* activity on their land. It must be taken as given that due consideration must be made of the continued, viable involvement of people with their land as they see fit.

Sacred sites are not some peculiar characteristic of Aboriginal societies. Like people everywhere, Aborigines have thought about, classified and used the world around them. They have endowed the world with meaning. Areas of cultural significance are socially recognised and only can be fully known and used by people with the appropriate knowledge and rights. All societies have sacred sites in this sense. The specific form and meaning that Aboriginal sacred sites have for Aborigines is the result of their unique history and a perception of the environment which is distinctly their own. For the Pitjantjatjara, for example, sites are no more 'sacred' than the land in its entirety and the land is no less sacred to them than to other hunters and gatherers throughout the world. There is no room in the Aboriginal perception of the land to regard it as something to be mapped, coded, 'protected', bought and sold.

The second rule is that negotiations between Aboriginal groups and mining companies must be conducted on a professional basis. No negotiations with highly sophisticated parties such as transnational mining companies would be thinkable by anyone without legal advice and, in this specific case, anthropological advice as well. Strangely, the same lawyers a government might use are suddenly transformed into 'white stirrers' when acting in the interests of Aborigines. Pitjantjatjara people insist that all traditional owners hear the proposal and agree to it only upon legal advice. There is no way of short-cutting or by-passing this process. It is good business and common sense. In South Australia these basic premises have been translated into what has become known throughout the Mines Department and mining industry as the 'Pitjantjatjara model'. The process is as straightforward as the principles which underly it.

The first agreements resulted from Pitjantjatjara Council initiative. The Council is now approached by representatives of a mining company interested in securing exploration licences on land which lies within the orbit of the Council's interest. Members of the Pitjantjatjara Council Executive, the Council lawyer and anthropologist initially meet with the company's and Mines Department representatives. At this time the Pitjantjatjara Council is told what the miner is looking for, the areas of interest, how many men will be involved during a specific period of exploration, the proposed activity and the likely scenerio should minerals or oil be discovered. The Company agrees to send a summary of its proposal to the Pitjantjatjara Council offices, along with photographs, maps and any information relevant to the proposed operations. A date is set for a field trip with Aboriginal people most knowledgeable in the cultural significance of the area.

After the Council anthropologist conducts initial fieldwork to obtain instructions from the Aboriginal people concerning the 'traditional owners' of the proposed area, an independent survey is made with the relevant Aboriginal advisors. Then, a second field trip proceeds involving company and, occasionally, Mines Department representatives, the Council anthropologist and Aboriginal advisors. Access roads are identified and approved for use during the operations, as well as planned seismic lines and drill sites. It might be the case that Aboriginal sites are within the exploration area, or nearby. At no time are the locations of sites revealed, and mining representatives are advised in the most general terms the areas of sensitivity. At the end of this field exercise, company representatives and the Pitjantjatjara Council have agreed to a programme and an area of activity within which the company will conduct its activities.

Other matters are also settled before exploration activities actually begin. Getty Oil, for example, has agreed to hire Aboriginal workers on the site, as they see it, for good public relations. Neither Getty nor Comalco[11] object to Aboriginal people visiting their operations at any time and actively promote Aboriginal monitoring of their activities. Comalco has taken the initiative to write provisions in the agreements made with their contractors, specifying that any breach of their agreement with the Pitjantjatjara Council will result in the immediate dismissal of those involved, but to date such action has not been required. Both the Council and the company agree that any alteration of the programme must be renegotiated and rechecked. Finally, all costs for Aboriginal approval and monitoring of a company's exploration activities are borne by the company.

One of the most significant applications of this process to date is the agreement reached between Shell Oil and the Ngaanyatjara members of the Pitjantjatjara Council. That direct negotiations were accepted by an oil company operating in Western Australia clearly indicates the position that some companies take on a Noonkanbah solution in gaining access to Aboriginal land. This has been accomplished despite the Western Australian Government's view on the matter.

In 1979 Shell's exploration programme in the Gibson Desert, west of the Aboriginal community of Warburton, was approved by the Western Australian Government. The company was informed by the Western Australian Museum, without any Aboriginal consultation, that no sacred site had been recorded within Shell's leases. On the basis of these instructions, the company decided that there would be no difficulty in accommodating Aboriginal interests in the area. A drilling rig and crew was contracted and in August 1980 drilling began on a site abandoned by a petroleum explorer some years before. Another contractor was sent into the area to begin line cutting and seismic surveying.

The Ngaanyatjara people, who live in the area and have sustained cultural and economic links to the land, were aware of Shell's presence but, apart from the obvious operation of the drilling rig, had no idea of the company's programme. More importantly, they knew nothing of seismic surveys or the potential threat these had to areas of religious significance. Bulldozers and graders had been seen but it was thought that they were needed to upgrade existing tracks.

At the first Ngaanyatjara Council meeting, Shell's work in the area was discussed. It soon became obvious to the 150 men and women gathered that very little was known about oil exploration. The Council instructed their lawyer to contact Shell and to seek an urgent meeting with the company at the drill site.

The Company agreed a day after the telex was sent. Two weeks later four company representatives met with 50 Ngaanyatjara men and their advisors in the bush. Shell's exploration programme was described in detail: 1400 kilometres of line were to be bulldozed and graded followed by seismic survey. The men wanted to know how Shell was going to avoid the possible destruction of sites along the Dreaming.

In the long discussion that followed, Shell agreed in principle to supply the funds and equipment to enable a scouting party of Aboriginal advisors, a Council anthropologist, a surveyor and support staff to screen and peg the future locations of Shell's seismic lines, well ahead of the bulldozers. The alignments would be approved by the Ngaanyatjara Council through its Aboriginal advisors and anthropologist. If sites were threatened the lines would be moved. The location of sacred sites would be mapped by the Council anthropologist for future reference, but not disclosed to Shell. Instead, the Council would indicate, in vague terms, areas to be by-passed and would suggest realignments. It was agreed that all information on secret/sacred sites was the Council's business, not Shell's.

Several weeks later, an agreement was worked out between the advisors of both the Council and Shell. The basic principles accepted in the bush were incorporated in the document. On one major point, however, there was serious difficulty. In case of dispute, no independent mechanism existed to settle the disagreement. What if Shell could not or would not move a line running directly into an area containing a sacred site?

Shell agreed that the protection of an area, *considered to be significant by the Aborigines,* came before the company's preference for the location of a bulldozed track; the Company agreed that should incompatible differences arise it would confer with the Council. Shell's operations would be conducted so as to avoid interference with areas which are of significance to the Ngaanyatjara people.

The agreement was signed by representatives of the two incorporations on 8 October 1980. For the next 24 months, in alternating fortnightly intervals, Shell's three seismic programmes—a total of 4800 km of siesmic lines—were scouted and approved. Technical difficulties were worked out in the bush and, after the initial two-week scouting session the practical applicability of the agreement was proven. In a few cases lines and water drill sites had to be moved but these changes presented no serious difficulties to the company.

Interestingly, not only did Shell enjoy uninterrupted activities on the land but it also received added benefits from the scouting party's work. Usually, the cutting of seismic lines involves limited on-the-ground reconnaissance; planned lines are drawn on maps in company offices on the basis of available geological information and a surveyor accompanies the bulldozer to assure that the line cut corresponds to the planned alignment. If the bulldozer encounters unforeseen topographical obstacles or if the planned line passes through critical points inaccurately located on maps, the line cutting crew must backtrack and recut a section of the line. Several days are lost, at a cost to Shell of $50 000 a day. In this case, the scouting party would not only relocate planned lines in order to avoid sacred sites but also to prevent wasted effort and expense to the company.

It appears as if a new relationship between Aboriginal groups and mining companies is emerging. This is not to imply, however, that all transnational corporations engineering Australia's 'resource boom' have accepted a Pitjantjatjara-type model of negotiation.[12] Other non-confrontationist strategies can be, and are being, developed whereby uninterrupted exploration is achieved and a good corporate image is preserved while, at the same time, Aboriginal opposition is effectively defeated. Negotiations then become little more than company-inspired public relations exercises designed at the expense of Aboriginal interests.[13] CRA's activity at Lake Argyle is one example of this type of strategy.

The Lake Argyle area, south of Kununurra in the Kimberleys of Western Australia, has become the centre of what may be one of the largest diamond mines in the world. Unlike Noonkanbah and the lands of interest to members of the Pitjantjatjara Council, initial exploration at Argyle has been completed and significant deposits have been located and verified. Feasibility studies are under way and may place the starting date for large-scale production before the end of 1982.

Most of the mineral claims in the area are held by Ashton Joint Venture of which CRA, a subsidiary of the British RTZ Corporation, owns a 58.6% share. As managing partner of the consortium, CRA stated in its 1979 annual report that Aboriginal interests are recognised and its activities only commence *after* Aboriginal people in an area are consulted.

As it happened, however, exploration at Argyle began before any Aboriginal group was contacted. In fact, it was the Aboriginal people from Turkey Creek, Dunham River and other communities who made the initial demands to meet with the company, after excavation at an important site was discovered.

Five months after the Warmun Community at Turkey Creek and the Kimberley Land Council, the regional Aboriginal political organisation, contacted CRA a company representative met with the knowledgeable Aboriginal people of the area. By this time, however, CRA's geologists had discovered a large, rich kimberlite pipe near a sacred site. The area had been identified by a Western Australian Museum anthropologist and was known to the company. The museum staff played an important part in identifying Aboriginal owners and sites in the area of CRA's major interest, and the company received a copy of the Museum's report, along with recommendations and warnings that activities in certain locations should cease because site damage was occurring and further research was needed to identify site boundaries. Apparently, CRA did not follow the recommendations. Consequently, the Aboriginal people were placed in the weak position of relying on government agency to take action, which it failed to do.

Not only had cultural information been traded for the dubious protection by the Museum, but the company could now use the Museum's report to redefine site boundaries. Advisors from the Kimberley Land Council and the Warmun Community were ignored by CRA; instead, the company chose one Aboriginal family with which to negotiate the 'Argyle Agreement'. In return for unrestricted access to the entire area, CRA agreed to undertake a capital works programme on the Aboriginal-run station of Glen Hill, supply four vehicles, offer Aboriginal employment and fund capital development on Glen Hill up to $100 000 (later increased to $250 000) if mining went ahead.

A few Aborigines from the Argyle area were flown to Perth by CRA where they were 'signed up' thousands of kilometres away from their community and the Kimberley Land Council. The company approached two Perth lawyers who were prominent in Aboriginal matters, and asked them to act for the Aboriginal party. They agreed to do so on condition that they travel to Turkey Creek to meet with the entire community and seek instructions. This, CRA refused. Consequently, the lawyers withdrew and their place taken by another lawyer who was willing to represent the Aborigines and accept the company's terms. Over the course of a single weekend documents were prepared and signed. Those Aborigines who agreed returned to the north to face the anger of their fellow countrymen.

The company not only had obtained an agreement but it also had divided Aboriginal opposition to its plans. Because only four Aborigines signed the agreement other 'traditional owners' for the area declared the entire outcome as invalid. In order to protect their benefits under the agreement, the few people who signed came into conflict with the majority of Aboriginal people who had an interest in the land but who were not party to the agreement. CRA continued dealing with the original negotiating team of Aborigines.

The events at Argyle point to several factors which limit the applicability and effectiveness of the Pitjantjatjara method of negotiation. At present the Aboriginal people who live in the desert regions of South Australia, Western Australia and the Northern Territory have the advantage of being members of organisations recognised by some governments and mining companies and with marginally sufficient resources to further and protect their interests. This is not so for many Aboriginal groups in Australia. Without the financial means, at least, to employ their own advisors and pay operating expenses, there is little choice left for these people and their organisations when mineral exploration begins on their land. Government assistance can be sought (if politically worth while) as well as independent support, often from churches and underfunded Aboriginal legal aid services. But the kind of assistance the Noonkanbah people received from the Western Australian Government cannot be considered reasonable from an Aboriginal point of view. Without specialist advice, there is little way of knowing how to deal with a mining company and almost no chance of obtaining critical information on the nature of an operation and, consequently, on the extent and kind of potential social impact. The implications of signing 'a paper' or giving cultural information to a museum (or a company anthropologist) are seldom realised.

Because of the financial weakness and non-recognition[14] of the Kimberley Land Council, CRA was able to negotiate the Argyle agreement for the benefit of the company and only a few Aboriginal people.

In South Australia the Southern Land Council, operating out of Port Augusta, has approached the State Government for funds to employ an anthropologist to assist it in the protection of sites in the Roxby Downs area, where Western Mining and British Petroleum are exploring for copper and uranium. They were refused. The Yalata community has experienced similar disregard in its attempts to gain protection from mineral exploration on the 'Maralinga Lands'. Other examples can be found throughout Australia. Faced with such 'choices', Aboriginal groups, like the Noonkanbah people, are *forced* into a situation of confrontation.

This is not the only consideration limiting the usefulness of the 'model' of direct negotiation which has been described. Specialist advice is a means to achieve Aboriginal aims, but lawyers and anthropologists are not magicians. Negotiation with mining companies works best during the initial stages of exploration on Aboriginal land not held in title. Miners are much more flexible in their demands and planned areas of activity are relatively easy to negotiate. But Aboriginal groups have been far less successful in reaching a fair settlement in cases where mining companies have identified a commercially viable deposit. The economic stakes become much higher. New strategies will be devised by both the company and government to balance economic and political risks and benefits. Given the vast resources of transnationals, accommodation of Aboriginal interests, such as providing compensation for social and environmental impact, may still be seen as necessary, particularly if the political climate has been judged to be 'sensitive'. But it is likely that companies will strive to limit Aboriginal opposition directly, and perhaps indirectly through government departments and the press[15] to cast doubt on the 'genuine' nature of a sacred site or claim that the interests of the state and nation are being frustrated by a small and unreasonable interest group.

It is fortunate for the Pitjantjatjara and many other cultural intact Aboriginal groups as well that the mineral potential of their land is largely unknown. When the time comes for planning mineral or oil extraction, 5–10 years after the start of exploration activities, a regularised relationship between land councils and mining companies will have been established. Designs for extraction will take as given the Aboriginal interest and presence on the land. The more difficult process of negotiating matters of social and environmental impact will, it is hoped, be made much easier.

Finally it cannot be overemphasised that these negotiations, however 'open and honest' they appear to be, are not land rights; agreements with mining companies do not alter their basic interests or replace the demand for inalienable freehold title, including ownership of all on and below the ground. There are no assurances and, as yet, no reliable way to determine *if* the information supplied by the companies *is* honest. Transnational corporations not only continue to retain control of their property but also their information. Moreover, for *all* agreements with mining companies to date, *every* land council, including the Pitjantjatjara and Northern Territory land councils, approaches the negotiating table from a position of considerable weakness; none has an irreversible choice to refuse access altogether.[16] Aboriginal people may not be, by some curious cultural quirk, bloody-minded in respect to activity on land held in freehold title, but neither are they able, even if they wished, to veto a totally unacceptable programme. Agreements under these constraints must be seen for what they often are: the result of Aboriginal people negotiating the best terms derived from a second, 'fall-back' position.

For Crown land, pastoral properties and reserve land the legal rights and protections of Aboriginal groups are considerably less. Only the legislation protecting 'sacred sites' or vague conditions on exploration licences provide the basis for most legal action. While admitting the advantages of direct negotiations, the very real danger exists that, should a major oil or mineral deposit be located, a company will reconsider unilateral action or legislation will be amended to serve company demands. 'Good business' through confrontation may then be viewed as economically, if not politically rational.

'THE BUSINESS' OF LAND RIGHTS

In 1974 Mr Justice Woodward concluded in his report that to deny Aborigines the right to prevent mining on their land is to deny the reality of land rights.[17] He based his conclusion on the fact that:[18]

> Aboriginal ownership was not expressed in terms merely of the land surface. In many of the legends which gave expression to mans' spiritual connection with his land, his mythical forbears emerged from the ground and returned to it at different points in their sagas. Their spirit essences still pervade those places and are retained in the soil and the rocks.

Throughout the Aboriginal literature one can find that a number of anthropologists have reached the same conclusion.[19] But anthropologists and judges do not make political policy, nor do they create the political and economic realities of the day. Woodward recognised the differences between political preferences and possibilities and seemingly contradicted his own recommendations by stating that 'minerals and petroleum on Aboriginal lands should remain the property of the Crown'.[20] His rationale was to place mining on Aboriginal land in a wider social and political context. Woodward believed that 'the general approach adopted in this country [is] that minerals belong to all the people'.[21]

Therefore, Aboriginal communities, like *any community,* should have the right to consent to any mining proposal likely to affect members of the community. However, Woodward added that, should consent be withheld, 'the Government must be able to act if it is, on balance, contrary to the national interest'.[22] If Aborigines were given powers exceeding those enjoyed by other Australians, he felt that this would be

> . . . unnecessarily divisive and could lead to reactions among other members of the community which, in the long term, would not be in the best interests of Aborigines . . . The whole of Australian mining law is based on the assumption that minerals belong to the Crown. To provide otherwise in a particular case could well create problems and sorting these problems out could delay necessary legislation.

Woodward felt that the Government, as the only agency available to balance all interests, should continue to decide if mineral exploration and extraction is to be approved, on what basis, and who should do it. As the final arbiter on a question of national interest, he suggested that an Aboriginal veto of an operation could only be overruled by both (Federal) Houses of Parliament. 'National interest' would be the subject of open, public debate; obviously, the proper forum to decide the fate of the 'peoples' resources', but an unappealing concept to mining companies. In response to the mining industry lobby, particularly the Australian Mining Industry Council (located in the Australian offices of Rio Tinto Zinc), a number of important amendments to the original Labor Bill were successfully introduced by the Liberal/Country Party (Fraser) Government,[24] including the provision that the Governor-General would determine a matter of national interest.[25] In other words, a closed meeting of the Federal Cabinet would decide if the 'public good' demanded the reversal of an Aboriginal veto.

This is not an isolated incident; the list of Government actions and policies designed to further and protect the interests of mining companies, particularly in Queensland and Western Australia, is a long one. If government does in fact decide on the benefits derived from developing a resource owned by 'all the people', vested in the Crown, then its ability to do so would need to be based on power which overrides all other interests, including mining companies. Perhaps the almost single-minded actions of some State governments to favourably respond to company demands can be explained on the basis of collusion with private interests by government officials. However, a more serious possibility presents itself: government control of resource development may be illusory and this is likely to be so for at least two reasons.

Firstly, practically all mining in Australia is conducted privately, and most of the major operations are either controlled or managed by trans-nationals; 38 companies generate 95% of the industry income.[26]

This situation has resulted, in part, from the policy assumption of State and Federal Governments that foreign investment, initiated privately, is an essential prerequisite for the development of Australia's resource industry. While it is true that governments will place various conditions on a mining or exploration lease, the fact remains that companies will exert their considerable influence in matters such as level of finance, market decisions and industrial agreements.[27] This bias towards corporate ownership means that 'the public' has little choice in essential questions of control. Thus, if minerals 'belong to all the people' this is purely an ideal right[28] since the economic (and political) reality is that ownership of Australia's resources is *practically* acted upon by a very few.

Secondly, multinationals mine for one reason above all others—maximisation of profit. There is no magic in this. The implications, however, are enormous. In brief, it is clearly the *company's* business, and *not* the government's, to decide if an operation *should* begin and when it will end (leaving aside the possibility of nationalisation). Regardless of the control governments say they have, no company will agree to engage its resources in any mining venture unless uninterrupted, long-term profitability is assured. Governments provide these assurances, on the one hand by underwriting a mining operation with infrastructure assistance (roads, harbours, power, etc.), deferred payment of taxes and royalties and a number of other *financial* concessions, and on the other hand by acting *politically* as a 'mediator' to assure that those interests which may effect profitability and uninterrupted production are 'accommodated'.

In Australia the links between government and the corporate interest are not yet as extensive as in the USA, for example, where top government officials have served on the boards of major corporations. Also, the exact nature of the relationship between governments and corporations will vary from state to state and from project to project. Very often, operations are legitimised as economic 'development' by the use of a number of strategies: from elaborate public-relations campaigns conducted by the company or government, to relatively low-cost, high appeal, private sponsorship of non-political public institutions and events.

But, in addition to various agreements with local public administrations, transnationals seek to assure continued maximixation of profit by developing strategies designed to *centralise* their power.[29] As often happens, these strategies conflict with local and regional interests since corporate power is attained, developed and protected by weakening local power structures and at the expense of local development. Amax might confidently assert, 'what is good for Amax is good for the world', but the Noonkanbah people obviously have no place in the world Amax intends to build. Indeed on a broader level, government can only consider the wishes of the public *after* corporate interests are satisfied, if not entirely, at least to a point where the company will judge a venture profitable.

It would be a mistake, in our opinion, to underestimate the opposition to Aboriginal rights, particularly in the land. If government control of mining is severely limited by corporate demands it is not surprising that no Aboriginal organisation has been able to exert full control over the mineral and oil developments on their land. Furthermore, it is unlikely that a State or Federal Government would willingly strait-jacket itself by giving Aboriginal groups the right to negotiate with miners without the usual 'arbitration' or 'national interest' provisions. Certainly, *no* government would legislate to prevent itself from furthering the interests of the most powerful section of society, for the simple reason that corporations, as they have done in the past, would organise themselves to prevent such a possibility. And if there is any doubt as to the extent of corporate strength, consider that at the end of 1979 the CRA group of companies *alone* employed an amount of capital which more than doubled the entire state revenue of South Australia in 1977-78.[30]

Aboriginal organisations, now more than ever, need to appraise themselves of corporate strategy and government policy towards 'development'. If land rights are to be won, and fundamentally this means the control of oil and mineral development, Aboriginal land councils, in particular, will need this knowledge in order to plan their own political strategies, to assess their strengths and weakness and to balance short-term and long-term interests. Knowledge is not enough, of course, and Aboriginal groups are already realising that alliances with common interests, however difficult, are essential.

Knowledge of changing corporate strategy in the aftermath of the events at Noonkanbah is particularly relevant here. There is little doubt that the national and international attention created by Noonkanbah has alerted all major corporations operating in Australia to the dangers of this kind of confrontation. Amax and the Western Australian government created difficulties which read like a list of corporate nightmares: revival of land rights as a public issue in a state which had previously been politically 'stable', a climate which aroused wide interest and debate in corporate strategy and corporate effects on local development, a broad-based alliance with the Noonkanbah people including, in particular, organised labour and the dangerous potential this had of becoming an *anti-corporate* alliance, and, most importantly, the possibility that successful demands be made to restrict *corporate freedom*—the freedom to invest, develop and maximise profit.

Consequently, the tactics of the Western Australian Government at Noonkanbah, while not directly and publically criticised by the mining industry, are being quietly replaced by less dangerous and more useful strategies. With the ability to act independently of governments and the inclination, paradoxically because of their overriding search for profit, to *recognise* rather than confront Aboriginal interest in the land, corporations are entering into their own agreements with Aboriginal groups. At first, as in the case of the Pitjantjatjara Council agreements, the initiatives came from the Aborigines themselves. But now, as the advantages of direct negotiation are becoming known throughout the industry, companies are taking the lead. Aboriginal land councils such as the Central and Northern land councils in the Northern Territory have been extended an invitation by the Northern Territory Chamber of Mines to attend their meetings so that an agreeable, long-term strategy can be worked out before differences reach the point of confrontation.

The Australian Mining and Petroleum Law Association has asked the two lawyers from the Central Land Council and the Pitjantjatjara Council to give papers at a special meeting on mining on Aboriginal land. Some companies are now *seeking* agreements with Aboriginal groups before they begin their activities regardless of official government policy towards Aboriginal rights to the land. Conceivably, the Western Australian Government would act against Shell, for example, if that company was conducting its affairs in a way which threatened corporate interests generally. But it is not likely that the present Western Australian Government will stop Shell from negotiating directly with the Ngaanyatjara Council, particularly if an agreement is acceptable to the company.

For Aboriginal organisations an obvious question arises: If the basic interest of corporations cannot be those of Aborigines, what then are the benefits and risks of direct negotiation if this now is becoming an accepted part of corporate strategy?

The dangers can be simply stated, for they are exactly the benefits of negotiation for mining companies: Aboriginal land rights are replaced by private compromise outside the political arena, Aboriginal unity is replaced by isolated, independent agreements, and business proceeds as usual. There is nothing to suggest that this new relationship between Aborigines and corporations has changed the basic structure of power. If the structure has not changed the companies cannot lose. On the contrary, the very real threat to corporate interests created by the Noonkanbah confrontation becomes defused, as a 'corporate/Aboriginal accord' develops. There is no doubt that corporations would be happy to see Noonkanbah forgotten, and recently the Federal Government indicated its endorsement for this position. The film *On Sacred Ground,* which contains scenes of the Noonkanbah confrontation with the Western Australian Government and Amax, has been banned for distribution by all Australian Embassies.[31]

Is there an alternative to direct negotiation? Most Aboriginal people have little, if any, power to prevent uncontrolled mining activity on their land. At this moment, the Queensland government is attempting to open all Aboriginal reserves in that State to mineral exploration.[32] In Western Australia the central reserves can be deregistered by a simple proclamation of the Minister.[33] For those Aboriginal groups in the Northern Territory who have limited powers over mining on freehold land, amendments designed to weaken the act are being discussed by the Northern Territory and Federal Governments.[34] Also, it is well known that any mining lease granted before 4 June 1976 cannot be refused by the traditional owners although conditions can be placed on the company's operations, as in the case of the Mereenie Gas and Oil fields west of Alice Springs. Finally, under the new Pitjantjatjara Land Rights Act, Aboriginal refusal of a mining lease on Pitjantjatjara freehold land can be reversed through arbitration, however, unlike the Northern Territory Act, 'national and state interest' must be determined by the judiciary.[35]

If miners are now on land which is of economic and cultural significance to Aboriginal people, but over which they have either limited or no legal rights, can they refuse to negotiate if the possibility presents itself? Another Noonkanbah confrontation is an alternative; but is it realistically possible for Aboriginal organisations with limited resources to sustain one Noonkanbah after another? *Will* Aboriginal groups refuse to compromise with corporations?

Aboriginal people may or may not realise that any attempt to negotiate with such powerful interests as transnational companies, particularly by weak organisations, is dangerous. Aboriginal people may want to win land rights, but what is to be done to protect their land and their interests in the meantime? Mining royalties, gifts (such as bores, jobs, housing, etc.) and agreements are hard to pass up but, often, cost little for CRA and Shell Oil. These arrangements tend to establish a cosy relationship between transnationals and Aborigines while, at the same time, they separate Aborigines from other allies. In other words, the very people who are at the point of contact with mining companies want only to protect their own interests. It is not surprising, that a strategy such as the 'Pitjantjatjara model' is acceptable to Aboriginal people. It might be shocking to some that Aborigines are taking the road of compromise and short-term benefit against the long-term and broader interests. But given that Aborigines have done little else but lose in the past, short-term benefit certainly becomes appealing. Aborigines *want* to place their own interests ahead of other Australians. They see white workers destroying their land, not the makers of corporate policy.

It would seem that the relations of some Aboriginal groups to their land will not be extinguished in the near future. While these relations remain Aborigines will try to protect their land and benefit from its wealth. In doing so, they may go against their long-term interests. On the other hand, if Aboriginal relations to the land were to disappear, or the interests derived from these ignored, there would be little substance to the demand for land rights in the first place. Therefore, given the present powerless situation for many Aborigines, the process of direct negotiation with miners is both a blessing and a potential disaster. For advisors, it must be a kind of juggling act. People will take real protection, they will accept royalties from mining, however dangerous, instead of vague promises.

This leads to, perhaps, the most essential point. If history has proven anything, it is that land rights can only be achieved through *political* action. Land rights are not based on promises nor will they be achieved through business deals. The Pitjantjatjara Council has defined what it considers to be the rules for proper negotiation with miners, but these negotiations however 'proper', cannot replace the political demand for the right of ownership and control over land and minerals. In the final analysis, although the process will neither be simple nor predictable, the *strength* of the political demand will depend upon the organisation of Aboriginal groups, the relationships among themselves *and* with non-Aboriginal organisations who are willing to support land rights. Direct negotiations must, therefore, be seen as a short-term strategy producing short-term benefit. Negotiated agreements between Aborigines and corporations will in the future be seen as unacceptable compromises if, as a result, Aboriginal unity becomes weakened to the point where there is nothing left but defeat when the next confrontation arises.

ACKNOWLEDGEMENTS

This article is an edited version of a chapter from the book *Not Passing Through: the Pitjantjatjara struggle for their land* by D.A. Vachon, P.H. Toyne & C. Forbes, to be published by McPhee Gribble, Melbourne (in press). The authors gratefully appreciate the helpful advice of Richie Howitt, Nick Peterson and Susan Woenne-Green in the preparation of this article.

NOTES

1. cf. *Milirrpum and Others v. Nabalco Pty Ltd and the Commonwealth of Australia* (1971) 17 FLR 141.

2. In Western Australia, for example, the Government's militant anti-union stance, reflected in the introduction of a number of repressive acts during the past several years, is discussed in *W.A. . . . State of Siege*, published by ASWU (WA), CARE and AUS (WA), cf. also Cooper, Steve, 'Repressive legislation and Australian Trade Unions' in: Greg Crough, Ted Wheelwright & Ted Wilshire (eds), *Australia and World Capitalism*. Ringwood, Vic. Penguin Books, 1980, pp. 101–105.

3. For a brief introduction on the effects of transnational penetration in the economies of various third-world countries, cf. Richard J. Barnet & Ronald E. Muller, *Global Reach; the power of the multi-national corporations*. New York, Simon & Schuster, 1974. Pt II, pp. 123–185; and cf. Jack Woddis, *Introduction to neo-colonialism*. New York, International Publishers, 1972. pp. 61–117.

4. Fitzgerald, T.M., *The contribution of the mineral industry to Australian welfare*. Canberra, Australian Government Printer, 1975, p. 93.

5. For more detailed accounts of the Noonkanbah dispute, cf. Richie Howitt, *The Impact of Transnational Capital on the Political Economy of North Australia*, vol. 1. *The Corporate Strategies of CRA Ltd and*

Amax Inc. (in press) pp. 59–72 and cf. Jeremy Salt, Australia: discrimination and human rights in the Kimberleys. *Iwgia Newsletter*, No. 25/26, March 1981, pp. 4–14.

6. cf., for example, *The West Australian* for 4 August and 12 September 1980, and cf. *The Advertiser* for 27 August 1980.

7. *Aboriginal Heritage Act (WA) 1972*, section 11; and *Aboriginal Heritage Act (No. 2) 1980*, section 3.

8. *Noonkanbah: the facts*, September, 1980, Western Australia, William Benbow, Acting Government Printer.

9. A description of this settlement and an account of the events which led up to it is contained in P. Toyne and D.A. Vachon, *Growing up the Country: land rights and the Pitjantjatjara*, to be published by McPhee Gribble, Melbourne. On 4 November 1981 the Pitjantjatjara received freehold title to over 102 630 km^2 of their traditional lands.

10. cf. *Report of the Pitjantjatjara Land Rights Working Party of South Australia*, Adelaide, SA Government Printer, June 1978, p. 94.

11. In part, Comalco's strategy of cooperation with the Pitjantjatjara Council can be explained by the fact that the company has wanted to explore on Granite Downs pastoral lease, an area which the Council had been negotiating for inclusion in the freehold lands under the Act. Now that exploration on Granite Downs requires the prior agreement of the land-holding incorporation, Anangu Pitjantjatjaraku, Comalco's good relationship with the Council will undoubtedly have a positive effect on the company's future plans.

12. Recently, two organisations within the petroleum and mining industry, the Australian Petroleum Exploration Association (APEA) and the Australian Mining Industry Council (AMIC), have published quite dissimilar guidelines for proper dealings with Aborigines. In the APEA pamphlet the emphasis is on accommodation. Aboriginal traditions, customs and culture should be respected and, where appropriate, assistance should be given to community development. The influence of Shell Oil in the preparation of the document becomes clear when APEA suggests proper face-to-face negotiations, disclosing exploration programmes in full and, most important, dealing through land councils, both statutory and non-statutory. The last recommendation is not acceptable to AMIC. Also, whereas the AMIC guidelines recommend that a plan showing the location of sacred sites be prepared, APEA does not. cf. *Aboriginal communities and petroleum and exploration development*, APEA, 1981, and cf, *Declaration of policy*, AMIC, 1981. pp. 20–21.

13. cf. Howitt, op. cit., 72–86.

14. On 18 July 1981, Administrative Instruction No. 210 was issued to all Western Australian Government Departments. It read, in full:

> Attention is drawn to the fact that the Aboriginal Lands Trust and its associated structures is the only Land Council in Western Australia recognised by the Western Australian Government. Government policy is that neither official nor unofficial recognition is to be given to the Kimberley Land Council and Departmental officers are not to be involved in dealings with that Council. Signed: Keith Maine, Director.

15. cf. Janine Roberts, *Massacres to Mining*. Blackburn, Vic., Dove Communications, 1981, pp. 125–36.

16. cf. below in text, p. 320.

17. *Aboriginal Land Rights Commission Second Report*. Canberra, Australian Government Printer, April 1974. p. 104.

18. ibid., p. 104.

19. cf., for example, Ken Maddock, *The Australian Aborigines: a portrait of their society*. Ringwood, Vic., Penguin Books, 1975, pp. 27–28.

20. *Aboriginal Land Rights Commission Second Report*, op cit, p. 127.

21. ibid., p. 115.

22. ibid., p. 115.

23. ibid., p. 115.

24. cf. Janine Roberts, *From Massacres to Mining: the colonisation of Aboriginal Australia*. CIMRA and War on Want, 1978, pp. 163–73.

25. *Aboriginal Land Rights (N.T.) Act 1976*, section 41(1)b.

26. cf. Greg Crough, Ted Wheelwright & Ted Wilshire, op. cit., p. 16.

27. cf. Howitt, op. cit., pp. 8–43 for a discussion of the corporate strategies of CRA and Amax.

28. The immediate objection here is that, as the collective owners of Australia's mineral wealth, the public does benefit by receiving royalties from mining. We refer again to Fitzgerald (1975) for a brief analysis comparing public benefits received from mining and public expense through various tax concessions to

mining companies and infrastructure development. Incidentally, Fitzgerald (1975: 75–77) describes the attitudes of Sir Harold Raggat, late advisor to the Chifley Government and first director of the Bureau of Mineral Resources. In his book, *Mountains of Ore,* Raggat assumes, as would many others, that mining companies own the minerals they find. After all, it was the company that stimulated capital investment and 'took all the risks'. As such, Raggat considered it outrageous that mining companies should need to pay royalties for activities 'which destroy *their* basic asset' (Raggat, as quoted in Fitzgerald 1975:77). A miner should be 'entitled to reap the reward of *his* discovery' (Raggat, ibid.: 77).

29. In the past 15 years a number of books have been written on the strategies of transnational corporations. For a non-technical introduction, cf. Paul A. Baran & Paul M. Sweezy, *Monopoly Capital: an essay on the American economic and social order.* New York, Modern Reader Paperback, 1966, pp. 14–51.

30. Figures are taken from CRA *Annual Report,* 1979, p. 31, and *Pocket Yearbook of South Australia,* Adelaide, South Australian Government Printer, 1978.

31. cf. *The National Times* for 5-11 July 1981.

32, cf. *The National Times* for 20-27 June 1981.

33. *Aboriginal Affairs Planning Authority Act (W.A.) 1972* section 7.

34. Recently, the Northern Territory land councils, the Northern Territory Government and the Commonwealth have been holding meetings to discuss possible amendments to the Act. cf. *Centralian Advocate* for 8 July 1981 and the Central Land Council press release in *The National Times* for 28 June-4 July 1981.

35. Judges must be of the High Court, the Federal Court of Australia, or the Supreme Court of a State or Territory. For the mining provisions of the Act, cf. *Pitjantjatjara Land Rights Act, 1981,* sections 20–24.

22

NOONKANBAH *Philip Vincent*

Noonkanbah Pastoral Station, a property comprising some 385 000 hectares, lies approximately 97 km south-west of Fitzroy Crossing in the Kimberley region of Western Australia. At present it is populated by some 150–200 Aboriginal people, the Yungngora Community Inc., who are of Walmadjari and Nyigina descent with some Bunapa and Djaru also. The station was bought for the Yungngora Community by the Aboriginal Land Fund Commission in 1976 in response to appalling social conditions experienced by the group which was then living in Fitzroy Crossing. The group's traditional association with the station area is, however, of much longer standing, pre-dating European arrival in the area.

Oral tradition at Noonkanbah tells of early conflicts between settlers and Aborigines and of mass killings and burnings of bodies. A number of burial sites on the station are said to contain the remains of those shot by European settlers but little work has yet been done on local history in the area. Suffice it to say that the interaction between the European settlers and the Aboriginal population at Noonkanbah resulted in a 'walk-off' by the latter in 1971 because of ill-treatment. The Aborigines moved to Fitzroy Crossing where they remained until 1976. The stay at Fitzroy Crossing had traumatic consequences for the group, which experienced the poverty and alcohol use attendant on life in the town.

The purchase of the station by the ALFC under the auspices of the State Aboriginal Lands Trust was accordingly seen by the Yungngora as a means of grasping a last chance for their very survival—free from the perceived pernicious influence of Europeans both in Fitzroy Crossing and on the station. Once returned to their land at Noonkanbah, the Community quickly proved to have a formidable combination of determination and capacity for hard work. The station, which had been badly run down and left derelict over a number of years by its previous European owners, was nurtured by the Yungngora to a viable stage. In this regard, recent cattle sales figures have been impressive in indicating how well the community has transformed the station into a successful enterprise.

A primary aim of the group has been to maintain its own culture, free from European influence. The result has been that morale has been high in the community, teetotalism has been established on the station, and a school, operating in the station's woolshed has become a model community-run school in which traditional culture, taught by members of the community, feature prominently in the curriculum.

The Yungngora's understanding that quiet possession of their land had been returned to them was shattered by the incursion of personnel from various mining companies during the diamond exploration boom of 1977–78. The miners' presence was significant and imposing, evidenced as it was by trucks, helicopters, bulldozers, white-tipped pegs, trenches and camps of what the Aborigines saw as loud-mouthed, alcohol-imbibing, uncouth Europeans.

Between 1977 and 1978 some 500 mineral claims were physically pegged on the station area by various companies. Little, if any, consultation with the community occurred. The Yungngora viewed this invasion of their territory with increasing concern. The situation was brought to a head in May 1978 during a bush meeting at Noonkanbah station, which involved Aborigines from throughout the Kimberley region and also some from the Northern Territory. Traditional songs and dances featured significantly in the bush meeting, which lasted several days, and discussions amongst those present concerning land rights led to the inauguration of the Kimberley Land Council. The Council was established with a view to providing a strong unified body to assist the various Aboriginal groups in the Kimberleys in their land rights struggles. During the course of the bush meeting it was drawn to the attention of those present that a bulldozer from one of the mining companies then on the station (Amax) was in the process of creating a new 'road' down to the Fitzroy River only a short distance away. The 'road' went through an important and sacred area. This news provoked anger and heated discussion amongst the group and a truckload of people was despatched with instructions to ensure that the bulldozer driver halted his acts of desecration. I am told that the bulldozer driver was so intent upon his work, so convinced of the rectitude of his course of action and yet so ignorant of the provisions of the Western Australian Aboriginal Heritage Act that, I regret to say, the group found it necessary to physically remind him of the illegality of his actions.

Alarmed by this incident and in the knowledge that mining companies on the station ultimately threatened the social cohesion of their people and also, and more immediately, sacred areas on the station, the Yungngora instructed the Aboriginal Legal Service of Western Australia to take legal action in an endeavour to stop further exploration on the station.

Pursuant to those instruction, on 16 June 1978 the Aboriginal Legal Service filed objections in the Broome Mining Wardens Court to the mineral claims which had been lodged by various companies including CRA. The grounds set out in the objections were that:

- One mining company had already been given mineral rights on the property and the activities of a multiplicity of mining companies could not be satisfactorily monitored by the Aboriginal lessees and occupiers;
- the sacred sites of the Aboriginal people would be endangered by such occupation;
- such occupancy would deprive the Aboriginal occupiers of the land from enjoying newly found self-dependence and freedom from alien cultural pressure; and that
- such occupation would interfere with their pastoral business and subsistence, cause roads and tracks necessary to their livelihood to deteriorate and generally cause the deterioration of scenery and environment.

The applications for mining tenements on the part of CRA and the objections thereto came on for hearing before the local Mining Warden, Mr D.A. McCann, SM, at Broome on 8 and 9 November 1978. Both CRA and Yungngora were represented by Queens Counsel at the hearing.

Two aspects regarding the jurisdiction of the Warden should be borne in mind when considering the outcome:

- Under the Western Australian Mining Act, the Warden has power merely to recommend to the Minister for Mines whether or not mineral claims should be allowed or refused or whether certain conditions should be attached to the granting of the claims. That is to say, the final decision rests with the Minister; and
- there is authority emanating from the Supreme Court of Western Australia for the proposition that the jurisdiction of Mining Wardens is restricted to examining the

formal aspects of pegging, such as compliance with the regulations, and questions of overpegging, and that they have no jurisdiction to examine equitable claims (which would include the matters raised by the Yungngora).

Notwithstanding this apparent limitation, Mr McCann embarked upon the hearing of evidence relating to the matters raised by the Yungngora and made a finding upon it.

In the event, he recommended that all but two of the CRA claims should be unconditionally approved, and that the other two should be approved subject to the condition that no mining take place until action was taken under the Aboriginal Heritage Act to identify and, where necessary, protect places and objects within the mining tenement.

In his decision Mr McCann referred to past objections in other cases based on the interference caused to pastoral activities by mining and noted that they had been rejected. He also held that such an objection was not valid. At the end of his decision however, Mr McCann stated:

> 24. I have written at some length rather than summarily dismiss the matters raised by the Objectors. It would be insensitive not to recognise the sincere and deep interest of these aboriginal people in the land they see as theirs. It is clear that they are worried and, to a degree, feel threatened by the mining development in the area. This concern and worry has manifested itself in the objections made to these claims. It is a matter of comfort that this manifestation has taken a lawful, as distinct from an illegal and hostile, form.
>
> 25. If only as a matter of self interest, the Government, the mining companies and the community at large would do well to look at the issues raised in these proceedings and take positive steps to attempt to abate the concern expressed by the Aboriginal people.

While the CRA claims were being heard in the Wardens Court, the petroleum division of Amax Iron Ore Corporation, a joint holder and the operator of petroleum exploration permit No. EP97, was preparing to drill a wild-cat oil exploration well on the station. Such exploration for oil was governed by the Petroleum Act of Western Australia rather than the Mining Act, and was not subject to the scrutiny of the Mining Warden.

The approximate location had been established by the company and was shown to the Western Australian Museum. Amax indicated to the Museum that it was not concerned to have an anthropological survey of the area carried out as one of their mining engineers, Mr Lyons, had already discussed the question of sites with an elder and there appeared to be no conflict of interest. The Museum decided, however, that a professional examination of the area should take place and an investigation was undertaken by Mr P. Bindon, a museum anthropologist, during April 1979. This immediately revealed that the proposed drill site was within a sacred site complex centred around 'P Hill', located approximately 5 kilometres from the station homestead.

The revelation that the miners intended to violate a significant sacred site virtually on the community's front door brought a strong reaction from the Yungngora. A series of talks with Amax and Mines Department personnel were held; however, the community was told that the drilling would proceed notwithstanding their objections. A petition in Walmadjari bearing 50 signatures of Yungngora people was forwarded from Noonkanbah on 17 May 1979 for presentation by Mr R. Davies, Leader of the Labor Opposition in the Western Australian Parliament. The official English translation of the petition rendered by Mrs Olive Bieundurry was as follows:

> We are sending this letter to you important people who can speak and who are now sitting down, talking in the big house.

> We Aboriginal people of Noonkanbah Station are sending this letter. We truthfully beg you important people that you stop these people, namely CRA and Amax, who are going into our land, which is at Noonkanbah.
>
> These people have already made the place no good with their bulldozers. Our sacred places they have made no good. They mess up our land. They expose our sacred objects. This breaks our spirit. We lose ourselves as a people. What will we as a people do if these people continue to make all our land no good.
>
> Today we beg you that you will truly stop them.

Press releases were sent by the Yungngora Community to the press of the world and representatives of the Community were sent to Perth to better acquaint the population of Western Australia with their views via the media of television, radio and public meetings. Amax personnel were told that should they violate the Yungngora sacred sites they would be in 'big trouble' with the law.

This response from the Yungngora prompted the Western Australian State Government to decide that a meeting should be convened at Noonkanbah to get the matter straightened out. Representatives from Amax, the Mines Department, and the Museum were to attend, and the Police Department was directed to send a contingent of police to the meeting on the purported grounds that they were required to prevent a likely breach of the peace. Having already had numerous meetings with Amax personnel, the Yungngora advised that they would meet with the Mines Department representative and the Museum personnel but not with Amax. Furthermore, they said, if police attended there would simply be no meeting whatsoever.

A compromise was eventually arrived at whereby on the day of the meeting, 28 May 1979, no police went to the station and Amax personnel stayed at the Noonkanbah airstrip for the duration of the meeting in case they were required to provide the Mines Department representative with information during the course of the meeting. At the meeting there was vigorous discussion between the various parties concerned. It was eventually agreed that a further Museum survey should be conducted, this time of a somewhat larger area within which Amax's surveys had indicated it would be worthwhile exploring further by drilling (the company's 'area of interest').

The Mines Department representative gave an assurance to those present at the meeting that his Department would not authorise drilling unless the Museum indicated that such drilling would not harm sacred sites. The Museum accordingly undertook a further survey this time of the Amax 'area of interest'. The survey, which took place during May and June 1979, was once again carried out by Mr P. Bindon of the Western Australian Museum.

The results of his investigation on the Noonkanbah location were noted by him as follows:

> The whole area within which any drill hole could be located by the Company falls under the influence of the special sites shown to me by the Aborigines of the clan descent group for that area.
>
> The site complex is significant in both a religious and economic context. Mythological connections are both authentic and ancient and are intimately linked to the economic present.
>
> It is currently the opinion of the Aboriginal community that any utilisation of the drill zone, particularly the substrata, by the company would be deleterious to the site complex.

Furthermore, it was proposed in the report that the 'P Hill' site complex and surrounding area be declared a protected area under section 19 of the Western Australian *Aboriginal Heritage Act*, 1972. This section provided that the Trustees of the Western Australian Museum may recommend that any Aboriginal site is of outstanding importance and the Governor may, by order in Council, declare that site to be a protected area.

Subsequent to the submission of Mr Bindon's report to the museum, it was considered by the Museum's Aboriginal Cultural Material Committee. This Committee was established by section 28 of the *Aboriginal Heritage Act* and vested pursuant to section 39 of the Act with the duty, inter alia, 'to evaluate on behalf of the community the importance of places and objects alleged to be associated with Aboriginal persons'.

The Committee, having considered the report, decided to seek Protected Area status for the area proposed by Mr Bindon. The Trustees of the Museum also considered the report and endorsed the decision of the Committee in that regard. This information was conveyed to Mr R.C. Old, then acting Minister for Cultural Affairs and being the Minister responsible fo the Aboriginal Heritage Act.

Meanwhile, the Minister for Mines, on behalf of the Crown, by letter dated 7 June 1979 to the Trustees of the Museum, gave notice that the Crown as 'owner of the land, required it for the purpose of having an oil exploration well drilled there by Amax Iron Ore Corporation on behalf of the holders of the exploration permit.' The consent of the Trustees to the use of the land for the purpose was requested. In making this request, the Crown was presumably following the procedures under section 18 of the Act, as it then was, whereby owners of land on which an Aboriginal site was located could apply to the Trustees of the Museum for permission to use the land for a purpose that would have a deleterious effect on the preservation of the site.

The Trustees replied, after consideration of the request by the Crown and further evaluation of the site (including a discussion with Mr Bindon concerning his findings), that not only did 'they consider it was inappropriate that the Crown should request consent, but in any event they would not consent and they would continue to make a recommendation for a protected area to be declared under section 19 of the Act.'

In a letter dated 14 June 1979, Mr Old wrote to the Trustees and advised that, after giving full consideration to their views and other views, it had been decided that, with all reasonable precautions being taken, such drilling could be carried out with a minimum of disturbance to the area and to the welfare and way of life of the Aboriginal community living there. The Trustees were thereby accordingly directed to consent to the use of the land contained in the Aboriginal site, the consent being subject 'to all reasonable precautions being taken to keep disturbance of the area and to the welfare and way of life of the community, to a minimum'.

On the same date, in a memorandum to the Minister for Mines, the Director of the Museum advised that, having regard to the direction given by Mr Old, the Trustees gave their consent to the use of the land as required. In doing so it is clear that the Trustees felt themselves bound to comply with the direction of the Minister, having regard to section 11 of the Aboriginal Heritage Act which states:

> The Minister, after consultation with the body concerned, may give to the Trustees, or to the (Aboriginal Cultural Material) Committee, directions of a general or a specific character as to the exercise of any function under this Act and that body shall give effect to any such direction.

By 7am on 15 June (the day after the directed consent) approximately 40 members of the Yungngora were at the front gate of the station. The gate had been padlocked shut to prevent the expected intrusion by Amax. At 8.35am Amax personnel and a Mines Department official arrived at the gate. It was made clear by Yungngora spokesmen that these officials would not be permitted to enter Noonkanbah, and they turned back after a short discussion. The next morning the Yungngora were still at the gate, waiting for whatever steps the Government and Amax might take. The situation

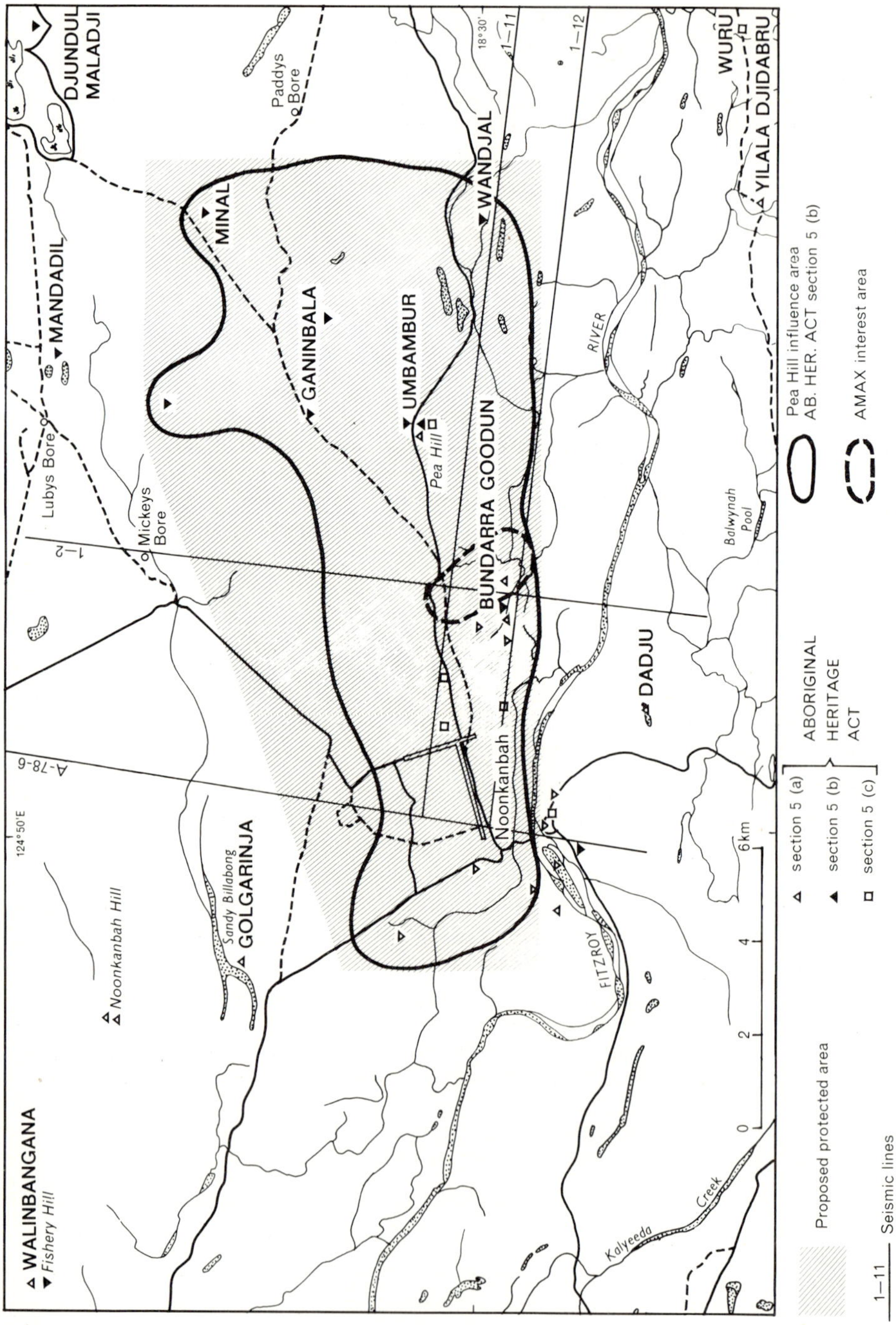

Fig. 1.
Aboriginal sites on Noonkanbah station (after P. Bindon).

was defused, however, with the announcement that the Yungngora, through the Aboriginal Legal Service, had been successful in obtaining an interim injunction from the Supreme Court of Western Australia restraining Amax 'whether by itself, its servants or agents, or otherwise howsoever, from or doing anything with respect to exploration or drilling on or with respect to the land within a radius of three kilometres of 'P Hill' near the Noonkanbah homestead'. The injunction was later extended by the court on the basis of grave doubts concerning the validity of the Minister's direction to the Museum.

These questions were argued more fully when an application by Amax (supported by the Crown) was brought to have the injunction discharged. This application came on for hearing on 19 and 22 June 1979 before Brinsden J. Questions raised by counsel for the Yungngora included the following:

- Was the Crown the appropriate party to apply to use the site for a deleterious purpose rather than Amax?
- As the Trustees had already decided to recommend that the area surrounding 'P Hill' should be proclaimed a protected area under the Aboriginal Heritage Act, how could it then be said that they 'consented' (albeit by direction) to the application for user of the site for a deleterious purpose under section 18 of the Act? The giving of consent is a concept particularly involving the free exercise of the will, therefore is it one of those functions which is capable of being the subject of direction by the Minister as referred to in section 11?
- Furthermore, does section 11 only refer to the administration of procedure under the Act or does it relate to the administration of the Act *in toto* such that the Minister may give directions to the Trustees either of a specific or a general nature as to how they should go about their duties under the Act?

With regard to the first question, Brinsden J. concluded that the Crown was an appropriate party to apply to the Museum for deleterious user of the site. Secondly, Brinsden J. held that the Minister's direction was in all aspects valid.

In holding that the Minister did have the power under the Aboriginal Heritage Act to control and direct the Trustees in all their functions including that of directing their consent to deleterious use of sacred sites, Brinsden J. made the following comment

> It is not for me to comment on the wisdom of the provisions of the provisions [sic] of this Act. Parliament has seen fit to pass an Act which provides for such control without setting out the criteria to be observed in the exercise of that control by the Minister other than by obliging him to consult with the Trustees or the Committee as the case may be before giving either of them a direction. Once of course a site is declared a protected area a greater restriction of control in the Governor is provided for because he may only vary or revoke the protected status, after consultation with the Trustees, and is satisfied that it is in the general interest of the community so to do, and not otherwise—s.25.

Thus not even the limited protection of 'community interest' consideration was available to the community to protect 'P Hill' and its environs, the Trustees' recommendation that the area be granted protected status not having been formalised by the Governor by Order in Council. (It is understood, incidentally, that there are 59 Aboriginal sites in Western Australia which have been granted protected area status under the Act.)

In the light of his findings upon the questions of law which were raised, Brinsden J. held that the interim injunction restraining Amax should be lifted.

The following morning, 28 June 1979, the gates of Noonkanbah Station were once again manned, this time by about 80 Aboriginal people from the station and Fitzroy

Crossing. Their determination was not, however, then put further to the test as on that day the Government announced that Amax would drill at Noonkanbah that year because of the impending wet season. The rest of 1979 and the wet season passed by without further incident.

On 6 March 1980 information was received that the Western Australian Government had directed Amax to proceed to Noonkanbah station during the following week in order to set up a camp and carry out preliminary drilling. The police had been instructed to attend with Amax in order to facilitate the action. They were to force the gates of the station if necessary. The revelation of this information brought a denial from the Premier of Western Australia, Sir Charles Court. A news release from the Premier's Department number P80/205 and dated 11 March 1980 stated:

> There is no suggestion that the company will enter the area to commence drilling without proper consultation between us and the local community. The company is anxious to respect the areas which can genuinely be classed as sacred sites—as is the Government.

The Yungngora Community, which had immediately re-manned the gates upon hearing of the Government's instructions to Amax, relaxed in the light of this assurance from the Premier, and waited for the consultation to eventuate. Senator Chaney, Federal Minister for Aboriginal Affairs, was, apparently, also relieved. In a press release of the same date he said:

> The rumour that the company would enter the property—without notice and with police protection—caused great consternation. It is good that the Premier has put that rumour to rest.

On 14 March 1980 three Ministers of the Western Australian Government flew to Noonkanbah for consultations. These were the Ministers for Cultural Affairs (Mr Grayden), Mines (Mr Jones), and Community Welfare (being the Minister responsible for the *Aboriginal Affairs Planning Authority Act, 1972,* Mr Hassell). The Meeting commenced by Mr Grayden praising the community in the following terms, as recorded in notes of the meeting made by the writer at the time.

> *Grayden*—'A few years ago Government gave station because it wants people like you on stations. You don't allow alcohol, that's good—we're proud of you. You have a strong culture—that's good. We want to see more Aborigines on stations. You're doing so well that the Government wants more Aborigines on stations'.

From that point the direction of the meeting moved to Mr Grayden then asking the community to accompany the Ministers and Mines Department representatives to the Amax area of interest (which, you will recall, was wholly within the area recommended by the Trustees of the Museum to be declared a protected area) and point to a spot where Amax could drill. After discussion, the community declined to do this. The point was made by community members that this was the very exercise which had been undertaken with the Museum representatives the previous year. The notes of the meeting reveal this curious exchange:

> *Nipper Tabagee:* 'It looks like people didn't believe what we told the museum—like we lied.'
> *Mr Jones:* 'No, we don't believe you lied, that's why we've come to ask where the company *can* drill.'
> *Nipper Tabagee:* 'But the museum told you.'
> *Mr Jones:* 'We want to make really sure.'

Apart from this attempted sleight of hand, nothing further was offered by the Ministers present by way of resolution of the issue and the 'consultations' broke down.

On 17 March 1980 Amax entered the property, without notice and with police protection. A party from the station moved to where the Amax personnel had situated themselves and were told that Amax intended to drill on one of the two places (both considered sacred and identified as such in the Museum report). The Yungngora Community was to tell Amax on which of the two places the company was to drill or, so the community was told, the company would immediately commence to drill on whichever of the two spots it pleased.

After seeking some time within which to make a decision, and such request being denied, the Yungngora advised Amax and the police party of their choice, which was, apparently, the lesser of two evils. Bulldozing of a camp area thereupon commenced immediately under the watchful eye of the five car-loads of police.

These acts of Amax were followed by yet another injunction from the Supreme Court upon the application of the community. In its haste to commence operations, the company had overlooked the necessity of obtaining consent from the Museum to deleteriously use the new location, it having not been part of the area the subject of the prior directed consent. The company was thus in breach of section 17 of the *Aboriginal Heritage Act,* which provides that it is an offence for any person to excavate, destroy, damage, conceal or in any way alter any Aboriginal site without the consent of the Museum Trustees.

Work on the site stopped with the granting of the injunction, but recommenced again when the injunction was lifted by the Supreme Court following, once again, the issuing of a direction by the Minister for Cultural Affairs (now Mr W. Grayden) to the Trustees of the Museum, and their acquiescence, to consent to the use of the sacred site for oil drilling.

Notwithstanding the lifting of the injunction, the Aborigines resorted to the processes of their own law. They set up camp adjacent to the workmen on the site. They danced through the night. They pointed out to the workmen the danger they had put themselves in from Aboriginal law by violating the site.

On 2 April 1980, for vague unexplained reasons, Amax personnel and contractors left the area and returned to Derby from whence they had come. The exploration well had not been drilled. A further reprieve had had been obtained.

Following the vacation of the area by Amax the Yungngora Community waited for some indication of the intentions of the company and the State Government. On 30 May 1980, aware that the question of drilling at Noonkanbah had become a highly political issue, the Western Australian Premier, Sir Charles Court, visited the station specifically to discuss the matter. The discussions, however, were not successful in resolving the issue, with the Premier maintaining adamantly that the proposed drill site was not on a sacred area and the community elders maintaining just as adamantly that it was.

Following the Premier's visit events moved rapidly. On 10 June 1980 the Government gazetted a Notice of Intention to compulsorily acquire the access road to the station together with the drill site. This was an obvious first step in the State Government's plan to force through the drilling programme on the station.

The issues surrounding Noonkanbah at that stage had been clouded by many unfortunate allegations emanating from the Western Australian State Government at its highest level. These included:

- That the Yungngora had been subjected to 'ideological penetration' by 'so-called advisers', the implication being that the sacred sites issue was fabricated by 'stirrers' and not one of real concern to the Yungngora themselves. It is disturbing that the apparent intention of this type of remark was to diminish in the eyes of the public the credibility and standing of those individuals and agencies who provide legal and other advisory services to the Yungngora and other Aboriginal communities.

- The coincidence of the emergence of the Noonkanbah controversy and the subsequent arrests, on charges under then recently introduced provisions of the Western Australian Electoral Act prohibiting the 'inducement' of persons to lodge postal votes, of advisers to the Yungngora and other Aboriginal communities speaks for itself in that regard.
- That the issue was not one of sacred sites but rather of 'land rights' (although one would have thought that the preservation of sacred sites is an important aspect of land rights).
- That the Yungngora were really only seeking royalties from the drilling (this had never been sought by or on behalf of the Yungngora).
- That the Yungngora were displaying 'raw racial hatred' in their stance.
- That it was the State Government's policy, and one which it would pursue with regard to the Noonkanbah issue, to protect 'genuine, identified' sacred sites. The innuendo being, of course, that the Noonkanbah site, which was recommended by the Trustees of Western Australian Museum to be accorded protected area status, was non-genuine and not identified.

Clearly, the Western Australian Government was simply not willing to accept that an Aboriginal sacred site could be anything other than a readily recognisable and readily fenced physical feature (preferably small and non-valuable). In this case, however, Bindon had recorded a rather more complex concept involving several distinct features or locations with related surrounding areas of influence. That this could be a sacred site was not acceptable to the Government.

Mr Bindon noted that there was, first, a series of initiation sites in the immediately adjacent area to the drill site related to the intersection of two routes followed by mythological figures and secondly found[1] that

> In addition the proposed AMAX drill site is within the sphere of influence of the site located by both Mr Lyons and Mr Palmer and which is commonly known as 'P' or 'Pea Hill'.
>
> This site contains two distinct central features both of which are concerned with the proliferation of species of animals and thus can be seen as sites involved with the perpetuation of the natural order of part of the animal world.

The Government's attitude, however, was not dictated by the provisions of the *Aboriginal Heritage Act*. Section 5 of the Act as it then stood provided that Aboriginal sites (i.e., sites which are protected by the Act) include *inter alia* 'any place, including any sacred, ritual or ceremonial site, which is of importance or of special significance to persons of Aboriginal descent'. and 'any place which, in the opinion of the Trustees (of the WA Museum), is, or was associated with the Aboriginal people and which may be of historical, anthropological, archeological and ethnographical interest'.

The sacred site at Yungngora, as described by Bindon, clearly came within the ambit of the Act; however, the Government was not, apparently, willing to employ the terms and spirit of the Act in what it obviously regarded as a dangerous precedent.

The ultimate State Government response to the Yungngora's stance on the issue was an awesome display of paramilitary might directed against this tiny Aboriginal community.

On 7 August 1980 a convoy of 45 trucks left Perth under a cloak of secrecy with a heavy police escort.

At Enneaba, north of Perth, an oil drilling rig owned by Richter Drilling was loaded onto the trucks and the convoy commenced its journey up the Great Northern Highway towards Noonkanbah.

By this stage, outrage at the actions of the Government had been voiced across the nation and the events provided banner headlines in many newspapers. The trade union movement had also stepped in to support the claims of the Aborigines.

Along the course of the route taken by the convoy, at towns such as Port Hedland and Broome, there were many arrests of unionists who formed picket lines in front of the oncoming trucks. Similarly, at the station itself, a large group of Aborigines together with four ministers of religion, sat on the access road to the station ahead of the convoy. Seventeen of the Aborigines and the ministers were arrested prior to the arrival of the rig. (Those arrested were charged with preventing free passage of vehicles on the road; however, at a subsequent court hearing, the charges were dismissed as the police could not prove the geographical coincidence between the spot where the group was sitting and the allegedly newly gazetted access road.)

A further brief reprieve in the drilling of the site was obtained when, after consultation with the ACTU, the drillers employed to work the rig agreed not to proceed. However, eventually a strike-breaking crew commenced the drilling operations on the 30 August 1980.

The day preceding the commencement of drilling a delegation from the National Aboriginal Conference left Australia for Geneva to attend the sittings of the United Nations Human Rights Commission's Sub-Commission on the Prevention of Discrimination and Protection of Minorities. The delegation was responding to a request to attend the sittings from the Yungngora Association in order to put its case on the drilling question.

This historic delegation, being the first delegation of Australian Aborigines to appear before the United Nations, comprised Messrs Jim Hagan, Chairman of the NAC; Jimmy Bieundurry, the NAC member for West Kimberley (in whose electorate lay Noonkanbah Station); and Reg Birch, the NAC member for East Kimberley and an executive member of the World Council of Indigenous People. The writer accompanied the delegation as legal counsel.

Mr Hagan addressed the Sub-commission to unprecedented attention (according to United Nations sources) by the world press and media. In his address Mr Hagan sketched the history of the treatment of Aborigines in Australia and highlighted the situation at Noonkanbah as an example of how their oppression has continued. He pointed to the failure of the Australian Federal Government to intervene in the dispute:

> The Noonkanbah Community have sought justice, and they have been given obstruction. They have sought peace and they have been given violence.
> The Australian Government's acquiescence in this continuing breach of human rights must see it stand condemned in the eyes of the world.

Notwithstanding a conciliatory reply by the Australian Government observer to the Sub-commission, a resolution was subsequently adopted by the Sub-commission in the following terms:

> *Having heard* the statement made by Mr Jose R. Martinez Cobo, Special Rapporteur for the study on discrimination against indigenous populations, *Thanking* the Special Rapporteur for his work in preparing basic materials for the above-mentioned study in accordance with the guidelines adopted on the matter and expresses regret that the report prepared for submission this year was not available in all the languages necessary for its consideration,
>
> *Recognising* the great importance of the subject and of the need to protect and promote human rights of indigenous populations,
>
> *Bearing in mind* the concern expressed in this regard at the World Conference to Combat Racism and Racial Discrimination in 1978,
>
> *Bearing in mind* also the statements made at the current session concerning the

situation of aboriginals in Australia and in particular at Noonkanbah in Western Australia by the National Aboriginal Conference and by the government of Australia,

Believing that special attention should be given to appropriate avenues of recourse at the national regional and international levels in order to advance the promotion and protection of the human rights of indigenous populations,

Having noted with satisfaction the progress report given by the Special Rapporteur, Mr Jose R. Martinez Cobo, on the matter,

1. *Expresses* its hope that the Study of the problem of Discrimination against Indigenous populations will be completed as a matter of urgency, in time for consideration by the Sub-commission at its thirty-fourth session,
2. *Decides* to this end to request the Secretary-General to provide all necessary assistance to the Special Rapporteur so as to facilitate his work.

The fact that the Sub-commission chose Australian Aborigines and, in particular, Noonkanbah, from all the other matters before it involving indigenous people is most significant. In diplomatic terms, it was a decided rebuke for the Australian Government over its handling of the affair.

Indeed, the Federal Government had failed to adequately deal with the issue. Requests had been made for Federal intervention by the Yungngora Community and the National Aboriginal Conference; however, whilst there were indications in the press of philosophical support by the then Minister of Aboriginal Affairs, Senator F. Chaney, the Federal Government declined to take any positive action in support of the community.

The United Nations and its member countries are well aware that the Australian Government has recently ratified the International Covenants on Civil and Political Rights, on the Elimination of all forms of Racial Discrimination and on Economic, Social and Cultural Rights. The onus now rests with the Government to see that its international obligations under those covenants are honoured in so far as they relate to the human, cultural and religious rights of Aborigines in the States. If the Government fails in that regard its record in the field of human rights will be irreparably damaged.

The members of the Yungngora Community have stood up to the massed might of commerce and government to defend what they have regarded as their basic cultural and religious rights. The aggressive stance adopted by the Western Australian Government has not only resulted in much harm to that community and to Australia's international image but was unproductive and wasteful in economic terms. No oil was found at Noonkanbah.

NOTE

P. Bindon, *Site investigation on Noonkanbah pastoral lease and adjacent areas, April–June.* Perth, Aboriginal Sites Department, Western Australian Museum, 1979.

23 URANIUM AND ABORIGINAL LAND INTERESTS IN THE ALLIGATOR RIVERS REGION

Peter Carroll

The Alligator Rivers region of the Northern Territory is the location of Australia's major uranium deposits. It is also an area of unique environmental significance, and the Commonwealth Government has nominated the Kakadu National Park for inclusion in the World Heritage list.[1] Throughout the region there are extensive galleries of Aboriginal rock art of international repute and significance. Archaeologists working in the region have discovered an ochre-impregnated grinding stone carbon dated to 18 000 years ago as well as edge-ground stone axes carbon dated to 22 000 years ago.[2]

Until very recently Aboriginal people have been a majority in the region but current developments will significantly increase the numbers of non-Aboriginal residents and visitors. This article outlines the history of the region, gives details of the first two uranium developments (Ranger and Nabarlek), the establishment of the Kakadu National Park, and other uranium developments and further mineral exploration. An appendix gives a summary of agreements concerning the Ranger and Nabarlek uranium mines and the Kakadu National Park.

EARLY EXPLORATION AND SETTLEMENT

Between 1825 and 1850 three different military settlements were established and later closed along the north coast of the Northern Territory:

- Fort Dundas at Apsley Straits on Melville Island, 1824–29 (Spillett, 1972:13–14),
- Fort Wellington at Raffles Bay on the Cobourg Peninsula, 1827–29 (Spillett, 1972:15–16),
- Victoria at Port Essington on the Cobourg Peninsula, 1838–49 (Spillett 1972:24, 166).

The Asian water buffalo was introduced from Timor, and small numbers were released at the close of the settlements. They thrived in the conditions and today thousands roam the coastal plains.

In 1845 Ludwig Leichhardt passed through western Arnhem Land *en route* from Moreton Bay (Brisbane) to the settlement at Port Essington. In his journal (Leichhardt, 1847:488–521) he reports numerous contacts with Aborigines in the region. Oral tradition among Oenpelli Aborigines recalls an early contact, drawing attention to the Aborigines' first encounter with flour and sugar. They regarded flour as useful only for body decoration, and sugar was identified with sand because of its granular appearance.

Following the establishment of the settlement at Escape Cliffs[3] in 1864 (at Adam Bay near the mouth of the Adelaide River, east of Darwin), John McKinlay was sent to explore the country to the east. His intention was to explore as far as the Liverpool River and the Roper River. They made no allowance for the Northern Territory wet season and, after leaving the Adelaide River in January 1866, finally reached the East Alligator River in June. Their situation was hopeless as their supplies had been used and the horses were exhausted. The horses were killed and their hides used to make an improvised raft in which they returned by sea to the Adelaide River. Miraculously, no lives were lost (McKinlay, 1866).

Aboriginal oral[4] tradition tells of a hostile encounter with Europeans near Oenpelli when spears were thrown. The tradition suggests it was Leichhardt's visit, but this is not confirmed explicitly by his diary; however, McKinlay refers to an attack by Aborigines.

In the latter part of the nineteenth century buffalo shooters came into the region after buffalo hides. Among these was Paddy Cahill who, in the 1890s was to settle in the Oenpelli area, having previously been at Delamere Station near Katherine. The Government Resident visited Cahill in 1893 and, among other things, reported on the incidence of leprosy amongst the Aboriginals. (South Australian Government Resident's Report, 1894:8):

> I was surprised and alarmed to find several undoubtedly suffering from leprosy. In one case the fingers of both hands were gone, merely the stumps remaining; in another the toes had all decayed away, and others disfigured about the face. They evidently understood the loathsomeness of the disease, and were afraid, for very soon after they disappeared. I am informed by Mr. Cahill that he has seen, during the few months he has been in the district, over fifty natives affected in the same way.

In 1901, the Government Resident drew attention to the reduction in numbers of a tribe in the region (South Australian Government Resident's Report, 1901: Appendix: 17):

> Mr. Cahill reports of the Alligator Rivers tribe that of about 190 members who composed it seven or eight years ago, only about sixty survive, a large proportion of the deaths having been due to the leprosy.

In 1906 Cahill took out a pastoral lease in the Oenpelli area and in 1912 was host to Baldwin Spencer, the newly appointed Protector of Aborigines following the takeover of the Territory from South Australia by the Commonwealth Government. Spencer refers extensively to the Kakadu nation (Spencer, 1914:275-312) and some have assumed that Oenpelli is Kakadu country. Aborigines now living at Oenpelli, including the traditional owners, are adamant that this is not the case. They maintain that Cahill brought Kakadu people with him to Oenpelli when he settled there. Kakadu land is between the East and South Alligator rivers, from the escarpment towards the coast. Aboriginal people in the region have established the Gagudju Association to assist them in dealing with land matters and mining payments. Speakers of the language insisted that 'Gagudju' and not 'Kakadu' is the appropriate spelling.

In 1916 the Government took over Cahill's property to establish an experimental dairy and butter factory to supply the Darwin market, with Cahill as manager initially. For a variety of reasons the project never developed as planned, despite an apparently successful trial shipment. Following the end of the First World War there was considerable trouble on the Darwin waterfront and, when it was realised that the butter shipment came from an Aboriginal area, it was declared 'black' and allowed to melt on the wharf. The dairy and butter project never developed further.

Black and white relations at Oenpelli at this time were not as ideal as is sometimes claimed. The Northern Territory Administrator recorded an attempt to poison Cahill (Administrator's Report for 1915-16 and 1916-17:13-14):

> Mr. Cahill, than whom no-one knows the native more thoroughly (speaking as he does more than one dialect) nor views him more sympathetically, informs me that, in spite

> of the defection of Romula in attempting to poison him and his family, he would gladly have the Aboriginal back at once, trusting him as fully as he did in the past. He is satisfied the aberration manifested was solely due to the bad influence exercised for a time by the other native 'Nipper' and as Romula had been his close companion during twenty-five years of an adventurous career it may be assumed that Mr. Cahill thoroughly understands the moral temperament of the man.

THE RESERVES

In April 1920[5] the Oenpelli Reserve was proclaimed, with an area of about 5180 square kilometres. The East Alligator River was its western border. After the failure of the dairy project the Government turned to the churches and invited a number of agencies to establish a mission at Oenpelli. The invitation was accepted by the Church Missionary Society, which commenced work at Oenpelli in October 1925.

The Arnhem Land Reserve was proclaimed in April 1931[6] but, in effect, the land reserved was up to and adjacent to the Oenpelli Reserve. In 1963[7] the various reserves were revoked and reproclaimed as one big reserve. The issuing of a lease of 518 square kilometres to the Church Missionary Society in 1946 (and other mission leases elsewhere) was to cause legal complications in relation to the status of part of the reserve so that, prior to the enactment of the *Aboriginal Land Rights (Northern Territory) Act 1976*, it was necessary to make a special proclamation to cover land contained in various mission leases.[8]

The Woolwonga Reserve of 505 square kilometres is located in the South Alligator River-Nourlangie area. It was first proclaimed in 1936[9] and redefined in 1968.[10] It was also proclaimed a wildlife sanctuary in 1964.[11] An earlier Woolwonga Reserve was originally proclaimed in 1892[12] approximately 100 kilometres to the south-west.

NATIONAL PARK

The proposal to establish a National Park in the Alligator Rivers Region of the Northern Territory has a long history (Ranger Inquiry Report, 1977:199-203). In 1965 the Northern Territory Reserves Board proposed an area of 6410 square kilometres between the East and South Alligator Rivers for a National Park. This included the Woolwonga Aboriginal Reserve and land that was to become the Mudginberri and Munmalary pastoral leases. In 1967 various modified proposals were made which mainly sought some accommodation with conflicting interests.

In 1968 the Commonwealth Government asked Mr Sam Weems (a Parks Adviser to the United States Government) to visit the area and report on proposals. In 1971 a planning team was appointed to prepare a master plan. This was led by Mr J. Bosward of the New South Wales National Parks and Wildlife Service.

In 1972 a wildlife sanctuary was declared with similar boundaries to those of stage 1 of the National Park, excluding the coastal area. In May 1975 the Australian Government announced its intention to establish a National Park in the region. No action was taken in this matter until the completion of the Ranger Inquiry.

RANGER URANIUM DEPOSITS

In September 1969 Geopeko Limited was granted Authority to Prospect No. 2362 of 2489 square kilometres between the South and East Alligator Rivers, outside the Arnhem Land Reserve. This area became Exploration Licences 219 and 220 following changes to the Northern Territory mining laws in the early 1970s. Early in the exploration programme a number of anomalies were located south of Mudginberri

Station. Further work in the 1970 dry season established the existence of a uranium ore-body. There are extensive reserves of ore and operations will continue for more than 20 years. Peko Mines Limited and Electrolytic Zinc Co. of Australasia Ltd formed Ranger Uranium Mines Pty Ltd to develop the deposit.

The Ranger deposits are located about 220 kilometres east of Darwin. They are in the catchment area of the Magella Creek, which flows into the East Alligator River after passing across extensive flood plains. The project area is of 78.6 square kilometres and the project has special authorisation under section 41 of the *Atomic Energy Act*. In October 1975 a Memorandum of Understanding had been entered into between the joint venturers—the Commonwealth of Australia (Atomic Energy Commission), Peko-Wallsend Ltd, and Electrolytic Zinc Co. of Australasia Ltd for the development of the deposit.

In July 1975 the Australian Government appointed a commission to conduct an inquiry in relation to the proposal to develop uranium deposits in the Alligator Rivers Region of the Northern Territory. This commission became the Ranger Uranium Environmental Inquiry under section 11 of the *Environment Protection (Impact of Proposals) Act* 1974. Mr Justice Fox was Presiding Commissioner with Mr G.G. Kelleher and Professor C.B. Kerr, Commissioners. Public hearings of the Commission of Inquiry commenced in September 1975 and continued until March 1977. Evidence was received from 303 witnesses over 121 sitting days in Sydney, Melbourne, Brisbane, Adelaide, Darwin, Gove and Mudginberri.

In Sydney in August 1976 the Commission received formal 'final' submissions from seven 'principal parties'—Ranger Uranium Mines Pty Ltd, Pancontinental Mining Limited, the Australian Atomic Energy Commission, the Australian Conservation Foundation, the Conservation Trust of South Australia, the Friends of the Earth, the Northern Land Council, and the Oenpelli Council.

Both the Northern Land Council and the Oenpelli Council submitted that the Ranger mine site should be regarded as if it were on Aboriginal land, and that royalties should be payable to Aboriginal people to assist them to strengthen their traditional culture, to aid in the development of Aboriginal communities, and to assist in establishing outstations. There had been preliminary talks between the two councils in June but the submissions were prepared independently.

The Aboriginal Land Rights (Northern Territory) Bill was amended to specifically exlude Ranger from the consent provisions of the Bill and also to allow the Inquiry to consider the Aboriginal land claims in the area west of the reserve. The Inquiry then took expert evidence on the claims and in its second report (presented in May 1977) recommended that certain vacant Crown land should be granted to an Aboriginal Land Trust, and that this land should be leased as proposed by the Northern Land Council for a National Park.

The adoption of these recommendations by the Government in August 1977[13] meant that although the Ranger deposit was outside the Arnhem Land Aboriginal Reserve the Aborigines would be in a position to negotiate terms and conditions of mining, though they could not veto the development.

In late 1977 the Northern Land Council presented a draft agreement to the Commonwealth in respect of the Ranger development. The Commonwealth responded in May 1978, and negotiations commenced between the Northern Land Council (on behalf of the traditional owners and other Aboriginals affected) and the Commonwealth of Australia on the terms and conditions for the development of the Ranger uranium deposit. The agreement, concluded pursuant to section 44 of the *Aboriginal Land Rights (Northern Territory) Act* 1976, was signed at Oenpelli in November 1978. Ratification of the agreement had originally been given at a full meeting of the Northern Land Council in August, but certain Aborigines took out an injunction to prevent the signing, alleging inadequate consultation with affected communities. The injunction was withdrawn following a number of discussions between the claimants and the Northern Land Council Executive. The project is authorised under section 41 of the *Atomic Energy Act* 1953. A brief summary of the agreement is to be found in Appendix 1.

Construction of a temporary township in the project area and the treatment plant commenced in 1979 and will continue through 1981. The construction work force in the project area built up to approximately 1100 during the 1979 dry season and peaked at about 1200 in the 1980 dry. In May 1981 the number was 950, but this will decrease significantly through 1981. It is planned that production of yellowcake will commence in September 1981. The operational work force is approximately 350.

During 1979 the Commonwealth Government announced its intention of divesting itself of its 50% share in the Ranger project. The Ranger partners (Peko-Wallsend Ltd and Electrolytic Zinc Co. of Australasia Ltd) took over the Commonwealth's 50% share of the development and during 1980 established Energy Resources of Australia (ERA) to own and manage the Ranger project. Provision was made for both local and overseas investment in the new company.

KAKADU NATIONAL PARK

An integral part of the Government's decision on uranium was the establishment of the Kakadu National Park in the Alligator Rivers region. The negotiations between the Northern Land Council and the Commonwealth of Australia concerning the Ranger project proceeded at the same time as negotiations concerning a lease to the Australian National Parks and Wildlife Service. The Park was seen by the Ranger Inquiry as a buffer zone to protect the environment and Aboriginal interests in the region and to provide recreation outlets (with necessary controls) for the increasing number of people coming into the region.

The agreement for the National Park was signed at Oenpelli in November 1978. The Kakadu Aboriginal Trust granted a lease for a period of 100 years to the Director of the Australian National Parks and Wildlife Service *(National Parks and Wildlife Conservation Act* 1975). A brief summary of the agreement is to be found in Appendix 2 on pp. 353–54.

Stage 1 of the park was proclaimed in 1979. It is an area of approximately 6000 square kilometres between the East and South Alligator Rivers. Most of the area of stage 1 is south of the sealed Arnhem Highway. Exceptions are a relatively narrow strip stretching northwards to Cannon Hill and the Border Store area adjacent to the East Alligator River, and an area along the coast north of the former Mudginberri and Munmalary pastoral leases.

It is proposed that stage 2 will include the area of these two former pastoral leases resumed by the Commonwealth in 1979 (approximately 2000 square kilometres) with extensions westwards, providing a total area of approximately 7000 square kilometres. The lease area is the subject of a land claim, which was heard in 1980–81, and proclamation of stage 2 could follow negotiations between the land council, the parks service and government, once the outcome of the land claim is known.

The Jabiru regional town is within the Kakadu National Park but is not Aboriginal land. The mine sites at Ranger and Koongarra are within, but are not part of, the National Park but are Aboriginal land. The National Park has been established under Commonwealth legislation *(National Parks and Wildlife Conservation Act* 1975) to be operated and controlled by the National Parks and Wildlife Service. This reflects the wishes of the traditional owners and the Northern Land Council, as expressed during the negotiations with the Commonwealth.

The Northern Territory Government maintains that all National Parks in the Territory should be under the control of the Northern Territory Government, not a Commonwealth authority. In 1980 the Commonwealth Government nominated the Kakadu National Park for inclusion in the World Heritage List.[1]

JABIRU REGIONAL TOWN

This is situated about 10 kilometres from the Ranger mine site and is being developed by the Northern Territory Government through its specially created Jabiru Town Development Authority. The town is being constructed to provide accommodation for the employees at the Ranger mine and for the necessary government staff (both Commonwealth and Northern Territory). It was a recommendation of the Ranger Inquiry, accepted by the Government, that the town population should not exceed 3500.

The location of the town inside the National Park follows recommendations of the Ranger Inquiry. The Director of the National Parks and Wildlife Service will issue a lease to the Jabiru Town Development Authority for the town site. The terms and conditions of the lease depend on the Plan of Management for the Park. Until the Plan comes into effect the Director is authorised to issue licences for the carrying out of necessary work in the town. The Plan of Management came into effect in April 1981 and a lease is to be issued.

Construction commenced in 1979 and continued through 1980 and 1981 and into 1982. The first houses were completed in 1980 and were occupied by Ranger staff.

NABARLEK

In August 1969 Authority to Prospect No. 2046 was granted to an Adelaide woman (Mrs Stevens) who engaged Queensland Mines Limited to carry out an exploration programme. It was an area of 3320 square kilometres east of Oenpelli and inside the Arnhem Land Reserve. With the change in Northern Territory mining laws, this area became Exploration Licences 243, 244 and 245. Early in the exploration programme a number of anomalies were discovered by airborne survey and exploration work in the 1970 dry season indicated the richness of the Nabarlek ore-body. At one stage during the mineral boom of the 1970s it was claimed by some company officials that there were reserves of over 50 000 tonnes. Subsequent drilling led to a review of the reserve estimate to 10 000 tonnes, recently revised to approximately 12 000 tonnes.

Mr Justice Woodward presented some historical background to the Nabarlek situation (Aboriginal Land Rights Commission 1974: 117–24). He outlined aspects of the negotiations that had taken place between Queensland Mines, the Commonwealth Government and the Aboriginal people and stated (para 683:119):

> I have no hesitation in recommending that this is a case in which the Aboriginal view should prevail.

Mr Justice Woodward also recommended that mining development on Aboriginal land not occur without the consent of the Aboriginal land owners (para 708(ii):122):

> Aborigines should have the right to prevent exploration for them (i.e. minerals and petroleum) on their traditional lands.

Further (para 708(xxii):124):

> Queensland Mines Limited should not be permitted to develop mineral deposits in the Nabarlek area without Aboriginal consent.

During June 1974 the Prime Minister, Mr Gough Whitlam, visited the region having discussions at Oenpelli, Nabarlek and other places. In a very clear and direct manner the Prime Minister explained to the Oenpelli Council, the community and the traditional owners that Australia did not need to develop and mine the Nabarlek ore-body; there was sufficient uranium available elsewhere to meet Australia's commitments, and the ore-body would not be developed without the consent of the Aboriginal people.

It seems likely that in 1974, having had the support of both the Prime Minister and his specially appointed Land Rights Commissioner, Aborigines felt that they had made their point, that their opposition to mining was finally understood and that would be the end of the matter. But within a matter of weeks, Queensland Mines officials asked to come to Oenpelli for further talks about the development of Nabarlek. This incident highlights some of the differences between Aboriginal and European methods of decision-making. On the one hand, the Aborigines had maintained their opposition and finally told the highest authority in the land of their opposition, and this was accepted by him. On the other hand, for the mining companies this was only a statement of opinion and a basis for further negotiations and compromise if necessary.

As a result of the approach by Queensland Mines discussions began between Queensland Mines and the Aborigines leading to the negotiations later carried out by the Northern Land Council with Queensland Mines on behalf of the Nabarlek traditional owners. One can only speculate as to why the Aborigines concerned changed their attitude. My observation is that both the key members of the Oenpelli Council and the traditional owners of Nabarlek decided that opposition to the development of Nabarlek was futile and that development would occur sooner or later, irrespective of Aboriginal opinion (Carroll, 1978:7-8).

Negotiations between the Northern Land Council and Queensland Mines Ltd were held during 1978 and the main negotiations were completed by November. Some Aboriginals from Oenpelli and the Northern Land Council were pressing for early approval from the Minister for Aboriginal Affairs. The company was equally concerned to have early approval so that they could commence development as soon as possible and meet contractual obligations to supply yellowcake in 1980. It was envisaged that development would begin during the wet season, making it necessary to bring material in through the Wunyu Beach barge landing, not by road from Darwin across the East Alligator River. But the actual signing did not take place until late March 1979 because of necessary procedures under the *Aboriginal Land Rights Act* (See section 43(3)) and the *Environment Protection (Impact of Proposals) Act* 1974. A brief summary of the agreement is to be found in Appendix 3.

An early end to the 1978-79 wet season meant that road access was available almost immediately and the company was able to use the road and not the barge landing. Some traditional owners resident at Oenpelli and Goulburn Island maintain that they were not consulted about the use of access roads between Nabarlek and the barge landing and between Nabarlek and the East Alligator crossing. A group of traditional land owners of the country through which the road from the East Alligator River to Nabarlek passed took legal action against Queensland Mines, revoking permits and claiming that approval for the use of this road was neither sought nor given by them. The case was adjourned indefinitely following the announcement of proposed changes to the land rights legislation.

The amendments were introduced into Parliament in April 1980 were subsequently passed and received Royal Assent in May (No, 72 of 1980). There were two main purposes:

- to facilitate the registration of titles to Aboriginal land in the Northern Territory, and
- to provide for the security of agreements entered into between a land council and a miner.

It is the second purpose that is relevant here and the aim, as stated in the Minister's second reading speech, was:

> . . . to ensure that once an agreement has been concluded between a land council and a miner in accordance with procedures set out under the Act, both parties will be in a position to honour the agreement and will be bound by it. [14]

Special provision was made so that an agreement concluded between a land council and a miner cannot be invalidated on the grounds of non-compliance with the provisions of the Land Rights Act concerning consultation with traditional Aboriginal owners (sections 23 and 48). In his second reading speech, the Minister for Aboriginal Affairs, Senator Chaney, acknowledged the complex responsibilities of a land council, and the amendments included a specific provision requiring:

> . . . the Minister for Aboriginal Affairs to withhold his approval under Section 27 of the principal Act unless he is satisfied that the Land Council concerned has complied with any duty imposed on it by sub-section 23(3).[14]

Nabarlek is the only current uranium development located inside the Arnhem Land Reserve. The deposit is situated about 280 kilometres east of Darwin. It is close to tributaries of Coopers Creek, which enters the East Alligator River near its outlet to the sea. It is about 30 kilometres by road from Oenpelli. The project area is approximately 13 square kilometres in size and includes the mine site, as well as a small area at the Wunyu Beach barge landing on the north coast. Queensland Mines Limited holds Special Mineral Lease No. 94 under Northern Territory mining legislation.

The ore was excavated and stockpiled during 1979. Treatment of the ore and production of yellowcake commenced in 1980. The yellowcake was transported to Darwin by road during the 1980 dry season and by aircraft during the 1980–81 wet season.

JABILUKA

In August 1969 Air Navigators Pty Ltd was granted Authority to Prospect No. 2013 of 186 square kilometres between Mudginberri and the Border Store. This area was subsequently taken over by Pancontinental Mining Limited. This area was, like Ranger, outside the Arnhem Land Reserve and became Exploration Licence No. 12. The company also held a smaller area inside the reserve which became Exploration Licence No. 13, and was subsequently relinquished.

Jabiluka deposit is located 230 kilometres east of Darwin, within the catchment of the Magella Creek and on Mudginberri pastoral lease, 20 kilometres north of the Ranger deposits. The proposed project area covers approximately 105 square kilometres and the company has applied for mining and other leases. There are extensive ore reserves and mining operations could continue for more than 20 years.

Intensive exploratory drilling was commenced in 1971. Concentration was on areas of land adjacent to the sandstone escarpment. (Each of the proven ore-bodies in the Uranium Province is relatively close to the escarpment.) The exploration programme proved the Jabiluka 1 ore-body in 1972 and the Jabiluka 2 ore-body in 1973. The No.

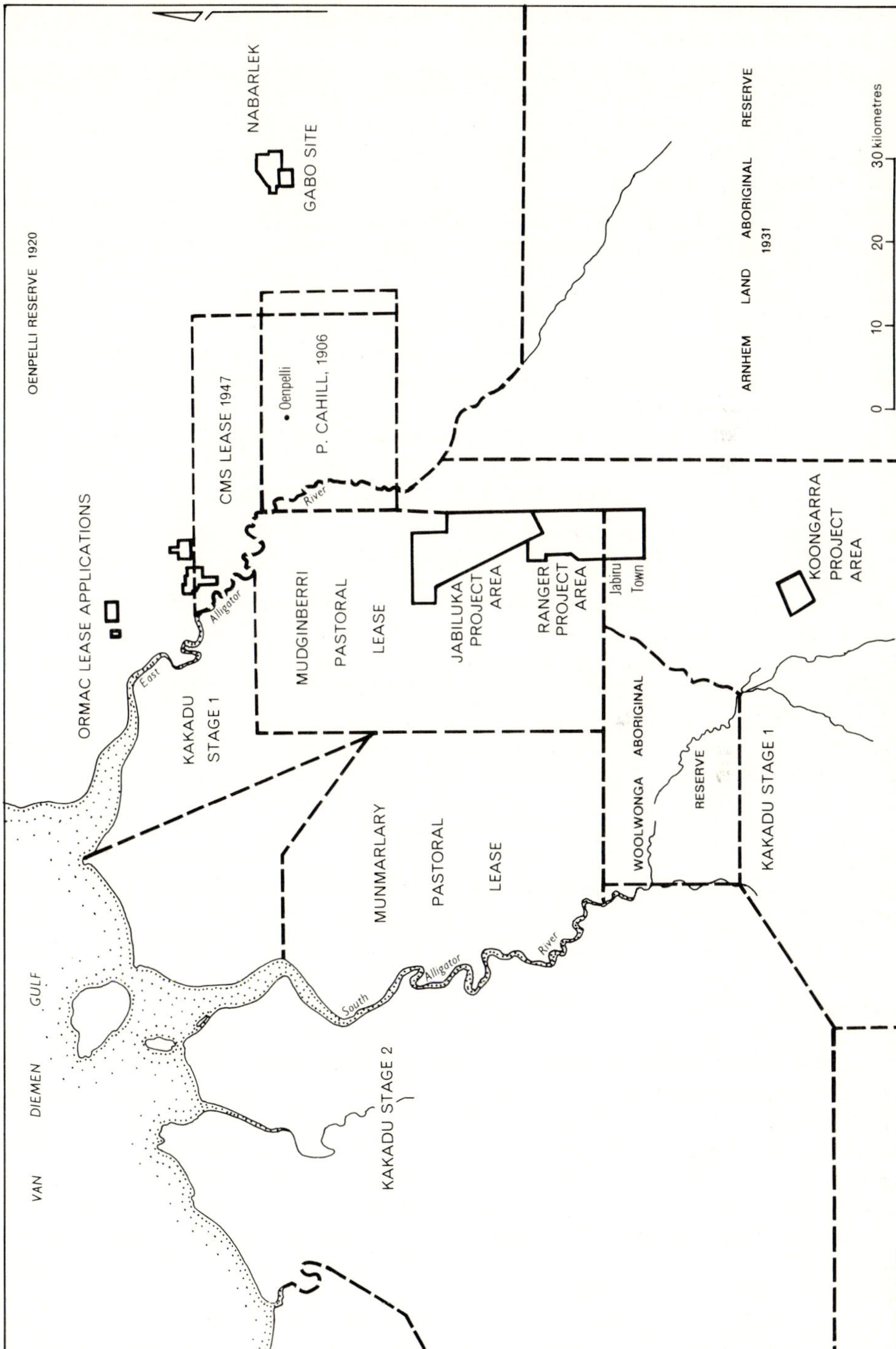

Fig. 1
Lease areas.

2 ore-body contains gold-bearing uranium ore which Pancontinental proposes to extract and market. Finance has been provided by Getty Oil of America and the development proposals for Jabiluka are a joint venture between Pancontinental Mining Limited and Getty Oil Development Company Limited.

The Ranger Inquiry received evidence from Pancontinental and made some comment on the project, recommending generally that there should be a sequential development if projects other than Ranger were approved. The Government did not accept this recommendation and decided it would not be appropriate to specify the sequence of mining either as to order or timing, but noted that the environmental requirements and procedures set down, as well as the processes of negotiation which must be carried on between the mining companies and Aboriginal land-owners, would in fact lead to any development being of a sequential nature.

In December 1977 the Jabiluka Project Draft Environmental Impact Statement (Pancontinental, 1977) was released. It proposed open cut mining of the two ore-bodies with the larger pit being approximately 1000 metres wide and 1600 metres long with a depth of 300 metres. The development would have included extensive dams and ponds as well as massive waste rock dumps all in the narrow corridor between the Magella flood plain and the sandstone escarpment. The tailings dam would have covered 192 hectares and been approximately 2000 metres long and 1400 metres wide. The waste rock dumps would have covered an area of approximately 250 hectares with a final height of about 125 metres.

In the Final Environmental Impact Statement (Pancontinental, 1979) the company changed its proposals significantly and met many of the objections raised against the Draft Impact Statement. The new proposal involved under ground mining with return of tailings to the mine shafts. The ore would be taken by conveyor to the treatment plant over a distance of approximately 8 kilometres.

The tailings dam will be adjacent to the treatment plant and will cover an area of 182 hectares. It would be about 2 kilometres in length and 1.5 kilometres at its greatest width and in the final stage the wall will reach a height of 30 metres.

After considering the statement the Minister for Science and the Environment recommended that the project should not be approved unless certain conditions are satisfied. These include additional design and operational information, further environmental investigations, satisfactory arrangements with the Northern Land Council concerning consultation with Aboriginals as well as acceptable environmental requirements. Considerable progress has been made in meeting these conditions. Discussions between the Commonwealth and Northern Territory governments concerning the environmental requirements for the Jabiluka project are at an advanced stage. Both the Commonwealth and Northern Territory governments need to be satisfied that, having regard to the total land of activity in the region as a whole, the impact on the environment and on the Aboriginals is acceptable.

The location of the Jabiluka project area is outside the former Arnhem Land Aboriginal Reserve. The additional land that was declared Aboriginal land in 1978 following the Ranger Inquiry's recommendations on the Alligator Rivers Land Claim Stage 1 brought Aboriginal land closer to, but still separate from, the ore-body.

Pancontinental had applied for leases for some of their project area prior to June 1976 and, if the land claim is successful, are in part protected from the current provisions of the Land Rights Act, but this does not apply to the whole project area.

An important recommendation of the Ranger Inquriy was that the Mudginberri and Munmalary pastoral leases be resumed by the Commonwealth Government for inclusion in the National Park and that the Northern Land Council be able to lodge a land claim on behalf of the traditional land-owners. If the claim is successful the Jabiluka project area would be on Aboriginal land and, once the environmental requirements were met and government approval to proceed given, it would be necessary for the company to negotiate with the Northern Land Council.

The Alligator Rivers Stage II Land Claim was heard between October 1980 and March 1981. At the time of writing (April 1981) the Aboriginal Land Commissioner (Mr Justice Toohey) is preparing his report to the Minister for Aboriginal Affairs. During the course of the hearing the Northern Land Council announced that the traditional owners had given approval for talks with Pancontinental to commence.[15] The company had supported the claim made by the Land Council on behalf of the traditional owners to land in the Jabiluka area.

During 1982 it was announced that the land claim was successful in part only. Land belonging to the Mirarr and Bunidj clans on the eastern side of the claim were recommended for granting as Aboriginal land. These areas include the Jabiluka project area. Title for the land of the Project area was presented to Toby Gangale by Senator Kilgariff in June, 1982. Toby is a key traditional owner for the area and leader of the Jabiluka Land Trust.

The agreement between the Northern Land Council, on behalf of the traditional owners, and Pancontinental Mining Limited for the development of the Jabiluka uranium deposit was finalised in July 1982, and subsequently a mining lease was issued to Pancontinental by the Northern Territory Minister for Mines in August.

KOONGARRA

Noranda Australia Limited was granted Authority to Prospect No. 1964 of 699 square kilometres in the Nourlangie Creek area in June 1968 outside the Arnhem Land Reserve. This became Exploration Licence No. 281 with the change of Northern Territory mining laws in the early 1970s. The Koongarra anomaly was located by airborne survey in the 1969 dry season. Further exploration and drilling proved an economic ore-body.

The Koongarra deposit is located approximately 225 kilometres east of Darwin close to Nourlangie Rock. It is about 25 kilometres south of the Ranger deposits. The proposed project area covers approximately 10.5 square kilometres. A Special Mineral Lease has been applied for. Koongarra is a relatively small ore-body with reserves of approximately 12 000 tonnes with mining proposed for a period of about 10 years. The project area is on the Aboriginal land that was granted in 1978 following the land claim heard by the Ranger Inquiry. This land has been leased as the Kakadu National Park but the Park lease excludes the Koongarra Project Area.

Noranda had applied for mineral leases for some of their project area prior to June 1976 and in part is protected from the consent provisions of the Land Rights Act but this does not apply to the whole project area. Noranda released its Draft Environmental Impact Statement in December 1978 (Noranda, 1978) and submitted a Final Environmental Impact Statement in November 1979 (Noranda, 1979).

In 1980 Denison Australia Ltd (100% Canadian owned) bought the Koongarra prospect from Noranda Australia Ltd. In January 1981 the Northern Land Council announced that initial approval had been received from the traditional owners of land in the Koongarra project area. Instructions were given that the Council begin formal negotiations with the company.[16]

Complications have arisen because Denison wishes to modify the boundaries of the project area that had been previously established by Noranda. The Aboriginal people are not happy with this variation and discussions between the Northern Land Council and Denison Mining are continuing.

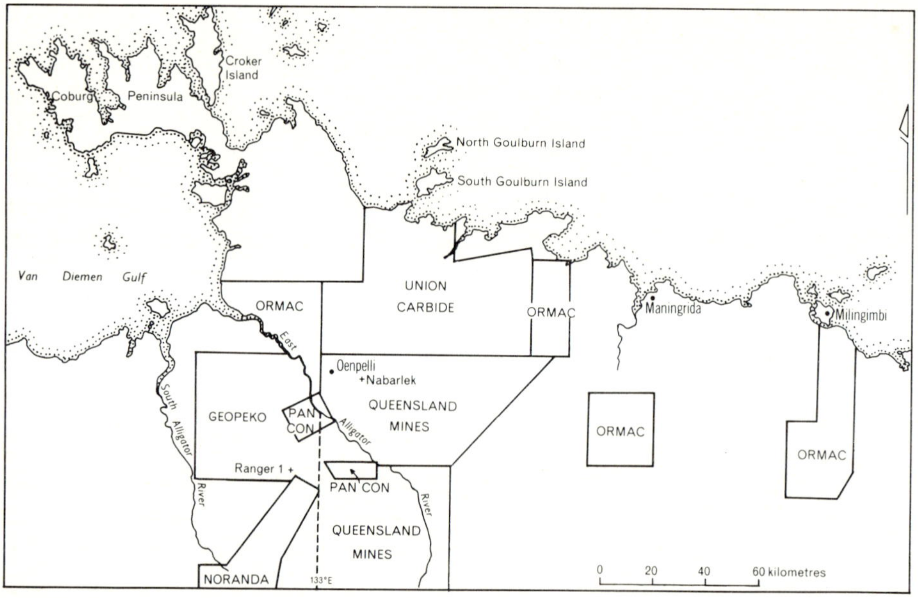

Fig. 2
Mining exploration areas, c.1970.

ORMAC

In November 1970 a group of Aborigines from Goulburn Island was granted Authority to Prospect No. 2859 of 1554 square kilometres within the Arnhem Land Reserve. This was for two separate areas, one south of Goulburn Island and the other north-west of Oenpelli. Aboriginal groups at Maningrida and Milingimbi also held Authorities to Prospect for country south of their respective communities and joined with the Goulburn Island group to participate with the ORMAC consortium in 1971. ORMAC is a consortium of companies including Ocean Resources, Pancontinental, Canadian Superior, and MacIntyre Mines. Membership of the consortium has varied from year to year. After twelve months all areas were relinquished, except the one closest to Oenpelli and nearest the Uranium Province. This area became Exploration Licence No. 130.

The Aboriginal participants in the Joint Venture held Exploration Licence No. 130 which covered country north-west of Oenpelli between the East Alligator River and Coopers Creek (1018 square kilometres). The exploration Licence has expired and applications were made in November 1976 and in May 1977 for a total of 76 mineral leases. Aboriginal progress associations at Goulburn Island, Maningrida and Murwangi (Ramangining) are partners in the Joint Venture with ORMAC. Generally, the traditional owners of the land involved live at Oenpelli and Croker Island and were not directly involved as participants in the Joint Venture. In recent years they have refused permission for further exploration work.

Ocean Resources, an exploration company and one of the companies in the ORMAC consortium, negotiated directly with individual Aborigines and Aboriginal communities in Arnhem Land. The first agreement for mineral exploration was signed in July 1971 (Ocean Resources, 1971). The mineral lease applications were made in November 1976 and May 1977 so that the consent provisions of the land rights legislation do apply.

FURTHER MINERAL EXPLORATION

At the time of the Woodward Land Commission Inquiry a 'freeze' had been placed on the granting of exploration licences for Aboriginal land. Applications were received by the then Mines Branch of the Department of the Northern Territory, but were not processed. This freeze was continued by the Northern Territory Government after July 1978. By 1981 several hundred applications for exploration licences were held by the Northern Territory Department for Mines and Energy in respect of Aboriginal land. If there are competing applications for the same area of land the Department makes an assessment to determine the most suitable applicant. The Northern Territory Mining Act provides various procedures to be followed in processing applications. These procedures include newspaper advertisements, and during 1981 such advertisements have appeared for applications in the Alligator River locality.[17] When the Department has chosen the most suitable applicant and completed the necessary procedures the applicant is referred to the land council, which must consult the traditional Aboriginal owners and any other Aborigines interested in the land applied for.

By mid 1982 the Northern Land Council had been asked to process 54 such applications for exploration licences.

CONCLUSION

The Aboriginal land rights legislation of the Commonwealth Government established land councils in the Northern Territory with responsibilities for Aboriginal land. Much of the pressure for mineral development is in the area of the Northern Land Council, and it has been acknowledged that the Council has not had adequate resources to effectively carry out its responsibilities. Legal action by two different groups of Aborigines who claimed inadequate consultation by the Northern Land Council concerning both the Nabarlek and Ranger agreements indicates something of the problem. A management consultant has been appointed to work with the Land Council for twelve months to effect a reorganisation. In April 1981 recruitment of six senior management positions in the reorganised bureau of the Northern Land Council had commenced. By mid 1982 the bureau had a staff of 65 working at the direction of the Northern Land Council which comprises 51 Aboriginal members. Strong and effective land councils are vital for the long-term protection of Aboriginal land interests.

ACKNOWLEDGEMENTS

The comments and suggestions made by Messrs J. Long, J. Wauchope and W. J. Gray of the Department of Aboriginal Affairs are gratefully acknowledged.

APPENDIX 1

AGREEMENT BETWEEN THE NORTHERN LAND COUNCIL AND THE COMMONWEALTH OF AUSTRALIA CONCERNING THE RANGER URANIUM PROJECT

Summary

1. *Environmental Aspects* (clauses 5, 6, 8 and 9)
   — The Joint Venturers have agreed with the Commonwealth to observe all environmental requirements specified or imposed by law.

— 'Best practicable technology' as defined, shall be employed in the design of the plant and mine, and in the mining, milling and related operations.

— The Commonwealth is to arrange for health monitoring programs which will continue for as long as the authority conducting them considers them to be effective.

2. *Liaison* (clauses 10 and 11)

— The Joint Venturers are to provide for the formation of an Aboriginal Liaison Committee; members shall be the mine manager, one person appointed by the Manager and two appointed by the Northern Land Council.

— Functions of the Committee are primarily:

- to receive and hear representations of local Aboriginals on the one hand, or by an employee, agent, or contractor of the Commonwealth or the Joint Venturers on the other;
- to make recommendations to the Manager as to which Aboriginals are available for employment; the Manager will not employ any Aboriginal without first consulting the Committee.

3. *Employment and Training* (clause 12)

— The Commonwealth shall require the Joint Venturers to ensure that

- as many local Aboriginals as is practicable are employed where those Aboriginals are capable of carrying out in a satisfactory manner the particular work required;
- an 'operator training scheme' for Aboriginals be established with a view to the Manager employing trained Aboriginals;
- by agreement with the Northern Land Council further employment training schemes are sponsored;
- all practical steps are taken to adjust working hours and conditions to suit the needs and culture of Aboriginal employees, through consultation between the Joint Venturers, the Northern Land Council and trade unions;
- working conditions for Aboriginals shall be as for any other workers under the appropriate awards in force in the Northern Territory.

4. *Local Business Development* (clause 13)

— The Commonwealth shall support, encourage and advise local Aboriginals wishing to establish enterprises and businesses for the purpose of providing goods and services to the Joint Venturers.

— The Commonwealth shall require the Joint Venturers to make maximum use of Aboriginal subcontractors where their goods and services are competitive. The Joint Venturers, however, shall not be required to employ any subcontractor unless the subcontractor is capable of carrying out the work in a satisfactory manner and work is available.

— The Commonwealth shall require the Joint Venturers to ensure that appropriate training facilities are made available where skills are not sufficient for the satisfactory performance of subcontracting tasks, if the circumstances reasonably so require.

5. *Control of Liquor* (clause 14)

— The Commonwealth shall ensure that no liquor is brought onto, or sold or consumed within, the Ranger Project area, except through the Jabiru Sports and Social Club and subject to the rules detailed in the agreement.

6. *Rights of Traditional Owners* (clause 16)
   — Traditional rights to use and occupation of land may be exercised subject only to specified restraints to avoid interference with the Project.
7. *Sacred Sites* (clause 17)
   — Commonwealth to act to protect any sites not adequately protected by legislation, on NLC request.
8. *Instruction in Aboriginal Culture* (clause 18)
   — Commonwealth and Joint Venturers to promote 'knowledge, understanding and respect for the traditions, languages and culture of the Aboriginal people' among employees and contractors, in consultation with NLC.
9. *Review and Term of Agreement* (clauses 20 and 21)
   — Every five years the parties shall meet to discuss the operation of the Agreement and may agree to changes.
   — The Agreement to continue for 26 years unless sooner terminated, renewed or extended.
10. *Payments* (clauses 3 and 25; annexure B)
   — Agreed amounts to be paid by the Commonwealth to the NLC on signing of the Agreement and when the project is authorised and at designated stages of the construction.
   — Additional annual amounts of $200,000 to be paid during the currency of the Agreement.
   — Amounts of up to $150,000 annually for the first four years to meet NLC costs associated with the Ranger Project.
   — Payments in the nature of royalties at 4¼ per cent to be made to the Aboriginals Benefit Trust Account for distribution in accordance with the Act: Land Councils (40%), communities affected by the Project (30%) and Aboriginals in the Northern Territory generally (30%).

APPENDIX 2

KAKADU NATIONAL PARK: AGREEMENT BETWEEN THE NORTHERN LAND COUNCIL (NLC) AND THE DIRECTOR, NATIONAL PARKS AND WILDLIFE SERVICE (NPWS) FOR LEASING OF ABORIGINAL LAND AS NATIONAL PARK

Summary

1. *Employment and Training*
   — NPWS will run a programme for local Aboriginals to train them in the necessary skills to assist in the management and control of the Park.
   — NPWS will employ as many of the traditional owners as practicable in the running of the Park.
   — Where possible, working times and conditions will be changed to suit the needs and culture of the Aboriginal workers.

— NPWS will endeavour to make use of the traditional skills of Aboriginals residing in the Park.

2. *Aboriginal Sacred Sites, and Instruction in Aboriginal Culture*
   — NPWS will help the NLC to identify and record Aboriginal sacred sites and it will provide equipment and facilities to do this.
   — NPWS will promote among non-Aboriginals living in the area knowledge, understanding and respect for Aboriginal traditions, language and culture.
   — NPWS will arrange instruction for non-Aboriginal people on local customs, geography, plants and animals, where possible by Aboriginals.

3. *Traditional Aboriginal owners*
   — Traditional Aboriginal owners will be able to enter and move freely in Kakadu National Park except for some restricted areas which NPWS may designate after consulting with, and having regard to the views of, the NLC.
   — Traditional owners may bring into or use in the Park any vehicle, boat or aircraft subject only to reasonable conditions.

4. *Consultation*
   — NPWS must consult with the NLC about the management plan for the Park; NLC will consult with the traditional owners.
   — NLC has agreed if any 'Kakadu Stage 2' land becomes Aboriginal land, it will be leased to NPWS on the same conditions.
   — NLC and NPWS will make available to each other all information and reports they have on the area except specific material that must be kept secret.
   — Duly authorised officers of the NLC may enter and move freely in the Park while on NLC business and will observe any reasonable directions concerning the use of any vehicle, boat or aircraft.

APPENDIX 3

AGREEMENT BETWEEN QUEENSLAND MINES LIMITED (QML) AND THE NORTHERN LAND COUNCIL ABOUT MINING AT NABARLEK

Summary

1. *Protection and Rehabilitation of the Environment* (clause 13)
   — QML must do all things required by the Government to protect the environment.
   — QML will backfill the opencut mines after mining and milling is finished; all the affected land will be returned as near as possible to its natural state, except the airstrip, access roads, and areas with facilities acquired by the Northern Land Council.
   — QML will use all reasonable means to make sure no non-Aboriginal under its control obtains access to Aboriginal sites of significance, without proper permission; QML will put up signs and fencing around Aboriginal sites if the Advisory Committee (see below) thinks it necessary.
2. *Safety and Health* (clause 16)
   — QML will follow all the statutory safety and health rules.

— All Aboriginal and non-Aboriginal workers will have medical examinations before starting, and during their employment.

— QML will give free medical treatment to all their workers, their families and any NLC officers doing work related to the Project.

3. *Liaison* (clause 17)

— An Advisory Committee to be established with representatives from QML (including the Resident Manager), the NLC and the traditional owners; non-members can be invited only as observers or spokesmen.

— Some of the functions of the Committee will be to:
- liaise between QML and local Aboriginals;
- review the Agreement as necessary;
- decide upon Aboriginal applicants for employment with QML on the Project;
- make recommendations about any workers not following the rules in the Agreement.

4. *Employment and Training* (clause 14)

— QML will employ as many local Aboriginals as practicable providing they can do the work or they can be trained to do it in a satisfactory way.

— QML will establish an 'Operator Training Scheme' and provide later 'on the job' training and employment on the Project.

— QML will make sure that all non-Aboriginal workers are told about Aboriginal history and culture.

— QML will try to adjust working times and conditions of its Aboriginal workers to suit the local Aboriginal way of life, and QML and the NLC will try to get the trade unions to agree to this; but except as agreed, conditions of work will be the same as for other workers under awards.

5. *Local Business Development* (clause 15)

— QML will help and encourage local Aboriginals who want to provide goods and services to the Project and will help Aboriginals who want to start a business for that reason.

— QML will make maximum use of Aboriginal subcontractors provided they are competitive with other subcontractors on price, etc.

— Together with the NLC, QML will prepare and review a 'business development program' for Aboriginal businesses.

6. *Social Club* (clause 18)

— The Social Club will be able to sell beer for drinking at the Club only.

— During the Project construction period, QML must do everything reasonable to stop alcohol going onto Aboriginal land unless permission has been given.

— QML will provide a recreation area including a swimming pool, tennis court and outdoor movies for use of all local people as well as QML workers.

7. *Permits to enter Aboriginal Land* (clause 9)

— NLC will be responsible for issuing entry permits, and will not refuse or delay permits to persons employed on the Project unless there is a good reason.

— If anyone with a permit breaks the rules, the Aboriginal members of the Advisory Committee can tell the NLC to take the permit away; the Advisory

Committee can recommend that the person breaking the rules be removed from the Project area, if the Committee thinks the matter is serious enough.

— The NLC has the right to inspect land used by the Project; for safety reasons a QML officer must go with the NLC officer if the mine site or the mill are to be inspected.

8. *Roads and Buildings, etc.* (clause 10)

— QML will build (or improve) and maintain access roads, an airstrip, a barge landing, water supply, housing (including an Aboriginal Permanent Camp) for the Project.

— When milling has finished, QML will leave many of these roads and buildings, etc., for the use of the NLC and the Aboriginal people without payment.

— Local Aboriginals, and the NLC will be allowed to use the main roads, the airstrip and the barge landing site so long as this does not interfere with the running of the Project, or cause too many costs or interference with the environment.

9. *Payments* (clause 4)

— Agreed payments to be made by QML to the NLC on approval of agreement and after mining titles were granted, and annually thereafter in the 'construction and mining' phase and in varying amounts in the 'operational' phase; these payments to be divided between the traditional owners and others interested in the Project area (mine and barge landing sites) on the one hand, and the traditional owners of land generally affected by the Project on the other.

— Payments equivalent to royalties of 2½ per cent to be paid to the Aboriginals Benefit Trust Account for distribution in accordance with the Act between Land Councils (40 per cent), communities affected by the Project (30 per cent) and Aboriginals in the Northern Territory generally (30 per cent).

— Royalties and additional payments combined to amount to approximately 4½ per cent of the value of the uranium.

(*NOTE*: Under the terms of the Act (ss 16, 35(4)) mineral lease rentals are paid by the Crown to land councils to be paid to traditional owners of the land.)

NOTES

1. Australian National Parks and Wildlife Service, 1980
2. C. White (1967, vol. I: 188, 251); Kamminga & Allen (1973: iv, v).
3. Kerr (1971): 16–20, 27–28); Bauer (1964: 52–57).
4. Personal communication.
5. *Commonwealth of Australia Gazette* No. 36 of 22 April 1920, p.595.
6. *Commonwealth of Australia Gazette* No. 33 of 16 April 1931, p.643.
7. *Commonwealth of Australia Gazette* No. 95 of 7 November 1963, p.3871.
8. *Commonwealth of Australia Gazette* No. G50 of 14 December 1976, p.2.
9. *Commonwealth of Australia Gazette* No. 95 of 3 December 1936, p.2177.
10. *Commonwealth of Australia Gazette* No. 60 of 4 July 1968, p.3654.
11. In the Fourth Schedule of the *Wildlife Conservation and Control Ordinance* 1964 (No. 60 of 1964).
12. *South Australian Government Gazette* No. 19 of 28 April 1892, p.940.
13. Commonwealth of Australia 1977.
14. Australian Senate 1980, p.1364.

15. *Northern Territory News (Darwin)*, 28 January 1981.
16. *Northern Territory News (Darwin)*, 23 January 1981.
17. *Northern Territory News (Darwin)*, 23, 25, 26 March 1981.

REFERENCES

Aboriginal Land Rights Commission (A.E. Woodward, Commissioner). *Second Report April 1974*. Canberra, Australian Government Publishing Service, 1974.

Australian National Parks and Wildlife Service. *Nomination of Kakadu National Park for inclusion in the World Heritage List*. Canberra, Australian National Parks and Wildlife Service, 1980.

Australia Senate. *Commonwealth of Australia Parliamentary Debates, Weekly Hansard, No. 6, 2 April 1980*. Canberra, Australian Government Publishing Service, 1980.

Bauer, F.N. *Historical Geography of White Settlement in part of Northern Australia. Pt 2. The Katherine-Darwin Region*. Canberra, CSIRO, 1964.

Carroll, P.J. *'Uranium Mining: an Oenpelli viewpoint'*. Darwin, Nungalinya College, 1978. Nungalinya Occasional Bulletin No. 1.

Commonwealth of Australia, Northern Territory. *Report of the Administrator for the Years 1915–1916 and 1916–1917*. Melbourne, Government Printer, 1918.

Commonwealth of Australia. *Uranium—Australia's Decision*. Canberra, Australian Government Publishing Service, 1977.

Kamminga, J. & Allen, H. *Alligator Rivers Environmental Fact Finding Study — report of the archaeological survey*. Darwin, 1973. (mimeo).

Kerr, M.G. *The Surveyors*. Adelaide, Rigby, 1971.

Leichhardt, L. *Journal of an Overland Expedition in Australia*. London, T. & W. Boone, 1847.

McKinlay, J. *McKinlay's Northern Territory Explorations, 1866*. Adelaide, South Australian Government Printer, 1866. (South Australian Parliamentary Paper No. 82).

Noranda. *Koongarra Project—Draft Environmental Impact Statement*. Melbourne, Noranda Australia Ltd, 1979.

Noranda. *Koongarra Project—Supplement to Draft Environmental Impact Statement*. Noranda Australia Ltd, 1978.

Ocean Resources NL. *First Annual Report and Notice of Meeting 1971*. Brisbane. Ocean Resources, 1971.

Pancontinental Mining Ltd. *The Jabiluka Project Draft Environmental Impact Statement*. Sydney, Pancontinental, 1977.

Pancontinental Mining Ltd. *The Jabiluka Project Environmental Impact Statement* (3 vols). Sydney, Pancontinental, 1979.

Ranger Uranium Environmental Inquiry (R.W. Fox). *Second Report*. Canberra, Australian Government Publishing Service, 1977.

South Australia. *Government Resident's Report on the Northern Territory for the year 1894*. Adelaide, Government Printer, 1895.

South Australia. *Government Resident's Report on the Northern Territory, 1901*. Adelaide, Government Printer, 1902.

Spencer, B. *Native Tribes of the Northern Territory of Australia*. London, McMillan, 1914.

Spillett, P.G. *An Illustrated History of the Settlement of Victoria, Port Essington, North Australia 1838–1848*. Melbourne, Lansdowne, 1972.

White, C. *Plateau and Plain: Prehistoric Investigations in Arnhem Land, Northern Territory*. (2 vols). PhD Thesis, Australian National University, Canberra, 1967.

24

THE EFFECTS ON ABORIGINAL COMMUNITIES OF MONIES PAID OUT UNDER THE RANGER AND NABARLEK AGREEMENTS

Sue Kesteven

The Ranger agreement[1] and the Nabarlek agreement[2] are the first mining agreements to have been negotiated with Aborigines since the passing of the *Aboriginal Land Rights (Northern Territory) Act* 1976[3], and hence royalty rates in these two agreements differ from those in previous agreements in that they are negotiated and not merely statutory. Much publicity has been given to the fact that Aborigines will be receiving sums of money as a result of signing agreements with mining companies for the mining of uranium ore in the Alligator Rivers region. Comments centre on the large sums of money which will be received by people popularly seen by the press as having a Stone Age technology.[4] Opponents of land rights have also used the payment of money to Aborigines as evidence of Aborigines receiving favoured treatment.

This paper is based on two years' fieldwork in the Alligator Rivers region,[5] as part of a project to monitor the social impact of uranium mining on Aboriginal communities in the Northern Territory. Financial matters are only one of the fields of study of the project, but many things hinge on money. Facts mentioned in this paper derive from personal observations, conversations with people, reportings from Aboriginal co-workers and information collected during four censuses (dry seasons: August 1979, November 1980; wet seasons: February 1980, April 1981).

At the time this paper was originally written,[6] there had been very little serious examination of the amounts of money which had been disbursed to Aborigines under mining agreements, and of the uses to which this money has been put.[7] As to the Ranger and Nabarlek agreements, there had been no examination of the structures which were created to channel the sums of money, nor of the failings of these structures.

It is not possible at this stage to disclose the financial clauses of the Nabarlek agreement since the signatories to that agreement, Queensland Mines Limited and the Northern Land Council, will not agree. The Ranger agreement, however, is a public document so the financial details are readily available. But in both cases there are difficulties in discussing sums of money which individuals have received as Aborigines understandably consider this to be their own business and nobody else's.[8] 'Large' and 'small' obviously, however, do not adequately describe the sums. The advertised 'millions' certainly have been greatly exaggerated and it can be said that most beneficiaries have received less than $3000 in the two and a half years since the Ranger Agreement was signed.

BRIEF SUMMARY OF THE FORMAL ECONOMY OF THE REGION

As is typical of most Aboriginal settlements and reserves, the formal economy of the Alligator Rivers region is very lop-sided, the value of imports far exceeding exports. The formal economy depends to a large extent on government grants of various sorts. Employment can be found at settlements with councils, schools, health centres, etc, and more recently in the Alligator Rivers region with the Australian National Parks and Wildlife Service and with mining companies. The mining companies have not proved to be popular sources of employment among Aborigines of the immediate area.

At present there is only a limited opportunity for small-scale private enterprises in the region; these centre on buffalo shooting and cattle raising and abattoirs, and tourist-oriented occupations such as safari guides or the making of artifacts and bark paintings. This, very briefly, is the background to the formal economy of the Alligator Rivers region.

Now, for the first time in the area, with the export of yellowcake starting, substantial amounts of money are coming in which are completely at the disposal of Aborigines, to do with as they like, and which are not tied to particular projects.

However, it should be stated at the outset that at the time of writing no actual royalties have been paid out to Aboriginal communities. To date (April 1981) some money has been paid out to Aboriginal communities under clauses in the agreements made with Ranger and with Queensland Mines; these monies are referred to as 'up-front monies' and do not pass through the Aboriginal Benefit Trust Account. The amounts are not large. Royalties are not expected in the case of Ranger Uranium Mines Pty Ltd until 1982, and in the case of Queensland Mines Ltd at Nabarlek until mid 1981. However, up front monies from Nabarlek are offset against royalties. Thus royalties will not be paid to groups who receive up-front monies from this agreement until the value of royalties exceeds the amount of up-front monies paid out.

All up-front monies deriving from these agreements pass through the Northern Land Council for disbursement to Aboriginal bodies. A major point in any discussion of the effects of mining revenues on Aboriginal communities must be that all structures evolved for the purpose of dealing with such revenues have been imposed on Aboriginal communities from the outside. The complexity of the structures would be great enough in any case, but to add to the problems different agreements have been drawn up for the two companies which have received the go-ahead. There is little in parallel between the financial clauses of the Queensland Mines and the Ranger agreements.

PAYMENTS TO ABORIGINES FROM RANGER[9]

The agreement made between the Commonwealth of Australia and the Northern Land Council with respect to the Ranger Uranium Project specifies that the Commonwealth shall pay the Northern Land Council $200 000 annually during the currency of the agreement, and that the Commonwealth shall also pay the Council $1 300 000 as follows:

- $200 000 within 7 days after the execution of the agreement,
- $200 000 within 30 days after the date of issue of the Authority,
- $300 000 within 30 days after the date on which the last pour of concrete for the primary crusher concrete structure at the truck tipping level is made,
- $300 000 within 30 days after the completion of commissioning of the power generation plant,
- $300 000 within 30 days after the date on which the total quantity of U_3O_8 in uranium concentrates produced in the first treatment plant to be constructed in the Ranger Project Area reaches:
  (i) 500 tonnes of U_3O_8 in uranium concentrates of designated specification, or
  (ii) 1000 tonnes of U_3O_8 in marketable uranium concentrates, whichever is earlier.

(These latter sums are specified in section 3.2 of the agreement.) In addition, the

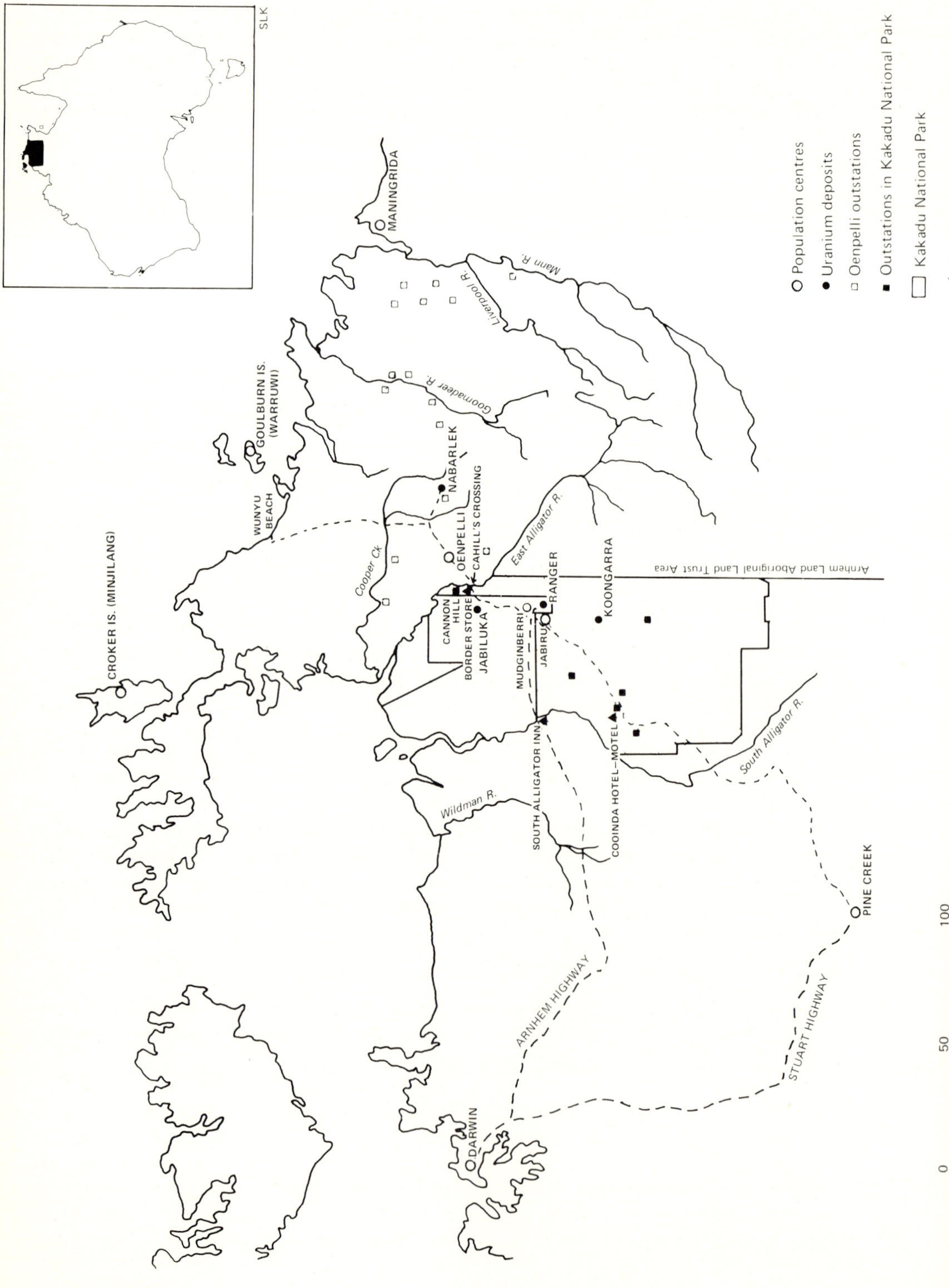

Fig. 1
The Alligator Rivers region

Commonwealth is to pay the Northern Land Council $150 000 annually for four years to meet administrative costs in relation to the functions of the Council in relation to the Ranger project. Royalty payments have been fixed at 4¼% of the production value and are made up of a 2½% statutory royalty and a 1¾% negotiated royalty.

The agreement does not specify how up-front monies are to be distributed; this is specified by section 35(3) of the Land Rights Act:

> Moneys paid to a Land Council under an agreement made under section 43 or 44 shall be applied by the Land Council in accordance with the agreement or, if the agreement makes no provision in relation to the application of the moneys, shall be paid to—
>
> (a) Aboriginal Councils of the Aboriginals in the areas which are affected by the agreement; and
>
> (b) any incorporated Aboriginal communities or groups the members of which are affected by the agreement, in such proportions as the Land Council determines.

The Northern Land Council determined in December 1978 that 'the Kakadu Land Trust No. 2 be registered as a trustee for the traditional owners of the Kakadu Region and that the beneficial interest in the Kakadu Land Trust be held by such traditional owners, and that it becomes an incorporated association'. The Northern Land Council also directed that the $1 300 000 up-front money should be transferred to this Trust as it is received by the Council.

STRUCTURES ESTABLISHED TO CHANNEL RANGER MONEY

The incorporated association set up to receive the up-front monies from the Ranger agreement was the Gagudju Association. It was finally incorporated under the *Associations Incorporation Act (Northern Territory)* 1978 in September 1980 although it had been functioning since October 1979.

Adult land owners of the 'Kakadu Region' are members of the Gagudju Association; children who own land in the area are beneficiaries also, but cannot become members until they are 18 years old. The business and management of the Association is carried out by a Committee of 10 people, all of whom must be members of the Association.

In September 1979 the Association decided at a general meeting that some of the money then held was to be distributed in equal proportions to all beneficiaries (adults and children). Two vehicles were also bought (see below). A further sum of money which was received by the Association was put on short term deposit, at least until a meeting to be held as early as possible in the dry season of 1980. This meeting was held in May 1980. A further 30 people were made beneficiaries, and there was a second share out of money. The sum was smaller than it had been the first time; children's shares were put into a trust. The Association also decided that pensioners should wait until the first day of the new financial year (1 July) to receive their share so their eligibility to receive pensions would not be affected.

In 1980 a decision was also made to buy the Cooinda lease.[10] The purchase of the lease was finalised in September, and the purchase of the hotel sublease in December. This means that the Gagudju Association has not only bought a pocket of land which was within Aboriginal land but not Aboriginal owned, but also now controls the availability of liquor in the southern end of the Kakadu National Park. A hearing regarding alterations to the liquor licence is in train, and the Association is hoping to stop take-away sales. The purchase of the hotel lease means that the Association now owns a business and has a source of income additional to mining revenues. Money has already been earmarked to improve facilities for tourists.[11] A manager was appointed in March 1981.

In 1979 two men were singled out as being senior members of outstation communities which required vehicles. They were each provided with a four-wheel-drive vehicle. In 1980 four further vehicles were bought for communities in the Kakadu National Park area, and two other vehicles were purchased for the Association to be used as supply vehicles for supporting outstations in the Park area. The allocation reflects a slight male bias, and the tendency is sometimes for those individuals who have access to the vehicle keys to enjoy a greater part of its use.

There are several points to be made about the setting up of the Gagudju Association. It took a long time to establish a mechanism to distribute the money, and there was jealousy when people could make the comparison with the speed with which the Nabarlek money was distributed. The explanation of the rules of the Association when they were finally decided on was too rushed; as a consequence some people are not fully aware of their rights and responsibilities.[12] When the first money deriving from the Ranger agreement was finally disbursed, several problems became immediately apparent:

- Because of the large number of people who had been included as beneficiaries, the payments made to individuals were very small compared with payments made under the Queensland Mines agreement. Not only are there the usual problems that people feel cheated, but if this disparity continues then pressure may well be put on people to accept more mining developments since they feel that they are getting too thin a slice of the present mining operations cake. Then if that becomes the case, i.e., more mining operations come into being, all the stresses that arise from increased numbers of Europeans, more complex administrative arrangements and more meetings will need to be dealt with.

- With some exceptions, money from the payment in 1979 which was intended for children was not put into a trust account of some sort to be held for them, but was instead included in the amount of money made out in a cheque to the father; children had little say in how that money was spent. This not only raises the point of how children are to be accommodated in the scheme of things, but also of providing for future generations. In some of the cases of children who benefited under the agreement but have no father the money was not made out to their mother, but to some male relative. That male relative need have very little to do with the children, and so their chances of benefiting even indirectly (e.g., in having rides in a vehicle which was bought with money intended for them) was much reduced. Great acrimony arose as a result of this practice.

These last two problems were obviated by the establishment early in 1980 of a trust fund for children's money, as were the next two potential problems.

- There was potential for trouble in the matter of adopted children if the practice outlined above continued. If both natural and adopting fathers were due to benefit as members of the Gagudju Association each would want to claim the child as his if it increased the money coming to the person classified as his or her male parent. If only the natural parent were to benefit, he may still have wanted the child back if it increased the amount of money coming to him. If only the adopting father was due for money, then the natural father may still have demanded a portion of the money intended for the child. There appeared to be a considerable scope for manipulation and complaint.
  When adopted children became aware of the ramifications outlined above, they too may have wished to manipulate circumstances to make sure that they got some money.

Two further matters were raised in 1980. The first concerns the ages of children. Ages were roughly calculated and included on schedule 3 of the Gagudju Association following the first meeting of the Association at Muirella Park in September 1979. No actual birth dates were given. Hence some people who were listed as being 17 years old then may or may not have been 18 for the payout in 1980 (remember that money for children, i.e. those under 18, was put in trust that time). Also in some cases ages were only guesses, and some complaints were made (as it happens, all by women, who have very accurate memories for ages, expressed in such ways as: when X was born, Y was already walking) that some people are several years older than the age they are listed as, and are in fact adults. (The converse is also true.) Some people were not aware that they were listed as children, and were perplexed when they did not receive money when others they knew were younger did. It was explained that their money was not 'lost', but that it was being held for them, and all that was needed was for the Association to be informed of their true age and an application made for them to become (adult) members of the Association. A programme of consulting birth records started, and the problem should no longer exist.

The second matter was the question of including in the list of beneficiaries people who are of the same clan (i.e., bear the same clan name) as people whose land lies in the Kakadu area but whose estate in fact lies well to the east, inside Arnhem Land; members of intervening clans are not listed as beneficiaries. Whether this is equitable or not is a matter for the Association to decide.

In August 1980 the Gagudju Association appointed a full-time resource officer/manager. The Association also appointed an outstation resource officer, has engaged its own lawyer, and has appointed accountants. Moves are under way to appoint financial advisers.

One problem the Association still has is that of budgeting and forward planning: because of the imprecision of the dates for payments of up-front monies[13] it is difficult to make definite commitments about investments and purchases, and make loan repayments.

Although the Gagudju Association was set up primarily to distribute money from Ranger, it is rapidly growing into an organisation which is felt to be representative of Aborigines in the area. As such it is frequently consulted by government bodies, especially the Australian National Parks and Wildlife Service. As is suggested by the titles of Association employees, the range of activities of the Gagudju Association far exceeds that of the handling of money from the Ranger agreement. A present priority is the development of outstations in the park area, and providing services to them.[14]

The last 18 months has shown both a period of growing confidence in the Association and an assumption of responsibility by the Association Committee for the affairs of the Association. The functioning of the Association appears to be proceeding smoothly. There is a minimum of outside interference; decisions are made by Aboriginal people, but they have European advisers whom they can consult as the need arises.

STRUCTURES ESTABLISHED TO CHANNEL NABARLEK MONEY

Under the Nabarlek agreement, the up-front monies from the Queensland Mines Project are divided equally between two groups of people. One group comprises traditional owners and other Aborigines interested in the project area. The other group consists of traditional owners of land affected by the project.[15] For payments made in 1979, these two groups were known as 'traditional owners' and 'affected communities' respectively.

The 'traditional owners' consist of two groups. The first was determined to consist of the clan which owns the Nabarlek area where the mine is situated, a man who has the role of 'caretaker', some people considered to be 'company', and members of the same clan whose estate lies a short way to the east of Nabarlek. The second consists of the owners of Wunyu Beach where the Company was to build a barge landing. The former group decided to use Gunbalanya Nominees (see below) to channel their money. For the Wunyu Beach owners, the Mangarnwal Association Pty Ltd was established.

The 'affected communities' were determined to be Oenpelli together with its outstations (one of which is Nabarlek), Croker Island and its outstations, and Goulburn Island and its outstations. The Marryalayala Association was set up to represent these communities. It consisted of two representatives from each of Oenpelli, Nabarlek, Croker Island, Goulburn Island. (see Fig. 2).

Several points can be made: No formula was devised for the splitting of money within the two groups, traditional owners (Nabarlek/Wunyu) and affected communities (Oenpelli/Croker/Goulburn). In other words, each time that a sum of money was 'released' a meeting had to be held to decide on who got how much. This had two results; firstly, there was an unnecessary addition to the surfeit of meetings that people were obliged to attend; and secondly, there was acrimony each time, the subgroups accusing each other of being greedy.

Why Oenpelli, Croker Island and Goulburn Island were picked as being affected is not clear, nor, for that matter, why only those three were chosen. Maningrida, for instance, and especially some Maningrida outstations, would have had a good case for considering themselves to be affected. There was also a suggestion from communities to the south that they should be compensated for disturbances to Dreaming or ceremonial tracks they are responsible for looking after which pass through the Oenpelli area.

The singling out of the Wunyu Beach barge landing site owners for specific sums of money led to acrimony. Why, people asked, should they have been given special consideration and consulted frequently when owners of other affected portions of land had not been? Land through which the roads used by the mining company pass is a case in point; inconvenience stretches beyond the heavy use of the roads to land required for borrow pits, dams and for road maintenance camps. The owners of the land between

Fig. 2

Structures for channelling Nabarlek monies.

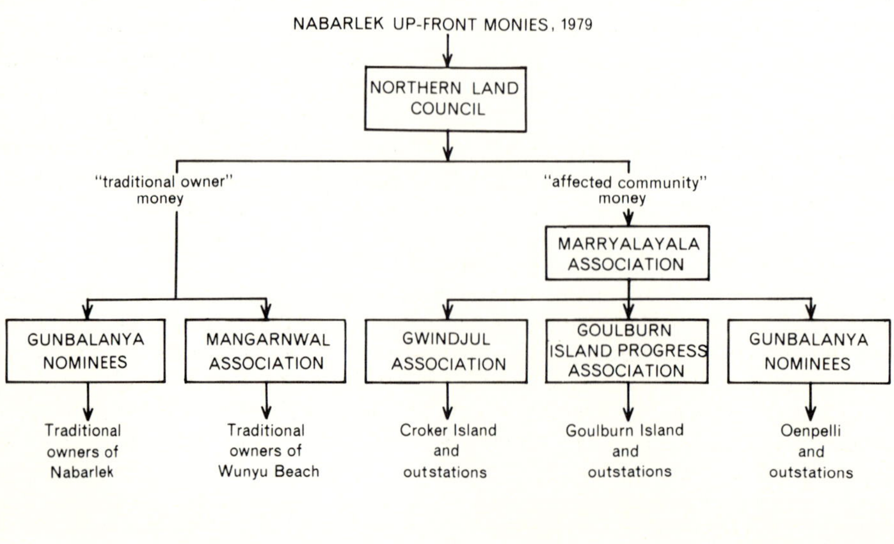

Nabarlek and Wunyu received no special mention, and great bitterness arose during 1979 over the use of Cahill's Crossing[16] -Oenpelli-Nabarlek road; this road was used to bring in heavy equipment and housing to Nabarlek before the barge landing was even constructed, and the owners of that stretch of road had not given their consent to the use of what they consider to be a private road.

The division of the money paid out by Queensland Mines in 1979 was as follows:

- the traditional owners of Nabarlek—37.6%
- the Nabarlek community—1%
- the Wunyu Beach traditional owners—11.85%
- the Oenpelli community—31.75%
- Goulburn Island—8.4%
- Croker Island—8.4%
- the Northern Land Council—1%

Oenpelli is reported to have spent just under three-quarters of its money on providing four-wheel-drive vehicles for all of its outstations, amounting to $226 000. This indicates how far Oenpelli was prepared to interpret the 'affected community' category. But as a consequence of a re-examination[17] of the Nabarlek agreement in the first half of 1980 the 'affected communities' clause was reinterpreted as *people who are traditional owners of land affected by the project,* and this was interpreted in a very concrete way, with the visible physical disturbance of land the criterion.

Money is still split evenly between the two categories of beneficiaries (now called 'traditional owners' and 'people affected'), but the category of 'people affected' is now taken to include:

- traditional owners of Nabarlek,
- traditional owners of Wunyu Beach,
- traditional owners of the land over which the road passes between Nabarlek and Cahill's Crossing (the Oenpelli road),
- traditional owners of the land over which the road passes between Nabarlek and Wunyu Beach (the Cooper Creek road).

There is no formula for dividing the money between these four groups. In theory the distribution of money from the Nabarlek agreement should flow as shown Fig. 3. However, because there is no incorporated group comprising the 'people affected', the actual distribution flows as in Fig. 4.

For the first sum of money released to the 'traditional owner' category in 1980, the division between the amount to go to the owners of Nabarlek and the amount to go to the owners of Wunyu was made on the basis of land affected and this was calculated on the basis of the size of the areas leased by Queensland Mines. By this formula the owners of Nabarlek got a sum slightly more than 50 times greater than that received by the Wunyu Beach owners. As a consequence, the Wunyu Beach owners were somewhat upset by the exceedingly small amount each received.

Then lobbying began as certain individuals tried to manipulate the 'people affected' money. What follows is the bare bones of a sordid story. People, Aboriginal and European, whose right to intervene was questionable, put pressure on the Northern Land Council and individual Aboriginal people in attempts to have the money divided up. At first the course of action was to use the Marryalayala Association, but this organisation had not been incorporated and so was easily circumvented. (And as yet no incorporated body has been set up to replace it.) At the end of this wrangling the division of money was:

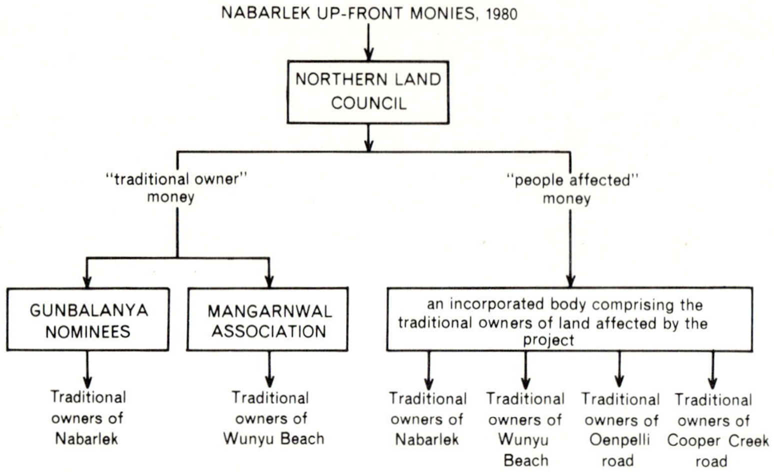

Fig. 3
Theoretical distribution of monies from the Nabarlek agreement.

- half to Wunyu Beach traditional owners,
- one-quarter to Nabarlek traditional owners,
- one-quarter to the Oenpelli road owners.

This division was disproportionate to the amount of land affected on an area basis. The Oenpelli road owners are quite severely affected by the Nabarlek project, and the traditional owners of Nabarlek and Wunyu Beach are already beneficiaries under the 'traditional owner' category. This was not the end, but the start, of the wrangling within the three groups. A handful of individuals, most of them not traditional owners of

Fig. 4
Actual distribution of monies from the Nabarlek agreement.

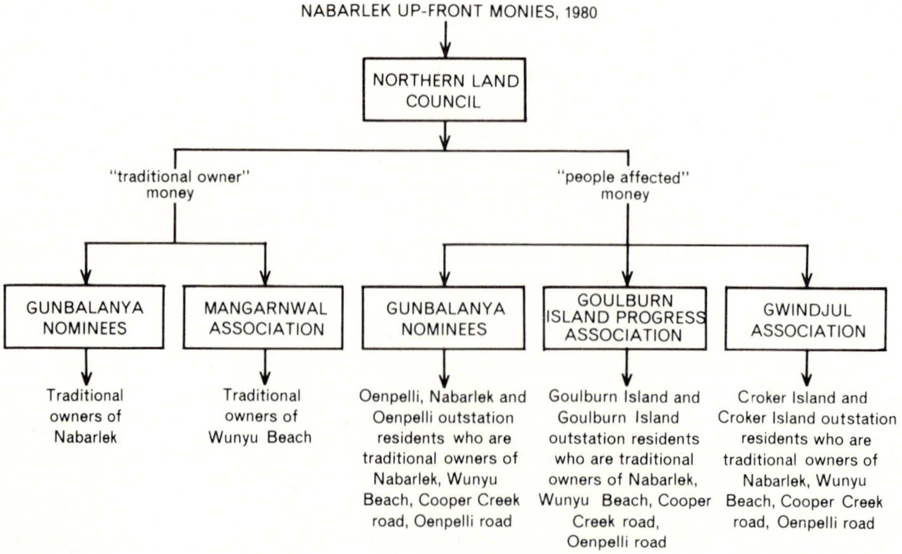

Wunyu Beach, made off with the lion's share of the Wunyu money. It seems pointless to add that there was great anger about this. One woman has openly said that she was robbed.

Initially the money allotted to Nabarlek was going to be kept to hire a person to work for the community as an independent adviser. [18] The community had a husband and wife team in mind. The remainder of the money was to have been used to buy another community vehicle. The vehicle was bought; the rest of the money was divided up among the traditional owners, and none remained to hire the community adviser (and so the Nabarlek Aboriginal community continues to be dependent on Queensland Mines' liaison officer).

The money allotted to the Oenpelli road owners was divided up among the adult owners in something of a hurry. At least one adult traditional owner was left off the list because that person was absent from Oenpelli the day the list was compiled. Children were discounted altogether and no money was put aside for them. The Cooper Creek road owners were not happy about being left out. There were greedy moves by certain individuals also: (successful) claims to be included as land owners on spurious grounds, a (successful) attempt to double up on land owned, and the use of past and present community Council-derived power, family connections and an ability to pressure Europeans in key organisations in (successful) attempts to deflect money from others to themselves. It has become clear that aggrieved individuals find it very difficult to seek redress, in the sense that they are unaware that rules can be altered to close loopholes, and of possible legal action.

Subsequent to these episodes, lists have been drawn up of all the traditional owner groups that benefit under the Nabarlek agreement to prevent the expropriation of funds that has occurred. Still, some irregularities remain. At a further meeting in November 1980 the 'people affected' money was split:

- half to the traditional owners of Nabarlek,
- one-sixth to the traditional owners of Wunyu Beach,
- one-sixth to the traditional owners of the Oenpelli road,
- one-sixth to the traditional owners of the Cooper Creek road.

Again, all the money was handed out to individuals and again no money was put aside for children.

As a consequence of the reinterpretation of the 'people affected' clause of the Nabarlek agreement, and because of the lack of an incorporated body to represent this category of beneficiaries, 1980 saw a greater proportion of money going to individuals than 1979. No money has been invested on behalf of the groups in this category.

Some 'affected community' money which was to have been paid in 1979 was not paid out until late 1980. The sum to Oenpelli was swallowed up in commitments made when it was thought 'affected community' money would be a continuing source of income for the community. There still remain debts for such projects. The Nabarlek community's share of the money was not committed and became the subject of a number of squabbles; not over how it should be used for the community but over which people were going to have it for their personal use.

Under one proposal Oenpelli residents were to get 80% of this money, and Nabarlek residents 20% (traditional owners of Nabarlek would have been getting 60% of the money). But the division of the money in December 1980 was 87.5% to Nabarlek residents and 12.5% to Oenpelli residents (traditional owners of Nabarlek got 50% of the money). Although most of the money went to Nabarlek residents none of the money was spent on the Nabarlek community as such.

Episodes such as these throw into relief the conflicts that arise between ownership, residence and brokerage. In this particular example the principal traditional owner was able to bolster his legitimate authority by using European connections to thwart stand-over tactics on the part of the 'brokers', whose power lies exclusively in their knowledge of how to use white structures for their personal ends.

Movements are under way to form a 'West Arnhem Association' akin to the Gagudju Association, but operating to the east of the East Alligator River, taking in the western part of what was the Arnhem Land Reserve. Its principal purpose would be to function as an incorporated body for the purpose of receiving *royalties* when they are issued (*vide* sec. 35 of the Land Rights Act) and possibly also 'people affected' monies. It would also serve the function of rationalising structures in the western Arnhem Land area.[19] In that respect the Gagudju Association enjoyed *carte blanche*; there were no organisations directly serving Aborigines in the Kakadu National Park area before the formation of the Gagudju Association. In the area between the East Alligator and the Mann rivers, however, there are myriad organisations associated with the various settlements, and several church organisations. The Department of Aboriginal Affairs has a continuing presence there, whereas prior to 1978 the Department had no responsibility for the Kakadu area.[20]

The initial idea was for the 'West Arnhem Association' to be land-based like the Gagudju Association so that the membership would depend on clan and not on residence. But now it seems that the criterion for membership will be residence. It was proposed that the clans should be grouped into areas and each area would have a representative on the committee which would be the decision-making body. So far a working party consisting of clan members of the area in question has been elected, and the working party is now to work out the guidelines for the formation of the association. There is some evidence that there is more lobbying going on for this association than there was for the formation of the Gagudju Association. People have become aware of its potential power and wealth; manoeuvring by the 'brokers' is apparent already and there is an undercurrent of suspicion in some people's minds. However, if the teething problems are overcome and the ideals realised, the association may enjoy the same stature in Aboriginal minds that the Gagudju Association has attained.

CONSEQUENCES OF THE DIFFERENCES BETWEEN THE NABARLEK AND RANGER AGREEMENTS

In summary, the main consequence of different agreements having been drawn up for Queensland Mines and Ranger are:

- People receiving money under the Queensland Mines agreement got their money long before the people who benefit under the Ranger agreement. (The first Nabarlek money was disbursed in June 1979; the first Ranger money was disbursed in October 1979, and this in spite of the fact that the Ranger agreement was signed in November 1978, while the Nabarlek agreement was not signed until March 1979.)

- People benefiting under the Queensland Mines agreement have to date received much greater sums of money than those benefiting under the Ranger agreement[21] because of the differences in the amounts paid out and the different numbers of beneficiaries amongst whom they have to be divided. Ranger money is spread very widely: the number of Ranger beneficiaries (including children) is more than 10 times greater than the number of people listed as traditional owners of Nabarlek, and about three times greater than the total number of people who benefit[22] under the Nabarlek agreement.

- There is a great deal of confusion since people do not understand the reasons for the discrepancies in the date of initial payments, and in the amounts paid out. People have given up trying to understand and—although they still make comparisons between the two agreements—limit their inquiries to when the next lot of money is to be paid out. (It should be noted that inquiries come not only from those who are destined to receive money.)

A great number of people still do not know the Associations that handle the mining revenues; not even, in some cases, recipients of these monies. One recipient even denied that she was receiving mining money. But in general people know which members of their families are getting money.

While the people who benefit under the Nabarlek agreement have a fairly accurate picture of when money is due to be paid, it is quite evident that people who benefit under the Ranger agreement have no notion whatever of the timing of payments. For Ranger, the nature of the scheduling is so complex that the beneficiaries do not understand it. There are, in any case, no *fixed* dates for payment of up-front monies.[23] (See above, also, for problems the Gagudju Association has with respect to budgeting and forward planning.)

Nevertheless, Ranger recipients know how much they have received so far (the sums were small, there have been only two payouts, and the distribution ensured each person's share was the same). Nabarlek recipients have only a hazy idea of how much they have received, if they know at all.[24]

In general people do not think the mining agreements are 'fair' with respect to money, or say they are not sure because 'nobody ever tells us anything'. Some Nabarlek recipients say the money they have had is enough, some say not.[25] No Ranger recipient has said the money received has been enough. None of the recipients questioned so far knows how much he/she will get next year, let alone how much they will have after five years. This is understandable in view of the imprecision of the scheduling of up-front monies from Ranger, but also demonstrates that people are unaware of likely royalty amounts as well as not being able to predict the allotment of monies.

SOURCES OF ACRIMONY

The point which has been raised time and time again is that the potential for acrimony and jealousy is very very high. There is mistrust and jealousy arising between communities. One manifestation of this is that those communities and groups receiving money have not used the same mechanism for the distribution of money. Even the communities which comprised the Marryalayala Association did not deal directly with that Association, but fed the money due to them into three separate accounts.

All the communities and groups benefiting under the two uranium mining agreements could have used Gunbalanya Nominees, a holding company, which was in fact established in 1972 with a view to catering for development in the area. Its activities are diverse: money going through the company comes from the Department of Aboriginal Affairs for outstation support and for specific DAA purposes (e.g., payment of salaries to staff), money goes through the company from the Oenpelli store, the company maintains a cash float to cater for outstation needs, and so on. The directors of the company, now numbering 16, represent all the areas of the Trust territory; this extends from the South Alligator River in the west to the Mann River in the east (though it does not take in Maningrida) and as far south as 13°50' latitude.

The Nabarlek traditional owners and Oenpelli (and outstations) residents who benefit under the 'people affected' category use Gunbalanya Nominees for the distribution of their money, as did Oenpelli for its 'affected community' money; none of the other groups have. Oenpelli and the Nabarlek owners were the first to have money available for use; Croker Island waited almost ten months for money to be channelled to it.

I am not sure that people were aware that they could use Gunbalanya Nominees to channel money. Even if they were, however, I feel that rivalry is growing between the different groups that receive money, and they want to preserve separate identities. People west of the East Alligator River and on Croker and Goulburn islands have a suspicion of Oenpelli and, for that reason, Gunbalanya Nominees may appear tainted in their eyes. (Oenpelli was consistently rejected as a site for the meetings to set up the Gagudju Association.) In 1979 the Kakadu Park area used Gunbalanya Nominees for the distribution of buffalo royalties; in 1980 the Gagudju Association was used to distribute these royalties. Nevertheless, if people had realised how long it was going to take to set up the Gagudju Association they may have wanted to use Gunbalanya Nominees to speed up the process of getting their money.

The effects of certain communities having money can now be seen; the reactions differ from place to place. Maningrida people have expressed jealousy at the numbers of new vehicles coming into Oenpelli and want to enjoy similar benefits. They have made moves to be included in any allocation of money that is being made. At a public meeting at Nabarlek in November 1980 some Maningrida people threatened to stop bringing their ceremonies to the Oenpelli area if they were not given a share of the money from Nabarlek. Milingimbi, on the other hand, is reported not to care in the least; they have no motor vehicles but they still have their land intact and undisturbed by invasions of white workers. It may be the case that the closer a non-recipient community is to the visible effects of increased income, either physically or in terms of social ties, the more prone it is to jealousy.

It is possible for people to play on the divisions that arise as a result of the allocation of money. An example is the Oenpelli road case; a tactic used to try to get the court case dropped was to tell the people at Nabarlek that if the road owners won their case no more royalties would be given out.[26] In other words, there was an attempt made to play off one Aboriginal group against another, adding to the fragmentation that already exists. The promoting of dissension started with mining companies making 'gifts' to certain land-owners. This has been particularly noticed as the date for the first payments of mining revenue came due ('no matter he got car/tent/(etc.), I'll get my money now').

On an individual level, jealousy can arise in several ways:

- Between the recipients of mining money. This can arise because different agreements specify different things. It can also arise among people benefiting from the same agreement because of extras going to certain people. I mentioned the case of cars being allocated in 1979 to two individuals under the Ranger agreement; this has also happened in the case of money arising from the Queensland Mines agreement, one individual being given a car before anybody else received any money at all, which made for a great deal of bitterness.

- Between recipients and non-recipients. The obvious point here is that some are getting money and others not. But the ramifications of this spread further. There are now pockets of affluence at Oenpelli. With more cars coming into the community the police are becoming stricter about cars being roadworthy before they will register them. Obviously, a person who has plenty of money has the option of buying a new car and would have no problem getting it registered. Those who receive lesser sums of money, or who through saving or gambling have amassed a small amount of money, buy used cars, often dubiously roadworthy, and have trouble getting them registered. I have observed a great deal of curiosity on the part of people who are not getting money as to when money is due, and in what amounts. This last point has bearing on the next point.

- Between non-recipients, in that there is a scramble to make connections with 'monied' families, possibly even through marriage. Such accusations have been made (by Aboriginal people).

Some 'grey areas' that need exploring are in the realm of adoptions and other multiple affiliations to land. Some cases are clearcut and there is no argument about including these people as beneficiaries under a mining agreement; the same goes for certain 'company' relations. There would seem to be no problem where traditional owners are happy to include these people as beneficiaries. Problems arise when there is disagreement as to whether a claim is spurious or not—and the proponents and opponents in these cases are not entirely disinterested either.

For example, in one specific case a woman, now widowed, asked why she was not benefiting under the Ranger agreement. It became evident that she fully realised that her clan was not entitled to money under this agreement; she was claiming as a widow of a man who would have benefited under that agreement (indeed, her children are beneficiaries).

CONSEQUENCES OF ACRIMONY

A consequence of all the rivalry mentioned thus far is that there is an increase in stress:

- People have to devote time and energy to ensure that they get the money that they are entitled to. This involves not only attending meetings but trying to understand the implications of the foreign structures that are being set up (see fifth point below).

- They have to devote time and energy to ensure that those people they feel are not entitled to benefit do not receive any money. A watch also has to be kept for 'strong-arm' tactics by people who are not entitled to mining revenues, but use past and present power derived from European structures (e.g., settlement councils) to skim off some money.

- In the case of those who do not have such a strong claim to be included, they must constantly be on the lookout for moves to strike them off the list, or must put in extra energy in promoting good grounds for their inclusion in the list. When this point is taken with the one above, it can be seen that there is the possibility of a vicious circle being established during the negotiation stage, and bitterness after the decision, then irrevocable, has been made.

- People may have to spend extra effort to ensure that relatives are included as beneficiaries. In some cases this may mean that there is a potential for contradiction; a person may not want the cake sliced too finely and will want to exclude all those without a strong claim and yet may want to include a relative who is in a 'weak' category.

- Stress can result from a feeling of not being in control of the necessary knowledge and information necessary for manipulating the rules established by a white administration. There is a constant fear that rules will be changed behind people's backs. While this obviously extends beyond the matter of money, control of information relating to money matters is crucial.

- Also leading to stress is that the method used for clearing up any contentious issues *is the public meeting.* There, for example, final lists of beneficiaries are drawn up. To air publicly a person's claim to land is to shame them. Mutterings of bad feelings are very evident at such meetings. (And yet this must be contrasted with some of the secret manipulations which have been attempted.)

SOME FURTHER SOURCES OF STRESS, AND SCOPE FOR MANIPULATION

The range of the struggle for access to and control of money goes beyond the individual to the Territory-wide level. Under sections 62-65 of the Land Rights Act the Aboriginals Benefit Trust Account (which superseded the Aborigines Benefits Trust Fund in 1978) handles money from mineral royalties. In all, 40% of this revenue is passed on to the land councils (24% to the Northern Land Council, 14% to the Central Land Council, 2% to the Tiwi Land Council, on a population basis) for administration costs; 30% is passed on to the land council of the area in which that mining project is taking place, to be shared among incorporated groups and councils in areas affected by the project,[27] and 30% is available to communities in the Northern Territory on application for a specific undertaking.

The first point that should be made is that the land councils have, by this arrangement, a vested interest in mining operations.

The second point that should be made is that the land councils have amassed debts in the early stages of their existence because of the enormous costs of undertaking land claims. At present, loans are being made which are to be repaid when royalties start coming from uranium mines.

A third point is that although money such as royalties is thought of as *compensation* some people fear a decrease in government expenditure on Aborigines as mining money starts to come into communities. If the same amount of money is coming in, but Aborigines now have total say in what is spent on what, then I feel that there would be little disruption *so long as the money is sufficient for their needs and aspirations*. The danger lies in overall amounts of money to Aborigines being reduced, or in some communities getting more than is necessary, to the exclusion of others, who are worse off than before. The unevenly balanced distribution of monies to communities must be corrected before any decision is made on a Territory-wide basis to reduce government money allocated to Aboriginal communities. A careful examination of the money inflow and outflow is necessary to ensure that equity is maintained, otherwise Aboriginal communities will have to agree to mining (or other) ventures on their land just to remain financially secure; nevertheless, communities on land of no material benefit to European Australians will still suffer unless they get a share of the money generated.

SUMMARY: THE NATURE OF THE STRUCTURES ESTABLISHED TO DISBURSE MINING REVENUES

The struggle for the control of mining revenue is fought at every level, and to add to the complexity the structures evolved for the purpose of dealing with mining revenue have little relevance in traditional terms. Furthermore, the structures were not well-thought out before being imposed, and so they have had inconsistencies, gaps and unfortunate effects. Because there has been no precedent for these structures the people having to deal with them cannot be said to have had any experience in manipulating similar circumstances, whether financial, bureaucratic or political. Because of their *ad hoc* nature, the structures are patched up as effects are noticed; again, this leads to complications and a lack of understanding. And because the various agreements and financial structures are all different, the *ad hoc* nature of each is different, distorting the differences even further.

Because implications of the Land Rights Act have not been thoroughly considered essential devices for the distribution of money are missing. But there is delay before the lack is acknowledged, and then more delay while the lawyers work out some arrangement for the necessary formation of the association (or whatever) to be formed. The waiting period is extremely frustrating for Aborigines, especially when they do not understand the reasons for delay.

USES TO WHICH MINING REVENUES HAVE BEEN PUT

I turn now to the uses to which these sums of money have been put. It should be noted that money has gripped the imagination of Aborigines, just as it has gripped the possibly jealous minds of Europeans. Money for Aborigines is also a source of power, but the nature of that power is very likely to be misunderstood by Europeans. Certainly, Aborigines want to be independent of outside interference, but they can also use money to amass social capital in their own terms. This not only involves acquiring credit in the social system by spreading favours among close and distant kin, and thus establishing a form of social security, but also involves expenditure for ceremonial purposes. The major priority of this area is cultural maintenance, and there are some indications of a cultural resurgence west of the East Alligator River, made possible by money deriving from the Ranger agreement.

The author is in the process of conducting interviews to examine attitudes to, and understanding of, money. The study is not complete as yet, but tendencies are discernible. Observations of behaviour patterns complement and confirm the information obtained in interviews. Money is well-understood as a means of satisfying wants (there are very concrete responses here) and as a means of indebting others and thus gaining status. People are well aware of relevant minutiae such as pay-days for Council workers, pension days, etc., and the cost of items frequently bought, e.g., $80 for a drum of petrol.

There is no knowledge of matters such as the source of money, both in general and as a source to the community and mining companies. The 'government' is seen as the source of all money (including that for mining companies); other responses indicate that money is entirely a *balanda* (white) business. There is no knowledge of fiscal matters such as interest rates. There is no knowledge of money as a rationing system or as a means of establishing worth or value, or as a means of transferring value.

Money is well understood as a compensatory mechanism in Aboriginal realms (e.g., if one gets the wrong relative to cut one's hair one has to compensate the person who should have cut it), but not in European realms (e.g., reasons for awarding a widow's pension, and reasons for not awarding a 'widower's pension', or reasons for receiving the unemployment benefit).

INDIVIDUALS' MATERIAL OBJECTIVES

In material terms there appears to be a limited set of objectives that people have. People's immediate desires seem to be a vehicle, followed later by clothes, food, bedding and alcohol.[28] There are also individuals with specific desires; a young man may want an electric guitar, someone else may want a boat. The current craze is for expensive billiard cues. In general, women's material aspirations may be more limited than men's.

Having more money than is required (certainly not the case as yet) could have the following consequences:

(a) the excess could be spent on non-durables, e.g., drink, food, clothes, with possible attendant waste;

(b) durables could be treated as non-durables; in other words, care need not be taken with, for example, a car, since if it breaks down or is seriously damaged one need only wait for the next allocation of money to get a new one;

(c) the excess could be channelled into maintaining a mobile lifestyle by extending the range of places visited; in other words, the money could be used to finance trips and holidays;

(d) the excess is given away;

(e) the money could be invested.

With respect to points (a) and (b), it is possible that individuals will quickly reach saturation point, and have no further desires, apart from a regular income for food, clothing and other necessities of life (e.g., petrol). Then the extra money may well be useless from a personal point of view (though not necessarily from a community point of view, or from the point of view of succeeding generations). The problem is partly that *individuals* are allocated sums of money, as well as certain groups and communities. This is considered later.

With respect to point (c), the great desire for mobility can be seen in the use to which Oenpelli's share of community money was put: it was spent almost entirely on vehicles. Each outstation was allocated a vehicle, Oenpelli itself was provided with a vehicle, and a vehicle was purchased to enable people to maintain a road patrol. Moves are being made to establish a commercially oriented workshop at Oenpelli to service and repair vehicles. But because 'affected community' money ceased to exist as a category there is not as yet enough money available to finish carrying this out.

With respect to point (d), it is already the case that beneficiaries give some of their mining money away. This is expected of them by their kin and is not to the disadvantage of the person giving away the money because he or she is then given 'social credit' in Aboriginal terms (see above). The same can be said for using one's money to finance ceremonies. About half of beneficiaries asked have said that they have used at least part of their mining money to finance ceremonies.

With respect to point (e), the limitations on this course of action are discussed below (pp.375–76)

Recurrent needs of people in the Oenpelli area might be:

food and utensils such as billycans, cups, water coolers;
tobacco;
clothing;
mattresses, sheets, blankets, pillows;
petrol, diesel, oil;
car repair/maintenance;
soap, shampoo, washing powder;
torches, batteries;
aspirin, cough mixture;
cassette tapes;
alcohol;
toys;
fishing lines, lures, bullets, cartridges;
playing cards, comics.

Many items are recurrent costs because they are either lost or broken very soon after purchase. It has been the practice to deduct money for firewood, rent, movies and town services from wages and pensions and hence these items are not so much a recurrent cost to Oenpelli residents as a form of local tax.

Artists and basketmakers are likely to have recurrent costs for:

needles,
files and sandpaper,
glue,
axes.

Outstation communities will have all the costs outlined above, plus special needs such as tarpaulins for shelter.

Other items which will count as recurrent costs but probably would not be purchased quite so frequently are for example:

cassette players, radios;
rifles, shotguns, wire (for fishing spear prongs);
electric guitars, drums, amplifiers;
electric jugs, grills, electric frying pans, washing machines, refrigerators, electric fans;
Avon products (jewellery, scent);[29]
children's bicycles;
mosquito nets;
rakes, hoses, axes, brooms.

LIMITATIONS OF USES TO WHICH MONEY CAN BE PUT

For money to be used to its best possible effects certain ingredients must be available. These include knowledge and information about investments, interest rates and a variety of other matters,[30] and then availability of advice. This also presupposes an interest in financial matters, which is lacking at present in almost all forms except gratification of personal wants.

An adequate information flow must also be established (and it must be borne in mind that access to information is tied in with positions of power and authority, whether traditional or European-derived). This will involve examining access to information, control of information, possible means for information spread, and also the reasons for misinformation. The last of these is common, and can arise in various ways, from deliberate withholding or manipulation of information, to conjecture becoming fact, to an inability to translate from the European structure to traditional structures.

At present there is nobody to offer financial advice to individual Aborigines, other than casual contacts, and friends. Some sort of advisory agency informing people on an individual basis, as well as a community basis, of what they can do with their money is urgently required. [31] Community advisers and adult educators have not taken on this role, and nor have banks taken up the opportunity to increase their business in the Alligator Rivers region.

No Aboriginal organisation in the area other than the Gagudju Association has a financial adviser. The Gagudju Association has a manager with some experience in financial matters, and is about to appoint financial advisers.

Aborigines will also have to be taught that they have bargaining power. At present they are unable to use this to advantage because they are unfamiliar with the world of business. An example would be the purchase of the vehicles with the "affected community" money which went to Oenpelli from the Nabarlek agreement. The community wished to buy vehicles to a total value of $234 000. A discount of merely $8000 was negotiated on the grounds that no more money was really required (and it would probably only be spent on another vehicle). The person bargaining on behalf of the Aborigines, however, failed to look further afield to see if there were other things that could be included in the deal: special insurance, extended warranties, free servicing for a certain period, and extras for the vehicles (e.g., roof racks, radio/cassettes).

There have also been some examples of unscrupulous dealing by whites and, latterly blacks, taking advantage of the Aborigines' lack of knowledge of the state of the market for used cars. The scope for this sort of business chicancery would seem to be unlimited, and the sooner there is an agency offering advice to people in the area, the better.

CONSEQUENCES FOR LOCAL SERVICES

Together with a lack of structures for giving financial advice (see above), there are few of the facilities needed to deal, directly or indirectly, with increased amounts of money in the community. Most money which comes into the Oenpelli community from mining revenues is not circulated but goes straight outside the area, mostly to Darwin. Some reasons are obvious. For example, there is very little that one can buy at Oenpelli, and virtually nothing at places like Cannon Hill. Major purchases, such as vehicles, can only be made in Darwin. Alcohol can be bought in only limited quantities for limited hours at Oenpelli, and people seek alternative outlets, for example, the South Alligator Inn.

But there are also less obvious reasons. The Commonwealth Savings Bank has agencies in Arnhem Land and is the only bank at Oenpelli. The float for such agencies is $2000. [32] This is obviously not enough to deal with the large number of large cheques coming into Oenpelli. The Oenpelli Council (accountant) has undertaken to provide the community with cash, by 'buying' money from Darwin occasionally, from the shop or social club, by issuing a Gunbalanya Council cheque. The money is deposited in the Council's account at the agency; this provides the agency with the large sums of cash that are occasionally needed. It should be noted that this is necessary not only because of the money generated by the mining agreements; the $2000 float does not even cater for Council's wages bill. In spite of a verbal assurance in 1980 that the float would be increased to $5000, this has never been implemented (it would, in any case, still be insufficient to cater for people's needs when mining payments are made). The Northern Land Council has undertaken to warn the Oenpelli bank when cheques from mining revenues are about to be issued. [33]

If the money withdrawn from the agency were spent at the shop, workshop and social club only, then that money would be deposited back in the agency at the end of each trading day. However, money leaves the community because the shop and social club have to buy provisions from Darwin. Then there is the fact that large cheques can only be cashed in Darwin; the maximum that could be withdrawn at the Oenpelli agency in one day was $300-$400; now it is $200.

The amount of money going out of the community can be judged by the fact that the Council usually buys $20 000 from Darwin once a month. In November 1979, however, which was the time for the first Ranger payments, the Council bought three lots of $20 000. (It must be remembered that this does not reflect the total amounts of money leaving the community, since many people chose to cash their cheques in Darwin and buy vehicles instead of depositing money at the Oenpelli agency.)

The pattern of circulation of money at Oenpelli during the wet season is different to that of the dry season; for any money to be spent directly outside of Oenpelli a plane trip or a charter is necessary, so less money needs to be ordered from Darwin.

Banking provisions for other communities in the immediate area are even more primitive. All outstations rely on Oenpelli. Social security cheques can be collected at Oenpelli or exchanged for provisions when the outstation is serviced. A float is maintained by people doing the servicing to help outstation people do their banking.

The construction camp at Nabarlek had a bank agency for the duration of the construction phase. Bank hours were set to coincide with contractors' wishes. At the end of the mining period the hours were cut down. The bank 'arrived' on Thursday afternoons and departed Friday mornings. Banking hours were therefore restricted to about three hours on a Thursday evening. A few people at the Aboriginal camp at Nabarlek used the agency, although the hours did not suit them at all since the workers there are paid on a Friday. A DAA officer located at Nabarlek acted as an informal bank, keeping money for people. There no longer is a bank at Nabarlek. The Aboriginal people there can cash social security entitlements at the canteen, otherwise they have to rely on Oenpelli banking facilities, and, in one case at least, on a Darwin account.

The mining township at Ranger has agencies of the Bank of New South Wales and the Commonwealth Bank. The latter has normal bank trading hours, the former operates three days a week. Approximately 30 Aborigines in the Kakadu National Park area have savings accounts at the Ranger township,[34] these are handled for them by Gagudju Association and DAA staff resident in the township.

There are problems associated with entry to the Ranger project area, and hence access to the Banking facilities there. There is uncertain access and/or restricted access to the mining township for those people who are not employees of Ranger Uranium Mines. The township is, in any case, cut off from most Aboriginal communities in the wet season.

Cannon Hill people (and others) can cash cheques for modest amounts at the Border Store, thus pension cheques present no problems. For slightly larger amounts some notice has to be given.

The regional township of Jabiru will have a full range of banking facilities provided by the Bank of New South Wales. This is expected to open in January 1982. There have been suggestions that it should be approached to provide a 'travelling bank' to serve the wider area.

In the meantime there is need for more sophisticated machinery to deal with mining revenues. For a start, the agency at Oenpelli could be upgraded to have a larger staff, a bigger float, tighter controls over access to savings books, a range of high interest investment possibilities and larger opening hours. In 1979 it was open only 6 hours over three days a week, which was extended to 10 hours over five days in March 1980, and later that year to 20 hours over five days. The upgrading of banking facilities is desirable both to provide Aborigines with the same sort of investment possibilities that most white communities have and also to cater for Aboriginal interests. One way to keep money for oneself in an Aboriginal community is to feign not having any; having it in the bank or not physically on one's person counts as not having any (at least to give away).

Further, an example of the consequences for local services of an increase in personal and community affluence is the lack of facilities for servicing the new vehicles purchased from mining revenues. There is no real workshop at Oenpelli for individuals to get their cars serviced; everyone goes into Darwin. The petrol selling outlet at Oenpelli is also limited. Most of the new vehicles purchased with mining money have had diesel engines. However, no one thought to increase the amount of diesel fuel ordered for the workshop, and the supply almost ran dry one weekend with the increased demand. There is no diesel mechanic at Oenpelli. The same general comment applies to servicing of cassette players, washing machines and other electrical appliances.

CONSEQUENCES TO INDIVIDUALS OF INCREASED PERSONAL INCOME

The consequences of individuals getting money is that their rights to other incomes may be affected. There are problems especially with social security entitlements.

Income earners are not affected. Money received from mining agreements is taxed before it reaches the traditional owners (a form of withholding tax) and it does not affect income tax assessment *(Income Tax Assessment Amendment Act (No. 2)* 1979).

To date there seems to have been no change in employment patterns in the area. There has been no abandonment of work by recipients of mining revenues.[35] The pattern for production of bark paintings and baskets also continues to be the same: high production in the wet season, low production in the dry season.[36] The quality of artefacts has not deteriorated. Artists are asking, and getting, higher prices than they did a year ago. This is more a demand for a fair price than a result of 'money hunger' from seeing some people with increased personal income from mining revenues.

Contrary to statements of likely impacts of mining on Aborigines in the Final Environmental Impact Statements of Pancontinental Mining Limited for the Jabiluka project, Queensland Mines Limited for the Nabarlek project and Noranda Australia Limited[37] for the Koongarra project, employment patterns have not changed in response to compensation payments (see, for example, pp 8:37–8:40 of Pancontinental' Final Environmental Impact Statement). The suggestion seems to be that Aborigines will take up entrepreneurial activities and invest their money in businesses serving the mining industry. There has been no hint of such developments as yet.

Mining money will not affect the receipt of child endowment payments and it appears that pensions or supporting mother's benefits of people who receive mining revenue will not be affected. However, pensioner members of the Gagudju Association decided to delay their receipt of the second payment from Ranger so that was not made in the same financial year as the first payment.

If the policy changes, and pensioners are assessed on, for example, yearly income, the effects will soon be felt. Pensions are of importance in Aboriginal communities. Old people are dependable sources of income and can usually be relied on to help out in looking after children, making sure that they are adequately fed and clothed; widows are made independent of men and may choose not to remarry. Since this source of income has been made available to them they can now manage quite well on their own, and can also support their children. Invalid pensions provide incomes for many Oenpelli people because large numbers have been badly disfigured and incapacitated by leprosy.

Mining money comes in large blocks and at irregular (or erratic) times and is quickly dissipated, either by a major purchase such as a car or by spreading it among relatives. If a pensioner's money is cut off, then the individual will be left with no regular income, and in the lulls between the disbursement of monies he or she will have no income whatsoever. This is obviously the consequence of depending on a system of security which is not based on a planning in detail of credit and debit, and does not depend on saving. Old age and invalid pensioners will lose the the security they once had.

At present there are no people at Oenpelli receiving unemployment benefits. Two people at Croker Island and eight at Goulburn Island receive this benefit. In the Kakadu National Park area, including the Jabiru township and Mudginberry Station, 22 people receive the unemployment benefit. The current attitude of the Department of Social Security is that any person receiving the unemployment benefit will lose it for that period (assessed over a month) in which he or she receives mining revenue.[38]

The matter of *individuals* (as opposed to groups of Aborigines) receiving money deserves some comment. The Woodward Commission into land rights[39] specifically stated that individuals should not receive money. The report says (1973 section 131) '. . . it would seem unfortunate that some groups of Aborigines, which might be quite small, should become extremely wealthy while others are comparatively poor—the difference being represented by the presence on their land of a metal or fluid which had probably no significance at all in traditional Aboriginal society'.

As recently as October 1978, in an address to the National Press Club, Mr Stephen Zorn, special negotiator employed by the Northern Land Council, said:

> It should also be noted that none of the revenue from mining projects will go to individual Aboriginals. The newspaper cartoons portraying Aboriginals as some sort of equivalent of Arab oil sheiks are misleading and dangerously racist. Such conceptions encourage racial antagonism, and do little to promote any possibility of good long-term race relations. Under the Land Rights Act, all money received by Land Councils must either be spent by the Councils themselves, for their own performance of the functions required of them by statute, or must be passed on to local Aboriginal councils or other groups of Aboriginals for community purposes. Once again, none of the money will go to individuals.

In a note in the same volume (1978) of the *Northern Territory Newsletter* in which Zorn's speech is reproduced there is a note on the tax scheme for mining revenue (author's emphasis):

> From July 1, 1979, revenues received by *Aboriginal groups* from mining operations on Aboriginal land anywhere in Australia will be taxed on the basis of the standard rate of personal income tax (32 per cent) applied to 20 per cent of gross revenues . . . the tax would be collected by the withholding system, that is, it would be deducted before the payments were made.
>
> The withholding would be made at the first payment point. The tax deducted would be the final tax—there would be no subsequent tax assessment process. This means that *Aboriginal groups* will not have to bring the amounts they receive to account for income tax purposes.
>
> Distribution by the groups would also be free of any further income tax in the hands of the recipients . . .

Now, either there has been some change in policy and the Land Rights Act is not in the same form that Zorn saw it, or the Land Rights Act is not clear enough and not stringent enough in its clauses to preclude the distribution of mining money to individuals. The Land Rights Act does not specify the *use* to which revenue from mining is to be put once it has been transferred to Aboriginal groups. If the money is given to a community, then the latter is free to decide not to undertake any community projects or develop an investment portfolio, but can instead divide the money between all the members of that community. People are then free to do with their portions as they see fit. It is true to say, however, that mining monies are not paid *directly* to individual Aborigines.

Whatever the intentions of the Land Rights Act and the people who drafted it, a precedent has been set in the Alligator Rivers region, and it will be difficult to alter matters now. People will again feel that they have been 'tricked' if no more sums are given to individuals; they will still want their own vehicles, etc and they will not be so happy to have 'communal access' to 'communal property' (whatever that may mean in Aboriginal terms).[40]

If future agreements affecting the Alligator Rivers region are to differ from the two already established in the matter of individuals getting money, there will again be jealousy in that the people benefiting under current agreements get individual property but others benefiting under the new agreements only get communal goods (and this implies that those things which cannot be communal goods cannot be bought with that money, it would appear).

SOCIAL RAMIFICATIONS OF INCREASED INCOME

People in the area are affected in different ways in terms of access to money, representation on bodies that make decisions about money, access to goods, whether they are put in control of goods, the priorities they make in expenditure, and so on. While a study detailing such matters is desirable, here I will give only one example, mentioning in broad terms the position of women.

It appears to me that there is a male bias in the way that money has been allotted; indeed, in the very fact that mining has been allowed to proceed. Women are generally not represented on bodies which make decisions about the area, and where they are they do not participate to the extent that men do . . . In other words, men dominate these structures. The Northern Land Council currently has no female field officers. There are no female DAA staff in the field. There are no women among the senior staff running Oenpelli.

In negotiations with traditional owners bodies such as the NLC tend to address themselves to men for decisions and tend to allot more goods to men, or at least place these in the control of men. People may object that Aboriginal society is male-biased and hence the distribution, etc, of money is merely following traditional lines. This may be so (though I have strong doubts about the strength of this argument), but if the consequences of money being distributed are so non-traditional in terms of bad feelings generated, increased accidents, a rise in stress, then it only seems fair that those who bear the brunt are allowed to have a say in how things are managed.[41] Since women are depended on to maintain the social fabric of a community, an extra burden is placed on them to alleviate the effects of mining in the vicinity.

Women seem to have a more socially responsible view than men of what they can do with money; buying things for their children is a reflection of this.[42] The limited set of material objectives (see above) is especially true of women, who seem to put their money in the bank and wait to think of something to spend their money on. Women often express no idea of what they might do with money beyond buying a car; clothing for children is a frequent response. They are often observed buying household goods such as saucepans, mattresses, electric grills and frying pans.

If numbers of self-indulgent women increase, because the receipt of mining money makes them independent, the stability of the society which requires an unselfish and responsible attitude from women may be put into jeopardy. As it is, nepotism and selfishness are evident in the area. Now, these two words have negative connotations in English, which they probably do not have in the Aboriginal world view. Indeed, a good man is one who looks after his family to further its interests above all others. This sort of behaviour is evident in all fields, but is becoming evident in the uses to which 'community' money is being put. A vehicle intended for a community is usually taken over by a particular family and used for that family's convenience. Jealousy is evident here too, and stress can arise from the manipulation of circumstances and power to attain those goods to the exclusion of others, or to wrest goods away from the group which now controls them.

But sometimes even the rights of an individual's children have been disregarded (as the case with the first payment of the Ranger money and with payments of the 'people affected' money). Now this may just be the first grand scramble for all the sorts of things which Aborigines have desired for a very long time but which until now have been totally beyond their means. If that is so, then after these desirable objects have been bought the individual will have no further use for large sums of money.

Although at the moment the social discount rate appears to be 100%, I hope that this is just the reaction to having sizeable sums of money for the first time at the entire disposal of the individual. But unless money is invested in communities, then it is unlikely that the social discount rate will be lowered substantially, and later generations of Aborigines of the Alligator Rivers region will have been totally sold out: the power that Aborigines might gain from having financial clout, and hence power in the white community, will never come to pass.

Of the direct needs in the Alligator Rivers region that must be catered for, one could cite again the necessity for some sort of advisory agency informing people, on an individual as well as a community basis, of what they can do with their money. This should be a priority in any case, since there is often confusion surrounding money, with sums intended for communal use being viewed as belonging to individuals. One should examine the sorts of rights that an individual has in the resources which belong to the group of which he is a part; strict delineation may be an ill-advised imposition, especially in terms of the Aboriginal understanding of the working of structures. This view, however, should be contrasted with the potential for selfishness.

The favourable effects of increases in the amounts of money available are obviously that desired material objects are now attainable by some individuals, and that also there is an increase in independence as far as community needs are concerned. This is only limited as yet, but the promise of independence is obviously felt. For example, the Department of Aboriginal Affairs sent officers out to Oenpelli to visit outstations to determine their needs. Oenpelli has had a surfeit of people visiting the community to 'consult', and invasions of 'government men' are deeply resented; this is even more true of outstations to which people have withdrawn so that they can—at least as one objective—diminish their contact with the white community. On this particular occasion the DAA officers were refused permission to visit the outstations, and the reason given was that their money was no longer needed.

Already there are promising signs that people's priorities are being re-ordered. The Gagudju Association has invested a fair part of its money in a business venture, which not only 'buys back' some land for Aborigines, but can also serve as a satisfactory source of employment to them. Also as being an ambition of people is the appointment of a travelling teacher for outstation schools[43] and ultimately the establishment of a private school in the area to cater exclusively for Aboriginal needs. These include a curriculum suited to Aboriginal desires and expectations, catering for post-primary education (so that children are no longer required to attend a boarding school far from their own community, away from the control of their parents) and organising time and space to suit Aborigines.

Yet another desire is for independence in the fields of legal, financial and planning advice, so the community can hire and fire as it likes, and be free to run its own affairs in a manner which suits it. The communities will only be happy when they have achieved this state, with a balance between societal and long-term needs, and individual and short-term needs.

ACKNOWLEDGEMENTS

I have been helped in many ways by the director of the project, John von Sturmer. I have also benefited from discussions with, and material sent by, staff of the Northern Land Council, notably Mark Dreyfus, Wesley Lanhupuy, Gavin O'Brien, David Rourke, Philip Teitzel and Gerry Thomas. Ross Hebblewhite (Resource Officer/Manager, Gagudju Association) was a cheerful source of information on developments in the Kakadu National Park area. Len Richardson (Northern Territory Division of the Department of Aboriginal Affairs) allowed me to pick his excellent memory. Alf Wilson and Donald Gumurdul provided me with information on Gunbalanya No minees. Robert Tyrell and Roger Pink gave me information on cash-related matters. Bob Beedman of the Department of Aboriginal Affairs provided information on the Aboriginals Benefit Trust Account (ABTA). The Hon. W. C. Wentworth provided me with his calculations on payments from the Nabarlek agreement.

I would also like to express my appreciation to Nathanael Maralngurra and Jacob Nayinggul for going through this paper with me. Their comments made publication of this article possible.

NOTES

1. The full title is: *Ranger Uranium Project, Agreement under S. 44 of the Aboriginal Land Rights (Northern Territory) Act 1976 between the Commonwealth of Australia and the Northern Land Council*, signed November 3, 1978.

2. The full title is: *Mining Agreement between Queensland Mines Limited and the Northern Land Council*, signed March 22, 1979.

3. Henceforth this Act is referred to as the Land Rights Act.

4. Ironically, the word for 'money' in Kunwinjku (Gunwinggu), the dominant language of the area, is *kunwarde*, 'stone'.

5. A general physical description of the Alligator Rivers region is given in *The Ranger Uranium Environmental Inquiry Second Report*, Australian Government Publishing Service, Canberra, 1977, pp.15-21. The accompanying map shows the features of the area mentioned in this paper. The Aboriginal population of the area between the Mann River and the South Alligator River is approximately 1300. This breaks down as follows:

Oenpelli, 450 (350–500)

Oenpelli outstations, 300 (250–350)

Nabarlek, 30–50

Croker Island, 170

Goulburn Island, 200

Ranger Township, 30–50

Mudginberri, 35

Kakadu National Park communities, 100

Exact figures for the location fluctuate greatly because of high mobility between settlements. (See also J.R. von Sturmer, *Uranium Mining and the Aborigines of the Alligator Rivers Region: a review*, paper given at the UNESCO Regional Seminar on Technological Impact on Culture in the Pacific, Sydney, 19–24 January 1981.)

6. This is an up-dated version of a paper presented at the Australian Institute of Aboriginal Studies Symposium on Land Rights in May 1980, which was in turn a slightly modified version of an information paper prepared for the Steering Committee for the Project to Monitor the Social Impact of Uranium Mining on Aboriginal Communities in the Northern Territory.

7. *The Ranger Uranium Environmental Inquiry Second Report* examines the clauses in the Land Rights Act which apply to royalties and other payments (pp.240–42), but in the section Impacts on Aboriginal society (pp. 225–33) there is no mention of the impact of royalties on communities in the area. This Report is referred to henceforth as the Fox Inquiry.

8. Many people in the area are becoming very conscious of being scrutinised; apart from monitoring activities, there has also been a major investigation for a land claim (the Alligator Rivers Stage II Land Claim). One or two Aborigines have even suggested that anthropologists should be licensed before they are allowed to do any work which involves matter of a personal nature.

9. For the following financial details I am indebted to the Northern Land Council.

10. The Cooinda Hotel-Motel is located on a special purpose lease within the Kakadu National Park. It is not Aboriginal Land under the meaning of the term in the Land Rights Act.

11. The Hotel-Motel currently has 30 beds, plus camping facilities. A conservative estimate is of 40 tourists a night from May until the end of September (the dry season).

12. It would have been possible for the people benefiting under the Ranger agreement to use an already existing mechanism—namely, by using Gunbalanya Nominees (see below), as some of the people benefiting

under the Nabarlek agreement had chosen to do. However, there are reasons why people benefiting under the Ranger agreement may not have wished to use Gunbalanya Nominees.

13. For example, the commissioning of the power-plant at Ranger was expected in November-December 1980. The current projection for its commissioning is late May 1981.

14. While the development of communities in the Kakadu area is no doubt a proper function of the Association, some emphasis in the future may have to be given to traditional owners of the area who live outside the park in such places as Bamyili, Pine Creek, Humpty Doo, Darwin, etc.

15. The project areas consist of the mining lease at Nabarlek and the lease for the barge-landing site at Wunyu Beach. If a distinction can be made, the first group mentioned above owns the land which is leased and the second group owns land which is affected by the project; these definitions have been subject to a number of interpretations, and have led to some of the difficulties outlined below.

16. On the East Alligator River.

17. Outside legal advice was given to the Northern Land Council.

18. In response to an approach by Queensland Mines, a community development officer was appointed to Nabarlek by the Department of Aboriginal Affairs in October 1979. He resigned six months later. In September 1980 a community adviser was appointed to Nabarlek, but he is based at Jabiru and unable to travel to Nabarlek in the wet season. Queensland Mines itself has an Aboriginal liaison officer. These government and mining company positions are not subject to the same control by the Aboriginal community at Nabarlek as its own employees would be.

19. See J.R. von Sturmer, *The Distribution of Nabarlek Moneys: towards a structural solution,* 1980 (mimeo).

20. The West Arnhem office of the Northern Regional Office of the DAA, which has responsibility for the Kakadu National Park area, was set up in January 1978. The impetus for setting up this office was the Fox Inquiry.

21. Because of differences in the two agreements, when royalties are paid, beneficiaries under the Nabarlek agreement will receive a greater *proportion* of the royalties from the Nabarlek project than that received by Ranger beneficiaries from the Ranger project.

22. Or who should benefit, since children who should benefit under the 'people affected' category have not had any money put aside for them yet.

23. See *Payments to Aborigines from Ranger,* above, p.

24. Questions about mining revenues are included in the author's interviews to do with perceptions, and understanding, of money (see below).

25. The Nabarlek project is short-term compared to Ranger (mining and processing the Nabarlek ore will take about 8 years), and there is a sense that the money from Nabarlek, is, or will be, running out.

26. Needless to say, this was erroneous information.

27. The decision on which communities or associations receive this money is determined *by the relevant land council.* See Shann Turnbull, *Economic Development of Aboriginal Communities in the Northern Territory,* Australian Government Publishing Service, Canberra, 1980, pp. 23–25, for possible consequences of this.

28. There is a general desire for better housing in the area, but with the exception of one individual no one has indicated that a house would be bought with mining money (with the provision that there is enough to do so). The expectation seems to be that 'government' or the Council provides houses and undertakes repairs.

29. The demand for these products disappeared when the Avon lady left Oenpelli.

30. At present literature available on fiscal matters seems to be confined to 'The Beagle Boys versus Uncle Scrooge'.

31. The Australian Institute of Aboriginal Studies raised the lack of structures offering financial advice in the Alligator Rivers region as a matter of urgency in its *Report to the Minister for Aboriginal Affairs on the Social Impact of Uranium Mining on the Aborigines of the Northern Territory (for the period 1 October 1979 to 31 March 1980).*

32. The burglary cover is for $4000.

33. These matters were raised by the Australian Institute of Aboriginal Studies with the Minister for Aboriginal Affairs, and his response is summarised in the *Report to the Minister for Aboriginal Affairs on the Social Impact of Uranium Mining on the Aborigines of the Northern Territory (for the period 1 April 1980 to 30 September 1980).*

34. Some Aborigines at Ranger have a Bankcard.

35. There is at least one case of a beneficiary under Ranger who was formerly receiving the unemployment benefit but is now employed by Ranger.

36. This has to do not only with a greater set of activities for people during the dry season, but also a lack of availability of materials (bark, pandanus), especially towards the end of the dry season.

37. On 14 September 1980 the Federal Government announced the approval of an application by Denison Australia Pty Ltd to acquire the Koongarra Uranium Deposits and associated Territory from Noranda Australia Ltd.

38. It will seem inequitable if this policy continues but the policy on eligibility for pensions is altered so that it is assessed on yearly income.

39. *Aboriginal Land Rights Commission, first and second reports,* Australian Government Publishing Service, Canberra, 1973, 1974.

40. Answers to the questions on money in the author's interviews suggest that people have little idea of what should be bought for communities; answers seem to reflect personal desires and inclinations e.g., mothers want fences keep their children penned up or washing machines, pensioners want a bus to take them shopping.

41. It is interesting to note in this connection that when Oenpelli bought vehicles for outstations with its 'affected community' money, two of those vehicles were placed under the control of women, even though only one of them could drive.

42. One woman was worried about her sons and other young men driving around in cars and getting drunk. She wanted to buy them something that would also keep them at home. So she bought electric guitars, amplifiers, drums. Their interest was evident. The community's ears, however, were punished—one did not have to be particularly close to the practice sessions—and the equipment has languished in a locked room for the last year.

43. At present an outstation has to be stable and have a person trained and willing to be a teaching assistant before the Department of Education will appoint a visiting teacher to it.

25

A NATIONAL STRATEGY TO DEAL WITH EXPLORATION AND MINING ON OR NEAR ABORIGINAL LAND

Marcia Langton

This paper attempts to elucidate some of the issues surrounding proposals for exploration and mining on or near Aboriginal land. First, I discuss the Commonwealth Government's role in exploration and mining situations where Aboriginal interests are jeopardised. Secondly, I present a case study of how exploration was experienced by one Aboriginal group. This case study underlines the need for a rational approach to consultation and negotiation. Thirdly, I suggest a national strategy which may improve the Aboriginal position and which could bring about a more constructive approach to the inevitable series of consultations and negotiations between Aboriginal groups, and mining and exploration companies and the Federal and State Governments.

A national strategy should enable the public, both Aboriginal and non-Aboriginal, to assess more realistically the important issues at stake in such situations; in particular such a strategy should enable the public to understand the relative weakness of the Aboriginal negotiating position and to accept that guidelines and precedents for regulating the situation are essential if 'fair play' is to prevail.

MINING AND LAND RIGHTS

There is more than sufficient evidence to support the contention, often expressed by Aboriginal people, that exploration and mining can present dangers for the survival of Aboriginal cultures and societies. Various committees of inquiry appointed by the Commonwealth Government have documented Aboriginal opposition to and concern about the dangers posed by exploration and mining for their well-being. The most striking example is the social monitoring programme of the Australian Institute of Aboriginal Studies in the Alligator Rivers Region, which has brought to light not only the advantages but also the disadvantages of mining for Aboriginal people in that region.

A common theme in these conflicts is the fact that although various inquiries have recommended that the Commonwealth must be involved as an arbitrating presence, the Commonwealth has been reluctant to assume its full role in the States in relation to its responsibilities in Aboriginal affairs. Another theme is the unsatisfactory nature of the communication and information flow between Aboriginal groups, on the one hand, and the mining companies and State governments, on the other.

The interests of Aboriginal people and those of the State governments in relation to mining are in conflict over some important matters. While Aboriginal groups throughout the country are attempting to establish viable and worthwhile life-styles, economic pursuits and a stable niche within the Australian milieu, State governments support a 'development' strategy that is largely dependent on the exploitation of non-renewable resources, particularly minerals, with little concern for the problems they pose for the attempts by Aboriginal communities to reconstruct their societies.

For Aboriginal people the most desirable alternative to the present situation is complete ownership of minerals since this would give Aboriginal groups the maximum degree of control over the impact of mining on their communities. This is the situation in the United States of America for all land-owners, with the result that American Indian groups in areas of mineral wealth have an assured economic and thus social future. For Aboriginal Australia complete ownership of minerals would restore rights that closely resemble traditional ownership and make possible the reconstruction of Aboriginal society without further unwanted intrusion on our lands and compromise of our interests.

THE RECOMMENDATIONS OF THE ABORIGINAL LAND RIGHTS COMMISSION

Mr Justice Woodward (Australia 1974:104) in the Second Report of the Aboriginal Land Rights Commission found that with regard to the position of mineral rights, traditional laws and customs could be interpreted as follows:

> . . . It is clear that Aboriginal ownership was not expressed in terms merely of the land surface. In many of the legends which gave expression to man's spiritual connexion with his land, his mythical forbears emerged from the ground and returned to it at different points in their sagas. Their spirit essences still pervade those places and are retained in the soil and the rocks.

He found that the 'two Land Councils have each pressed for the grant to Aborigines of full ownership of minerals on their traditional lands. They say that anything less than this would simply not satisfy the people they represent' (Australia, 1974). He concluded (Australia, 1974:104) that:

> . . . to deny Aborigines the right to prevent mining on their land is to deny the reality of their land rights. I find it quite impossible to inspect developments on Groote Eylandt or the Gove Peninsula or proposed works on uranium deposits in Arnhem Land and to say that such developments, without consent, could be consistent with traditional land rights for Aborigines . . .

However, he recommended in the end that 'minerals and petroleum on Aboriginal lands should remain the property of the crown' (Australia, 1975:127). He gave a number of reasons for this decision (Australia, 1975:115):

> In particular I feel that the Government must be able to act if it is, on balance, contrary to the national interest . . . The chief of these is my belief in the general approach adopted in this country that minerals belong to all the people . . . Secondly I think that the legitimate objectives of Aborigines in this connexion would be met if the recommendations I have made were accepted. To go further would be unnecessarily divisive and could lead to reactions among other members of the community which, in the long term, would not be in the best interests of Aborigines . . . Thirdly, the whole of Australian mining law is based on the assumption that minerals belong to the crown. To provide otherwise in a particular case could well create problems and sorting these problems out could delay necessary legislation.

However, other provisions have been made in law without the detrimental results predicted by Woodward. The legislation establishing the Aboriginal Lands Trust of New South Wales gives the Lands Trust, which is not for any purpose the Crown, or an instrumentality of the Crown, full possession of mineral rights in relation to its land with the exception of rights in gold and silver. But the amount and size of the parcels of land owned by the Trust are very small as compared with those in the Northern Territory.

It is worthwhile here to briefly look at Aboriginal rights in minerals in other States. Nowhere else do Aboriginal people own the minerals. However in South Australia those areas under the Lands Trust receive 50% of the royalties paid to the Government while the other 50% is kept by the Lands Trust. For the area held under the *Pitjantjatjara Land Rights Act* one-third of the statutory royalties go to the Pitjantjatjara, one-third to benefit all other Aborigines in the State and one third into general State revenue. The Pitjantjatjara cannot veto mining but they may negotiate reasonable royalties above the statutory payment in proportion to the disturbance to the land and people.

In Western Australia there is a complex formula for the proportion of statutory royalties to be paid to the Aboriginal Lands Trust (see McDonald, 1981:226) which despite all the mining activity in that State only generated $7926 in the year ended 30 June 1980.

In Victoria mineral rights remain with the Crown, but the *Archaeological and Aboriginal Preservation Act* 1972 may be relevant in restricting exploration and mining operations if they endanger land where there are sites of scientific interest. The provisions do not extend to Aboriginal land.

In Queensland the regulation of mining on reserves is entirely in the hands of the Director (as trustee of the reserves) and the State Minister for Aboriginal and Islander Advancement under the terms of *The Aborigines Act*. They can grant leases for mining purposes and exploration on Aboriginal reserves without consulting Aboriginal residents. The State Government can make agreements with mining companies and the trustees of the reserve giving the Director, a share in the royalties from mining. Such royalties may be spent for the benefit of Aborigines on reserves, but as far as I can ascertain there is no public statement of such expenditure.

While Mr Justice Woodward was considering communities in the Northern Territory he may well have been referring to any Aboriginal community with traditional links to land in Australia. As well, it is important to note that his arguments apply equally to Aboriginal communities with links to land which may not be defined as traditional in his terms, but perhaps, with rights in land by virtue of occupation or historical circumstances. Often, traditional rights to land coexist with rights acquired by historical occupancy. 'Conception' rights are recognised in reserve areas, for instance. The two arguments Woodward advances in this respect are stated thus (Australia 1975:110, 115):

> . . . it is necessary that *any community likely to be affected by a substantial mining development* should also consent. It is they who would be affected by a substantial influx of non-Aboriginal workers and, to my mind, these consequences can be even more serious than the devastation of an area of land. They should not be forced on an unwilling community. (emphasis added)

and

> I have made it clear that . . . Aborigines should be able to exercise most of the rights of an owner of minerals—particularly the rights to decide when exploration for minerals should not take place . . . I think Aborigines should have special rights and special compensations because they stand to lose so much more by the industrial invasion of their traditional lands and *their privacy* than other citizens would lose in similar circumstances. (emphasis added).

Woodward (1974:109–10) set out the terms under which Aboriginal consent to exploration and mining should be sought. Clearly, he felt that Aboriginal groups and communities were not in a sufficient position of power to cope with the demands of consultation and negotiation. His recommendations on impact statements, the need for consent of traditional owners, communities, land councils, and as well, the approval of the Minister for Aboriginal Affairs, before any exploration licence is granted, show his concern for a process of consultation and negotiation with checks and safeguards to protect the interests of Aboriginal people. Other reports have also urged a Commonwealth role in negotiations and the overseeing of Aboriginal interests.

HOUSE OF REPRESENTATIVES STANDING COMMITTEE ON ABORIGINAL AFFAIRS: REPORT ON THE PRESENT CONDITIONS OF YIRRKALA PEOPLE (1975)

The first of the principal recommendations of this committee states (1975:12):

> the Government should take a positive role in working out with the Aboriginals and Nabalco Pty Ltd a satisfactory formula whereby the Aboriginal community can freely exercise its proprietary rights to the land . . .

The committee also recommended that 'the Government should play a positive role in supporting the Aboriginal interests' (1975:33). It found (1975:33):

> . . . *effective consultation did not take place with the community in 1968 and that its interests in the final agreement with Nabalco were not fully taken into account.* This lack of understanding of Aboriginal rights and aspirations has given rise to feelings among the people of indifference towards them by Government, the Administration and business interests. This state of affairs should not be allowed to recur nor to continue (emphasis added).

That Aboriginal people in the States, as well as in certain areas of the Northern Territory, feel that Government, administrators and business interests are indifferent to their rights and aspirations is evident in their organisation of independent, non-statutory land councils and in the international campaign currently being conducted to draw attention to the reprehensible activities of mining companies.

The Committee accounted for the Aboriginal response to mining in this way (1975:57):

> *More than anything else, the fears and suspicions about the effect of the new mining complex upon their land explain the uncertainty within the community and apprehensions about the future.* In the short space of five years the Aboriginal people have seen large tracts of their traditional land transformed in a way they never envisaged. (emphasis added).

THE RANGER URANIUM ENVIRONMENTAL INQUIRY

At least a third of the Ranger Inquiry's second report deals with the effect of mining on Aboriginal people, their land and rights in it, and related matters. It is not necessary here to refer in detail to most of their many recommendations but it is relevant to refer to the statements of the Commissioners on Aboriginal rights and aspirations (1977:9):

> . . . there was a general conviction that opposition was futile. The Aboriginals do not have confidence that their own view will prevail; they feel that uranium mining development is almost certain to take place at Jabiru, if not elsewhere in the Region as well. They feel that having got so far, the white man is not likely to stop. They have a justifiable complaint that plans for mining having been allowed to develop as far as they have without the Aboriginal people having an adequate opportunity to be heard. Having in mind, in particular, the importance to the Aboriginal people of their right to self-determination, it is not in the circumstances possible for us to say that the development would be beneficial to them.

The Commissioners continued in a later section of the second report (1977:269-70):

> The great need, constantly explained in the evidence before us, is to provide them with the means of making their lives meaningful in their own terms, and of thus restoring

> their own dignity and self-assurance. It is thought that a recognition of their association with the land and the grant to them of title to it, albeit in white man's terms, are basic means to that end . . . It is possible that if part of their land is to become subject to mining the spiritual satisfaction and psychological benefit will be lost. This is not an argument for rejecting their claim; what it does point to is the desirability of recognising their title as fully as that can reasonably be done . . .

The various recommendations fears and rebukes that have been quoted here indicate that the Commonwealth has not fully accepted its responsibilities to protect Aboriginal interests in relation to mining. In particular, the Commonwealth has not, from an Aboriginal point of view, granted title to land 'as fully as that can reasonably be done'. (This is especially true of the State Governments' recognition of Aborignal entitlement to land.) Nor has it acted upon Woodward's recommendations regarding exploration and mining on or near Aboriginal communities.

The Woodward Commission made it clear that exploration and mining should not proceed without Aboriginal consent, and that Aboriginal consent should only be overridden if 'the government of the day were to resolve that the national interest required it' (Australia, 1975:104). Mr Justice Woodward stated:

> In this context I use the word 'required' deliberately so that such an issue would not be determined on a mere balance of convenience or desirability but only as a matter of necessity.

It is probable that the conclusion of the Commissioners of the Ranger Uranium Environmental Inquiry that Aboriginal 'opposition should not be allowed to prevail' (1977:9) has the intention of declaring uranium mining on Aboriginal land in the Alligator Rivers Region to be in the so-called national interest. But it is also possible, in view of the debates about the provisions of draft legislation being prepared at that time, particularly over whether 'consent' or 'consultation' should be the condition for mining, that the Ranger Commissioners were creating an exception to the asserted need for the consent of the Land Council and traditional owners. While the land councils in the Northern Territory seem to have achieved a measure of satisfaction in their dealings with the Commonwealth Government in relation to mining, and indeed seem to have obliging relations with mining companies, the same cannot be said for Aboriginal groups and organisations in general in the States.

Mr Justice Woodward recommended that, on the application of his terms of reference outside of the Northern Territory, the approach he had instigated in the Territory be followed in the States: 'By this I mean that regional councils of Aborigines, if not already in existence, should be encouraged to establish themselves' (Australia, 1975:135). He also stated:

> . . . I have borne in mind the probability that what is done in the Territory will be regarded by many as setting some sort of precedent for action elsewhere. I have therefore tried, so far as possible, to frame my recommendations in such a way that they could be adapted for use beyond the Territory in any case where that was thought to be appropriate.

Clearly, these recommendations have been in the main acceptable to Aboriginal people in the States. The establishment of the North Queensland Land Council, the Kimberley Land Council, the Victorian Land Council and the New South Wales Land Council is evidence of this. The continuing obstacles to the successful representation of their constituents on matters of land rights, mining and others, is largely the result of the failure of the Commonwealth Government to grant them full and statutory recognition and adequate funding. It is clear from the policy of these land councils that they are not satisfied with the State governments' policies on mining on Aboriginal land (with the possible exception of New South Wales), and that they desire to have the Commonwealth exercise its powers to protect Aboriginal interests in exploration and mining.

There is, then, a need for full recognition of Aboriginal land councils and for adequate guidelines to enable Aboriginal groups, mining companies and government to negotiate more effectively; it is also important that procedures are established which take account of certain inequalities in the bargaining positions of Aboriginal communities, mining companies and government. These issues affect the lives of many people. Just how this happens and what the consequences are are shown in the case study on the Argyle Prospect, to which I now turn.

CRA (EXPLORATION) PTY LTD AND THE ARGYLE PROSPECT: A CASE STUDY

This case study is a chronological account of the events surrounding the discovery by CRA (Exploration) Pty Ltd of diamond-bearing alluvial deposits and kimberlite pipes in the country of the Mirriwung-Kitja, now known as the Argyle Prospect, south-east of Kununurra in the Kimberley region of Western Australia. It underlines the arbitrary, *ad hoc* and insensitive approach to the Aboriginal community practised by exploration and mining companies and the inadequacy of the Aboriginal responses in a situation where they were largely powerless to shape events or prevent intrusions.

Ashton Mining NL, a consortium, whose largest shareholder, Conzinc Riotinto of Australia, is the manager, released an interim report in Melbourne on Sunday 21 October 1979 about the discovery of alluvial deposits in the area now called the Argyle Prospect in the Glenhill-Lissadell border area *(The West Australian,* 22 and 23 October 1979). Further reports on the yields were released on Monday 5 November 1979 *(The West Australian,* 6 and 12 November 1979, 12 December 1979, and 10 January 1980; *The Sydney Morning Herald,* 5 and 12 November 1979).

Press reports varied as to the quality of the yield and extent of the deposit. *The West Australian* of 10 January 1980, for example, stated that 'alluvial diamonds found at Argyle extended up to 32 km from their scource'. Information given in that report indicated that there may be more than four kimberlite pipes (these are the ore-bearing deposits). The main pipe was said to cover 45 hectares (approximately 5½ square miles) and has yielded 750 carats per 100 tonnes, which is 'extremely rich by world standards'. Press reports compared the Argyle Prospect with one of the highest carat-value producers in South Africa, the Koffiefontein pipe, which averages only 9 carats per 100 tonnes. CRA (Exploration Pty Ltd.) labelled this pipe 'AK1'. The report continued:

> It is believed these values fell away to as low as 60 to 65 carats a 100 tonnes of material at more than 30 km (approx. 19 miles) from the pipe.

Clearly, the area of mining operations will be enormous. About 25% of the diamonds are of gem quality and a large proportion are industrial stones. In pipe 'B' diamonds have been found at a depth of 175 metres (about 600 feet) and a sampling showed 13.6 carats per 100 tonnes.

The West Australian of 6 November 1979 reported that CRA intended to crush and sample 25 tonnes of material in a secondary deposit before the 1979/1980 wet season alone. The full extent of crushing and sampling in the area since then is not indicated in media reports.

By excavating many hundreds of tonnes of earth, crushing it and estimating the yield of diamonds over many square kilometres CRA (Exploration Pty Ltd) intended to find out for the consortium of companies how feasible the establishment of a mine would have been. The decision to mine became public the following year in July 1980, althought it was obvious that mining would eventually proceed.

Bill Gossan writing in *The Miner* in November 1978 indicated the voraciousness of the mining companies:

> To evaluate kimberlite pipes large tonnages of material have to be tested . . . In yesteryear, mining went ahead on the basis of near-surface promise, but today this is not on. It is well to recall the maxim that originated in the South African diamond fields which states 'the grade of a kimberlite pipe is not known until the last diamond is removed' . . .
>
> Many of the smaller outfits that have pegged claims or obtained reserves do not have the financial resources or expertise to evaluate their holdings.

The Bulletin of 15 January 1980 set out in an article, 'Who's who in the Great Diamond Rush', the companies involved in the diamond search and their interests. Several hundred had joined the spree.

At the time of the first announcement of the discovery, the then Minister for Mines, Mr Mensaros, was reported in *The West Australian* as saying that:

> . . . the W.A. Government was pleased that the exploration by the Ashton joint venturers had resulted in further promising prospects for the Kimberleys.

He could not have been referring to the prospects for Aboriginal people in the Kimberley. In November 1979 the Minister for Mines, Mensaros, had approved 25 temporary reserves to the Ashton consortium thereby securing for them most of the ground they had been seeking. David Haselhurst in *The Bulletin* of 15 January, 1980, explained the extent of the *gadeya*[2] rush for Aboriginal land:

> The diamond rush began after the Ashton Syndicate reported in early 1978 its initial discovery of kimberlite pipes and associated diamonds at Ellendale station . . . In that year a frantic claim-pegging spree developed. West Australian Mines Department records show 5775 mineral claims were lodged in 1978 totalling as much as 693 000 hectares . . . Apart from the vast tracts of land now held under mineral claims, more than 270 temporary exploration reserves have been let for diamond prospecting in the past two years—an area that could total as much as 54,000 square miles.

Apart from the glee of greed, the carefully timed and spaced reports to the press from Ashton and CRA brought to public attention the extent of the diamond find and the unprecedented opportunity to exploit the country's 'wealth' and they brought to the Western Australian Government's attention the need to quell Aboriginal opposition or at least divert it, as Noonkanbah so successfully did. The media hysteria was felt in every quarter, and if the claim-peggers lounging in the hotels and bars throughout the Kimberleys were not as excited as the Pierponts, it was because they knew that they could sell their claims at astoundingly inflated prices and leave the Kimberley with the fortunes that shareholders dream of.

The Australian Financial Review reported the Premier of Western Australia, Sir Charles Court, as stating that, 'Development would begin within 12 to 18 months on the Argyle diamond prospect in the Kimberley region', and that, 'his government would "expedite" a study of environmental and associated matters'. The deposit, he stated, 'lent itself to progressive development in logical steps'. What he meant was that the mine would be developed to its maximum capacity.

The Premier welcomed the likelihood of an increase in the white population and the real possibility of higher living standards for the whites as a result of mining development. However, he had nothing at all to say about the problems that Aboriginal people would face when the mining at Argyle got under way. Since then, the 15 000 or more Aboriginal people in the Kimberley region have returned an Aboriginal member to the Legislative Assembly of the Western Australian Parliament, Mr Ernie Bridge, a first in the Aboriginal history of Western Australia (see Langton, 1980).

As late as 19 January 1980 the company's reports referred only to sampling although the tone of their reports was one of feverish optimism. Shares in Ashton Mining NL reached a record in November 1979 at $1.76, while CRA shares rose $3.80 after publication of their report on the Argyle prospect. On 16 January 1980 Ashton shares were listed in the Perth Share Quotes in *The West Australian* at $3.35 and CRA shares were listed at $5.76. The shares had almost doubled in two months.

It was admitted by representatives of mining companies that the extent of exploration in the Kimberley was far beyond the ability of the companies to follow through with proposals for establishment of mines. The main reasons were financial (pers. comm., February 1980). Throughout the Kimberley region there has been a spate of exploration, most of which cannot for the immediate future be followed up by adequate investment in mining. This 'booty' or 'raider-type' exploration causes inestimable damage to areas of great religious significance to the Aboriginal people and to the natural environment. Exploration is not of the type imagined popularly. It is not simply the brave geologist with a hammer and bag but as with the Argyle exploration activities, hundreds of tonnes of earth are excavated after a promising find, roads are cut, and camps established

CRA feared the effect of speculative investment and the creation of an artificial boom, and so until April 1980 they barred journalists from the Argyle prospect and forbade direct coverage of the exploration activities and taking of photographs. J. N. Pierce of *The Sydney Morning Herald* was forcibly ejected from the area in November 1979. There may well have been other reasons such as fear of public objections to uncontrolled exploration, crushing and sampling and the environmental damage and of Aboriginal reactions to the social and physical effects of mining on their communities. As exploration and other activities proceed at Argyle, CRA may use their secretive behaviour of early 1980 as a basis for denying Aboriginal people access to the land they do not already inhabit or use.

At Turkey Creek the Mirriwung-Kitja traditional owners had been worried about the extensive exploration activities and site damage that had occurred in the area of the Argyle prospect. One man, John Toby, was particularly concerned. When I met him in January 1980 at Turkey Creek he gave the impression of being a hard-headed businessman as he explained his plans for developing his 'grandfather's run' as a viable economic base for the community of people he felt responsible for. In late 1979 he began re-establishing the Glenhill pastoral property on the 'run' which had been incorporated with the Dunham River lease, an Aboriginal-owned and controlled venture. The Woolah people at the Dunham River homestead had established a successful pastoral operation. They were mustering cattle and horses and were experimenting with grasses to rejuvenate the land which had been severely over stocked by the previous owners.

Toby and others at the station, had learnt that a large-scale exploration project was operating in the area near their pastoral lease and that sacred sites had been desecrated and roads and machinery established in the area only when they went to investigate what they thought was the work of cattle thieves. On 7 November 1979 the manager of the Dunham River station, Jimmy Smith, with his book-keeper, Tom Stevens, the Kimberley Land Council anthropologist Kim Akerman, and Peter Bindon from the Human Studies section of the Western Australian Museum, flew over Glenhill to investigate roads that had recently been put through the area. It had been thought that these roads were established by cattle thieves, who, in the Kimberley, have sophisticated techniques. The inspection revealed, however, that considerable roadworks combined with test trenches were linked with mining exploration. Sites in the vicinity of Devil Devil Spring had been desecrated to the horror of the men. John Toby immediately contacted the then Chairman of the Kimberley Land Council, Jimmy Bieundurry, to complain about CRA's activities. Bieundurry then contacted the traditional owners to propose an immediate survey of the damage and to locate further sites in the area. CRA was loathe to use the Kimberley Land Council's resources for the proposed survey as their representatives felt that the Land Council staff would be biased against the company. CRA (Exploration Pty Ltd) agreed to a proposal that the Western Australian Museum do the survey at CRA's expense.

The Aboriginal Sites Department of the Museum, realising the importance of the involvement of the Kimberley Land Council, particularly as traditional owners requested its participation, asked that their anthropologist, Kim Akerman, be seconded to the project. On 14 November 1979 Peter Randolph and Kim Akerman began the survey with a brief visit to the CRA camp. There they met with CRA's senior personnel, Warren Atkinson and Frank Hughes. CRA provided helicopter time of about three hours over the next two days. Aboriginal consultants accompanied the two researchers and located and mapped the sites in the immediate area of Smoke Creek. This was an initial survey and then *only* in the area of the most intensive exploration. The other temporary mining reserves had yet to be surveyed after the wet season. A report and map were produced by the Western Australian Museum. However, both are closed documents. Further, the community requested that the report contain only a broad, general outline of the mythological significance of the sites in the area. The community requested that the report be made available only to the Kimberley Land Council, the Western Australian Museum and CRA.

The policy of the Kimberley Land Council in such survey work is to undertake total coverage of the general area rather than to confine surveys to areas for which mining is known to be proposed. This policy has been adopted to counter the growing tendency for mining company representatives to suggest that sites have been 'invented' to thwart mining. Jokes about 'mobile sites' are common in the Kimberley mining circles. In this case the Kimberley Land Council, an underfunded and understaffed grassroots organisation, had found out too late about the desecration of sites in the Mirriwung-Kitja country.

Most Aboriginal people do not foresee any benefits accruing to them from mining. Nor do they expect that it will stabilise their already precarious social and economic situation. On the contrary, they are concerned that even more fragmentation and bureaucratic manipulation from mining and government officials will deprive them further. John Toby stated to Kimberley Land Council field staff at Turkey Creek on 20 January 1980:

> The white man takes away our land. Then he might give the blackfella back a little bit of country. Then he wants it back because he find a bit of mineral. When are they going to give us a fair go . . . The white man pushes us from pillar to post. A man hasn't even got a home. I've gone back to my country. Then this thing came up. I'm a bit worried I'm trying now to find some way to stop this. (pers.comm., 1980)

It was not only the 50 traditional owners who were concerned about the exploration and the proposed mining venture. People as far away as Wyndham, Halls Creek, Mistake Creek and Mount House have traditional associations with the country because of the Dreaming tracks that pass through it. The people at Glenhill, Dunham River Station, Turkey Creek and Guda Guda, numbering some 400 people, knew too that they would be affected by the inevitable dispossession, intrusion and destruction of Aboriginal land.

In April 1980 the Turkey Creek community requested the Australian Institute of Aboriginal Studies to prepare a comprehensive report on their traditional associations with the land. Williams and Palmer, anthropologists commissioned by the Institute for the work, reported that there were 48 traditional owners as well as a large number of other people with inchoate rights in the land through maternal links. They documented the mythological significance of the area and the attachment of the people to the land maintained through their religious law and ceremony. This report resulted in the recommendation by the Aboriginal cultural material committee through the Western Australian Museum Trustees to the relevant minister for the protection of a number of traditional and religious sites.

On 6 July John Toby and the Warmun community at Turkey Creek called on the Museum to prosecute CRA for desecration of sites under the terms of the *Aboriginal Heritage Act*. By late July John Toby had withdrawn the court action against CRA and was ready to negotiate with them; thus he forsook his and every other Aboriginal owners' rights to the sites under Western Australian law.

The West Australian announced on 26 July under the heading, 'CRA CASH OFFER SPLITS ABORIGINES', that:

> A group of Kimberley Aborigines is set to sign a compensation agreement for land containing a sacred site at the Ashton Joint Venture's Argyle diamond find.
>
> The proposed deal—understood to involve a payment of $100 000 and possible further payments during the life of any mining operations at Argyle—has angered other Aboriginal groups in the Kimberleys . . . CRA Exploration Pty Ltd has flown six members of the Aboriginal family group to Perth in a charter plane to sign the settlement.
>
> However, a meeting of members of the local Aboriginal community and other involved elders has called on the family group not to sign any deals and to return for further talks. That meeting has also sent a telegram to CRA saying that Aborigines would not be bound by any agreements signed by the family group.

On 28 July *The West Australian* continued its report following the conclusion of the agreement:

> The Ashton joint venturers have agreed to make long-term payments to a group of Kimberley Aborigines for disruption caused by the operations at the Argyle diamond find . . . It is understood that 20 of the traditional owners were signatories to a telegram on Thursday calling on the family group not to sign the agreement.

The majority group of traditional owners, the Kimberley Land Council and the Aboriginal Legal Service felt utterly betrayed. They reported (pers. comm.) that CRA had apparently given John Toby a rented vehicle and possibly cash sometime before, allegedly as an inducement for him to sign the 'agreement'. It was further alleged that CRA staff in a company helicopter had flown into Turkey Creek to 'round up' one afternoon some prospective signatories. They had reportedly asked one woman if she was Toby's sister, to which the woman had replied 'yes'. The KLC staff believed that she was a classificatory or 'skin' sister rather than a sibling. Five people were collected and flown to Perth by charter plane. Their legal representatives were commissioned by CRA. The signatories were John Toby, Peggy Pat, Evelyn Hall, George Dixon and Tim Timms. It appears that this report may be correct. Cross-checking of the list of signatories against the list of traditional owners reveals that one of the women signatories is not in fact a traditional owner. The CRA men had 'rounded up' a 'skin' sister and not a sibling.

The newspapers reported that 'confusion still existed on the validity of the agreement' (*The West Australian,* 28 July 1980). The Aboriginal objections were that all the traditional owners had not been consulted, that there was no consensus that the 'agreement' should be signed, nor that talks so far had amounted to negotiations. The consortium justified its conclusion of the 'agreement' in the following way to the press on 28 July:

> In a press release, the Ashton Joint Venturers refer to the family group as the recognised Aboriginal custodians of the Argyle sites.
>
> The custodians had wanted to avoid a dispute at Argyle such as the one that occurred at Noonkanbah, the release said. The operations at Argyle would have a disturbing effect on areas of recognized interest to the custodians.
>
> The press statement said that the joint venture would undertake a capital-works programme on Glen Hill to upgrade the road to the station, supply and erect fencing, provide improved buildings and services including septic tanks, showers and ablutions and supply an administration building. It would provide a water bore, windmill and pump, help to erect stockyards, provide a station generator and supply three station vehicles and a cattle truck.
>
> If mining went ahead, the joint venture would fund capital development on Glen Hill to the value of $100 000 a year, increasing to allow for inflation.
>
> The joint venturers have agreed to seek to provide employment for Aborigines from Mandanagala community, both in the mine and in the work of Glen Hill.
>
> The agreement means that the family group has ended its interest in the sacred sites covering the geological formation that is the source of diamonds at Argyle.

The Aboriginal Legal Service of Western Australia came to the defence of the majority group of traditional owners, saying amongst other things, in a series of press statements: 'Kimberley Aborigines thought that CRA was buying off a small, vocal minority from the diamond find'. (*The West Australian,* 28 July 1980). The then Minister for Mines, Mr Jones, denying any State involvement in the 'agreement', accused the Aboriginal Legal Service and Kimberley Land Council of 'pressuring the family group' (*The West Australian,* 28 July 1980). That kind of accusation against organisations which have developed to protect Aboriginal interests has become the typical red herring used by politicians wherever their own group's interests lie with 'development' through exploitation of minerals. The accusation seems rather like stating that a solicitor is attempting to convince the court that his client is not guilty.

The Premier, Sir Charles Court, the following day, stated to the press that he 'welcomed moves by the Ashton Joint Venturers to work out "good-neighbour arrangements" with Kimberley Aborigines' and that 'the Government had told the venturers there was plenty of scope for them to talk to local Aborigines and to do things that a good neighbour would do' (*The West Australian,* 29 July 1980). He said that he:

> and the Minister for Mines, Mr Jones, had talked with CRA and had said that it would be all right with the Government if suitable arrangements were worked out. But we have to make it clear that there is no question of compensation and no question of royalties . . .

On 30 July members of the Warmun community and the traditional owners who had not been consulted sought legal advice on the 'agreement' and decided to take action to have it invalidated. Their commitment to traditional Aboriginal Law was evident in their comments on the behaviour of the Mandangala people. They warned of 'likely reprisals' and that 'they would be dealt with by tribal law'. They accused them of 'placing Aboriginal law to one side and not knowing the culture'. 'The elders are responsible for the law', they said. They warned that people would die because of indefensible behaviour (*The West Australian,* 30 July 1980).

The furore that had followed the 'agreement' caused the Ashton Joint Venturers to further defend themselves in the Press. *The West Australian* reported on 31 July:

> The Ashton Joint Venturers yesterday defended their compensation agreement with Kimberley Aborigines. They said they had dealt with members of the tribes most closely associated with sacred sites on the Argyle diamond prospect.

> In a statement, the Joint Venturers said they believed that they had acted in good faith. They had entered into an agreement with those Aborigines with an independently identified direct affinity with the Argyle sites.

The Ashton Joint Venturers gave the following account of their dealings with the Mandangala community leading up to the conclusion of the 'agreement'. The Warmun community disputed the facts and the impression of reasonableness and good faith that the Ashton representatives had attempted to portray, (*The West Australian,* 31 July 1980):

> . . . the agreement was with the Gidja and Mirriwung tribes—the recognized custodians of the Argyle Aboriginal sites. The WA Museum had identified four members of those tribes as the Aboriginal core-group directly designated by Aboriginal lore [sic] as the principal custodians of the Smoke-Argyle area.
>
> Mr. John Toby, the leader of the community at Glen Hill station, had approached the Ashton joint venturers for a meeting. This took place on July 22 with more than 30 adult Aborigines attending, the statement said. The meeting had reached agreement and the Aborigines attending had acknowledged the right of the four core-group custodians to enter into an agreement. The Aborigines had expressed a wish to seek legal advice on the format of the agreement and this was why a group was flown to Perth.
>
> The statement said that three of the four core-group custodians were signatories to the agreement. The other was unable to travel to Perth for family reasons. The fourth signatory was one of two Aborigines nominated at the July 22 meeting to sign in addition to the core-group custodians.

Ashton personnel thus attempted to convince the public that they had the anthropological knowlèdge and sufficient understanding of Aboriginal land tenure systems to justify their actions.

On 10 September, the Warmun community, still incensed at the conclusion of the 'agreement' and their loss of control over the sites, wrote the following open letter to set the record straight. The letter was addressed to the Trustees of the Western Australian Museum:

> Dear Sirs,
>
> RE : Sites of Significance to Aboriginal
> People Near CRAE's Argyle Prospect
>
> At a meeting with members of our community on September 3, 1980, Dr. Crawford and Mr. Wright made a number of points concerning the Australian Institute of Aboriginal Studies Report by Kingsley Palmer and Dr. Nancy Williams entitled *Aboriginal relationships to land in the Southern Blatchford Escarpment area of the East Kimberleys,* and the likely response of the Museum to subsequent events in this area.
>
> One of their points was that the Museum understood that the Agreement between CRAE and the group at Mandangala was the result of meetings with the traditional owners, and that the traditional owners agreed for mining to go ahead on sacred sites.
>
> We wish to make it quite clear that this view is only partially correct. We have appended lists [not reproduced here] showing traditional owners, as specified in the AIAS Report who attended meetings where the Agreement was discussed, and those who were not in attendance at such meetings. To our knowledge, 19 of the specified adult traditional owners were present at such meetings, while 16 were not. Of the former group, six persons are resident at Turkey Creek; of the latter, thirteen are resident at Turkey Creek. Roughly half (18 out of 35) of the adult traditional owners are resident at Turkey Creek and members of the Warmun Community, quite a few others reside at Kununurra, yet all financial benefits arising from the Agreement, which will amount to millions of dollars over the life of the mine will go to Mandangala (Glen Hill) for *capital* items.

Yet it is claimed that all the traditional owners were fully cognizant of the Agreement and its implications! In fact the situation as its stands to this day is that the contents of the Agreement are yet to be made known to all the traditional owners, let alone ratified by them.

In view of the Museum's possible misunderstanding of the circumstances in which the Agreement was signed, and the unwanted consequences of an adverse recommendation to the Minister about our sites, we feel it may also be worth pointing out to you that the traditional owners and others who attended the meeting with CRAE at Mandangala did not have the benefit of legal advice. Solicitors were retained on their behalf only when the individuals who were to sign the Agreement reached Perth. Consequently, there was no opportunity for these individuals to discuss the legal advice they received with all the people they claim to have signed for, namely, the 'traditional owners'.

It is interesting to note that CRA's solicitors approached one solicitor who was known to members of the Mandangala group. That solicitor set the following as the conditions under which he would act for the traditional owners of the sites in question:

(a) that he receive "direct instructions from appropriate Aboriginal clients"
(b) that he would "then act as an advisor to those clients"
(c) that he "would not take instructions from meetings which had not been notified well in advance to concerned Aboriginal people"
(d) and "did not see how the matter could be concluded quickly if it were to be concluded by agreement at all".

In the event, those conditions were not acceptable to the Mandangala group, and as mentioned above, a Perth solicitor was retained for the group. It seems likely that CRA paid the legal costs of both parties to the Agreement.

The reasons for making this information available to you are firstly, to set the record straight, since comments of Dr. Crawford and Mr. Wright at Turkey Creek last Wednesday indicated that you had been misinformed; and secondly, and more importantly, to request that your recommendation to the Minister be based on the underlying traditional significance and continuing importance of the sites in question to Aboriginal people. Our understanding is that the Museum's statutory responsibility is to recommend wether [sic.] a site is of such significance that it should be protected from use for other purposes. It is not a valid approach to recommend that a site should not be protected simply because the Aboriginal people concerned have been convinced that the site will not be protected!

Dr. Crawford's remarks to us were: "We've come to find out where you stand for those places now that John Toby has made an Agreement." This and other comments by Dr. Crawford and Mr. Wright indicated that you as the Trustees may in fact be taking an approach which takes into account factors which are clearly irrelevant to the Museum's job of assessing the significance of the sites. If this is the case, we ask you to reconsider, especially in the light of the way the Agreement came about.

Our response to Dr. Crawford and Mr. Wright was to ask that the 'main springs' (involved in *djundungal)* be protected: Wesley, Devil Devil, Flying Fox, Hot Water and Billygoat Yard Springs, plus springs on both sides of Mt. Pitt; and for access to these places to be guaranteed.

This is clearly not our most favoured position, which remains set out in the AIAS Report. It has been adopted as a result of (a) the Museum's inability to prevent disturbance and desecration of sites to date, and (b) the apparently successful signing of the Agreement in the unacceptable circumstances outlined above.

We feel that it is important that you should also note that the signatories to the Agreement have apparently either agreed to allow mining on sacred sites, or at the least, agreed not to oppose mining on the sacred sites. If the former is the case, the Agreement may be illegal on the basis that only the Minister may allow mining on registered sites. In either case, CRAE has entered into the Agreement while their application to use the sites for another purpose (under s.18) was being evaluated and considered. We note that it is also an offense under s.54 of the Aboriginal Heritage Act to wilfully obstruct any person acting in the execution of the Act.

We request that both your evaluation of CRA's application to use the sites for mining and your recommendation to the Minister take into account the conclusions of the AIAS Report which you commissioned. In particular, we request that you note that the four areas of importance to Aboriginal people in the vicinity of the mining activities are all :

(a) given specific geographical locations, or defined by geographical features; and
(b) said to be of importance to Aboriginal people and groups other than the traditional landowners particularly Devil Devil Springs which is "a site of importance to *all* men in the area who have experienced the post circumcision rituals sometimes referred to at Turkey Creek as *djundungal.* Such rituals remain a part of current ritual and religious significance." *(AIAS Report:68)*

We should also briefly note that due to the short notice given us of the visit by your staff, only one woman was present at last Wednesday's meeting. As the AIAS Report makes it clear that the site known as 'Dayiwul Gap' is a "site of importance to Aboriginal women in the area", the Trustees should be cautious of assuming that there has been a radical change of opinion without consulting them.

Finally, in view of the length of time that CRA's application to use the sites in question has been before you, our strong suspicions of Ministerial involvement in your evaluation of the application, and our agreement with the *West Australian* editorial comment of September 4, 1980 that the public should be more fully informed of Museum deliberations, we have decided to make this letter available to the public. We hope you will give favourable consideration to our request.

Yours sincerely,
(snd.) Bob Nyalcas
Chairman, Warmun Community Inc.

Meanwhile the Oombulgurri community, formerly the Forrest River Mission and situated on an Aboriginal Lands Trust reserve near Wyndham, had watched the events at Turkey Creek and responded to a call for assistance from the Warmun community. They rejected the application by CRA (Exploration Pty Ltd) to renew its entry permit for diamond exploration in the Forrest River reserve, protected by the Aboriginal Lands Trust. Under the heading 'TRIBAL LAND CLOSED TO CRA', *The West Australian* of 2 August 1980 reported:

> Its decision is partly in protest against the handling of an agreement on the Argyle diamond prospect between a Kimberley Aboriginal group and the Ashton joint venturers, of which CRA is the manager . . . In a press release issued through the land council, the Oombulgurri people—who occupy the reserve in the far north of WA—said they feared that they might be treated by CRA in the same way as the Warmun community.

This action by the Oombulgurri people may have been a catalyst for a statement from the Minister for Cultural Affairs, Mr Grayden, a few days later, appearing in *The West Australian* on 5 August. His statement was an exposition of the peculiar racist views of some sections of the white population of Western Australia—an attempt to blame the Government's failure at Noonkanbah and its embarrassment over the Argyle 'agreement' on the evil, Marxist plans of the yellow horde or 'part Aboriginals'.

The West Australian reported:

> Mr Grayden said yesterday that any undesirable precedent set at Noonkanbah or Argyle could develop overnight into a situation that would extend throughout WA . . .
>
> 'The once laudable objective of land rights for Aborigines has now degenerated into a mineral rights trading racket that has serious implications for all Australians . . .'
>
> 'Anyone who can claim a trace of Aboriginal blood—and their European hangers on—are now vying with each other in claiming alleged Aboriginal sites under the pretence of being traditional owners of the areas involved . . .'

> Mr Grayden said it would make a mockery of existing statutes if the Government tolerated such claims.

The West Australian of 5 August 1980 saw his statement as an attempt by the Government to distance itself from the 'agreement'. Following Oombulgurri's rejection of CRA's exploration lease as a gesture of support to Warmun, the Premier's chortlings about 'good-neighbour' relations seemed vacuous.

By early September six Aboriginal land councils from around Australia had galvanised their support for the beleaguered Kimberley people. They placed a ban on all mining talks at the historic inaugural meeting of the Federation of Aboriginal Land Councils at Noonkanbah where Omen Pty Ltd was still drilling into sacred land. The meeting released a statement explaining its retaliation against mining companies. It condemned the State Government for its actions in the Noonkanbah dispute and condemned the Federal Government for refusing to use its powers to stop the desecration. The ban on negotiations between Aborigines and mining interests would remain in force till meaningful negotiations began between the State Government, AMAX Petroleum Pty Ltd and the Yungngora community to move the drill site. The Warmun representatives present at the meeting explained their case, and although the press doubted that the ban would affect the Argyle 'agreement', plans were made to assist the East Kimberley people.

On 22 September the press reported a serious traffic accident involving signatories to the Argyle 'agreement' and family members. Turkey Creek people believed it to be retribution for their decision to sign and failure to protect sites. Those injured were taken to the Darwin and Wyndham hospitals. John Toby said that he 'was tired of fighting for his sacred places'. On 26 September the Western Australian Government gave the 'all-clear' to Ashton. Permission to use the Argyle area was granted by Grayden following the amendment of the *Aboriginal Heritage Act*.

This case study exposes the unenviable position of an Aboriginal community, Warmun at Turkey Creek, who in a few months lost their traditional religious sites and legal protection over them through the unscrupulous activities of a powerful and ruthless mining consortium, the State Government and a few targeted Aboriginal people who gave up the fight.

A NATIONAL CONFERENCE

In his second report, Mr Justice Woodward recommended that a mineral survey should be conducted (Australia, 1975:108–109):

> I . . . see considerable merit in a planned approach to the whole subject of mining on Aboriginal lands, beginning with a survey conducted by mining experts appointed by the Government. They should be accompanied in the field by Aboriginal representatives, so that the Land Councils, and through them the communities, would know just what was happening . . .
>
> With the results of such surveys available, Aborigines would be in a much better position to make considered decisions about mining developments . . . If such survey work on behalf of government is not practicable or is thought to be undesirable, this leaves the Aboriginal people in the position of being asked to consent to mineral search with very little idea of the chance of mining later taking place or of the likely impact on them of such developments.

However, no such government-community mineral survey has occurred. There is still merit in the idea of a mineral survey conducted on behalf of the Commonwealth Government for the reasons stated by Mr Justice Woodward. But since Woodward proposed the idea, the activities of exploration and mining companies have proceeded apace; mining proposals that Woodward referred to in his report are now in the initial stages of development, and the land councils in the Northern Territory have reached agreement on the terms on which a number of mining ventures may proceed.

Because of these developments in the Northern Territory, and because the issues have not been clarified in the States, a more appropriate response at this stage would be for the Commonwealth Government to convene a national conference of Aboriginal land councils, land trusts and other organisations directly involved with mining and land rights, the mining and exploration companies with interests on or near Aboriginal land, and State governments. The national conference would work towards establishing the guidelines for a statutory framework which would create a process of continuous consultation. In the initial stages at least, consultation could be organised on a regional basis focusing on the areas represented by official and unofficial land councils. Such a regionalised approach would strengthen the possibilities for a rational, planned approach. The advantages would accrue not only to Aboriginal communities, but as well, to non-Aboriginal communities, local governments, government and non-government bodies concerned with the protection of the environment, and those bodies which would service the mining industry. Regionalisation would also lessen the possibilities of anarchical and unrestrained exploration and mining, which can only have adverse effects socially, economically and environmentally.

IMPACT STATEMENT PREPARED BY EXPLORATION AND MINING COMPANIES

Woodward also indicated the need for a form of impact statement for all exploration and mining proposals, the need for consent of communities and land councils, and again the final approval of the Minister for Aboriginal Affairs before any exploration licence is granted. Mining and exploration companies should make available to Aboriginal interests the exact nature and extent of their involvement on Aboriginal land, the location of their exploration licences, mining reserves, tenements, etc., and their purposes and what they hope to achieve.

Woodward (Australia, 1974) recommended that:

- each company should make a proposal to the regional Land Council, setting out clearly the area to be searched and the terms it is proposing. These terms should include:
  — any payments offered for the right to explore,
  — the royalty payments proposed in the event of the search being successful and mining taking place;
- in order that the people can be shown as clearly as possible what they are being asked to agree to, the company should supply a form of impact statement, setting out what its purpose is, what it hopes to achieve, what will be involved at the exploration stage by way of road or airstrip construction, test drilling, seismic surveying, tree felling, ground clearing, bulldozing and building construction. The statement should then go on to give the best possible picture of activities and land and water requirements in the proving, developmental and production stages if the search is successful. It would need to set out the likelihood of any processing works being located in the region (ibid, 109);
- for all these stages, estimates should be given of the number of employees likely to be involved and the works required for their maintenance (ibid, 109);
- this presentation should be illustrated with such maps, photographs and diagrams as may be necessary to convey a clear picture of what is proposed (ibid, 110).

I would suggest further requirements of exploration and mining companies in preparing impact statements are:

- that all impact statements, consultations and negotiations be *interpreted and/or translated* and produced on audio tapes and video tapes where necessary;
- that communities should be provided with the resources to monitor the effects of mining on the people as mining progresses;
- that Aboriginal communities be funded by the Commonwealth Government in order to produce/commission impact statements in reply to mining company statements prior to approval for mining to go ahead.

It is imperative that Aboriginal communities and groups be given the opportunity to reply to mining company impact statements setting out the advantages and disadvantages as they see them. Commonwealth funding is essential for this so that expert staff, such as anthropologists, economists and others, can formulate their statements.

It is considered of no consequence that Aboriginal hunting and gathering activities or social and religious activities are disrupted by mining. Nor is it considered of consequence if Aboriginal economic ventures, such as cattle stations, are disrupted. Rarely is exact information about such disruption recorded in the way that mining company interests in an area are recorded. This imbalance of representation should be corrected.

No exploration or mining licences should be issued before the impact statements from both mining companies and Aboriginal communities are produced and *consent* of Aboriginal communities is obtained. Measures to ensure an adequate information flow must be established. If consent to exploration and mining is not given by Aboriginal communities a *judicial inquiry* should be appointed to determine whether that exploration or mining is 'in the national interest'. Mr Justice Woodward recommended that either House of Parliament could override the Government's decision on 'the national interest'. But in my view this is not sufficient. The matter should be determined by the judiciary independent of the political institutions of the day. Such a judicial inquiry should be appointed by the Commonwealth Government in all cases.

Other problems could be dealt with by the establishment of a Commonwealth statutory body composed of Aborigines to oversee the consultation and negotiation process with mining companies. Such a body could provide professional services, including legal advisers, interpreters, translators, economists, negotiators and other people as required, and report to Parliament on the quality of such consultations and negotiations. Possibly the Aboriginal Development Commission could perform this function or alternatively a body based on land council representatives might be preferred. The personnel of such a body would be present at all consultations and negotiations and be responsible for ensuring that Aboriginal people fully understood the process and were adequately represented. This body could also consider general policy in respect of the payment and disbursement of royalty and up-front monies. Disputes between Aboriginal communities or bodies and mining companies or government agencies should be dealt with by an independent inquiry.

CONCLUSION

I propose this national strategy, not as a final formula to resolve the problems Aboriginal people face from exploration and mining activity but as a starting point for further debate. Aboriginal land councils and land trusts will be able to make more detailed and up-to-date contributions on these matters as Aboriginal thinking on these matters develops. It can only be hoped that the Commonwealth and State governments and mining and exploration companies will respond to the suggestions set out here and participate in the establishment of a more rational approach to the problems created by resource development.

NOTE

1. The opinions and information I offer here are the result of experience in working with the North Queensland Land Council, the Kimberley Land Council, the New South Wales Land Council, the Federal Council for the Advancement of Aborigines and Torres Strait Islanders, other Aboriginal organisations and as a research officer for the Select Committee of the Legislative Assembly Upon Aborigines in New South Wales.

2. Pan-Aboriginal word used in the Kimberleys and parts of the Northern Territory (with variations) for white people.

REFERENCES

Australia (1974) *Aboriginal Land Rights Commission: second report.* Canberra, Australian Government Publishing Service.

Australia (1975) *House of Representatives Standing Committee on Aboriginal Affairs: Report on the present conditions of Yirrkala people.* Canberra, Australian Government Publishing Service. (Parliamentary Paper 227).

Australia (1977) *Ranger Uranium Environmental Inquiry: second report* Canberra, Australian Government Publishing Service.

Langton, M. (1981) Bridge to parliament. *Identity,* 4(1):30–32.

McDonald, G. (1981) Western Australia. In: *Aboriginal Land Rights: a handbook.* N. Peterson (ed.), Canberra, Australian Institute of Aboriginal Studies, pp.221–53.

Nyalcas, B. (1980) Open letter from Warmun Community to the Trustees of the Western Australian Museum, 9.10.80. *Anthopology News* (Proceeding as the Anthropology Society of Western Australia) 17:124–27.

PART FIVE

CANADIAN PERSPECTIVES

26

THE NEGOTIATION OF INDIAN TREATIES AND LAND RIGHTS IN SASKATCHEWAN

Noel Dyck

During the 1970s aboriginal rights and Indian land claims became controversial political issues in Canada. The struggle by Indians in, to name but three examples, the James Bay area, the Northwest Territories and British Columbia to establish their rights to traditional lands attracted the attention of politicians, the news media, and Canadians as never before. One relatively little publicised development in this field was the negotiation in 1977 of an agreement between the federal government, the Province of Saskatchewan and the Federation of Saskatchewan Indians to settle outstanding Indian land entitlements dating from the nineteenth century. Under the terms of the entitlement formula the provincial government undertook to transfer approximately one million acres of land to 15 bands that had not received their full allotment of reserve lands as provided for in treaties and land surrenders signed during the previous century. By entering into this agreement the Saskatchewan Government formally recognised the treaties as legally binding commitments, an admission that other provincial governments have carefully avoided making.

The legal implications of the Saskatchewan agreement are restricted to existing Indian treaties; thus, it does not directly contribute to furthering recognition of aboriginal rights *per se*. Yet, the Indian and government negotiators of the agreement contend that it constitutes a major advance, not only for Saskatchewan Indians and 'treaty' Indians in other provinces but for all Canadian Indians. They argue that the good faith and flexibility exhibited by the federal and provincial governments in settling this one area of Saskatchewan Indians' land claims stands in stark contrast to government-Indian dealings elsewhere in Canada.

The Saskatchewan entitlement formula does, in fact, represent a rare instance in which Indians have not been forced either to take the ponderous, expensive and uncertain course of seeking recognition of their land rights in the law courts or of having to accept land surrenders bargained for under the threat of massive energy development projects that will proceed whether or not agreement is reached with Indians. Government spokesmen in the neighbouring provinces of Manitoba and Alberta have been critical of the Saskatchewan agreement, suggesting that it is an overly generous and awkward precedent that exceeds what was legally or politically required under the circumstances. Both governments have petitioned the Federal Government to reconsider its endorsement of the Saskatchewan agreement.

This paper examines the structure and operation of the Saskatchewan settlement and attempts to locate it within a broader political and historical context. It considers different explanations of why and how the agreement has been achieved at a time when other provincial governments have been unwilling even to enter into serious discussions with Indians about land claims. It also identifies some of the agreement's shortcomings and raises questions about its long-term benefits to Saskatchewan Indians, especially with regard to its affects on their claims for other as yet officially unrecognised land and treaty rights. The paper begins with a brief overview of Indian treaties and federal Indian administration in Saskatchewan.

THE HISTORICAL SETTING

In the twenty years following the annexation of Rupert's Land and the Northwest Territories to the Dominion of Canada in 1870 the basic task of settling and developing the prairie west consumed a major portion of the young nation's energies. The most immediate and potentially the most difficult issue to be dealt with in the Canadian west involved the management of relations between the indigenous Indian peoples and the growing white population. In a matter of two decades western Canada underwent a profound transformation; the region that in 1871 had been characterised as 'the great lone land' (Butler, 1871) had by 1890 been connected by rail to both the Atlantic and Pacific oceans. The vast plains that 20 years before had been inhabited by magnificent herds of buffalo were by 1890 dotted with towns and settlements. In less than two decades the nomadic way of life of plains Indians in Canada had been terminated and the critical features of their new relationship with the Canadian Government had been determined.

The treaties entered into by the federal government and prairie Indians during the 1870s contained far more specific terms than those negotiated by the Imperial government in its eastern colonies.[1] In return for relinquishing aboriginal land title to the prairies, Indians were granted reserves (at a rate of 640 acres per family of five), hunting rights on all Crown lands, and the promise of government assistance in the form of education, health care and agricultural development.[2] The extent of the assistance promised and, at least initially, provided by the Canadian Government in order to aid the transition of the plains Indians from a nomadic to a sedentary and agricultural way of life following the disappearance of the buffalo in 1879 was quite unlike anything which had previously occurred in the administration of Indian affairs in North America. In exchange, however, the violence and bloodshed which had characterised the settlement of the American West was, for the most part, avoided in the prairies.

The relationship established between the Federal Government and the Indians of the prairies differed from those between government and Indians in other parts of Canada. To begin with the treaties made here were negotiated in advance of large scale immigration of settlers. Unlike the United States Government, which possessed both the resources and a continued willingness to put substantial military forces into the field to subjugate any Indian bands that threatened the advance of American settlement, the Canadian Government initially lacked both the capital and the manpower to undertake sustained warfare against its western Indians. The costs of constructing a transcontinental railway would absorb the greatest part of the government's finances, and in any case the British imperial practice of colonising with a minimum of military force and expense offered a preferable alternative. At the time of the negotiation of the prairie treaties, the Northwest Mounted Police with its 300 men constituted the total might which the Canadian Government could bring to bear on the 26 000 Indians in the area. As a result, the treaties signed between the plains Indians and the Federal Government were, in fact, the product of negotiation between the Indians and the Government and were not merely terms dictated to a defeated aboriginal population after the fact of settlement or defeat. The negotiated treaties contained explicit acknowledgement of original aboriginal title to the land surrendered. Moreover, the location of reserve lands allocated to individual bands was for the most part chosen by the Indians themselves.

When the two major prairie Treaties (number six and seven) were negotiated, the Indians anticipated the imminent disappearance of the buffalo and insisted upon the inclusion of several special conditions in these treaties. One of these demands was the provision of medical care by the government, another was an undertaking from the government to assist them when the buffalo were finally exterminated. In the terms of Treaty six this last item became:

> That in the event hereafter of the Indians comprised within this treaty being overtaken by any pestilence, or by a general famine, the Queen, on being satisfied and certified thereof by her Indian Agent or Agents, will grant to the Indians assistance of such character and to such extent as her Chief Superintendent of Indian Affairs shall deem necessary and sufficient to relieve the Indians from the calamity that shall have befallen them. (Morris, 1880:354)

When calamity befell the plains Indians some three years after the signing of treaty six, when the buffalo herds did not return from their wintering grounds in the United States, the Federal Government unwillingly, but none the less promptly, provided food rations in plenty for the Indians and prepared a programme to introduce farming on the reserves as quickly as possible. The reserve agricultural policy was almost adequately funded for a period of some three years, even though the expense of this undertaking along with that of rationing the Indians was disconcerting, to say the least, to federal members of parliament. Yet, under the circumstances the completion of the railway, the settlement of the prairies and indeed the very integrity of the Dominion depended upon peace in the West and thus necessitated these huge expenditures.[3] While considerable progress was made towards the end of transforming the plains Indians into self-sufficient farmers, the reserve agricultural programme did not, ultimately, succeed.

Limited knowledge about the kinds of crops and agricultural practices best suited to the prairie climate rendered farming a difficult business even for the experienced Ontario farm instructors appointed by the Department of Indian Affairs. But the gravest shortcoming of the programme was the government's willingness to realise false economies and to underfinance the programme, particularly once the rail link between Ontario and the prairies was completed (Dyck, 1970). Indian leaders employed a variety of tactics in seeking better treatment of their people during this difficult period. The government, however, steadfastly refused to increase rations or to improve other unpopular aspects of its administration of the programme and replied by dispatching more Mounted Police to the west. In the spring of 1885 an uprising fomented by Metis or half-breed inhabitants of the northwest (in pursuit of their particular interests) erupted,[4] and there was limited participation in this action by a handful of Indian bands. Government reaction to the Metis uprising and Indian involvement in it was swift: troops were rushed to the West, and in less than two months the resistance was entirely suppressed. After the Metis principals had been punished, eight Indians were hanged for their part in the rebellion and several other Indian leaders were sent to prison. Most significantly, the fabric of government-Indian relations which had developed in the northwest during preceding years was destroyed. Thereafter, the nature of Indian administration across the West was drastically realigned. After confiscating Indian horses and firearms and prohibiting Indians from travelling away from their reserves, federal officials instructed field officers of the Department of Indian Affairs that they were to be absolutely certain in the future that every Indian worked for every pound of provisions given to him; moreover, 'all future grants should be regarded as concessions of favour, *not of right* and . . . Indians should be made to understand that they have forfeited every claim as a matter of right' (ibid:76).

After 1885 the administration of Indian affairs in Canada, and particularly in western Canada, assumed a format which endured with few changes until the period following the Second World War. The legislative basis of federal Indian policy and administration was—and still is—the *Indian Act*. First compiled in 1876 from an amalgam of Imperial and colonial legislation and administrative practices, the *Indian Act* was amended extensively in the 1880s to take into account the exigencies of government-Indian relations in the northwest Territories. The Act provided the Department of Indian Affairs with exclusive jurisdiction over Indians, and armed officers of the Department with immense authority to supervise the lives of individual Indians. The Act not only defined in detail which persons were and were not Indians but also divided Indians into bands, each of which constituted a discrete and separate politico-administrative unit. Each band occupied one or more reserves of land set aside in perpetuity for the use of its members. The Act permitted the Minister of Indian Affairs to manage Indian lands and trust funds which accrued to individual bands through the surrender and sale of various reserve lands.

Under the terms of the *Indian Act* and accompanying sets of regulations established by the Minister, Indians were subjected to a range of prohibitions: they were denied the franchise; they were not allowed to leave their reserves without obtaining a pass from the Indian agent which specified the destination, purpose and period of their travel; they were unable to purchase or to sell stock, personal possessions or any other commodity without the written permission of the agent; and they were forbidden to possess or to consume alcohol. In addition, the Act provided for the suppression of aboriginal religious ceremonies such as the plains sun dance and the potlatch of the Pacific coast. Appropriate punitive means for the enforcement of these and other prohibitions were contained in the Act.

These were the parameters within which Canadian Indian administration, particularly in western Canada, was conducted. In short:

> . . . Indian administration was a version of colonialism. The[Indian Affairs] Branch was a quasi-colonial government dealing with almost the entire life of a culturally different people who were systematically deprived of opportunities to influence government, a people who were isolated on separate packets of land and who were subject to different laws. (Hawthorn, 1966:368)

The expressed aim of the government's Indian policy was essentially the same in 1945 as it had been in 1885, although in the interim it had been added that the ultimate hope was that Indians would achieve full citizenship and be assimilated into Canadian society. The segregated and regulated reserve, which imposed serious limitations on the personal and property rights of Indians, was intended to serve as the 'cradle' of the realisation of these ends:

> . . . [the reserve] fixes the Indian to one place where the hard lessons of self-support may be imparted and where the influence of Christian civilisation may be brought to bear. The reserve is also designed to protect his rights and property from the whites. . . . Although the government imposes arbitrary guardianship, she does so in order to implement the promise of an equal place in a free society. (Harper, 1945:132)

In reality, however, the Federal Government's administration of Indian affairs up to 1945 failed miserably to achieve these ends, except to the extent that today there are relatively few Canadian Indians who have not been baptised by one or more Christian denominations. Few Indians were self-sufficient by 1945, although the reserve lands which the Federal Government had been entrusted to administer in perpetuity for Indians had shrunk markedly in area from those originally granted. While the pass and permit systems had been abandoned by the 1950s when Indians also received the franchise and the right to consume alcohol in a number of provinces, a number of government commissions and inquiries were established to examine various means of promoting equal and full participation of Indians in Canadian society. It becomes obvious, even to Federal Government officials, that contrary to earlier expectations the system of Indian administration being practised was not notably successful in guiding

Indians towards 'civilisation', 'progress', and participation in 'mainstream' Canadian life.

Successive minority governments in the 1960s placed a low legislative priority on reforming Indian administration, but in 1969 the newly elected Trudeau Government proposed a genuinely radical 'solution'—outright abolition of federal Indian administration within 5 years. The Trudeau Government sought to sever the Gordian knot of a century of Indian administration by the simple expedient of terminating the special legal and constitutional status of registered Indians and declaring them to be 'equal' to other Canadians. Indians would be granted title and control of their lands and would become ordinary citizens who received services from, and paid taxes to, provincial and municipal governments. Federal funds normally spent on Indian administration would be transferred to the provinces although this subsidy would be phased out eventually. Other proposals included a $50 million economic development fund and appointment of an Indian Claims Commissioner.

Indian associations across Canada denounced the White Paper in the strongest possible terms to the amazement of the Government, news media and Canadian public. Harold Cardinal's best seller, *The Unjust Society* (1969), delivered a scathing critique that summarised Indians' fears about the White Paper. For several months the Minister of Indian Affairs sought to discuss the proposals with Indians and their representative associations; he repeatedly denied that the White Paper was either a programme for 'cultural genocide' or a device for robbing Indians of their lands. Finally, in June 1970 the Prime Minister formally withdrew the White Paper and announced that his government would not implement proposals unacceptable to the Indian people.

The White Paper controversy renewed the determination of associations such as the Federation of Saskatchewan Indians (FSI) to protect Indian treaty rights and special status. The National Indian Brotherhood (NIB) accepted the government's conciliatory offer of financial support to enable Indians to conduct research and prepare their claims. As the differing concerns of treaty Indians and Indians without treaties surfaced within the NIB, individual provincial Indian associations applied to the Privy Council and the Indian Claims Commission for funds to establish separate provincial and territorial research projects. By the summer of 1972 different associations had retained legal advisers, dispatched researchers to archives and sent fieldworkers to collect elders' recollections of treaty negotiations and promises. Research carried out by FSI personnel led to the development of 15 band entitlements claims that eventually precipitated the 1977 agreement with the Federal and Provincial governments. Before proceeding to examine this agreement, however, we should summarise the key features of the Indian-government relationship that has evolved in Saskatchewan (and other parts of western Canada) during the past century.

First, the negotiation of treaties in the nineteenth century and the limited, but none the less continuing recognition of special status and treaty rights by government, have been inspired as much as political considerations as by acknowledgement of lasting legal obligations to Indians. Traditionally the Federal Government has justified its special relationship with Indians in terms of the social and administrative ends it was intended to further—namely, the eventual assimilation of a culturally distinct people into Canadian society. Implicit in this approach was the assumption that special status and special privileges for Indians were not as much binding contractual responsibilities as temporary measures that would at some future time no longer be required. There has, in other words, always been a close connection between federal social policy objectives for Indians and continued recognition of Indians' special status and rights.

Second, the protection of Saskatchewan Indians' communally held reserve lands and treaty rights (in the areas of education, health care and hunting and fishing rights) has depended directly upon the maintenance of their special legal and constitutional status. The abolition or erosion of the *Indian Act* and other legislation that explicitly recognises their special status would undermine both the legal and political bases of their treaty rights and would jeopardise the rationale for maintaining reserve lands outside the normal system of property ownership in Canada.

Third, Indians' special legal status as wards of the Crown has historically subjected them to an arbitrary form of federal administration that has been both offensive and detrimental to them in most respects; nevertheless, from the 1870s to the present day Saskatchewan Indians have been unswerving in their efforts to maintain their special constitutional status, social identity and treaty rights as Indians within a non-Indian nation. With few individual exceptions they have, generation after generation, resisted government inducements that would have freed them individually or collectively from federal tutelage by stripping them of their special status as Indians. In short, the continued existence of a legally distinct Indian population in Saskatchewan today is in no small part a manifestation of Indians' lasting determination to remain a distinct people within Canadian society.

SASKATCHEWAN INDIAN LANDS ENTITLEMENTS

The treaties signed in western Canada during the nineteenth century provided for the granting of reserve lands at the rate of 1 square mile or 640 acres per family of five. When the federal government transferred western Crown lands and natural resources to the provinces in 1930 it was known that some northern bands had not yet selected reserves; in consequence, the transfer agreement obliged the provinces to make unoccupied Crown land available to Canada when required to fulfil any outstanding Indian land entitlements. Research conducted by the FSI during the 1970s revealed that in addition to five northern bands known to have outstanding entitlements for approximately half a million acres that there were a further 10 bands in the southern part of the province with claims for another half million acres. These southern entitlement claims were based variously on (1) errors made in surveying reserves, (2) oversight on the part of government, and (3) the past amalgamation of bands with unextinguished entitlements with bands that had already selected their reserve lands. While there were ample Crown lands available in northern Saskatchewan for discharging entitlement claims, it would be a good deal more difficult to find half a million acres of suitable Crown land in the southern agricultural part of the province. Moreover, there was also the question of whether the province would agree to assume responsibility for fulfiling Indian land entitlements that were thought to have been discharged at the time of the natural resources transfer agreement.

The timely agreement reached with the Saskatchewan Government on a formula for settling both the northern and southern entitlement claims departed substantially from the usual Western position on Indian land rights. Faced with similar entitlement claims the Alberta Government, for example, has adopted a 'we will see you in court' stance in dealing with Indians (Price, 1977:151). Yet, while the representatives of all three parties involved in the Saskatchewan agreement have claimed credit for its achievement, it is useful to take a somewhat broader view of the matter.

Sources close to the Saskatchewan negotiations suggest that the agreement resulted from particularly favourable circumstances that brought together certain 'key factors' to represent the province and the FSI. It has also been alleged that there are strong political sympathies as well as concrete linkages between FSI leaders and the ruling New Democratic Party (NDP) in Saskatchewan (ibid:209 ff.). Without wishing to deny the significance of the mutual respect that Indian and government negotiators may have had for one another, it should be recognised that there was a basic continuity between the 1977 agreement and a long-standing pattern of Indian–Provincial Government relations in Saskatchewan. Since the 1950s the Provincial Government has awarded an annual grant to the FSI and has respected the association's position that the province ought to avoid jeopardising Indians' special relationship with the Federal Government. Moreover, this policy has been honoured by successive ruling parties since that time. Thus, the relatively cordial relationship that the FSI enjoys with the Provincial Government is not a new and fortuitous development; it is instead the product of a patient and perceptive strategy of succeeding generations of Saskatchewan Indian leaders to seek support for maintaining their special status and treaty rights by lobbying all potential allies.

Under the terms of the agreement the Saskatchewan Government made all of its lands, occupied or vacant, available for entitlement selection subject to the following conditions: (1) that the Federal Government also made available its lands in Saskatchewan on the same basis; (2) that where occupied lands were selected by bands that the lessees' interests would be discharged satisfactorily either through compensation or other arrangement; and, (3) that acreage for the settlement of treaty entitlements would be based on band populations at 31 December 1976. Provision was also made for the striking of an intergovernmental joint committee (with FSI participation) to develop appropriate mechanisms for assisting bands to select lands. Finally, the Department of Indian Affairs undertook to ensure that land selection would be carried out in conjunction with appropriate community development plans for each band.

For its part the FSI made three major compromises in accepting the terms of the agreement. First, the FSI and the bands agreed to establish 31 December 1976 as the date for determining band populations and, hence, for calculating final reserve land entitlements. Yet, by the beginning of 1980 it was apparent that differences of interpretation of the entitlement formula and selection procedure would delay the transfer of Crown lands to Indian bands for an indefinite period. Since Saskatchewan Indians have the highest rate of population increase of any segment of the province's population, it is clear that the Provincial Government had much to gain by reaching early agreement on binding terms of land entitlement that did not, however, specify a final date by which the land transfers would have to be completed.

Second, FSI acceptance of the terms of the agreement obliged the association to recognise non-Indians' occupation rights on Crown lands, an action that may well detract from other FSI claims that Saskatchewan Indians enjoy usufructuary rights on all Crown lands as a treaty right. Third, the FSI committed itself to procedures for ratification of entitlement claims and procedures for ensuring satisfaction of both lessees' (individual and corporate) and third parties' interests in Crown Lands that in effect subordinate the interests of bands to those of virtually all other parties.

But perhaps the most costly compromise made by the FSI Executive was not one of legal advantage but of political judgement. FSI leaders interpreted the situation as one that although temporarily favourable to Indians might soon be reversed if the reigning MDP government was by chance defeated in the coming provincial election. Thus, they advised bands that if they did not make certain compromises in order to reach a quick agreement with a friendly provincial government the opportunity to settle outstanding land entitlements might be lost.

In fact, the Provincial Government was easily re-elected and as time goes by the pressure on bands to take what they can get now steadily increases. Given that more valuable Crown lands are encumbered with more government, lessee and third-party interests than are less valuable lands, it is obvious that bands that are not prepared to wait for as many years as it takes to satisfy all other parties' interests in the more valuable lands will be required to settle for less valuable lands. Already this is happening; several bands in southern Saskatchewan are in the process of selecting community pasture lands that are, in agricultural terms, of marginal value. Moreover, the provincial Department of Mineral Resources and several mining corporations have so far demonstrated an unwillingness to permit northern bands to select Crown lands that hold significant mineral deposits.

At this point it is important to recall that treaty land entitlement claims represent only one of several different kinds of treaty rights and land claims being put forward by the FSI. In addition the FSI argues that:

(1) substantial portions of reserve lands have been illegally and improperly surrendered in the past and that it is the responsibility of the federal government to compensate Indians for these losses;

(2) treaty eight did not constitute a land surrender but was only a treaty to establish a peaceful relationship between the Indians who signed it and the government; thus, it is argued that the federal and provincial governments have yet to extinguish the aboriginal rights of Indians over this area of the province;

(3) the rights of Dakota Indians in Saskatchewan to land and to other privileges have not been adequately recognised or fulfilled;

(4) Saskatchewan Indians, by the terms of the treaties, enjoy pre-eminent usufructuary rights over all Crown lands in the province; in short, that Indians never surrendered their rights to any of the elements essential to their livelihood, namely, land, water, animals and the forests; instead it is contended that Indians only agreed to share these resources with non-Indians.

Besides these and other claims (which neither the Federal nor the Provincial governments show any likelihood of accepting—even in principal—in the near future) there are a further 20 bands that are in the process of preparing treaty entitlement claims. Validation of each of these band's claims will be left to the discretion of the Department of Indian Affair's Office of Native Claims. In the event that any or all of these claims are validated by federal authorities, these bands will be expected to abide by the selection procedure that has been established. Thus, the legal and political precedents created by the FSI's handling of the first 15 band entitlement claims will have a far wider and lasting significance than was at first apparent.

Hindsight is, of course, easy. Moreover, from the perspective of Indians in other parts of Canada and of indigenous peoples in other nations it may seem indulgent to suggest that the Saskatchewan agreement gave Indians rather less than they had coming to them. Yet, retrospectively, there are sound reasons for arguing that Saskatchewan Indians ought to have held out for a better kind of settlement, especially in the case of treaty land entitlement claims. There have been many suggestions concerning how the bands might have been better served. Non-Indian farmers using community pastures that may be taken over by bands have recommended one obvious measure: that the federal or provincial governments could have purchased first-rate lands from retiring farmers nearby reserves and transferred these to the bands. In addition, the inclusion in the agreement of a clearly stated mechanism for resolving differences of interpretation would have provided a much needed means for avoiding protracted delays in implementing the agreement.

It would be gratuitous to second-guess the FSI leaders' 1977 decision to endorse the entitlement formula, but it would be foolish not to recognise some of the lessons that have emerged in the wake of that decision. Moreover, there is no reason why the FSI should not insist upon a more satisfactory means of settlement in the case of upcoming entitlement claims. In any case, fundamentally better agreements and settlements with government will be achieved only if and when FSI and band leaders recognise that their bargaining position on entitlement claims and other treaty rights is far stronger than they evidently judge it to be. Rather than concerning themselves unduly with what might have happened if the NDP Government had been defeated, it would now be more useful, perhaps, for Indian leaders to wonder why the Provincial Government was prepared to recognise any obligations to Indians and to come to any settlement at that time.

Viewed from this perspective, the province's decision to enter into the 1977 agreement is far less a voluntary act of charity and far more an act of self-interest. Today it is more obvious than it was three years ago that the Provincial Government wishes to undertake massive resource development in the north and that the existence of any lingering Indian claims to land and resources there might one day result in court actions that could not be readily controlled by the province. What is more, *any* doubt about the extent of Indians' potential land rights in the north—as has been demonstrated in the case of James Bay[5]—could well dampen the enthusiasm of foreign investors and bond-buyers for projects in northern Saskatchewan.

Furthermore, there is evidence that suggests that both Federal and Provincial governments are not now and in the past never have been as certain of the legal and constitutional limitations of special status and treaty and aboriginal rights as they have professed to be in their dealings with Indians. For example, in the early part of this century Indians in southern Saskatchewan were placed under enormous pressure to surrender particularly valuable portions of their reserve lands in order to accommodate the land requirements of incoming settlers (cf. Raby, 1973). If the legal rights of Indians were as limited as government spokesmen before and after that time have claimed that they are, surely the Federal Government could have acted unilaterally to achieve this end. Yet, in spite of the power that federal authorities wielded over Indians, recalcitrant bands that refused to part with their lands were not subjected to expropriation or arbitrary government actions to strip them of their lands.

A more recent example of this muted recognition of Indians' rights is provided by the James Bay Agreement which pointedly refused to admit the existence of aboriginal rights but which required the Indians to renounce any hypothetical or supposed aboriginal rights to the area that they might be said to possess. Finally, the Saskatchewan Government has recently entered into an agreement with Indians in the north-eastern part of the province to co-manage wildlife resources in that area. In view of the province's refusal to extend the arrangement to include local Metis people, it would appear that Indians' treaty rights serve as the basis for their involvement in the scheme.

CONCLUSION

It can, therefore, be argued that there may be a more solid legal and political foundation to Indians' claims about the nature and extent of their treaty and aboriginal rights than is commonly recognised and, further, that governments are more cognisant of this than ever they admit in their words and actions. Nevertheless, contentions such as these provide scant encouragement for Indians who are seeking to realise some more tangible recognition of their rights in their lifetime. They might well respond to such contentions by asking when and under what circumstances one might reasonably expect governments to see the error of their ways and give appropriate recognition to Indian rights that they may or may not privately believe to be legitimate claims?

If the historical record in Saskatchewan is a reliable guide, then the answer is that governments will begin to honour Indian rights when they are convinced that Indians will not be content with anything less. Saskatchewan Indians have been talking about government's commitments to them since the signing of the treaties, and over a century they have gradually succeeded in bringing successive provincial governments part of the way round to their point of view. Of course, governments and lawyers can be exceedingly adept at delaying action long enough to convince people that their interests would be better served by compromise than by persevering with their full original claims. In the end, questions of when and under what circumstances Indians should or should not compromise any aspects of their treaty rights claims must be decided by Indians on pragmatic grounds.

Bargaining and negotiating have been essential and continuing aspects of Indian-government relations in Saskatchewan during the past century. Morris's account (1880) of the making of the western treaties shows that prairie Indians have been making limited compromises in order to attain particular commitments from government since the 1870s. Still, it is worth recalling that one of the options that Indians have frequently exercised during the past is to refuse to enter into negotiations when they have occupied too weak a political position to bargain effectively. What is more, in light of recent provincial government recognition of particular treaty rights that authorities once scoffed at, it is appropriate to observe that Saskatchewan Indians have been slowly but steadily winning ever greater government acceptance of their interpretation of the place and the privileges they deserve within Canadian society.

Finally, it should be noted that in recent years the only substantial erosion of aboriginal and treaty rights that has taken place in Canada invariably has resulted from surrenders and agreements that Indians have been placed under considerable pressure to accede to lest a 'last' opportunity to receive some 'concession' from a government temporarily willing to negotiate be lost. Historically the hardest Indian bargainers in Saskatchewan were those leaders who in the late nineteenth and early twentieth centuries endured the hardships of arbitrary and often harsh federal Indian administration without endangering their peoples' belief that the treaties guaranteed them a special place and special rights within Canada, whether or not the governments of the day chose to honour those rights.

ACKNOWLEDGEMENTS

I would like to acknowledge the generous manner in which Peter Brook, Peter Legg and John R. McLeod shared information and insights with the author. At the same time they must be absolved of responsibility for any of the statements made in this paper.

NOTES

1. See Cumming & Mickenberg (1972) for a thorough account of the "numbered" treaties signed on the prairie provinces. The treaties that pertain to Saskatchewan Indians and the years that these were negotiated in are as follows: No. 2 (1871), No. 4 (1874), No. 5 (1875), No. 6 (1876), No. 8 (1899) and No. 10 (1906).

2. For the full written text of the treaties and a partial account of the negotiation sessions (see Morris, 1880).

3. The Province of British Columbia threatened to leave Confederation and apply for annexation to the United States unless the transcontinental railway link between the Atlantic and the Pacific was completed by the early 1880s.

4. The interests of the Metis or 'half-breed' population in the North-West Territories were quite different than those of Indians because of differences in their social, political and legal situations. For further details on the Metis demands in the 1885 Rebellion (see Stanley, 1961).

5. Price (1977:176) reports that when in 1973 Premier Bourassa of Quebec travelled to New York to have a bond issue floated for the James Bay Development Corporation that, 'New York financiers informed Bourassa, in no uncertain terms, that Indian land claims must be settled before James Bay Development could be considered a safe, economically viable investment'.

REFERENCES

Butler, W.F. (1881) *The Great Lone Land.* Toronto, Musson.

Cardinal. H. (1969) *The Unjust Society: the tragedy of Canada's Indians.* Edmonton, Hurtig.

Cumming, P.A. & Mickenberg, N.H. (eds) (1972) *Native Rights in Canada.* Toronto, Indian–Eskimo Association of Canada and General Publishing Company.

Dyck. N.E. (1970) *The Administration of Indian Aid in the North-West Territories, 1878–1886.* Unpublished MA Thesis, Department of History, University of Saskatchewan, Saskatoon.

Harper, A.G. (1945). Canada's Indian Administration: basic concepts and objectives. *America Indigena,* vol. 5.

Hawthorn, H.B. (ed.) (1966) *A Survey of the Contemporary Indians of Canada: a report of economic, political and educational needs and policies,* vol. 1. Ottawa, Queen's Printer.

Morris, A. (1880) *The Treaties of Canada with the Indians.* Toronto, Bedford & Clark.

Price, R.T. (1977) *Indian Land Claims in Alberta: politics and policy-making.* Unpublished MA Thesis, Department of Political Science, University of Alberta, Edmonton.

Raby, S. (1973). Indian Land Surrenders in Southern Saskatchewan. *Canadian geographer,* vol. 17, pp. 36–52.

Stanley, G.F.G. (1961) *The Birth of Western Canada.* Toronto, University of Toronto Press.

27

NEGOTIATING RECOGNITION OF ABORIGINAL RIGHTS: history, strategies and reactions to the James Bay and Northern Quebec Agreement

Harvey Feit

Discussions of the means available for gaining recognition of the aboriginal rights of indigenous populations within nation states have often tended to centre around discussions of the relative merits of reaching negotiated settlements with responsible governments or of seeking judicial determination of the rights, usually through initiation of court actions. While these do not exhaust the possibilities the aim of this paper is to reflect on the nature of these two options, and more specifically to indicate how these options are not so much alternatives as complementary means, each appropriate at various points in the process of defining and gaining recognition of aboriginal rights. I will suggest in this paper that negotiation may in many cases be the best of the means available for defining and recognising such aboriginal rights, and that other means such as legal action and political mobilisation may generally be more effective as levers for a negotiation process. The demands of negotiation are, however, heavy and they must be understood. The potentials of negotiation in a given situation, therefore, need to be examined to see if they offset these demands when actual strategic planning and decisions are taken.

My evaluation of the possibilities is based on an account of the court cases and the negotiations initiated by the indigenous peoples of the northern portion of the Province of Quebec, Canada following the announcement that the provincial government would build the largest hydro-electric project in the free world on the lands of the Cree Indian and Inuit (Eskimo) peoples of that region.

The indigenous peoples' responses to the project led, eventually, to the first modern comprehensive land claims settlement in Canada. Signed in 1975, the James Bay and Northern Quebec Agreement (JBNQA) has since then been given legislative form and is now in the process of being implemented. My own first-hand experience of these processes has involved assisting the Cree Indians as an expert witness in court, as an adviser helping to develop the social inputs to the court case, as an assistant and adviser to the Cree negotiators and their lawyers during negotiations, and as a Cree appointee to several official bodies concerned with the initial implementation of the JBNQA.

INITIAL RESPONSES TO THE JAMES BAY HYDRO-ELECTRIC PROJECT: FROM GOVERNMENT TRUSTEESHIP TO NEGOTIATIONS TO THE COURTS

The decision to build the James Bay Hydroelectric Project was announced in April 1971 at a massive political rally called by the then Premier of Quebec, Robert Bourassa.

The initial Cree reaction was one of shock: at not having been informed and consulted; at the size of the project which was then expected to flood 8800 km^2 of the approximately 363 000 km^2 of Cree hunting lands; at the impact the project would have on the wildlife that still provided an essential and substantial portion of the Cree diet; at the impact of the project on the hunting activities of the Cree; which were central to their culture and social organisation; at the social consequences of a massive influx of non-indigenous workers to the territory; at the uncertain economic benefits for

Cree; and, at the possible difficulties for the continued maintenance of the Cree communities and villages.

At the time of the announcement the Cree were grouped into eight distinct communities, called 'administrative bands' or just 'bands', which ranged from about 250 to 1500 people each at eight major settlements, and some 10 small summer encampments. In winter, about half the adult population and one-third of the children dispersed to 150–200 smaller encampments of one to five families each, from which subsistence hunting and fishing as well as commercial trapping activities were conducted. Children who were not in the bush went to local schools up to high school and some continued their education in urban centres. Those adults who hunted depended on fur pelt sales, some summer employment and government transfer payments. Those living in the settlements depended generally on transfer payments, intermittent employment and limited local subsistence hunting and fishing. The Cree population of Quebec shared a mutually intelligible series of dialects of the Montagnais language and had some kinship and friendship linkages across band boundaries, based both on former commercial fur trade networks and on more recent schooling in a few large residential schools. However, the Cree had no unifying administrative or political organisation that united them as a distinctive population. The only cohesive structure was an association of all Quebec Indian bands, which held several meetings a year of the administrative chiefs and band councillors.

The first response of the Cree to the announcement was to use friendship linkages to establish informal communications among the eight Cree bands potentially affected by the project, and call a meeting of the administrative chiefs plus some of the traditional and young leadership from each band to discuss possible responses. The provincial association was invited to send representatives and legal counsel.

This June 1971 meeting was the first unified response by the Cree, and it was the beginning of a long process that developed an effective unified political organisation and leadership. Finding an adequate response to the hydro electric project was not, however, easy. The recently passed Alaska Native Claims Settlement Act was known about, but the Cree were not initially seeking a settlement of aboriginal rights, they were seeking ways to oppose a specific development project. The Cree leadership agreed to ask the federal government to intervene on their behalf to protect Cree lands (Diamond, 1977). It is not clear whether this resolution ever reached the Minister of Indian Affairs, but it was announced over the media. The federal government decided not to intervene on behalf of the Cree, apparently because action against the provincial government would work against its general political strategy for dealing with a province where separatist sentiments were active. It adopted a position of 'alert neutrality', which while it clearly violated the spirit if not the letter of the trust mandate of the federal government, guided federal policy throughout most of the successive events (cf. Bird, 1972).

Up to this time many Cree had considered the federal government a benevolent protector, if often ill-informed and somewhat erratic. The preceding events clarified for the leadership, and later for the population as a whole, how the federal authorities could not be counted on to actively assist the Cree to protect their interests.

At the same time (early 1972) the federal government began to provide interest-free loans to the Cree, beginning with small grants to pay for communications workers and some basic research. These later grew to substantial sums to cover the costs of the court case and succeeding negotiations. Part of the impetus for the initial financial commitment by the federal government appears to have been the public support for the plight of the Cree and Inuit people by a small but vocal sector of environmental, Church and critical social organisations which organised in the southern urban centres, and which were partly based in the universities.

Thus, while the initial Cree response to the James Bay project failed to make direct headway, it did gain the financial means to develop a more autonomous response. It must be noted, however, that the failure of the federal government to actively support the indigenous peoples deprived them in large measure of an important potential avenue of political action, namely using differences of bureaucratic and political interests between the federal and subordinate levels of government as a lever against one or the other. This is the type of political action which has been at the core of developments in Alaska (Brelsford, 1980).

In 1972, (a chronology of events is given in the Appendix)[1] the Cree used their new funding to conduct information and research programmes, and to initiate trilateral negotiations with Quebec and Canada. Quebec appointed a negotiator and a series of initial meetings were held. The position of the Government of Quebec at the time was that the plans for the project were not negotiable, and that the indigenous peoples had no special rights, or at least none that warranted anything more than an expropriation of their interest in the land and monetary compensation for that interest. This position was completely unacceptable to the Cree, who insisted that they did have rights; and, although they were told the project would be hard to stop permanently, they were adamant that it be modified so as to affect them less.

During the spring and summer of 1972 the Cree, now joined by the Inuit, took out a court action against Quebec and the state-controlled development corporations, an action which the Cree hoped would put pressure on the government to discuss serious project modifications and remedial actions that were necessary to maintain the hunters' way of life. To give further impetus to these demands, the Cree and Inuit hired several scientists to document their dependence on wildlife resources and on the land and to assess potential effects of the project on these (Salisbury et al., 1972b; Spence, 1974). Using the results of these researchers, the Cree and Inuit again pursued negotiations with Quebec but they were met with a continued refusal to modify the project, and with assurances that effects of the project would be easily remedied and the environment could be protected using environmental management techniques. It was actually argued by some scientists that the environment would be improved by the ecological management that would accompany development.

Unable to make headway, the Cree and Inuit leaders attempted to have their case heard at the highest level of provincial government. They arranged a meeting with the provincial premier, but it lasted only 15 minutes; Premier Bourassa cut off the presentations made by the Cree and Inuit leaders and reiterated the basic government positions, before rushing off to other business.

After this meeting the Cree and Inuit leaders decided they had to accelerate legal proceedings. The Cree legal advisors thought the Cree had a very good legal basis for the action because their rights had never been extinguished, and because of the particular legislative provisions affecting the territory, discussed below. However, they were not optimistic about stopping the project permanently, nor about whether a court would rule strongly in their favor given the size and the political dimensions of the project.

This initial stage of negotiations demonstrated the impossibility of negotiations without each party having some perceived power to influence the actions of the other. Quebec saw no threat from the indigenous people, no realistic means by which they could alter the course of action which the Quebec government was pursuing, and it therefore felt no need to give up anything it valued, no need to compromise. In short, it really was not ready to negotiate.

Quebec maintained this intransigent position despite the fact that in 1971 a royal commission on the territorial integrity of the boundaries of Quebec had reported on the potential rights of the indigenous peoples, and had pointed out the need to recognise those interests and to obtain their surrender in accordance with the 1912 act of parliament transferring most of northern Quebec from the federal to provincial Crown. This explicit legislated obligation to settle any aboriginal rights which might exist, which applied to about 78% of the territory of what is now northern Quebec, was one of the unique features of the land claims proceedings in this region. Quebec also maintained its position despite the conclusions of a joint federal-provincial task force, established to report on the environmental impacts of the project, which stated that the major impacts would be those experienced by the indigenous populations (Joint Federal-Provincial Task Force, 1971).

These circumstances point up the significance of the federal government's refusal to intervene actively, and the insignificance of the aboriginal rights issues in the particular context of Quebec politics, where strong and vocal support from a minority of the population did little to raise public opinion, or to sway government policy.

In order to accelerate court action, the Cree and Inuit inscribed an interlocutory injunction against the governments and the state-controlled corporations to stop construction work which had been going on for a year. This injunction was sought on the grounds that the indigenous peoples would suffer irreparable damage while awaiting the hearings and decisions on their main court injunction.

After a brief hearing before Mr Justice Malouf, who ruled that the case for an interlocutory injunction should be heard, actual court hearings began in a matter of weeks rather than having to wait months or years for the main injunction hearing. Furthermore, whereas the main injunction would be a hearing concerned primarily with the legal basis for and nature of the claimed aboriginal rights, and would therefore concern Indian life mainly from the perspective of the historical and archaeological evidence for occupancy and use of the land, the interlocutory injunction would focus on how people were living today, and how the project would affect them in the immediate future.

In order to get an interlocutory injunction the Cree and Inuit had to prove precisely the points which the Quebec government did not accept: that there was a *prima facie* aboriginal right which allowed the Cree and Inuit people to stop the project; and that there were real, serious and immediate impacts of this development on the indigenous peoples, which were irreversible and unacceptable.

Part of the verdict would hang on the question of the 'balance of convenience', i.e., on which party would suffer the most damages, if the project was allowed to continue, or if it was stopped. Thus, the interlocutory hearing resembled in some respects an impact assessment evaluation focusing on the impact on Cree and Inuit ways of life as well as on the economic and social needs for the project in Quebec (Penn, 1975).

These questions provided opportunities for extensive Cree and Inuit inputs into the court case, which thus became a forum in which representatives from the Cree and Inuit communities could articulate their own experience and concerns. It also stimulated extensive discussions in the villages that helped to formulate a consensus about what the people wanted for the future. The court case thus became a means for political mobilisation.

The interlocutory injunction hearing lasted six months, and heard testimony from 167 witnesses, many of them Cree and Inuit. The presiding justice took five months to prepare his judgment.

Quebec argued in court that the indigenous peoples had no rights, that there was only a moral obligation to deal with them, and that even if the court decided they did have rights these would simply be the rights to provisions such as are found in the old treaties: small reserve lands, an annual *per capita* token cash payment, and the right to hunt on unoccupied Crown lands until they were needed for development. Quebec also argued that the indigenous people were just like Euro-Canadians now, they no longer had a distinctive way of life, that the land was under-utilised, that the indigenous people were totally dependent on government transfer payments and investments, and that therefore there were no irreparable damages from the project.

The indigenous people argued that Euro-Canadians were trespassers and Quebec had to settle the aboriginal title before using the territory. They argued that the Cree and Inuit had definite rights, that they had occupied the land from time immemorial, that they had been exercising their rights, that their hunting and land use activities were important and constituted a way of life people wanted to continue, that their diet was dependent in part on animals and the sale of furs, that they had a unique concept of the land, and that any interference would compromise their existence as a people.

Mr Justice Malouf released his surprise ruling in November, 1973, granting the interlocutory injunction and ordering work on the project stopped immediately. Furthermore, the judge ruled there was clear evidence that the Cree and Inuit had exercised personal and usufructory rights over the territory and had possessed and occupied it since time immemorial. As a result 'the Province of Quebec cannot develop or otherwise open up these lands for settlement without the prior agreement of the Indians and Eskimo' (Malouf, 1973:38). This was the strongest recognition and interpretation of an aboriginal right rendered judicially in Canada up to that time, and indeed since. It was a stronger interpretation than many lawyers thought possible, and stronger than some thought could be defended.

CHOOSING HOW TO DEFINE AND SEEK RECOGNITION OF ABORIGINAL RIGHTS

The province moved to suspend the injunction immediately, pending an appeal of the first judgment to higher court. Within a week the Court of Appeal had ruled to suspend the injunction and allow the project to continue while it held hearings and considered the appeal of the first judgment, a procedure which took over a year. This suspension was as sudden as the initial judgment, but it could not completely undo the effects of the earlier ruling, for two reasons.

First, the Cree and Inuit had demonstrated that they could effect governmental activities. By November 1973, possibly a thousand million dollars had already been spent, and some 4000-6000 workers were on site. Even temporary disruptions of a project of this scale are massive, costly, and disruptive of operations over a much longer period than the actual period of the work stoppage; With two appeal rulings to be made before final determination of the interlocutory injunction, and three rulings yet to come on the permanent injunction, as well as various procedural and jurisdictional appeals, there was a clear possibility of further disruptions and stoppages.

This point was not lost on potential investors. Although clear data are hard to come by, it appears likely that while funding for the expected 12 thousand million dollar project from USA and European sources was not cut off, funds available at relatively acceptable rates were limited, and those available cost more than they otherwise would have. In consequence, Quebec apparently tried to use internal funding to keep the project going, which affected government investments in other economic sectors and made government financial administration difficult.

While these factors had all been at work to some degree since legal action began, the court judgment now made it impossible for Quebec to ignore the Cree and Inuit case. Within five days of the first court judgment Quebec announced it was ready to negotiate, and within two weeks it presented the Cree and Inuit with a proposed settlement.

Up to this point the Cree and Inuit leaders and lawyers had claimed an aboriginal right in order to strengthen their claim that the government had to modify the project. The judgment pushed into the forefront the possibility of defining and seeking recognition of aboriginal rights in northern Quebec, which the court had unexpectedly gone so far towards claiming existed.

However, this new possibility developed slowly, even though it was consistent with the consensus that had developed within and among the indigenous communities during the court proceedings. The extensive discussions had, on one hand, led to a revitalisation of people's commitment to pursuing and maintaining a hunting way of life. On the other hand, discussions led also to a consensus that the Cree and Inuit people needed a clear recognition of their distinctive ways of life and communities and more extensive control over their villages, the services they used, and the land and wildlife on which they depended. There was, in short, a consensus developing for a general redefinition of the relationship of the Cree and Inuit communities to the governments and Euro-Canadian society.

This consensus was consistent with the negotiations proposal made to the Cree and Inuit peoples by the Quebec Premier shortly after the announcement of the court ruling (Bourassa, 1974). The 11-point proposal, based on some indirect discussions with the Cree, emphasised two things: the offer of a renewed relationship between the indigenous peoples and the government through their active involvement in the development of the region; and modifications to the project. The latter were essentially changes warranted by the continuing engineering and cost optimisation studies, but some did reduce impacts on areas critical to the Cree. However, the Cree and Inuit found the proposal unacceptable, and told the federal Minister of Indian Affairs so that he privately suggested it could be the basis for a rapid settlement of their dispute with Quebec.

The central choice now confronting the Cree and Inuit leaders was whether to recommend to their people to continue with their opposition to the project and attempt to gain recognition of their aboriginal rights primarily through continued court action, or to renew negotiations. It is worth recalling that the Cree and Inuit already had experience with trying both means, although under different circumstances than now existed. A third possibility they had to consider was an imposed settlement.

Pursuing the court cases had several advantages, and risks. First, if the courts upheld the position of the first judgment they would provide the strongest possible definition of aboriginal rights. However, it was considered most likely that a final court ruling would be weaker, and there was a real risk of gaining little or no recognition at all.

Second, the court definition of an aboriginal right was likely to involve usufructory interest in the land, and possibly an interest that would be strong enough to control or exert power over some outside development projects. But, it was less clear whether a judicial determination of the aboriginal right would include actual control of resources and development. And it was less likely that such a determination would include other elements which the indigenous people now saw as critical to their futures, such as increased control over social services, and participation in regional and supraordinate administrative, economic and political structures. While it was possible that some or all of these rights could be attained through political manoeuvring based on a clear judicial recognition of aboriginal rights, this emphasised that a judicial determination was likely to be incomplete by itself, and that at one point or another, court action would have to lead to political negotiations.

Negotiations, on the other hand, had the essential advantage that the indigenous people would be looking neither to Euro-Canadians, nor to an alien judicial system, to take the decisive role in defining an aboriginal right or what were acceptable project modifications or remedies. In negotiations, the indigenous peoples would take the active role in defining what they wanted recognised as their aboriginal rights, how they wanted to exercise them, and how the project could be made less damaging. And, they could do this in the light of present problems and future aspirations.

But, this advantage required that they assume the difficult responsibilities for creating consensus about what they wanted. Furthermore, negotiation also imposed the burden of compromise, because each side must not only have power it must be prepared to give something up in an exchange. Assuming the responsibilities of a negotiation included taking the often heavy responsibilities of striking the compromises. Finally, there was a real chance negotiations would not produce acceptable results because the compromises might be so burdensome as to be unacceptable.

The advantage of negotiations, as opposed to a settlement imposed by a court or by parliament, in addition to the effective inputs of the native people into the provisions of the former was the greater acceptance and willingness of all parties to work and live with the provisions of a negotiated agreement. Where settlements are imposed, or parties forced into an agreement, the outcome is usually neither accepted nor workable, and the settlement is frequently undermined by bitter opposition or passive subterfuge, or both.

The Cree and Inuit decided that renewed efforts at negotiations would be an essential means of taking a maximally active role in determining their own future, and of effectively re-defining for Euro-Canadian society and governments how they wanted to live in the future.

The key question then was when to re-open negotiations. Under the circumstances existing at the time immediate negotiations seemed the best choice. The court case had brought about a consensus in the Cree villages on major problems and components for discussion, a consensus that could now be developed toward a consensus on solutions and possible compromises. Such consensus is essential for success, and it can easily lead to disillusionment and demoralisation if it is not enhanced and pursued at a reasonable pace.

The court decision seemed more likely to be eroded in successive court appeals than to be fully maintained. The year-long interlocutory injunction procedure augured for a long string of court battles over 4 or 5 years before a final judicial determination on the question of an aboriginal right would be rendered. Such delayed legal action would not permit rapid resolution of the community and economic problems the Cree and Inuit wanted improved. Also because construction of the hydro-electric project would probably continue during legal actions, a final judicial declaration stopping or modifying the project would be meaningless; the damages would already have occurred.

The massive commitment of capital to the project also made successive judicial declarations less likely. It was thought that the governments could not permit a judicial decision to require abandonment of the project once construction was well advanced because the economic and political consequences would be too severe. The parliaments would probably legislate a land claims settlement, in order to pre-empt a possibly adverse judicial decision. The indigenous peoples thought they would probably have very limited input to such a settlement act, certainly less than in negotiations.

The Cree and Inuit therefore decided to recommence negotiations immediately. But because they had already experienced difficulties in establishing meaningful negotiations, they decided not to abandon their court cases, but to hold them in reserve should negotiations prove fruitless.

In summary, the Cree decided to start negotiations for three kinds of reasons. First, negotiations were seen as preferable to court actions in the process of seeking project changes and a definition and recognition of aboriginal rights because they provide the greatest input by indigenous people into the definition of those rights and their adaptation to modern conditions. Second, the prerequisites for serious negotiation were present, including (1) consensus on issues and general goals, (2) a substantial power base, recognised by the governments, that was judged to be high and probably at its peak, and (3) a willingness to compromise existed on both sides. Third, the costs of not attempting a fairly rapid settlement were high in terms of continuing impacts, delayed benefits, and declining opportunity for effective inputs to a settlement.

SOME REACTIONS TO THE NEGOTIATED RECOGNITION OF ABORIGINAL RIGHTS

The announcement that the Cree and Inuit were prepared to negotiate with the government and, by implication, to reach certain compromises, had serious implications for relations between the Cree and Inuit and their supporters. While public support had so far played a limited role, the Cree and Inuit of Quebec had been a *cause célèbre* during the court case. Two books were published on their struggle against the project (Richardson, 1972, 1975), and a series of films and articles had been circulated (cf. bibliography in Feit, 1976).

The core of the Euro-Canadian supporters were environmentalists for whom the massive hydro-electric project was a monstrosity. They supported the Cree and Inuit struggle against the project largely in the hope that they could stop it entirely. Their desire for opposition at any cost was not dampened by the lesson of the initial court victory and its reversal, which indicated that stopping the project permanently was unlikely. The aboriginal rights issues were not of primary interest to them, and they tended to see adaptations and changes of the indigenous population to the Euro-Canadian presence as losses of integrity and principles. Their opposition to negotiations developed with time, and when the first agreements were announced to the media, many of the former Euro-Canadian supporters labelled the Cree and Inuit sell-outs.

The experience was a sad one for the Cree and Inuit leadership, and it suggests a possibly general instability of alliances between the indigenous people and environmental and conservationist movements. These groups were not generally informed about the conditions of the indigenous peoples, and neither shared nor understood the concerns and priorities of the Cree and Inuit. Many could not see that the Cree and Inuit did not face a single-issue problem but rather the complicated issues of how to redefine their relationships to Euro-Canadian society and how to strengthen and continue their culture and society. The Cree and Inuit could not simply move away from the project if they lost the battle. For them, the chance of a partial victory, and therefore a partial loss, could well be more attractive than the risk of an all or nothing strategy, because they would suffer the human cost of a complete defeat.

Equally sad for the Cree and Inuit were the divisions that occurred between themselves and other indigenous peoples in Quebec and Canada. The initial court judgment was perceived as a victory for all indigenous peoples in Canada, many of whom wished to see the court case pursued to completion, in the hope of establishing a strong judicial recognition of aboriginal rights that would form the basis for court actions and negotiations elsewhere. The Cree and Inuit had always supported the common interests of indigenous peoples, but they felt that their own interests, and those of others as well, could best be served by a successful and innovative negotiated agreement which redefined and specified their aboriginal rights.

Other indigenous people had either not yet reached a consensus of their own on the contents of aboriginal rights or had different priorities and objectives than the Cree and Inuit of Quebec. This became apparent early in the negotiations as a growing separation, but not a complete split, developed between the Cree and Inuit of northern Quebec and the other Indian peoples of Quebec and Canada.

From my personal perspective, these differences centred around four areas. First, the northern native peoples differed from southern Indian peoples because the former had a viable hunting way of life and an important subsistence economy which they wished to maintain and develop. This priority led to a series of trade-offs which must have looked anachronistic to many southern Indian peoples near or in urban areas, for whom aboriginal hunting rights played an important role but not an immediate role in their economic welfare. This was the basis of significant differences on how land, mineral resources, and economic provisions of the negotiations should be viewed and valued.

The priorities and trade-offs the Cree and Inuit made could be understood only in the light of their efforts to maintain an economy balanced between subsistence production and locally controlled economic enterprises and employment. And, they also could be understood only in the light of the slow *de facto* erosion of the land base on a day to day basis which the Cree and Inuit were determined to reverse.

Second, the Cree saw themselves as a people who had maintained extensive autonomy in the face of earlier intrusions by Euro-Canadian interests, and they saw themselves neither as losing their distinctiveness as a people, nor primarily as victims, although they did see themselves as having been treated unjustly by Euro-Canadians. The court case had strengthened their indentity, and was seen as a partially successful confrontation with governments and outsiders that set the stage for new responses designed to increase their autonomy. Thus, they were willing to see the vague and unspecific aspects of their claim for an aboriginal right extinguished, so long as the aboriginal right was defined to include the specific rights which they felt would help assure their continued existence as a people. They therefore tended to view the recognition of aboriginal rights as a recognition of the specific rights that would allow them to deal with the immediate problems they were encountering. The key rights they wanted recognised were the traditional hunting, fishing, trapping, and land use rights; but they also insisted on inclusion of rights not traditionally included in the aboriginal rights concept, such as rights to services and government and administrative powers.

This was in contrast to other indigenous peoples who saw recognition of a general aboriginal right as essential to maintenance of their identity, and who saw their ties to the land as dependent on such recognition. This was especially the case where a distinctive economic adaptation, such as hunting, was no longer practiced; or where indigenous peoples had already had their rights extinguished by treaty, or *de facto* by being driven off much of their land by encroaching Euro-Canadians. In these cases, and especially where there is a long established claim to have extinguished aboriginal rights, a generalised recognition of the aboriginal right is an essential step to get the government to open new negotiations. Therefore, the process of claiming such a general right may be essential to political action, to maintenance of an identity vis-á-vis Euro-Canadians, and to continued cultural survival.

The Quebec Cree and Inuit were not in the same circumstances; their rights had not been extinguished, they had not been driven off the land, and their identity as native people was not threatened. They therefore sought, and would only accept, a negotiated agreement which recognised the specific rights they felt would prevent them from being driven off the land and having their hunting society and culture destroyed. They were ready to trade off the general and vague aspects of an aboriginal right for an explicit definition of these rights. Although such an agreement might not be just, it could assure their future as a people.

Third, the Cree and Inuit of Quebec differed from some other Indian and Inuit peoples with respect to the political structures they sought. The Cree sought local and regional autonomy and self-determination through encapsulation of their communities within ethnic structures but by also building extensive administrative, consultative and political linkages to provincial and national institutions. They also sought to limit the authority of the provincial and national institutions through a series of legally binding principles and operating procedures. The northern Quebec Inuit sought to establish both ethnic and non-ethnic regional structures in which Inuit control would continue for the foreseeable future. This difference in approach was due, in part, to the fact that the Cree population was a minority in its territory, approximately 6500 compared with about 20 000 Euro-Canadian and eight villages, as opposed to seven Euro-Canadian settlements. The Inuit, in contrast, numbered approximately 4500 as opposed to 500-800 Euro-Canadians, and inhabited 12 villages as opposed to one predominantly Euro-Canadian mining settlement.

The position of both the Cree and the Inuit, however, contrasted with that developed in some other parts of the Canadian north where indigenous peoples appear, if I understand their position correctly, to want more extensive governmental powers and sovereignty, falling somewhere between those of a provincial government and those of the federal government. Such an objective seemed to imply an administrative and bureaucratic structure that would, at least in the northern Quebec case, be substantially out of proportion to the size of the indigenous populations. Furthermore, the Cree had experienced some success at maintaining their autonomy within the framework of the state apparatus; although not without conflicts and some losses which they sought to reverse through negotiations. Finally, in my view, the evidence that macrostructures would be substantially more autonomous from national political and international economic interests than the enclaves linked to macrostructures sought by the Cree and Inuit is uncertain in the light of the contemporary plight of small third world nations. Whichever view is correct, at the time of the northern Quebec negotiations the Quebec government was seeking increased autonomy within Canadian confederation, and such broad sovereignty for the Cree or Inuit at a provincial or regional level was non-negotiable. However, at a local level, extensive autonomy was imperative and was achieved. The Cree and Inuit, therefore, did not seek the broader range of regional powers, and chose instead to negotiate for certain restrictions on macro-administrative and legal powers; in the expectation that they would demand extensive local powers which could provide an adequate basis for effective autonomy.

There was considerable debate and compromise on the actual type of decision-making and consultative powers to be given to the regional structures linking the Cree and Inuit to provincial and national institutions, and this formed a core of the negotiations process. (For a discussion of the results in the sector of hunting see Feit, 1979.) As these compromises became public, and as the specific objective the Cree and Inuit had set for themselves became clear, the issue of governmental power and sovereignty became an important point of disagreement between the Quebec Cree and Inuit and several other indigenous populations in the Canadian north.

Fourth, as I have indicated, the Quebec Cree and Inuit were dealing with the problem of the definition and recognition of aboriginal rights within the context of an ongoing project. The presence of a project affects the strategies and options available, and the choices made. The project and the aboriginal rights objectives were intimately related because the Cree and Inuit were being asked, in effect, to permit the construction of the hydro-electric project and other development of the territory as a concession in the settlement. Thus, the process proceeded in the shadow of a pending threat. Much of the discussion of aboriginal rights negotiations has evisaged a situation where native peoples would not incur heavy costs if a settlement were delayed, and it therefore often does not take sufficient account of the trade-offs and priorities under circumstances where this is not the case.

On the other hand, it is possible to overemphasise one side of this complex issue because it must be noted that there would have been no negotiations without the project. From a James Bay perspective it sometimes looks as if the same pattern is occurring elsewhere in Canada; that there is real activity only in the face of threatened developments. Where no development is proposed governments appear to be extremely slow to respond seriously to aboriginal rights claims. Indeed, it sometimes appears as if this kind of a threat is essential to both sides for negotiations to proceed to conclusions.

These differences between the Quebec Cree and the Inuit and many of the other indigenous peoples of Canada point out the diversity of historical experiences and contemporary circumstances that both unite and distinguish indigenous peoples within the country. The northern Quebec Cree and Inuit people remained true to their own understandings of contemporary circumstance and historical experience, and chose to pursue a negotiated recognition of specific aboriginal rights and new rights. In the process they were alienated from some, indeed many, of the other indigenous peoples. It was an unfortunate, but apparently unavoidable consequence of events. This experience runs counter to many of the efforts to define all Indians as having common interests, and it reflects real differences that are often glossed over or denied.

While this is an important conclusion it is also worth noting that the variety of ideas, analyses and values which disagreements among indigenous peoples expose, indicate the complexity of the choices that must be taken, and the difficulty of the consensus that must be developed whenever a group undertakes to define what the aboriginal right will mean in its own case. And, they show that there is no single answer to this formulation, each group being challenged to remain true to, and thereby gain its strength from, its own history, experience, knowledge and values.

THE ORGANISATION OF AND STRATEGIES FOR THE NEGOTIATION PROCESS

Once the Cree and Inuit had approved the decision to re-initiate negotiations, they began by rejecting the government's proposal. They rejected the inadequate land provisions of the proposal, the inadequate recognition of hunting, fishing and trapping rights and environmental protection, the inadequate modifications to the project and proposals for remedial and compensatory measures, and the failure of the proposals to provide for sufficient local or regional autonomy and self-determination (Diamond, 1977).

The Cree immediately drew up a position paper called 'Our Land, Our Demand' in order to take the initiative and define the scope and contents of the negotiations.

Negotiations were organised as a two-stage process, with the goal of reaching an agreement in principle first, and then, if this was acceptable to all parties, proceeding to a final agreement. If the Agreement in Principle was unacceptable, then it was back to the courtroom.

Early in the negotiations the Cree formed their own political association, the Grand Council of the Crees (of Quebec), with the administrative chief and another leader from each community on its board of directors, and an executive group of four regional leaders. The Grand Council took over the organisation of the negotiations. However, the Cree people remained the final decision-makers; they gave the GCCQ a mandate to negotiate, but retained the right to decide whether the results of those negotiations were acceptable.

Day to day negotiations were carried on by Cree and Inuit teams consisting of a maximum of 20 persons each. By my estimate, the government negotiating teams reached a maximum of about 200 people at one point in the two-year process. The Cree team consisted of the four Cree executive members who took strategy and policy decisions, four to six senior and junior Cree negotiators, and approximately eight Euro-Canadian lawyers and consultants with diverse professional experience in biology and ecology, geography, engineering and anthropology. The small size of the Cree negotiating team facilitated coordination and an integrated approach in the diverse range of issues discussed. Most of those involved had worked with the Cree during the court cases, and when additional assistance from Euro-Canadians was needed, an effort was made to find individuals with some experience in the Cree communities. A group of Cree and Inuit communications workers kept information linkages open between the negotiating group, working in urban centres, and the Cree communities. Progress of the negotiations was regularly reported in the villages, but such information was effectively kept out of the mass media because experience indicated that public opinion would not, at that time, support a negotiated settlement.

The negotiations were organised around seven parties, the Cree, the Inuit, the governments of Quebec and Canada, and the three Quebec state-owned corporations responsible for the development of the territory. While the presence of the corporations was an unusual feature, it made it possible for the Cree and Inuit to deal with them directly, rather than having them play a behind-the-scenes role. Although it complicated the process, and cost certain objectives, their presence was sometimes an assistance because conflicting interests between them and government agencies helped negotiating Cree and Inuit objectives which did not threaten their immediate and relatively narrow interests.

Negotiations were conducted by a main negotiating committee and several subcommittees. The main committee consisted of the senior negotiators and lawyers for each party as regular members, and various specialist advisers as part-time participants. It drafted some of the general provisions of the agreements, and edited the texts of the drafts negotiated in the subcommittees. Some substantial revisions of drafts were made by the main committee, but an effort was made to have strong mandates for effective negotiations by the smaller subcommittees. The subcommittees were typically comprised of Cree and Inuit negotiators, and one or more lawyers and professional experts, on one side, and senior government or corporate administrators from the departments most directly involved in the specific subject matter, on the other.

It was considered important that senior administrators form the departments that would have a role in administering an agreement be involved so that the agreements reached be perceived as practicable. Negotiations also aimed at creating a core of informed administrators who would know something about the indigenous peoples, and about the compromises involved in, and the meaning of, the agreements that were finally reached. At the same time, the negotiations were directed toward solutions to problems which did not assume that an informed government administrator would necessarily be involved in their implementation.

A basic strategy of the Cree and Inuit negotiating team was to keep the initiative by drafting a constant flow of position papers and working documents, and tabling these in the appropriate subcommittee prior to the formulation of government positions. This put a heavy workload on the small staff, but it directed the negotiations to critiques, defenses, and modifications of Cree and Inuit positions, rather than of government positions. This procedure tended to retain the internal logic and assumptions of the Cree and Inuit positions in the final documents, although in many cases the text resulting from negotiated compromises had inconsistencies in logic and assumptions.

The Cree and Inuit strategy assumed neither all-pervasive conflict nor cooperation with governments. Each party was seen as self-interested, self-organised, and willing to make trade-offs; widespread, underlying shared interests were not assumed to exist. Despite the limited range of shared interests the pattern of conflict was not monolithic; there appear to have been several sets of relatively self-consistent assumptions, bodies of knowledge, and interests, each unique to a party and each having specific areas of conflict or overlap with those of other parties. The parties involved differed not only across levels, the self-interested and self-organised organisations within levels differed (for example, the diverse departments, agencies and corporations within each government). Thus, conflicts occurred within as well as across levels. Each agency sought its highly valued goals and exploited the areas other parties or units undervalued relative to the agent.

The negotiation was constrained by the historical conditions and the powers of the parties; however, these came into play only in the areas of direct conflict, which while critical were limited. All parties had minimum positions which were unchangeable. These became clear early in the negotiations. As they proceeded a central strategy was to specify and thereby narrowly focus the areas of direct conflict, and also to find alternative ways in which goals were unacceptable in one form could be accepted.

The process required careful thinking out of positions and tactics, based on the clear identification of objectives and priorities, and the anticipation of counter positions. The Cree and Inuit teams identified immediate objectives, fallback positions and trade-off alternatives prior to each negotiating discussion. Planning thus played an essential and critical part in determining the course and outcome of the negotiating process.

In consequence, the course and outcome of negotiations were not solely and objectively determined by power in the wider political and economic spheres; the outcome was significantly, but not entirely, determined in the series of strategic decisions taken in the course of negotiations. Nevertheless, important areas remained in which a satisfactory set of provisions could not be reached, given the positions of each party.

The Government of Quebec had six firm negotiating positions: (1) that it maintain and extend its jurisdiction and authority over the northern regions of the province; (2) that the territory be opened for controlled development; (3) that the settlement create no more than a politically acceptable level of opposition among Euro-Canadians; (4) that any outstanding aboriginal rights claims be extinguished; (5) that the economic viability of the hydro-electric project not be compromised, and the economic costs of concessions be minimised; and (6) that there be no royalties provisions, although a lump sum compensation in place of royalties was acceptable. The corporations shared these positions, especially the second and fifth.

The Government of Canada was represented but not active during most of the negotiations. It only intervened at the end to impose a series of conditions by which it sought to protect its interests. These were (1) that the final jurisdiction of the federal government over Indian affairs be maintained although it was preferable if continued federal jurisdiction was coupled with a turning over of administrative responsibilities, including some sharing of administrative responsibilities, including some sharing of financial responsibilities, to subordinate levels of governments or to the indigenous peoples themselves; (2) it was essential not to reduce federal jurisdiction within Quebec; (3) no precedent should be set in the northern Quebec negotiations that would compromise the federal government in the settlement of land claims elsewhere in Canada.

For the Cree and Inuit the essential positions were (1) that the provisions make possible the continuation of hunting and subsistence economy, and the regulation of future development; (2) that project modifications be made and remedial measures taken to reduce the impacts of the hydro-electric project; (3) that land be set aside for the Cree and Inuit sufficient to protect their communities, and some of their most important wildlife harvesting sites and activities; (4) that control over basic administrative services, programmes and new regional structures be turned over to the Cree and Inuit with extensive local autonomy well beyond that normally given municipal governments, but with funding from provincial or federal governments; (5) that a balance be struck between rights and benefits in the land rights and benefits flowing to people who no longer depended on the land but who needed new economic opportunities; and (6) that there be sufficient monetary compensation so that funds could be invested and protected for future generations, while providing adequate incomes for the costs of implementing the other objectives.

While this over-simplifies the positions, it does show that there were points of agreement, areas where the interests of one party were unopposed by another, and areas of general or direct conflict. The key areas of general conflict were: control of development activity; project modifications; transfers of land from Quebec to Cree and Inuit control; transfer of regional administrative powers and control over basic resources (such as wildlife) from Quebec to Cree and Inuit institutions; royalties; and an adequate protection of hunting rights, resources and opportunities. This paper does not review the specific provisions of the Agreement relating to these and other issues.[2] As indicated above, satisfactory solutions were found for some, but not all of these conflict areas. The Cree and Inuit had to decide whether the package as a whole was sufficient to protect and build their future.

THE DECISION TO SETTLE AND IMPLEMENTATION

The first set of negotiations lasted about eight months, but most of the work on the Agreement in Principle was completed in the last two months. This Agreement spelled out the broad outlines of the positions all parties could agree upon. The main legal provisions provided for eventual Cree and Inuit withdrawal of opposition to the hydroelectric project and of claims to other undefined rights and recognition by both governments of the rights spelled out in the agreement. Four sections were eleborated in some detail: the general principles for a hunting, fishing and trapping regime; the new modifications to the hydro-electric project and the associated compensatory and remedial measures; the size and principles for land allocations and the associated regime; and the compensation to be paid.

The Agreement in Principle was taken back to each of the Cree communities, where the provisions were outlined in detail. The outcome was summarised by Chief Billy Diamond of the Grand Council of the Crees, in his speech to the press, announcing that all Cree communities had accepted the Agreement in Principle and that it would be signed on the first anniversary of the court judgment on the interlocutory injunction. After outlining the provisions of the Agreement in Principle, Chief Diamond said:

> The Cree People were very reluctant to sign an Agreement in Principle. However, after many meetings and many hours of meetings, the Grand Council of the Crees has received a mandate to sign an Agreement in Principle with the Quebec Government. Our mandate is also to see that the Quebec Government lives up to its obligations and we have a mandate to suspend court proceedings. We also have a mandate to carry out future negotiations with the Quebec Government.
>
> We feel, as Cree People, that by coming to an Agreement in Principle, that it is the best way to see that our rights and that our lands are protected as much as possible from white man's intrusion and white man's use. We have always said that we wanted to maintain our way of life. We have always said that we want to pass the land on to our

children. Now we believe that this Agreement in Principle will maintain our way of life and that we can also pass the land on to our children, just as it has been done in the past. It guarantees the future of our children. It also guarantees that we can continue to live in harmony with nature. We believe that even though we practised the traditional way of life, the aboriginal way of life, we believe this agreement supports and strengthens the hunting, fishing and trapping rights in/over all of the territory, and restricts non-native activity in that area.

By the proposed agreement, we feel we have removed the worst effects of the Project to our way of life and the Cree People. The Treaties in the past that were signed have always been to settle land claims and land uses and land rights once and for all. However, we believe that the Cree People have not settled their land claims once and for all; other negotiations will continue after the Agreement in Principle.

We realise that perhaps we will disappoint many of the public by signing an Agreement in Principle with the Quebec Government. We realise that many of the friends that we have made during our opposition to the project will label us as 'sell-outs'.

However, we have come to a decision together, and we intend to carry-out that decision, and also we consider it a victory. A BIG VICTORY FOR US, because there are only 6 000 Crees and there are 6 million Quebecers here in this Province. It is also a big victory because there are not very many people that can persuade the best engineers in the world to change the location of a major dam and to change their plans such that our way of life will be less harmed.

I hope you can all understand our feelings, that it has been a tough fight, and our people are still very much opposed to the project, but they realise that they must share the resources. That is why we have come to a decision to sign an Agreement in Principle with the Quebec Government. (Diamond 1974)

One provision of the Agreement in Principle was that a final agreement would be signed within a year. During the next 12 months extensive and intensive negotiations continued in order to give detailed specifications to the rights agreed upon during the first phase of negotiations, and to provide a legally explicit and binding framework for recognising and exercising such rights. More than 15 subcommittees and task forces were established covering: project modifications; hunting, fishing and trapping; environmental protection; land selection and regime; local and regional government; economic development; income security for hunters; legal entities; taxation and compensation; education; health; police and justice; and eligibility. Each subcommittee drafted a section of the final agreement for approval or revision by the negotiating committee. The texts were drafted in both English and French, and the aboriginal peoples had to work in their second language, English. The final agreement, read out in the villages and translated into the native languages, was ratified by vote. Only after it was legislated did the Cree and Inuit finally drop their court cases.

A key decision was whether or not the agreement should be dependent upon legislation, that is, did it have to be enacted into law to have effect. The Cree and Inuit, on legal advice, decided to have legislation, and negotiate an agreement in great detail to assure that the changes needed to pass legislation giving legal force to the various sections would require a minimum of interpretation and leave a minimum of room for later change; and that there be a relatively clear basis for legal recourses to the courts if the governments did not live up to the terms of the agreement.

The final agreement took an intensive year of work to draft. It needs to be stressed that it simply took an enormous effort to keep the process going, and a total committment of those involved to bring it to completion. There was considerable pressure on and by government parties to withdraw from part or even all of the agreement, because it was felt the native people had gotten too much. Thus, without a massive effort by the Cree the final agreement would never have been completed and approved by all parties.

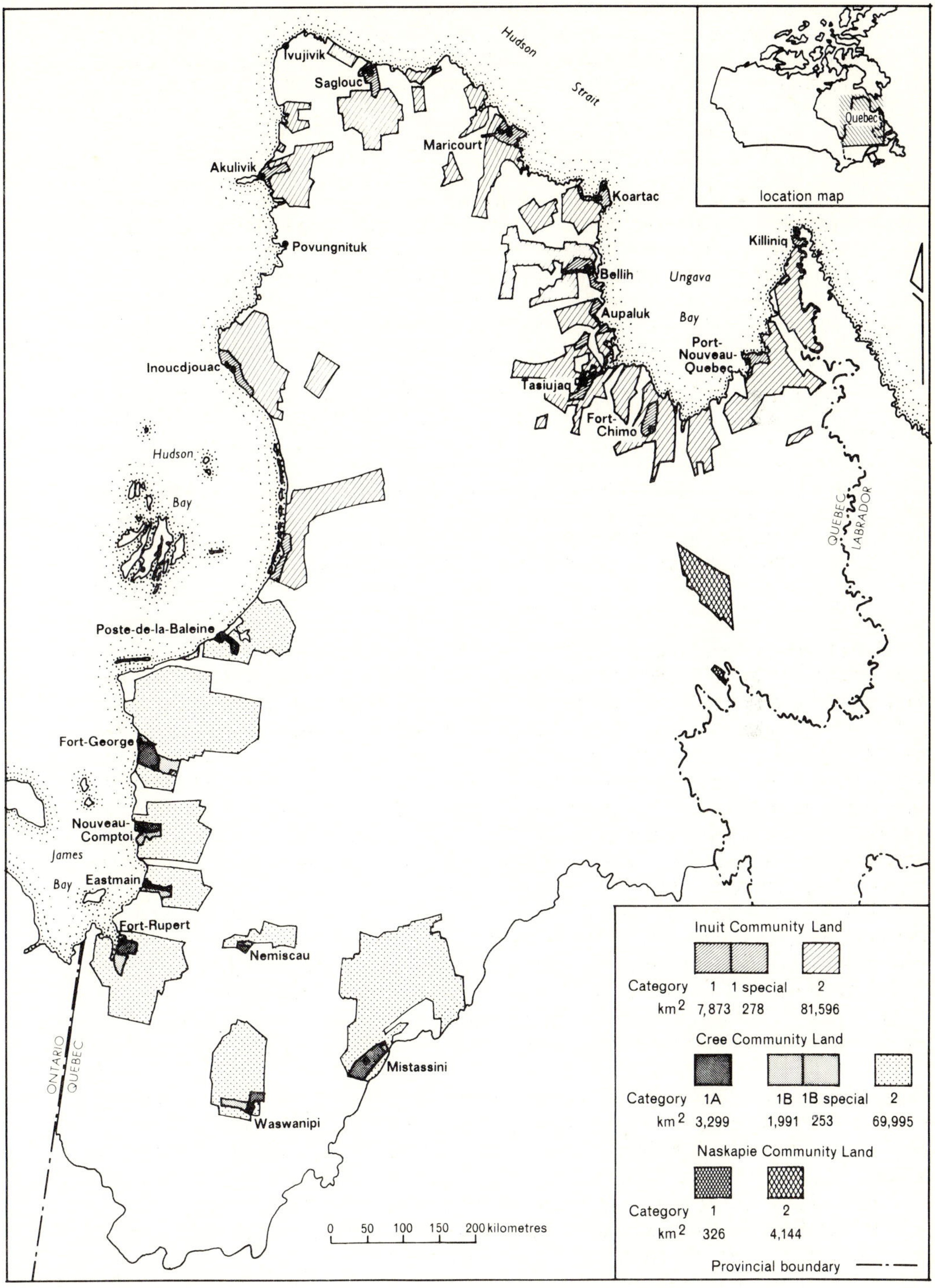

Fig. 1
Division of lands under the James Bay and Northern Quebec Agreement.

The agreement was given legal force by general government legislation two years after it was signed, and shortly before the deadline which the agreement specified for such legislation. Altogether 20 Legislative bills were necessary to implement all the provisions of the agreement, particularly from the Quebec government, and some are still being revised. The governments have, as expected, often tried to turn the legislative drafting itself into a renegotiation of the provisions. This process has been resisted but not entirely prevented. The governments have also tried to delay implementation and considerable effort has been necessary to force implementation. Nevertheless, implementation is proceeding, and in many areas it is proceeding as rapidly as the Crees and Inuit respond to the opportunities. In addition, negotiations continue on certain topics which were not settled in the final text. The Cree are now drafting the actual legislation in the outstanding areas where negotiations continue.

The final agreement was signed in November, 1975, and despite the slow passage of the legislation various provisions were, by the terms of the agreement, implemented immediately by provisional orders-in-council and regulations under existing laws. As a result, nearly all the provisions are now implemented, in whole or in part, permanently or temporarily.

The agreement contains a number of relatively innovative measures and provisions, and these in particular will need close evaluation. Among these are: a guaranteed income security programme for people who live by hunting, fishing and trapping as a way of life; establishment of a series of permanent, preferential, exclusive and mandatory consultative bodies of government and Cree and Inuit experts to supervise and implement specific hunting, fishing and trapping, and environmental provisions of the agreement, legally binding principles and operational rules to govern the exercise of governmental authority over wildlife and the environment; recognition of the Cree system of land use and control; a guaranteed allocation of wildlife to the indigenous peoples; Cree and Inuit administration and control of social services and local governments and structures; and new legislation replacing the federal Indian Act with a Cree-designed Cree Act.

Experience with these provisions is just beginning to accumulate, and I believe it may be several years before it will be possible to evaluate either the effectiveness of the provisions of the agreement in general, or whether the agreement will meet the specific expectations and objectives of the Cree and Inuit of northern Quebec. Nevertheless, some initial assessments have been undertaken (cf. Salisbury, 1979; Scott, 1979; Scott & Feit, in press, LaRusic, 1979; and LaRusic et al., 1979). It is already clear that the negotiations did not take sufficient account of the financial and human burden of legislating, implementing and operating the provisions of the agreement. The human and monetary costs to the Cree and Inuit are heavy and should have been more carefully considered, and more appropriate provisions should have been made. Furthermore, it is clear that in some areas there is considerable government resistance to implementing the agreement in full, and judicial and political initiatives have been required to try to bring compliance. The critical tests of the process are now occurring.

It is clear, however, that the process of reaching the agreement has strengthened the Cree and Inuit peoples of northern Quebec because they have successfully fought for and achieved many of their objectives. Furthermore, it has given them new resources, organisations and experience which they are now using to implement and pressure for respect of the agreement, and to initiate new consultations, court actions, and negotiations in order to further their rights, protect their land, and determine their futures. Serious modifications to the agreement are also now being given some initial consideration.

CONCLUSION

A land claims agreement, however important it may be, should, I suggest, be seen as but one critical step in the process by which indigenous peoples can redefine their relations to encapsulating societies, and thereby attempt to ensure their own futures. The settlement establishes structures and means for a continuing relationship between the indigenous peoples and the government and it provides the resources with which the indigenous peoples can actively pursue their own interests. An agreement does not answer or foresee all the problems. It is a tool in ongoing processes in which the agreement itself will have to be changed and modified.

Gaining recognition of aboriginal rights is a dynamic and continuing process in which court battles, political action, legislation, and negotiations must be used and coordinated. Any aboriginal rights negotiation offers lessons that should be of use for the continuing efforts of all those engaged in seeking recognition of aboriginal rights. The critical evaluation of aboriginal rights agreements will be whether they enhance the ability of indigenous people to determine their own lives and futures, and whether they respond to the new opportunities for achieving those objectives.

ACKNOWLEDGEMENTS

This article has been prepared with the assistance of a Killam Post-Doctoral Research Scholarship from the Canada Council. The author also wishes to thank Peter W. Hutchins for his valuable suggestions on an earlier draft of the paper. The article was originally published in the *Canadian journal of anthropology,* 1980, pp. 159-72, and appears here, with slight alterations, by permission of that journal. *The Cree and James Bay Agreement: A Chronology of Events* is reprinted as an appendix with permission from LaRusic et al. (1979).

APPENDIX:

THE CREE AND THE JAMES BAY AGREEMENT: A CHRONOLOGY OF EVENTS[1]

KEY: Announcement and early reactions (Roman type)
The court case (Bold type)
Negotiations and Agreement (Italic type)

February 1971. Publication of the Dorion Commission Report on the territorial integrity of the province; the Commission recommends the extinguishment of aboriginal rights, which were described as partial and private, by the recognition of certain proprietal rights and compensation.

30 April 1971. Prime Minister Bourassa announces plans for the James Bay Hydro-electric Development Project. The project was justified on the basis of job creation and the need for electricity.

May 1971. Cree, though Attorneys, alert the Minister of DINA to issues of Indian land rights posed by the project.

June 1971. Minister of DINA makes known his concerns about Indian Rights to the Provincial Minister. As a result, the work of a Tripartite Committee on general issues, formed in 1969 of Fed/Prov IQA representatives, is accelerated.

1 July 1971. First of meetings of the Cree to discuss the Project, held in Mistassini.

July 1971. Bill 50 in National Assembly of Quebec constitutes the SDBJ; the SEBJ is subsequently incorporated in December 1971.

October 1971. DINA extends a subsidy to IQA for purpose of informing the population of James Bay about the Project.

January 1972. Provincial Minister of National Resources refuses to discuss a claim for compensation put forward by IQA.

February 1972. Joint (Fed/Prov) Committee on Ecological Effects of the Project publishes report, notes a substantial impact on Indians.

April 1972. Meeting of Cree, under IQA auspices at Fort George. Billy Diamond raises possibility of a court case to stop project and a general mandate for this purpose is extended to IQA. Cree set up Cree community liaison workers.

May 1972. Minister of DINA meets with Province to talk of impacts of the Project on Indians.

3 May 1972. IQA forms a Task Force and calls upon a number of McGill University researchers to conduct ecological and social studies.

5 May 1972. **Indians and Inuit initiate action in injunction.**

8 May 1972. **DINA reveals subsidy to IQA for preparation of Court case and other research.**

16 May 1972. Province announces switch from NBR to La Grande (LG) as the first phase of the Hydro developments.

23 October 1972. Province announces policy of no modifications.

23 October 1972. Meeting in Montreal of Cree Chiefs, Inuit representatives and Executive of IQA, to review work of Task Force.

25 October 1972. **This group meets with Bourassa; very unsatisfactory meeting; Cree resolve to pursue court actions including interlocutory injunction.**

7 November 1972. **Indians and Inuit file an amended writ seeking interlocutory injunction.**

8 December 1972. **Mr Justice Malouf of Quebec Superior Court grants a hearing on the petition by the Cree and Inuit.**

11 December 1972 through 24 May 1973. **The trial on the interlocutory injunction begins. It will see 71 days of testimony including 167 witnesses of whom nearly 100 were Inuit and Cree hunters.**

15 November 1973. **Mr Justice Malouf accords the interlocutory injunction on the basis of 'prima facie' evidence of Indian rights over these lands effectively occupied by the Cree and Inuit in the pursuit of their traditional subsistence activities.**

19 November 1973. Bourassa submits his 11 point proposal for a settlement to the IQA executive and the Cree and Inuit representatives.

22 November 1973. **Quebec Court of Appeals suspends the Malouf Judgment on the basis of the 'balance of convenience' without specifically treating issues of Indian title to lands.**

10 December 1973. Cree chiefs meeting in Val d'Or agree to enter negotiations, extend a mandate to the IQA to seek funds for and to undertake negotiations. Cree also set requirement that IQA must consult with the villages prior to negotiations.

21 December 1973. **The Cree make a request to the Supreme Court for leave to appeal the suspension of the Malouf Judgment. This leave is denied.**

1 January 1974. **The Indians and Inuit request leave from Quebec Court of Appeals to proceed with matter of permanent injunction.**

24 January 1974. Bourassa makes public his 11-point provincial offer.

January 1974. Cree Chiefs meet in Fort George, develop counter position entitled 'Our Land, Our Demand' (undated). Diamond then announces to press that Cree reject the offer, that the 'lands are not for sale'.

January 1974. The Minister of Indian Affairs threatens to cut off funds if the Cree do not seriously consider the Bourassa proposal, but he later backs down.

13 February 1974. **Mr Justice Crete refuses leave to proceed with permanent injunction until the full appeal on the Malouf Judgment has been heard.**

February 1974 through July 1974. Negotiations undertaken; Cree represented on IQA team. Negotiations proceed by main committee and subcommittees.

March 1974: IQA undertakes consultations with all communities regarding offers and negotiation positions.

2 April 1974: **On petition from Indians and Inuit, Supreme Court of Canada refuses leave to appeal Mr Justice Crete's ruling.**

April 1974: Cree Chiefs meet in Fort George. As a result of dissatisfaction with IQA in the negotiations, mandate withdrawn and three-man Cree negotiation team is constituted. 'Our Land, Our Demand No. 2 for Crees' is drawn up.

10 June 1974. **Quebec Court of Appeals proceeds with the matter of the appeal of the Malouf Judgment.**

July 1974 through November 1974. Major work of main committee completed, work proceeds by subcommittees.

16 August 1974. Cree Chiefs form 'The Grand Council of the Crees (of Quebec)'.

14–15 October 1974. Final offers between Cree and Province exchanged.

October 1974. Cree undertake another extensive consultation with communities.

15 November 1974. Signature of Agreement in Principle. Cree leaders call it a victory for the Cree. IQA denounces Agreement in a press conference.

21 November 1974. **The Quebec Court of Appeals overturns the Malouf Judgment, based on the 'balance of convenience'. The justices hold that Indian rights were extinguished at the time of HBC Charter or were at best 'rights to live on the territory'.**

January 1975 through July 1975. Negotiations start on Final Agreement taking the form of subcommittees, working groups and task forces.

August 1975. General Assembly of Crees decides to proceed with Negotiations to reach an Agreement and GCCQ is empowered to sign on behalf of the Cree.

September 1975. Main committee moves to a Montreal hotel to review, edit and negotiate final matters prepared by the sub-committees and working groups.

15 October 1975 through 11 November 1975. All Cree Band Councils converge on Montreal for close review of Agreement and signature of Agreement.

11 November 1975. After last minute negotiations, the James Bay and Northern Quebec Agreement is signed in Quebec.

15-18 December 1975. Cree communities circulate a 70-page text of the Agreement and hold ratification vote: 24% of population voted, 922 for, 1 against.

NOTES

1. I am indebted to Ignatius LaRusic for permission to reprint this chronology from LaRusic et al. (1979).

2. For a discussion of some aspects see Diamond (1977), Feit (1979, 1980, 1982) LaRusic et al, (1979), Scot & Feit (in press); and from the point of view of 'selling' the agreement to the Quebec National Assembly and the public, see Ciaccia (1976).

3. This paper does not review the specific conditions under which the Northeast Quebec Agreement was completed, so as to integrate with and extend the JBNQA to the Naskapi of Quebec.

REFERENCES

Anon. (1974) *Agreement in Principle, Between the Grand Council of the Crees (of Quebec) and the Northern Quebec Inuit Association and the Government of Quebec and The James Bay Energy Corporation and the James Bay Development Corporation and the Quebec Hydro-electric Commission (Hydro-Quebec) and the Government of Canada.*

Anon. (1974) Texte intégral de l'entente de principe signée le 15 novembre 1974 par les Cris de la Baie James, les Inuit du Québec et les gouvernements provincial and fédéral. *Recherches Amerindiennes au Quebec,* 4(4-5):79-94.

Anon. (1976) *The James Bay and Northern Quebec Agreement.* Quebec, Editeur officiel.

Anon. (1971) La Baie James des Amérindiens. *Recherches Amerindiennes au Quebec,* 1(4-5).

Anon. (1979) Autochtones: luttes et conjonctures I. *Recherches Amerindiennes au Quebec,* 9(3).

Anon. (1980) Autochtones: luttes et conjonctures II. *Recherches Amerindiennes au Quebec,* 9(4).

Bird, M.J. (1972) *An Analysis of Federal Interest Affected by the Proposed James Bay Hydro Development.* Ottawa, Environment Canada.

Bourassa, R. (1974) Robert Bourassa announces proposals made by Quebec to the Indian and Inuit people of the James Bay area. (See 'Schedule A' in Anonymous, Agreement in Principle, 1974).

Brelsford, T. (1980) *Subsistence Protections: the political and administrative struggles in Alaska and James Bay, Quebec.* Paper presented to the Second International Conference on Hunting and Gathering Societies. Quebec, Sept. 19-24, 1980.

Ciaccia, J. (1976) The Philosophy of the Agreement. In: Anon. (1976), The James Bay and Northern Quebec Agreement, xiii-xxiv.

Diamond, B. (1974) A time of great decision has come for the Cree People. (press statement).

Diamond, B. (1977) *Highlights of the negotiations leading to the James Bay and Northern Quebec Agreement.* Val d'Or; Grand Council of the Crees (of Quebec).

Environment Canada (1975) *James Bay Hydro-electric Project. A statement of environmental concerns and recommendations for protection and enhancement measures* (mimeo).

Feit, H.A. (1972) The Waswanipi of James Bay. *Canadian Dimension,* 8(8):22-25.

Feit, H.A. (1973) Twilight of the Cree Hunting Nation, *Natural History,* 82(7): 48-57, 72.

Feit, H.A. (1974) Review of *'Derivation Eastmain-Opinaca-La Grande—Premier Rapport D'Environnement sur les Parties aval des Rivieres Detournees',* Cultural, Social and Economic Aspects. Montreal, Grand Council of the Crees [of Quebec] (mimeo).

Feit, H.A. (1976) Bibliographie concernant la Baie James. *Recherches Amerindiennes au Quebec,* 6(1):61-64.

Feit, H.A. (1979) Political Articulations of Hunters to the State: Means of Resisting Threats to Subsistence Production in the James Bay and Northern Quebec Agreement. *Etudes Inuit Studies,* 3(2):37-52.

Feit, H.A. (1980) The James Bay and Northern Quebec Native Harvesting Research Project: the basis for establishing guaranteed levels of harvesting by native peoples of Northern Quebec. Montreal, Cree Regional Authority.

Feit, H.A. (1982) The future of hunters within nation states. Anthropology and the James Bay Cree. In: E.B. Leacock & R.B. Lee (eds.), *Politics and History in Band Societies.* Cambridge, Cambridge University Press.

Feit, H.A. (unpublished a) Restructuring linkages between James Bay Cree hunters and the State. Paper presented at the Second International Conference on Hunting and Gathering Societies, Quebec, 19-24 September 1980.

Feit, H.A. (unpublished b) Protecting indigenous hunters' ways of life: the social and environmental protection regime in the James Bay and Northern Quebec Aboriginal Rights Agreement. Paper presented at a conference on Social Impacts of Natural Resource Development on Indigenous People, Ithaca, NY, 19-20 August 1980.

Feit, H.A. & Penn, A.F. (1975) Guaranteed Harvests for the People of Eastmain and Paint Hills Possibly Affected by the Project. Montreal: Grand Council of the Crees [of Quebec] (mimeo).

Inuit Studies, Revendications autochtones/Native Claims. *Etudes Inuit Studies,* 3(1). (1979).

James Bay and Northern Quebec Native Harvesting Research Committee (1976a) *Research to establish present levels of harvesting by native peoples of northern Quebec. Part I. A report on the harvests by the James Bay Cree.* Montreal.

James Bay and Northern Quebec Native Harvesting Research Committee (1976b) *Research to establish present levels of harvesting by native peoples of northern Quebec. Part II. A report on the harvests by the Inuit of Northern Quebec.* Montreal.

James Bay and Northern Quebec Native Harvesting Research Committee (1978) *Interim report for phase II, year 1, Research to establish present levels of harvesting by native peoples of northern Quebec. Part I. Harvests by the James Bay Cree.* Montreal.

James Bay and Northern Quebec Native Harvesting Research Committee (1979a) *Harvests by the James Bay Cree, 1976–77. Third progress report (phase II, year 2). Research to establish present levels of harvesting by native peoples of northern Quebec.* Montreal.

James Bay and Northern Quebec Native Harvesting Research Committee (1979b) *Research to establish present levels of native harvesting. Harvests by the Inuit of northern Quebec, phase II (1976).* Montreal.

Joint Federal-Provincial Task Force (1971) *A Preliminary Study of the Environmental Impacts of the James Bay Development Project,* 56 pp.

LaRusic, I.E. (1979) *The Income Security Program for Cree hunters and trappers. A study of the design, operation, and initial impacts of the Guaranteed Annual Income Programme established under the James Bay and Northern Quebec Agreement.* Montreal, McGill University, Programme in the Anthropology of Development.

LaRusic, I.E., et al. (1979) *Negotiating a Way of Life. Initial Cree experience with the administrative structure arising from the James Bay Agreement.* Montreal, SSDCC.

Malouf, A.H. (1973a) *Judgement. Superior Court No. 05-04841-72. Chief Robert Kanatawat, et al. vs the Attorney General of Canada.*

Malouf, A.H. (1973b) *La Baie James indienne. Texte integral du jugement du juge Albert Malouf.* Montréal, Editions du Jour.

O'Reilley, J. et al. (1974) Respondents Factum vol. I and vol. II. Court of Appeal, Montreal. 09-000890-73; 09-000896-73; 09-000906-73. In: *appeal from an interlocutory judgement of the Superior Court of the District of Montreal rendered on November 15, 1973 by the Honourable Mr Justice Albert H. Malouf.*

Owen, G.R.W., Turgeon, J., Lajoie, F., Créte, M. & Kaufman, F. (1974) *Judgements. Court of Appeal Nos. 09-000890-73. The James Bay Development Corporation, et al. vs Chief Robert Kanatewat et al.*

Penn, A.F. (1975) Development of James Bay: The role of environmental impact assessment in determining the legal right to an interlocutory injunction. *Journal of the Fisheries Research Board of Canada,* 32(1):136–60.

Penn, A.F. (1979) The James Bay and Northern Quebec Agreement: Its Design and Execution (manuscript in preparation).

Penn, A.F. & Feit, H.A. (1974) *The northward diversion of the Eastmain and Opinaca rivers as proposed: An assessment of impacts on the native community at Eastmain Village.* Montreal, Grand Council of the Crees [of Quebec], (mimeo).

Richardson, B. (1972) *James Bay—The plot to drown the north woods.* Toronto, Clarke, Irwin & Co.

Richardson, B. (1975) *Strangers Devour the Land.* Toronto, Macmillan.

Rouland, N. (1978) *Les Inuit du Nouveau-Quebec et la convention de la baie James.* Québec, Association Inuksiutiit Katimajiit et Centre d'Etudes nordiques, Université Laval.

Salisbury, R.F. (1976) The Anthropologist as societal Ombudsman. In: David Pitt (ed.), *Development from Below. Anthropologists and development situations.* The Hague, Mouton, pp. 256–65.

Salisbury, R.F. (1977) A Prism of Perceptions: The James Bay Hydro-electricity Project. In: Sandra Wallman (ed.), *Perceptions of Development*. Cambridge, Cambridge University Press, pp. 172–205.

Salisbury, R.F. (1979) Application and theory in Canadian anthropology: the James Bay Agreement. *Transactions of the Royal Society of Canada*, series IV, 17:229–41.

Salisbury, R.F. (1980) The North as a developing nation. In: *At the Turning Point*. Proceedings of the Eighth Northern Development Conference, November, 1979. (in press).

Salisbury, R.F., Filion, F., Rawji, F. & Stewart, D. (1972a) *Development and James Bay: social implications of the proposals for the Hydro-Electric Scheme*. Montreal, Programme in the Anthropology of Development, McGill University.

Salisbury, R.F., Hyman, J. Hyman, K., Elberg, N., Tanner, A., Elliot, R.D. & Spence, J.A. (1972b) *Not by Bread Alone*. Montreal, Indians of Quebec Association.

Scott, C.H. (1977) *The Income Security Program for Cree Hunters, Fishermen and Trappers—an initial field report on impacts and reactions in four James Bay coastal settlements*. Montreal, Grand Council of the Crees [of Quebec], (manuscript).

Scott, C.H. (1979) *Modes of Production and Guaranteed Annual Income in James Bay Cree Society*. Montreal, McGill University, Programme in the Anthropology of Development.

Scott, C.H. & Feit, H.A. (in press). *Income Security for Cree Hunters: Initial socio-economic impacts and long term considerations*. Montreal, McGill University, Programme in the Anthropology of Development.

Société de Développement de la Baie James, Société d'Energie de la Baie James (1974) *Developpement hydro-electrique de la Baie James Description de l'environnement*. Montreal, SDBJ, SEBJ.

Société d'Energie de la Baie James (1978). *Connaissance du milieu des territoires de la Baie James et du Nouveau Quebec*. Montreal, SEBJ.

Spence, J.A. (1974) *Summaries of research carried out in 1972 and 1973 by the James Bay Task Force of the I.Q.A. and N.Q.I.A.* Montreal, Indians of Quebec Association (mimeo).

Spence, J.A. & Spence, G.C. (1972) *Ecological Considerations of the James Bay Project*. Montreal, The James Bay Committee.

Weinstein, M. (1976) *What the Land Provides. An examination of the Fort George subsistence economy and the possible consequence on it of the James Bay Hydro-electric Project*. Montreal, Grand Council of the Crees [of Quebec].

28

THE INCOME SECURITY PROGRAM FOR CREE HUNTERS IN QUEBEC, CANADA: an experiment in increasing autonomy of hunters in a developed nation state[1]

Harvey Feit

The Income Security Program for Cree Hunters, Trappers and Fishermen (ISP) was negotiated and established under the James Bay and Northern Quebec Agreement (JBNQA) as one of an integrated set of provisions of that aboriginal land claims settlement which were designed to assure the continuation of hunting, fishing and trapping as a viable option and means of livelihood for those Cree who practise these activities as a way of life, and for members of future generations of Cree who may wish to pursue that way of life. ISP is an experiment in increasing the participation in and intensity of hunting activities in the face of powerful disincentives to hunting created by external conditions affecting the Cree population for whom hunting is a core of social, cultural, economic, personal and religious life. Where hunting is essential to the maintenance of societies and cultures like those of the Cree, and in so far as hunting is still a valued and important means of locally providing for subsistence needs such means of assuring the continuation of the hunting way of life may serve more generally to protect and increase the autonomy and self-determination of contemporary hunting peoples.

In this respect the ISP experiment is one with potentially broad implications. Nevertheless, ISP was designed not as a general solution, but as a historically specific one. ISP was designed as a response to conditions which were seen as endangering the continuation of a particular hunting society although many of these conditions are in some degree common and widespread. The generalisations that may be drawn from the experiment must therefore be drawn carefully, and they must be accompanied by specific descriptions of the conditions under which the experiment is being conducted.

Thus, ISP cannot be understood if separated from the historical situation of Cree hunting society or if examined in isolation from the range of programmes and benefits the Cree sought and obtained in the JBNQA in order to assure the future viability of intensive Cree hunting activities. In societies where hunting activities do not play a similar role, in which hunters do not have comparable problems, or in which income security is not to be part of a similar package of remedies, a quite different programme would probably be needed.

ISP was negotiated in 1975 as part of the comprehensive aboriginal claims negotiations between the Cree and Inuit people of Quebec and the governments of Quebec and Canada and their state corporations. It came into effect with the signing of the JBNQA in November 1975. Originally intended to be a guaranteed annual income programme, ISP is one of the first such programmes implemented in North America and the first to be established on a permanent basis. However, in the negotiation of the Program the Cree insisted that the ISP not be bound by the classical conceptions of guaranteed annual income programmes, and they developed a specific series of proposals intended to make sure that ISP responded effectively to the needs of Cree hunters. ISP therefore was designed as a distinctive and innovative programme that cannot be said to conform to the usual criteria of guaranteed annual income programmes.

A discussion of its origins, purpose, design and structure is therefore as essential to an understanding of ISP, as is a simple description of its eligibility and benefits rules. This paper, therefore, provides descriptions of both. The impacts of ISP to date and an evaluation of its success are beyond the scope of this paper, although a few indications and a set of references are appended by the way of conclusion. The paper begins by setting Cree hunting in its historical context.

THE PROBLEMS OF CREE HUNTING SOCIETY IN THE 1960s

While many problems confronted the efforts of the Cree people to maintain hunting, fishing and trapping activities as a central part of their society and of their economy, these efforts had been generally successful throughout the 300-year history of involvement with agents of the world markets and the three decade history of involvement with agents of nation state administrations. There were real threats to the integrity of their hunting society, and there were real dependencies on external markets, but nevertheless their subsistence production activities remained a central part, and the most important part, of their economic activities. And, as suggested above, their hunting society is still integrated by a powerful cultural belief system, a continuing system of social and economic relationships and an effective system of ecological knowledge, all based on hunting, which have secured the society to date and which by most indications are viable for the foreseeable future. Despite the general success, however, there were new and serious challenges to the Cree in recent decades.

During the 1950s and 1960s the pace of change in regional environmental and socio-economic conditions was accelerated and Cree hunters began finding themselves in an increasingly difficult situation. One range of problems arose from the increasing physical intrusion of Euro-Canadians into Cree territory. A second range of problems focussed around the economics of hunting.

Mining centres were opened in the 1950s bringing roads and rail communication links into the southern portion of the Cree territory and opening the well-forested southern portion to commercial forestry operations. Along with the generally adverse but initially limited impacts this activity had on the wildlife and ecological systems of the territory, the new communications links made the region significantly more accessible to Euro-Canadian sportsmen. Competition for those wildlife species of interest to sport hunters and fishermen rapidly developed, and as a response to this problem the Government of Quebec implanted conservation officers, then called game wardens, in the southern portion of the territory.

The conservation officers began to impose provincial game laws, regulations and policies on the Cree hunters for the first time as part of their response to the growing wildlife conservation and management problems. These policies were based on a recognition that standard game laws could not be inflexibly applied to Indian populations, who hunted and fished for subsistence, who extensively depended on the food of the animals they harvested for nutrition, and whose whole culture and society were integrated with and by hunting activities. The Government did not, however, recognise a basic right to hunt and it viewed the special exclusions from the laws of general application as a privilege granted by government to the Crees. The Government therefore reserved entirely to itself the formulation of the extent of special privileges to be accorded indigenous peoples. Under these circumstances some of the new regulations which it imposed had the effect of limiting Cree hunting in areas most accessible to sportsmen.

The active involvement of government agencies in aspects of Cree hunting activity was not new; the governments of Quebec and Canada had given recognition to the traditional system of Cree hunting territories, now called traplines, in the 1930s and

1940s, and had instituted programmes for improving beaver populations, preventing excessive harvests, and improving the trappers' returns on the sales of fur pelts. These programmes were provided in response to the decimation of the beaver populations in the 1930s. Beaver was both an important source of meat and of fur pelts for sale. Its decimation in the Cree territory was caused primarily by pre-emptive hunting by the Cree in response to the intrusions of Euro-Canadian trappers who began intensive trapping to clean out beaver populations on parts of the Cree territory and who left the Cree with little choice other than taking the beaver before the Euro-Canadians got to them (Feit, 1978).

The Government programmes of this period were distinguished by the fact that (1) they excluded Euro-Canadian trappers and protected Cree interests; (2) the entire system was cooperative, encouraging Cree inputs; and (3) in so far as it involved Cree compliance it was self-regulated. In fact, the system had as its model the indigenous Cree system of territorial organisation and wildlife management. The involvement of the Quebec Government in the 1960s was therefore a radical break with previous practice because the existence of an aboriginal right to hunt was explicitly denied; the Government acted to protect the interests of Euro-Canadian hunters and restricted some Cree activities, and the Cree were no longer consulted in the formulation of new policy nor involved in its implementation.

The change of position by governments may be related to changes in the relationship of the Crees and the non-native population to the Government, as well as to a change in government objectives and priorities. In the 1930s and 1940s, government support to maintain Cree hunting was a way of keeping Cree demands for government welfare assistance limited. By the 1960s the Cree were receiving extensive welfare payments, for reasons I describe below, and this use was by then irreversible. On the other hand, white trappers in the 1930s were a frontier group without special linkages to or commitments from governments, whereas in the 1960s sportsmen were an urban-based population with effective pressure group organisations. Finally, in the 1960s the Government itself desired a public presence in the newly opened territory in order to promote publicity for the supposed widespread benefits of its economic development programmes in the region. Data are not available to assess the relative importance of these factors, but *prima facie* the change in government objectives would appear likely to be the most influential.

These developments, along with growing impacts of development activities on the wildlife, created new problems for Cree hunters. The announcement of the James Bay Hydro-electric scheme in 1971 foreshadowed the extension of regional infrastructures and the problems related to development throughout the Cree territory, and an intensification of the multi-faceted conflicts with Euro-Canadian society. This range of hunting problems had four foci for which the Cree sought solutions when the JBNQA was negotiated in 1974 and 1975; recognition of aboriginal hunting rights; effective involvement of the Cree in management of wildlife and the environment; regulation of the allocation of wildlife between indigenous hunters and sportsmen, including priority allocation to the former; and regulation of the environmental impacts of developmental activity.

The second range of problems the Cree encountered with increasing frequency during the 1960s and early 1970s were related to the growing difficulty of meeting the economic costs of hunting.

In the 1940s the Government of Canada had started giving welfare to Cree hunters in response to the crises in subsistence and incomes caused by the decimation of beaver populations during the preceding decade. The Government responses to the decimation were highly successful and included the provision of welfare rations, first in kind and then in money, to help the Cree hunters meet subsistence and cash needs during the period of low beaver harvests. At first, welfare was given as a temporary measure but the introduction of universal transfer payment schemes in the late 1940s assured that at least some payments would continue on a permanent basis.

When beaver trapping recommenced in the early 1950s pelt prices were relatively high, and the combination of incomes from the sale of beaver pelts and government welfare provided an adequate income. Furthermore, the incomes were well integrated with the specific scheduling needs of hunters; the welfare ration was given out monthly in summer, when hunting is more limited, and in a lump sum in the fall; the fur income came in winter and in spring. The fall lump sum payment was needed to facilitate purchasing the goods—food, supplies and equipment—for the 6–9 months of living in isolated bush camps between September and June. These camps of from one to five families were the locations from which intensive fall, winter and spring hunting and trapping were traditionally practised. The welfare payment complemented and partially replaced the credit given by the fur trader in the fall, which was traditionally repaid when the pelts were sold in winter and spring. With fewer beaver, and with stricter debt policies imposed by the main trading firm, the Hudson's Bay Company, credit was limited and welfare rations took up the slack in the fall. By giving out a lump sum fall ration, equivalent to about three months' welfare payments, the Government kept people productive in the bush in winter and off welfare for part of the period from September to June. From a Cree perspective cash incomes appear to have been abundant during this period.

The cash available was used by many hunters to reduce some of the most onerous aspects of the heavy work load required of intensive hunters living in a highly unstable, relatively unproductive, and rigorous subarctic environment. While certain components of this work could not be reduced, given the nature of the animal distributions and abundance and given the technology available, there were some components which could be eased. Most important for present puroposes were the possibilities of more extensive use of chartered bush aeroplanes as a means of improving transportation to and from those winter camp locations which were not readily accessible from the summer settlements by waterway or by newly established road network. Air transportation eliminated the need to carry families and winter supplies to bush camps by canoe. Travel by canoe usually involved paddling one or more heavily packed canoes, and then frequently portaging the supplies and canoes between water bodies. While the time saved by flying varied widely, the more isolated hunters could save 2–4 weeks' travelling time, and over 100 portages needed to reach winter camps.

Given this situation, the practice of chartering bush aircraft rapidly became commonplace, and did itself have ramifications creating other new labour-saving uses for cash incomes. Use of chartered aircraft made possible the transporting of larger quantities of supplies to the bush, including the liquid fuels needed for more extensive use of equipment such as outboard motors and snowmobiles. Thus, by the 1960s both summer and winter travel were being transformed through the introduction of new equipment into the bush. All these changes involved significant new annual cash expenditures, both as capital investments and for operations and maintenance (Feit, 1978).

The period of adequate funding therefore led to the kinds of transformation which have been found widespread in subsistence economies, the use of available cash to improve labour efficiency, possibly to improve productivity, and to improve security and comfort through a limited use of productive and consumer goods. But these desired improvements brought with them an increased, but possibly not yet apparent, dependency, not only on the world market (the Cree had been selling furs for 300 years) but also on the governmental welfare system. This dependency existed despite the fact that the Cree themselves often perceived the welfare payments as compensation for past profits by whites at Cree expense, and therefore as 'due', and despite the fact that the actual levels of cash incomes being received were modest by the standards of an affluent nation state.

During the middle and later 1960s the consequences of these increased and new dependencies became apparent as conditions changed. First, the credit system was curtailed by the Hudson's Bay Company. The growing Cree demands for consumer goods made it more profitable for the Hudson's Bay Company to shift its emphasis in much of the region from running fur-trading posts to becoming general merchants. This, plus the growing Euro-Canadian presence, which brought in a competition among merchants, made them less willing and able to issue large credit amounts in many communities. Second, the managers of the stores were replaced along with this change and few experienced fur buyers remained, so the prices paid for fur pelts declined.

The Cree, in general, attempted to use the growing opportunities for summer employment to increase their incomes and to offset these other restrictions on access to cash because summer wage labour could be integrated with the maintenance of winter hunting and trapping. Summer employment, however, also increased expenses because less fishing was done and more foods were purchased to meet family needs during the summer itself. To meet their winter needs, many Cree would therefore work later into the fall, when possible almost until the freeze-up, and then fly to the bush. And they would come out of the bush earlier in the spring as well (Feit, 1978).

These changes led the Government of Canada's representatives in the southern part of the region to decide the Cree were on the way to abandoning hunting and becoming wage labourers. As a result, they started cutting off lump-sum payments to hunters in the fall, and offered a standard monthly welfare cheque while introducing various make-work programs to reduce the apparent unemployment.

This change of policy deprived many hunters in some communities of the cash to charter aircraft in the fall, and it encouraged people to stay near the towns to pick up their monthly cheques. The final result was that many hunters were forced to abandon intensive hunting from isolated bush camps within a few year period, although the numbers did increase somewhat after a Cree-initiated reorganisation.

These problems were accompanied by other changes related to the costs of hunting. The lack of fur trade posts in some areas meant that the specialised goods needed for trapping were often unavailable. Similarly, changes in the demand for air services often meant planes were not available when needed. And the increased services available in the settlements increased demands for improved services in the bush camps; but these had to be entirely funded by the individual hunters, as opposed to having government assistance, under existing government policies.

Thus, the Cree were trying to maintain a subsistence economy in the midst of an increasing interaction and dependence on government programmes, on cash, and on goods, services and employment in the regional market economy. The results were mixed, and a significant number of people were being driven out of subsistence production in the process.

Nevertheless, in some communities at least overall subsistance production did not decline, as those remaining in hunting produced more. Thus, in the late 1960s and early 1970s it was estimated that families, when living in the bush, were providing 90% of the food potentially available to them, and a clear surplus over their immediate needs. For the communities as a whole it is estimated that between 40% and 60% of annual caloric nutritional requirements were being produced from subsistence activities, and a much higher proportion of protein and most other nutritional needs (Feit, 1978). Their success was partly due to the hunters using new technology and altered hunting patterns and partly due to local Cree welfare administrators reinstituting some lump-sum payments, contrary to the rules. The lesson of economic dependency and of the need to have greater economic autonomy was, however, made clear by these events, and it is a general lesson.

To summarise then, there were two groups of problems: those directly related to the intrusion of Euro-Canadians into the region and focusing on hunting rights, regulation of sport hunting, management of wildlife, and the regulation of the impacts of development; and those that were more directly economic, involving assurance that there would be adequate cash flows at the critical times of the year, and provision of necessary goods and services for efficient use of those cash incomes. These common problems called for new means of solving the hunters' problems that would not enhance the process of growing dependency on external conditions, resources and people.

THE RELATIONSHIP OF ISP TO THE JAMES BAY AND NORTHERN QUEBEC AGREEMENT AND ITS RELATED PROVISIONS

The negotiation of a comprehensive aboriginal and land claims settlement during 1974 and 1975 provided the Cree people with the first opportunity to deal with these problems in a relatively extensive and co-ordinated fashion. It was one of their assumptions during the negotiation of the agreement that hunting was a central force of Cree life and society and that in the future they desired to build a society based on a balance among the population of participation in subsistence activities and in economic enterprises and employment. To achieve this goal the two sets of problems which confronted those Cree who engaged primarily in the subsistence sector had to be resolved.

The first set of problems of the hunters was addressed in the hunting, fishing and trapping regime, and the environmental and social protection regime of the JBNQA. Very generally, they provide for: a recognition of a Cree right to hunt, fish and trap at all times of the year over all Cree territory, called a right to harvest, subject to a principle of conservation, and certain other limited restrictions; a clear and binding principle of the priority of indigenous harvesting over sport hunting and fishing, and operational procedures for implementing such a principle; certain binding principles for regulating the government's exercise of wildlife management authority in favour of protecting indigenous peoples, communities, economies and activities, and an obligatory consultative participation of the indigenous peoples in that management; and, a similar set of binding principles and obligatory consultation and participation for protecting and limiting the effects of development activity on the indigenous people and the environment. I have reviewed these measures in another paper (Feit, 1979), and only note their existence here and their importance below.

The economic problems of hunting were addressed in the JBNQA sections dealing with ISP, a Cree Trappers Association (CTA), and the provision of a corporation to undertake remedial works relevant to the impacts of the first stage of the hydro-electric development (SOTRAC). ISP is the key provision here, intended to provide sufficiently generous cash payments to Cree hunters to effectively reduce their dependence on fur prices in the world economy, and on government controlled transfer payments programs. The explicitly stated objective of ISP is (JBNQA, section 30. 1.8):

> The program shall ensure that hunting, fishing and trapping shall constitute a viable way of life for the Cree people, and that individual Crees who elect to pursue such a way of life shall be guaranteed a measure of economic security consistent with provisions prevailing from time to time.

ISP could only be used to accomplish this objective, however, because it was integrated into the JBNQA, which contained the other provisions briefly cited above. The effectiveness of a cash payment to hunters depended on hunters having a right to hunt that could not be removed at the initiative of governments; it depended on a continued priority access to wildlife resources and on limiting the impacts of sports hunters and fishermen; it depended on full participation in wildlife management; and it depended on regulation of the impacts of future development. ISP payments themselves, however, could contribute to such regulation of impacts, by providing the funds for Cree hunters to increase access to other unaffected resources by means of additional travel or equipment.

The general effectiveness of ISP payments also depends on there being available the goods, services and infrastructures necessary to make effective use of the funds available to hunters. This is the role of SOTRAC and the CTA within the framework of the agreement. These organisations, individually and jointly, can provide infrastructures (including access routes, improved bush camps, and bush communications systems); and needed goods and services (including fur sales cooperatives, bulk purchasing and distribution facilities, bush pick-up and delivery facilities, aeroplane dispatching services, and wildlife and harvest monitoring services). SOTRAC is funded by the hydro-electric development corporation, the CTA will be funded by joint contributions from the governments of Quebec and Canada and from the Cree themselves.

Without these other provisions of the JBNQA, ISP could not contribute effectively to reduce the dependency of the Cree hunters on world economic conditions and government welfare policies. Even with these other provisions it clearly can only reduce and not eliminate such dependencies.

The ISP is also an integral part of the JBNQA in the sense that its incorporation into the framework of that claims settlement made it possible for ISP to be structured in such a way that it could limit some of the dependencies inherent in usual transfer payment programmes. The costs of ISP, both Program benefits costs and administrative costs, were to be paid for by Quebec under the terms of the agreement. In this sense ISP is another transfer payment programme, and it ran the risk of creating dependencies of the kind experienced by the Cree under the previous welfare programmes, that is, dependency on funds controlled by changing government policies and politics.

When the Cree negotiated ISP as part of the JBNQA they attempted to use the negotiations and the agreement itself to limit these kinds of dependency. First, ISP exists both through the Agreement and through Quebec law which is to give legislative force to the terms of the Agreement. The legislation is subject to parliamentary politics and discretion. But because this legislation does not replace the agreement, and because the agreement states the legislation must reflect the provisions of the JBNQA, and because the agreement is a legally binding contract between the Cree and the governments, any change in the Program must involve changes in the Agreement, and this can only be done with Cree consent. A recourse for breach of this contract would lie with the courts. This was intended to assure, in effect, that ISP is not treated as a standard government programme, which would be unilaterally changed by the government. It is intended to insure, with certain specific exceptions[2], that changes to ISP require the approval and consent of the Cree.

This is especially important because recent studies of welfare systems have shown that programme and policy changes tend to be systematically related over decades to the need to support unemployable labour during recessions, and to bring labour back into the market during boom cycles (Cloward Piven, 1971; Gough, 1981). A programme designed to support subsistence producers working largely outside the market must, of course, be isolated from such state control.

Second, unlike most welfare recipients the beneficiaries of ISP have the right to benefit from ISP, so long as they meet the fixed criteria for eligibility in the Program, and based on fixed criteria for calculating the size of benefits to be paid. And they can appeal or take legal action if those rights are violated.

Third, ISP is not administered by the government that funds it but by a separate corporate entity, the Cree Income Security Board, comprising equal numbers of Quebec and Cree appointees, with a rotating chairmanship: The board hires and employs its own staff, although those hired may be civil servants if the board so decides. The obligation of Quebec is to transfer the funds needed each year to the accounts of the ISP Board. In practice, the board members and the staff are either closely associated with the CRA or with the Quebec government, and the balance is and has been maintained. The board is therefore not bound by the full range of government administrative norms and it is given considerable authority to implement, and where necessary interpret and review, the Program and its operations, consistent with the legislation and the agreement.

Fourth, the board operates out of a regional office, but it must also maintain staff and offices in each Cree community to assure access of the beneficiaries to the administrators of the Program.

In summary, the incorporation of the negotiations over ISP within the framework of the comprehensive aboriginal and land claims negotiations permitted ISP to be integrated into packages of regimes, programmes, organisational structures and benefits thought to be necessary to assure the viability of hunting as a way of life. It also made it possible to establish a programme that, although funded by government, was significantly independent of government policy and politics; is jointly controlled and administered by the Government and the representatives of the beneficiary population; and that legally encodes the specific rights of the individual beneficiaries.

Thus, the unique features essential for the ISP to increase the economic and political autonomy of Cree hunters depend, in part, on a closely integrated package of rights, policies, programmes, institutions and benefits, and also on the relative autonomy of the program itself from government control. These features may well be essential wherever such a program is established with the intention of assisting a hunting population to limit its dependency.

THE STRUCTURE OF ISP: ELIGIBILITY CRITERIA AND THE CALCULATION OF BENEFITS

While specialised income security programmes are probably among the most desirable and advantageous forms of transfer payments to individuals, and while many indegenous peoples may wish to seek to establish such programmes of various forms, the eligibility criteria and benefits formula of the Income Security Program for Cree Hunters, Trappers and Fishermen were designed for the specific circumstances of the Cree and probably are not a model easily transferable to situations where similar conditions do not exist. Indeed, any such programme must be designed for specific populations and conditions if it is to be effective.

As has already been indicated, ISP was designed for a society in which a significant proportion of the adult population had maintained continuous and viable hunting activities, which were at the core of the social fabric of the communities. Furthermore, hunting was still at the core of religious knowledge and experience. It was in this context that the desire of a large sector of the Cree adult population to maintain hunting as a way of life, and to have some of their children follow in their footsteps, must be understood. There was an ongoing tradition and practice into which new participants could be integrated. This consideration significantly affected the detailed structure of ISP.

A key part of this tradition was a system of management of the social relations of hunting and of conservation of key game animal populations. The entire Cree territory was divided up into hunting territories to which various community members had specific usufructory rights and privileges. These rights, in effect, provided that intensive hunting on any piece of land was to be done under the stewardship of an individual 'owner' responsible for the long-term protection and management of the most intensively used wildlife, and also responsible for distributing social access to such resources so as to serve broad community needs.

Thus, in the case of the Cree, at least five conditions were present which were essential to the form ISP took during negotiations: the social fabric and contemporary practice of hunting was intact and did not have to be rebuilt; these traditions included means for the general management and conservation of wildlife; hunting involved extensive absences from settlements; the sector of the population which hunted intensively organised its annual cycle and other activities such as employment around hunting; and the people who hunted intensively required modest but not insubstantial cash incomes. The significance of these conditions will be readily apparent from a description of the conditions for eligibility and the formula for calculation of benefits.

Eligibility to the ISP is based on a beneficiary unit, defined as being either an adult individual or a family of one adult with consort and/or one or more dependents. Consorts and dependents are defined according to Cree traditions. The age of adulthood is 18 years but there is no age limit, retirement being self-defined. The beneficiary unit so defined coincides with the only social grouping in contemporary Cree society which generally stays together throughout the year and over the course of years. It is also the social unit which extensively shares all goods, including cash, purchased items, and subsistence produce. While sharing and coordination are also extensive in larger social units, the actual on the ground composition of larger units typically varies significantly from season to season and year to year. The small scale of this social unit reflects both a traditional emphasis on adult autonomy in Cree culture and long-term pressures toward individualisation in the interaction with a capitalist economy and state.

In the 1960s a new social pattern of splitting families in winter began to develop in a few settlements. Some adult men would join others to form all-male bush camps, leaving their wives and children behind in the settlement. This pattern developed as a response, however inadequate, to the shortage of funds to pursue hunting. When ISP was being designed, it was not only adapted to the then existing social units, the Cree also decided that it should provide incentives that would directly counteract the new trend toward splitting families. The eligibility and the payments structures were therefore designed to reflect these social objectives, as I indicate below.

There are two general criteria, and five exceptional and time-limited criteria, for determining the eligibility of potential beneficiary units to the ISP. The first general criteria is based on the amount of time devoted to harvesting and related activities. Single individuals and families, the heads of which spend *more* days in a given *year*, in harvesting and related activities than they spend in salaried or wage employment, *and* who spend at least 120 days in the former activities, *of which* at least 90 are spent away from the settlement, are eligible to be ISP beneficiaries for the *next* year. Harvesting activities are defined as all activities involved in the exercise of hunting, fishing and trapping rights established by the JBNQA and over all traditional hunting, fishing, trapping and gathering activities. Related activities are defined as women's and men's activities associated with the former, including travel, travel preparations, camp and household maintenance, food preparation, equipment construction and repair, pelt preparation, the making of handicrafts, etc. In the calculation of eligibility, days spent guiding, outfitting, or commercial fishing, and days spent in receipt of unemployment insurance, workmen's compensation for injuries, and of manpower training allowances are not counted as either harvesting and related activities, or as salaried or wage employment. Almost all beneficiaries establish their regular eligibility under this criterion.

A second general criterion provides eligibility for those who derive the greater part of earnings from harvesting and related activities. Under the present economic conditions, the latter group is effectively a subset of those meeting the first criterion.

Five exceptional criteria provide continued eligibility for up to two future years for individuals, or heads of families and their families, who are already on the Program but who due to specified special circumstances fail to meet either of the regular criteria for eligibility for a coming year. The failure may be due to injuries resulting from accidents during either harvesting or related activities, or seasonal employment or due to other illness-induced disabilities; a voluntary decrease in harvesting activities in order to permit animal populations to increase to a harvestable level, i.e., wildlife conservation practices; involvement in a manpower, upgrading, training, or other self-improvement programme; or temporary employment on a community improvement programme or project. It should be noted that these exceptional provisions provide for continued eligibility to ISP, but they do not change the basis for calculating the actual benefits to be paid to the beneficiaries to be described below. It was assumed that while beneficiaries would receive less ISP benefits under these exceptional circumstances they would be in receipt of other sources of income during the period. The key here was to prevent them from losing eligibility, for reasons which I elaborate below.

ISP eligibility is established by the actual hunting and related activities of the potential beneficiaries and not simply by an intention. As a result, eligibility for one year is determined by activities in the previous year. The actual time that must be spent hunting is not unreasonable, given the diverse Cree hunting practices, but the fact that performance must be demonstrated to gain admission, is strict. It is a provision that made sense given the on-going nature of Cree participation in hunting, and given an exception that was made for the first year of ISP operation, see below. It would not make sense as an eligibility criterion for a population trying to re-establish hunting activities.

The exception in the Cree case applied only to the first year, because it was recognised that many Cree people had abandoned intensive hunting in the 1960s and early 1970s as a result of the conditions described previously, and there was therefore a need for special admissibility criteria to start up full participation in the first year. Potential beneficiaries were therefore given eligibility for the first year of ISP if their local band council declared that they practised harvesting as a way of life, or if they declared an intention to do so during the first year of the Program. After the initial enrolment, these criteria no longer applied.

One consequence of the regular criteria for enrolment is that for a new or former beneficiary to join ISP they must practise harvesting or related activities for one year previous to becoming beneficiaries. Many young people hunt with their parents, and are eligible on turning 18 to become separate beneficiaries. This provision, therefore, mainly restricts those adults who want to try intensive hunting, or who want to hunt in intermittent years when not employed. The former must try hunting without ISP assistance for one year. The Program intentionally discouraged intermittent use becuse it was designed for those who practice harvesting as a continuing way of life. This provision follows from the objectives of and justification for the Program cited above. If this justification had not been followed consistently in the negotiations. It is likely that the Program would not have been acceptable to governments, or that the benefits paid would have been lower than those agreed upon.

Nevertheless, this provision does create a problem, because during the first year of hunting, or renewed hunting, a man encounters especially high costs for new or replacement equipment and supplies. It is precisely this first year in which ISP benefits are not paid, while eligibility is being established, except in the case of beneficiaries who have just turned 18 and who were in the bush the previous year.

One final point with respect to eligibility is that the potential beneficiary reports the time he or she spends in harvesting and related activities each year in an interview with his or her local ISP administrator, and keeps his or her own records and may report them verbally, by means of a diary, or by such other means as he or she finds suitable.

The ISP has the legal power to get information from other government agencies, employers, etc. However, it was believed, and it has been demonstrated, the self-reporting generally works in this case. There are some difficulties with accuracy of recall of some income figures, and rare breakdowns of an intentional nature do occur, but these clearly do not warrant the substantial administrative, financial and social burdens that alternatives to depending on beneficiary reporting would require.

The determination of the benefits payable to an eligible beneficiary is based on two calculations. The first is a *per diem* payment made to an individual or a head of family and to the consort of family head, for every day the greater part of the daylight hours of which is spent outside a permanent settlement in the pursuit of harvesting or related activities. The payment is made for single days spent outside the settlement even though the beneficiary returns in the evening, and it is made for each and every day during stays in isolated bush camps.

The actual amounts paid each year are indexed to the cost of living, and in 1978–79 they amounted to $15.96 Canadian per adult individual, or per head and per consort. The minimum number of days that can be paid to an indidual or head of family is, in effect, 90 and the Program establishes a limit of 240 paid days per recipient. An individual beneficiary would therefore receive between $1436.40 and $3830.40 Canadian, in *per diem* payments, and a family in which the consort accompanied the head would receive between $2872.80 and $7660.80. In fact the average number of days payable per beneficiary was 181 during 1978–79, so an average individual beneficiary received $2889, and the average family $5778, in *per diem* payments. The average *per diem* payment per beneficiary unit (including individuals and families) was $4709.

It is worth noting that the average of 181 days is a measure of the commitment of beneficiaries to harvesting. On average, six months of the year were spent outside the settlements in harvesting activities. The provision for a calculation of benefits based on the activities of the consort, as well as those of the head, was designed to encourage consorts to participate in harvesting activities with the head of the family, as indicated above.

The *per diem* payments are the largest portion of the total payments made under ISP, accounting for over 75% of all payouts. This makes it clear why ISP is not a classical guaranteed income scheme, its main payment is based on performance and not simply on income and family size. In some ways it may be better described as a cash support for performance of subsistence activities. Such support is needed because the activities are highly productive in terms of production of food, housing, clothing, equipment, medicines, heating, etc., but they do not produce sufficient income in the form of cash to permit full participation by those who want and who can be fully employed in such activities.

The Program is often justified by government literature because it has reduced welfare payments, and at the same time increased productive employment. It should be noted though that the employment it creates is effectively outside the labour market.

The second calculation of ISP benefits more closely approximates a guaranteed income programme. A basic amount is calculated from which 40% of incomes are deducted, and the balance, if any, is paid to the beneficiary in addition to the *per diem* amount. The basic amount is based on the size of the family. It was during 1978-79 the total of: $1351 Canadian each for an adult, a head or a consort; $540 for each child (dependent) in a family; plus $540 for each family. From these amounts 40% of all income is deducted, except certain universal transfer payments; and except the first approximately $320 of fur sales income for each adult. Included in the income, and counting towards the 40% reduction of the basic amount, is the *per diem* payment.

The guaranteed minimum amounts were intended to make substantial increases to the *per diem* payments received by the numerous large families (approximately 10% of biparental beneficiary families have seven or more children) and to small families and individuals who spend near the minimum amounts of time in the bush, and who therefore have relatively low *per diem* payments. The guaranteed amounts therefore supplement the payments to families with high expenses and they provide a supplement to those individuals and young, small families who may have recently entered the Program by just meeting the minimum time criteria. For these new beneficiaries it was to provide a bridge from welfare to Program benefits, on the assumption that once on the Program they would have an incentive to increase participation in harvesting, and therefore their *per diem* payments.

Once on the Program the structure of the *per diem* benefits encourages beneficiaries to increase the number of days they spend in harvesting and related activities. This again emphasises the relationship of Program structure to an assumed intensive involvement in harvesting. It should be noted that payments are not directly linked to actual kills of animals, but to the pursuit of the whole range of bush activities. The Program does not therefore directly require or encourage increases in wildlife harvests, although it does encourage more time be spent in the bush. The Cree system of wildlife management was taken into account in programme design in the expectation that increased time would not be directly linked to increased harvests; that is, that regulation by the socially recognised hunting leaders would occur. The available data on yearly harvests confirm this expectation despite the fact that a year of adjustment was required, as indicated by a significant increase in harvests during 1976-77, when the Program first came into operation.

ISP payments are made four times a year on or about 1 September, 2 January, 1 April, and after the end of the Program year in July. There is provision that beneficiaries planning to spend all winter in the bush may receive half the annual payment in September and no January payment.

ISP benefits are based on beneficiaries' estimates of their activities during the coming year. It was deemed essential that while eligibility was based on past performance, payments should not be based on activities of the previous year but on current year activities, so they could respond to current needs. This requires that anticipated activities be reported in July each year and that actual performance be monitored and benefits calculations updated during the year, when possible, to try to avoid overpayments. Overpayments in the first or second quarterly cheques result in reductions in subsequent payments in the current or the next year. While this system still seems the best available, it has been found in practice that overpayments and subsequent reductions are relatively frequent, given the contingencies of hunting patterns, and reduction of subsequent payments often causes further disruptions to hunters' plans.

The average total benefits paid during 1978-79 amounted to $5763 per beneficiary unit. With 901 beneficiary units, this amounted to a total cost of $5 250 000. It is difficult to compare this with welfare payments, but welfare would maximally amount to 60% of what beneficiaries receive from ISP for one year. However, because of the time spent in the bush few hunting beneficiaries get welfare all year, so ISP is probably two to three times what beneficiaries would get from welfare if they maintained their present harvesting patterns.

Beneficiaries cannot combine benefits from welfare programmes and ISP, but they can receive certain other transfer payment programme benefits of general application. In addition, the beneficiaries retain other earned income.

It was estimated that beneficiary units had total cash incomes of $7680 in 1978-79. To evaluate the standard of living this would provide, the value of domestic production in kind would have to be added, especially food but also housing, equipment, clothing, medicine and heating. While no detailed evaluation of those items has been made, a rough estimate of their 1976-77 value totalled some $6110 (GCCQ, 1977). Against the total income in cash plus kind, however, one must deduct the costs of producing that income, especially the costs of hunting. These have been similarly estimated for the pre-1975 period of $3700 per adult hunter per year, leaving a net income equivalent of $10 090. However, the mean number of days spent in hunting and related activities has increased since 1975, as has the cost of intensity of equipment and transportation used, partly as a result of the introduction of ISP, see below. Furthermore, it is not clear how this standard of living valuation in dollars and cents is related to the Crees' own standard of evaluation. These figures should therefore be used with care.

In relation to the costs of hunting (c. $3700 plus), ISP payment levels do not appear to be excessive to the Cree (c. $5700), especially when it is recalled that welfare is no longer received. Most beneficiaries now feel that a further substantial increase in the level of benefits would be warranted and would improve hunting related goods, services and security. It is also clear from Cree statements and from the data available that some erosion of the benefits levels is taking place with time. The Program itself has led to substantial increases in the use of motorised and commercial transportation, the costs of which are tied to oil prices and which have consequently risen quicker than the general cost of living. It is on the basis of the latter that annual Program increments have been calculated to date. The JBNQA provides for the establishment of a local cost of living index, taking account of actual expenditure patterns, which would better reflect real cost increases to hunters. Such an index will need to be initiated in coming years. Overall, the Program appears also to have led to an increase in the levels of need and expectation. Substantial increments to its benefits structure would therefore appear to be appropriate now, although care will need to be taken if an ever-accelerating consumerism that could not be permanently maintained is to be avoided.

THE INITIAL IMPACTS OF THE OPERATION OF ISP

Participation in ISP has been high from its first year, declining only about 13% to the second year, and remaining relatively stable in its two succeeding years. In 1978-79 there were 901 beneficiary units, comprising 1478 adults and 2086 children. This represents 51% of the total registered population of the eight Cree bands. The intensity of participation varies between villages, from 34% to 70% of the population of each village. The proportion of potential beneficiary units is considerably lower, however—approximately 35%. This reflects the fact that a higher proportion of the larger families are represented in the ISP beneficiary population than of smaller, and generally younger families and individuals.

The initial impacts of ISP can best be seen in the original enrolment statistics. The first year of full operation, 1976-77, began with 1021 beneficiary units. Of these, 717 were enrolled because they were considered to be people presently practising harvesting as a way of life. The remaining 304 beneficiary units were admitted to the Program because they declared an intention to practise harvesting as a way of life. Thus, 30% of the initial beneficiary units decided to try intensive hunting because of the initiation of ISP. The considerable majority of these beneficiaries were people who had experience as intensive hunters in the past but who were not practising harvesting as a way of life in the years immediately prior to 1975. Following the first year, most of these have stayed in the Program. About 75 units from the 304 units admitted on the basis of an intention to practise intensive harvesting dropped out, and the remainder retained eligibility under the regular criteria, to participate in ISP the next year. Some of those registering in the first year were people without intensive hunting experience, and it appears this group was most heavily represented among the drop-outs.

These data suggest that there was a significant sector of the Cree population that wished to pursue intensive harvesting and who were not able to do so without the economic resources provided by ISP. For these people, ISP has re-opened the choice of and commitment to hunting.

ISP also was effective in encouraging hunters to spend additional time in their harvesting and related activities outside the communities. During 1976-77, the heads of beneficiary units averaged 214 days in harvesting and related activities in the bush. This can be compared to the estimates of hunters' times in the bush made by the band councils of the Cree communities in the last weeks of the negotiation of the JBNQA, which indicated an average of 170 days per head of potential beneficiary units for 1974-75. This represents a 26% increase of time in the bush.

The immediate impact commencement of actual ISP payments had on beneficiaries is reflected in the time spent hunting during the first two years of operation of the Program. ISP legally commenced on 11 November 1975, with the signing of the JBNQA, but 10 months of intensive preparations preceded the first payment to beneficiaries at the beginning of the intensive hunting period in September 1976. The Program was therefore legally in operation for nearly eight months during 1975-76, from 11 November until the end of ISP's fiscal year, 30 June. During that period, while it is likely that ISP payments were anxiously awaited, the Program itself had little impact on beneficiaries' behaviour, because the payments for the period were only made retroactively in September 1976, when the first payment for 1976-77 was also made.

The time spent by beneficiaries in the bush during these nearly eight months of 1975-76 can therefore be compared to the time spent in the bush during the same eight months of 1976-77, after the commencement of ISP payments. ISP Board data indicate an average of 124 days were spent in the bush in harvesting and related activities during this period in 1975-76, and 154 days during the same period in 1975-77, an increase of 24%.

The number of days spent in the bush in harvesting and related activities therefore increased significantly upon commencement of operation of the Program, and data for 1977-78 and 1978-79 indicate that this increased intensity of involvement has been maintained in succeeding years (Scott & Feit, in press). Finally, it is interesting to note that data gathered on the time spent in various seasonal hunting, fishing and trapping activities indicate that the largest increase occurred in winter trapping activities, the physically hardest of the seasonal activities, and the one which was most subject to limitation due to inadequate economic resources (James Bay and Northern Quebec Native Harvesting Research Committee, 1979).

Data for the broader range of social impacts of ISP are at present being prepared for publication by Colin Scott and the author (in press), and are not to be reviewed here. Another study of the administrative aspects of the operation of ISP has been prepared by Ignatius LaRusic (1979), and it is now being updated. These studies will provide the detailed data for a comprehensive analysis of impacts. A key question for analysis will clearly be the longer term recruitment patterns.

What is clear now is that ISP has been well received by Cree hunters, presumably because the intensive Cree participation in its conception, design, negotiation and implementation assured it was well adapted to the specific conditions encountered by Cree hunters, the specific aspirations they had, and the specific problems they faced. It appears to now be accepted as a key component of the JBNQA and of hunters' planning, although certain complaints are also made about the Program structure and operation.

The economic stability and assurance of future incomes ISP provides appears to be having an impact on Cree hunters' commitments. There are some indications that the stabilisation of economic conditions by ISP after the unpredictable economic conditions for hunting during the previous two decades has led some hunters to consider hunting as a way of life as a more viable option and to offer greater encouragement to their children to stay in the bush and learn the hunting ways. The transition that has occurred may be subtlely reflected in a series of rumours, which were common during the initial year or two of ISP operation, to the effect that the JBNQA really established the ISP only for a short term, two years, or five years, or 10 years. One man is reported to have refused to apply for eligibility the first year because he did not believe the Program would actually come into operation. The assumptions behind these rumours and anticipations were, of course, well-founded on previous experience. However, it may be significant that such rumours are given less credence today and that the number of children being taken to the bush appears to have increased.

While it is clear that some adjustments and improvements now can and should be made to the Program, the increases in the number of people hunting and in the time spent hunting, as well as the readily apparent improvement in the standard of living of the hunters, are clear testimony to the positive initial impacts of ISP. These factors indicate a generally positive long-term direction for the Program and the hunters.

Given the level of self-reliance and control of one's own activities inherent in the pursuit of intensive hunting from bush camps, ISP has by inference already resulted in an increased level of autonomy for beneficiaries, and for the community as a whole, and with adjustments, it appears likely to continue the trend in the future.

NOTES

1. This paper is part of an ongoing analysis of the sociopolitical implications of the James Bay and Northern Quebec Agreement, funded in part by a Killam Post-Doctoral Research Scholarship from the Canada Council. Some of the data have been extracted from a report of research which is presently in press and which was funded by the Quebec, Ministère des Affaires Sociales, Comite de la Recherche Socio-Economique.

2. The major exception was the inclusion of a means of establishing an upper limit on the cost of the Program to Quebec. The Government insisted on this protection during the negotiations because the innovative nature of the Program made predictions of actual costs very difficult, prior to commencement of the Program. The limit was to first apply after a several year 'shakedown' period, and Quebec retained certain authority to impose changes on the ISP administration to assure the limit was not exceeded. In the event, ISP costs did exceed the limit during the initial years, and Quebec and the Cree negotiated a revised limit, based on the success of the Program in meeting its stated objectives.

REFERENCES

Anon. (1976) *The James Bay and Northern Quebec Agreement*. Quebec, Editeur officiel.

Cree Hunters and Trappers Income Security Board (1981) *Annual Report, 1978–79*. Quebec.

Gough, I. (1979) *The Political Economy of the Welfare State*. London, MacMillan.

Feit, H.A. (1978) *Waswanipi realities and adaptations: resource management and cognitive structure.* PhD Dissertation, Department of Anthropology, McGill University.

Feit, H.A. (1979) Political articulations of hunters to the state: means of resisting threats to subsistence production in the James Bay and Northern Quebec Agreement. *Etudes Inuit Studies,* 3(2):37–52.

Feit, H.A. (1982) The future of hunters within nation states: anthropology and the James Bay Cree. In: E.B. Leacock and R.B. Lee (eds), *Politics and History in Band Societies.* Cambridge, The University Press.

Grand Council of the Crees (of Quebec) (1977) *Position of the Grand Council of the Crees (of Quebec) and the James Bay Crees Respecting the Possible Imposition of a 150,000 Man/Day Limit on the Income Security Program for Cree Hunters and Trappers Established by Section 30 of the James Bay and Northern Quebec Agreement.* (restricted document, 104 pp).

LaRusic, I.E. (1979) *The Income Security Program for Cree Hunters and Trappers. A study of the design, operation and initial impacts of the Guaranteed Annual Income Programme established under the James Bay and Northern Quebec Agreement.* Montreal, McGill University, Programme in the Anthropology of Development.

James Bay and Northern Quebec Native Harvesting Research Committee (1976) *Research to Establish Present Levels of Harvesting by Native Peoples of Northern Quebec. P1. A report on the harvests by the James Bay Cree.* Montreal, 2 vols.

James Bay and Northern Quebec Native Harvesting Research Committee (1978) *Interim reports for phase II, year 1, Research to establish present levels of harvesting by native peoples of northern Quebec. P1. Harvests by the James Bay Cree.* Montreal.

James Bay and Northern Quebec Native Harvesting Research Committee (1979) *Harvests by the James Bay Cree, 1976–77. Third progress report (phase II, year 2). Research to establish present levels of harvesting by native peoples of northern Quebec.* Montreal.

Piven, F.F. and Cloward, R.A. (1971) *Regulating the Poor: The functions of public welfare.* New York, Vintage.

Quebec, Province of (1977) *Rapport preliminaire d'evaluation sur le programme de securite du revenue pour les chasseurs et trappeurs Cris.* Quebec, Ministère des Affaires Sociales.

Scott, C.H. (1977) The Income Security Program for Cree Hunters, Fishermen and Trappers—An initial field report on impacts and reactions in four James Bay coastal settlements. Montreal: Grand Council of the Cree [of Quebec] (manuscript).

Scott, C.H. (1979) *Modes of Production and Guaranteed Annual Income in James Bay Cree Society.* Montreal, McGill University, Programme in the Anthropology of Development.

Scott, C.H. and Feit, H.A. (in press) *Income Security for Cree Hunters: Initial socioeconomic impacts and long-term considerations.* Montreal, McGill University, Programme in the Anthropology of Development.

29

THE ABORIGINAL LAND RIGHTS (NORTHERN TERRITORY) ACT 1976: AN OUTSIDER'S PERSPECTIVE

Constance Hunt

This paper is intended to serve as a critique of the *Aboriginal Land Rights (Northern Territory) Act* 1976 (hereinafter referred to as the Act), written by an interested outsider. One of the difficulties of such an approach is that the 'insiders' may not appreciate the perspective from which the analysis is offered. While the Canadian and Australian Norths superficially at least have a great deal in common, it is indisputable that there are fundamental historical, social, political and cultural differences that make the drawing of comparisons somewhat dangerous. Nevertheless, the writer remains convinced that there are many similarities between the situation of Australian Aborigines in the Northern Territory and that of native groups in northern Canada, and that the similarities outweigh the differences. Thus, it is hoped that an analysis of the 1976 legislation by a non-Australian will serve to highlight aspects of it that Australians may have overlooked or ignored.

Perhaps a very sweeping view of the current Canadian situation will help to set the stage for the analysis that follows. Canada's aboriginal population consists of three major groups: the Indians, Métis and Inuit (or Eskimo). They are scattered throughout the country, forming a majority of the population only in our northern areas, the Yukon and the Northwest Territories. The aboriginal rights of certain southern Indian groups were recognised historically: these settlements took a form that is viewed by many as grossly inadequate, generally consisting of the swapping of land rights for small areas of reserve lands and tiny monetary payments. The ignored claims of other groups have been a festering sore that erupted over the past decade and a half, and that gained public recognition primarily as a result of a series of lawsuits launched by different native groups.[1] The actual results of the lawsuits have been mixed, but it is now clear that the essentially positive view toward aboriginal rights taken by the Supreme Court of Canada has been a major factor behind our government's approach to the issue. In 1973, following the first major aboriginal rights case in the Supreme Court, the federal government adopted a policy of negotiating settlements with native peoples in areas of comprehensive claims (essentially, areas such as northern Canada where no settlements had been reached previously). Progress has been slow. In part, this may reflect the fact that the Canadian Government has refused consistently to put even a temporary halt on industrial and other development in the disputed areas. Indeed, it has actively promoted the search for oil, gas and other minerals and encouraged proponents of pipelines and other forms of oil and gas transportation. It has engaged in the building of roads to previously isolated native areas, and authorised the prosecution of full-scale mining projects. This had led many native groups to adopt a position of 'no development until settlement of land claims', resulting in an impasse between government and natives and a labelling of native organisations as anti-development. Moreover, the Federal Government has generally refused to concede that there is anything at issue other than a pure question of property rights. Since a bottom line of many native groups' negotiating stance has been that political rights and arrangements are fundamental to a resolution of the issue, there has been little satisfactory communication between the Government and a number of native groups. Differences of opinion among the natives themselves, and the fact that the federal government has changed four times in the past decade, have exacerbated inherent difficulties in the negotiating process.

In only two parts of the country have there been concrete steps to resolve the aboriginal land rights issue. In November 1975 two native groups in northern Quebec signed an agreement with the Federal and Provincial governments, which was later enacted into legislation.[2] This settlement (referred to hereafter as the James Bay Agreement) was considered by some to provide a model for arrangements to be reached later with other natives. It extinguishes native title except in tiny areas where ownership of the surface is formally granted to the natives. In larger areas the natives have been accorded certain rights, notably rights to hunt, fish and trap, and to participate in institutions such as hunting advisory boards and school boards. The sum of $225 million will be paid to native-run corporations, part to be invested in 'blue-chip' securities, and the balance to be devoted to the establishment of social and cultural entities and business enterprises.

The James Bay Agreement was negotiated between the Government and natives at a time of great stress for the natives. A major hydro-electric project was proceeding at their back door, and their efforts to halt it through the courts were not expected to succeed. The other major breakthrough in the land claims area in Canada took place under rather different circumstances. This was an Agreement in Principle[3] negotiated by the Committee for Original People's Entitlement (COPE) on behalf of the Inuvialuit, a small group of Eskimos in the western Arctic. The future of the COPE Agreement is currently uncertain; at the time the final agreement was to be signed the federal government had changed and the Conservative party, then in power, refused to proceed with the Agreement.[4] At the time of this writing, the Liberals have been returned to power, and negotiations toward the signing of a final agreement are being pursued. The COPE Agreement in Principle is startling, in Canadian terms, because it dedicates relatively large areas of land to native ownership.[5] About 19% of the surface area of their traditional lands is to remain in the ownership of the Inuvialuit, with both surface and subsurface ownership formally recognised in relation to an additional 3%. The Inuvialuit would be empowered to negotiate certain types of agreements (excluding royalties) with those who develop resources under their lands. A cash payment of $45 million would be made for social and economic development; and the Inuvialuit would be entitled to participate in certain forms of decision-making in the western Arctic area.

It is in contrast to the James Bay and COPE agreements that the following analysis is offered. It focuses upon those aspects of the Australian legislation that strike a Canadian as unique or unusual.

THE DECISION AND THE PROCESS

The above overview may help to explain why, to a Canadian, the most surprising thing about Australia is that concrete steps have been taken to respond to land rights in the Northern Territory. Without suggesting that there is any intrinsic merit in a too-hasty resolution of this important issue, a Canadian cannot help but feel some admiration for a government that was prepared to take some hard decisions and get on with the process. The Canadian Government has tended to waffle about land rights and refuse to give the issue any legislative or other priority. There seems to be an attitude that the matter will resolve itself if it is ignored. Or, alternatively, there may be a feeling that if enough time passes the opposition of native people to the kind of settlement the Government favours will be ground down. Since the Canadian Government has always refused to impose any form of a freeze on northern development there is no incentive for it to find a solution to the issue. The incremental process of northern development in Canada is gradually weakening the life-style and the land that the natives seek to protect. If enough time goes by without a settlement it will become irrelevant. Thus, the Australian Government must be applauded for the fact that it has tr eated land rights as a serious legislative priority, and has committed itself to an implementation of the Act.

One feels greater doubts about the process followed by the Australian Government in determining the contents of the legislation. On the one hand, the appointment of the Woodward Commission to canvass the possible approaches, with the Aboriginals represented before him, suggests a careful and thoughtful consideration of the issues. The fact that non-Aboriginal interests were also represented, it may be postulated, may have served to make the eventual legislation more widely accepted. Moreover, the openness of the process must have succeeded to some degree in defusing possible complaints that decisions were being taken behind closed doors. In addition, the fact that the process occurred during a land freeze must have enabled the Aboriginal owners to participate in circumstances of less stress and pressure than, for example, existed during the James Bay negotiations. That the final legislation, largely modelled upon the Woodward recommendations, was enacted into law even after the fall of the Labor government that had appointed Woodward and had promoted the concept of Aboriginal land rights, suggests that the hearing process fostered a degree of momentum that transcended strict political lines.

On the other hand, one wonders how influential the Aborigines really were in this situation. Did they feel that their interests were clearly represented before the Woodward Commission? Did they feel that they had any points at which to apply pressure against the Woodward recommendations they opposed? Most importantly, did they feel that they had truly been involved in determining the form that the legislation ultimately took? Was the influence of non-Aboriginals perceived to be unfair, since basically the issue was one of Aboriginal land rights? From a different viewpoint, did non-Aboriginal interests perceive the Woodward process to be so stacked that they could not influence the outcome, no matter how meritorious their arguments?

These questions are raised because it seems that the process is often as significant as the end result it leads to. If there are objections to the process, or if it is perceived to be inequitable by key actors, this may have a negative impact upon whether or not the result is felt to be acceptable. What lessons about the process of resolving Aboriginal land rights can be drawn from the Northern Territory experience? This Canadian is driven to the conclusion that the process adopted by the Australian Government in the Northern Territory is both more effective and has led to a more generous result than the negotiating process being used in Canada.

LAND OWNERSHIP

It is surprising to a Canadian that the Australian Government was willing to turn over such relatively large areas of land to the Aboriginal claimants. While the final extent of Aboriginal ownership is still dependent on the processing of claims before the Aboriginal Land Rights Commissioner, some estimate that up to 45% or 50% of the Northern Territory's land area may eventually be under Aboriginal control. Critics point to the fact that much of the land in question is unproductive and economically valueless. Nevertheless, the fact remains that no North American Government has dared to even contemplate this degree of ownership being vested in native claimants.

Even more striking is the fact that in so doing Aboriginal rights were not extinguished. The concept of an Aboriginal Land Rights Commissioner to deal with detailed claims in the future, is also a novel one. This suggests a recognition of a fundamental point, namely, that the land rights issue is not simply a matter of property ownership to be resolved once and then forgotten. In fact, the land issue reflects profound questions about on-going relationships between Aboriginal peoples and others, and about the extent to which the dominant society will be prepared to permit the survival of alternative life-styles and values. These are not questions that are capable of instant answers but must engage both groups in a long-term process of communication and discussion. The concept of the Land Commissioner seems to recognise this reality, and provides a forum which, among other things, can help to educate the European population about their Aboriginal countrymen.

The legislation itself sets no 'cut-off date' by which the processing of claims must be completed. The Commonwealth Government's policy of extending the freeze on alienations of Crown land in the Northern Territory gave Aboriginal owners some breathing space in which to prepare claims. Self-government in the Northern Territory, resulting in land and resources being turned over to the Northern Territory Government, arguably has altered the situation. With the Northern Territory Government's announcement that the freeze on Crown alienations would be terminated in August 1980, time pressures were placed upon those Aborigines whose claims had not yet been presented since claims can only be brought in relation to unalienated Crown lands, there is now a *de facto* cut-off for Aboriginal claims. To some extent, this flies in the face of the long-term on-going process philosophy which, on paper, seems to underlie the legislation. Perhaps it also highlights the fact that, whatever form an approved land rights may take, there are always going to be development and other interests pressing for certainty as to who owns what land. The Australian approach seems to have postponed final determinations for several years after the passing of the legislation, but it also suggests that there must ultimately be a time beyond which claims will not be heard, simply because there is no more unalienated Crown land against which to lodge them.

Also of interest is the approach governing the Land Commissioner's deliberations, namely the fact that s.50(3) requires him to consider the attachment of the claimants to the land in question, not the attachment of their ancestors. This is in stark contrast to the 'museum culture' approach followed in the Canadian legal system which has, for instance, led the judiciary to define the scope of aboriginal rights in terms of the practices of the claimants' ancestors at the time of European contact.[6] One obvious result of the latter approach is to stifle the dynamic nature of the culture which the natives seek to protect. The Australian approach appears to facilitate changing and developing cultural needs. Moreover, the view that the Commissioner[7] has taken of s.50(3), namely, that it requires him merely to comment upon certain issues such as 'the detriment to persons or communities . . . that might result if the claim were acceded to', emphasises the fact that it is the legal right of the Aborigines at stake.

There have been many complaints and criticisms in Australia about the operation of the claims process. Development interests argue that it is nearly impossible to disprove evidence of Aboriginal attachment to land. For one thing, there are relatively few anthropologists in the country qualified to prepare evidence in this regard, and most of those prefer to work for Aboriginal organisations. Moreover, Aborigines themselves are unwilling to talk to anthropologists not employed by their organisations, so it becomes a Herculean task to discount the validity of claimants' evidence. In contrast, other critics complain that it is demeaning and unnecessary to require Aborigines to participate in a claims process that, although informal by European standards, is alienating and frightening to Aborigines. Moreover, Aboriginal traditions and taboos sometimes make it difficult or embarrassing for claimants to give the evidence required as proof of ownership under the Act. Such critics often favour a process that would start from the presumption that Aborigines are the owners of all land, and that would place the obligation to rebut the presumption on Europeans who are interested in the land.

Clearly, the claims process under the 1976 Act is imperfect and works certain hardships upon both groups. It is a compromise solution designed to recognise Aboriginal ownership when it can be established within certain parameters, yet to formalise the means of establishing ownership so as to prove to Europeans that there are valid reasons for recognising Aboriginal ownership in relation to particular pieces of land. When one considers the widely divergent interests of different groups in the Northern Territory, this accomplishment is not to be dismissed lightly. Moreover, the success or failure, and fairness or unfairness, of the claims process cannot be evaluated finally until the ultimate land ownership picture in the Territory becomes more clear.

The form of ownership which the Act dictates, the land trust, seems another example of legislative support for Aboriginal culture. Compare, for example, the institutional form of ownership adopted in Canada under the COPE and James Bay settlements. Although there has been a recognition that the ownership must be collective, in Canada the corporation has been selected as the appropriate institution. Indisputedly, the corporation has no counterpart in native society, and is basically a southern institution designed to facilitate profit-making. Canadian settlements have not reflected the consensus form of decision-making which characterises many native communities; instead, southern models of decision-making have been imposed. The Northern Territory legislation goes much further toward supporting and promoting current practices among Aboriginal communities, and, as a result, should be less disruptive and divisive. That the land councils can help resolve any disputes as to traditional ownership under s.24[8] would seem to encourage hard decisions being taken by the Aboriginals themselves with a minimum of outside interference.

The fact that subsurface rights were not granted to the Aboriginals undoubtedly weakens the sphere of their ownership rights. However, there are other trade-offs in the Act that appear to counteract this. For instance, the near-veto in relation to mining which s.40 gives the Aboriginals makes them a powerful factor in resource developments. While their veto can be overridden by a proclamation by the Governor-General, the procedures to be followed guarantee, at minimum, an opportunity to expose the issue in a very public way. Moreover, their power to negotiate agreements with mining companies theoretically gives them a major voice concerning the type and form of development on their lands. It is true that Aborigines have much less influence in situations where mining rights predated the 1976 legislation. Even in those circumstances, however, mining-interest-holders are required to negotiate agreements with the owners. The success or failure of agreements negotiated to date is a matter upon which opinion is sharply divided.[9] Even so, it must be emphasised that this formal recognition of the Aboriginal role has no counterpart in Canadian settlements, and, to this outsider, implies a commitment to their on-going involvement in matters affecting their lives. Compare, for instance, the Canadian Government's approvals of major mining projects, with no prior discussions with nearby Inuit communities.[10]

In summary, the Act has turned over ownership of relatively large tracts of land to Aborigines, in a form that recognises and is compatible with customary concepts. It accepts the reality that the ownership issue cannot be finally resolved overnight but needs to be placed in the context of an on-going process; and it enables the Aboriginal owners to exert some influence in relation to subsurface developments on their lands.

ABORIGINAL INVOLVEMENT IN PARKS

Another interesting offspring of the legislation from a comparative viewpoint is the acceptance of the recommendations by Mr Justice Woodward and the Ranger Inquiry[11] that Aboriginal ownership of land in Kakadu National Park be recognised. That the government is prepared to amend national park legislation in order to facilitate aboriginal ownership of parklands[12] presupposes a flexibility of approach that does not exist in Canada. It also reflects some commitment to the notion, put forward by Mr Justice Woodward, that since parks might provide a land use compatible with Aboriginal goals, park dedications ought to be pursued in a manner that would most fully involve the Aboriginal owners. Recently, the first training course for Aboriginal rangers has been completed, with apparent success. The philosophy upon which the training programme was based, and the methods employed, provide a model which ought to be the envy of parks departments in other countries.

In Canada, too, there has been some feeling that native people and parks could prove an attractive combination. Indeed, as part of the COPE Agreement-in-Principle, the federal government undertook to dedicate some 5000 square miles of traditional Inuvialuit land for the purposes of a 'national wilderness park'. The land is located on the northern coast of the Yukon and has been the subject of intense conservation interest because of its ecological significance for a large herd of caribou, the Porcupine. The COPE Agreement required the establishment of a group (with Inuvialuit representation) to advise the Minister of Indian and Northern Affairs as to details of management and other issues relative to the area. The success of the working group process is debatable. The group submitted an interim report to the Federal Government but, since the group could not reach a consensus on a number of important issues within the time it had been given, the final report to the government was prepared by the Chairman, based upon his view of what course ought to be followed.[13] One of the points of dispute was whether or not natives ought to have 'equal' participation in land and wildlife management of the park.

The advisory group has suggested, however, that the reserve be implemented through the *Canadian Wildlife Act*[14] rather than the *National Parks Act*.[15] One reason for this recommendation is the interpretation that the latter legislation, in its present form, does not permit non-government ownership of parklands, and is less susceptible to formal Inuvialuit involvement in management arrangements. Parks Canada has adopted the policy that national park lands must be vested in the Crown,[16] and will not support the notion of leasehold or other arrangements with aboriginal owners.

The experimental and more open approach that seems to exist in Australia on this question is attractive, and the results will be watched with interest by those in my country who favor the possibility of long-term native participation as owners and managers of parks and other conservation reserves.

ABORIGINAL RIGHTS IN RELATION TO NON-ABORIGINAL LANDS

Another aspect of the Act deserving comment are provisions protecting certain Aboriginal rights throughout the Northern Territory, in particular s.69, which prohibits entrance on sacred sites except under certain conditions. The effort to protect those widely scattered pockets of land that are deeply significant to Aborigines appears to be another step fundamentally supportive to Aboriginal culture. The Northern Territory's companion ordinance,[17] requiring that 7 of the 12 members on the Aboriginal Sacred Sites Protection Authority be Aboriginals selected from nominations submitted by the land councils, should help to ensure a strong Aboriginal voice in the selection and methods of protecting sacred sites.

It is recognised that this potential sphere of influence could be thwarted through under-funding of the Authority, or through the Administrator ignoring the wishes of the Authority. Nevertheless, it should be pointed out that in Canada no land settlements have made any attempt to protect areas of particular religious or cultural significance to natives, except to the extent that such lands could be selected as part of the native-owned allotment.

Some steps have been taken to protect Aboriginal use of lands and waters for hunting, food gathering, and ceremonial and religious practices, specifically through 1978 amendments to the *Territory Parks and Wildlife Conservation Ordinance* authorised by s. 73 of the Act. Section 73 of the Ordinance, which contemplates the entering into of management agreements between Aborigines and the Commission, is similar to the kinds of arrangements typically found in Canadian agreements, and designed to ensure participation by natives in management of wildlife resources. One difference is that the Canadian agreements tend to set out in much greater detail the role that natives will play. This has led to a plethora of formal committees and advisory groups that, some fear, will place heavy numerical burdens on the native population. These administrative and advisory burdens may leave few natives with sufficient time to pursue the traditional activities that are supposed to be protected. The Australian legislative arrangements pose the other danger, namely[15] that Aboriginals may not ultimately have an effective voice in wildlife management. For example, what mechanisms will there be for resolving differences between administrators and Aborigines concerning the meaning of s. 122(2) of the Ordinance, which preserves the validity of 'regulations made for the purposes of conserving wildlife in any area and expressly affecting the traditional use of the area by Aboriginals'? That such disputes may arise seems obvious; and while the Canadian settlements have been perhaps too extreme in describing the precise means of resolving them, one wonders if the Australian legislation goes far enough.

POLITICAL ASPECTS OF THE LEGISLATION

Canadian natives have been adamant that land claims settlements go hand in hand with the evolution toward self-government in the Yukon and the Northwest Territories. They seek protection from an erosion of their political strength by non-native residents, through residential requirements in relation to voting and the like. It is surprising that this issue does not seem to have emerged in the Northern Territory. Indeed, s. 73 of the Act specifically authorises the Northern Territory government to pass ordinances in relation to matters ancillary to land rights. Canadian natives would have found this unacceptable, and would be surprised that broader political matters had received so little emphasis. It should be mentioned, however, that the Canadian Government's refusal to negotiate the political side of land rights seems to have drawn native leaders into the existing political institutions. A majority of the current membership of the Northwest Territories Council are natives, many of whom have previously held leadership posts with native organisations. This one effect of the insistence of Canadian natives on political rights has been their increasingly effective participation as politicians themselves, a development that seems almost non-existent in Australia.

SUMMARY

There are aspects of the land rights issue that seem to be universal, and to cut across national and geographical boundaries. There are difficult questions that will arise no matter what form a land rights settlement takes.

Nevertheless, the Northern Territory legislation appears to accede much more than any Canadian settlements to fundamental aspects of Aboriginal culture. Its on-going process approach underscores a recognition that there are no instant or easy answers to the land rights issue. It seems to inaugurate greater respect for the Aboriginal ways and less mania for making them like us.

This is not to suggest that the legislation is perfect, or to ignore the very real problems of implementation that exist. It is, however, to commend Australia for having taken a bold step to deal with the land rights issue, many aspects of which strike me as being in the correct direction.

NOTES

1. The major cases are *Calder v. A.G.B.C.* [1973] S.C.R. 313; *Re Paulette and Registrar of Titles (No. 2)* [1977] 1 W.W.R. 321 (S.C.C.); *Kanetewat v. James Bay Development Corp.* [1974] R.P. 38 (Que. S.C.); [1975] C.A. 167; (1974) 41 C.L.R. (3d) 1 (S.C.C.); and most recently *Hamlet of Baker Lake v. A.G. Canada* (Fed Ct., 14 November 1979, not yet reported). While this litigation has been of some use to the natives asserting Aboriginal title, there remain many unanswered legal questions concerning Aboriginal title in Canadian jurisprudence; and given the enormous cost of this type of litigation and the apparent judicial reluctance to provide firm answers to the complex questions raised, one is left with grave reservations about the institutional appropriateness of the courts in resolving these important issues.

2. *The James Bay and Northern Quebec Agreement.* Quebec, Editeur Officiel du Quebec, 1976.

3. *Inuvialuit Land Rights Settlement Agreement in Principle,* 31 October 1978.

4. Letter from Sam Raddi, President, COPE, 30 August 1979, to the Honourable Jake Epp, Minister of Indian and Northern Affairs.

5. An analysis of the COPE Agreement is found in C.D. Hunt, Inuvialuit Land Rights: A Commentary, *Northern Perspectives,* vol. 6, No. 4 (1978).

6. A good example of this kind of approach is found in Mr Justice Mahoney's judgment in the Baker Lake case, *supra,* note 1.

7. Land Claim by Warlpiri and Kartangarurru–Kurintji, p. 2.

8. Land claim by Alyawarra and Kaititja, p. 20.

9. A recent article suggests that there are still many outstanding questions about these processes. See B.A. Keon-Choen, A Progress Report on Land Rights in the Territory, *Legal Service Bulletin,* 4:236 (1979).

10. Nansivik mine, located on Baffin Island, was approved by the Canadian Federal Government in the mid-1970s. Arvik mine, on Little Cornwallis Island, has recently been approved.

11. *Ranger Uranium Environmental Inquiry: Second report.* Canberra, Australian Government Publishing Service, 1977.

12. *Australia and Uranium 9* (ISBN 0 642 03258 0).

13. An interim report was submitted to the Minister of Indian and Northern Affairs on 4 December 1979. A final report was submitted by the Chairman, Lloyd Brooks on 1 May 1980.

14. *Canada Wildlife Act,* S.C. 1973,c. 24.

15. R.S.C. 1970, c. N 12 as amended.

16. *Parks Canada Policy,* 39 (1979).

17. *Aboriginal Sacred Sites Ordinance* 1978, s. 5.

INDEX